Teaching American History in a Global Context

Teaching American History in a Global Context

Carl Guarneri and James Davis, Editors

M.E.Sharpe
Armonk, New York
London, England

Library of Congress Cataloging-in-Publication Data

Teaching American history in a global context / [edited by] Carl Guarneri, James Davis.
    p. cm.
  ISBN 978-0-7656-2079-8 (cloth : alk. paper)
  1. United States—History—Study and teaching. 2. History—Study and teaching. 3. United States—
History—Philosophy. 4. Teaching—United States—Philosophy. 5. Global method of teaching.
I. Guarneri, Carl, 1950– II. Davis, James, 1949–

E175.8.T39 2007
973.007—dc22   2007047206

Printed in the United States of America

The paper used in this publication meets the minimum requirements of
American National Standard for Information Sciences
Permanence of Paper for Printed Library Materials,
ANSI Z 39.48-1984.

BM (c)   10   9   8   7   6   5   4   3   2   1

No man is an island, entire of itself; every man is a piece of the continent, a part of the main.

—John Donne

For John Gillis, builder of bridges between islands and continents, scholarship and teaching

Contents

Acknowledgments

Studying and teaching history is a collective endeavor, and an anthology like this by definition builds upon the contributions of our colleagues. The editors are grateful to the organizations and individuals who graciously gave permission to reprint their work. All are named in the source notes on the first page of each contribution. Particular thanks go to the Organization of American Historians and to its publications editor, Michael Regoli, for their generosity in allowing their magazine's lesson plans to reach more teachers through this book. Thanks also go to teachers who contributed unpublished syllabi, along with apologies to those whose course descriptions we were unable to include in the final draft of this book.

A grant from the Saint Mary's College Alumni Faculty Fellowship Fund helped to defray the expenses of preparing the manuscript.

At M.E. Sharpe, Niels Aaboe first proposed the idea for this book, and after he moved to another publisher the project passed to the equally enthusiastic and supportive Steven Drummond. Nicole Cirino, Katie Corasaniti, and Stacey Victor played important roles in the publication process, and Susanna Sharpe did a careful job of copyediting.

Particular scholars and teachers deserve special mention for their inspiration or assistance. Michael Adas, Laura Belmonte, Thomas Bender, Avi Black, Ed Davies, Alan Dawley, Ellen DuBois, Eliga Gould, John McNeill, Thomas Osborne, Daniel Rodgers, Andrew Rotter, and Ian Tyrrell have provided ideas, suggestions, and sources that improved this book. Tom Bender directed the La Pietra conferences on Internationalizing American History (1997–2000), where one of us (Carl Guarneri) gained many insights about reframing American history in global terms. In 2005 Guarneri co-directed a National Endowment for the Humanities (NEH) summer institute, "Rethinking America in Global Perspective," co-sponsored by the American Historical Association and the Library of Congress. James Davis was a participant in this institute, and both Guarneri and Davis owe a profound debt to the NEH, our guest lecturers, and two dozen faculty participants for the insights generated, projects hatched, and friendships begun there. John Gillis, the institute's co-director, has been a warm friend, a champion of dialogue between American and world history, and an exemplary builder of community among scholars and teachers. This book's dedication is our token of appreciation.

Introduction

If you are a history teacher or training to become one, you cannot help noticing that in most American schools the history curriculum is stuffed into two boxes: the United States and the rest of the world, or "us" and "them." In middle and high schools, American and world history are normally taught in alternate years and carefully segregated in content. In colleges, the history departments' course offerings are often organized by nations or continents in a way that keeps courses on the United States separate from the others. These courses usually assume a distinctive national experience without testing that premise or integrating the American story into larger world patterns.

This separation of national from world history stems partly from the special civic agenda that teachers of American history are asked to promote. Parents, school boards, and state standards expect these teachers to provide students with detailed information about the nation's history and to instill in them a sense of national pride and civic responsibility. Yet the divided history curriculum also reflects—and reinforces—mythic ideas about American national uniqueness and separateness that have deep roots in our culture. The idea that Americans have built a unique nation with a special destiny has been voiced in so many ways by politicians, preachers, and teachers that it has become part of the air we breathe. It is an assumption that has been challenged and tested only recently. The related belief that two oceans separated America from the rest of the world and thus allowed it to develop blessedly apart from global trends also became conventional wisdom. Even though two world wars, a global depression, and the tragic events of 9/11 periodically jolted Americans from this complacency, it is still unclear whether most Americans have internalized the conviction that their nation's fate is inextricably connected to that of all the world's peoples.

The truth is that the United States does not exist apart from events and trends in the larger world, and it never has. As it developed from a frontier outpost of Europe into an independent nation and then a world power, the United States was enmeshed in global ties of all kinds. The colonies that became the nation were products of the "first globalization," an era of European overseas expansion during which distant peoples and ecosystems were mingled and a global trade network was established. Those colonies evolved into a nation-building project that depended on foreign ideas, capital, migrants, and technology. Industrial growth and imperial designs culminated in a superpower nation that owns its own colonies, operates military bases overseas, intervenes in regional conflicts, and influences the lives of people everywhere. To be accurate, America's history must be told with these global connections and impacts in mind.

Highlighting the global context of American nation building also invites comparative analysis. The United States has not been unique in witnessing conflict between settlers and indigenous peoples, importing African slaves, declaring independence, expanding toward a frontier, industrializing, taking in millions of immigrants, and debating the "welfare state." These experiences link America's history to those of other settler colonies, industrialized nations, and multiethnic societies, opening up opportunities to explore family resemblances and to construct thoughtful comparisons that can replace simplistic dichotomies between "us" and "them."

More and more American history teachers are now paying attention to the nation's global ties. A movement to "internationalize" the study of American history has been gaining ground among scholars and teachers since the 1990s. It stems from several sources. Many originated outside the academy, such as the persisting debate over American uniqueness or "exceptionalism," curiosity about the origins and dynamics of globalization, and concerns about the impact of American power abroad—an issue that predated the events of 9/11 but was heightened by them. The post-1965 surge in non-European immigrants to the United States, which coincided with debates over "multicultural-ism," brought new attention to Americans' global roots. Since the past is always reinterpreted in light of the present, it is not surprising that these issues have cropped up in history courses. Immigration, environmentalism, religious fundamentalism, transnational feminism, the globalized economy, and U.S. foreign policy are hot public topics that readily lead inquiring history students beyond the nation's boundaries. All of these subjects can be illuminated by a more global approach to U.S. history; all are obscured by anything less than that. In the twenty-first century, informed American citizenship requires greater global knowledge and a commitment to the common concerns of humanity.

Within the educational community itself, probably the most important globalizing impulse has come from the dramatic rise of world history in the core curriculum at all levels. As world history courses replace offerings in Western Civilization, and as more and more instructors are asked to teach both American and world history, linking the United States and the world offers a pedagogical benefit as well as a public good. In recognition of this, the National History Standards (1994) urged teachers to integrate U.S. and world history, and the College Board has announced plans to include questions on their AP U.S. history exam that internationalize the scope of American history. The idea, as a recent report from the Organization of American Historians declares, is not to absorb American history into world history but to enrich it through global contexts and connections.

For teachers, it is one thing to recognize the need to inter-nationalize U.S. history courses, and another to accomplish it effectively. Are there ideas, models, and materials that can help? This was the dominant question that emerged during a recent month-long forum on the History Matters website (http://historymatters.gmu.edu/) entitled "Internationalizing U.S. History." Despite the strong desire among teachers to enlarge their approach to U.S. history, there is a shortage of pedagogical aids to guide them and their students. The historical profession is beginning to respond, however. American history textbooks have been revised to enlarge their treatment with features on "Links to the World" or "Voices from Abroad." A few supplementary readers have been published to parallel traditional topics in the introductory U.S. survey course (see Part V of this book for these and other resources). Articles supporting globalized approaches have appeared in journals such as *The History Teacher* and the Organization of American Historians' *Magazine of History* along with specific lesson plans, while calls for curricular change and teachers' testimonials are scattered through the website and journal literature.

This resource book gathers many of these article-length materials and adds original ones to bridge the gap between historical theory and classroom practice. Its contributors discuss the larger issues involved in studying American history in global perspective and offer practical guidance for teachers about topics, organization, and pedagogy. It includes a variety of ideas, materials, sources, syllabi, and lesson plans that should prove useful to history teachers who want to create a global context for their U.S. history courses.

Part I, "Calls for Change," reprints reports and position statements from the Organization of American Historians, the American Council on Education, and other professional groups. These initiatives have advanced the international-izing trend in two important ways. First, they provide an educational and civic rationale for enlarging the spatial and temporal contexts of American history. Second, they focus attention on the introductory U.S. history course as the primary lever of change, offering specific suggestions for reframing its topics in international perspective.

Part II, "Widening the Horizons of American History," reprints seminal essays by historians that showcase the ways in which comparative and transnational approaches lead to new questions and important discoveries about U.S. history. The articles in this section also discuss how new spatial frames such as Atlantic and Pacific history, and important transnational topics such as migration, the environment, and globalization, are redefining the boundaries of American history. By implication, the approaches advocated here of-fer a variety of themes and methods for organizing courses in U.S. history.

Part III, "Teaching American History in a Global Con-text," contains more than thirty practical resources for teachers. These include articles that offer conceptual mod-els for a globalized U.S. history course, syllabi that place U.S. history in global context, and essays that illustrate the international dimension of specific teaching topics. In the final section we describe or reproduce nearly twenty lesson plans covering international or cross-cultural episodes in American history.

A key component of a globalized U.S. history—exam-ining how others see us—is the subject of Part IV, "Views from Abroad." Those outside the national community can offer revealing insights on the United States and help us to map areas of commonality and difference between societ-ies. As Americans travel globally and their nation flexes its economic or military muscle abroad, foreign views of the United States take on heightened importance. Accordingly, this section includes materials on how foreign textbooks, teachers, and students view American history.

Finally, Part V, "Additional Resources," contains an annotated directory of printed and Internet resources for teachers to consult beyond this anthology. These resources offer ideas, documents, syllabi, lesson plans, and videos that support the teaching of U.S. history in global context.

The time is right to adopt more globally informed approaches in American history classrooms. More than ever before, our students come from diverse cultures and their lives are shaped by developments that cross national borders. Learning to exercise responsible citizenship will require understanding Americans' place among the world's peoples. And success in business and professional life will increasingly depend on our graduates' ability to understand, compete, and collaborate with their counterparts abroad. With globalizing trends increasingly influential in society and the schools, we believe that the movement to internationalize American history will win over more and more educators.

This movement is open to many methods and shades of opinion. It is not an attempt to generate a new historical specialty or subfield. Nor does it have a particular political ax to grind: there is no single method, theory, or "master narrative" that is being proposed. Instead, those who advocate a globalized American history seek to develop a new habit of mind, a disciplined way of inquiring that challenges what Thomas Bender calls the "default narrative" of American exceptionalism and opens new vistas on an artificially insulated subject. Our goal is to have students instinctively ask how America's history relates to what happened elsewhere in order to tease out its distinctive features and to understand the full range of its causes and effects. We hope that the materials we have collected here inspire teachers to enlarge the spatial and temporal contexts of American history and assist them in reshaping their courses to make it happen.

Teaching American History in a Global Context

PART I

CALLS FOR CHANGE

Position statements by history organizations have played an important role in the movement to internationalize American history. These statements construct an authoritative rationale for enlarging the context of our history teaching, one that includes disciplinary, pedagogical, and civic components. Moreover, thanks in part to these organizations, the introductory U.S. survey course has become a focal point for reform. How should the American history survey relate to world history surveys? How might its topics, themes, and periods be reshaped by transnational and comparative perspectives? Can globalized introductory courses become levers of change for the entire history curriculum? Reports from history organizations have stimulated discussion of such questions at teacher workshops and department meetings around the nation.

One shot across the bow of tradition was fired in 1994 by the *National History Standards for Grades 5–12,* the result of a collaborative effort among scholars, teachers, and educational organizations funded by the National Endowment for the Humanities and the U.S. Department of Education. Intended only as voluntary guidelines, the *Standards for United States History* were pounced on by traditionalists for belittling America's achievements and paying inadequate attention to such figures as Paul Revere, Robert E. Lee, and Thomas Edison. Amid the furor over the *Standards'* emphasis on social history and their alleged demotion of the Founders, their innovative call for a closer relationship between U.S. and world history was ignored. Even within the *Standards,* this call was honored more in principle than practice. In the specific content standards for each period, the era of exploration and settlement was envisioned in international and Atlantic terms, but after the American Revolution the *Standards* retreated inside U.S. borders in quite conventional ways, at least until World War II.

A more sweeping reform in the direction of internationalizing American history was envisioned by participants in the La Pietra project of New York University and the Organization of American Historians (OAH). In the 1990s the OAH, led by *Journal of American History* editor David Thelen, began a drive to internationalize its membership and publications that culminated in the La Pietra project. More than seventy-five scholars and teachers met in a series of conferences held in Italy from 1997 to 2000. The report they issued aimed to enrich the scholarship and teaching of American history by suggesting ways in which many U.S. history topics could be reenvisioned in light of their connections to global forces and trends. It provided a list of teaching objectives for a globalized U.S. history, concluding that "broader-gauged historical training . . . will . . . better prepare students to understand not only American relations to the rest of the world, but . . . the everyday life of Americans within the borders of the United States, past and present." The report suggested various reforms in history education, including more foreign-language study, better teacher preparation in world history, and reorganized history major requirements. Perhaps most important, the *La Pietra Report* specifically highlighted the introductory American history course as the logical place to instill habits of global awareness in students.

One hoped-for result of the reforms proposed at La Pietra is a concept of American citizenship informed by global knowledge and committed to "a global human commons." "Preparing Citizens for a Global Community" is what the National Council for the Social Studies (NCSS) had in mind in its position statement first approved in 2001. Without specifically addressing American history, the NCSS endorsed two versions of a more globalized education: "international education," which involves studying a non-U.S. world region in depth, and "global education," which entails studying transnational issues and problems and their potential solutions. Both are reference points for an internationalized American history to connect to and compare with.

During the 1990s, the American Council on Education (ACE), the coordinating body for American institutions of higher education, undertook a series of projects to promote the internationalizing of American colleges. The approach was multifaceted, including reports on internationalizing the faculty, student body, and curriculum and suggestions for engaging American campuses with overseas partners and problems. An ACE initiative on internationalizing teaching and learning at American universities enlisted a task force of historians appointed by the American Historical Association. Their report to the ACE, "Internationalizing Student Learning Outcomes in History" (2006), is a remarkably useful document for U.S. history teachers. It picks up where the *National History Standards* left off by providing a global context for developing students' historical skills. The report also seconds the La Pietra group's call for globally informed citizenship. Most important, it develops the *La Pietra Report*'s focus on the American history survey course. Declaring that the U.S. history survey can be a "vital building block" for further curricular changes, the AHA/ACE group offers insights about the scales, boundaries, and periods of American history. Within each period of U.S. history, the report offers specific suggestions about topics, themes, and comparisons that connect local, regional, and national developments in the United States with global trends. Although these suggestions are meant to differentiate college from secondary-school history courses, there are good pedagogical and civic reasons why the foundation for these "building blocks" ought to be laid in earlier grades.

CHAPTER 1

The National Standards for History (Excerpts)
National Center for History in the Schools

The development of national standards in United States and World History presents a special challenge in deciding what, of the great storehouse of human history, is the most significant for all students to acquire. Perhaps less contentious but no less important is deciding what historical perspectives and what skills in historical reasoning, values analysis, and policy thinking are essential for all students to achieve.

The following criteria, developed and refined over the course of a broad-based national review and consensus process, were adopted by the National Council for History Standards in order to guide the development of history standards for grades kindergarten through 12.

1. Standards should be intellectually demanding, reflect the best historical scholarship, and promote active questioning and learning rather than passive absorption of facts, dates, and names.
2. Such standards should be equally expected of all students and all students should be provided equal access to the curricular opportunities necessary to achieving those standards.
3. Standards should reflect the ability of children from the earliest elementary school years to learn the meanings of history and the methods of historians.
4. Standards should be founded in chronology, an organizing approach that fosters appreciation of pattern and causation in history.
5. Standards should strike a balance between emphasizing broad themes in United States and World History and probing specific historical events, ideas, movements, persons, and documents.

6. All historical study involves selection and ordering of information in light of general ideas and values. Standards for history should reflect the principles of sound historical reasoning—careful evaluation of evidence, construction of causal relationships, balanced interpretation, and comparative analysis. The ability to detect and evaluate distortion and propaganda by omission, suppression, or invention of facts is essential.
7. Standards should include awareness of, appreciation for, and the ability to utilize a variety of sources of evidence from which historical knowledge is achieved, including written documents, oral tradition, quantitative data, popular culture, literature, artifacts, art and music, historical sites, photographs, and films.
8. Standards for United States History should reflect both the nation's diversity, exemplified by race, ethnicity, social and economic status, gender, region, politics, and religion, and the nation's commonalities. The contributions and struggles of specific groups and individuals should be included.
9. Standards in United States History should contribute to citizenship education through developing understanding of our common civic identity and shared civic values within the polity, through analyzing major policy issues in the nation's history, and through developing mutual respect among its many people.
10. History standards should emphasize the nature of civil society and its relationship to government and citizenship. Standards in United States

From *National Standards for History: Basic Edition* (Los Angeles: National Center for History in the Schools, UCLA, 1996), pp. 43–46. Reprinted by permission.

History should address the historical origins of the nation's democratic political system and the continuing development of its ideals and institutions, its controversies, and the struggle to narrow the gap between its ideals and practices. Standards in World History should include different patterns of political institutions, ranging from varieties of democracy to varieties of authoritarianism, and ideas and aspirations developed by civilizations in all parts of the world.

11. Standards in United States and World History should be separately developed but interrelated in content and similar in format. Standards in United States History should reflect the global context in which the nation unfolded and World History should treat United States History as one of its integral parts.

12. Standards should include appropriate coverage of recent events in United States and World History, including social and political developments and international relations of the post–World War II era.

13. Standards in United States and World History should utilize regional and local history by exploring specific events and movements through case studies and historical research. Local and regional history should enhance the broader patterns of United States and World History.

14. Standards in United States and World History should integrate fundamental facets of human culture such as religion, science and technology, politics and government, economics, interactions with the environment, intellectual and social life, literature, and the arts.

15. Standards in World History should treat the history and values of diverse civilizations, including those of the West, and should especially address the interactions among them.

Developing Standards in United States History

Periodization for U.S. History

Students should understand that the periods into which the written histories of the United States or the world are divided are simply constructions made by historians trying to impose some order on what is inherently an untidy past that can be read and conceptualized in a variety of ways. In a nation of such diversity as the United States, no periodizing scheme will work for all groups. Native American history has benchmarks and eras that sometimes but not always overlap with those of European settlers in the colonial period. For that matter, Iroquois history would have to be periodized differently from Sioux or Zuni history. African

American history would have its own watersheds, such as the shift from white indentured servitude to black slave labor in the South, the abolition of the slave trade, the beginning of emigrationism, and so forth. So also with women's history and with Mexican American history.

Nonetheless, we believe that teachers will appreciate a periodization that attempts to blend political and social history. For this purpose, political events in United States history such as the American Revolution, the Constitution, the Civil War, Progressivism, the New Deal, and the Cold War—all of which have fairly definite beginning and end points—continue to provide breakpoints in the United States History curriculum. The Industrial Revolution, the labor movement, environmentalism, shifts in childrearing and family size, and so forth have no such precise beginning and end points and cut across eras defined by revolution, civil war, depression, and the like. In fact, none of the college texts in United States History that have tried in recent years to infuse social history into political and institutional history have been able to get around the general determinacy of wars and political reform movements and the indeterminacy of demographic, cultural, and social transformations.

We have tried to overcome, in part, the difficulties inherent in periodizing history by overlapping eras to demonstrate that there really is no such thing as an era's beginning or ending, and that all such schemes are simply the historian's way of trying to give some structure to the course of history. The ten eras selected for periodizing United States history are presented below:

Era 1: Three Worlds Meet (Beginnings to 1620)
Era 2: Colonization and Settlement (1585–1763)
Era 3: Revolution and the New Nation (1754–1820s)
Era 4: Expansion and Reform (1801–1861)
Era 5: Civil War and Reconstruction (1850–1877)
Era 6: The Development of the Industrial United States (1870–1900)
Era 7: The Emergence of Modern America (1890–1930)
Era 8: The Great Depression and World War II (1929–1945)
Era 9: Postwar United States (1945–early 1970s)
Era 10: Contemporary United States (1968–present)

Approaching World History

These standards rest on the premise that our schools must teach a comprehensive history in which all students may share. That means a history that encompasses humanity. In writing the standards, a primary task was to identify those developments in the past that involved and affected relatively large numbers of people and that had broad significance for later generations. Some of these developments pertain to particular civilizations or regions. Others involve patterns of human interconnection that extended across cultural and political boundaries. Within this framework, students are encouraged to explore in depth particular cases of historical change that may have had only regional or local importance, but that exemplify the drama and human substance of the past.

These standards represent a forceful commitment to world-scale history. No attempt has been made, however, to address the histories of all identifiable peoples or cultural traditions. The aim, rather, is to encourage students to ask large and searching questions about the human past, to compare patterns of continuity and change in different parts of the world, and to examine the histories and achievements of particular peoples or civilizations with an eye to wider social, cultural, or economic contexts.

Periodization for World History

As in United States History, arranging the study of the past into distinct periods of time is one way of imposing a degree of order and coherence on the incessant, fragmented flow of events. Historians have devised a variety of periodization designs for World History to make it intelligible. Students should understand that every one of these designs is a creative construction reflecting the historian's particular aims, preferences, and cultural or social values.

A periodization of world history that encompasses the grand sweep of the human past can make sense only at a relatively high level of generalization. Historians have also worked out periodizations for particular civilizations, regions, and nations, and these have their own validity, their own benchmarks and turning points. The history of India, for example, would necessarily be periodized differently than would the history of China or Europe, since the major shifts in Indian history relate to the Gupta age, the Mughal empire, the post-independence era, and so on.

We believe that as teachers work toward a more integrated study of world history in their classrooms, they will appreciate having a periodization design that encourages study of those broad developments that have involved large segments of the world's population and that have had lasting significance. The standards are divided into nine eras of world history. The title of each era attempts to capture the very general character of that age. Note that the time periods of some of the eras overlap in order to incorporate both the closure of certain developments and the start of others. The beginning and ending dates should be viewed as approximations representing broad shifts in the human scene.

Era 1: The Beginnings of Human Society

Era 2: Early Civilizations and the Emergence of Pastoral Peoples, 4000–1000 B.C.E.

Era 3: Classical Traditions, Major Religions, and Giant Empires, 1000 B.C.E.–300 C.E.

Era 4: Expanding Zones of Exchange and Encounter, 300–1000 C.E.

Era 5: Intensified Hemispheric Interactions, 1000–1500 C.E.

Era 6: Emergence of the First Global Age, 1450–1770

Era 7: An Age of Revolutions, 1750–1914

Era 8: A Half-Century of Crisis and Achievement, 1900–1945

Era 9: The 20th Century Since 1945: Promises and Paradoxes

The La Pietra Report: Internationalizing the Study of American History (Excerpts)

Organization of American Historians

The La Pietra Meetings, 1997–2000

In 1996, the Organization of American Historians (OAH) and New York University's International Center for Advanced Studies jointly established the Project on Internationalizing the Study of American History.

The initial planning for the project was undertaken by Thomas Bender of NYU; David Thelen, editor of the *Journal of American History;* and Linda Kerber, the President of the OAH. . . . Bender was designated director of the project, and he undertook to raise funds for it. The International Center for Advanced Studies, NYU's Faculty of Arts and Sciences, and the American Council of Learned Societies provided the funds for a planning conference, held in NYU's Villa La Pietra in Florence, Italy, in the summer of 1997. The participants . . . represented all continents, and they developed the plan for the next three conferences. Meanwhile, several major foundations provided the funds necessary for the project to go forward: The Gladys Kriebel Delmas Foundation, The Rockefeller Foundation, The Ford Foundation, and the Mellon Foundation.

The next three conferences (1998, 1999, and 2000) were organized in an unusual way. About half of the participants were invited by the director of the Project, and the remainder of the participants were selected by an annual competition administered by the Organization of American Historians. This enabled both a strong focus in the commissioning of papers and an openness that invited new ideas and welcomed self-selected participants. In both the process of commissioning papers and in selecting participants from among those who proposed papers, an effort was made to cover all continents, a variety of historiographical spe-

cializations, and a mix of different work settings: research universities, liberal arts colleges, community colleges, high schools, and public history institutions. In total, seventy-eight historians participated, about one-third of whom were foreign scholars of the United States. In order to insure some continuity of discussion from year to year, at least two foreign and two U.S. scholars, plus the director, were participants in one of the previous conferences, and the final conference, out of which these recommendations emerged, had strong representation by participants in each of the previous conferences, but it too had new voices in the interest of insuring that the project itself did not become self-referential.

Each conference had a special focus. The first, in 1997, was a planning conference that, as has been noted, set the agenda for the project. The second, in 1998, was concerned with the theoretical issues that attended the project's reconsideration of the assumptions that determined the temporal and spatial scales of conventional national historical narratives. It also considered the sociology of the profession—the history of its relation to the making of modern nation-states, its audiences in the academy and in the public realm, the relation of American history to other national histories in U.S. departments, and the moral and civic responsibilities of the historian. The third conference, in 1999, moved to exemplary essays probing either particular themes or reframing conventional historical movements or periods from a more international perspective. The final meeting, in 2000, focused its attention on the practical implications of the intellectual agenda developed by the project, and this report [written by Thomas Bender] is the product of those discussions. The Report should be understood, however, as a product of the whole project, and it has in fact been reviewed by all participants.

There was an annual report for each conference, and those reports are available on the Web pages of the OAH and the International Center for Advanced Studies at New York University. These are: www.nyu.edu/institutes/nyu and www.oah.org. A selection of the papers has been published in a book edited by Thomas Bender, *Rethinking American History in a Global Age* (University of California Press, 2002).

Rethinking American History in a Global Age

History is a contextualizing discipline; it explains social change by reference to temporal and spatial contexts. Since the professionalization of the discipline in the nineteenth century, the nation has been treated as both the principal object and the context for historical inquiry. Study of the United States offers no exception to this generalization. Its historiography may even offer a particularly strong example of this approach.

At present, however, intellectual trends in the general culture are pointing in a different direction. Recent discussions of "globalization," for example, may be uninformed by history, but they have nonetheless promoted important thinking about the historicity of the nation itself. These new understandings of the nation-state invite more complex understandings of the American nation's relation to a world that is at once self-consciously global and highly pluralized.

If historians have often treated the nation as self-contained and undifferentiated, it is increasingly clear that this assumption is true in neither the present nor the past. A history that recognizes the historicity of different forms of solidarity and the historical character of the project of nation-making promises to better prepare students and the public to understand and to be effective in the world we live in and will live in. A more limited history, one insensitive to a multiplicity of contexts and scales of experience, would be a partial and inadequate history, telling far less than the history of the United States.

Both the nation and the other historical phenomena we examine must be resituated in larger contexts because the movements of people, money, knowledge, and things are not contained by single political units. The lived and experienced connections in transnational space need to be explored—both the channels that facilitate movement and the ruptures, discontinuities, and disarticulations that structure inequalities and constitute the basis for national and other forms of differentiation.

Not all historically significant forms of power are co-terminous with nations. Historical inquiry must be more sensitive to the relevance of historical processes larger than the nation. Under the inspiration of social history, historians have in the past generation become aware of the importance of solidarities and processes smaller than the nation. Now we must extend our analysis of those histories to incorporate an awareness of larger, transnational contexts, processes, and identities. Many contemporary theories converge with this project, but it is not motivated by theoretical considerations. Its inspiration is empirical, the quest for verisimilitude.

This approach builds upon comparative history, a method of historical inquiry that has been developed by Americanists in the past generation. Yet what we propose here is a different project. Rather than comparing two national experiences, it relates national experiences to larger processes and local resolutions. The approach of this project is closer to and extends recent work in the study of the African diaspora, the creation of the Atlantic world, diplomatic history, the history of migration, environmental history, the study of gender, and intellectual history. One could extend the list of examples. Economic history, for example, is vital to this work, yet in recent years the number of its practitioners have declined. We hope that the historiography we propose will prompt renewed engagement with such essential fields and encourage work in some of the newer fields just mentioned. But our point here is to call attention to the evidence of an emerging trend in historiography. This developing work, which we seek to advance, promises to enhance our capacity to explain past and present social change.

That the nation is historically made, not a natural or socially inherent unit, is today easily grasped by historians as well as by our students and the public. Boundaries are increasingly understood as being relatively permeable, more like "zones of contact" than firm lines of division. There is a greater awareness that the people, institutions, and cultures of America are entangled in multiple narratives both larger (e.g., migration systems or capitalism or democratic revolutions) and smaller than the nation (e.g., local, regional, and sometimes ethnic).

An internationalized history will, we think, make students and the public more fully aware of the presence in their lives of histories larger than the nation and smaller than the nation. It will also reveal various Americans being participants and even agents in a world larger than the United States. By recognizing the complexity of American relations and identities both within the bounds of the nation and beyond it, one is better able to understand the lines of division or dimensions of otherness within and beyond the nation, as well as the sources of solidarities within and beyond the nation.

While this approach seeks to contextualize the United States on a global scale insofar as such a scale is pertinent to the questions at hand, it does not propose to subsume United States history under the umbrella of world or global history. We would not have United States history thus erased; rather the aim is to deepen its contextualization and to extend the transnational relations of American history.

We are therefore urging historians self-consciously to rethink the scales, temporalities, and networks of historical transformation. For this work, the revitalized discipline of geography, once a close partner of history, will no doubt be valuable, and we urge a renewal of that collaboration.

The modern, professional discipline of history, reflecting the larger cultural assumptions of the nineteenth century, initially excluded large parts of the world from its purview. The study of these non-Western "peoples without history" was relegated to the discipline of anthropology. Today, however, that divide has largely dissolved, and the discipline of history has incorporated the whole globe into historiography. This expansion of the territory of history not only demands inquiry into many more nations and cultures, but it enables history to make available as a human resource the whole of human cultures. History thus has the capacity vastly to enlarge the meaning of a liberal arts education and to provide students with richer access to a living culture, a resource that will sustain their own future cultural creativity and social invention.

To make these much enlarged cultural resources part of the working knowledge of American students and the public at large, it is essential that we not isolate the knowledge we acquire about the rest of the world. Our offer of the gift of cosmopolitanism depends upon our capacity in our teaching and research to connect a more extensive and worldly knowledge to our particular history and everyday life. Connections and comparisons in our thinking about nations and cultures beyond the borders of the United States are essential. American history, so often sharply distinguished from the histories of the wider world, must be connected to that world, as the experiences of Americans have been for centuries.

Caution is in order here. By simply extending the domain of American history one might unthinkingly produce a form of historiographical imperialism or an ideological justification for globalization and American hegemony. We must resist the error of making world history a mere extension of a triumphalist narrative of the American experience. The point of the project is to produce a much more nuanced understanding of the place of the United States in the world in all periods of its history. Such a history must attend to the complexity and contexts of relations and interactions, including the ways in which they are infused with a variety of forms of power that both define and result from the interconnections of distinct but related histories.

As they grasp the relevance of widening the lens of social analysis, students and the public should better understand the processes, the possibilities, and the limits of social change. Such a reframing of American history invites a welcome sense of defamiliarization that will, in turn, prompt a new and more inquiring curiosity about the American past. There is thus something vital to be gained in the acquisition of the cosmopolitan feeling once described by Williams James as a sense that "one's native land seems foreign."

Much that previously has been assumed about the nation thus becomes the subject of historical curiosity and inquiry: not only the American project of nation-making, but as well the analysis of identity formation, the sources and conditions of multiple identities and solidarities, the role of various heritages in institutions and everyday life, the sources and consequences of power and privilege, and much else. By contextualizing the nation and comparing it with other nations, one may better appraise the nature of its particular, even exceptional qualities, while avoiding simplistic assertions of American exceptionalism.

One cannot claim a master narrative for American history, but there are a series of themes and issues that are especially pertinent and likely to be illuminated by the study of the United States in a context larger than itself. The U.S. has been, as Alexis de Tocqueville proposed, a site for the study of historical phenomena that have a significance beyond itself. In many cases, the United States has a role in either extending or limiting the transnational significance or success of some of these phenomena, and relations with the larger world often serve to modify them within the United States. Besides democracy, we note such historical phenomena as Christianity and/or religious pluralism, modernization and modernity, racial hierarchy, migration, environmental change, capitalism, slavery and freedom, technology, community formation, empire and colonialism, cultural modernism, identity formation, and others that could be added to a longer list.

National history remains important, and will of course continue to be so in the future. But the national history we are describing resituates the nation as one of many scales, foci, and themes of historical analysis. Our students and public audiences will gain a heightened sense of nation-making. And they will be invited to consider in a more acute way the relations of underlying structures and processes, human agency, and contingency in historical change. The history curriculum, individual courses, and historical writing we anticipate, the exhibits we envision, the films that will be produced, will all be marked by the recognition of a plurality of narratives, as well as the contingency, incompleteness, and interdependence characteristic of any social practice at whatever scale of analysis, even at the level of the individual.

Such a history will also connect the United States and United States history to other histories, making it a part of world history. Broader-gauged historical training at the undergraduate and graduate levels will, we hope, better prepare students to understand not only American relations to the rest of the world, but it ought to enable them better to understand the nature of American nation-building and the everyday life of Americans within the borders of the United States, past and present.

By looking beyond the official borders of the United States and back again, students, we anticipate, will better understand the emergence of the United States in the world and the significance of its direct power and presence. We expect them to understand the controversial power and presence of the United States as a symbol beyond our borders. We hope students will gain a historical comprehension of the difference between being a peripheral colony and a powerful nation, and they will be introduced to some of the large historical processes, not all contained within the nation, that might explain such a shift in the geography of global power.

An international history not only requires a wider vision by United States historians; it requires in them a firmer knowledge of the histories of other peoples, nations, and transnational regions of the world. It points toward and strongly encourages expanded participation in the substantial international historical scholarship and teaching on the history of the United States. Among U.S.-based historians, knowledge of foreign scholarship on the United States is distressingly limited. Ways must be found to extend and expand the international initiatives already undertaken by the Organization of American Historians, the American Studies Association, and various activities already being undertaken at various universities and historical organizations in the U.S. and abroad.

Foreign scholars of the United States are a rich resource for novel and provocative perspectives on American history, interpretations that depend upon the different intellectual traditions out of which they work and the different contexts within which they write and teach American history. It is important that students and faculty have the experience of intellectual engagement with international colleagues and that we develop a genuinely international community of Americanist teachers and scholars. Colleagues teaching in different national contexts might, in fact, be invaluable collaborators in the work of revising the U.S. history survey or the curriculum more generally. Such joint projects should be given serious consideration.

We believe that there is a general societal need for such enlarged historical understanding of the United States. We hope that the history curriculum at all levels, not only in colleges and universities but also in the K–12 levels, will address itself to these issues. Indeed, in recent years state education departments have mandated world history, and the National History Standards for world history rightly urges the integration of United States history into courses in world history, though of course retaining United States history as a field in its own right. It is essential that college and university departments—which carry the responsibility for training historians who will teach at the K–12 levels—begin this work of integration.

The obligations of a professional discipline are substantial.

College and university history departments are responsible for the creation and transmission of the new knowledge, not only for the schools but also for museums, historical sites, historical societies, and the media. As professionals, historians have a responsibility to advise state education departments and textbook publishers as well as to write textbooks that reflect the best current historical scholarship.

The more specific recommendations that follow are intended to stimulate a variety of local conversations and varied strategies for addressing these issues. The world and the discipline are changing, and this report seeks to call attention to the implications of these changes for the next generation of scholarship and teaching. In a general way, this report seeks to encourage a particular orientation to these challenges and opportunities. We do not propose another "new history"; nor do we dismiss any existing practices. We wish history to be more inclusive, not less. Such inclusiveness will, we think, eventually result in a substantial reframing of the basic narrative of American history. But we understand the process as incremental and ongoing, working in distinctive ways in different institutions. The specific suggestions elaborated below are not to be taken as a checklist of reform, but rather as a tool kit that may be useful for a variety of local experiments.

Teaching Objectives

- Better prepare students to understand the contemporary world and its historical development;
- Develop in them a fuller sense of the historicity of nation-making;
- Enable students to recognize the multiple spatial and temporal contexts of American History;
- Help students to understand better the processes of identity formation, exclusions, boundaries, and different forms of solidarity;
- Enrich student understanding of the perceptions and imaginations of America from beyond its borders and promote in students a more informed sense of and commitment to a global human commons;
- Develop in students habits of historical analysis sensitive to context, interrelations and interactions, comparison, and contingency, always with an awareness that such sensitivity might well require rethinking assumed or traditional historical categories;
- Integrate U.S. history more effectively into world history;
- Encourage greater study of languages and foreign study.

Curriculum: Undergraduate

Since the recontextualization of the national history of the United States that is envisioned here establishes new relations with other national and regional histories, our proposals about American history invite reconsiderations of the undergraduate history curriculum more generally. If the American nation is understood as one of many forms of solidarity, if the American nation is more extensively contextualized, if transnational courses are conceived as vital to the study of American history, it may be necessary, or at least advisable, to rethink the interrelations of all aspects of the history curriculum and its pedagogical strategy.

Changes may range from the modest to the more substantial. One can encourage revision of the U.S. survey course, and one might provide more room in the curriculum for courses that are transnational and comparative in character. Such self-contained innovations do not disrupt the general organization of the program. Those with a special interest would prepare the courses in question. Departments must, however, be sure that such courses are allowed to fulfill departmental requirements. Many departments require a distribution of courses—for example, a number in American, European, and so-called "other" fields, and a course or more in early history. Either a transnational/international distribution requirement could be added, or a transnational/international course could fulfill some element of the existing distribution requirement rather than falling between them, as sometimes happens at present.

More ambitious revisions of the history curriculum are imaginable. One might, for example, move away from the usual organization of the departmental "map." Most departments organize the courses around nations and regions, with a progression from broad or "survey" courses to more specialized ones. As well, there is usually an implicit, if not explicit, division between the U.S. (or U.S. and Europe) and the rest of the world. In recent years, the development of thematic courses has begun to confuse the legibility of this map—a sign that perhaps it is time to redraw the map. There have been surprisingly few efforts to consider a different presentation of the divisions and genres of historical inquiry. The following alternative map is offered as an example. Its purpose is not prescriptive, and adoption is not the object intended. Rather it aims to stimulate a critical conversation about existing organizations of the field of historical knowledge and to prompt still more alternative conceptions.

This proposal divides the field into four rubrics, and students would be required to take at least one course in each division, one of which must be before 1500 A.D.

I. Nations and Empires
II. Multi-sited histories (transnational, comparative, or international)
III. Themes, Groups, and Institutions
IV. Periods: Early (before 500 A.D.); Middle (500–1500); Late (1500–)

A department could decline to demand a specific distribution, though there are probably reasons for some distribution. Or one could reduce the organization to three rubrics, with an additional requirement that at least one course be taken in each of the three periods, whatever the rubric.

The point here, again, is neither the precise structure nor the distribution, but rather the way the field of history is represented. It is not nation-centered. The nation is one of the units of history or approaches to the study of change over time rather than the "natural" unit for historical concern. By getting outside of the nation in this fashion, students will in fact better understand the nation.

Inquiry will replace unstated premises. The result will encourage more reflexivity about the object of inquiry, about spatial relations, scales of time and space, the uses and rigor of categories and concepts, and the connections between different histories. Emphasis is on a multi-faceted approach to history that stresses various transnational and international connections and comparisons.

Such an internationalist approach will encourage study abroad, even for students especially interested in American history. Likewise, history teachers, even those in the American field, would become strong advocates for serious language study.

Such a history curriculum as is being suggested here, whether in its modest or more ambitious version, contributes more broadly to education in the liberal arts by locating American history in its largest historical and geographical settings. Indeed, it would give American history a larger place in liberal arts education, both for its temporal and geographical contextualization and for its greatly enhanced contextualist interpretations of culture and explanations of social change, an approach less and less available in the social sciences generally.

The U.S. History Survey Course

The United States history survey course is properly a focal point for the creation of an internationalized American history. If in the survey course one embraces the simple advice to follow the people, the money, the knowledge, and the things, one would quite easily—on the basis of pure empiricism—find oneself internationalizing the study of American history. One might reasonably anticipate that constructing and teaching such survey courses would stimulate new research and interpretations, as has happened with world history.

A variety of approaches might be pursued to connect American history more strongly to historical themes that are not exclusively American. Some examples:

• British America can be located within the context of other worldwide colonial empires and native Americans. It can also be understood in relation to the Pacific Rim, for the social groupings that became the United

States were formed by more than westward movements. There were also southern, eastern, and northern migrations of peoples, elaborations of labor systems, and movements of culture and capital.

- The early history of the Americas can be analyzed as part of an Atlantic-wide contest over the control of labor, a complex bundle of histories involving migration, enslavement, and the historical fusing of notions of free labor, freedom, and capitalism.
- The American Revolution and its aftermath need not be treated as a singular event, but a part of a global system of empires that over the next two centuries would be challenged by democratic revolutions. The American Revolution in this context was the initiating event of that age of revolutions, and the United States was an actor—on various sides—in many of the later revolutions.
- The Civil War can be examined as an episode in an international process of consolidating national territories and empires, all of which was entangled with the reorganization of systems of labor on a global scale.
- The Industrial Revolution was not local, or even Anglo-American. It was sustained by the emergence of a global economy, significantly dependent on New World slavery and worldwide colonial systems. In time industrialism was itself a global phenomenon.
- The Progressive Movement and New Deal might be contextualized as part of an international age of social politics.

One could explore even larger categories: modernity, for example, of which the United States was early recognized as a prominent and influential example; or democracy, capitalism, or nation-making. One might, to take a different kind of example, explore the proposition that the transnational African diaspora provided the foundation for American nation-making and national identity or nationality. Or one might frame the historical development of the United States within the context of global systems of trade, both before and after European arrival in the Americas. The point, again, is not to push any of these points of view in particular, but rather to suggest the richness of possibilities as one extends and rethinks the contexts of American history.

Master's Degree

In recent years, particularly at research universities, the M.A. degree has been undervalued. In fact, it deserves our fullest attention. It is mostly at the level of the Master's Degree that History Departments perform their work of training K–12 history teachers, one of the discipline's most important responsibilities. The M.A. degree is also pursued by students pursuing a variety of public history careers.

Few M.A. degree programs have complex requirements,

and the M.A. degree usually demands less specialization than the Ph.D. degree. Both structure and purpose, therefore, make the M.A. program a valuable opportunity to develop the broader education in history that we are proposing. Within the framework of the M.A. degree, a department can mount the courses that will allow for a global contextualization of American history, ideally in conjunction with an M.A. degree or concentration in world history.

At the level of the M.A. degree one cannot, of course, provide in-depth preparation for teaching world history (including U.S. history) or broadly contextual approaches to U.S. History in K–12 or in a museum. But it is both possible and desirable to provide the examples and conceptual formulations for such courses, curricula, and exhibitions.

Ph.D. Degree

Enhancing Research and Teaching Capacities

Whatever the structure of requirements in a given department, we propose that specialists in American history develop reasonable command of the history of at least one other area, whether a nation or a transnational region or themes. The paths to this competency are various, but the intention is that they be integral to the research agenda or teaching fields of the student, not some added-on set of course requirements or exams.

While it is essential that the structure of Ph.D. requirements not hamper the development of a transnational or comparative study of American history, it is equally vital that some courses be available to engage students in broader conceptions of American history. Most crucial to the work of reorienting the intellectual aspirations of Americanists may be faculty encouragement both by precept and, even more important, by example. In fact, the departmental culture—whether it nourishes and supports the ambition for an enlarged understanding of American history—may be the decisive factor in the success or failure of efforts in this direction. Surely nourishing such a culture is more important than ever more elaborate requirements.

In this spirit, we encourage a methodology or historiography course that considers current historical writing about societies on all continents, representing a good sample of the variety of historiographical traditions being pursed in the department. Both faculty and students will have a richer and more immediate sense of the larger territory of the discipline. Students will recognize one another as colleagues and the various historiographies as a part of their scholarly armamentarium, thus enlarging their sense of the discipline beyond the community of Americanists and the literature of American history alone.

In order to engage this international historiography and scholarly community, students in American history will need greater language proficiency than has usually been required. If they are asked to acquire reading knowledge of a foreign language, it is essential that they be asked to use that knowledge as part of their training, in course work and in research. Ideally, they might have an opportunity to examine foreign archives as part of their training or dissertation, which would enrich that specific work and lay a foundation for developing larger perspectives on American history. . . .

It is important to emphasize that our recommendation is not to train Americanists as global historians or even comparative historians. Rather it is to help them acquire the capacity to explore the full dimensions of their research and teaching interests, by following them beyond national borders when the question at hand invites or requires it. Studying the international economy and the changing place of the United States in it is one example of the history being proposed here, but so is a narrative history of a community or even that of a single person whose life can be understood only in a context larger than its immediate context, whether a city or nation. . . .

The Department

A history department less tightly organized around the nation as the object and context of inquiry will doubtlessly have a greater sense of shared interests and intellectual connections among its members, which might invite more collaborative research and teaching. It will also exemplify to students the fullness of the discipline, beyond any one specialization or theoretical orientation.

Such a department will, we hope, encourage and sustain work that breaks traditional spatial and temporal boundaries, recognizing that such work often requires more demanding preparation, more complicated and therefore longer research agendas, and more complex historical narratives. To encourage such work, department personnel committees may have to think seriously about reward structures that emphasize "originality," even if of trivial import, and "productivity," even if it confuses quantity with quality.

Breadth and significance, even complexity and ambition, reflected in problems addressed (rather than ambition as measured by simple output) must be fairly rewarded. So must experiments in novel forms of historical narratives and types of presentation. There must be recognition of the value of innovative teaching, teaching that moves beyond the comfort zone of specialization and teaches a more extensive, synthetic, and richly contextualized history of the United States.

One might reasonably expect that a department moving in this direction would have a commitment to the teaching of World History. Americanists should be invited into that work, and they should be willing and able to contribute to such courses.

The department would do well to consider the development of bilateral exchange programs for both faculty and students, with selected and familiar counterparts abroad. Specialists in the American as well as in foreign fields, could, of course, participate. We encourage special efforts to bring foreign visitors to teach American history, whether as visiting professors or on exchange programs. Likewise, an effort can be made to enable Americanists to teach American history abroad, whether with outside funding (as in a Fulbright) or through exchanges. . . .

Release time for course development and encouragement of team-teaching would considerably advance faculty capacity for such research and teaching. The development of such courses will not only enrich the teaching curriculum but it will build a foundation for research. We urge both encouragement and the allocation of resources (release time, research assistance, team-teaching) that would enable Americanists to participate more fully in world history courses at the departmental level or in general education programs. Work on textbooks in the field will contribute both to teaching and to the intellectual foundations of a more international history of the United States, and we urge appropriate professional recognition for such scholarship and for course development as a form of scholarship.

CHAPTER 3

Preparing Citizens for a Global Community

National Council for the Social Studies

The National Council for the Social Studies believes that an effective social studies program must include global and international education. Global and international education are important because the day-to-day lives of average citizens around the world are influenced by burgeoning international connections. The human experience is an increasingly globalized phenomenon in which people are constantly being influenced by transnational, cross-cultural, multicultural, and multiethnic interactions. The goods we buy, the work we do, the cross-cultural links we have in our own communities and outside them, and increased worldwide communication capabilities all contribute to an imperative that responsible citizens understand global and international issues. The increasing globalization in the human condition has created additional opportunities and responsibilities for individuals and groups to take personal, social, and political action in the international arena.

Global education and international education are complementary approaches with different emphases. The integration of both perspectives is imperative for students to develop the skills, knowledge, and attitudes needed for responsible participation in a democratic society and in a global community in the twenty-first century. International studies focuses on the in-depth study of a specific area or region of the world to develop knowledge and understanding of another culture. A global perspective is attentive to the interconnectedness of the human and natural environment and the interrelated nature of events, problems, or ideas. An important characteristic of global studies is the analysis of problems, issues, or ideas from a perspective that deals with the nature of change and interdependence.

Approved by the NCSS board of directors, May 2001.

CHAPTER 4

Internationalizing Student Learning Outcomes
in History (Excerpts)

A Report from the American Historical Association
to the American Council on Education

Committee Members:

Noralee Frankel (American Historical Association); Kevin Gaines (University of Michigan); John Gillis (Rutgers University); Dane Kennedy (George Washington University), Chair; Patrick Manning (Northeastern University); Sonya Michel (University of Maryland at College Park); Kevin Reilly (Raritan Community College); and Peter N. Stearns (George Mason University).

A. Introduction

Now, more than ever, the cumulative effects of global exchange, engagement, and interdependence make it important that we provide our students with an international perspective on the past. Such a perspective is essential if they are to make sense of the world they confront.

An international perspective can be integrated into the history curriculum in various ways. This committee chose to focus on the general education courses in history, particularly the American history survey. These introductory courses communicate with the largest number of college students, and successful internationalization at this level will have its widest impact. Moreover, it may help to differentiate these courses—particularly the U.S. history survey—more effectively from their high school counterparts, reducing the sense of repetition for students and providing them with a more challenging educational experience.

Three history survey courses—world history, Western civilization, and U.S. history—are variously deployed to serve the purposes of general education at the college level, and all three of them warrant some scrutiny with interna-

tionalization in mind. **World History** courses, though international by definition, often need further attention to ensure appropriate inclusion of the United States, which helps to make global issues more meaningful to students. **Western Civilization** courses must frequently be challenged to open out to wider comparisons and wider consideration of the interactive nature of contacts; though international in one sense, such courses sometimes encourage narrowly ethnocentric thinking. The **American History** survey courses present more obvious challenges to "internationalization," evident in what critics have referred to as their insular, exceptionalist orientation. By the same token, they hold the greatest potential for reconstitution along lines that would provide students with an accessible entry point into the analysis of larger global forces in the modern era.

This report addresses both the general challenge of internationalizing history survey courses and the particular challenge presented by the American history survey. The first section identifies the themes, skills, and outcomes that are applicable to all three of the general education history surveys. The second section focuses on the American history survey, offering specific recommendations for internationalizing its curriculum. It should be added that these recommendations also carry implications for the history major. The measures taken to internationalize the survey courses should be explicitly reiterated in the courses and sequences of the history major as well.

The committee appreciates the complex web of factors that affects any curriculum change. These include the intellectual, content-driven issues entailed in making the general education survey more genuinely international in focus, the pedagogical challenge of making such a survey course more meaningful to students, the institutional issues arising from state educational requirements, the graduate training of faculty who teach the survey course, the tendency by universities to resort to part-time faculty to teach introductory courses, and so on. The report also reflects some thinking about who the ideal student is, the "new" American whom we would like to see emerging from this process.

Finally, the committee understands that some caution is necessary in using the term "internationalization," particularly in contexts such as the American history survey, lest it privilege national terms [units] of analysis even as it seeks to transcend the nation as its focus. We also want to stress that "internationalization" need not merely signify the global. It can refer to other units of analysis, which are larger than the nation but still smaller than the world itself (the "Atlantic world," for example). The type of inquiry being undertaken determines the size of the analytical unit.

B. General Goals

1. Knowledge:

Historical knowledge can be specific or general, descriptive or interpretive. It may apply to a particular locality, a specific moment, or a given topic, but it also may reference wide regions, long time periods, and a range of topics within the human experience. Descriptive knowledge operates on multiple scales, providing information on events, characters, and processes at levels from local to national to comparative to global. Interpretive knowledge works on multiple scales as well, integrating descriptive evidence into causal or correlative analyses. The study of history should emphasize linkages between the local and the global, the immediate and the long-term, the topically specific and the civilizationally general.

The topics and themes identified below are, in our opinion, those that will bring a substantial re-contextualization of the history survey. (Here "topics" are taken to mean statements of subject matter, and "themes" are taken to mean relationships within the subject matter of a topic.) They address major historical issues that are equally applicable to the World history survey, the Western Civilization survey, and the American survey. Balancing the coverage of these challenging issues confronts both teacher and student with the problems of selection, reasoning, and memory. Yet the additional effort of choosing and linking selected areas of knowledge brings, in compensation, a higher level of student involvement in historical analysis through their participation in the choices. We encourage teachers of the history survey to address these topics and themes on varying scales: through comparative studies of communities and nations, through investigation of global patterns, and

through study of links and interactions among communities or between local and global levels.

- Political institutions and practices: empires, states, and nations; imperialism, colonialism, nationalism
- Wars and revolutions
- Structures of governance, constitutional and legal developments
- Modes of production, exchange, and consumption (agriculture, industry, trade, etc.)
- Migrations and diasporas
- Culture contact and exchange; cultural transfers and innovations
- Systems of labor and social inequality and their rationales (notably race, class, and gender)
- Social movements, social reform, emancipation
- Impact of environment and disease
- Sodalities of belief: religions, ideologies, educational practices
- Science, technology, and the manipulation of nature
- Frontiers and borderlands

2. Skills for Students:

The skills acquired in the introductory survey course constitute the building blocks of a liberal education. They can be applied not only to upper division history courses but across the entire curriculum. Chief among these skills are the ability to recognize and analyze change over time and space, to handle diverse forms of evidence, and to master forms of written, oral, and visual expression that facilitate communication with peoples of other regions and cultures. The goal should be to provide all students with ways of approaching the world and thinking about themselves in the dimensions of time and space. These are skills that will both enhance their own lives and enrich the global communities of which they are a part:

- Identify how causation relates to continuity and change in global frameworks
- Recognize connections between the past and the present; i.e., locate both self and others in time and spaces
- Acquire familiarity with the uses—and the limitations—of historical comparison as an analytic tool
- Appreciate the constructed nature of geographical categories when thinking about geographical space
- Grasp temporal relationships and integrate multiple chronologies within the same analytical frame of reference
- Demonstrate the capacity to deal with differences in interpretation
- Critically analyze narrative structures and construct narratives

- Demonstrate an ability to recognize and interpret multiple forms of evidence (visual, oral, statistical, artifacts from material culture)
- Recognize the distinction between primary and secondary sources, understand how each are used to make historical claims . . .

3. Outcomes for Students:

In addition to its goals of increasing knowledge and developing the skills that mark a liberal education, the general education course in history has traditionally had the goal of creating engaged and responsible citizens. Yet the purview of that civic goal has broadened with America's place in the world. Nineteenth-century American history gave the children of immigrants a national identity. Twentieth-century "Western Civilization" courses taught Americans to participate in an Atlantic community. More recently, the world history survey has arisen in response to the increasingly globalized character of the American experience. The "new" American faces a smaller, but vastly more complex and interdependent world than any previous generation. American actions, private and public, leave larger footprints than ever before. The lines between foreign and domestic, international and national, even global and local, diminish and blur. Consequently, the introductory history course must prepare future citizens to understand and navigate a far greater kaleidoscope of cultures and countries. Among the outcomes of such a course will be the following:

- Ability to see contacts among societies in terms of mutual (though not necessarily symmetrical) interactions, benefits, and costs.
- Ability to look at other societies in a comparative context and to look at one's own society in the context of other societies.
- Ability to understand the historical construction of differences and similarities among groups and regions.
- Ability to recognize the influence of global forces and identify their connections to local and national developments.

C. The American Survey: Rethinking Periodization

The American (U.S.) survey course can become a vehicle for students to rethink (or begin thinking about) basic tools of historical analysis, not only with regard to the U.S., but also more generally. These tools include periodization, territorial boundaries, and causation. From the outset, the field of U.S. history has operated on (and reinforced) a set of unquestioned assumptions: that U.S. history and the existence of the nation itself are more or less co-extensive (the colonial period is included as a run-up to "the birth of the nation"); that the boundaries of the nation have been determined by nature; and that it makes sense to examine the history of the rest of the world from the perspective of the United States.

Internationalization of the course would help students become aware that these assumptions are themselves intellectual constructs by asking some of the following questions: When does American (U.S.) history start? Why does it start when it does? Where does it start? How, and why, have its boundaries shifted over time? In what ways would a history of the North American continent look different from U.S. history? What ethnographic divisions of space existed prior to the colonial era? What nations existed before the American nation? What is the relationship between land and sea as human spheres of interaction and connection? How has the U.S. appeared to the peoples and governments of other nations (e.g., Britain, France, Germany, Cuba, Nicaragua, Iraq, Vietnam, the Soviet Union/Russia, Japan, China, South Africa, etc.) at particular points in time? How is the U.S. discussed in the histories of these nations?

A more self-consciously internationalized U.S. history survey offers an escape from the tyranny of "coverage," with its obligation to take up an ever-expanding range of topics. An international approach encourages a more rigorously thematic orientation, requiring the identification of and concentration on topics that open up U.S. history to comparative scrutiny. The proposed outline that follows is meant to signal some of the ways that the survey can be connected to historical patterns that transcend the nation. Several points should be noted about the outline. First, our intent in preparing it is to be illustrative, not prescriptive. Second, we have sought to stress both continuity and change by dividing the outline into sections that are thematically distinct but overlap in periodization. Third, we have taken care to ensure that all of the bulleted items in the following sections correspond to one or more of the general themes listed in B1. Fourth, we have concluded each section with a brief consideration of some of the many ways that U.S. history can be framed in comparative perspective.

1. Themes for the Colonial Era (1400s–1770s):

- The existence of an "international" system of national polities of indigenous peoples before—and during—the colonial period
- European imperial expansion and the creation of settler states
- The Columbian exchange of microbes and plants, and their environmental consequences
- Slavery and other forms of unfree labor
- Mercantilism and state-regulated trade, markets and consumption
- Cultural encounters and exchanges among Europeans, Indian, Africans—religion and missionaries; sexuality and creole populations; pidgin languages

- Invention and institutionalization of race and racism
- Demographics, sexuality, and marriage patterns
- Technologies of production and destruction
- Democratization, freedom, citizenship, social mobility, written constitution

Comparisons can be made to patterns of European settlement, systems of production and trade, and uses of slave labor in other parts of the Americas and Africa. The English American colonies were part of a much broader Atlantic and, indeed, world economy, and their development should be framed in these contexts. Similarly, the issue of cultural encounters and their ideological and demographic consequences opens up fruitful comparative possibilities regarding religious conversion, race mixture, and more in English, French, and Spanish colonial territories. Another prominent theme in U.S. history that has parallels elsewhere is the frontier, which plays a comparable role in the histories of Russia and other states that expanded at the expense of neighboring peoples.

2. Themes for the Age of Revolutions and Nation-Building (1760s–1860s):

- The influence of liberal political philosophy on revolutionary thinking and its role in the construction of a national ethos and identity
- The American Revolution as a political and social upheaval
- Redefining relations between Euro-Americans and American Indians; American Indian removal
- Growth of a market economy and urbanization; transnational trade and migration
- Expansion of system of African-American slavery; creation of free African-American communities
- Poverty, charity, and public assistance
- The Great Awakening, Abolitionism, early feminism, utopian socialism, and other social movements
- The challenge of nation-building: Civil War
- The challenge of nation-building: politics, public schools, and the creation of a public sphere

The American Revolution, its ideological foundations, social character, and political consequences, can be compared to the Haitian, Latin American, and French revolutions, among others. The territorial and political processes of nation-building in the United States occurred in an environment that generated similar dynamics in other parts of the globe, from France to Japan. Attention could be given to ways that slavery in the U.S. resembled coercive labor systems like Russian serfdom. By the same token, the abolition of slavery in the U.S. occurred in conjunction with similar shifts to free labor in Brazil, Russia, and elsewhere. While the Civil War figures prominently in the story of abolition, it also bears notice as an event comparable to other bloody upheavals in the mid-19th century, such as the 1857 uprising in India, the Paraguayan War, and the Taiping Rebellion.

3. Themes for the Age of Industry and Empire (1840s–1920s):

- Post-slavery system of social inequality: Jim Crow and sharecropping, sweatshops and ethnic labor ghettos
- Urbanization and immigration, assimilation, shift from rural to urban-oriented society and economy
- Industrialization, mass production, mass consumption, mass culture, and the rise of leisure
- Rise of an industrial working class: labor unions and social protest
- Commercialization of agriculture: meat-packing industry, export production of grains
- Technological change: railways, electricity, medical advances
- Feminism and changes in family demographics
- Progressivism and social welfare: public education, land grant colleges
- Internationalization of banking and trade
- Continental expansion: the Mexican War, the destruction of American Indian nations, and the closing of the frontier
- Manifest Destiny, the missionary impulse, and American ambitions abroad
- U.S. involvement in world politics: the Spanish American War, World War I, intervention in Latin America, the treaty system
- National, industrial, and imperial forms of culture

Many of the themes of U.S. history in this period—mass migration, urbanization, industrialization and technological change, labor struggles—correspond directly to processes elsewhere across the globe. The comparisons are not merely structural, but instrumental: they reflect the increasing social and economic interactions that we refer to as globalization. Patterns of production and consumption in the United States can be compared to—and considered in interaction with—countries such as Britain, France, Germany, and Japan. Their impact on gender roles and the impetus they gave to international feminism also deserve consideration. Politically, too, the United States becomes an increasingly active participant in international affairs, culminating with its involvement in World War I. It increasingly assumed the characteristics of an empire, both in its expansion across the continent and with its claims to overseas territories. The former process, which included the destruction of autonomous American Indian polities, can be considered in the context of developments in Australia, New Zealand, and other settler states. The latter process, which resulted both in the political integration of Hawaii and the military subjugation of the Philippines, offers interesting points of comparison to the European colonial empires.

4. Themes for the Age of America as a World Power (1898–present):

- Growth of the modern American state: bureaucracy, militarism, mass politics
- Rise of the corporation and welfare capitalism; rise (and demise?) of the labor movement
- Depression and prosperity: production, consumption, and the redistribution of wealth
- U.S. involvement in international agreements and organizations: from isolationism to United Nations, NATO, and NAFTA
- Planes, trains, and automobiles: suburbanization, the expansion of the highway system, and the making of mobile America
- Changing role of women in the public sphere, the workplace, and politics
- Export of U.S. commodities and culture, contestation over its influence
- Identity politics and civil rights/human rights movements: non-violent social change among African-Americans, Native Americans, others
- Cold War: global ideological struggle, interventions and conflicts (Korea, Vietnam, Latin America, etc.)
- Environmental politics: the struggles over water in the West, the use and abuse of natural resources, environmental contamination and human health
- The struggle between secular and religious views on education, the family, and sexuality
- Demographic shifts: aging and the "Latinization" of the U.S. population

The synergistic expansion of state, corporate, and technological power in the United States intensified its involvement in global affairs and brought it into a series of collisions with other countries, making American history an integral element of world history in the 20th century. How the United States came to conceive of its interests and obligations as a global power should be juxtaposed to the aims and ideological claims of its rivals, ranging from Britain to the Soviet Union. Many of the social, economic, and political movements that shaped the American domestic experience had their counterparts elsewhere, opening up a range of opportunities for comparative consideration of civil and human rights struggles, environmental movements, ideological clashes over capitalism and state power, the rise of international corporations, and more. The rise of an American consumer culture and its contested impact abroad bear particular attention.

D. Connecting to Other Disciplines

In considering ways in which survey courses can be infused with an international perspective, the committee was conscious that the role of history as a discipline in advancing the internationalization of student learning outcomes must be carefully connected with similar efforts in other disciplines as well, where, for example, data and habits of mind relevant to comparison or to the relationships between the local and the global are developed. By demonstrating how change and continuity affect global patterns and also how larger constellations of global forces like migration and cultural diffusion influence regional patterns, the history survey can be a vital building block for internationalization efforts in the curricula of higher education more generally. . . .

F. Selected Bibliography

Anderson, Fred, and Andrew Cayton. *The Dominion of War: Empire and Liberty in North America 1500–2000* (Viking, 2005).

Bayly, C.A. *The Birth of the Modern World, 1780–1914* (Blackwell, 2004).

Bender, Thomas, ed. *Rethinking American History in a Global Age* (University of California Press, 2002).

Burton, Antoinette, ed. *After the Imperial Turn: Thinking with and through the Nation* (Duke University Press, 2003).

Christian, David. *Maps of Time: An Introduction to Big History* (University of California Press, 2004).

Degler, Carl. *Neither Black nor White: Slavery and Race Relations in Brazil and the United States* (Macmillan, 1971).

Drescher, Seymour. *From Slavery to Freedom: Comparative Studies in the Rise and Fall of Atlantic Slavery* (New York University Press, 1999).

Fernandez-Armesto, Felipe. *The Americas: A Hemispheric History* (Modern Library, 2003).

Frederickson, George. *White Supremacy: A Comparative Study of American and South African History* (Oxford University Press, 1981).

Guarneri, Carl J. *America Compared: American History in International Perspective*, 2 vols. (Houghton Mifflin, 2005).

Hartz, Louis. *The Founding of New Societies: Studies in the History of the United States, Latin America, South Africa, Canada, and Australia* (Harcourt, Brace, 1964).

Hemphill, C. Dallett. *Bowing to Necessities: A History of Manners in America, 1620–1860* (Oxford, 2002).

Kocka, Juergen. *White Collar Workers in America, 1890–1940: A Social-Political History in International Perspective* (Sage, 1980).

Kolchin, Peter. *American Slavery and Russian Serfdom* (Belknap, 1990).

Laslett, John. *Failure of a Dream? Essays in the History of American Socialism* (Anchor Press, 1974).

Lepore, Jill. *The Name of War: King Philip's War and Origins of American Identity* (Vintage Books, 1999).

Lipset, Seymour Martin. *Continental Divide: The Values and Institutions of the United States and Canada* (Routledge, 1991).

Manning, Patrick. *Navigating World History: Historians Create a Global Past* (Palgrave Macmillan, 2003).

McNeill, John, and William McNeill. *The Human Web: A Bird's-Eye View of World History* (Norton, 2003).

Moore, Jr., Barrington. *The Social Origins of Dictatorship and Democracy: Lord and Peasant in the Making of the Modern World* (Beacon Press, 1966).

Siegel, Micol. "Beyond Compare: Comparative Methods after the Transnational Turn," *Radical History Review*, 91, 1 (2005), 62–90.

Stearns, Peter N. *The Industrial Revolution in World History,* 2nd ed. (Westview, 1998).

———. *Global Outrage: The Impact of World Opinion on Contemporary History* (One World, 2005).

Stoler, Ann Laura. "Tense and Tender Ties: The Politics of Comparison in North American History and (Post)Colonial Studies," *Journal of American History*, 88, 3 (2001).

Wigen, Kären, and Martin Lewis. *The Myth of Continents: A Critique of Metageography* (University of California Press, 1997).

PART II

WIDENING THE HORIZONS
OF AMERICAN HISTORY

The path between scholarship and teaching has been different for American and world history. In the case of world history, the demand for a new, globally encompassing survey course preceded most of the scholarly books and articles that provided its themes and questions. By contrast, the list of scholarly works that treat American history in comparative and cross-national terms has expanded over the past two decades without substantially affecting the existing U.S. survey. Today's movement to internationalize American history courses promises to change that. As the work of globally minded U.S. historians is disseminated and its implications are developed, teachers can select from a varied menu of concepts and approaches for classroom use.

One methodological distinction lies between comparative and transnational approaches. The internationalized American histories that first appeared following World War II studied the frontier, slavery, and race relations in comparative perspective by examining parallel features in other nations. Comparative studies continue to be developed in these fields and have extended to immigration, industrialization, the welfare state, and other topics. Meanwhile, a new body of scholarship has emerged that examines flows of people, money, goods, and ideas between Americans and others, including commodities and corporations, transnational social movements, and ethnic diasporas. These exchanges are seen not only as important factors in U.S. history but as evidence that Americans, like other peoples, have forged their individual and national lives through their negotiation with processes larger than the nation. As it turns out, as American historians "go global," their debates have begun to echo those in world history between "comparativists" and "interactionists," those who emphasize distinctive regional institutions or civilizations and those who emphasize exchanges, conquests, and migrations as the key levers of change. Teachers who internationalize

their U.S. history courses face a similar pair of options—or the possibility of blending these approaches, as most world history textbooks now do.

These are not the only choices. Other interpretive strategies for teachers to consider involve crucial decisions about time, place, topics, and themes. If we are to expand the temporal frame of American history, when do we begin the story? The options range from Asians' crossing the Bering "land bridge" 20,000 years ago to Columbus's landing in 1492, with many critical dates between. Alternatively, widening the spatial boundaries of American history poses the question of *where* to begin. It also requires teachers to select appropriate geographic scales for the story—regional, continental, hemispheric, Atlantic, Pacific, and global—and to rotate among them deftly. As for topics and themes, among the triad of people, place, and nation—all seen in international contexts, of course—which should take center stage as the survey course's main subject? Is nation-making the primary story of the introductory course, or is the nation simply a particular place to chart peoples' lives or to watch regional and global processes at work? Should teachers choose a specific internationalizing theme, such as trade, migration, or war, to thread through their course, or should they sketch an overall trajectory for American history, such as the nation's move from the margins of global power to the center? Should American history narratives (and courses) work their way outward from traditional topics and events to explore their global setting, or should they move inward from world history to highlight American variations or innovations on major global themes?

The essays that follow illustrate particular internationalizing approaches and in various ways offer direct or implied responses to these questions. They represent a sample of ongoing historical discussions and debates. Two pioneering articles set the stage by staking out polarized positions.

Carl Degler proposes that the study of American history be widened to include other parts of the world, but that it remain centered on comparisons that reveal what made the American experience unique. Laurence Veysey, by contrast, finds that the dominant—but almost unspoken—trend of American history has been its immersion in the large social transformations of modern history and thus the gradual loss of its national distinctiveness.

From these opening gambits the discussion moves beyond the dichotomy of sameness and uniqueness into more grounded accounts of Americans' connections to other lands, including reflections on the patterns and variations that emerge from such studies. Thomas Bender urges us to rethink central episodes in American history—the age of exploration, the Revolution, the Civil War, imperialism, and reform—by placing them in their global setting. Alison Games explores the growing literature on Atlantic history, asking by implication how it might transform our approach to early American history. Ian Tyrrell uses American links to his native land, Australia, to undertake four tasks at once: (1) to propose a Pacific-based perspective to supplement Atlantic history, (2) to suggest the British "settler societies" (Canada, Australia, New Zealand, and South Africa) as an appropriate comparison group for the United States, especially for the American West; (3) to examine, albeit briefly, the relevance of Immanuel Wallerstein's "world-system theory" for locating these societies in world history; and (4) to show how the new environmental history compels us to see the nation as only one among the multiple geographic scales—global, national, regional, and local—on which our lives are lived and our stories must be told. His essay is full of suggestions for scholars and teachers to take up.

Besides the environment, another transnational topic drawing growing attention among historians is migration. In separate essays, Henry Yu and Robin D.G. Kelley suggest how two migrations, Asian "sojourning" and the African "diaspora," have transnational dimensions that enlarge nation-centered perspectives on ethnic and immigrant history. Yu highlights the multiple destinations of Asian migrants and the racial basis of citizenship that the United States shared with other immigrant receivers. At the same time, his essay connects transnational with local history: he shows how different patterns of group identity and discrimination took shape regionally in the United States based on the migrants' homeland, the composition of other ethnic groups in the region, and their order of arrival. Kelley examines the implications of the African diaspora for the development of hybrid African/American identities and black internationalism. His final section sketches what might happen if the concept of diaspora were applied more widely to reshape our notions of American history and identity.

Finally, Eric Foner's eloquent presidential address to the American Historical Association brings up two essential topics of an internationalized American history: foreign policy and globalization. According to Foner, America's sizable global impact since 1900 should radically alter our ideas about the scope of American history. In line with recent trends among foreign-relations historians, he uncovers mutual influences between U.S. domestic and foreign policy. His particular subject is how the idea of freedom has influenced Americans' view of their place in the world—and other peoples' views of them. In brief outline he shows that U.S. relations with the rest of the world have continually revised the ideas of freedom that Americans have debated and applied at home and abroad. Concentrating on the post–World War II era, Foner offers pointed remarks on what he sees as the dangerous implications of globalization for freedom—both the idea and the reality. His essay confirms that the many facets of globalization are a proper subject for an enlarged view of American history.

A variety of other topics, themes, and approaches have surfaced in the growing conversation about placing American history in a global context. These readings represent a small sample of historians' contrasting views, but they do illustrate important topics and issues for teachers to engage. Other topics, such as race and gender, and other spatial frameworks, such as a hemispheric approach to U.S. history, will appear in Part III. Despite their different emphases and interpretations, the historians represented here agree that an accurate understanding of our past requires teachers and students to study what happens beyond the nation's borders and to reattach America's history to the world, where the facts of geography, if not Americans' mental maps, tell us it has always been.

CHAPTER 5

In Pursuit of an American History

CARL N. DEGLER

Over the last twenty years, American history has splintered. Indeed, the fragmenting has become so obvious that it is a commonplace in discussions of the state of the American field.[1] The principal source of that disarray has been an explosion of historical information, particularly in social history. The seminal work on the history of slavery in the 1960s stimulated historians to take the same imaginative and probing approaches to the history of cities, blacks, Chicanos, Indians, immigrants, families, and women, and even to transform the history of the economy and politics. Groups and subjects ignored in traditional history suddenly became visible, clamoring for inclusion in a historical framework that once had no place for them. On one level, this informational explosion is what we expect in history, a subject well recognized for changing its content as the society it serves asks new questions and makes new demands. That is the good side of the splintering. On the less appealing side, we have no clear way of determining how this new knowledge will be integrated into what we call the history of the United States. Simply to tack the new information onto the old story disrupts the organizing framework and renders the new version disjointed and incoherent.

Perhaps the most successful and enduring of the framing interpretations for the United States was that created by the "Progressive" historians: Carl L. Becker, Frederick Jackson Turner, Charles A. Beard, and the literary historian Vernon Louis Parrington. The heart of their story was the conflict between democracy and privilege, the poor versus the rich, the farmers against the monopolists, the workers against the corporations, and, at times, the Free-Soilers against the slaveholders. That pattern of interpretation came under attack in the 1950s and has been falling into disuse ever since. Its successor, which has been called the "consensus" school of interpretation, had hardly been put into place before it was shot down by a profusion of new research emphasizing the divisions and conflicts in the American past and by actual social and political conflict in the American present of the 1960s and 1970s.

Thanks to the sophistication of the questions we now ask about the American past and the greater care we now take in arriving at answers, we know more today that is significant about the history of the United States than ever before. But the general history we purvey to our students and to the public lacks central themes or a framework. The history of the United States at the present time does not seek to answer any significant questions, such as those the Progressive historians posed when they, perhaps naively but certainly interestingly, asked how "the people" had been treated, or been frustrated, or had triumphed over the special interests. History today, to be sure, no longer seems simple to us; that is a measure of our achievement. But history serves a more vital social purpose than simply documenting the complexities of human behavior, although it certainly ought to do that. If we look to the purposes of history, I think we may discover a framework that not only encompasses the new information but also more effectively achieves those social ends that history alone can fulfill. I am recommending that we begin to shape our presentation of American history around the question, "What does it mean to be an American, that is, a citizen of the United States?" The word "mean" in this context, I hasten to add, should not imply what ought to be or who is a "proper" or "true" American. Rather, I use it in an effort to define us historically. The implicit, but operative, assumption is that Americans differ in some important ways from people of other nations.

From *American Historical Review* 92 (February 1987): 1–12. © American Historical Association. Reprinted by permission.

The justification for following this line of interpretation rests on two purposes of history. These are not the only uses or purposes, and by advancing them I betray my personal biases. But biases are surely excusable in a profession that no longer expects objectivity. First, history is socially useful. To ask "Who are Americans?" is to raise a question of central importance to citizen and society alike. It is especially relevant to a nation as extensive, as diverse, as recent, and as susceptible to change as ours is. Second, our identity, whether national or individual, comes primarily from history, from the past. The present, after all, is merely a nation's skin, its body is the past. . . .

If we take these two purposes of history as given, where do we go from there in seeking to describe what an American is? One way is to identify the nature of America today and then to trace through the past the sources of its present identity. I once took that route myself in trying to define how Americans came to be the way they are. The practice has been condemned as Whig history, but it does have the advantage of following the sound historical principle of process or continuity. It does little, however, to enlighten us as to what distinguishes us from other peoples. This weakness proved to be nearly lethal to many of the works of American studies that were influential in the 1950s. These studies assumed that, by closely examining some aspect of the American past, historians could identify the traits and values that characterized Americans. Thus articles and books on the American West, the American novel, American pastoralism, and the American cult of violence tumbled from the presses. If the point or outlook that scholars took to be American could be documented from American sources, then the identity of Americans had supposedly been delineated. But, by failing to look beyond the United States, these studies could not distinguish between those traits or developments that were peculiar to Americans and those that other peoples may have experienced.

When one advocates, as I do here, that the United States be compared historically with other societies, the specter of American exceptionalism inevitably floats before us. During much of our history, the idea that America was somehow outside European patterns of development was almost a truism, beginning with Crevecoeur's famous question, "Who is this new man, this American?" and running through Goethe's "Amerika, du hast es besser" to Tocqueville's conclusion that Europe should look to America for a picture of its own future.[2] More recently, starting with Marxists in the early twentieth century, writers have increasingly abandoned the idea that America was an exception to European patterns of development, partly because exceptionalism called into question, at least for Marxists, the idea that there were universal laws of historical development, and partly because it encouraged American chauvinism. Marxists, to be sure, have not been alone in decrying American exceptionalism, especially during the Great Depression, when it seemed obvious that the United States was hardly an exception among the company of industrial nations of European heritage. As one recent critic of American exceptionalism remembered, such an interpretation of American history "made little sense" to him as a junior in college in the 1940s, since the depression's devastation of his family situation and the outbreak of war effectively belied the image of America as the "land of peace and economic plenty."[3] The eclipse of exceptionalism was nowhere more clearly measured than in the assault in the scholarly literature during the 1940s on Frederick Jackson Turner's frontier thesis, which, of course, was an application of exceptionalism.

After World War II and during the cold war years, the idea of American uniqueness was reborn in the form of the concept of "national character," also of ancient vintage. During the 1930s and early 1940s, the assumption that it was legitimate to refer to the character of a whole people had come in for sharp criticism, principally because of the insistence by the German Nazis of the superiority of the so-called Aryan peoples and of Germans in particular. Although the idea of national character had been widely and freely, if loosely, used through a substantial part of the nineteenth century, it began to smack of extreme nationalism, racism, and German Nazism. The work that brought about a reversal in attitude toward the concept was David M. Potter's *People of Plenty,* published in 1954.

Early in his book, Potter spelled out why the idea of national character arose. "The history of American events would be devoid of intellectual challenge if it were merely a literal recording of any events that chanced to occur within American territorial limits. The purpose of history," he emphasized, "is not simply to show that events which might have happened to anyone did happen to someone, but rather to explain why a special sequence of events befell a particular aggregation of people." He went on to say that, to accomplish this goal, the historian must find "what is distinctive in the circumstances, the condition, and the experience of the aggregation in question. But unique circumstances, conditions, and experiences are apt to produce unique traits and attitudes among the people as a whole. To recognize such collective traits and attitudes," he concluded, "is to embrace the concept of national character."[4]

Potter was defending the concept of national character, not exceptionalism, and with good reason. To ask what differentiates one people from another does not mean one has to insist on deviation from a norm, which is clearly implied in the term exceptionalism. In fact, a much sounder approach admits that each nation is unique or exceptional, that there is no general law of historical development, as Marxists implied when they coined "exceptionalism." Recently, for example, German historians have also been debating their version of exceptionalism: the concept of a German *sonderweg,* or "separate way." Like Turner's version of exceptionalism, the German *sonderweg* was once a positive idea, a way of asserting German national superiority. After 1945, the term took on a much less flattering meaning.[5] In itself, the German *sonderweg* reminds us that, in various ways, the history of each nation is unique, which is but another way of recognizing the concept of national character.

Some historians spurn nationally organized history because it is outdated, indeed, moribund, in the face of the pervasive and overpowering forces of technology, urbanization, and industrialization that they perceive as homogenizing the societies of our planet. "The real trend of American history," wrote Laurence Veysey, "is toward a loss of whatever distinctiveness the society once possessed. . . . For over a hundred years, and in some respects for much longer, the merger of America into a common pattern of modern life has been the great underlying tendency."[6] On a narrowly practical level, this rejection of national differences seems premature, in view of the difficulties even the advanced industrial nation-states of Europe are experiencing in trying to create a truly common market, not to mention a common parliament. Industrialism may once have been thought to make internationalism inevitable, but, as Ernest Gellner has pointed out, the spread of industrial culture has probably done more to entrench nationalism than any other single force.[7] On a more theoretical level, historians in particular ought to be suspicious of any notion that implicitly denies the role of the past in shaping the present, as Veysey's remarks seem to do. The past as a molder of the present should not be written off just because the forces of modernity seem pervasive. Experience warns us that the past penetrates the present whether we like it or not. No nation escapes its past even when it deliberately seeks to transcend it, as in the ideological revolutions in Russia in 1917 and China in 1948. Nor does a nation necessarily lose its past when foreign conquerors attempt to obliterate it, as the history of Poland reminds us. The ways in which a people adapt to the forces of modern technology or organization are, surely, the product of their history.

But, some of you will undoubtedly object, why should we study how national societies differ from one another? Does not such a procedure overemphasize nationalism and other forces that divide rather than unite peoples? Professional students of nationalism themselves have raised these objections. "I make no secret of my belief," wrote Boyd C. Shafer some years ago, "that nationalism, especially when carried to extremes, leads to war and destruction." Shafer looked forward to the day when it would be shown "that men in every nation are basically more like men in other nations than they are different," and that their "*human* likenesses are possibly much more significant than their *national* differences."[8] It is worth recognizing, nonetheless, as Marc Bloch emphasized half a century ago, that the identification of differences is a primary reason for historical comparison. Through this process, we learn what national events or developments require explanation and how we might explain them.[9] More important, nationalism, though rightfully charged with many sins, is a deep-seated institution of our time, shaping and vivifying the lives of people throughout the world.[10] We can write history that implicitly denies or ignores the nation-state, but it would be a history that flew in the face of what people who live in a nation-state require and demand. As Potter wrote, the "study of the American people holds little intellectual attraction if the American people are merely an undifferentiated mass of humans fortuitously located in America."[11] We want to know what there is about them that makes them Americans. If we historians fail to provide a nationally defined history, others less critical and less informed will take over the job for us.

A further objection needs to be addressed. Does not the approach I am suggesting ignore conflicts within American society? Was it not this very neglect of internal differences that delivered the coup de grace to the "consensus" interpretation of American history in the 1960s? And has not that lack of recognition of conflict been a legitimate objection to the concept of national character? Conflict or diversity need not be ignored in the approach I am suggesting. On the contrary, any divisions within the nation, by invoking comparison with other countries, would be given a historical measure instead of a subjective one. For example, by comparing cross-nationally the activities of labor unions and radical groups or the extent and character of urban riots over a period of time, we would avoid the ahistorical subjectivity inherent in making judgments about the degree of class consciousness in this country, judgments that are implicitly comparative but which are arrived at from within the experience of the United States. Indeed, studies of social mobility in the United States, on which much scholarly energy has been expended, have suffered from a lack of just this kind of cross-national comparison. Only comparison, after all, can answer the question that prompted the investigations in the first place, namely, was America the land of opportunity that the national myth proclaimed?[12]

It is often said that an emphasis on differences between one national experience and another, such as I am proposing, encourages national hubris. A danger does lurk here, but not an inescapable one. We need to recall that the comparative method is used just as often by critics of a given society as it is by those who would extol it. The comparative study of race relations has certainly not resulted in a new sense of pride for Americans. If both critics and champions of a nation use comparison, there is a very good chance the story that emerges will indeed have the critical bite indispensable to any sound national history.

I suggest, then, that we put the history of the United States quite self-consciously, and as consistently as the overall historical account permits, into comparative perspective. This method requires that we raise our eyes from the narrow American scene and ask if what happened here may have differed from what happened elsewhere, and, if so, why? Seeking differences will not overturn the traditional story, for the continuity between past and present—how the past became the present—will remain as pertinent as ever. But comparison will emphasize aspects of our past that may have gone unnoticed before, just as it will call for explanations where none was thought necessary before. The purpose, I emphasize, is not to praise us, but to understand who we are. By asking what is American about us, we will also begin to construct a framework that could provide the integrating pattern or synthesis that, at the moment, seems to elude us. In effect, we will be reversing the process that Turner followed when he assumed the differences between American and European history and then called on the frontier to account for them. I am suggesting instead that we ascertain what is distinctive about the United States in the surest way we can: by finding out how we have differed from others.

How should the comparison be carried out? With what countries, for example, should the United States be compared? The comparison should be neither random nor global. Comparisons have traditionally been with Europe, more specifically, Western Europe, for most American immigrants came from that region, and almost from the beginning, Americans have sought, in one way or another, to differentiate themselves from Western Europeans. Comparisons would not necessarily be with all of Western Europe but only with those nations that seem to have shared with us the same historical developments. The purpose of comparison would be to see aspects of our history that differ where we might have expected similarity. For example, the character of American politicians, the nature of our political parties and constitutional practices, the extent of suffrage and popular participation, might be compared with those of England, from which our own political and constitutional practices largely derive. Similarly, our processes of economic growth might be compared with those of Germany, a nation that, like the United States, came late to industrialization.

Some differences in economic development are already known and are suggestive: the absence in Europe of an antitrust movement comparable to that in the United States, and the absence in the United States of a socialist movement comparable in strength and influence to those in most Western European nations. This second difference can be further explored by contrasting the fragility and narrow base of the American labor movement over the past century with the experience of organized labor in most industrial states of Western Europe. State-owned economic enterprises are common in Western European economies while almost absent in the United States, another difference in economic life that seems worthy of detailed comparative study.[13] Most significant, the possibility exists that, behind these differences (once they are examined together and in detail),

we may identify national values that can be legitimately described as "peculiarly American."

European societies are obvious comparisons for this purpose but so are the nations of the New World, for they share with us a European heritage and a novel environment in the western hemisphere. This basis of comparison with the New World has been drawn on before, notably by Latin Americanists such as Herbert Eugene Bolton and Frank Tannenbaum.[14] Most recently, comparisons of slavery in the United States with that in some of the nations of Latin America have yielded valuable insights into the special character of bondage in the United States. Only a beginning has been made in exploring the differences in the reactions of Europeans in the New World to open land, or the frontier. Turner accurately singled out the frontier as a prime source of American identity, but for the wrong reasons. He was right, not because the frontier explained us, as he contended, and not simply because its absence from the history of modern Europe differentiated us. He was right because the frontier experience in the United States differed from that in Canada and in Latin America. We know from comparison with Canada, for example, that the long, drawn out, and bloody conquest of native peoples that stained the history of the United States during the nineteenth century had no counterpart across our northern border. When we ask why the difference, we begin to recognize what is distinctively American about our ways of settlement, our forms of frontier government, and our practices of federalism, a recognition that without comparison would have escaped our attention.[15] That in Latin America there are no equivalents of Daniel Boone and Kit Carson, and that *frontera* carries none of the meanings and connotations that cluster around "frontier," alerts us again to the different character of the American frontier and the forces that went into the making of Americans.[16] The peculiarly American values that may lie beneath these and other differences can only be uncovered by looking again at the frontier, but this time in comparison with the ways other societies confronted open land and native peoples.

The frontier is one situation in which comparison with New World nations would help to identify those elements that went into the making of an American nationality. Equally distinguishing is another, the presence of slavery, which set apart the United States not only from Europe but also from those Latin American nations in which slaves were as economically and demographically important as they were in the United States. By bringing Africans to the colonies, slavery left an impress on the social, economic, and cultural history of this country that, even with limited comparison, hints at underlying values and traits unique to Americans. No other society in the western hemisphere in which black people were introduced in bondage equals the record of racism of the United States. No other New World country instituted the social and legal segregation of blacks from whites that, until recently, was endemic here. Although at this point we cannot be sure, it also seems likely that no other New World country counted anything near the almost 2,000 lynchings of blacks recorded in the United States between 1882 and 1902.

Yet, at the same time, no other New World country has mounted a revolution like the Civil Rights Movement of the 1960s and 1970s in the United States. The contrast is most obvious when the sounds of that upheaval are placed beside the almost total silence on the question of racial prejudice in Brazil, where, even today, only weak and peripheral organizations speak out against the racial discrimination that the social order has long ignored and frequently denied.[17]

More important is the recognition that the Civil Rights revolution was not simply a modern outburst of rage against injustice. Its roots ran deep into the American past. Throughout our national history, the role of black people has been a social issue of import, even though hostility of whites toward blacks has, at the same time, been almost an American trademark. Some white Americans always stood with black Americans and denounced racial hostility as un-American. Again and again in the course of our history, the place of blacks in U.S. society has been a subject of dispute and debate. During and after the American Revolution, the question of race divided Americans. In the middle decades of the nineteenth century, it disrupted the Union and transformed the South and, in the second half of the twentieth century, tore apart the nation's cities and reordered its social agenda. Political leaders from Thomas Jefferson to Lyndon Johnson have had to confront it, while American prophets from Anthony Benezet in the eighteenth century to Martin Luther King, Jr., in the twentieth have used their moral eloquence to keep us from forgetting it. The salience of the issue cannot be explained by force of numbers. All through our history, no more than one American out of eight has been black and often fewer than that. The special place of blacks in the American past is further highlighted when we recognize that no comparable concern was displayed toward the struggle of women for political and social equality. Unlike blacks, women have been left, until very recently, to fight their own battle.

An additional sign of the special role of blacks in the making of America is the distinctive cast that blacks have given to American culture by insisting on being a part of it, as, for example, American Indians have not. Blacks have advanced our economy, inspired our literature, energized our reforms, shaped our music, and redirected our politics. The special place of blacks in our national culture and the accompanying ambivalence of whites toward blacks—that odd combination of appreciation and hatred—are not easy to explain, but, as Gunnar Myrdal contended over forty years ago, they still seem distinctively American.[18]

Deliberate historical comparison would surely throw new light on the meaning of the ethnic diversity that has long been regarded as distinctively American. It is true that England has had its massive Irish immigration and Germany its Polish, but it is the New World countries, with their heavy dependence on European immigration, that offer the most fruitful way of determining if the ethnic past of America is in fact distinctive. We already know that the range of immigrant nationalities and the total number who came to the United States distinguish us from the other nations in the western hemisphere. It is also true that the United States received a substantially greater proportion of European immigrants than any other nation. At the same time, however, the proportion of immigrants in the population of the United States was less than that in several other nations that received immigrants.[19] Yet historians frequently point to the high proportion of foreign-born people as an explanation for the several upsurges of nativism, or opposition to immigrants, in the United States. Comparison with South American societies that received large numbers of immigrants but experienced very little nativist activity might be revealing, not only in regard to the reception accorded foreigners in the United States but also in ascertaining the roots and meaning of American nativism. At least two recent studies, for example, have concluded that opportunities for and acceptance of Italian immigrants were better at the turn of the century in Argentina than in the United States.[20] Comparisons of the social reception and public policies on immigration in the United States and other New World countries would let us ascertain if there was indeed anything that could be termed American about our response to immigrants.

Finally, one difference that seems to identify us but which has rarely been studied comparatively is religion. On the face of it, religion is a distinguishing characteristic of Americans. Today, according to recent public opinion polls, we are the most religious people in the Western world.[21] Religion, usually in the form of Puritanism, has been amply acknowledged in our traditional history. This early Protestantism undoubtedly separates us from any nation to the south of us and from most of those across the Atlantic. I am thinking, however, of more enduring aspects of religious life, those that are still operative, such as the principle of separation of church and state, the wide diversity of sects in the past and present, the voluntarism of Protestant churches, and the relatively recent and massive growth of Catholicism and Judaism. Nor should we forget the founding within our boundaries of two world religions, one frontier and one urban in origin: the Church of Jesus Christ of Latter-day Saints, and the Church of Christ, Scientist. Such obvious differences suggest that cross-national comparisons of public religious policy, church organization, and the place of religion in the social order would tell us much about what it means to be an American.

The limits of your patience and the extent of my ignorance do not permit me to spell out here other ways we might learn about what it means to be an American if we would look beyond our borders and shores. Some limited comparative studies in a variety of fields already promise that systematic comparison will provide fresh and revealing ways of defining Americans. We know, to mention four recent examples, that big business came to the fore in the United States long before it did in the first home of the Industrial Revolution,[22] that American wives were much less likely to work outside the home during the nineteenth and early twentieth centuries than were wives in Britain,[23] that public education encountered almost no objections in the United States as compared with the stiff, vocal resistance it met in England,[24] and that reformers during the Progressive era in the United States were much less theoretical than were their counterparts in Britain.[25] Until we look outside ourselves, we neither know who we are nor what we need to account for in our becoming Americans. The job of comparison is, to be sure, arduous and continuous, though, as Fritz Redlich reminded us some years ago, comparison need not be entirely or mainly archival work.[26] Much secondary literature already exists from which valuable comparisons may be drawn.

If we begin to look at our history as comparatively as we can, it will place us, sometimes with pride, sometimes with embarrassment, and sometimes with shame, in the midst of other nations' histories, clearly identifying who we are. Inasmuch as all nations require a past to obtain the identity history alone can provide, this approach is applicable to any nation. It is, however, especially appropriate to Americans. Our ethnic, racial, and religious diversity help to define us as a people, but diversity, by its centrifugal nature, continually threatens to attenuate, even to dissolve, the identity it helped to define. To shape our past around the ways in which we differ from other peoples will assist us in escaping that danger while articulating what it means to be an American. Finally, in pursuing our historical identity, we obtain a framework that can encompass and integrate the new knowledge garnered from the explosion of research in the last two decades. This pursuit will gain for us a history that is distinctively American, not simply because it happened to us, but because it did not happen to others.

Notes

1. See, for example, Herbert G. Gutman, "The Missing Synthesis: Whatever Happened to History?" *Nation* 233 (November 21, 1981): 521, 553–54; "Interview with Herbert Gutman," *Radical History Review* 27 (1983): 217–22; Olivier Zunz, "The Synthesis of Social Change: Reflections on American Social History," in Zunz, ed., *Reliving the Past: The Worlds of Social History* (Chapel Hill, N.C., 1985), 60, 80; and Thomas Bender, "Wholes and Parts: The Need for Synthesis in American History," *Journal of American History* 73 (June 1986): 120–36. European historian Peter N. Stearns has suggested that the disarray extends beyond American his-

tory. See his "Social History and History: A Progress Report," *Journal of Social History* 19 (Winter 1985): 3, 19–34. I fully recognize that other peoples in the New World have as good a claim to be known as Americans as the citizens of the United States. I have nevertheless followed throughout this essay the standard practice of referring to the history of the United States as "American" because only that term can describe the people of the United States. No one, so far as I know, has suggested an alternative term, such as "United Statesian."

2. Tocqueville apparently believed that the term "exceptional" would apply to the United States even when compared with later societies: "The position of the Americans is . . . quite exceptional, and it may be believed that no democratic people will ever be placed in a similar one"; Alexis de Tocqueville, *Democracy in America,* Phillips Bradley, ed., 2 vols. (New York, 1948), 2: 36–37.

3. David W. Noble, *The End of American History: Democracy, Capitalism, and the Metaphor of Two Worlds in Anglo-American Historical Writing, 1880–1980* (Minneapolis, Minn., 1985), 141. Interestingly enough, Daniel Bell's effort to declare an end to exceptionalism did not quite succeed when he considered the American political system. See his "The End of American Exceptionalism," *Public Interest* 41 (Fall 1975): 222–24.

4. David M. Potter, *People of Plenty: Economic Abundance and the American Character* (Chicago, 1954), 29–30. The sociologist Alex Inkeles has continued to emphasize psychological traits in delineating national character. See his essay, "Continuity and Change in the American National Character," in *The Third Century: America as a Post-Industrial Society,* Seymour Martin Lipset, ed. (Chicago, 1979), 390–416.

5. For recent literature on the *sonderweg* debate, see Theodore S. Hamerow, "Guilt, Redemption, and Writing German History," *American Historical Review* [hereafter *AHR*] 88 (February 1983): 53–72; Robert Moeller, "The Kaiserreich Recast? Continuity and Change in Modern German Historiography," *Journal of Social History* 17 (Summer 1984): 655–83; David Blackbourn and Geoff Eley, *The Peculiarities of German History: Bourgeois Society and Politics in Nineteenth Century Germany* (Oxford, 1984); and Hans-Ulrich Wehler's review of the German edition of Blackbourne's and Eley's book, in *Merkur* 35 (May 1981): 478–87.

6. Laurence Veysey, "The Autonomy of American History Reconsidered," *American Quarterly* 31 (Fall 1979): 477.

7. "The nationalist principle as such, as distinct from each of its specific forms . . . has very very deep roots in our shared current condition, [and] is not at all contingent, and will not easily be denied"; Ernest Gellner, *Nations and Nationalism* (Oxford, 1983), 118.

8. Boyd C. Shafer, *Faces of Nationalism: New Realities and Old Myths* (New York, 1972), xiii, 340. Emphases in original.

9. Marc Bloch, "Toward a Comparative History of European Societies," in *Enterprise and Secular Change: Readings in Economic History,* Frederic C. Lane and Jelle C. Riemersma, eds. (Homewood, Ill., 1953), 507.

10. Gellner, *Nations and Nationalism,* 56, 125.

11. Potter, *People of Plenty,* 29. Thomas Bender, who also is interested in the creation of a fresh, interpretive synthesis of American history, concluded that national history is not likely to disappear in the near future. "Professional history

has been institutionalized on the basis of national cultures as well as states," he wrote. "Anyone with a sense of history must recognize that such associations are contingent, but there is little evidence at the moment of the emergence of any new transnational cultural or political formations to sustain a history that will transcend nations"; Bender, "Wholes and Parts," 125.

12. One German historian who has a strong interest in the investigation of social mobility has complained that U.S. historians began to lose interest in the question of social mobility when their studies began to reveal more social mobility in the American past than they had anticipated. See Hartmut Kaelble, "Foreword," *Journal of Social History* 17 (Spring 1984): 406. For a statement on the unfinished state of comparative studies of social mobility, especially between the United States and European societies, see Kaelble, *Historical Research on Social Mobility: Western Europe and the USA in the Nineteenth and Twentieth Centuries* (New York, 1981), 34–57.

13. A table in the *Economist* for December 21, 1985, p. 72, shows that, among seventeen industrial nations, the United States was unique in having a dearth of state-run economic enterprises. Other New World countries such as Mexico, Brazil, and even Canada were conspicuous in their departures from the U.S. pattern.

14. It is worth noting that Bolton's use of comparison was quite the opposite of Tannenbaum's (and mine). Bolton was interested in identifying similarities, Tannenbaum in differences.

15. The explanations are advanced in Mary Floyd Williams, *History of the San Francisco Committee of Vigilance of 1851: A Study of Social Control on the California Frontier in the Days of the Gold Rush* (Berkeley, Calif., 1921), 424–27, and Paul F. Sharp, *Whoop-Up Country: The Canadian-American West, 1865–1885* (Minneapolis, Minn., 1955), chaps. 5 and 12.

16. Alistair Hennessy, *The Frontier in Latin American History* (Albuquerque, N.M., 1978), 11, 158–59. A Briton, Hennessy identified a specific value of North-South comparisons when he pointed out that, if such comparisons were made, "there may be a better chance of getting [British] students to realize that the United States is a foreign country and not just an eccentric version of the British experience"; p. 5.

17. See, for example, the recent survey of Brazilian race relations and organizational opposition to racial discrimination in Pierre-Michel Fontaine, ed., *Race, Class and Power in Brazil* (Los Angeles, 1985).

18. Myrdal provided a striking measure of the American concern when he wrote, "Wandering around the stacks of a good American library, one is amazed at the huge amount of printed material on the Negro problem. A really complete bibliography would run up to several hundred thousand titles. Nobody has ever mastered this material exhaustively, and probably nobody ever will. The intellectual energy spent on the Negro problem in America should, if concentrated in a single direction, have moved mountains"; Gunnar Myrdal, *An American Dilemma: The Negro Problem and Modern Democracy,* 2 vols. (New York, 1944), 27.

19. J.D. Gould, "European Inter-Continental Emigration 1815–1914: Patterns and Causes," *Journal of European Economic History* 8 (Winter 1979): 604.

20. Samuel L. Baily, "The Adjustment of Italian Immigrants in Buenos Aires and New York, 1870–1914," *AHR* 88 (April 1983): 281–305; and Herbert S. Klein, "The Integration of Italian Immigrants into the United States and Argentina: A Comparative Analysis," *AHR* 88 (April 1983): 306–29. In the absence of any systematic comparative study, an emphasis such as David A. Hollinger placed on the relatively high degree of ethnic acceptance in the United States is questionable. We just do not know that Americans are more accepting than other immigrant societies are until we make the comparisons. Hollinger, "Two Cheers for the Melting Pot," *Democracy* (2 January 1981): 89–97.

21. John M. Benson, "The Polls: A Rebirth of Religion?" *Public Opinion Quarterly* 45 (Winter 1981): 578, 582.

22. See Alfred B. Chandler and Herman Daems, eds., *Managerial Hierarchies: Comparative Perspectives on the Rise of the Modern Industrial Enterprise* (Cambridge, Mass., 1980), 3, 36–39; and especially the essay by Morton Keller, "Regulation of Large Enterprise: The United States Experience in Comparative Perspective," 161–81.

23. In his comparative study of Pittsburgh and Birmingham, England, Peter Shergold noted that married women in the British city were four times as likely to work outside the home as wives in Pittsburgh were. Less than 50 percent of unmarried women under the age of twenty in Pittsburgh were employed as against 89 percent in Birmingham. Shergold, *Working-Class Life: The "American Standard" in Comparative Perspective, 1899–1913* (Pittsburgh, Pa., 1982), 74–76. Michael Katz, *People of Hamilton, Canada West: Family and Class in a Mid-Nineteenth-Century City* (Cambridge, Mass., 1975), 273, noted that only 2 percent of married women with husbands present were employed as against 28 percent in Preston, England. Richard J. Evans noted another striking difference between women in America and women in other countries: "The feminist movement in the United States began earlier than elsewhere; and by the end of the nineteenth century, the Americans' domination of international feminism was unchallenged"; Evans, *The Feminists: Women's Emancipation Movements in Europe, America and Australasia, 1840–1920* (London, 1977), 44.

24. Carl F. Kaestle, "Between the Scylla of Brutal Ignorance and the Charybdis of a Literary Education: Elite Attitudes toward Mass Schooling in Early Industrial England and America," in Lawrence Stone, ed., *Schooling and Society: Studies in the History of Education* (Baltimore, Md., 1976).

25. Morton Keller, "Anglo-American Politics, 1900–1930, in Anglo-American Perspective: A Case Study in Comparative History," *Comparative Studies in Society and History* 22 (July 1980): 458–77; and Melvyn Stokes, "American Progressives and the European Left," *Journal of American Studies* 17 (1983): 3–28. As Ross Evans Paulson's book, *Women's Suffrage and Prohibition: A Comparative Study of Equality and Social Control* (Glenview, Ill., 1973), makes evident, a cross-national study of temperance would give us novel insights into one of the most important aspects of American reform.

26. Fritz Redlich, "Toward a Comparative Historiography, Background and Problems," *Kyklos* 11 (1958): 385–87. As Redlich pointed out, some historians have been so committed to archival work that they "have tended to forget that work in archives is not the purpose of historical research but a means toward the end of describing, explaining, and, as I would add, 'understanding' the historical process"; p. 385.

CHAPTER 6

The Autonomy of American History Reconsidered

LAURENCE VEYSEY

The increasing global awareness of our age enables us to view national differences with a new sophistication. . . . A new, more cosmopolitan approach to the entire American past is marked by the use of broader reference points outside the nation-state, by the constant questioning of American uniqueness even as regards the most traditional and hitherto "sacred" topics, and by a self-conscious hesitation before applying the adjective "American" to anything. This approach emphasizes awareness of relevant occurrences in other societies, no matter what the concrete subject of inquiry, so as to avoid the elementary logical error of ascribing a particular phenomenon to a distinctly American chain of cause and effect when its appearance was not limited to America.

Transatlantic Connections and Similarities

A few examples drawn from familiar topics within American history will help show what this difference in perspectives can mean. Some of these instances may lead us to question American uniqueness altogether; others may instead suggest a more genuine and refined sense of what the national differences were. However, the overall effect of such an exercise will be to diminish the degree to which American history appears to have operated in a vacuum.

It is agreed that evangelical Christianity, moral prudery, and more sharply defined sex roles were interrelated rising tendencies in early nineteenth-century America. But it happens that the same trends appeared strongly in England at the same time.[1] Hence these subjects, of great import in defining central areas of American behavior as well as values or character in a more nebulous sense, turn out not to be exclusively American subjects at all, but Anglo-American. Explanations limited to trends in either particular nation, British or American, will by their nature be deeply suspect, once the total extent of these unfolding social patterns has been grasped. The bare mention of this case reminds us how closely intertwined American and British domestic social history remained (far transcending such an episode as the antislavery movement) in a period often thought of as the crucial heartland of the argument for a unique American character and destiny.

Or consider the subject of how Americans evoked nature—their own virgin land—in the same decades. The point often missed by students of such literature is that early nineteenth-century Americans from Cooper and Thoreau on down saw nature through the lens of romanticism, a novel mode of perception that was of course European in origin. Only an arriving romantic sensibility enabled the "howling wilderness" of the Puritans and the utilitarian forests of Benjamin Franklin (whose first thought on seeing them was to measure how long it took to cut down a tree)[2] to be replaced by the passionately heroic imagery of the Leatherstocking tales or by the organicist contemplations, seasoned by classical allusions, at Walden pond. Americans viewed their own landscape in ways borrowed from an international literary movement, and the true pioneering was done by Rousseau, Goethe, and other members of a European intellectual elite. To be sure, the American environment held peculiarities (such as its natives) that could be seized upon by the imagination, and these are a genuine element in the emerging story. Yet at the most basic level the heroic individualism offered in variant versions by Daniel Boone legends, by images of pioneer farmers, and

From *American Quarterly* 31, no. 4 (Fall 1979): 459–477. © American Studies Association. Reprinted by permission.

by Transcendentalists must all be traced to new ideas that had floated westward across the Atlantic. Without those ideas, the nineteenth-century American landscape would have seemed unrecognizably different.

Again, what are called recurrent populistic tendencies have been looked at from many angles in America, as if they expressed a characteristically native theme. Here the international frame of reference is less clear-cut. Yet, through the investigations of Laurence Wylie and others, we are aware of a deep-seated strain of skeptical suspicion of official authority at the grassroots level in much of France, occasionally erupting to the surface.[3] Again, it is interesting to explore parallels between the American notion of "the people" versus "the interests" and the British working-class concept of "us" and "them."[4] These and other social environments abroad need to be carefully considered before we can ascertain what is specifically American in an attitude of active (or cynical) resentment against elites.

Americans have also been credited with an unusual degree of aloofness or outright hostility toward institutions of all kinds. On the other hand, we know that church attendance has been far higher in America than in most European nations for a very long time, and that individuals will far more readily join neighborhood associations in American suburbia than in similar British surroundings.[5] Does the usual Tocquevillean interpretation of this evidence, distinguishing between voluntary and legally established institutions, form a meaningful explanation of these differences? Then why have Americans been relatively punctilious about their tax returns as compared with Frenchmen? Why was anarchism a smaller movement here than in much of Europe? There are arguments and counterarguments, of course, but they will never be settled without a much more extended look at the attitudes of great numbers of people toward institutions of all kinds in a multinational setting, both for the nineteenth and twentieth centuries.

The same searchlight might be turned on the question of political democracy itself. Here lies the very core of the popular account of American uniqueness, yet from a larger vantage point the movement toward giving every adult human being the vote was the central political tendency throughout the Western world in the period since 1800. When Richard Hofstadter once was asked just what he considered to be unique about American political institutions, with wise caution he replied that mass suffrage arrived here in the 1820s and 1830s as compared with 1867 in England and that popularly based political parties were also first developed in the United States.[6] Yet Hofstadter's statement unthinkingly neglected the denial of the suffrage to a majority of the adult population in England until 1918 and in America until two years later. As for parties, Hofstadter failed to mention the emergence of certain surprisingly modern precursors in the England of the 1780s, not only the following of John Wilkes but also the Yorkshire

Association.[7] Quarrels can go on endlessly over these details, but one wonders whether a few decades' precedence in similar tendencies is enough contrast on which to hang a theory of distinctive national development, when it is set against the record of forces leading everywhere in the same direction.

What about the failure of radicalism in America? Revolutionary Marxism failed in England, France, and the smaller states of Western Europe as well. This basic similarity of outcome has been lost from view in concern for a somewhat higher percentage of Communist voting, in France for example, over the years. But one cannot ignore the question of the nature of French Communism, as it arguably developed into something surprisingly non-revolutionary and establishmentarian. Crucially, in the critical year of 1919, when revolutionary hopes were at their peak throughout the Western world, a decisive majority of Frenchmen as well as Americans reacted with counterrevolutionary alarm, chaining themselves to unimaginatively orthodox political leaders rather than risk their existing property-oriented way of life.[8] We forget that France has not had a successful revolution in over a century, and indeed not since 1848 except in the special context of a military defeat. The difference between a lingering heritage of what Louis Hartz called "feudalism" and its absence in America has been no more than the survival in France of a minority faction, itself composed of persons deeply attached to the bourgeois style of living.

The blunt fact is that socialist agitation everywhere failed to achieve its original goals, while various relatively similar versions of the welfare state were achieved throughout Western Europe, the British Commonwealth, and Japan, as well as in the United States. National variations seem distinctly minor in comparison with that single overall result. Not just Americans, but Englishmen, Australians, and Western Europeans proved decisively loyal to a modified version of the existing social system as the twentieth century advanced, and so-called American exceptionalism has not been as exceptional as all that.[9] Truly militant leftism comprises a tiny minority everywhere within the post-industrial group of nations, though it can become briefly conspicuous, as in 1968, almost anywhere—in France or America alike. Only by emphasizing the milder parliamentary leftism of certain European and Japanese parties can the weakness of the American left be made to stand out as unique.

The closely related subjects of immigration and social mobility deserve attention, as they directly pertain to the legendary "American dream." Scholarly work on mobility has advanced along quantitative lines. The recent studies of Stephan Thernstrom and Thomas Kessner reveal impressively high rates of mobility in major American cities in the late nineteenth and early twentieth centuries, though European mobility rates do not seem as low as they were once pictured, and some questions remain regarding limitations in the data.[10] The argument for American uniqueness as a "land of opportunity" is on still firmer ground if it centers upon the bedrock fact of consistently higher real wages, especially in occupations toward the bottom of the social scale that were filled by white people. In this respect there was indeed a continual contrast in America's favor from colonial times forward, as the result of a real or perceived labor shortage.

Not so clear, when set against this, are the possible later effects of the grandiose mythology of "from rags to riches," operating as an irrational lure in the migrant's mind. Increasingly we question the actual prevalence of such high-flown expectations, and possibly the intensity of the work ethic itself.[11] Perhaps the romanticized verbal expressions of the American dream of success only represented the ideology of some sectors of the nineteenth- and twentieth-century male middle class. There is a growing case for seeing an overwhelming share of the initial movement to America and later movement within city neighborhoods as based upon logical calculations including knowledge of wage rates, employment opportunities, transportation and housing costs, and the availability of kin on the scene to cushion the change. At the bottom layer of the society, these considerations shade off into the more desperate form of movement that randomly seeks bare survival.[12]

Such calculations are set in motion by the basic belief in the possibility of improving one's life-chances through a change in location. And this has been the most general trend throughout the industrializing world. A belief of this kind, which is a component even in moves described as sheer necessity, appears to have impelled Englishmen to move into the new factory towns during the industrial revolution.[13] Alien immigrants, moreover, became a standard part of the English scene in those early days of factory production. In Manchester by the early 1840s, some 24 percent of the entire city population was Irish, and the Irish there were subject to the same intensity of scornful dislike as in the Eastern seaboard cities of the United States.[14] Though the volume and diversity of this migration into England does not compare with the American at so early a time, clearly the contrast is less absolute than it has often been pictured.

Again, the sheer degree of physical or geographical mobility within the United States has been one of the most astonishing discoveries of recent social historians. Yet European nations have not had such locally fixed populations as was long believed.[15] Behind the architectural facade of a "traditional" and picturesque Southern French village, for example, lies the reality of a high degree of in- and out-migration of people, starting in the late nineteenth century.[16] The degree of American peculiarity in this respect must be defined with greater care.

One does not want to simplify the explanatory account of migration unduly, whether it is within or between countries, and objective economic appraisals hardly explain all decisions to move or to stay put. For certain groups, especially the Jews, the factor of religious persecution, and of

America as a nation peculiarly mild in its expression of it, was very real. But the lure of the city, whether in Europe or America, and of a change of neighborhoods within cities later on, seems for most people to have been the lure of one concretely envisioned step upward.[17] The reading of a novel such as Emile Zola's *L'Assommoir* in conjunction with such American novels as William Dean Howells' *A Modern Instance* or Frank Norris' *McTeague* can raise anew the question of certain basic similarities in the lives led by newly arrived rural folk in large city neighborhoods, whether in Paris, Boston, or San Francisco at the end of the nineteenth century.

At the level of the mythology itself, though we have had several penetrating studies of American "success" literature considered in isolation, more attention could be paid to the impact of such a writer as Samuel Smiles in conjunction with the rise of a similar thrift ethic among British workers in the 1850s and 1860s.[18] In all this increasingly careful examination of life patterns, beliefs, and motives, room remains for an appreciation of American differences, especially centering on higher real wages and somewhat higher social mobility, but the added context clarifies their nature and reduces them to proper scale.

As a final thematic example of the use of international reference points in the reconstruction of American history, one might consider the topic of nationalism and imperialism. Here also the similarities between American and European state histories have gained increasing attention.[19] Is the imperial dream so very different when it is pursued in contiguous territory rather than overseas? From the natives' point of view, the American policy of equal citizenship in the states formed by expansion or conquest merely fastened alien rule upon them all the more vigorously—nor were Indians soon given full citizenship rights. Was the pseudo-idealism that attended our territorial outreach of a genuinely different caliber than French dreams of spreading their "civilization," as it was called, in Africa and Asia? To what extent were we directly imitating European models of imperialism in the 1890s? In this area there are again counterarguments, but the internationalization of the discussion creates the very dialogue that allows possible genuine American peculiarities to come into focus. A cross-national exploration of such attitudes may lead us to the insight that a national sense of mission and destiny paradoxically forms one of the great common qualities of the major nations in the modern world—indeed, that intense popular nationalism, stressing claims to superior collective virtue of some kind, is one key attribute of any modern society, frequently finding an echo in its historians' interpretations.

Divergence and Convergence with Europe

Here, then, are some major instances of topics that might profitably be explored in a less traditional light. Beyond them, however, lies the deeper concern over how one should now conceptualize the entire course of American history as it unfolds chronologically, in relation to the trend of the other industrializing nations. For the early colonial period, the central issue is whether, as it has been phrased, we were "born modern."[20] That is, did American society begin on a basis already very much unlike that of Western Europe? This is the kind of question that Frederick Jackson Turner appeared to have confidently answered long ago, and it is also a broader version of the question of consequences stemming from the absence of "feudalism" in America, posed in the 1950s by Louis Hartz.[21] Certainly the conventional view of American distinctiveness required us to have been unique almost from the very beginning. But then was American uniqueness heightened or dampened during the course of the eighteenth century—both as regards the trend of the society in the decades just before the Revolution, and as a result of the Revolution and Constitution? How was the picture affected by the supposedly greater isolation of America from Europe in the nineteenth century? Did this isolation actually intensify after 1815 in any sense beyond that of mere political caution? Did the United States drift further apart from Europe as a result of its own internal westward movement? With the coming of the industrial revolution a whole new range of questions appears. Industrialization is now often regarded as the single most fateful event of recent human history. America was the second major nation to industrialize—after England and ahead of Germany. Is there anything in this timetable, or in the way in which industrialization proceeded here, which would add to a sense of American distinctiveness? Finally, according to what processes did America come more closely to resemble other nations as we move into the twentieth century, with its global wars and rapid communications?

In brief space it is possible only to sketch some major aspects of an argument that would address itself to this theme, and to take note from time to time of a few of the complexities of interpretation.

Insights into the earliest divergences between European and American society have appeared in recent writings of social historians. An initial abundance of land in America had numerous effects, only some of which Turner recognized. Because people spread out on the land, they lived farther apart from each other than in Europe, and this meant a gain in life expectancy, as they were somewhat insulated from epidemics. Available land made for an initial social structure far more egalitarian (among white males). Sheer distance from England meant that all sorts of burdensome institutions were not transported over here, or, if they were, like the Anglican church in Virginia, they took on untraditional meanings.[22] Ironically, these structural differences were at their greatest in the very same period, immediately after the foundings of colonies, when the settlers had had the least time to evolve distinctive ways of thinking.[23]

From a point of view that emphasizes demography and social stratification, the very fact of denser development within a limited Eastern seaboard terrain over the course of the eighteenth century meant that colonial American society grew in some respects once again to be more like the European. Land was parceled out, until by midcentury a flow of younger sons toward the frontier was under way, leaving older communities stranded in a state of incipient decline. Greater population density in them had already moved disease rates up toward European levels, thereby curtailing the biggest single advantage of living in America—a longer span of life.[24] Meanwhile, American society was becoming more unequal. Every quantitative study of wealth distribution shows a growing inequality as one moves forward in time and especially as one moves from the rural areas to the more dynamic towns.[25] The well-to-do colonial elite dramatized this tendency by directly imitating the styles and customs of the English gentry, thereby emphasizing a gulf between rich and poor. By the time of the American Revolution, Richard D. Brown argues, America was fast losing its earlier distinctiveness.

Was America then growing toward England, rather than away from it? A seemingly rival interpretation points to the emergence of an American cultural consciousness in this same period, culminating quite naturally (if only after some prodding by events) in political independence. Yet, from a cosmopolitan perspective, this may not after all be so inconsistent. For the sense of an American identity meant paradoxically that in still another respect America could be like Great Britain. That is, it could attain the dignity that went with national status.[26]

The arrival of nationalism on a popular level is usually associated with Napoleonic Europe. Erratic British policies may have brought about its birth in America at a slightly earlier time—prematurely, so to speak. For a long time after the 1770s it flickered somewhat fitfully, only barely surviving during the Articles of Confederation. Not until the 1820s did it take all but universal root in the truly modern fashion. By then it was a rising force in Europe as well. The fateful propensity of the ordinary man to identify himself with the nation-state occurred at nearly the same historical moment on both sides of the Atlantic. What was important about the beginnings of American nationalism was not so much that it was American as that it was nationalistic. Americans, like Europeans, had adopted the primary religion of the soon-to-be industrial world.[27]

In other respects, as we move forward into the early nineteenth century and westward across the Appalachians, it may become necessary to concede more to traditional arguments about American distinctiveness. The extremely rapid push into the wilderness brought a temporary return to some of the same conditions that had initially marked the Atlantic seaboard—above all, a staggering abundance of land (needing only to be cleared of troublesome natives). A thin spreading out once again created more equalitarian daily circumstances even if land titles this time fell in large share to advantaged speculators. A national ethos of republicanism (born in the improvisational heat of the Revolution, while looking back to the memory of the far earlier English Commonwealth) now gave ideological sanction to impulses that were somewhat leveling.[28]

A society with these values that is engaged in the rapid occupation of enormous tracts of land will no doubt possess important characteristics that set it sharply apart from all long-settled societies, whether agrarian or industrial, even if (as earlier seen) it borrowed its vision of itself from European romanticism. In this sense Turner was right.[29] And there remains in some major respects an argument for the exceptional character of American life in those times and places where such factors have been present—mainly in the seventeenth and again in the early nineteenth centuries. But, of the total number of Americans who have ever lived, very few of them breathed under such pure frontier conditions. No less startling than the rapidity of the westward push was the quick trend toward urbanization, even in the western regions themselves.[30] And again, as in the eighteenth century, greater population density—now accompanied by technological improvements sweeping Europe and America, and by the beginnings of industrialization—turned the society in directions that would make its differences with other dynamic societies increasingly ephemeral.[31] This time there would be no turning back.

The most characteristic experience of modern people is to live inside dense, large-scale communities, whether these are towns, cities, or their suburbs. The cultural historian who is bent on squeezing atmospheric symptoms of uniqueness out of particular national environments in this primarily urban world must at least recognize that the total context in which such subtle embellishments can be made has been set everywhere in these fundamentally given terms, and that these terms furnish an enormous contrast with the experience of most peoples (including Americans) in all earlier centuries. Diversities abound, of course, within cities. But the most important sources of variation—between rich and poor, white and black, men and women—do not usually lend themselves to analysis along neatly national lines. We go on studying such topics as the working class within particular countries because the customary forms of graduate education channel us in nationally defined directions, but it is the intrinsic state of being poor, female, or socially excluded (in the context of an urban cash economy) that primarily serves to excite our attention. The backdrop of similarity concerning life circumstances and aspirations among ordinary people within a great number of modern nations must not be lost from sight in the continued pursuit of finer distinctions. . . .

Marxism, Modernization Theory, and the Post-Industrial World

If the older concept of distinct, autonomous national cultures surviving in the modern period deserves critical scrutiny, the attempt to define a suitable alternative conceptual framework immediately lands us in a snake's nest of contending partisanships. It is far easier to urge that traditional programs in American history or American Studies are obsolete than to specify what should replace them. I have put forth the view that the natural unit of study comprehends the industrialized, non-socialist nations. But such an avoidance of provincialism is only a beginning. What, in the way of substantive guiding conceptualizations, should infuse such study?

In fact, several well-marked traditions of inquiry beckon us, seeking to make us converts. Marxism, internally divided as never before, tries at bottom to promote our sympathy for oppressed groups within these societies and our estrangement from the thought processes of their decision-makers. Most of all at present, in the writings for instance of Immanuel Wallerstein,[32] it attempts to imbue the entire Western intelligentsia with a sense of guilt over the dealings, past and present, of industrial nations with the rest of the globe. National differences are assessed primarily in terms of commercial patterns, and those nations which are "core" rather than "peripheral,'" in Wallerstein's vocabulary, are those which eventually comprise very much the same group as I have envisioned forming a natural collective unity for analysis in the modern period.

An alternative perspective that likewise focuses upon economic development is the now familiar theory of modernization, developed by Walt W. Rostow and others in an explicitly anti-Marxist spirit.[33] Unfortunately, the polemics of advocacy—that is, a defense of capitalist industrial development—infused the notion of modernization from the very first. It thus became difficult to argue both that the concept of modernization might have value as a major tool for historical analysis and that one might not entirely like the fruits of capitalist industrialism. The concept has also been plagued by troubles of another sort, purely on the analytical level. It seems notoriously hard to define just what it means. And historians have not always been able to pinpoint economic "take-offs" with precision. For these reasons the concept has come under an increasing cloud. . . . Yet to abandon it would be a grave mistake if it meant lapsing back toward the routine nationalism of earlier scholarship in such fields as American history. Modernization theory has been important, at least historically, in helping to pry us loose from the crushing provincialism of the early Cold War period—an effect that Rostow may not have intended. . . .

I am impressed by the major points of agreement between modernization theorists and many Marxists, despite their intense mutual hostility. They agree—aside, oddly enough, from Wallerstein—in seeing the arrival of industrialism as the key turning-point in the history of mankind, the creator of the kinds of cities, landscapes, and patterns of human interaction which we experience today. From both traditions we obtain our sense of the fundamental break in human history that occurred during the nineteenth century. And as for the substantive definition of what distinguishes the modern period, when taken together the factory, the impersonal, meritocratic bureaucracy, and technology that permits rapid travel over distances would seem to be the essential components. For cities had always existed, although their size and character greatly changed with the coming of the electric streetcar and the automobile.

Modernization theory rather than Marxism directs our attention to the recent arrival of a post-industrial stage, marked by widespread affluence, a shortening of the workweek, and an emphasis in most people's lives upon consumerism and leisure. In America this stage may have begun as early as the 1920s; in Europe it arrived in the 1950s. The shift from industrialism to post-industrialism is surely less profound than the break that occurred at the outset of industrialism, yet it is real enough to have altered the grounds on which such societies are both attacked and defended. In the early industrial period, the attack focused upon the flagrancy of human misery and the defense upon laissez-faire individualism. Now the attack is made upon the psychological consequences of monotony in work and of media-fed leisure, and upon discrimination against minorities rather than the earlier majority, while the defense points to what might be called the flagrancy of affluence and the survival of considerable liberty, especially in comparison with other sections of the world. But the proper term to describe this latest, inescapably real social stage has not yet been coined. Post-industrial is ungainly. Along with deeper analysis of its nature, as a topic in recent history rather than in futurology, should come a better label for it.

The post-industrial world, though it has a clear identity, is by no means entirely a monolith. My argument is that until lately, we have too greatly ignored its transnational similarities. . . . [A]mid the continued exploration of differences, it should not be lost from sight that the texture of life as it affects most industrialized peoples becomes increasingly uniform. The division of daily and weekly existence into separate spheres of work and leisure, each now almost equally important, the bureaucratized and rationalized content of the former, the travel- and gadget-oriented content of the latter, seem strikingly similar in the various developed nations. Large-scale organizations play the major role in economic life, whether nominally they are termed public or private. Yet in the non-work realm, the individual gains certain private choices through somewhat wider moral tolerance as well as such practices as birth control. Attitudes—at least as revealed in the quantitative cross-national studies we have—do not become utterly identical. But neither are they as dissimilar as stereotypes would often propose.[34]

On the cultural side, to ignore these trends and to continue dwelling instead upon contrasts between England and America, or between Los Angeles and San Francisco, as ritualistically conjured wholes increasingly comes to seem like a merely pleasant diversion, a conversational resource among the advantaged. It is not only to fly in the face of all the evidence concerning basic life-patterns and the spread everywhere of hedonistic values, but to obscure (by inattention) the glaring differences, for instance of income, which indeed remain. The very fact that climate now becomes an important consideration to many people in evaluating differences among cities, leading to the growth of the so-called sun belt in America (and to British workers' annual vacations in Spain) reveals a post-industrial level of expectation from life which has its roots in these spreading uniformities of attitude. (Nineteenth-century British novels do not complain about the amount of rain.) Yet economic disparities still prevent large numbers of Americans or Europeans from enjoying the newly prized rewards of escape from grayness.

Devaluing American "Firstness" and Uniqueness

In taking the path that has brought us where we are, the United States sometimes led the way. It often set the pace and other nations, originally less affluent on a mass level, followed a bit later on. But if the forms of change, and the hungers they seem to satisfy, turn out to be so similar, then why should it matter all that much which particular segment of the industrially developed world happened to display them first? Moreover, the United States was by no means always first in important phases of these developments. We were not the first country to industrialize; we did not go as far as Germany in the direction of corporate monopolies; we were not the first country to achieve a comprehensive welfare state (indeed we have not done this even now); we were not the first major country to give women the vote; we were not the first to build subway lines under cities.

We were the first to build skyscrapers, the first possibly to have recognizably modern political parties, and so on. And yet this record is very mixed, and one wonders, anyhow, just what could seem alluring about basing an historical account on "firstness" of this sort. The kind of a race we have all been in, not the relative standing of the competitors, should matter to us most, as historians or as students of contemporary society. Especially is this so when the lag between first and last nation (within this group) seems to amount usually to no more than half a century, while the common course of development—the race itself—poses grave dangers for the ecological survival of the planet.

We are now witnesses to the late twentieth-century

outcome of the industrial process, and it is our most important task to try to understand this outcome and the ways in which it came about. American uniqueness in certain respects during relatively brief periods of the increasingly remote past no longer matters much except as a curiosity. It has long since largely been swallowed up in the common processes of industrialization, large-scale urbanization and suburbanization, and the frequent movements of peoples across national borders (as job-seekers or as tourists), which produce the characteristic patterns of life in the twentieth-century world.

The real trend of American history—no less so for usually being unacknowledged—is toward a loss of whatever distinctiveness the society once possessed. It is a trend that gives scant comfort either to mainstream nationalists or to leftists (who commonly have their own strongly held alternative ideal "America," replete with its sense of an influential mission to perform in the world).[35] But for over a hundred years, and in some respects for much longer, the merger of America into a common pattern of modern life has been the great underlying tendency.

David Potter, after years of reflection on the subject, warned that "the close relation between nationalism and the political state warps the historian's view" in certain ways, among them that the evaluative use of the concept of nationalism "impels him to explain the origins of nationalism in terms of deep-seated, long-enduring cultural affinities among a people, or in other words to rely too heavily upon cultural factors in his explanation, even where they are tenuous."[36] One might go a step further and ask whether the study of any particular society—and its diverse internal components—can advance any longer except in the context of studying other closely related societies. . . . To make sense of America may require the act of reaching at least some distance beyond it.

Notes

An earlier version of this essay was written while the author held a Senior Fellowship from the National Endowment for the Humanities and was concurrently a fellow of the Charles Warren Center at Harvard University. The author greatly benefited from the advice (often strongly critical) given various versions by James M. Banner, Jr., Carl Degler, David Hackett Fischer, Jack P. Greene, David D. Hall, Hugh Hawkins, John Higham, David Hollinger, H. Stuart Hughes, William R. Hutchison, Carl Kaestle, Paul Koistinen, Henry F. May, David Riesman, and Robert Wells.

1. Concerning the intensification of sex roles for middle-class women, the British and American trend seems so chronologically similar as to becloud the interpretation that it stemmed directly from the industrial revolution, for the latter occurred so much later in America. See Nancy F. Cott, *The Bonds of Womanhood: Woman's Sphere in New England, 1780–1835* (New Haven: Yale Univ. Press, 1977), and the argument (uninformed by an American comparison) in Harold Perkin, *The Origins of Modern English Society. 1780–1880* (London: Routledge and Kegan Paul, 1969), 157–60.

2. John Bigelow, ed., *The Autobiography of Benjamin Franklin* (New York: G.P. Putnam's Sons, 1909), 283.

3. Laurence Wylie, *Village in the Vaucluse* (Cambridge: Harvard Univ. Press, 1957); and "Social Change at the Grass Roots," in Stanley Hoffman et al., *In Search of France* (Cambridge: Harvard Univ. Press, 1963), 159–234. Wylie himself tries to emphasize contrasts between American and French realities, yet in revisiting France more recently he is reluctantly much impressed by evidences of convergence. "The New French Village, Hélas," *The New York Times Magazine,* Nov. 25, 1973, pp. 63ff.

4. E.g., see Richard Hoggart, *The Uses of Literacy* (New York: Oxford Univ. Press, 1970), 62–63, 71–72, 87. Hoggart (p. 99) also develops a case for the pragmatism of the British working class. The American idea of "the interests" no doubt carried more of a tone of geographical remoteness than the British idea of "them."

5. Howard Edwin Bracey, *Neighbors: Subdivison Life in England and the United States* (Baton Rouge: Louisiana State Univ. Press, 1964). Yet a middle-class observer like Bracey ignores the traditional vogue of voluntary institutions such as the workingmen's clubs and brass bands, widespread through the north of England. See Brian Jackson, *Working Class Community* (New York: Praeger, 1968), 21–68.

6. John A. Garraty, *Interpreting American History: Conversations with Historians* (New York: Macmillan, 1970), 1: 160.

7. E.g., see Ian R. Christie, "The Yorkshire Association, 1780–84: A Study in Political Organization," *The Historical Journal,* 3 (1960), 144–61.

8. Robert Wohl, *French Communism in the Making, 1914–1924* (Stanford: Stanford Univ. Press, 1966), 121, 150.

9. The issue of the nationalization of basic industry, in England as well as France, is of course more divisive than in the United States. But the experience of Britain since 1945 shows such nationalization to have little effect either upon international political alignments or the daily lives of most people. . . .

10. See Stephan Thernstrom, *The Other Bostonians* (Cambridge: Harvard Univ. Press, 1973), 258–60; Thomas Kessner, *The Golden Door* (New York: Oxford Univ. Press, 1977). Older studies emphasized similarities among social mobility rates in industrial countries: e.g., Seymour Martin Lipset and Reinhard Bendix, *Social Mobility in Industrial Society* (Berkeley: Univ. of California Press, 1959); S.M. Miller, "Comparative Social Mobility," *Current Sociology,* 9 (1960), 1–89; Kaare Svalastoga, "Social Mobility: The Western European Model," *Acta Sociologica,* 9 (1965), Fas. 1–2, 175–82; and Alan C. Kerekhoff, "Stratification Processes and Outcomes in England and the United States," *American Sociological Review,* 39 (1974), 789–801. . . . The figures for the United States in Thernstrom do not place America in a range beyond Miller's data for France. There is, however, a running criticism of "grand comparative exercises" in this vein: e.g., see G. Payne, G. Ford, and C. Robertson, "A Reappraisal of Social Mobility in Britain," *Sociology* (London), 11 (1977), 299.

11. E.g., see David Brody, *Steelworkers in America* (Cambridge: Harvard Univ. Press, 1960), 99; Herbert G. Gutman, "Work, Culture and Society in Industrializing America, 1815–1919," *American Historical Review,* 78 (1973), 531–88.

12. Stephan Thernstrom and Peter R. Knights, "Men in Motion," in Tamara K. Hareven, ed. *Anonymous Americans* (Englewood Cliffs, N.J.: Prentice-Hall, 1971), 17–47.

13. E.g., see Phyllis Deane, *The First Industrial Revolution* (Cambridge, England: Cambridge Univ. Press, 1965), 145–46.

14. Asa Briggs, *Victorian Cities* (New York: Harper and Row, 1963), 85, 130; Friedrich Engels, *The Condition of the Working Class in England* (Stanford: Stanford Univ. Press, 1958), 27, 80, 104–7. Engels' estimate of the share of the Irish in the Manchester population at that time is still higher.

15. Concerning England in this respect, see E.A. Wrigley, ed., *An Introduction to English Historical Demography* (New York: Basic Books, 1966), 17–18, 21–22; R. K. Kelsall, *Population* (London: Longmans, 1967), 41–46.

16. Wylie, *Village in the Vaucluse,* 19–24.

17. E.g., see Sam B. Warner, Jr., *Streetcar Suburbs* (Cambridge: Harvard Univ. Press, 1962).

18. Samuel Smiles, *Self-Help: With Illustrations of Character and Conduct* (London: John Murray, 1859); Aileen Smiles, *Samuel Smiles and His Surroundings* (London: Robert Hale, 1956), 88–90. See Asa Briggs, *The Age of Improvement, 1783–1867* (New York: David McKay, 1959), 440, 451.

19. See in particular Ernest R. May, *American Imperialism: A Speculative Essay* (New York: Atheneum, 1968).

20. E.g., (for the claim), see Edward Shorter, *The Making of the Modern Family* (New York: Basic Books, 1975), 14.

21. Louis Hartz, *The Liberal Tradition in America* (New York: Harcourt, Brace, and World, 1955).

22. These points emerge in Richard D. Brown, *Modernization: The Transformation of American Life, 1600–1865* (New York: Hill and Wang, 1977), and (on disease) in James A. Henretta, *The Evolution of American Society, 1700–1815* (Lexington, Mass.: D.C. Heath, 1973).

23. So far as the rise of individualistic attitudes is concerned, a recent brilliant essay by Michael Zuckerman, "The Fabrication of Identity in Early America," *William and Mary Quarterly,* 34 (1977), 183–214, places the crucial turning point back in English history before colonization. Much argument remains, however, about the pace of its further intensification both in England and America.

24. On these points see, e.g., Philip Greven, *Four Generations: Population, Land and Family in Colonial Andover, Massachusetts* (Ithaca: Cornell Univ. Press, 1970), 175–258; Richard L. Bushman, *From Puritan to Yankee* (Cambridge: Harvard Univ. Press, 1967), 257; Henretta, *Evolution of American Society,* 15. For the situation in eastern Pennsylvania, only somewhat less extreme than in New England, see James T. Lemon, *The Best Poor Man's Country* (New York: Norton, 1972), 83–97.

25. Jackson Turner Main, *The Social Structure of Revolutionary America* (Princeton: Princeton Univ. Press, 1965), 286; Henretta, 103–6.

26. In India, members of the native elite were similarly to imitate British upper-class styles, forging an Indian nationalist identity modeled in many central respects on European lines.

27. To be sure, American nationalism was non-monarchical, but so by this time was at least one version of the French.

28. It is important, however, to understand the limits of American "democratic" tendencies in the early nineteenth century, and their only partial relation to what may be unique American characteristics. Much of their import centered upon acquisitiveness toward property. As an idea, laissez-faire philosophy gained ground rapidly in England as well as in the United States during the same period. Genuinely unique to America, in all likelihood, was the expectation of the ordinary farmer that he could hope to obtain expansive rewards in such a landscape. . . . [Yet] at the very top of the social structure in this period, Edward Pessen has documented the existence of a continuous elite of established wealth, surprisingly "European" in character and socially isolated from everyone else. See Edward Pessen, *Riches, Class and Power Before the Civil War* (Lexington, Mass.: D.C. Heath, 1973).

29. The use of Siberia and Spanish America as counterexamples to discredit this insight about the nature of frontiers disregards the differences between zones of light versus extremely heavy inflow of population. But it would be wrong to downplay the memory of the earlier colonial experience and the sanction of the republican ideology, both of them leading to the farmer's belief that it was his "right" to own increasingly large tracts of land, in producing the cultural style of the West. French peasants were also tenacious landowners, but without the scale of appetite whetted by the frontier.

30. See Richard C. Wade, *The Urban Frontier* (Cambridge: Harvard Univ. Press, 1959).

31. I am not persuaded that evidence concerning a mad social scramble, or the boorishness and naive pretension of the newly rich in American cities of the early nineteenth century, . . . indicates distinctively American traits. In traditional interpretations, such evidence has usually been linked to a view of total fluidity in the upper reaches of the society, such as Pessen has now refuted. A similar sector marked by an intense striving for position, along with a rapid learning of manners, may well have existed in many countries in this and other periods, occupying a niche just below the quieter established wealth.

32. Immanuel Wallerstein, *The Modern World System* (New York: Academic Press, 1974).

33. W.W. Rostow, *The Stages of Economic Growth* (Cambridge, England: Cambridge Univ. Press, 1960). For a thoughtful, up-to-date discussion of the concept of modernization, see Brown, *Modernization,* chap. 1.

34. Quantitative cross-national studies of attitudes and of revealing items in personal behavior emerged in large numbers in the early 1960s, culminating in such volumes as Richard L. Merritt and Stein Rokkan, eds., *Comparing Nations: The Use of Quantitative Data in Cross-National Research* (New Haven: Yale Univ. Press, 1966), and Alexander Szalai, ed., *The Use of Time: Daily Activities of Urban and Suburban Populations in Twelve Countries* (The Hague: Mouton, 1972), where sex-role differences emerged as more important than national differences. . . .

35. E.g., see William Appleman Williams, *The Tragedy of American Diplomacy* (Cleveland: World, 1959), 212.

36. David Potter, "The Historian's Use of Nationalism and Vice Versa," in *History and Society: Essays of David M. Potter* (New York: Oxford University Press, 1973), 84–85. This essay first appeared in 1962.

CHAPTER 7

No Borders
Beyond the Nation-State

THOMAS BENDER

I want to propose the end of American history as we have known it. "End" can mean both "purpose" and "termination," and I have in mind both those meanings. I want to draw attention to the end to which national histories, including American history, have been put. They are taught in schools and brought into public discourse to forge and sustain national identities, presenting the self-contained nation as the natural carrier of history. That way of writing and teaching history has exhausted itself. In its place, I want to elaborate a new framing for U.S. history, one that rejects the territorial space of the nation as a sufficient context and argues for the transnational nature of national histories.

The nation is not free-standing and self-contained; it is connected with and partially shaped by what is beyond it. Nineteenth-century nationalist ideology, which became embedded in the development of history as a discipline, has obscured the actual experience of national societies and has produced a narrow parochialism. I want to encourage a more cosmopolitan sense of being an American, to have us recognize the historical interconnections that have made America's history global history even as it is national, provincial even as it shares in the general history of human beings on this planet.

National histories, like nation-states, are modern developments. The first national history of the United States, David Ramsay's *History of the American Revolution,* was published in 1789. In fact, Ramsay held off publishing it until the Constitution was ratified. History—and especially history in the schools—contributed mightily to the acceptance of the nation during the next two centuries. It became the core of civic education in schools and other institutions devoted to making peasants, immigrants, and provincial peoples into national citizens. That category of citizen was supposed to trump all other sources of identity. Regional, linguistic, ethnic, class, religious, and other forms of solidarity or connection that were either smaller or larger were to be radically subordinated to national identity. To sustain the idea of a national citizen, the national space was to be firmly bounded, and population and culture were presumed to be homogeneous. In return, the modern nation-state promised to protect its citizens at home and abroad. One artifact that marks both the importance of borders and the promise of protection is the passport—a 19th-century innovation.

If this concept of the nation is specific to the past two centuries, still we are so comfortable with it as to refer routinely to events that occurred a thousand years ago within the present borders of France, for example, as "medieval French history." In this age of talk about globalization, multiculturalism, and diasporas, clearly our experience does not match up to such nationalist assumptions. Life is simply more complex.

In the past few years, some of the most innovative and exciting scholarship in American history has been framed in ways that do not necessarily tie it to the nation-state—work on gender, migrations, diasporas, class, race, ethnicity, and other areas of social history. If that scholarship has not succumbed to the nationalist framing, neither has it altered nor displaced it. It has grown up beside the older default narrative that we all carry around in our heads. It has brought forward new knowledge about previously unstudied or insufficiently recognized groups and themes

From *The Chronicle of Higher Education* (*Chronicle Review* section) 52, no. 31 (April 7, 2006): B6. Adapted from *A Nation Among Nations: America's Place in World History,* published by Hill and Wang, a division of Farrar, Straus and Giroux. Copyright © 2006 by Thomas Bender. Reprinted by permission.

in American history, but it has not changed the dominant narrative structure. The unitary logic of national history seems to have kept at bay new scholarship that could be transformative. Too often, new scholarship is bracketed (literally so in textbooks) rather than integrated. Much is added, but the basic narrative stays the same. That is why textbooks get longer and longer, more and more ungainly, and less and less readable.

About a decade ago, I began to think more seriously and quite differently about the way American history has been written, to say nothing about the way I was teaching it. What concerned me was not the then much-contested question of the politics of history, at least not in the narrow sense of supporting or opposing this or that side in the so-called culture wars. Nor was it about favoring liberal or conservative interpretations, for on the issue that concerned me there was no difference. The problem was more fundamental and methodological: it seemed to me that the default narrative limited my capacity to understand the central themes of American history. What were the true boundaries of America's national experience? What history did the United States share with other nations? How would the use of a wider context change the core American narrative?

Recent changes in the school history curriculum highlight the problem of teaching American history as a self-contained story. In the interest of better preparing our youth for citizenship in a multicultural nation in a globalized world, most states now require schools to offer world-history courses. That appears to be an effective curricular change, but in practice the new curriculum subverts the good intentions that prompted it. Most world-history courses do not include American history. Somehow the world is everything but us. America's interconnections and interdependencies beyond its borders are rarely captured, and the revised curriculum reinforces the split between America and the world that contemporary citizenship must overcome.

Strangely enough, many scholars who study foreign nations and regions—area-studies specialists—have shared and reinforced the approach that puts the United States and the rest of the world in two different boxes. American-studies and area-studies programs developed at the same time in American universities, but until very recently they did not acknowledge that each was an interacting part of the same global history.

I want to make two nested arguments. The first is that a common global history commenced when American history began, in the decades before and after 1500. The second follows directly from the first: American history cannot be adequately understood unless it is incorporated into that global context. It then becomes a different kind of history, with more explanatory power. It reconnects history with geography. It incorporates causal influences that work across space as well as those that unfold over time. It enriches our understanding of the historical making and remaking of the United States. It is, moreover, the only way to map and appraise the changing position and interdependencies that connect the United States today to the other provinces of the world.

The American nation-building project has been unusually successful. But the history of that success cannot and ought not be used to sustain a claim of historical exceptionalism or of categorical difference. Whatever the distinctive position of the United States today, it remains nonetheless only one global province interconnected with and interdependent with every other one. The history of the United States is but one history among histories.

At the same time—despite the clamor of debate about multiculturalism and globalization that has encouraged talk of the decline of the nation-state and the possibility of a postnational history—I do not believe the nation is likely to soon disappear. True, nation-states have done terrible damage to the human community, but they are also the only enforcer available to protect human and citizen rights. The nation must remain a central object of historical inquiry so long as we understand history to include both the analysis of power in society and the clarification of ethical responsibility within the human community. My purpose is not to dismiss national history but to propose a different mode for it, one that better respects the empirical record and better serves us as citizens of the nation and the world.

The story I want to tell begins around 1500, when oceanic seafaring for the first time connected all the continents and created a common history of all peoples. The beginning of American history was part of the event that made global history. This perspective redefines the "New World." It was not "America," which did not exist. Nor was it the European discovery of the Western Hemisphere. Rather the ocean was discovered to be a connector of the continents and a common carrier of peoples, money, things, and knowledge. The result was a "new world" for the peoples of every continent, and the American "founding" was embedded in the resulting global economy. There were two sequential dimensions to that base economy, and both depended upon global networks. The gold and silver that enriched the Spanish empire and invited further exploration and settlement was dependent upon an Asian market, hence the founding of Manila in 1571. North America depended upon the "plantation complex," which in turn exploited enslaved Africans. Its cash crops—mildly addictive drugs and sugar—required oceanic trade, since they lacked nutritional value and thus could not contribute to a local subsistence economy. Emergent capitalism and slavery (and the connection between them), not a band of Pilgrims, mark the American beginnings. This perspective also partially displaces the founding as a European event. In fact, before 1800 more Africans than Europeans made the Atlantic transit.

While the movement of Europeans to the Western Hemisphere vastly extended European civilization, the new global interactions produced a demographic catastrophe among the indigenous people of the Americas and in Africa, with devastating and long-term consequences in both places. Thus, while the American founding was not without the oft-rehearsed aspirations for religious freedom and to extend Christianity, utopian ideals, and the ambition for economic opportunity, it was also a story of death, slavery, exploitation, and the construction of racial identities.

Taking a cue from a comment made by James Madison at the Constitutional Convention, my framework extends the chronology and geography of the American Revolution, placing it in the context of the competition among the great 18th-century empires and, especially, the "Great War," the global conflict between England and France that lasted from 1689 to 1815. The American Revolution was an episode in that war, and French resentment over Britain's overwhelming victory in the Seven Years' War that preceded it brought an absolute monarchy into alliance with the republicans across the Atlantic. Like the Seven Years' War, the War for American Independence was a global war; the French, who had no specific North American objectives save for weakening Great Britain, hoped to regain trading posts in Africa and India that they had lost in the previous war.

Developments outside the territorial United States were not only decisive in the American victory against Great Britain, but in the development of the new nation. The emergence of political parties, something not envisioned in the Constitutional Convention, was largely the product of American division over the post-1789 conflict between France and Britain. The fall of the Bastille, which occurred four months after Washington's inauguration, and the Haitian Revolution of 1791 had profound consequences in shaping political conflict during the first four American presidencies. When the world war ended, internal conflict in the United States ended, economic development accelerated, settlers moved west in rapidly increasing numbers, and a new nationalism emerged, marking the completion, finally, of the long quest for actual independence. The war that made independence possible needed to end before independence became real.

Although the Civil War is the moral core of American history, it was nonetheless part of the larger history of the invention of the modern nation-state. The immediate context was the European revolutions of 1848. Lincoln watched and admired the European liberals who were forging a link between nation and freedom. He also absorbed their redefinition of the meaning of national territory, demanding homogeneity within the territorial borders. That new understanding of nation transformed the political meaning of slavery and established the logic of Lincoln's famous "House Divided" speech. The house had always been divided, and maintaining political stability had been a matter of negotiating compromises. By the 1850s, however, a nation had to be all one or the other. I do not think we can quite recognize the passions of Lincoln, as well as of ordinary soldiers, without taking account of the ideals of 1848 and the novel understanding of the nation then in circulation around the globe. That framing also provides an essential context for understanding the road to reunion that achieved national solidarity at the cost of removing American Indians and denying African-Americans rights. The link between nationalism and freedom was broken, as Americans embraced a conservative nationalism—partly sustained by academic and judicial theorists who were influenced by German concepts of the state—that weakened rights claims.

For European liberals, including John Stuart Mill, Giuseppe Mazzini, and Giuseppe Garibaldi, the American Civil War was a central episode in the history of liberal reform. New understandings of nation, freedom, and national territory were played out on every continent. The crisis of union in the United States was part of a larger "federative crisis" in which nations, from Argentina to Japan, from Germany to Siam, from the Russian and Ottoman Empires to the Hapsburg, were participants. All were recalibrating the relations between national and local authority. In most cases, wars were part of the story. So was emancipation. While the United States emancipated four million slaves, another 40 million serfs were freed in this era. Nation-making was a global phenomenon with distinctive local results.

Most Americans hesitate to acknowledge the centrality of empire in their history, let alone to see that the American empire was one among many. The imperial adventure of 1898 was not, as is often argued, an accidental and unthinking act; empire had been on the national agenda for decades. There is a striking continuity in purpose and style from America's westward expansion to its overseas colonization in 1898. If we prefer the euphemism of "westward expansion" to obscure the link with 1898, the participants had no such need. In 1900, Theodore Roosevelt, in a new preface to his *Winning of the West,* explicitly declared the Philippine venture to be a continuation of his story. When the rapid military victory in the Philippine war dissolved into a decade of insurgency, many Americans, including Roosevelt, looked toward commercial and cultural extensions of American power rather than territorial ones. But that, too, was continuous with American policy from the time of Thomas Jefferson. He had fought our first foreign war in the eastern Mediterranean in order to protect American trade, and by the middle of the 19th century American farmers were clamoring for policies that would make the world their market. Later industrialists and financiers would demand the same. Empires that seek investment opportunities, natural resources, and cheap labor abroad risk deeper entanglements than the simple trading empire Jefferson had envisioned. The internal affairs of other nations become vital; property rights, security of loans, and much else became the business of the United States, and that has resulted in innumerable "interventions." It has also meant competition with other empires: Germany and Japan early in the 20th century and the Soviet Union in the second half.

Looking at American progressive reform, social liberalism, and the claims of social citizenship in the decades following 1890, one cannot but recognize that such reform was part of a global response to the extraordinary expansion of industrial capitalism and of large cities. A global menu of reform ideas was available to all. They were selectively and differently adopted and adapted, nation by nation; the United States moved beyond laissez-faire liberalism toward a social liberalism by way of the teachings of German social scientists, particularly historical economists. Japan followed the same mentors, while Latin Americans came to understand social interdependence and the need for social insurance through the influence of French positivism. The politics of social policy varied. In Russia and Latin America, for example, the landed classes opposed industrial legislation to protect workers, while in the United States and Japan, it was business that opposed such legislation.

Nations kept their eyes on each other; none wanted to lag too far behind. As Roosevelt said in his 1908 annual address to Congress: "It is humiliating that at European international congresses on accidents the United States should be singled out as the most belated among the nations in respect to employer liability legislation."

What we call the welfare state is actually a social-insurance state, one that recognizes that modern society brings with it a variety of new risks—industrial accidents, unemployment, illness, old age. In the age of laissez-faire, industrial accidents were often blamed on the victim. Toward the end of the century, the concept of risk changed the moral meaning of the liabilities inherent in urban and industrial society. Novel theories were developed first in France and Belgium, but they soon spread. Instead of blaming worker or capitalist, the new understanding saw statistical probabilities of injury, unemployment, and the like. Those were conditions of modern society, and governments turned to various forms of social-security insurance. In the United States, however, the notion was slow to be accepted, and the moral approach lasted well into the 20th century.

Jane Addams, like Roosevelt, was distressed that the United States was "unaccountably slow" in responding to the challenges of modern industrial society. She was right, yet it may be more useful to say that the United States chose differently than other nations. Notions of individualism, given peculiar force by the strength of legal formalism in American law, made Americans less willing to interfere with contracts or legitimate collective bargaining. Yet Americans were quick to protect women and the domestic environment. Moreover, American unions had independence that eluded

unions granted greater rights in Mexico and Argentina, but that paid the price of co-optation. In the 20th century, the late-forming American welfare state may have benefited from its Anglo-American commitment to individual rights. Though there were worrisome illiberal and proto-fascist movements in the 1920s—the Ku Klux Klan, the Veterans of Foreign Wars, and, a little later, Father Coughlin—the United States was one of very few industrial nations to survive the interwar years without succumbing to fascist government.

One of my purposes is to argue against American exceptionalism, and in doing that I emphasize a world of difference. The problem with the idea of American exceptionalism is that it erases difference. There is only the United States and a homogenized "other" that is the rest of the world. The argument here is that, while there is a common history that includes us all, it plays out in many local variations. Hence I am not saying that the global history I invoke is a universal history, or that the American Revolution is just like other revolutions of its time. Nor do I say that the Civil War was no different from the emancipation of serfs in the Russian and Hapsburg Empires or the unification of Germany and Argentina. Nor do I argue that the American empire was indistinguishable from those of England, France, or Germany; or that progressivism in the United States was like progressivism in Japan or Chile. But I am saying that there are family resemblances we have missed, and we have also missed the self-aware communication about common challenges that historical actors on every continent had with one another.

More important, the extension of context enables us to see more clearly and deeply exactly what is unique about the national history of the United States. Its major events and themes look different; their causes and consequences get redefined. The United States has always shared a history with others. To acknowledge that literally makes us more worldly, and it makes our history more accessible to foreign scholars and publics. It makes us more open to interpretations of our history coming from historians and others beyond our borders. It will, I hope, better educate us and our children to the kind of cosmopolitanism that will make us better citizens of both the nation and the world.

This kind of history is not entirely novel. It is a recovery of history as it was envisioned by some of my predecessors a century ago. In the 1890s, when, as in the 1990s, Americans and others were intensely aware that new forms of communication and transportation made the world smaller, historians, too, thought beyond the nation in framing their histories. Henry Adams's great *History of the United States of America* was so framed, as was W.E.B. DuBois's Harvard dissertation on the suppression of the Atlantic slave trade. While Frederick Jackson Turner is most remembered for his famous address on "The Significance of the Frontier in American History," we should also recall his rich essay on "The Significance of History," presented to Wisconsin teachers two years earlier, in 1891. There he insisted that the history of every nation is connected to the history of all other nations. A history of any local place, he said, cannot be isolated from the rest of the world.

Those historians were among the many intellectuals and men and women of good will who, over the next three decades, sustained a hopeful internationalism and cosmopolitan values, which resulted in the foundation of various international organizations devoted to peace and uplift. There was a great awareness of global connections, and global thinking was quite pervasive. For historians, those understandings sustained a presumption that national histories were part of a larger universal history. Yet their history was, in fact, often parochial and race-based. They included in the domain of history only those parts of the world that were organized into nation-states, thus leaving out Africa, most of Asia, and what we now call the Middle East.

Still, that first generation of professional historians trained in the United States was more worldly than the post–World War II group, who emphasized American "exceptionalism." That earlier generation was typically trained in European as well as American history. With their passing, American history became more self-enclosed, a development accelerated by the cold war. Much was lost when a more worldly perspective atrophied in the interwar and war years and was dismissed after World War II.

It is important to recover it for the civic and historiographical reasons, and to renew it with the historical questions of our time. If we can begin to think about American history as a local instance of a general history, as one history among others, not only will historical knowledge be improved, but the cultural foundations of a needed cosmopolitanism will be enhanced. We do not want to reinforce a narrow and exclusive notion of citizenship, but to encourage and sustain a cosmopolitan citizenry, at once proud nationals and humble citizens of the world.

CHAPTER 8

Atlantic History
Definitions, Challenges, and Opportunities

ALISON GAMES

Fernand Braudel launched his massive history of the Mediterranean with an epigraph by the sixteenth-century priest José de Acosta. "To this day," wrote Acosta in his own equally massive *Natural and Moral History of the East and West Indies,* "they have not discovered at the Indies any mediterranian sea as in Europe, Asia and Affrike."[1] The irony is delicious in hindsight. While Europeans never found their own Mediterranean in the Americas, historians have since discovered the Atlantic as a unit of historical analysis. The very ocean that Acosta crossed to undertake missionary work in America has become an organizing principle through which scholars investigate the histories of the four landmasses it links. Yet the Atlantic does not have the coherence that Acosta first identified for the Mediterranean, nor that Braudel proposed and delineated centuries later; nor, indeed, is it possible to speak with confidence of an Atlantic system or a uniform region. Attempts to write a Braudelian Atlantic history—one that includes and connects the entire region—remain elusive, driven in part by methodological impediments, by the real disjunctions that characterized the Atlantic's historical and geographic components, by the disciplinary divisions that discourage historians from speaking to and writing for each other, and by the challenge of finding a vantage that is not rooted in any single place. . . .

If the Atlantic is a less obvious and coherent unit than the Mediterranean, it is also an anachronistic one. Historians have first had to invent the region: the emergence of the Atlantic as a single unit of analysis reflects trends in historical geography. What we call the Atlantic Ocean, our ancestors perceived as several distinct seas. The regions we have since labeled the North and South American continents are similarly modern creations.[2] Well into the nineteenth century, no one had an accurate idea of what these landmasses looked like or whether they were even connected to the Eurasian landmass. The components of Atlantic history—two of the four continents and even the ocean itself—are modern impositions.

And yet this unit of analysis, however artificially constructed it might be from the perspective of historical geography, has become sufficiently compelling to drive historical scholarship. Who are these scholars, and what is their impetus toward an Atlantic perspective? In one of the first efforts to articulate the history of this emerging field and to explain the origins of the current interest in the region, Bernard Bailyn argued that Atlantic history was a product of twentieth-century political developments.[3] But it is also possible to identify other converging strands of historical inquiry. Indeed, this North Atlantic diplomatic *longue durée* cannot alone explain the passion that has developed for all things Atlantic. Three converging strands have delineated different and sometimes incompatible Atlantics. First and foremost, historians of the transatlantic slave trade have been especially insistent about putting an Atlantic perspective at the center of their work, starting with Philip D. Curtin's painstaking efforts to calculate the size of the trade, and continuing with the innovative and extensive research on the African diaspora.[4] This vital field has opened up the ocean as a coherent unit of study by following the captives who moved across it, fanning out to Europe, to the islands of the Caribbean and the Atlantic, and to the American landmasses, especially Brazil. This approach, unfettered by state borders, pursues the logical lines of the trade, and puts people at the center, tracking the transmission of all

From *American Historical Review* 111 (June 2006): 741–757. © American Historical Association. Reprinted by permission.

elements of culture, from political identity to material goods to language to religion, all around the Atlantic basin. No other field has been so aggressively engaged for so many decades in pursuing an Atlantic vision and in framing the field as a whole. One of the most important conceptualizations of the Atlantic emerged from this vantage in 1993, when Paul Gilroy published *The Black Atlantic: Modernity and Double Consciousness.*[5]

A second source of energy toward Atlantic perspectives comes from historians of colonial societies in the Americas. Three factors have prodded their geographic expansion into and across the ocean. First, colonial historians are often trained in early modern European history, in addition to the history of the region of their research, and thus an Atlantic perspective can be a natural outgrowth of graduate training and reading. Second, historians of colonial societies often take comparative approaches to their subject, reading, for example, about colonization in other European empires in addition to their own, thus opening up possibilities of at least hemispheric connections. A third impetus comes from the frustration of trying to write a colonial history within historiographic traditions centered around modern nation-states. In this respect, the Atlantic potentially shares what Peregrine Horden and Nicholas Purcell, in their essay on the Mediterranean in this forum, describe as the political neutrality of these new regions. It is precisely this political neutrality that encouraged scholars seeking to escape the restrictions of the nation-state to move toward the border-less world of the Atlantic. For them, the Atlantic offers the liberation of the promised land.

Finally, historians of empires have long encompassed the Atlantic (among other ocean basins) within their purview.[6] The main constraint these approaches impose on the Atlantic is their tendency to see the region primarily from the perspective of Europe and to look mainly within a single imperial geography, an approach that can divvy up the world in strange ways—most apparent, perhaps, in studies of the islands of the Caribbean, each of which existed within its own imperial trajectory even while sometimes sharing space with a rival power and participating in common regional transformations. These two approaches (colonial and imperial) have converged most vigorously among historians of the British Atlantic. Both British historians and historians of colonial British America work within national paradigms characterized by exceptionalism: Britain's relationship to the European continent and the mythical exceptionalism of the United States traditionally set these two nations apart from their neighbors. Atlantic history offers scholars in both fields intellectual solutions to the burden of exceptionalism by privileging interactions and comparisons and by rejecting nationalism altogether for new analytic categories. It is no accident that the sole recent volume that exists for any single empire's Atlantic is David Armitage and Michael J. Braddick's edited collection *The British Atlantic World,*

1500–1800, which offers a thematic analysis of subjects ranging from the economy to politics to race, all investigated deliberately within an Atlantic framework.[7]

Although the existence of explicit Atlantic orientations dates from the middle of the twentieth century, it was not until the 1970s that a cadre of scholars emerged who self-consciously embraced Atlantic projects. In that decade, the Johns Hopkins University Press launched a series, the Johns Hopkins Studies in Atlantic History and Culture. But it was the 1990s that saw the greatest explosion of Atlantic scholarship. Greatly bolstered by the support of Harvard University's International Seminar on the History of the Atlantic World under the direction of Bernard Bailyn,[8] historians who are engaged in different aspects of Atlantic history—particularly those at the beginning of their career, for whom the seminar is intended—find regular opportunities to present research at seminars, colloquiums, and workshops. International conferences, particularly in North America and Europe, bring together scholars who investigate different aspects of the subject.[9] A new interdisciplinary e-journal, *Atlantic Studies,* published its first issue in 2004. Colleges and universities advertise for positions in Atlantic history. Atlantic history is taught at the college level in both introductory and advanced classes. Graduate students at some institutions, including New York University, Michigan State University, Florida International University, and the University of Texas at Arlington, can pursue degrees in Atlantic history, and elsewhere students can cobble together informal fields in Atlantic history. . . .

All this activity is a surprisingly recent phenomenon, given how long ago historians such as Curtin delineated some of the potential for a transoceanic history. These indicators may suggest that Atlantic history is hale and hearty. But there continue to exist a range of impediments to an oceanic history. Atlantic history means different things to different people, and it is for the most part appropriate that this breadth of opinion and perspective exists. But the Atlantic history that many historians produce is rarely centered around the ocean, and the ocean is rarely relevant to the project. Horden and Purcell point to the difference between history *in* and history *of* the Mediterranean. For Atlantic history, the relevant distinction is between a history of places *around* the Atlantic versus a history of the Atlantic. Of the former, there is an abundance. Of the latter, there are far fewer examples.[10] In fact, a survey of work that professes to be Atlantic reveals a lot of exclusively land-based (and sometimes landlocked) history, material that looks, as James Williams has said, like old wine in new bottles, or in this case the old colonial history repackaged as Atlantic history.

In a forum on oceans-based history, the Atlantic lurks on the sidelines like a surly middle sibling, tagging along behind the Mediterranean and the Pacific . . . and in the throes of an adolescent identity crisis. Atlantic history is all the rage, yet very few works exist that have attempted to capture the entire Atlantic across imperial, regional, and national boundaries.[11] It is time to restore the ocean to Atlantic history: if circulation around and across the ocean—not simply north-south hemispheric connections between Africa and Europe or within the Americas, but transatlantic connections—is not a fundamental part of historical analysis and does not in itself provide explanatory power to the subject under discussion, then we would do well to define these projects by some other name. To be sure, a history that requires attention to the Atlantic ends up privileging certain kinds of interactions (the migration of people and commodities, for example), but many historians have also effectively traced the circulation of ideas, tastes, preferences, and other less easily calculated and quantified aspects of exchange.

Assessing the different ways in which historians approach the Atlantic, David Armitage has identified three types of Atlantic history: "circum-Atlantic history," which takes the Atlantic unit as a whole; "trans-Atlantic history," which emphasizes a comparative approach; and "cis-Atlantic history," which looks at a particular place within an Atlantic context.[12] Cis-Atlantic history is the most accessible way for historians, particularly graduate students eager to research and write a manageable dissertation, to get into an Atlantic perspective, since it is less likely to require archival research in multiple languages and countries. There are numerous good examples of local histories oriented toward the Atlantic. April Lee Hatfield's *Atlantic Virginia: Intercolonial Relations in the Seventeenth Century* privileges English, Dutch, and indigenous economic and cultural interactions, depicting a Virginia vastly different from the one that has emerged over the past three decades from a historiography addicted to tobacco.[13] Hatfield argues that we cannot understand the development of one place, in this instance colonial Virginia, without looking well beyond that place, across the Atlantic, to the complex variables and interactions that converged to produce a particular set of local conditions. Armitage's "trans-Atlantic history" focuses on comparisons, and there is certainly a distinguished history of such approaches, long predating the current self-conscious passion for Atlantic history, and especially focused on some of the common processes and developments of societies in the Western Hemisphere.[14] These works have tended to focus on the western Atlantic, comparing labor systems and colonial societies, and fall into an established tradition of a history of the Americas, something Herbert Bolton identified back in 1933 as "The Epic of Greater America."[15]

It is circum-Atlantic history that remains the most challenging enterprise for Atlantic historians. From a circum-Atlantic perspective, Atlantic history is most literally the study of a large geographic region: the four continents that surround the Atlantic Ocean and the people contained therein. It especially focuses on those people whose societies were transformed by the intersection (or what Alfred W. Crosby referred to so memorably as the Columbian exchange) of the four landmasses after Christopher Columbus's momentous voyage in 1492.[16] These societies are not necessarily places along the Atlantic Ocean itself: one thinks immediately, for example, of Peru, or of the western coast of North America, or of the region surrounding the North American Great Lakes, or of the river deltas and valleys reaching deep into Africa and South America. Places and people on the Pacific coast of the Americas were engaged in processes originating from the Atlantic, regardless of their actual geographic location. Africans who lived hundreds of miles from the Atlantic coast were nonetheless ensnared in the slave trade and its varied economic, social, demographic, and political repercussions, while diets everywhere were altered by the new products of the Americas. Many Native Americans found their world transformed by pathogens, animals, and plants well before they laid eyes on a European. Nor is Atlantic history only about the literal points of contact (ports, traders, or migrants, for example), but rather about explaining transformations, experiences, and events in one place in terms of conditions deriving from that place's location in a large, multifaceted, interconnected world.

If the beginning point of Atlantic history is relatively fixed, with European and African trade interactions in the mid-fifteenth century and especially Columbus's 1492 voyage generally providing a good starting point for an exploration of the emergence of an Atlantic world, its terminus is more fluid and contested, shaped largely by one's perspective on the Atlantic. The so-called age of revolution and independence (through 1825) marks one possible ending, and the abolition of slavery (by 1888 in the Western Hemisphere, but not until the middle of the twentieth century in parts of Atlantic Africa) provides another: from a circum-Atlantic perspective, neither is entirely satisfactory, since both reflect developments of only local or hemispheric significance.[17]

This single region enjoyed a coherence for almost four hundred years, creating a viable unit of analysis within which we can understand the destruction and emergence of empires, the movement of people, the evolution of new cultural forms, and the circulation of ideas. This coherence, however, has a specific chronology, and by the middle of the nineteenth century, the region was being drawn more fully into a world system even as patterns specific to the intellectual currents and political dynamics of the region (such as abolition) continued. The Columbian exchange illustrated this balance between the regional and the global from the first return trips across the ocean. The unique American commodities that crossed the ocean transformed diets not only in Europe and Africa, but in Asia as well. Silver from American mines traveled to Europe, but it moved in equal amounts west across the Pacific, into Asian economies.[18]

Europeans who occupied and profited from territory in the Americas were similarly, and often more fully, engaged in commercial and extractive enterprises around the globe. These global ties intensified in the nineteenth century. The nineteenth-century post-emancipation labor crisis illustrates three core features of these new webs of connection: sugar production and marketing in a world economy, a world labor market and transoceanic labor migrations, and global imperialism. The expanded need for labor derived from the continued global migration of sugar. The plant's journey out of the Mediterranean and into the Atlantic continued into the Indian and Pacific oceans, and the deployment of Indian indentured migration was linked to efforts by British sugar planters to expand production to new regions, including some in the Atlantic (Guiana and Trinidad) and others around the globe (Mauritius, Natal, and Fiji). The continuity and intensification of migration across the Atlantic continued to reinforce the region's ties, always numerically eclipsing the newcomers from Asia; yet these new laborers from outside the Atlantic indicated the global economic and imperial forces that would ultimately reposition the region within a world system.

Atlantic history, then, is a *slice* of world history. It is a way of looking at global *and* regional processes within a contained unit, although that region was not, of course, hermetically sealed off from the rest of the world, and thus was simultaneously involved in transformations unique to the Atlantic and those derived from global processes. The Atlantic, moreover, is a geographic space that has a limited chronology as a logical unit of historical analysis: it is not a timeless unit; nor can this space fully explain all changes within it. Nonetheless, like other maritime regions, the Atlantic can offer a useful laboratory within which to examine regional and global transformations.[19]

This lengthy exploration of the region's geography and chronology, and of the shifting balance within the Atlantic between global and regional catalysts for change, points to the importance of flexibility in understanding and interpreting changes within the region. Some pointed critiques of Atlantic history have originated from scholars who insist on the superiority of world history perspectives, most notably Peter A. Coclanis.[20] But historians should work on geographic units that make sense for the questions they ask; the Atlantic is obviously not an appropriate laboratory for exploring all types of historical change. April Lee Hatfield has vigorously made the case for the necessity of multiple perspectives for Virginia in the seventeenth century. "Each of these constructions—Atlantic world, Virginia, local region, international colonial America, North America, and English Atlantic—functioned in slightly different ways, and each was relevant under different circumstances. They coexisted and intersected. All are necessary for understanding the reality of life in seventeenth-century Virginia that was connected to different parts of its wider world in very different ways."[21] Her refreshingly sensible and expansive methodology offers a model worth emulating.

By any number of measures, this Atlantic world was interconnected, and indeed historians have relied on the metaphor of the bridge to make sense of these links.[22] We know that the diseases that ravaged American populations came from thousands of miles away in Europe and Africa; we know that the political opportunities that indigenous people in strategic locations enjoyed derived from imperial rivalries elsewhere; we know that demographic transformations in Africa that led to the practice of polygyny were consequences of the transatlantic slave trade and its gender imbalances; we know that new staple crops in Africa (the peanut or the yam) and in Europe (the potato) were species unique to the Americas that traveled across the ocean on European vessels. The Atlantic, in short, was linked in ways that disregard the modern political boundaries that have defined departmental field structures and specializations. Atlantic history ultimately privileges and requires history without borders. In this respect, it joins other challenges to conventional geographic regions as units of analysis. Martin W. Lewis and Kären E. Wigen have argued this point most forcefully in *The Myth of Continents.* They illustrate the intellectual histories (often self-serving to people with political power) of continents and the conflation of geography with politics and culture. While we might find ourselves moving someday toward a corollary "myth of oceans," we are not there yet, and a history centered on the region of the Atlantic offers a logically viable space of analysis for particular questions with a range of methodological and pedagogical benefits.[23]

Atlantic history is more than simply the study of a geographic unit; it is also a style of inquiry that reflects the impulse that drew historians in specific fields to Atlantic history in the first place.[24] Within the space of these four centuries and these four continents, historians who adopt an Atlantic perspective explore commonalities and convergences, seeking larger patterns derived from the new interactions of people around, within, and across the Atlantic. The large geographic unit requires a different approach, one that by necessity deemphasizes any single place, although obviously some regions within and around the Atlantic enjoyed disproportionate political power at different points in time. If this is history without borders, then it should also be history without an imperial perspective. It thus implements some of the arguments about the intellectual construction of geographic space that Lewis and Wigen make in *The Myth of Continents:* Atlantic history can offer a case study of the ways in which historians can break down not only old regional barriers and paradigms, but also modes of analysis based on modern cultural and political hierarchies. Atlantic history may deal with European dominion, but it should not be Eurocentric. It may cover a space dominated numerically by African migrants, but it need not be Afrocentric. The most dynamic changes of the period of contact may be most immediately evident in the Americas, but it should not be an expanded history of the colonial Americas. It requires a different kind of perspective, one ideally not fixed in any one location. Atlantic history poses paired challenges: linking several regions, in which no one historian can have the competence or expertise that scholars desire, and doing so through multiple perspectives.

This problem of perspective is only one of many impediments that hinder efforts to craft a genuine oceanic history of the Atlantic. A second challenge derives from the uneven interest in Atlantic history among scholars who work on the individual regions of the early modern Atlantic world. Some fields of history have been more aggressive than others in attempting to convey an Atlantic vision. The working papers presented at the Harvard Seminar on the History of the Atlantic World offer one rough indicator of this pattern and reveal a preponderance of scholars from the British Atlantic.[25] . . .

A number of unintended consequences have resulted from the disproportionate intellectual energy expended by historians of the North Atlantic. Jorge Cañizares-Esguerra has faulted these historians for merely creating what he calls a "new paradigm [which] in fact sanctions Eurocentric cultural geographies for North America." He also rejects an emphasis on transoceanic ties in favor of hemispheric connections and comparisons.[26] His complaint obliquely addresses an important issue: the Atlantic tends to look very different when viewed from different vantages and within different imperial or commercial frameworks. . . .

It would be a mistake to assume that the ways in which people in one part of the Atlantic were transformed by their engagement with a larger unit would necessarily apply elsewhere: Africans and Americans had diametrically different experiences with European incursions. In Africa, Europeans traded at the largesse of African merchants and rulers, and secured political power in only a few places. In the Americas, Europeans occasionally replicated the culture of the trade factory, but they also pursued more bellicose styles of displacement and benefited from the demographic catastrophe visited on Americans. Some Europeans never pursued large-scale migration as part of their settlement strategy. The French and Dutch regions were characterized by tiny European minorities and large indigenous, African, subject, enslaved, or allied populations. Some European powers, especially the Dutch, were equally or more occupied by commercial activities elsewhere around the globe. If historians of the Anglophone world rarely doubt the existence of a British Atlantic, Pieter C. Emmer and Willem W. Klooster have argued that there was no Dutch Atlantic.[27] There was, moreover, no uniform style of cultural encounter or exchange around or within the ocean, even within a single imperial entity. The French along the St. Lawrence River valley and those in Saint-Domingue interacted differently with the non-French people around them. It is impossible to talk about an "Atlantic" style of interaction, or a single "Atlantic" culture, or even, as Pieter Emmer has argued, an Atlantic "system."[28] As these comments suggest, historians who work on the Atlantic have been sensitive to the complexity and variety within it, and this careful appreciation of diversity is essential.[29] Wim Klooster, building on Braudel's multiple "skeins of history," has proposed at least eight zones of Atlantic influence for the Americas alone.[30]

The Harvard sample notably demonstrates the special enthusiasm of colonial historians for Atlantic history. An inadvertent consequence of this admirable initiative is that "Atlantic" and "Americas" have become conflated. Thus Atlantic history may resemble or mirror the history of colonial societies writ large. We can see this tendency in a number of indicators, most vividly in the ways in which historians have tried to conceptualize the period from 1775 to the 1820s as the age of revolution and the end of empire. This characterization is certainly appropriate for several places in the Atlantic, but not for all. Many of the colonies on the American landmass had achieved their independence by 1830, but many colonies remained (including Canada and the colonies on the northern coast of South America). Brazil was a kingdom, not a colony, and with the exception of Haiti, every single island in the Caribbean remained subject to a European power. And that is only in the western Atlantic, where clearly fewer than half of all colonies achieved independence in this period. In the eastern Atlantic, Europeans increased their trade presence in parts of Africa; and in some regions, outside powers (the French in Senegal, the British in Sierra Leone, the United States in Liberia) enhanced their political dominance. But in the Eastern Hemisphere, this age was neither one of the end of empire nor distinguished by the emergence of independence. Viewed from an Atlantic perspective, the period evokes themes of political redefinition for some and of political subordination for many. Revolution and independence cannot do the period justice.

Closely linked to this tendency to let one small part of the Atlantic define the whole are barriers caused by terminology. Both problems derive from the challenge of perspective: How do we escape historiographic conventions to find a language and a framework that encapsulates the whole Atlantic? Words get in the way. Historians continue to invoke the Americas with the Eurocentric "New World," despite the logic they may apply as Atlantic historians that, in fact, if the entire region is a logical unit of analysis, it is so precisely because it was a new world for all involved in it. Historians who approach the region from colonial or imperial perspectives are similarly inclined to slip into the language of imperial dynamics, speaking, therefore, about centers, peripheries, and margins. It is difficult to identify processes shared by the entire Atlantic region, and this challenge speaks both to the *lack* of coherence of the region and to the continued difficulties of assimilating so many different fields of scholarship.

All of these geographic markers reflect perspectives rooted firmly in national, regional, and imperial, not Atlantic, historiographies. It is similarly difficult to find models that are easily portable from one historiographic tradition to another. Take Ira Berlin's concept of the "Atlantic creole," an imaginative and original formulation of the Atlantic and its inhabitants.[31] Berlin coined the term to describe those polyglot Africans who moved so adeptly among different societies in the early decades of the slave trade. Derived from linguistics and employed to highlight cultural mixture, fluidity, and innovation, "Atlantic creole" generates some confusion for historians of the Americas, who generally have employed "creole" to describe people of European or African descent who were born in the Americas. "Atlantic creole" poses a second challenge viewed in an Atlantic context: it replicates many of the cosmopolitan characteristics that historians of the Americas have come to attach to the term "cultural broker," those people in the Americas, indigenous, European, or of mixed race, who moved freely between cultures and who played important roles in mediating the moments when mutually incomprehensible societies conflicted or engaged in any number of ways. Just like "Atlantic creoles," "cultural brokers" were people who were culturally bi- or multilingual. They also looked like *lançados* or Eurafricans. Words to describe indigenous people, African or American, constitute another semantic stumbling block, including "tribe," "Indian," "First Nation," and "native," which can raise hackles in one place while being commonly used elsewhere. Atlantic historians need to think more self-consciously about the possibility of a common language. . . .

[F]or Atlantic historians it is especially urgent to delve into historiographies of other regions and people in order to sketch the patterns contained in the Atlantic. Our failure to do so produces some peculiar disconnects, easily illuminated by thinking about migration in the Atlantic. This gap between fields that are so logically connected is readily illustrated by looking at the ways in which historians of English and early American social history engaged in a protracted dialogue of the deaf in the 1970s and 1980s, a period characterized by an explosion of scholarship in early modern British social history. This was the great age of demographic history. English historians, starting with Peter Laslett, delineated an early modern English world characterized by high rates of migration.[32] Laslett demonstrated that the world we have lost was one of high mobility. At the very time that historians uncovered this unexpected world of high migration within England, historians who investigated migration from England to North America emphasized the static nature of relocation. They turned these migrants into "settlers" or "colonists," as if this one transatlantic

migration were an anomaly in otherwise sedentary lives. While historians of British parishes and towns employed local records to identify mobility, historians of British North America used town and church records to privilege stability and generated a score of town studies.[33] Far more troubling is another failure to communicate in the study of Atlantic migration. Some 12 million Africans and maybe 3 million Europeans in the same period migrated west across the Atlantic. Yet until the efforts of David Eltis to integrate multiple incompatible historiographies, these populations were treated separately, with "migrants" shaping one set of historiographic questions, and "slaves" another. Moreover, historians have been slow to pursue the implications of Eltis's arguments and evidence.[34]

In light of these many challenges, will the Atlantic find its own Braudel? If so, s/he is likely to approach the Atlantic from a few distinctive vantages, not necessarily geographic locations but rather methodological perspectives. Some of the most exemplary works in Atlantic history have been written by historians whose topics have no necessary connection to or investment in a single nation or empire—environmental history, historical geography, the African diaspora, migration, economic history, the history of commodities. These fruitful approaches give us hints about what a Braudelian Atlantic might look like. It will be archival, not synthetic, because the most innovative work on the Atlantic continues to be anchored in original research. It will set the Atlantic more explicitly in the context of global transformations, thus emphatically embracing the cosmopolitanism that Peter Coclanis has called for, even if it does so within a single slice of the world, helping us to identify what exactly was particular to the Atlantic world and what this region shared with other ocean basins. It will be transnational, transregional, oceanic, and integrative.[35] . . .

The study of people and the study of products suggest how historians might capture the whole Atlantic in their research, thus sketching a region that is liberated from any single national, colonial, or imperial framework. Both subjects open themselves to the full methodological richness that historians savor, leading scholars toward culture, environment, ideology, quantification, or whatever one might wish to pursue. They also, moreover, put the ocean at the center of the analysis, since people moved around the Atlantic, and commodities did as well. The ocean was not only the vehicle of circulation, but also the unique space within which goods and people were created, defined, and transformed.

People, especially migrants (European, African, or American), offer useful ways to see tangible evidence of the utility of a history without borders. Studies of migration across the Atlantic (almost invariably from east to west) have for decades offered large-scale assessments of one of the important processes by which the Atlantic became a region of study. The generation of computer-aided databases such as the monumental slave trade database further refined these studies, with the result that historians of European and African migrations have been able to delineate specific patterns of migration and settlement and to trace the migration not simply of people, but of distinctive cultures and subcultures.[36] Studies of return and repeat migration demonstrate how individuals knit the Atlantic world together and illustrate the cultural impact that even a very small contingent of return migrants had on their former home cultures.[37]

There has also been an enhanced interest in the experiences of individuals who themselves lived in different parts of the Atlantic. These biographies help readers grasp the vitality and variety of the Atlantic. Some of these individuals circulated within single imperial systems. Such was the case for Ayuba Ben Suleiman, Little Ephraim Robin John, and Ancona Robin Robin John. All three men were ensnared in the slave trade in the eighteenth century; all three circulated in the British colonies; all three found their way first to England and then home again. Sir Walter Raleigh hosted several Native Americans at his home in England: some of these interpreters assisted English settlement efforts in the Americas, while others were more hostile to their erstwhile hosts.[38] Other individuals crossed imperial and national lines. Mahommah Gardo Baquaqua did just that. Enslaved in Africa, he was shipped to Brazil, escaped in New York, and lived in Cuba, the United States, and Canada before traveling (as far as his biographers can tell) across the Atlantic to Europe. These are, admittedly, picaresque tales.[39] Throughout their travels, these men, and others like them, had experiences that altered them. They learned new languages, they converted to new religions, and they made new friends and new enemies. The ocean was not just a place within which people circulated: it was itself the place within which they had transformative experiences.[40] And this oceanic movement also permitted the circulation of news with each newly arrived ship and each garrulous passenger. With enough such stories, we might piece the Atlantic together in new, richly detailed, complex ways, putting people in the middle of a chaotic kaleidoscope of movement.

Like people, commodities link the Atlantic in distinctive ways, through production, consumption, and commerce. They reveal the movement of people to produce them, the emergence of new or revitalized commercial centers whose fortunes rose and fell with single commodities in all places of the Atlantic, and the evolution of tastes and fashion. They can help us reach deep into households (European, African, and American alike) and factories and plantations and ranches and mines far from the ocean itself. Commodities are not necessarily Atlantic in scope, but they can be; and several illustrative studies argue forcefully that the Atlantic is the most appropriate context within which to understand certain products in specific historical periods.

We can, moreover, see distinctive aspects of Atlantic history in the different goods that circulated within the ocean. Chocolate, of course, like so many other delectable and addictive American plants and products, came to have a career well outside the Atlantic. But its initial introduction in Europe was shaped by the unique context within which some Europeans—particularly Spaniards—encountered cacao and the many beverages with which it was made. Marcy Norton argues that the Spanish had to learn to like chocolate, and that they did so within the specific context of Spanish occupation and settlement in the Indies. The asymmetries of conquest, the peculiar demography of early Spanish migration to central America, the reliance of Spanish men on indigenous women, the challenges of Atlantic transport: all shaped the ways in which Spaniards learned to like chocolate and what kind of chocolate they would consume in Europe.[41] Madeira offers a second example of a product that emerged in a uniquely Atlantic setting. David Hancock has set the wine's "product innovation" in the context of the eighteenth-century Atlantic: Madeira was invented as a result of conversation and exchange around and across the Atlantic between 1703 and 1807. Producers and consumers learned how to communicate tastes and preferences, and the result was a new drink.[42]

If chocolate emerged in a unique colonial dynamic, and if Madeira wine resulted from communication within the Atlantic, sugar created an entire world in the tropics, but it was one that affected places far from the site of production.[43] The study of sugar links plantations to coffee houses, and slave ports in Africa to the rum used in European-Indian diplomacy in North America. Commodities and plantation production also wrought unique changes. Sugar, of course, nestled in the Atlantic as only part of its protracted world tour. But within the Atlantic, it generated its own peculiar world. This world of sugar production, J.R. McNeill argues, required the transformation of the tropics to make them more conducive to sugar cultivation and processing. Sugar created an unprecedented demand for plantation labor, which was met almost exclusively through the transportation of African captives. The unique convergence of European and African immigrants and creoles and a new disease environment characterized by mosquito-borne illnesses transformed the tropics and shaped the rise and fall of Atlantic empires.[44] Tracing products and people within the Atlantic introduces us to the rich and varied world that the region contained and suggests ways in which the region emerges as a logical unit of historical analysis, providing a geographic space, for a fixed period of time, within which we can understand processes and transformations that otherwise might remain inexplicable.[45]

Although there are numerous impediments to a Braudelian vision, more oceanic histories of the Atlantic are yet to be written. They will be generated by historians who work deliberately to integrate their particular findings into a larger unit, who read broadly, who are open to interdisciplinary approaches, and who are committed to moving beyond parochial frameworks dictated by conventional historiographic divisions toward an Atlantic perspective. Writing Atlantic history requires considerable optimism, fearlessness, and the conviction that a leap into the ocean will not end tragically in a wrecked heap in the Bermuda triangle, but rather will land you safely in a new, unexpected, and stimulating place. Jump in. The water's *great*.

Notes

I wish to thank readers who looked at earlier versions of this article, especially Wim Klooster and the anonymous reviewers for the *AHR,* and colleagues who heard and commented on aspects of this piece at conferences. I also thank Douglas Egerton, David Hancock, Kris Lane, John McNeill, Jennifer Morgan, Marcy Norton, Adam Rothman, John Tutino, Jim Williams, and Donald Wright for many helpful conversations on the challenges of teaching and writing regional, Atlantic, and global histories.

1. Fernand Braudel, *The Mediterranean and the Mediterranean World in the Age of Philip II,* trans. Siân Reynolds, 2 vols. (New York, 1973), 1: 19. This precise phrasing is from José de Acosta, *The Naturall and Morall Historie of the East and West Indies* (London, 1604), 151. Braudel cited the 1558 edition, p. 94.

2. Martin W. Lewis and Kären E. Wigen, *The Myth of Continents: A Critique of Metageography* (Berkeley, Calif., 1997).

3. Bernard Bailyn, "The Idea of Atlantic History," *Itinerario* 20, no. 1 (1996): 19–44. William O'Reilly shares Bailyn's emphasis on the link between twentieth-century politics and diplomacy and the emergence of Atlantic history. See O'Reilly, "Genealogies of Atlantic History," *Atlantic Studies* 1 (2004): 66–84.

4. Philip D. Curtin, *The Atlantic Slave Trade: A Census* (Madison, Wis., 1969).

5. Paul Gilroy, *The Black Atlantic: Modernity and Double Consciousness* (Cambridge, Mass., 1993).

6. The classic and seminal works include Charles Andrews, *The Colonial Period of American History* (New Haven, Conn., 1934–1938), and Clarence Haring, *The Spanish Empire in America* (New York, 1947).

7. David Armitage and Michael J. Braddick, eds., *The British Atlantic World, 1500–1800* (London, 2002). Benjamin Schmidt's *Innocence Abroad: The Dutch Imagination and the New World, 1570–1670* (New York, 2001) is a rare and exemplary study from the vantage of the European mainland.

8. http://www.fas.harvard.edu/~atlantic/index.html.

9. The University of Leiden hosted one of the earliest such conferences in 1999, at which participants were invited to summarize different aspects of Atlantic history. The papers were published as "Round Table Conference: The Nature of Atlantic History," *Itinerario* 23, no. 2 (1999): 48–173.

10. For exemplary studies of Atlantic history, see David Hancock, *Citizens of the World: London Merchants and the Integration of the British Atlantic Community, 1735–1785* (New York, 1995), and David Eltis, *The Rise of African Slavery in the Americas* (New York, 2000).

11. The few works that profess to describe the entire Atlantic tend to have perspectives very firmly rooted in one place. Paul Butel's *The Atlantic,* trans. Iain Hamilton Grant (London and New York, 1999), for example, neglected to engage the relevant and abundant literature on Africa.

12. David Armitage, "Three Concepts of Atlantic History," in Armitage and Braddick, *The British Atlantic World,* 11–27.

13. April Lee Hatfield, *Atlantic Virginia: Intercolonial Relations in the Seventeenth Century* (Philadelphia, Pa., 2004).

14. Slavery and labor systems are among the most typical points of comparison. For early examples of scholarly interest in these approaches, see, for example, Carl N. Degler, *Slavery and Race Relations in Brazil and the United States* (New York, 1971), or Richard R. Beeman, "Labor Forces and Race Relations: A Comparative View of the Colonization of Brazil and Virginia," *Political Science Quarterly* 86 (1971): 609–636.

15. Herbert Bolton, "The Epic of Greater America," *AHR* 38, no. 3 (April 1933): 448–474. See also Silvio Zavala, "A General View of the Colonial History of the New World," *AHR* 66, no. 4 (July 1961): 913–929.

16. Alfred W. Crosby, *The Columbian Exchange: Biological and Cultural Consequences of 1492* (Westport, Conn., 1972).

17. For a plea for an Atlantic history that moves into the modern era, see Donna Gabaccia, "A Long Atlantic in a Wider World," *Atlantic Studies* 1 (2004): 1–27. One of the rare books oriented toward the classroom that takes Atlantic history through the late nineteenth century is Alan L. Karras and J.R. McNeill, eds., *Atlantic American Societies: From Columbus through Abolition, 1492–1888* (London, 1992).

18. Dennis O. Flynn and Arturo Giráldez, "Cycles of Silver: Global Economic Unity through the Mid-Eighteenth Century," *Journal of World History* 13, no. 2 (2002): 391–427.

19. Jerry Bentley, "Seas and Ocean Basins as Frameworks of Historical Analysis," *Geographical Review* 89, no. 2 (April 1999): 215–224.

20. Peter A. Coclanis, "*Drang Nach Osten:* Bernard Bailyn, the World-Island, and the Idea of Atlantic History," *Journal of World History* 13, no. 1 (Spring 2002): 169–182.

21. Hatfield, *Atlantic Virginia,* 227.

22. Hancock, *Citizens of the World,* 8–9.

23. On the creation of oceans, see Martin W. Lewis, "Dividing the Ocean Sea," *Geographical Review* 89, no. 2 (April 1999): 188–214.

24. For a thought-provoking view of the Mediterranean as process, see David Abulafia, "Mediterraneans," in W.V. Harris, ed., *Rethinking the Mediterranean* (Oxford, 2005), 64–93.

25. My own rough calculations suggest that out of 268 papers presented between 1996 and 2004, 115 focused on the British Atlantic (including non-British subjects in British territories, such as Dutch- or German-speaking or African inhabitants of British colonies), 57 on the Spanish Atlantic, 18 on the French, 12 on the United States, 9 on Portugal or Portuguese Brazil, 8 on the Dutch Atlantic, 5 on Africa, and 1 on the Danish. Of the remaining 43 papers, a few are explicitly comparative across national and imperial borders, some are topical (demography and commodities), some are centered on Europe, and a still larger number take a single land-based region as their unit of analysis but investigate it over a period of multiple imperial invasions. In North America, Louisiana and

the region of New Netherland/New York fall into this category, as does Panama in central America.

26. Jorge Cañizares-Esguerra, "Some Caveats about the 'Atlantic' Paradigm," *History Compass,* www.history-compass. com.

27. Pieter C. Emmer and Willem W. Klooster, "The Dutch Atlantic, 1600–1800: Expansion without Empire," *Itinerario* 23, no. 2 (1999): 48–69. See the different Atlantics that emerge through approaches centered around imperial expansion in the accompanying essays by Silvia Marzagalli, Carla Rahn Phillips, and David Hancock, ibid., 70–126. In the same issue, Debra Gray White explores the Black Atlantic (127–140), and David Eltis sets the Atlantic in global perspective (141–161).

28. Pieter Emmer, "The Myth of Early Globalization: The Atlantic Economy, 1500–1800," *European Review* 11, no. 1 (2003): 37–47.

29. In *"Drang Nach Osten,"* Peter Coclanis has criticized those who work on the Atlantic for overemphasizing unity and integration.

30. Wim Klooster, private communication with the author.

31. Ira Berlin, "From Creole to African: Atlantic Creoles and the Origins of African-American Society in Mainland North America," *The William and Mary Quarterly,* 3rd series 53, no. 2 (April 1996): 251–288.

32. Peter Laslett, *The World We Have Lost* (London, 1965).

33. Virginia DeJohn Anderson was one of the first scholars to break through this impasse by putting mobility at the center of her history of New England. See Anderson, *New England's Generation: The Great Migration and the Formation of Society and Culture in the Seventeenth Century* (Cambridge, 1991).

34. Eltis, *The Rise of African Slavery.* See also James Horn and Philip D. Morgan, "Settlers and Slaves: European and African Migrations to Early Modern British America," in Carole Shammas and Elizabeth Mancke, eds., *The Creation of the British Atlantic World* (Baltimore, Md., 2005), 32–74. Wim Klooster and Alfred Padula, eds., *The Atlantic World: Essays on Slavery, Migration, and Imagination* (Upper Saddle River, N.J., 2005), is an excellent example of an essay collection that explicitly connects a range of historiographic problems often regarded separately.

35. Coclanis, *"Drang Nach Osten,"* 181.

36. David Eltis, Stephen D. Behrendt, David Richardson, and Herbert S. Klein, *The Trans-Atlantic Slave Trade: A Database on CD-ROM* (Cambridge, 1999).

37. Kristin Mann and Edna G. Bay, eds., *Rethinking the African Diaspora: The Making of a Black Atlantic World in the Bight of Benin and Brazil* (London, 2001); Alison Games, *Migration and the Origins of the English Atlantic World* (Cambridge, Mass., 1999).

38. Alden T. Vaughan, "Sir Walter Raleigh's Indian Interpreters, 1584–1618," *The William and Mary Quarterly,* 3rd series 59, no. 2 (April 2002): 341–376.

39. "Ayuba Suleiman Diallo of Bondu," in Philip D. Curtin, ed., *Africa Remembered* (Madison, Wis., 1987), 18–59; Robin Law and Paul E. Lovejoy, eds., *The Biography of Mahommah Gardo Baquaqua* (Princeton, N.J., 2001); Randy J. Sparks, *The Two Princes of Calabar: An Eighteenth-Century Atlantic Odyssey* (Cambridge, Mass., 2004).

40. On the unique maritime and class cultures of the Atlantic, see especially Peter Linebaugh and Marcus Rediker, *The Many-Headed Hydra: Sailors, Slaves, Commoners, and the Hidden History of the Revolutionary Atlantic* (Boston, 2000).

41. Marcy Norton, "Conquests of Chocolate," *OAH Magazine of History* 18, no. 3 (April 2004): 14–17.

42. David Hancock, "Commerce and Conversation in the Eighteenth-Century Atlantic: The Invention of Madeira Wine," *Journal of Interdisciplinary History* 29, no. 2 (1998): 197–219.

43. Sidney W. Mintz, *Sweetness and Power: The Place of Sugar in Modern History* (New York, 1985); Philip D. Curtin, *The Rise and Fall of the Plantation Complex: Essays in Atlantic History* (New York, 1990).

44. J.R. McNeill, "Yellow Jack and Geopolitics: Environment, Epidemics, and the Struggles for Empire in the American Tropics, 1650–1825," *OAH Magazine of History* 18, no. 3 (April 2004): 9–13; McNeill, *Mosquito Coasts: Plantation Ecology, Disease, War and Revolution in the American Tropics, 1640–1920* (forthcoming).

45. Studies of rice and corn suggest a new interest in studying commodities and the environment within the Atlantic. See, for example, James C. McCann, *Maize and Grace: Africa's Encounter with a New World Crop, 1500–2000* (Cambridge, Mass., 2005), and Judith A. Carney, *Black Rice: The African Origins of Rice Cultivation in the Americas* (Cambridge, Mass., 2001).

CHAPTER 9

Environment, Settler Societies, and the Internationalization of American History

IAN TYRRELL

American historiography was born in Europe, not America. It was Europeans who conceptualized the American continent as exceptional, and projected onto it all of their hopes and dystopian fantasies.[1] Although American historiography became separated from Europe progressively from the late nineteenth century through to the 1940s, the European legacy remains strong in the notion of American difference, established, more often than not, by comparison with Europe. The call for a reorientation of American history toward transnational themes is as timely as the claims of Frederick Jackson Turner one hundred years ago on the frontier thesis, yet incomplete if it remains a view within Euro-America. The new transnational initiative proposes quite rightly to contextualize American development, to make the boundaries between local, regional, national, and transnational less rigid. It is understandable that the search for a more cosmopolitan American historiography should lead back to Europe, building upon obvious networks of comparative history and manifest evidence of transatlantic economic, demographic, intellectual, and environmental influences. To take that direction would not be enough.

Any plan to internationalize American history must draw on the histories of people from outside of Europe. Atlantic perspectives must be part of this maneuver, but they, too, are not enough. The importance of southern Africa and the African diasporas for the study of race relations in the United States is already well established.[2] These subjects are heavily researched, partly because they are contained within the Atlantic world and within the commerce of those European empires based especially upon the Atlantic region.[3] While it is important not to forget the wider concept of the Americas implied in any Atlantic perspective, it is equally vital to consider "new worlds" beyond the Americas that can open new questions about American history. These may concern matters currently central to historical debates, such as race and slavery, or other, more neglected topics, such as environmental history.[4]

Settler Societies

One way of widening the frame of reference involves looking at similar experiences to American development that occurred in the so-called "settler societies." These, mostly within the British empire, concerned large areas of the globe in lands where whites came to dominate and in some cases almost obliterated indigenous occupation. These societies shared (but to different degrees and in different combinations) a similar cultural inheritance, ideas of racial superiority, parliamentary traditions (for whites), capitalist markets, and the institutions of the common law.[5]

Parallels between these societies were well understood in the nineteenth century and much discussed by a range of public commentators. Comparisons of settlement colonies undertaken by J.A. Froude, Anthony Trollope, Sir George Dilke, Richard Jebb, J.R. Seeley, James Bryce, and others explored a range of similarities to—and differences between—the new lands and the "motherland." This genre frequently put the history of the United States in the larger context of British expansion. But the settlement society model was gradually dropped in the twentieth century as nationalism replaced shared imperial loyalties in the think-

From Ian Tyrrell, "Beyond the View from Euro-America: Environment, Settler Societies, and the Internationalization of American History," in *Rethinking American History in a Global Age,* ed. Thomas Bender (Berkeley: University of California Press, 2002), 168–191. Reprinted by permission.

ing of the leading historians of Canada, Australia, and other former British possessions. An evolutionary and comparative framework had influenced American colonial studies too, but, by the 1920s, American historians had rejected it as a model for postcolonial developments.[6] Revolution and republicanism had severed the imperial link and appeared to many historians to make the American case distinctive among settler societies.

To restore this wider context of European expansion and settlement processes would contribute greatly to the transnational agenda. It would involve comparative as well as transnational history and conform to the strictures on comparative history set out long ago by that doyen of the *Annales* school, Marc Bloch. Comparative history was most likely to lead to fruitful explanations, Bloch stated, when it involved "a parallel study of societies that are at once neighboring and contemporary, exercising a constant mutual influence, exposed through their development to the action of the same broad causes just because they are close and contemporaneous, and owing their existence in part at least to a common origin."[7] With the exception of geographic propinquity, a point diminished by improved communications in the late nineteenth and twentieth centuries, the settler societies fulfill these conditions. Differences of substance could, as Bloch argued, be better discerned within common patterns, and hypotheses more readily developed to explain observed differences than in cases that are radically unlike in the first place.

There are signs today in historiography of a revived interest in comparisons of this type, with calls for a reconsideration of what the nineteenth-century English historian R. Seeley called "Greater Britain"[8] But the limitations of the settler society model must be confronted.[9] Such an approach cannot provide an adequate alternative transnational framework unless it combines comparisons of settler societies with analysis of the systemic relationships between the "new worlds" and "old." These relationships were determined by the process of European, and particularly British, imperial expansion, and the economic relationships of trade and investment in a developing global economy that accompanied that process.

These transnational amendments are made essential by several cogent analytical and empirical objections to the settler society agenda. Postcolonial scholarship in the 1990s became critical of the "settler" formula as Eurocentric and oblivious to the realities of race and gender. These conquered territories were, the critique goes, always "settled," and the role of the indigenous in resisting Western penetration and challenging the colonialism of white settlers must be acknowledged.[10] Yet using the conceptual framework of settler societies need not deny imperial conquest, resistance, or the realities of race and gender (or class, for that matter). What the concept does stress is difference from those countries where extraction of wealth rather than a staking of a permanent claim to the land was a more prominent feature of colonialism.

Perhaps the best way to capture the complexities of the situation would be to acknowledge similarities and continuities with Patrick Wolfe's formulation in a study of the anthropological profession and its complicity in the making of the Australian nation, when he writes of "settler colonialism."[11] Such societies may have had more transformative effects through what Alfred Crosby calls the "demographic takeover" of indigenous peoples than occurred under classical imperialism. Settler societies represented a particularly complex and resilient form of European colonial expansion often not recognized as imperial conquest by its own agents precisely because they claimed to do more than extract wealth and then return to the metropolitan space.[12]

A settler society framework can be subtle and dialectical enough to incorporate the insights of postcolonialism. Taking the example of Australia, the work done on settler societies may be able to convey the double identity of European settlers as colonized and colonizer; as "new" land transformed by Europeans and derivative in many ways of European culture, and as a polity that has itself become a colonizer in its own country, as Wolfe stresses. Even the spread of American empire abroad has resonances with Australian and New Zealand roles in the South Pacific. Especially in Fiji, Samoa, and New Guinea, these have been imperial roles involving not only the formal attributes of imperial power but also the gender and racial hierarchies of power that typically reinforce and even express imperial/colonized power relations.[13]

A second and more serious problem with settler societies as models for any transnational agenda in American history is that they may not challenge the national framework of traditional comparative analysis. Under the sway of the latter, these societies have tended to be treated as self-contained, to be compared with one another. The work of Louis Hartz and other contributors to *The Founding of New Societies* (1964) fits this type of comparative history. Hartz used the opportunity to expand upon his theme of the United States as a unique "liberal society" and sought to validate the thesis he had put forward in *The Liberal Tradition in America* (1955) about the development of historical fragments of European political ideology and culture as part of a general theory of national development. The fragments, whether liberal, as in the American case, or radical Chartist, in the Australian, develop in a state of autonomy once spun off from their European origins. Comparisons of this type do not question the national unit or the characterization of the United States as a unique society, distinguished chiefly by its difference from Europe.[14]

The opposite extreme to this national comparative approach to the history of settlement societies is one in which all societies of settlement in the "new worlds" can be depicted as having common patterns that differ from those of the "old" world. The environmental historian Stephen Pyne's analysis of common trends in the use and control of fire by European settlers is an example. New fire regimes replaced the fire-stick farming of indigenous peoples, and settlers used fire in similar ways in a number of New World societies. Pyne's approach is superior to national comparisons, but assimilates American experience to that of other settler societies and homogenizes a European experience, in this case in environmental management, to be contrasted with New World experience.[15] The binary concept of Europe versus America, common in theories of American exceptionalism, is not entirely overcome by this approach; rather, the polarity is simply displaced, and the connections between old worlds and new are not explained.

What is needed is the linking of comparative analysis of settler societies with transnational contexts of imperial power and the expansion of global markets under capitalism. With this modification, settler society models can be useful for enriching American historiography. The result would not be to provide ready-made reinterpretation of American historiography but, rather, to open up new questions and challenge unthinking assumptions concerning unilinear and homogeneous national patterns. American history from this perspective looks different than it does from within, and from that of a purely European or Atlantic re-take on American events.

Environmental History

Such assertions about the theories and methods of history need to be backed by concrete examples. Nowhere was the shared experience of European expansion more obvious than in the confrontation between settlement processes and the physical environments of "new" lands. This type of comparative and transnational history has not always been pursued in environmental analysis. Even though geographical influences rarely coincide with national boundaries, and transnational approaches appear to be a natural concomitant of environmental history, in this subfield, the boundaries between U.S. and other histories remain remarkably intact. It must first be conceded that when humans' interaction with their environment becomes the history of state policy, national boundaries must constitute one of the fundamental features of that history to be confronted. Yet the laws and policies of nation-states reflect only part of the interplay of forces that contribute to environmental history. American environmental history has inherited the traditions of American difference viewed in contrast with Europe, and has produced, as one Australian scholar has remarked, work that is "surprisingly nationalistic."[16] Great originality has been attributed to American development of national parks, wilderness ideas and ideals (including respectful studies of the iconic figure John Muir), western conservation, and frontier themes.[17]

These topics have been analyzed critically, but often in a way isolated from developments elsewhere. As a key example, American historians have seen the conservation movement of the early twentieth century as a pragmatic response to conditions in the western part of the United States in the 1890s; or as the work of a political, business, and scientific elite associated with the Progressive Era of national reform. Either way, the conservation movement began in the United States and stemmed from American conditions. The prodigious research of Richard Grove, among others, has since provided non-American perspectives on this issue.[18] Grove shows that seventeenth- and eighteenth-century colonial experience in such places as Mauritius, St. Helena, and the Caribbean led to concern with deforestation and species extinction long before the American George Perkins Marsh published *Man and Nature* in 1864. Not only did the first American efforts at conservation postdate those in some other places; the United States also drew upon this international scholarship on environmental degradation, as Michel Girard has shown for Marsh's own intellectual development.[19]

This is not simply a question of what came first, or even of the flow of intellectual influence. It also affects the content of environmental thinking. In the American West there was much borrowing from foreign sources conceptualizing the environment in broader and more complex terms than the wilderness versus rational conservation perspective. From the international debates concerning the transformation of nature came ideas of environmental restoration, and what others call rectification, before the emergence of the modern American conservation movement around 1900.[20]

The failure to appreciate this international context highlights a narrow frame of reference in American history. Despite the valiant efforts of some to adopt global approaches, much American environmental scholarship has focused on, or been influenced by, concepts of wilderness, as in the evidence presented by Roderick Nash's *Wilderness and the American Mind* (1967). Europeans as well as Americans have contributed to this special focus. English commentators such as Peter Coates and D.J.S. Morris have, while differing in their interpretations, drawn upon this American tradition in a debate that attributed to American green politics an entirely different ethos from the European sensibility. These differences were said to be grounded in ideas of American exceptionalism and to have stemmed from the "crucible" of the frontier experience.[21]

Did no other nation have a sense of wilderness parallel to the one that touched the United States and that gave rise to the great national parks? Given that Australians (and South Africans) established a number of national parks during the late nineteenth and early twentieth centuries, including the second "national park" in the world in Australia (1878), on lines similar to those of Yellowstone and later Yosemite, assertions of American uniqueness are dubious.

The Australian experience has not been as intensively studied as it ought to be, but from the available evidence, it appears to have paralleled the American example rather than derived from it.[22]

Underpinning wilderness ideas is the suggestion that American landscapes confronted by Europeans were unique. That is, because Europeans had turned "first nature" into manicured farms and fields, "America" was truly foreign to Europeans. Australian experience helps to put this set of perceptions into better perspective. Both European settlers in Australia and American visitors found the arid landscape and the flora and fauna to be truly unique. American trees—pines, oaks, and firs—were familiar to Europeans and could be assimilated to European ideas of beauty. Australian trees, the eucalypts, or gum trees, in particular, shed bark instead of leaves, and did not develop the riot of deciduous color that Americans and Europeans rejoiced to see across their autumn landscapes. Much of the Australian vegetation was scrub, rather than cathedral-like forest, and Australia's aridity did not help either. The twisted shapes of many eucalypts, such as the dwarf mallee varieties of the arid zone, added to the perception of the Australian environment as strange. European perceptions derived from Romanticism could accommodate redwoods, but not river red gum. Australia, not the United States, was profoundly foreign to Europeans in environmental terms. Americans, too, eventually found landscapes within their own expanding national ambit that deeply challenged their inherited environmental sensibilities, but this did not happen until they confronted the dry and often inhospitable Southwest, conquered from Mexico, where the land began to resemble that encountered in Australia.

But this uniqueness of Australia's "natural" environment has not been invested with the connotations of exceptionalism that have often greeted America's frontier and wilderness of abundance. It might be argued that it was not the American wilderness that was unique, relative to places in Europe, but the quantity of resources to be transformed. Europe had long since squandered its environmental largesse. Now it was America's turn.

Australia, in comparison, proved to be poorer in terms of its ability to fulfill these Euro-American fantasies about material abundance. Because of severe shortages of water and poorness of soil—measured in terms of the needs of European-style agriculture—much of Australia had more limited potential to be transformed into European-style gardens, farms, and parks. But all this places a very different construction upon the meaning and significance of wilderness in American culture, and upon an American exceptionalism grounded in material conditions. . . .

To make confident statements about American exceptionalism in this or any other area requires much more extensive research than hitherto undertaken into the histories of a range of other countries that have absorbed American influences, paralleled American innovations, and also perhaps even influenced American developments. Part of the problem of encouraging a transnational approach to American history lies in the thin knowledge of American historians concerning the pasts of those other countries whose history might provide a fuller transnational context. To conceptualize American history better, U.S. Americanists need, paradoxically, to study the history of other countries more than they do, and possibly as much as they study their own national past.

This is not to say that Americans are ignorant of foreign histories. In fact, it has been cogently argued by some that America's colonial past has made U.S. historians more receptive than most to the study of foreign cultures. But the countries studied (traditionally those of western Europe) and the ways in which they are studied (as separate nations or regions) may promote consideration of the United States in isolation from wider intellectual, economic, and social currents. All this implies that internationalization of American history must include, rather than supersede, comparative history. Comparison of parts of nations, and of particular movements and issues, is absolutely essential to an internationalizing project. Comparative history must be set within broader themes of transnational history, so as to demonstrate the contingent and ever-changing character of the nation.[23] One example illustrating the possibilities for such transnational comparisons is presented by the environmental connections between California and Australia.

The Viewpoint of the Periphery

The Australian colonies and nineteenth-century California were both frontier regions influenced by the process of settlement, but they also shared geographic distance from the main centers of capital and cultural influence. Both, I argue, were peripheral places.[24] Both places have their distinctive features, but their histories are part of larger movements to dominate native peoples on the edge of European expansion and to transform local environments through economic activity based on staple exports of primary products and the raw exploitation of natural resources. The approach I propose draws upon Australian and American historians' theories of economic peripheral status and social geographers' theories of cultural landscape that enable us to see how the confrontation of European peoples with new environments played out on the edge of empire.

We can reinterpret American history using the vantage point of peripheries, just as Frederick Jackson Turner utilized the role of its internal "peripheral" zone, the frontier, in domestic American development of the eighteenth and nineteenth centuries. The United States itself was once peripheral; part of a great empire, it has become an empire in its own right. Its mentality as a nation has been profoundly influenced, even forged, by this transition. Thus the United

States must be seen in relation to its changing role within the world system of capitalism from periphery to metropolitan power, with all of the effects that the latter can have on other more marginal places.

The comparison and contextualization I am suggesting derive partly from the work of Immanuel Wallerstein and his disciples in the United States, which originated in Latin American dependency theory. The capitalist world economy is an important frame of reference for studies of the development of class relations and state developmental policies. Wallerstein's notion of a world system of capitalism is a powerful tool with which to assess "conventional comparative methods based on modernization's theory of relatively uniform and discrete national societies."[25] But the historical sociologist Phillip McMichael has noted that the crucial weakness of world-systems theory is its formalism: "Like formal comparison, it presumes a whole, an historical system 'whose future is inscribed in its conception.'" Or, to put the matter another way, "the unit of analysis is equated with the object of analysis. . . . By merging the concept of the world-system . . . with its empirical scope, the world-system perspective has no choice but to prefigure history."[26] McMichael's interest lies in the bearing of empirical cases upon the global framework of political economy, but his research project, which includes a major emphasis on Australia's social and economic development as a primary producing and exporting nation, also suggests that Latin American–derived models may not be enough to reveal the complexities of power relations between conquerors and conquered in the settler societies of the white, Anglo-American diasporas. Especially important is the need to realize that Europeans subjugated native peoples and other races on the periphery even where whites were simultaneously being controlled in some measure by the metropolis, either economically or politically.

Theories of staple export-driven economies, neglected in recent years, help to illuminate the problem of peripheral position. Staple theory is not the only example of how economic analysis can be used in the study of transnational history, to be sure. International capital flows, for example, can be charted to show how the trade cycles have operated transnationally, with great social as well as economic effects on employment, migration, and natural resource use.[27] But for peripheral societies, where the conquest of land and the extraction of raw materials were vitally important, staple theory allows us to deal with the unique relationship between colonies, their resources, and metropolitan centers, and to link this to the struggle of social classes over the course of economic development in peripheral zones. Criticisms of staple theory come from economic historians, yet the theory's heuristic value can be rescued when treated not simply as an explanation in which the world economy operates as some exogenous force upon society; rather, social relations within the settler society need to be seen as part of the struggle to define the relationship between local and world economies. Class tensions and struggles have to be built into the analysis of staples by looking at the way in which social aspirations about the distribution of resources are shaped by and shape the focus on distant markets. Within any particular society, social classes have struggled over how to utilize their given environment to meet markets.[28] In both California and Australia, a prominent economic and social problem before 1900 was how to cater to the aspirations of the large numbers of people who came in the wake of the mining booms of the 1850s but who did not profit from gold; instead of accepting the domination of the land by capital-intensive mining and large-scale wheat, sheep, or cattle farming, social reformers dreamed of establishing a democratic, small-scale agriculture, centered on horticulture. The choice was not purely an economic one but an environmental one as well. Reflecting the settlers' European and eastern American aesthetic, horticulture involved the imposition of mixed or "garden" landscapes on parts of California and Australia.

In neither Australia nor California did the advocates of small-scale agriculture succeed, but circumstances enabled California to overcome its peripheral status and make fruit growing—operated eventually as a mass-production industry—a highly profitable and major part of California's long economic climb, beginning in the 1880s. The successes of one socioeconomic interest over another in this struggle over the course of economic development were determined partly by the available soil, water, forests, and other basic resources, but these environmental constraints did not operate in a vacuum. In California, transport and marketing opportunities, the influence of the railroads and other entrepreneurial interests, and eventual incorporation into the larger political economy of the American nation-state, with its vast internal market, allowed some basic environmental constraints to be overcome, at least in the short to medium term.

In Australia, small-scale agriculture suffered from much greater distance from markets and lack of available entrepreneurial capital, as well as greater environmental obstacles posed for any group seeking to reproduce European styles of agriculture. Studying attempts of this sort to shape the relationship with external markets may explain how a vision of the reordering of the landscape succeeded in one settlement society but not in another.

The Spaces of Transnational History

These economic forces and cultural and social contests operate in and on particular places, and this process raises the issue of the precise spatial units of analysis within which American history might be situated. The idea of different spatial scales of human history, reminiscent of Fernand Braudel's levels of historical time in *The Mediterranean and the Mediterranean World in the Reign of Philip II,* has been advanced in relation to the environment by Richard White, who emphasizes the interaction of these levels—the spaces of history—with the relationships between them changing over time.[29] This fits well with the history of Australian and Californian contacts in the nineteenth century. Generally speaking, the problems of distance and European encounters with colonial environments created the space for innovation in environmental policy in peripheral zones of European capitalism. Frontier settlers were innovative in environmental policy because they were at the cutting edge of loss of environmental sustainability. Yet that space for regional autonomy did not last.

In the twentieth century, we witnessed a strengthening of nation-state powers, with environmental policy becoming more highly regulatory, centralized, and professionalized. Since the 1960s, however, we have seen the beginning of an international regime in environmental reform, with a series of UN conventions on the environment, such as the World Heritage Convention of 1972 and that on the Law of the Sea, which "finally came into effect" in 1994.[30] This transnational framework has produced a resurgence of international influences on environmental issues, but these have to take effect on and in different regions. International conventions do not override national interests, but provide sites for transnational organizations to lobby both international bodies and national governments for enforcement of conventions governments have signed. Thus it is important, as Richard White urges, to keep in view all of the levels on which environmental policy operates.

Global

At their broadest level, developments in California and Australia in the nineteenth century could be situated within a global context, commonly studied in the United States as "world history." Environmental history is an important part of the American movement to create a true world history, but even here the pull of Atlantic-focused work is strong, and it is difficult to feed back work by non-Americanists—for example, on Australian or British imperial environmental history—into these models. The idea of ecological imperialism, pioneered by Alfred Crosby, is a classic case of the application of an Atlantic model to explain global patterns, whereas consideration of the settlement societies on their own terms reveals more complex interactions between various new worlds. Crosby's interpretation of these ecological transformations as one-way and biologically deterministic looks different when we examine the cross-fertilization between Australia and South Africa, South America, New Zealand, and California.[31] These cases emphasize the need to temper the impulse toward global themes.

Globalization focuses on the world economy and economic integration of nation-states within its tentacles, yet these influences are often none too specific. In environmental history, some recent and contemporary problems are global, such as climate change and ozone damage, but the incidence even of large transnational influences such as acid rain has not been felt uniformly across hemispheres or regions. In economics, too, these global patterns have often been unevenly experienced. Flows of trade, people, and capital across the globe require rules to police markets, but these rules reflect the asymmetric power of the imperial centers of constantly shifting global systems. The nation-state is not withering away amid these global flows—certainly not in the case of the contemporary United States, which exercises disproportionate power in the setting of global rules but refuses in many cases to submit to conventions perceived as compromising its sovereignty and national interests. Because U.S. national actions are crucially important to global changes, it seems necessary to specify the links between national actions and events, on the one hand, and transnational processes, on the other. Such explanatory frameworks as staple economics and imperialism are useful in providing a historically grounded theory and may specify key changes in regional differences in position and environment.

Yet the long view on these changes is vital to understanding American history. The links between national and transnational influences must be shown in a historical way, since the changing trajectory of nation-state power rather than the legal position is at issue. The General Agreement on Tariffs and Trade (GATT) threatens aspects of U.S. environmental regulation today through the newly established World Trade Organization, as David Vogel shows.[32] Technology and tourism also threaten modern standards.[33] Conversely, the new international trade regime has changed the relationship between environmental lobbying groups and the state. For example, Greenpeace can use international public opinion to influence the policies of nation-states on climate change, oil spills, or the trade in endangered species.[34] How common was such action in the past? It is often forgotten that strong environmental regulation depends on a strong state, something the United States did not have in the nineteenth century. Proper national quarantine, for example, was not established until 1912, and before that time, environmental regulation of imported pests was minimal and chaotic, involving squabbling between the states and the federal government. Interest in international agreements for the protection of flora and fauna goes back to the first decade of the twentieth century and included American involvement.[35] Today, there is a focus on global instruments of cooperation, but most of these are of relatively recent origin. There is a long, underexplored history of efforts of particular lobbying groups to influence international policies over environmental diplomatic issues such as the protection of wildlife and the conservation of ocean fisheries since the Progressive Era. These have typically occurred in a regional setting, especially between the United States and Canada.[36]

Region

This raises the issue of transnational regional influences within American historiography. Regional perspectives, apart from that of the South, appear to be neglected because of the Euro-American and Atlantic bias in historical scholarship. Western American scholars still chafe at the inadequate incorporation of their regional specialization within American history, and trans-Pacific regional contacts, too, have partly been neglected in comparison with the Atlantic, because a majority of the American population (including African Americans) came across that ocean; but new economic development around the Pacific and large numbers of new immigrants to the United States from the region are now changing this. Yet if the recognition is new, the pattern can be traced back to nineteenth-century California and the impact of Asian immigration in the 1850s and 1860s. . . .

The gold rushes of the second half of the nineteenth century provide evidence of these transnational exchanges. From California, people and goods flowed to the Klondike; from Australia to California and back; from Victoria to northern Queensland and to other parts of Australia; and from Chile and Peru to the southwestern United States.[37] The technology and customs of the miners crossed national boundaries and left traces both in the material culture and demographically, in the shape of ethnic diasporas, especially a Chinese diaspora. Americans imported their mining technology into Australia, along with mining personnel, including Herbert Hoover, who served for several years as an engineer on the Western Australian mining fields in the 1890s. American mining machinery, as well, had spin-off effects through its use for artesian bore (groundwater) pumps, which by the 1890s were vital to the cattle industry in the arid Australian Outback. Looking at American history from the vantage point of the Pacific would no doubt reveal other connections such as these.[38]

For the United States, Pacific connections involved, in many social processes, movements from west to east that, in the view of some, render irrelevant the teleology inherent in ideas of Manifest Destiny and a movement "west." Indeed, the very meaning of the American "West" is in question from this standpoint. Migration history is richly suggestive of a more complex process of interaction of cultures in North America from different regions of the western hemisphere and East Asia.[39] These migration patterns have been tied up with racism and war in the twentieth century. Discriminatory land-ownership, immigration, and citizenship laws, anchored in geopolitical anxieties, were widely canvassed and passed in the white settler societies of the Pacific Rim. Similar policies toward Chinese and Japanese settlers were adopted at about the same time in Australia, Canada, the United States, and New Zealand. The international diplomacy of this fear of Asia's "Yellow Peril" in the early twentieth century has been partly covered by historians, but the comparative history of the impacts of these policies on peoples and on the individual nation-states is only beginning to be understood.[40]

Border Crossings

As part of the wider study of regions such as the Pacific coast, specific cultural links between borderlands have received some recognition in American historiography in recent years,[41] but the focus has been on geographic contiguity, and again the perspective of the British settlement colonies is valuable in broadening this concept. Not just the interfaces between the United States and Mexico and Canada, but other kinds of border crossings need to be investigated. Settler societies such as those on the Pacific coast of the United States and Canada and in Australia and New Zealand, which underwent similar, although not identical, processes of colonization, shared ideas, technology, and personnel on a number of issues relevant to transforming the land. Transnational exchanges occurred in dealing with the deforestation that apparently resulted from the introduction of European livestock, especially of sheep in West Coast Meso-America and Australasia;[42] in irrigation technology concerning California, Australia, and British Columbia, where similar problems of aridity were faced and shared concepts of an Arcadian, garden landscape were developed; and in the biological control policies fashioned by Australia, New Zealand, and California in the 1880s and 1890s.[43]

New Questions

Looking at the wider processes of colonial settlement may raise new questions about historical events and processes previously interpreted from a purely internal American standpoint. . . .

Attention to the history of other settler societies and to the impact of political and economic ideas of American origin abroad raises neglected questions as to the content of those American ideas. A prominent example concerns the work of Henry George, best known in the United States for *Progress and Poverty,* his extended and provocative commentary on the class conflicts of the Gilded Age and how to solve them. It must not be forgotten that George first worked out many of his ideas in California in an assessment of the relationship between land as a resource and political class struggle. George's ideas were taken up in terms of land politics more in Australia and New Zealand than in the United States. There has been a tendency, therefore, to forget just how much his political economy was concerned with environmental issues in the United States. George is seen as responding to class inequalities in industrializing society, and the environmental side of his thought concerning land tends to be forgotten. One might be able to look at other political economists and find a connection between land development on the periphery of European expansion, environmental thought, and radical social movements. We do know, for example, that in the 1880s and 1890s, farmers in the Middle West faced problems of drought and soil erosion as well as railroad discrimination. To what extent, then, were midwestern agrarian protests developing an environmental as well as an interest group or class critique of American society and its market economy?[44]

A [final] example is the role of the state. A pronounced tendency in American historiography has been to see the United States as a "weak" state political economy as opposed to the "strong" states of Europe. Comparison with the social democratic settler societies of Australia and New Zealand has seemed merely to confirm the exceptional status of the laissez-faire political economy of United States. But the histories of Australia and California in environmental policy in the nineteenth century show similar pragmatic patterns of use of state power combined with private innovation in each case. The choice of one over the other was not taken easily, and the variables dictating the combination are not what they are often thought to be.

The greater role played by the state in irrigation development and in other environmental policies in Australia should not, however, lead to ahistorical conclusions that contrast a laissez-faire and ideologically "liberal" America with a "socialist" Australia. The reality was always more complicated. One of the most striking aspects of environmental contacts between Australia and California from 1860 to 1900 was the interest in solutions derived from each other's experience. Greater Australian resort to government involvement in horticulture and irrigation after 1900 at the state level in Victoria, as opposed to California, reflected the failure of earlier, more hesitant strategies and private initiatives. Dictating the shift was a harsher natural environment relative to the demands of European-style agriculture, the lack of available capital, and the need for more cohesive and collective action to combat the advantages that competitors in other countries had in access to markets.[45] But the other side of the story was the considerable willingness of American westerners to resort to state power to alter their arid and harsh environments through irrigation. This story has been told in great detail by American historians, but rarely has the impact of Australian experiments in irrigation on these American cases been adequately assessed. That Elwood Mead, commissioner of irrigation in Washington, D.C., from 1925, brought experience to the job accumulated during eight years as state rivers and water supply commissioner in Victoria, Australia, is but one example of cross-fertilization and the use of Australian models to inspire state action in American irrigation policy.[46]

The patterns of state intervention in these roughly parallel cases of California and Australia seesawed over time. Ironically, it was in the United States, not Australia, that federal government intervention in environmental policy was greatest, once the Progressive Era and New Deal regulatory state had been created. Control of public land in the U.S. West, and hence major resource policy, was in federal hands, whereas in Australia, the states inherited control of the Australian equivalent, crown land, from the self-governing colonies at the time of federation. In Australia, fragmentation of environmental management persisted, and there was greater difficulty in developing major federal environmental initiatives such as those achieved in U.S. irrigation policy by the National Reclamation Act (1902), the Hoover Dam project of the 1920s and 1930s, and the even greater irrigation projects of post–World War II America.[47]

We can see from these brief examples how situating American history in the context of other societies that have undergone similar land transformations raises different questions. There is a need for American historians practicing outside the United States to take more account of work done on their subject in other countries, and European perspectives are not enough. Californian and other regional perspectives from the "new Western history" need to be—and are increasingly being—incorporated into mainstream American historiography, but viewing the history of the American West from comparative and transnational vantage points leads to the question of just how uniquely "western" that experience was. The Californian case illustrates the importance of Pacific connections in the further development of American historiography. Without Pacific perspectives—indeed, perspectives from every place touched by European expansion—the internationalization of U.S. history will reflect little more than Euro-American views.

Notes

1. Dorothy Ross, *The Origins of American Social Science* (New York, 1991), 475; Jack Greene, *The Intellectual Construction of America: Exceptionalism and Identity from 1492 to 1800* (Chapel Hill, N.C., 1993), 1.

2. *Modern American Landscapes,* ed. Mick Gidley and Robert Lawson-Peebles, *European Contributions to American Studies,* 26 (Amsterdam, 1995); *Representing and Imagining America,* ed. Philip John Davies, European Papers in American History (Keele, U.K., 1996).

3. See esp. James T. Campbell, *Songs of Zion: The African Methodist Episcopal Church in the United States and South Africa* (New York, 1995); Frederick Cooper, "Race, Ideology, and the Perils of Comparative History," *American Historical Review* 101 (October 1996): 1122–38.

4. For example, on slavery, the convict labor widely imported into North America prior to 1776 seems, from the perspective of a convict colony such as Botany Bay, unjustly neglected in American historiography as part of the range of labor used. Cf. A. Roger Ekirch, *Bound for America: The Transportation of British Convicts to the Colonies, 1718–1775* (Oxford, 1987), a book that partly fills the gap but raises as many questions as its analysis answers.

5. John C. Weaver, "Beyond the Fatal Shore: Pastoral Squatting and the Occupation of Australia, 1826 to 1852," *American Historical Review* 101 (October 1996): 980–1007.

6. Ian Tyrrell, "Making Nations, Making States: American Historians in the Context of Empire," *Journal of American History* 86 (December 1999): 1015–44.

7. Marc Bloch, "A Contribution towards a Comparative History of European Societies," in id., *Land and Law in Medieval Europe: Selected Papers by Marc Bloch,* trans. J.E. Anderson (London, 1967), 44–81.

8. See the *AHR Forum,* "The New British History in Atlantic Perspective," esp. David Armitage, "Greater Britain: A Useful Category of Historical Analysis?" *American Historical Review* 104 (April 1999): 427–45; and J.G.A. Pocock, "The New British History in Atlantic Perspective: An Antipodean Commentary," ibid., 490–500.

9. Louis Hartz, Kenneth D. McRae, et al., *The Founding of New Societies: Studies in the History of the United States, Latin America, South Africa, Canada, and Australia* (New York, 1964). For recent work, see, e.g., Weaver, "Beyond the Fatal Shore," 980–1007; Gary Cross, "Comparative Exceptionalism: Rethinking the Hartz Thesis in the Settler Societies of Nineteenth-Century United States and Australia," *Australasian Journal of American Studies* 14 (July 1995): 15–43; Aurora Bosch, "Why Is There No Labor Party in the United States? A Comparative New World Case Study: Australia and the U.S., 1783–1914," *Radical History Review,* no. 67 (1997): 35–78; Thomas R. Dunlap, "Australian Nature, European Culture: Anglo Settlers in Australia," *Environmental History Review* 17 (Spring 1993): 25–48.

10. Daiva Stasiulis and Nira Yuval-Davis, *Unsettling Settler Societies: Articulations of Gender, Race, Ethnicity and Class* (London, 1995); Phillip R. O'Neil, *Unsettling the Empire: Postcolonialism and the Troubled Identities of Settler Nations* (Ann Arbor, Mich., 1994); Donald Denoon, "Settler Capitalism Unsettled," *New Zealand Journal of History* 29 (October 1995): 129–41.

11. Patrick Wolfe, *Settler Colonialism and the Transformation of Anthropology: The Politics and Poetics of an Ethnographic Event* (New York, 1999).

12. Alfred Crosby, *Ecological Imperialism: The Biological Expansion of Europe* (New York, 1989).

13. Roger C. Thompson, *Australian Imperialism in the Pacific: The Expansionist Era, 1820–1920* (Carlton, Vic., 1980); Claudia Knapman, *White Women in Fiji, 1835–1930* (Sydney, 1986); Wolfe, *Settler Colonialism.*

14. Louis Hartz, *The Liberal Tradition in America: An Interpretation of American Political Thought since the Revolution* (New York, 1955); Hartz, McRae, et al. *Founding of New Societies.*

15. Stephen Pyne, "Frontiers of Fire," in *Ecology and Empire: Environmental History of Settler Societies,* ed. Tom Griffiths and Libby Robin (Melbourne, 1997), 19–34.

16. Tom Griffiths, "Introduction," to *Ecology and Empire,* ed. Griffiths and Robin, 10.

17. Alfred Runte, *National Parks: The American Experience* (New York, 1979), pp. xi, 1; Roderick Nash, *Wilderness and the American Mind* (1st ed., New Haven, Conn., 1967); in the revised 3d edition (1982), Nash added on a final chapter on international perspectives, but it does not sit well with the body of the text that precedes it. For examples of the continuing influence of American exceptionalism in assessing conservation policy, see Michael Kammen, "Culture and the State in America," *Journal of American History* 83 (December 1996): 793, and Marcus Hall, "Restoring the Countryside: George Perkins Marsh and the Italian Land Ethic," *Environment and History* 4 (1998): 100. See also the critique of Muir studies in Steven J. Holmes, *The Young John Muir: An Environmental Biography* (Madison, Wis., 1999), 54–58, 64–65, esp. concerning the Scottish inheritance and its influence on Muir.

18. Richard H. Grove, *Green Imperialism: Colonial Expansion, Tropical Edens, and the Origins of Environmentalism, 1600–1860* (Cambridge, 1995).

19. George P. Marsh, *Man and Nature, or, Physical Geography as Modified by Human Action* (New York, 1864); Michel F. Girard, "Conservation and the Gospel of Efficiency: Un modèle de gestion de l'environnement venu d'Europe?" *Histoire Sociale / Social History* 23 (May 1990): 63–80.

20. On rectification, see Alan Gilbert, "The State and Nature in Australia," *Australian Cultural History* 1 (1982): 9–28. Donald J. Pisani, "Forests and Conservation, 1865–1890," *Journal of American History* 72 (September 1985): 340–59, provided a path-breaking and superior survey of nineteenth-century American attitudes, but he too misses the strong transnational aspect to the movement. See also the perceptive remarks in Hall, "Restoring the Countryside," 91–103.

21. Nash, *Wilderness and the American Mind;* D.J.S. Morris, "'Help Keep the Peccadillo Alive': American Environmental Politics," *Journal of American Studies* 22 (December 1988): 447–55; Peter A. Coates, "'Support Your Right to Bear Arms (and Peccadillos)': The Higher Ground and Further Shores of American Environmentalism," *Journal of American Studies* 23 (December 1989): 439–46; D.J.S. Morris, "'Help Keep the Peccadillo Alive': American Environmental Politics: A Rejoinder," *Journal of American Studies* 23 (December 1989): 446.

22. Colin M. Hall, *Wasteland to World Heritage: Preserving Australia's Wilderness* (Carlton, Vic., 1992), 91–102, makes a start on what is a terribly neglected topic in Australian history.

23. Ian Tyrrell, "American Exceptionalism in an Age of International History," *American Historical Review* 96 (October 1991): 1031–55, 1068–72.

24. Ian Tyrrell, "Peripheral Visions: Californian-Australian Environmental Contacts, c.1850s–1910," *Journal of World History* 8 (September 1997): 275–302; id., *True Gardens of the Gods: Californian-Australian Environmental Reform, 1860–1930* (Berkeley and Los Angeles, 1999).

25. Philip McMichael, "Incorporating Comparison within a World-Historical Perspective: An Alternative Comparative Method," *American Sociological Review* 55 (June 1990): 395.

26. McMichael, "Incorporating Comparison," 391.

27. J.T.R Hughes, *American Economic History* (2d ed., Glenview, Ill., 1987), 298.

28. Philip McMichael, *Settlers and the Agrarian Question: Foundations of Capitalism in Colonial Australia* (New York, 1984), 38–39. A positive review of the value of staple theory for Australia can be found in W.A. Sinclair, *The Process of Economic Development in Australia* (Melbourne, 1976). See also Geoffrey Blainey, *The Tyranny of Distance: How Distance Shaped Australia's History* (Melbourne, 1966); Morton Rothstein, "West Coast Farmers and the Tyranny of

Distance: Agriculture on the Fringes of the World Market," *Agricultural History* 49 (January 1975): 272–80; Morris W. Wills, "Sequential Frontiers: The Californian and Australian Experience," *Western Historical Quarterly* 9 (October 1978): 483–94; Douglass North, *Economic Growth of the United States, 1790–1860* (New York, 1966). For a summary of arguments against the North thesis, see Stanley Engerman and Robert E. Gallman, "U.S. Economic Growth, 1790–1860," *Research in Economic History* 8 (1983): 1–46.

29. Richard White, "Where Is America?" Paper presented to the New York University / Organization of American Historians' Conference on Internationalizing American History, La Pietra, Florence, July 1998; Fernand Braudel, *The Mediterranean and the Mediterranean World in the Age of Philip II,* trans. Sian Reynolds, 2 vols. (1972–73; reprint, Berkeley and Los Angeles, 1995).

30. Ann L. Hollick, *U.S. Foreign Policy and the Law of the Sea* (Princeton, NJ, 1981); Lorraine Elliott, *The Global Politics of the Environment* (New York, 1998), 29, 36.

31. Crosby, *Ecological Imperialism.*

32. David Vogel, "The Environment and International Trade," *Journal of Policy History* 12, 1 (2000): 72–100.

33. Elliott, *Global Politics of the Environment,* 213–14, touches on this, but see also the *Sydney Morning Herald,* May 24, 1997, 35.

34. Elliott, *Global Politics of the Environment,* 136; Vogel, "Environment and International Trade," 72–100.

35. For a brief sketch, see Nash, *Wilderness and the American Mind,* 3d ed., esp. 358–61; on the British Empire's role in the pioneer international agreements on the protection of fauna, see John M. MacKenzie, *The Empire of Nature: Hunting, Conservation, and British Imperialism* (Manchester, 1988), 211; see also Elliott, *Global Politics of the Environment,* 8, on the range of international agreements.

36. Elliott, *Global Politics of the Environment,* 8; Homer E. Gregory and Kathleen Barnes, *North Pacific Fisheries: With Special Reference to Alaska Salmon* (New York, 1939); William F. Thompson and Norman C. Freeman, "History of the Pacific Halibut Fishery," *International Fisheries Commission,* Report no. 5 (Vancouver, 1930).

37. There is no adequate history of this subject. But for some indication of the possible scope, see Jay Monaghan, *Chile, Peru, and the California Gold Rush of 1849* (Berkeley and Los Angeles, 1973).

38. David Goodman, "Gold Fields / Golden Fields: The Language of Agrarianism and the Victorian Gold Rush," *Australian Historical Studies* 23 (April 1988): 21–41; and Goodman, *Gold Seeking: Victoria and California in the 1850s* (Sydney, 1994); for a valiant effort to incorporate the Pacific into world history, see Felipe Fernandez-Armesto, *Millennium: A History of Our Last Thousand Years* (New York, 1995).

39. Ronald Takaki, *A Distant Mirror: A History of Multicultural America* (Boston, 1993); id., *Strangers from a Different Shore: A History of Asian Americans* (Boston, 1989; rev. ed., 1998).

40. Charles Price, *The Great White Walls Are Built: Restrictive Immigration to North America and Australia, 1836–1888* (Canberra, 1974); see also, Sean Brawley, *White Peril: Foreign Relations and Asian Migration to Australasia and North America, 1918–1978* (Sydney, 1995).

41. David Thelen, "Of Audiences, Borderlands, and Comparisons: Toward the Internationalization of American History," *Journal of American History* 79 (September 1992): 436–44; Gerald E. Poyo and Gilberto M. Hinojosa, "Spanish Texas and Borderlands Historiography in Transition: Implications for United States History," *Journal of American History* 75 (September 1988): 393–416.

42. Elinor Melville, *A Plague of Sheep: Environmental Consequences of the Conquest of Mexico* (Cambridge, 1994).

43. Tyrrell, *True Gardens.*

44. Henry George, *Progress and Poverty: An Inquiry into the Cause of Industrial Depressions and of Increase of Want with Increase of Wealth—The Remedy* (San Francisco, 1879). See, on this, the suggestive remarks in Timothy W. Luke, *Capitalism, Democracy, and Ecology: Departing from Marx* (Urbana, Ill., 1999). The best available American discussions of these issues are in John Thomas, *Alternative America: Edward Bellamy, Henry George, Henry Demarest Lloyd and the Adversary Tradition* (Cambridge, Mass., 1987); and Charles Barker, "Henry George and the California Background of Progress and Poverty," *California Historical Quarterly* 24 (June 1945): 97–115.

45. Louis Hartz, *The Liberal Tradition in America* (New York, 1955); Cross, "Comparative Exceptionalism"; Gilbert, "State and Nature in Australia," 9–28.

46. Joseph Powell, "Elwood Mead and California's State Colonies: An Episode in Australasian-American Contacts, 1915–1931," *Journal of the Royal Australian Historical Society* 67 (March 1982): 328–53.

47. For Australia, see Alan Gilbert, "The State and Nature in Australia," *Australian Cultural History* 1 (1982): 9–28; Joseph Powell, *Environmental Management in Australia, 1788–1914* (Melbourne, 1976); for the extensive role of the state in the American West in irrigation policy, see Donald Worster, *Rivers of Empire: Water, Aridity and the Growth of the American West* (New York, 1985); Norris Hundley Jr., *The Great Thirst: Californians and Water, 1770s–1990s* (Berkeley and Los Angeles, 1992), 229–30; Marc Reisner, *Cadillac Desert: The American West and Its Disappearing Water* (New York, 1986). See also Kevin Starr, *Material Dreams: Southern California through the 1920s* (New York, 1990), 59–61.

CHAPTER 10

American Studies in a Pacific World of Migrations

HENRY YU

If, as George Lipsitz suggests, Los Angeles is a street corner, taking a trip along the streets that lead to and from this intersection might trace a larger world in which it, and this place called "America," are embedded. Like many before, I have come to Los Angeles from elsewhere and now call it home, but instead of seeing myself at the end of a one-way journey that has ended in Los Angeles, a migrant to this place from somewhere else, I think of Los Angeles as an intersection on a larger grid. In this world, migration is a process without end, comings and goings rather than the singular leaving of one place and arriving at another by which we mythically understand the immigrant's story. Los Angeles is one street corner, one intersecting node for many journeys, and if we follow the roads outward we find ourselves navigating the well-worn paths of a much larger world, where people riding buses and buggies (and planes and trains and automobiles), or finding passage in the holds of trans-Pacific ocean liners, or hidden in the back of a pickup truck, come to and from and through Los Angeles. Each of us in Los Angeles is tied in long links to other people in other places, drawing a map dense with the scrawling lines of our journeys.

Is Anybody in L.A. Actually from Here?

The strange thing about Los Angeles in its incarnation as the entertainment capital of the world is that the celebrities so powerfully associated with Los Angeles are usually not from here, fueling an impression that nobody is ever actually from Los Angeles. Of course, Los Angeles, like any place, can claim plenty of people who were born and raised here, but its image is strong as a city in which everybody is from

somewhere else. What if we were to export this particularly Los Angelean sense of imagined spatial belonging to the rest of the world? Rather than talk about how rooted the citizens of Los Angeles are to the physical space of the city, we could instead talk about how other metropolitan sites in the United States, North America, and perhaps around the world are actually more like Los Angeles in this aspect. Los Angeles, in other words, might not be the exception but the rule if we understand the history of the last two centuries as dominated by migration. First of all, we need to think about how we narrate migration. The actual movement of human bodies from one point to another has no inherent meaning, but is given meaning through the classifications of those movements. We imagine that going to work each day is one kind of movement, whether we walk two blocks to work or get on an airplane and fly across the continent. But if we get on a plane and "immigrate" to another country, even for job-related purposes, then this is a different kind of movement. My purpose is not to erase all distinctions between different forms of movement and migration, but to highlight how we categorize such differences. We should give more thought to the origins of our categories, and whether we should reclassify movements to achieve other political purposes. One of the most important benefits for American studies in placing migration to and from the Americas at the center of our scholarship, it seems to me, is to escape nationalism as our rationale.

So much of social scientific scholarship on migration for the last century has concentrated on "immigration," the influx of human bodies defined as foreign in origin to a nation. As Andreas Wimmer and Nina Glick Schiller have argued, this "methodological nationalism" has created

From Henry Yu, "Los Angeles and American Studies in a Pacific World of Migrations," *American Quarterly* 56 (September 2004): 531–543. © American Studies Association. Reprinted with permission.

generations of scholarship that have assumed the political interests of nation-states as the reason for the study of migration. Consequently, the question of assimilation into the host society dominated immigration scholarship from the earliest studies of the University of Chicago's sociology department, the foundational school for training social scientists in the United States.[1] Scholarship centered on national concerns has subsequently emphasized the crossing of national borders as the essential definition of what counted as immigration. The distance traveled or the existential experience of migration rarely determined the importance of migration. Michael Williams has labeled this a "border guard perspective," mocking how the study of migration so often took security and the control and incorporation of bodies as fundamental questions.[2]

There were many migrants at the turn of the twentieth century whose movements into the United States, for instance, provoked little concern: white, English-speaking Protestants from Canada were of little interest to most immigration scholars. Instead, immigration studies focused on groups that came to be defined as being a "problem" to the nation. Migrants from Asia, Latin America, and Southern and Eastern Europe needed to be studied and their movements observed. By the mid-twentieth century, the prevailing scholarship moved from a focus on these migrant groups as a problem to a study of their distinctive "cultures," shifting the question away from their desirability as foreigners to examinations of their lingering ethnicity within America. As exclusionary laws such as the 1882 Chinese Exclusion Act and the 1924 Reed-Johnson Act created categories of "illegal" immigrants, many migrants also assumed a "legal" identity defined by ever-changing legislation on citizenship and national status.[3]

Against this legacy of misapprehending migration, how should we instead understand it, and what might American studies learn from how Los Angeles has been shaped by migration? Following the authors of *Nations Unbound,* many scholars turned to the point of view of the migrants themselves to understand how the experience of migration is often a transnational process that ties together local places in more than one nation. Additionally, scholars traced the historical effects of colonialism in creating these linkages, recognizing how national belonging is no longer synonymous with residence in the geographic territory of the nation-state.[4] Other scholars have focused on the often circular networks created by labor migrants, with multidirectional flows that support national imaginings and nationalist political movements far away from "home" countries.[5]

The decentering of the nation within migration studies has helped release scholarship from the holding cells of the border guard perspective, but can we go further? There has been a tendency in studies of Chinese migration to Southeast Asia, for instance, to analytically blur the distinction between the "internal migration" within the Chinese nation-state and the "external" migration of overseas Chinese, emphasizing how the phenomenon of a laborer moving from an agricultural village to a nearby market town to find work is linked to the out-migration of the same kinds of laborers to Southeast Asia and across the Pacific to the Americas. The distinction of internal versus external migration is thus shown to obscure how the two rely on the same migration networks.[6] How are we to study migration in the nineteenth and twentieth centuries, periods marked by the expanding power of nation-states and of their control of migrating bodies, without assuming the analytical centrality of the very borders that such nation-states created? The distinctions between internal and external migration, between plain old moving around and immigration/emigration, between legal migration and illegal smuggling, have also been the product of the border guard perspective. While they have powerfully shaped migration patterns, we should avoid seeing migration exclusively through these categories.

What if we considered not just the migration of human bodies across national boundaries, but the movement of bodies throughout space as the basis of our studies? If we thought, for instance, of Los Angeles and Vancouver, British Columbia (two local sites in which I am particularly interested), as two nodal intersections, two street corners in a larger set of crisscrossing paths, we would see how these places connect with each other and with myriad other sites around the Pacific and the Americas. There would be some nodes that would be denser than others, cities and ports and gathering places, busy intersections with people coming and leaving and going through. "Illegal migration," rather than a category that extends outward from the moment of border crossing, infecting the way we understand the whole experience of the migrant, would become only one of the ways that migration has been shaped in the last two centuries. We would see how it intersects with other processes. For instance, after the Chinese Exclusion Act of 1882, Chinese workers shifted to Canada, Australia, and Mexico as destinations. They also continued to come into the United States, but the process had been changed—curtailed and constrained, driven into illegality. Their movements, however, remained embedded in larger networks of migration that continued to exist and in which the United States was only one location.

If we saw the world through the eyes of my great-grandmother, how different would it look? Lee Choi Yee was in her eighties when she left China in 1965. She had already been entwined in a network of family labor migration that had connected her home village in Guangdong province with Sydney, Australia, and Honolulu, Hawai'i, and all up and down the west coast of North America for almost a century. Generations of young males had left similar rural villages in Guangdong province to labor in distant places, sending money back to support families and occasionally returning home to find wives and sire children. If they were lucky, they retired wealthy men. My great-grandmother's husband spent his entire adult life in Australia, and although he had asked for her to join him and the Aboriginal second wife he had married in Sydney, she never did. He spent two extended trips to China with her, once between 1908 and 1911, and another between 1918 and 1919, each time fathering a daughter. After he left the second time, she would never see him again. Replicating her own married life, my great-grandmother would marry her youngest daughter off to another overseas laborer in 1937, this one in North America, who, along with his brothers had looked for their fortunes in the Pacific Northwest borderlands that straddled the U.S.-Canada boundary.

To see the world through my great-grandmother's eyes is to see a world both intimate and local—a farm, a village, your children and husband's relatives around you—as well as vast and linked to far-flung places. For years, her husband would send back, along with regular monetary remittances, fresh apples and oranges from his grocery in Australia. Her daughter married in anticipation of similar remittances from her own husband, who worked for much of his life as a butcher on an Alaskan cruise ship. When my great-grandmother mortgaged some of the family farmland to pay the passage for her brother to Trinidad, she continued the practices of borrowing and lending that girded a family economy of migration. His voyage was an investment, to be repaid with returns in long years of labor on plantations and then in a corner store. Well before my great-grandmother crossed the ocean to join her relatives in the Americas, she had been linked by migrant chains that anchored her existence there. When she went with my mother and my grandmother to join my grandfather in 1965, she traveled a route that was well worn, albeit traced across water. For generations her relatives had traveled trans-Pacific shipping lines; she flew in an airplane.

In the decades before her death, she continued to live in a world whose mental geography spanned great distances, celebrating grandchildren's birthdays in the United States, in Canada, in China and Hong Kong. My brother was the first to travel to Los Angeles, as an architecture student at UCLA and then an architect based in L.A., creating an initial space in my great-grandmother's imagination for "Loh Sung" as she called it, so that my decade here can trace its genealogy back through his presence and mine and tie her whole long history of migration to a place she had never been. Of course, Los Angeles has a history of Chinese migration, going back to its origins as an urban settlement. The original Los Angeles Chinatown was populated by people very much like my great-grandmother, peasants from rural areas of southern China near Hong Kong and Macau. More recently, just as in Vancouver, waves of migrants to Monterey Park and the San Gabriel Valley east of downtown L.A. have created new settlements that connect Los Angeles with Hong Kong, Shanghai, and Taiwan. The Chinese of Los Angeles are now linked with the migratory networks of people who have come from other areas in the United States and with places all through the Americas and Europe and around the Pacific and Asia.[7]

What lessons can we learn from such a life? Was my great-grandmother typical or not? Certainly she was representative of many women embedded in the migratory labor networks that tied the developing economies of the Americas to places of origin all around the Atlantic and the Pacific. The western coast of North America was not exceptional in this regard, attracting opportunistic migrants and laborers just as Argentina, Australia, South Africa, and the eastern United States had in the late nineteenth and early twentieth centuries. This period was marked by global flows of migration, and the chains of migration that linked disparate sites in Europe, Asia, Africa, and the Americas. Today, as my grandfather did decades ago, young Indonesian and Filipino cooks and waiters on Alaskan cruise ships spend long years away from their families, sending home remittances and connecting the places they visit to women and children in rural villages outside Jakarta and Manila. In Queens and Flushing, New York, workers from Fujian province in China mingle with those from Mexico, Pakistan, India, the Dominican Republic, El Salvador, and Guatemala, just as they do in downtown Los Angeles.

My great-grandmother's life was both typical and not, but the historical context of the migration networks in which she lived was and is a widespread phenomenon. Increasingly by the late nineteenth century, nation-states expressed their sovereignty by marking the bodies of those who crossed their borders. The Chinese Exclusion Act of 1882 necessitated a whole new bureaucracy to issue identification papers and control the movements of this newly created set of unwelcome migrants. Thus began a long process of differentiation between citizens and a class of perpetual foreigners that invested some bodies with privileges of national belonging while denying them to others defined as "aliens" and "ineligible to citizenship."[8] This process of national marking, with its demonization of some migrants as undesirable and the cementing of others into a common citizenry, paralleled similar processes in Canada, Australia, and New Zealand. Practices of white supremacy and new techniques of racialization helped legislate the uneven contours of national belonging around the globe.

In the United States, many of those who were defined by legislation as "aliens"—Chinese, Japanese, Filipino, East Indian, Mexican—found themselves, in the words of Mae Ngai, in the position of being "impossible subjects." However, we should be careful not to diminish the richness of these migrants' lives by seeing them only through the categories of their exclusion. They struggled despite the harshness of laws, defining in their own ways lives only partially encompassed by the category of "illegal" migrant.

From the point of view of border guards, they were engaged in smuggling and deception, telling lies in order to cross national boundaries. For those who saw immigration laws as unjust and discriminatory, breaking such laws involved no moral evasion, and the fictions they created became a part of the everyday fabric of their lives. Because of quirks in the exclusion laws, some Chinese were allowed to migrate even after 1882: merchants and scholars could still enter and leave, and those born in the United States were accorded citizenry and the privileges of border crossing. Acquiring the paperwork of a "legal" migrant became a route to the United States, and a lively trade in identity papers developed. The man my great-grandmother chose as her daughter's husband bought a fictive identity to enter the United States. For the rest of his life, his official name in English would be Low. The first time his real name, Yeung, appeared in English was on his headstone.

The granting of instant citizenship to those born within the geographic borders of the United States has had a tremendous effect on static conceptions of spatial belonging. For the first half of U.S. history, the possession of U.S. citizenship bore little relationship to the privileges of traveling across its borders—almost anyone was allowed in, and so citizenship was superfluous. As Erika Lee argues, excluding the Chinese forced the development and expansion of federal immigration law, so that what began as legislation aimed at restricting the border crossings of a specific group became entangled with definitions of national citizenry. In the Supreme Court case *U.S. v. Wong Kim Ark* in 1898, national belonging through nativity became automatic for everyone, even the Chinese. American-born Chinese possessed rights as citizens, including the privileges of border crossing, that were more important than their legal identity as a race "ineligible" for citizenship.

This automatic citizenry through nativity has reinforced birthplace as the most basic legal form of spatial identity, but it has also informed spatial identity in general. Native-born Angelenos, that seemingly rare breed, have staked a claim to belonging over those who have moved to Los Angeles. Being "raised" in a place is a secondary form of belonging, one that can be measured in multiple ways, from an emphasis on schooling and youth as formative stages, to others that mark the passage of time—how many years of living in a place does it take before you can call yourself a native? What if you never do? Sometimes claims of belonging are produced by longing and desire, a need to feel at home here, or a feeling of exile that longs for a home elsewhere. Spatial belonging can even be against someone's wishes, propelled by the need of others (or of nation-states) to claim someone even if he or she never felt at home, or to exclude someone despite that person's desire to belong.

If we move away from categories of belonging that emphasize static definitions of place and legal regimes of citizenry, we can see spaces not as geographically bounded (mirroring the territorial claims of nation-states), but connected in fascinating ways by the movements of human bodies. And if we follow the bodies, Los Angeles as a site of intersection leads us away from the East Coast, Atlantic-centered perspective of so much U.S. scholarship. We would see the United States embedded in a world in which the Americas are a part of both Pacific and Atlantic migrations.

Los Angeles and Regional Migrations

If we begin with Los Angeles, we will see how regional distinctions are so powerfully the consequence of regional migration networks. For instance, patterns of racialization and white supremacy are almost directly tied to regional migration flows. The vast bulk of scholarly work on racialization in the United States has been focused on the historical creation and maintenance of the dichotomy between black and white. However, if we understand migration flows as regional, we see that the American South might be better understood as a southeast region connected to the slave-holding societies of the Caribbean and the trans-Atlantic flows of enslaved Africans that populated the region. In the Northeast, a region dominated by large-scale European migration, the demonization of blacks helped mold together a diverse array of European migrants through the promised benefits of white supremacy. This was despite the fact that migrant flows of African Americans northward were relatively small until the twentieth century, but antiblack practices served a different purpose than in slaveholding regions in the Southeast. Understanding the dynamic of racialization in the Northeast as an outgrowth of the particular challenges of its migration history is crucial. Anti-Semitism and anti-Catholic practices dominated the region in the late nineteenth and early twentieth centuries, and the expansion of a generic Judeo-Christian whiteness to embrace Jews and Catholics was accompanied by a heightening of the racial divide between white and black, not its lessening.

The rise of ethnicity as a category was rooted in the migration patterns of the northeastern United States. Ostensibly, when W. Lloyd Warner and Leo Srole used the concept of ethnicity for the first time in the 1940s, it was to claim that racial groups were just one form of ethnicity. But the irony of the rise of the term ethnicity was that it came to describe migrant groups such as Irish, Italians, Slavs, and Jews that so recently had been vilified in the Northeast as inferior races. In separating out the intractable problem of African Americans as the primary remaining "racial" problem, Warner and Srole unwittingly recognized the process under way by which race as a concept was shifting in meaning in the Northeast; the expansion of white supremacy in the mid-twentieth century now allowed those willing and able to embrace it to erase problematic origins. Changes in clothing and manners, the adoption of English, the erasure of overt "ethnicity"—all created the illusion that ethnicity was somehow a choice, leaving behind those who could not pass for white in the dark cellar of a newly constricted category of race.

That this process was primarily focused in a northeastern region tied to trans-Atlantic flows of European migrants is quickly apparent when we compare it to the Northwest and the Southwest. These two regions were tied to trans-Pacific migrations and the conquest of formerly Spanish and American Indian territories. In the Southwest, the westward migration of European colonizers and the enslaved Africans brought along by the expansion of slavery crossed paths with Native Americans and the northern settlers of Spanish America. Most important, for much of the history of both the Northwest and the Southwest, Native American genocide and the labor politics of anti-Asian agitation, not antiblack practices, dominated processes of racialization. Early African American migrants who came to the western United States saw that another set of migrants was considered the primary problem, and before large numbers of African Americans arrived during World War II, it was the "Oriental problem" that dominated the racial politics of western cities such as Los Angeles, San Francisco, and Seattle. By the mid-twentieth century, Mexican labor migrations had come to replace the supply of Chinese, Japanese, Korean, Punjabi, and Filipinos cut off by exclusionary policies, and the racialization of Mexicans as eternal foreigners and cheap labor grafted onto similar representations of earlier Asian migrants.[9] In similar ways that antiblack politics helped amalgamate various Europeans into a common white supremacy, anti-Asian and anti-Mexican politics achieved a parallel result. Without an understanding of the consequences of regional networks of migration that brought migrants from Asia, Europe, Latin America, and the eastern United States to the Pacific coast, the very different patterns of regional racialization in the United States do not make sense.

More recently, scholarship focusing on imperialism and territorial expansion has placed areas such as the Southwest and overseas colonies such as Hawai'i and the Philippines at the center of U.S. history, in particular for the fifty years before and after the crucial date of 1898. The question of empire, it seems, has placed the West and the Pacific on the map.[10] The current scholarship of Vicente Diaz, Amy Stillman, and Damon Salesas at the University of Michigan, for instance, has the potential of reimagining the way that the United States has been engaged in the imperial contests of the region. Pacific studies scholars offer us a way of seeing the United States on the eastern edge of a world that has its own history, not autonomous and separate from the United States, but integral and intersecting, blending local and global connections.[11]

Most acutely, a century of recurring U.S. wars in Asia, from the conquest of the Philippines and Hawai'i through the conflict with Japan, with China in Korea, in Southeast Asia, and again in Central Asia now, has created a vicious dehumanization that sees in recurring cycles an Asian face of the enemy. We rarely consider military personnel migrants, but they are akin to the missionaries and civil servants who accompanied empire and in their own descriptions often described their travels in ways that any traveler going to a new land might. It is not surprising that the militarized migration of Americans into the Pacific created the mass tourism that would dominate sites such as Hawai'i, Bangkok, and Manila. Military expansion has been a particularly gendered form of migration, spawning a violent masculinity and accompanied by a sexual tourism replete with alluring images of Asian women as willing commodities. Between 1945 and 1965, when anti-Asian exclusion kept the borders of the United States closed to most Asian migrants, it was U.S. wars in Asia that were the direct source for many of those who did come: refugees and orphans from the Korean conflict or war brides of military personnel stationed in Japan and South Korea.

Differential migrations, in a sense, created the distinctiveness of the major regions of the United States by tying them into regional flows of human bodies. By following migrants as they move, we discover the local worlds in which they lived and see these sites of intersection as particularly generative places, with the capacity to create encounters and ideas and forms of social life that are bewildering in their complexity. Migrants create geographic space. Spatial imaginings are the product of movement, not of the static relationship between a body and the ground where it appears to root. Settlers are migrants who fantasize about stopping and making an organic tie between themselves and the land they occupy. A region is an act of imagination, an organizing and categorizing of a smaller subset of the ideas generated at these nodes of intersection, reflecting the density of migration routes and the pattern of connection between places. We might think of racial ideologies as one set of ideas generated at such sites, and nationalism as one particularly powerful mobilization of such regional cognition, produced by some migrants attempting to create and institute a shared sense of community with each other. In the historical case of the United States and other settler colonies, this often comes at the expense of other migrants or of aboriginal peoples. If we were to envision the Americas as a collection of intersecting nodes, connected with others around the world, we could reimagine this historical construct called "America" as the product of a limited number of these dense intersections.

Seeing American studies through the lens of migratory processes, then, foregrounds both the experience of individual migrants and the networks in which they are embedded. It also allows us to see how the ideas of "America" have migrated along these routes. If the question of "what is America" has been at the heart of American studies since its inception, here is a way that we can escape the parochial exceptionalism of too constrained a focus. If we see this imagined nation, and the border practices by which it is enacted, as the creation of the migratory networks that embed the Americas in a larger world, then the United States as a subject will not drive our scholarship like the administration of a citizenship oath. We can follow its travels, its appropriation and its reimagining, and recognize that it is just one of many ideas created out of the dense interactions that have occurred at nodal intersections. It might be one way by which we can truly forsake the political interests of nation building as the narrow rationale for scholarship.

"Life Differs from Death in the Matter of Movement"[12]

I will end by getting back to the places I live. After my great-grandmother migrated from her natal village to her husband's village in Zhongshan county, then to Shanghai, where her daughter worked in a textile factory, then across the Pacific to Canada, she embedded herself in her backyard garden in Vancouver. In this garden, she grew the vegetables of a time and place far away, offering them with friendly gestures to new neighbors who spoke English (or not) with Italian and Romanian and Punjabi accents. Afterward, she would watch wrestling on TV and mutter in frustration at the underhanded tactics of the bad guys (even in another language the simple dichotomies of professional wrestling are clear). Sometimes, after eating her daily dinner of salted fish, vegetables, and a bowl of rice, she would sit in her room patiently folding paper money festooned with bright gold and silver paint. She would fold paper for an hour here and an hour there, filling giant empty Pampers boxes that she had asked my mother to keep from the grocery store we ran. One day, in her late nineties, she decided to learn English. Day after day she repeated simple phrases such as "Good day" and "How are you?" When asked why she was trying so hard to learn a new language at her age, she replied that if she was going to be buried here, she wanted to know how to speak to her neighbors, just in case they did not speak Chinese. After she passed away, we opened up the dozens of densely packed Pampers boxes and burned all the hand-folded paper, sending to her the special ceremonial money that had value only in the afterworld.

We live here, in this world, but at any moment we don't know if this street corner that we call home will be the place we stop. There are roads that lead to other places, and people come and people go. We make friends and meet neighbors, and try to make our little corner a better place to live. All we can ask is that those who follow us remember the journeys we took, the people we knew, the places we were, and, if you're my great-grandmother, to send her some money at the end of the road so she can go hang out with her neighbors. Perhaps if historians followed these struggles

and built their histories out of them rather than out of the abstraction called America, we might see a history of lives lived well and stories worth telling.

Notes

My thanks to Katherine Kinney, George Sanchez, Marita Sturken, Raul Villa, and other readers at *American Quarterly* for their editorial suggestions, as well as special gratitude to Brandy Lien Worrall for a close reading and major revisions. Thanks also to Hokulani Aikau, Rainer Buschmann, Vince Diaz, Madeline Hsu, Adria Imada, Masumi Izumi, Kehaulani Kauanui, Erika Lee, Davianna MacGregor, Adam McKeown, Mae Ngai, Gary Okihiro, JoAnna Poblete, Robert Chao Romero, Damon Salesas, Christen Sasaki, Paul Spickard, Amy Stillman, Edgar Wickberg, and Michael Williams for conversations about mutual interests in this essay's themes.

1. Andreas Wimmer and Nina Glick Schiller, "Methodological Nationalism, the Social Sciences, and the Study of Migration: An Essay in Historical Epistemology," in a special issue on "Transnational Migration: International Perspectives," ed. Peggy Levitt, Josh DeWind, and Steven Vertovec, *International Migration Review* 37.3 (2003); an updated version of nation studies of incorporation, Richard Alba and Victor Nee, *Remaking the American Mainstream: Assimilation and Contemporary Immigration* (Cambridge: Harvard University Press, 2003); for Chicago sociology and migration, my *Thinking Orientals: Migration, Contact, and Exoticism in Modern America* (New York: Oxford University Press, 2001).

2. Michael Williams, "Destination Qiaoxiang: Pearl River Delta Villages and Pacific Ports, 1849–1949" (doctoral dissertation, University of Hong Kong, 2002).

3. For a number of works on immigration, in particular Chinese migrants, and exclusionary policies, see Lucy Salyer, *Laws Harsh as Tigers: Chinese Immigrants and the Shaping of Immigration Law* (Chapel Hill: University of North Carolina Press, 1995); Adam McKeown, "Ritualization of Regulation: The Enforcement of Chinese Exclusion in the United States and China," *AHR* 108.2 (April 2003): 377–403; Erika Lee, *At America's Gates: Chinese Immigration and American Exclusion, 1882–1943* (Chapel Hill: University of North Carolina Press, 2003); Mae Ngai, *Impossible Subjects: Illegal Aliens and the Making of Modern America* (Princeton: Princeton University Press, 2004). On the border patrol, see Kathleen Lytle-Hernandez, "Entangling Bodies and Borders: Racial Profiling and the U.S. Border Patrol, 1924–1955" (doctoral dissertation, University of California, Los Angeles, 2002).

4. Linda G. Basch, Nina Glick Schiller, and Cristina Szanton Blanc, *Nations Unbound: Transnational Projects, Postcolonial Predicaments, and Deterritorialized Nation-States* (Langhorne, Pa.: Gordon and Breach, 1994); also Linda G. Basch, Nina Glick Schiller, and Cristina Szanton Blanc, *Towards a Transnational Perspective on Migration: Race, Class, Ethnicity, and Nationalism Reconsidered* (New York: New York Academy of Sciences, 1992).

5. Donna R. Gabaccia, "Is Everywhere Nowhere? Nomads, Nations, and the Immigrant Paradigm of United States History," *Journal of American History* 86.3 (December 1999); Madeline Hsu, *Dreaming of Gold, Dreaming of Home* (Stanford, Calif.: Stanford University Press, 2000); Adam McKeown, "From Opium Farmer to Astronaut: A Global

History of Diasporic Chinese Business," *Diaspora* 9 (2000); "Conceptualizing Chinese Diasporas, 1842–1949," *The Journal of Asian Studies* 58.2 (May 1999): 306–37; and "Transnational Chinese Families and Chinese Exclusion, 1875–1943," *Journal of American Ethnic History* 18.2 (Winter 1999). On Chinese migrants in the border region of Southern California and northern Mexico, Robert Chao Romero, "The Dragon in Big Lusong: Chinese Immigration and Settlement in Mexico, 1882–1940" (doctoral dissertation, University of California, Los Angeles, 2003).

6. See the pioneering work of G. William Skinner on overseas Chinese in Southeast Asia, as well as that of Wang Gungwu, Anthony Reid, and Edgar Wickberg.

7. For the intersections between Asian Americans and Latinos in Monterey Park, see Leland Saito, *Race and Politics: Asian Americans, Latinos, and Whites in a Los Angeles Suburb* (Urbana: University of Illinois Press, 1998); for more on the "new" suburban Chinatowns, Wei Li, "Spatial Transformation of an Urban Ethnic Community: Chinatown to Chinese Ethnoburb in Los Angeles" (doctoral dissertation, University of Southern California, 1997); Laurence J.C. Ma and Carolyn Cartier, *The Chinese Diaspora: Space, Place, Mobility, and Identity* (Lanham, Md.: Rowman Littlefield, 2003).

8. Ngai, *Impossible Subjects;* Erika Lee, *At America's Gates.* See also John Torpey, *The Invention of the Passport: Surveillance, Citizenship, and the State* (Cambridge: Cambridge University Press, 2000).

9. Richard White, *It's Your Misfortune and None of My Own: A History of the American West* (Norman: University of Oklahoma Press, 1991); Patricia Limerick, *Legacies of Conquest: The Unbroken Past of the American West* (New York: Norton, 1987); and Donald Worster, *Rivers of Empire: Water,* *Aridity, and the Growth of the American West* (New York: Pantheon, 1985). For regional interpretations of race in the West, Tomás Almaguer, *Racial Fault Lines: The Historical Origins of White Supremacy in California* (Berkeley: University of California, 1994); Quintard Taylor, *In Search of the Racial Frontier* (New York: Norton, 1998).

10. Amy Kaplan and Donald Pease, eds., *Cultures of United States Imperialism* (Durham: Duke University Press, 1993); Lisbeth Haas, *Conquests and Historical Identities in California, 1769–1936* (Berkeley: University of California Press, 1995); John C. Rowe, ed., *Post-Nationalist American Studies* (Berkeley: University of California Press, 2000); Shelley Streeby, *American Sensations: Class, Empire, and the Production of Popular Culture* (Berkeley: University of California Press, 2002).

11. On Pacific Islander studies, Joanne Rondilla, Debbie Hippolyte Wright, and Paul Spickard, eds., *Pacific Diasporas* (Honolulu: University of Hawai'i Press, 2002). On oceans, Jerry Bentley, "Seas and Oceans as Frameworks of Historical Analysis," *The Geographical Review* 89.2 (1999): 215–24. See also Gary Okihiro's forthcoming book, which includes his unpublished essay "Towards a Pacific Civilization." For an interesting view on migration from the point of view of Pacific Island navigators, see Vicente M. Diaz, director/writer/coproducer, *Sacred Vessels: Navigating Tradition and Identity in Micronesia* (29 mins., 1997), a video documentary about the survival of traditional seafaring in Polowat, Central Carolines, and its revival in Guam and the Marianas.

12. Roderick McKenzie, "Movement and the Ability to Live," *Proceedings of the Institute of International Relations,* 1926, reprinted in McKenzie, *On Human Ecology,* edited and with an introduction by Amos Hawley (Chicago: University of Chicago Press, 1968), 134.

CHAPTER 11

The African Diaspora and the Re-Mapping of U.S. History

ROBIN D.G. KELLEY

What is the United States, if not a nation of overlapping diasporas? Perhaps this is the defining characteristic of the New World, if not the entire world—particularly in the age of modernity, when travel, discovery, settlement, and nation-building have been the order of the epoch. While historians have recognized and explored these overlapping diasporas, with roots in Europe, Asia, Africa, and Latin America, they tend to treat them as an assemblage of marginalized identities. Rarely has the concept of diaspora been employed as the central theme of American history.[1]

Part of the problem has been our conception of the United States as a discrete national entity, a social and political formation whose boundaries are clear, fixed, and traversed only in the most obvious ways (e.g., through immigration, international conflicts, movements of capital and labor, etc.). Our attachment as historians to nation-centered histories and our employment of categories such as "domestic" and "foreign" to frame historical processes and events limit our understanding of the international dimensions of American history. Diaspora as an analytical concept enables us to move beyond such neat divisions. Diasporan subjects are transnational subjects: their thoughts, desires, allegiances, and even their bodies are between and betwixt nations. They represent a wide range of transnational political relationships and international connections that belie the idea that "domestic" struggles can be studied in isolation from world events.[2]

Most students engaged in the interdisciplinary fields of ethnic studies have long drawn on diaspora models to understand the U.S. experience. Black studies, Chicano/Chicana studies, Asian-American studies developed an implicit diasporic perspective growing out of the social movements of the late 1960s and 1970s. Whether they are speaking of borderlands, migrations, or diasporas, ethnic studies scholars examine the connection between place of "origin" and America. For people of African descent, "diaspora" has served as both a political term with which to emphasize the unifying experiences of African peoples dispersed by the slave trade, and an analytical term that enabled scholars to talk about black communities across national boundaries. . . . Although the black studies conception of Africans and African descendants as one people (albeit diverse and complex, of course) has led to charges of essentialism, it is precisely this perspective of seeing black people in global terms that forced the field to be relentlessly international and comparative.[3]

Diaspora has recently returned to analytical prominence in both the humanities and social sciences, fueled in part by current debates about "globalization." Indeed, some of the latest efforts to develop a diaspora framework have profound implications, not only for our understanding of the black world, but for the way we write American history, if not the history of the modern West. The making of the African diaspora was as much the product of "the West" as it was of internal developments in Africa and the Americas. At the same time, racial capitalism, imperialism, and colonialism—the key forces responsible for creating the modern African diaspora—could not shape African culture(s) without altering Western culture.[4] The purpose of this essay, then, is to map out points of convergence where the study of the African diaspora might illuminate aspects of the encounter between Europe and the New World. At

From Robin D.G. Kelley, "How the West Was One: The African Diaspora and the Re-Mapping of U.S. History," in *Rethinking American History in a Global Age,* ed. Thomas Bender (Berkeley: University of California Press, 2002), 123–147. Reprinted by permission.

the same time, I want to draw attention to the ways in which specific formulations of the meaning of "diaspora" can also keep us from seeing the full range of black transnational political, cultural, and intellectual links. I end with a few speculative remarks on how we might broaden our understanding of black identities and political movements by exploring other streams of internationalism that are not limited to the black world.

Defining "Diaspora"

The term "diaspora" is essentially the Greek word for "dispersal," although its most common usage refers to the scattering of Jews throughout the world. For African Americans, however, the concept of diaspora and its particular meaning in New World black cultures has clear historical as well as biblical roots. Early activists, historians, and clergy frequently cited Psalm 68, verse 31, which prophesized that "Ethiopia shall soon stretch out her hands unto God." It has been used as a way of describing the black (world) condition and the source of liberation. This understanding of Ethiopia as the metaphor for a black worldwide movement against injustice, racism, and colonialism lay at the heart of the early historical scholarship on the role of African peoples in the making of the modern (and ancient) worlds.[5]

The metaphor proved especially powerful because African Americans practically had no "country" to speak of through most of the nineteenth century. Before the adoption of the Fourteenth Amendment, African Americans' citizenship status had not been legally established, and even a constitutional amendment was not enough to settle the matter. The implications of this condition for historical scholarship and national identity are enormous. While some black leaders insisted on their right to citizenship, others called on black people to leave the country and find a homeland of their own. African American leaders searched outside of the United States for political allies and often sought connections with North America's colonized people—the Native Americans.

Long after the ratification of the Fourteenth Amendment, the question of African American citizenship had hardly been resolved, and emigrationist sentiment remained a central issue in black political discourse, rendering both issues critical topics for early historical investigation. Black Americans were not willing to relinquish their claims to citizenship; yet, they reached a point of profound pessimism and began to deeply question their allegiance to and identification with the United States. In his 1921 essay "Fifty Years of Negro Citizenship as Qualified by the United States Supreme Court" (reprinted and widely circulated three years later as a small booklet), the historian Carter G. Woodson does not mince words: "The citizenship of the Negro in this country is a fiction."[6]

Woodson's criticisms help explain black historians'

early international perspective. Unlike the key figures in the U.S. historical profession, black historians tended to be critical of the nationalist, racist historiography of the era. In a measured but sharp critique of nationalism in the modern world, the historian Charles Wesley argued that imperialism was a natural outgrowth of nationalism. "Under the guidance of the national spirit," Wesley wrote, "imperialism made its way into Africa, Asia and the islands of the sea. The scramble for colonial empires was a distinct aspect of nationalism for the latter part of the nineteenth century. The glory of the nation seemed to be, in part, in its control of an overseas empire."[7]

Yet, for all their distrust of, or outright opposition to, U.S. nationalism, most of these early black historians were engaged in a different sort of nation-building project. Whether deliberately or not, they contributed to the formation of a collective identity, reconstructing a glorious African past to refute degrading representations of blackness and establish a firm cultural basis for a kind of "peoplehood." They identified with the larger black world in which New World Negroes were inheritors of African as well as European civilizations. To varying degrees, they were products of the same political imperatives that led to the formation of Pan-African, "Ethiopianist," and other black international movements. Thus, in assessing the political basis for black historians' peculiar internationalism, one might argue that it is a manifestation of a kind of "nationalism" or, rather, of a diasporic identity that might be best described as "imagined community."[8]

The term "African diaspora" in its contemporary usage emerges clearly in the 1950s and 1960s. It served in scholarly debates as both a political term emphasizing the unifying experiences of African peoples dispersed by the slave trade and an analytical term that enabled scholars to talk about black communities across national boundaries. Much of this scholarship examines the dispersal of people of African descent, their role in the transformation and creation of new cultures, institutions, and ideas outside of Africa, and the problems of building Pan-African movements across the globe.[9] A critical component of this work, as well as all diaspora studies, is the construction and reproduction of a diasporan consciousness. The main elements of such a consciousness (to varying degrees, of course) include a collective memory of dispersal from a homeland, a vision of that homeland, feelings of alienation, desire for return, and a continuing relationship and identity with the homeland.[10]

Although the analogies to studying nationalisms might seem obvious, we must remain cognizant of the distinct differences between nations, nation-states, and diasporas. First, the African diaspora is not a sovereign territory with established boundaries, although it is seen as "inherently limited" to people of African descent. Second, while there is no official language, there seems to be a consistent effort to locate a single culture with singular historical roots, no matter how mythical. Third, many members of this diaspora see themselves as an oppressed "nation" without a homeland, or they imagine Africa as home—either a place of return or a place from which they are permanently exiled.[11] They therefore understood their task as writing the "history of a race"—a people scattered by force and circumstances.

The Question of Africa

One of the foundational questions central to African diaspora studies is to what degree are New World black people "African," and what does that mean? It's an old question, posed as early as the publication of Sir Harry Johnston's amateur anthropological writings in a prodigious and enigmatic book, *The Negro in the New World* (1910), and explored more systematically in the pioneering work of anthropologists such as Melville Herskovits and Lorenzo Turner. Indeed, it could be argued that anthropologists have been central to the first wave of diaspora studies during the interwar years. Scholars from all over the Western hemisphere, including Nina Rodrigues, Arthur Ramos, Mario de Andrade, Edison Carneiro, Roger Bastide, and Gonzalo Aguirre Beltran, made the case that some aspects of African culture survived the Middle Passage and continued to exist in the New World.[12] . . .

Based on these initial anthropological explorations, a new generation of scholars sought to prove that much of West and Central African culture survived in the Americas. Focusing on music, dance, religion, and even linguistic patterns, dozens of historians and anthropologists extended Herskovits's initial findings and discovered many examples of continuity and the persistence of cultural memory.[13] On the other hand, scholars such as Sidney Mintz and Richard Price revised the cultural retention models, placing greater emphasis on discontinuity. In a fairly early and provocative position paper, Mintz and Price described New World Afro-American culture as a process of syncretism shaped by the context of "culture contact." The creation of New World cultures involved a kind of creolization of many different West and Central African cultures. Arguing that no single African culture survived the Middle Passage intact, they suggest that the enslaved forged new institutions, religious practices, and kinship roles out of a common experience and understanding of the crises created by the transatlantic slave trade and the plantation complex. The Mintz and Price position does not rule out African retentions, but they reject claims of a singular African heritage and place greater emphasis on the emergence of new dynamic cultures.[14]

These debates have hardly died. Recent work, in fact, has found continuity by paying closer attention to specific ethnicities, religions, and cultural identities within Africa itself.[15] Michael Gomez's *Exchanging Our Country Marks* (1998) is distinctive in that it is an Africanist's interpretation of the making of the African diaspora. He carefully and painstakingly reconstructs African culture and social life *in time and space* in those regions directly affected by the trade. After following these groups across the Atlantic and showing the degree to which concentrations of specific African cultures remained intact, he then charts what he argues is a transformation from specific ethnic identities to an internal black conception of "race," or rather a collective identity that regards African-descended people as a common community.[16] . . .

The movement and transformation of cultures, however, was never a unidirectional process. As J. Lorand Matory demonstrates in a recent article on the origins of the Yoruba nation, the diaspora profoundly shaped, and even gave birth to, new cultures on the African continent. He found that some of the most basic elements of Yoruba culture did not derive from the hinterlands of Lagos, Nigeria, but from Brazil, Cuba, Jamaica, North America, the Virgin Islands, and Sierra Leone.[17] . . .

Whether we employ metaphors of survival, retention, exchange, transformation, acculturation, or dialogue, the remaking of African New World cultures has enormous implications, not just for the study of the African diaspora but for the Atlantic as a whole. We can ask similar questions and consider similar methodologies for studying the making of New World European and even Native American cultures/identities/communities. The idea of a "European" culture or even "English" culture is often taken for granted and hardly ever problematized in the way that "African" is constantly understood as a social construction. For example, we might follow Nahum Chandler's lead and think of early New World Euro-Americans as possessing what DuBois called "double-consciousness": say, English and American, with whiteness as a means of negotiating this double consciousness.[18] Or we might consider the "New World" as a source of Pan-Europeanism in the way that it became the source of Pan-Africanism. In other words, insights drawn from cultural studies of the African diaspora may offer new ways of understanding New World identity formations as sites of both exclusivity and inclusivity, deepening our understanding of race, nationality, and culture.[19] . . .

On the other hand, the "Africanity" question has recently been met with caution, if not outright hostility, by scholars concerned with essentialism and interested in locating hybridity and difference within black cultures. This is understandable; thinking of cultural change as a process of "destruction" or loss does more to obscure complexity than illuminate the processes of cultural formation. Furthermore, emphasis on similarities and cultural continuities not only tends to elide differences in black cultures (even within the same region or nation-state), but it does not take into account the similar historical conditions in which African people labored and created/re-created culture. Forced labor, racial oppression, colonial conditions, and capitalist exploitation were global processes that incorporated black people through empire-building. They were never uniform or fixed, but they did create systems that were at times tightly coordinated across oceans and national boundaries. This raises a number of questions. Were the so-called cultural survivals simply the most effective cultural baggage Africans throughout the world used in their struggle to survive? Or were they created by the very conditions under which they were forced to toil and reproduce? Are the anthropological studies from which many of these scholars draw their comparisons and parallels valid in view of the fact that they were made under colonial domination? Is Pan-Africanism simply the recognition that black people share the same timeless cultural values, as some nationalists would have us believe, or is it a manifestation of life under racism and imperialism?

Leading the critical assault against racial essentialism in the study of black culture is a group of Afro-British scholars, most notably Stuart Hall, Kobena Mercer, Hazel Carby, and Paul Gilroy. They are less concerned with African cultural retentions than with how New World black cultures are made differently within different empires. Much of their work focuses on the twentieth century, thus emphasizing the modern and postmodern processes by which cultures are constantly being remade and commodified under capitalism. Paying attention to the rich diversity within black diasporan communities, they paint a complex portrait of African-descended people fractured by class, gender, culture, and space. Taken as a whole, they have produced a sophisticated body of work that attempts to understand the sources and range of black identities and how they operate in political struggle.[20]

Paul Gilroy's *The Black Atlantic* has received the most attention because it functions as a kind of manifesto for new studies of diaspora. *The Black Atlantic* is a collection of essays on nineteenth and twentieth century intellectual history that places slavery and race at the center of the Enlightenment and the dawning of modernity. Although he focuses exclusively on African American males (i.e., W.E.B. DuBois, Frederick Douglass, Richard Wright), by tracing their intellectual and cultural "routes and roots," he is able to explain how diasporic connections can be made and maintained through ideas and cultures that have little to do with Africa. He builds on DuBois's notion of "double-consciousness" to reveal how black intellectuals' radical critique of Western culture and domination was a product of their engagement with the West. Not only were these men betwixt and between "Negro" and "American," but travel generated transnational identities between Europe and the United States. Gilroy's subtle exploration of these men's lives and ideas also exposes the inescapable hybridity of Western civilization—the dark secret that the most avid defenders of the West refuse to acknowledge.[21] . . .

The Black Atlantic . . . ought to be read as a transatlantic philosophy of culture that draws insights from historical processes. In many ways, it builds on another, lesser-known text by the political scientist Cedric Robinson, *Black Marxism: The Making of the Black Radical Tradition.* Published a decade before *The Black Atlantic,* Robinson's book is a work of history and philosophy that pays attention to the political economy of slavery, feudalism, and capitalism. And whereas Gilroy limits his scope primarily to black encounters with England and the United States (with detours to Germany, France, and Israel), Robinson's ambitious project takes in half the globe, from western and eastern Europe to the Caribbean, from Brazil to the Middle East and the African continent.

Despite the title, *Black Marxism* is in part a history of the making of the Atlantic world—not simply the African diaspora. Just when European labor was being thrown off the land and herded into the newly formed industrial order, Robinson argues, African labor was being drawn into the orbit of the world system through the transatlantic slave trade. But political and economic interdependence did not translate into cultural assimilation. European civilization, whether in the shape of feudalism or of the nascent industrial order, simply did not penetrate African village culture. To understand the dialectic of African resistance to enslavement and exploitation, Robinson suggests, we need to look outside the orbit of capitalism, to West and Central African culture. The first African New World revolts were governed not by a critique of Western society but a total rejection of enslavement and racism as it was experienced. More intent on preserving a past than transforming Western society or overthrowing capitalism, Africans ran away, became outliers, created Maroon settlements (often with indigenous people and renegade whites), or tried to find a way home, even if it meant death.

However, with the advent of formal colonialism and the incorporation of black labor into a more fully governed social structure, Robinson detects a more direct critique of the West and colonialism, a revolt set on transforming social relations and revolutionizing Western society rather than reproducing African social life. The contradictions of colonialism produced native bourgeoisies intimate with European life and thought, whose assigned task was to help rule. But their contradictory roles as victims of racial domination and tools of empire, as Western-educated elites who felt like aliens in the dominant society as well as among the masses, compelled some of these men and women to revolt, thus producing the radical black intelligentsia. . . .

Both works agree that elite Europeans—the men of the Enlightenment—had no monopoly on the development of modernity. They view the modern world, and New World Atlantic societies in particular, as the product of numerous global encounters—through war, enslavement, cooperation and solidarity, intellectual and cultural exchanges, and so on—between Africans, Native Americans, and Europeans. Although Robinson examines the making of the English working class, the colonization of the Irish, and the myth of a unified "English" culture, neither book sets out to study all of the overlapping diasporas that have come to define the New World. A work that does—and does so brilliantly—is Peter Linebaugh and Marcus Rediker's *The Many-Headed Hydra: Sailors, Slaves, Commoners, and the Hidden History of the Revolutionary Atlantic*. It is an exemplar of transnational history, a model of how diaspora studies can be employed to construct a coherent, unified history of the Atlantic world. Building on the best traditions of "history from the bottom up," *The Many-Headed Hydra* is the story of the making of the modern working class—early capitalism's "hewers of wood and drawers of water." Born of dispossession—from the English countryside, the West African savannah, the North American forests—the Atlantic working classes were products of global revolutions in trade, industry, and colonization during the seventeenth and eighteenth centuries.

Challenging the kind of nation-bound formulations of English working-class history developed in the pioneering work of E.P. Thompson and Eric Hobsbawm, Linebaugh and Rediker argue that the English working class can only be understood as a transatlantic, imperial working class—one that includes Africans, Native Americans, and other transplanted Europeans.[22]

As much as the colonizers and adventure capitalists tried to control and divide this multiracial gang of laborers, the hewers and drawers found ways to communicate, expressed their desire for liberty, envisioned a different sort of New World turned upside down. From Barbados to New York, Liverpool to the Guinea Coast, they revolted. And it is through revolts and conspiracies that Linebaugh and Rediker are able to tell an international history of the formation of the United States. For it is in rebellion—whether in the form of an armed uprising or the formation of a Maroon village on the outskirts of the colonial settlement—that people from different parts of the world come together. The 1741 New York slave conspiracy, for example, turns out to be a critical event in Atlantic history, not just *American* history, or the history of Africans in the Americas. As the authors demonstrate, the conspiracy not only involved Irish and Native Americans, who identified as oppressed laborers and dreamers united in their hatred of "the whites," but its leaders included veterans of other revolts in the Western hemisphere. Some of the Africans had had experience organizing rebellions in the Caribbean and, for one reason or another, had been sold off to North America rather than executed.[23]

What most historians have understood as a local slave conspiracy, Linebaugh and Rediker reconceptualize as an example of working-class internationalism. Indeed, they have unearthed many other examples of workers' rebellions across the color line and the Atlantic Ocean, revealing how they shaped both the English and American revolutions. But finding such stories proved immensely difficult, because the laboring rebels were not the victors. The lack of sources documenting such movements, they remind us, is usually a by-product of suppression. The stories of revolt died with the rebels and were erased by the executioners: historical revision by way of the gallows, the rack, and the guillotine. Nevertheless, the failure of these uprisings and conspiracies helps us understand how the United States came into being as a "herrenvolk Republic" founded on capitalism, slavery, and the sanctity of private property. The outcome was hardly inevitable, nor was it some natural outgrowth of Western civilization. Rather, it was the product of a long and bloody struggle, from which a ruling class of white propertied men emerged victorious. In order to decapitate the "many-headed hydra," the new rulers sought to harden the color line and tighten the physical and ideological boundaries of the nation.

The Many-Headed Hydra, in short, reveals that American history is always international and diasporic history. At the very least, it is the story of how merchant and industrial capital, with its attendant maritime revolution, and the rise of the transatlantic slave trade, created a brand-new international working class and simultaneously gave birth to new, often suppressed, expressions of internationalism. In demolishing unilinear narratives that draw a line from, say, John Locke to the ideas of the American Revolution, Linebaugh and Rediker discover many competing ideas of liberty and freedom, derived from West and Central African religions, fugitive Maroon societies, various antinomian movements emerging out of Europe (the levelers, the diggers, the ranters), and other sources of Atlantic radicalism.

Likewise, Julius Scott's forthcoming book on New World black people in the age of the Haitian Revolution invokes the "sailing image" both literally and metaphorically to illustrate how networks of oral transmission and shared memory were the crucial dimensions of Afro-diasporic politics and identity. Black republicans not long out of Africa are its main characters, and they developed their own politically driven, relatively autonomous vision of an antislavery republicanism that in many ways was far more radical than anything being pursued in France or Philadelphia. Scott also demonstrates the level of ideological debate and international organization that existed among African Americans in the New World—a crucial element in the unfolding of the revolution. At the very least, Scott demonstrates how an Afro-diasporic approach can force us to rethink the history of the creation of New World republicanism, systems of communication in the eighteenth and early nineteenth centuries, the political and cultural autonomy of African people in the West, and the crucial role that black sailors played in the age of democratic revolutions.[24]

Scott's work more broadly echoes a tradition of scholarship that puts the end of modern slavery in global perspective. As W.E.B. DuBois, C.L.R. James, Eugene Genovese, and more recently Eric Foner, Robin Blackburn, Rebecca Scott, Thomas Holt, and Frederick Cooper have demonstrated, the transition from chattel slavery to freedom was a global process, in which the struggle over the reconstruction of the labor force had enormous implications for capitalism, democracy, liberal thought, and racial ideology.[25] Over sixty years ago C.L.R. James's *The Black Jacobins* argued that the slaves themselves shaped debates in the French National Assembly on the meaning of freedom and liberty as a natural right. More than any doctrine or speech, the revolt of African slaves themselves put the question of freedom before Paris radicals. Michel-Rolph Trouillot's book *Silencing the Past* goes further, demonstrating that at the start of the nineteenth century, the Haitian Revolution not only represented the only truly universalist claim to freedom and liberty for all of humanity but proclaimed the right of slaves (and colonial subjects) to win that freedom by armed struggle—an idea that no Western "free" nation ever accepted, not even during much of the twentieth century.[26]

Taken together, these studies move beyond unitary narratives of displacement, domination, and nation-building that center on European expansion and the rise of "racial" capitalism. The rise of the transatlantic system not only helped forge the concept of Africa and create an "African" identity but proved central to the formation of a European/ "white" identity in the New World. By seeing American history in a diaspora framework, the central role of African people in the making of the modern world becomes clear. Slave labor helped usher in the transition to capitalism; black struggles for freedom indisputably shaped discourses on democracy and the rise of republicanism; and cultures, ideas, and epistemologies taken from Africa or created in the New World have deeply influenced art, religion, politics, philosophy, and social relations in the West. Hence, just as Europe invented Africa and the New World, we cannot understand the invention of Europe and the New World without Africa and African people.

Not Out of Africa: Black Internationalism and the Limits of Diaspora

The concept of diaspora, as powerful as it is, falls short of illuminating all of the international dimensions and contexts of black identities. Too frequently we think of identities as cultural matters, when in fact some of the most dynamic (transnational) identities are created in the realm of politics, in the way people of African descent sought alliances and political *identifications* across oceans and national borders. We might follow Paul Gilroy's lead here and distinguish "identities" from "identifications"—the latter referring to the specific political choices people make in the context of struggle. Like identities, identifications are always contingent, transitory, and perhaps more than anything, strategic. By expanding the discussion from the question of black identity in the context of an African-centered notion of diaspora to black identifications—specifically questions of transnational political links and international solidarity—we open up new avenues for writing a world history from below.[27]

Consider the fact that black labor migrations (in slavery and freedom) were generally produced by many of the same needs of capital, the same empires, the same colonial labor policies, the same ideologies that forced so-called coolie labor from China and the Asian subcontinent to work on the plantations, mines, railroads of European empires and of the Americas. In fact, Pacific crossings and Asian migrations have profoundly influenced modern streams of African American nationalism, producing unique moments of black political identifications with Pan-Asian movements. We can point to numerous examples of black solidarity with various Pan-Asian movements or specific national struggles, particularly during the eras of Japanese imperialism in the Pacific, after the success of the Chinese Revolution and the emergence of Maoism, and during the war in Vietnam.[28] One excellent example of work that begins to do this is Vijay Prashad's *The Karma of Brown Folk,* which documents a long history of black and Indian solidarity. Despite deliberate efforts on the part of the colonial and nationalist states to foster anti-Asian sentiment among blacks in the Caribbean and Africa, there were dramatic moments of solidarity. Radical black intellectuals like DuBois recognized the racism suffered by Indians and promoted their struggle against British colonialism and South African racism.[29] On the other hand, Indians in India have occasionally found inspiration in radical movements in the African diaspora. For example, the black "untouchables" of India, known as the Dalits, developed an awareness of their African ancestry and have linked their struggle against racism to the struggle of all black people. Some have even compared their experiences with those of American blacks and formed organizations modeled on the Black Panther Party.[30]

Knowing that many peoples were migrating from all over the world, especially as industrialization and revolutions uprooted millions of people from Europe to Asia, what were the political implications of these overlapping migrations? This is a particularly important question, for it illuminates the degree to which the "black" world can only be understood in the context of the larger world and vice versa. During the first two decades of the twentieth century, for example, the world was marked by massive migrations on a global scale, rapid industrialization, the building of the Panama Canal, labor migration from Europe and Asia to North America, the Caribbean, and South Africa—these were developments that produced and were shaped by international wars, revolutions, famines, and violence. Indeed, this is precisely the context for international black movements such as Garveyism, the African Blood Brotherhood, the International League of Darker Peoples, and other black radical formations during the first part of the twentieth century.[31] . . .

My point here is that black internationalism does not always come out of Africa nor is it necessarily engaged with Pan-Africanism or other kinds of black-isms. Indeed, sometimes it lives through or is integrally tied to other kinds of international movements, such as socialism, communism, feminism, surrealism, and religion (e.g., Islam). Communist and socialist movements, for example, have long been harbingers of black internationalism and sources of radical Pan-Africanism that explicitly reaches out to all oppressed colonial subjects as well as to white workers. Although the relationships have not always been comfortable, the communist movement enabled new identifications with other oppressed peoples. Black people took up arms to defend the Spanish Republic in the late 1930s, traveled to Cuba and China in the 1960s, and made linkages with other radicals of the African diaspora in the most unlikely places—including the schools and streets of Moscow.[32] . . .

[M]ost of these encounters are seen in terms of how "Western" ideas have influenced black people as opposed to the other way around. The question we still need to grapple with is this: How have African American struggles for freedom shaped other national or international movements beyond the United States?

One area where these questions have been taken up recently is in the history of the Civil Rights movement and its relationship to anticolonialism. Of course, scholars have always been aware of these linkages since Civil Rights activists themselves identified with the independence movements in Africa, Asia, and the Caribbean. Recent books by Brenda Gayle Plummer, Penny Von Eschen, William Sales, Van Gosse, Timothy B. Tyson, Komozi Woodard, and others have gone even further, demonstrating just how fundamental Cold War politics and anticolonial movements were in shaping black domestic struggles for freedom. With Nazism barely in the grave, the horrors of European colonialism and U.S. racism came under closer scrutiny. Inspired by the anticolonial movements in Africa, Asia, and the Caribbean, African American activists found allies in the newly independent nations, sometimes turning to the United Nations to criticize U.S. race relations as well as colonial policies abroad. Between 1946 and 1951, at least three Civil Rights groups submitted petitions to the United Nations on behalf of the entire black world to draw attention to the denial of human rights to African Americans in the United States. On the other side, several leaders of independence movements cited the civil disobedience campaigns in the United States as models for their own political mobilization.[33]

The impact of anticolonial movements and the growing "Third World" presence in the United Nations was felt not only by Civil Rights activists but by the federal government. Indeed, the enormous impact international politics played in promoting federal policies on race is the subject of a recent book by Azza Salama Layton, who documents the State Department's active support for desegregation, prompted in part by incidents involving diplomats and students from Asia, Africa, and the Caribbean who had suffered the indignities of Jim Crow—most frequently in the nation's capital. The State Department and the Justice Department filed briefs on behalf of plaintiffs in most of the major civil rights cases, from *Shelly v. Kraemer* (outlawing restrictive covenants) to *Brown v. Board of Education.* Desegregation was in the State Department's interests because UN delegates from India, Pakistan, and Burma, not to mention the Eastern-bloc countries, relentlessly criticized the United States for allowing Jim Crow to persist at home while claiming to be a beacon of democracy for the world. In their brief in support of *Brown v. Board of Education,* State Department officials minced no words when explaining the reason for their intervention: "The United States is trying to prove to the people of the world, of every nationality, race, and color, that a free democracy is the most civilized and most secure form of government. . . . The existence of discrimination against minority groups in the United States has had an adverse effect upon our relations with other countries."[34]

Toward a Diasporic Approach to American History

If we employed a diaspora framework to U.S. history, what would change? What might result? First, we would be compelled to write the kind of history that follows people back and forth across the physical borders of the United States, a history in which the boundaries are determined not by geopolitics but by people and their movements—physical and mental, real and imagined. Of course, this idea, although still undeveloped, is hardly new. A quarter century ago, Herbert Gutman suggested that immigrant workers drew on "cultural baggage" from their homelands in their struggle to survive and shape American industrialization. Another labor historian, John Laslett, built on Gutman's insights and developed a general theory of American working-class history based on "overlapping diasporas." In other words, the politics and cultures of immigrant workers tend to be bound up with the politics of their home country. Peter Kwong's *Chinatown, New York: Labor and Politics, 1930–1950,* for example, demonstrates how impossible it is to make sense of Chinese working-class politics in New York City without reference to the Chinese Revolution of 1949. Likewise, Mexican-American politics and labor struggles in the Southwest during the early twentieth century are incomprehensible without understanding the Mexican Revolution.[35]

Second, processes such as "creolization," which we associate with the early period of "contact," would become a primary subject of investigation for all periods of U.S. history. Indeed, we may discover that the most dynamic moments of creolization, cultural transformation, and hybridization—if we can use those terms—might have occurred as a result of post-1965 immigration. We might even begin to think of the United States as a "home" country out of which reformations of Old World cultures travel throughout the globe. The movement of American cultural forms, such as jazz in the mid- to late twentieth century, might be studied not merely as another example of U.S. cultural imperialism but as an African American diaspora whose influence on Africa—the real and imagined place of black cultural "origins"—is itself profound. If we merely think of the impact of jazz and other black vernacular music as a return to the source, we miss the degree to which African American cultures are modern products of many overlapping diasporas. This way, the presence of Africa in America will not be limited to retentions during the period of early contact, but will be treated as a central question in the recasting of national history.

Finally, a diaspora framework ought to persuade scholars to revisit other intellectual traditions, other constructions of American history produced by so-called minority thinkers whose work consciously rejects the minority label. Here I am speaking of scholarship linked to social and political movements that have asserted global strength and significance through identification with a larger diasporic community. Whether independent activist/intellectuals or university-trained scholars, these scholars have much to teach us. Not only have they made marginalized groups visible, but their work has always started from the premises that history is global, and that in telling the stories of America, nothing is out of bounds.

Notes

I am deeply indebted to everyone who participated in the "internationalizing" seminars that met in New York City, Florence, Amsterdam, and Cambridge, England. I am especially grateful to Thomas Bender, who not only created the intellectual space to help me think about these issues, but understood better than I did the broader implications of what I was proposing. I have benefited immensely from the insights of Earl Lewis, George Lipsitz, Kwame Alford, David Thelen, Mauricio Tenorio, Alton Hornsby Jr., Marcellus Barksdale, and their wonderful students and colleagues at Morehouse College. I am also indebted to all who participated in the "Transcending Tradition" conference at the University of Pennsylvania, especially its distinguished organizers, Tukufu Zuberi and Farah Jasmine Griffin. Special thanks to Cedric J. Robinson, John Hope Franklin and the late John Henrik Clarke, without whom this essay could not have been written. Finally, I thank Tiffany Patterson; some of the ideas in this essay come out of my collaborations with Patterson, with whom I co-authored a longer piece about the African diaspora to appear in the *African Studies Review*.

1. There are some outstanding exceptions, including Earl Lewis, "To Turn as on a Pivot: Writing African Americans into a History of Overlapping Diasporas," *American Historical Review* 100, 3 (June 1995): 765–87; John H. M. Laslett, *Challenging American Exceptionalism: "Overlapping Diasporas" as Model for Studying American Working Class Formation, 1810–1924* (Chicago, 1987); Donna R. Gabaccia, "Is Everywhere Nowhere? Nomads, Nations, and the Immigrant Paradigm of United States History," *Journal of American History* 86, 3 (December 1999): 115–34; Donna R. Gabaccia and Fraser M. Ottanelli, "Diaspora or International Proletariat? Italian Labor, Labor Migration, and the Making of Multiethnic States, 1815–1939," *Diaspora* 6 (Spring 1997): 51–84.

2. Obviously, this is changing, as evident from recent issues of the *Journal of American History* and the *American Historical Review*. We have witnessed an explosion of transnational scholarship in American history, particularly in the areas of the Atlantic world, diaspora studies, environmental history, migration studies, intellectual history, and the history of political, social, and cultural movements.

3. See, e.g., Stuart Hall, "Cultural Identity and Diaspora," in *Identity: Community, Culture, Difference,* ed. John Rutheford (London, 1990), 222–37; Michael Hanchard, "Identity, Meaning and the African-American," *Social Text* 8, 24 (1990): 31–42; Kobena Mercer, *Welcome to the Jungle: New Positions in Black Cultural Studies* (London, 1994); several essays in *Black Popular Culture,* ed. Gina Dent (Seattle, 1992); E. Frances White, "Africa on My Mind: Gender, Counter Discourse and African-American Nationalism," *Journal of Women's History* 2,1 (Spring 1990): 73–97.

4. See Paul Gilroy, *The Black Atlantic: Modernity and Double Consciousness* (Cambridge, Mass., 1993); Peter Linebaugh, "All the Atlantic Mountains Shook," *Labour / Le Travailleur* 10 (Autumn 1982): 87–121; Cedric Robinson, *Black Marxism: The Making of the Black Radical Tradition* (Chapel Hill, N.C., 1983); and an excellent essay by Kim D. Butler, "What Is African Diaspora Study? An Epistemological Frontier" (forthcoming in *Diaspora*).

5. See George Shepperson, "African Diaspora: Concept and Context," and St. Clair Drake, "Diaspora Studies and Pan-Africanism," both in *Global Dimensions of the African Diaspora,* ed. Joseph E. Harris (Washington, D.C., 1982); for early examples of the Ethiopian analogy, see William Wells Brown, *The Rising Son; or the Antecedents and Advancement of the Colored Race* (Boston, 1876); Edward Wilmot Blyden, especially *Christianity, Islam and the Negro Race* (Edinburgh, 1967) and *Black Spokesman: Selected Published Writings of Edward Wilmot Blyden* (New York, 1971); Robert Benjamin Lewis, *Light and Truth: Collected from the Bible and Ancient and Modern History, Containing the Universal History of the Colored and Indian Race, from the Creation of the World to the Present Time* (Boston, 1844); J.E. Casely Hayford, *Ethiopia Unbound: Studies in Race Emancipation* (2d ed., London, 1969); Alexander Crummell, *Africa and America: Addresses and Discourses* (Springfield, Mass., 1891); Wilson J. Moses, *Alexander Crummell: A Study of Civilization and Discontent* (New York, 1989); Martin R. Delany, *The Condition, Elevation, Emigration, and Destiny of the Colored People of the United States* (reprint, New York, 1968); William Leo Hansberry, *Pillars of Ethiopian History,* ed. Joseph Harris, (Washington, D.C., 1974). See also William R. Scott, *The Sons of Sheba's Race: African-Americans and the Italo-Ethiopian War, 1935–1941* (Bloomington, Ind., 1993); Joseph E. Harris, *African-American Reactions to the War in Ethiopia, 1936–1941* (Baton Rouge, La., 1994); Wilson Jeremiah Moses, *Afrotopia:*

The Roots of African American Popular History (New York, 1998); St. Clair Drake, *Black Folk Here and There: An Essay in History and Anthropology, Afro-American Culture and Society,* 7 (2 vols., Los Angeles, 1987–90), vol. 1; *Imagining Home: Class, Culture, and Nationalism in the African Diaspora,* ed. Sidney J. Lemelle and Robin D.G. Kelley (New York, 1994); Robert Weisbord, *Ebony Kinship: Africa, Africans, and the Afro-American* (Westport, Conn., 1973).

6. Carter G. Woodson, "Fifty Years of Negro Citizenship as Qualified by the United States Supreme Court," *Journal of Negro History* 6, 1 (January 1921): 1. On the question of black citizenship, emigration, and political movements after the Fourteenth Amendment, see, e.g., Floyd Miller, *The Search for a Black Nationality: Black Emigration and Colonization, 1787–1863* (Urbana, Ill., 1975); Nell Irvin Painter, *Exodusters: Black Migration to Kansas after Reconstruction* (New York, 1977); Sterling Stuckey, *Slave Culture: Nationalist Theory and the Foundations of Black America* (New York, 1987); Hollis R. Lynch, *Edward Wilmot Blyden: Pan-Negro Patriot, 1832–1912* (London, 1964); William E. Bittle and Gilbert Geis, *The Longest Way Home: Chief Alfred C. Sam's Back-to-Africa Movement* (Detroit, 1964); Robert A. Hill, "Chief Alfred Sam and the African Movement," in *Pan-African Biography,* ed. Robert A. Hill (Los Angeles, 1987); Edwin S. Redkey, *Black Exodus: Black Nationalist and Back-to-Africa Movements, 1890–1910* (New Haven, Conn., 1969); V.P. Franklin, *Black Self-Determination: A Cultural History of African-American Resistance* (2d ed., Brooklyn, N.Y, 1992); Kevin Gaines, *Uplifting the Race: Black Leadership, Politics, and Culture in the Twentieth Century* (Chapel Hill, N.C., 1996).

7. Charles Wesley, "Three Basic Problems in Human Relations" (n.d., ca. 1950), reprinted in James L. Conyers Jr., *Charles H. Wesley: The Intellectual Tradition of a Black Historian* (New York, 1997), 191; see also L.D. Reddick, "A New Interpretation for Negro History," *Journal of Negro History* 22, 1 (January 1937): 18–19.

8. Benedict R.O'G. Anderson, *Imagined Communities: Reflections on the Origin and Spread of Nationalism* (1983; rev. ed., New York, 1991).

9. See George Shepperson, "African Diaspora: Concept and Context" and St. Clair Drake, "Diaspora Studies and Pan-Africanism," in *Global Dimensions of the African Diaspora,* ed. Joseph E. Harris (Washington, D.C., 1982); see, e.g., Robert B. Lewis's *Light and Truth: Collected from Bible and Ancient and Modern History* (Boston, 1844); William Wells Brown, *The Rising Son; or the Antecedents and Advancement of the Colored Race* (Boston, 1876); and, most important, the works of Edward Wilmot Blyden, especially *Christianity, Islam and the Negro Race* (Edinburgh, 1967) and *Black Spokesman: Selected Published Writings of Edward Wilmot Blyden* (New York, 1971). For more general works on the African diaspora, see *Out of One, Many Africas: Reconstructing the Study and Meaning of Africa,* ed. William G. Martin and Michaela West (Urbana, Ill., 1999); Aubrey W. Bennett and G.L. Watson, eds., *Emerging Perspectives on the Black Diaspora* (Lanham, Md., 1989); Jacob Drachler, *Black Homeland / Black Diaspora: Cross Currents of the African Relationship* (Port Washington, N.Y., 1975); St. Clair Drake, *Black Folk Here and There,* vol. 2; W.E.B. DuBois, *The World and Africa: An Inquiry into the Part Which Africa Played in World History* (New York, 1947); *Studies in the African Diaspora: A Memorial to James*

R. Hooker (1929–1976), ed. John P. Henderson and Harry A. Reed (Dover, Mass., 1989); *African Diaspora: Interpretive Essays,* ed. Martin L. Kilson and Robert I. Rotberg (Cambridge, Mass., 1976); Franklin Knight, *The African Dimension in Latin American Societies* (New York, 1974); *Imagining Home,* ed. Lemelle and Kelley; Vincent Thompson, *The Making of the African Diaspora in the Americas, 1441–1900* (White Plains, N.Y, 1987); Weisbord, *Ebony Kinship.*

10. William Safran, "Diasporas in Modern Societies: Myths of Homeland and Return," *Diaspora* 1, 1 (1991): 83–84.

11. James Clifford, *Routes: Travel and Translation in the Late Twentieth Century* (Cambridge, Mass., 1997), 249–50, 251.

12. For an interesting and fairly comprehensive discussion of these scholars and the attempt to coordinate research on an international scale, see Melville Herskovits, "The Present Status and Needs of Afroamerican Research," *Journal of Negro History* 36, 2 (April 1951): 123–47. Examples of this work include [Gonzalo] Aguirre Beltran, "Tribal Origins of Slaves in Mexico," *Journal of Negro History* 31 (1946): 269–352; Lorenzo Turner, "Some Contacts of Brazilian ex-Slaves with Nigeria, West Africa," *Journal of Negro History* 27 (1942): 55–67; E. Franklin Frazier, "The Negro in Bahia, Brazil," *American Sociological Review* 7 (1942): 465–78.

13. Melville J. Herskovits, *The Myth of the Negro Past* (Boston, 1941); id., *The New World Negro: Selected Papers in Afro-American Studies* (Bloomington, Ind., 1966); *Africa's Ogun: Old World and New,* ed. Sandra T. Barnes (Bloomington, Ind., 1989); Leonard Barrett, *Soul-Force: African Heritage in Afro-American Religion* (Garden City, N.Y., 1974); Roger Bastide, *African Civilisations in the New World* (London, 1972); Roger Bastide, *The African Religions of Brazil: Toward a Sociology of the Interpretation of Civilisations* (Baltimore, 1978); George Brandon, *Santeria from Africa to the New World: The Dead Sell Memories* (Bloomington, Ind., 1993); Margaret Creel, *"A Peculiar People": Slave Religion and Community—Culture among the Gullahs* (New York, 1988); Joseph Holloway and Winifred Vass, *The African Heritage of American English* (Bloomington, Ind., 1993); Joseph Murphy, *Santeria: African Spirits in America* (Boston, 1988, 1992); Joseph Murphy, *Working the Spirit: Ceremonies of the African Diaspora* (Boston, 1994); Karen Fog Olwig, *Cultural Adaptation and Resistance on St. John: Three Centuries of Afro-Caribbean Life* (Gainesville, Fla., 1985); Richard Price, *First Time: The Historical Vision of an Afro-American People* (Baltimore, 1983); Sterling Stuckey, *Slave Culture: Nationalist Theory and the Foundations of Black America* (New York, 1987); Jim Wafer, *The Taste of Blood: Spirit Possession in Brazilian Candomble* (Philadelphia, 1991).

14. Sidney Mintz and Richard Price, *The Birth of African American Culture: An Anthropological Perspective* (1976; Boston, 1992).

15. Robert Farris Thompson, *Flash of the Spirit: African and Afro-American Art and Philosophy* (New York, 1983); Michael Mullin, *Africa in America: Slave Acculturation and Resistance in the American South and the British Caribbean, 1736–1831* (Urbana, Ill., 1992); John Thornton, *Africa and the Africans in the Making of the Atlantic World, 1400–1680* (New York, 1992); Carolyn Fick, *The Making of Haiti: The Saint-Domingue Revolution from Below* (Knoxville, Tenn., 1990); João José Reis, *Slave Rebellion in Brazil: The Muslim*

Uprising of 1835 in Bahia, trans. Arthur Brakel (Baltimore, 1993); Gwendolyn Midlo Hall, *Africans in Colonial Louisiana: The Development of Afro-Creole Culture in the Eighteenth Century* (Baton Rouge, La., 1992).

16. Michael Gomez, *Exchanging Our Country Marks: The Transformation of African Identities in the Colonial and Antebellum South* (Chapel Hill, N.C., 1998).

17. J. Lorand Matory, "The English Professors of Brazil: On the Diasporic Roots of the Yoruba Nation," *Comparative Studies in Society and History* 41, 1 (January 1999): 72–103, quotation from p. 98. Of course, there are many other examples of Afro-Diasporan expatriates shaping political movements on the African continent, some of the most obvious being the African American missionaries and Garveyism. See, e.g., George Shepperson and Thomas Price, *Independent African: John Chilembwe and the Origins, Settings and Significance of the Nyasaland Native Rising of 1915* (Edinburgh, 1958); Alan Gregor Cobley, "'Far from Home': The Origins and Significance of the Afro-Caribbean Community in South Africa to 1930," *Journal of Southern African Studies* 18, 2 (1992): 349–70; Robert A. Hill and Gregory A. Pirio, "'Africa for the Africans': The Garvey Movement in South Africa, 1920–1940," in *The Politics of Race, Class, and Nationalism in Twentieth Century South Africa,* ed. Shula Marks and Stanley Trapido (London, 1987); Robin D.G. Kelley, "The Religious Odyssey of African Radicals: Notes on the Communist Party of South Africa, 1921–1934," *Radical History Review* 51 (1991): 5–24.

18. Nahum Chandler, "Force of the Double: W.E.B. DuBois and the Question of African American Subjection" (ms).

19. There is a growing literature on whiteness and new ways of understanding European identities. Some of the best work includes: Alexander Saxton, *The Rise and Fall of the White Republic: Class Politics and Mass Culture in Nineteenth-Century America* (New York, 1990); David R. Roediger, *The Wages of Whiteness: Race and the Making of the American Working Class* (New York, 1991); and *Black on White: Black Writers on What It Means to Be White,* ed. David R. Roediger (New York, 1998); Cheryl Harris, "Whiteness as Property," *Harvard Law Review* 106, no. 8 (June 1993): 1707–91; Grace Elizabeth Hale, *Making Whiteness: The Culture of Segregation in the South, 1890–1940* (New York, 1998); Matthew Frye Jacobson, *Whiteness of a Different Color: European Immigrants and the Alchemy of Race* (Cambridge, Mass., 1998); George Lipsitz, *The Possessive Investment in Whiteness: How White People Profit from Identity Politics* (Philadelphia, 1998).

20. Paul Gilroy, *"There Ain't No Black in the Union Jack": The Cultural Politics of Race and Nation* (1987; new ed., Chicago, 1991); and Gilroy, *Black Atlantic;* Mercer, *Welcome to the Jungle;* Hazel Carby, *Race Men* (Cambridge, Mass., 1998); and *Cultures in Babylon: Black Britain and African America* (New York, 1999).

21. Gilroy, *Black Atlantic.*

22. Peter Linebaugh and Marcus Rediker, *The Many-Headed Hydra: Sailors, Slaves, Commoners, and the Hidden History of the Revolutionary Atlantic* (Boston, 2000); Marcus Rediker, *Between the Devil and the Deep Blue Sea: Merchant Seamen, Pirates, and the Anglo-American Maritime World, 1700–1750* (New York, 1987, 1993).

23. Linebaugh and Rediker, *Many-Headed Hydra,* 174–210.

24. Julius Sherrard Scott III, "The Common Wind: Currents of Afro-American Communications in the Era of the Haitian Revolution" (ms, forthcoming).

25. Robin Blackburn, *The Overthrow of Colonial Slavery, 1776–1848* (London, 1988); W.E.B. DuBois, *Black Reconstruction in America, 1860–1880* (New York, 1935); Eric Foner, *Nothing but Freedom: Emancipation and Its Legacy* (Baton Rouge, La., 1983); Eugene Genovese, *From Rebellion to Revolution: Afro-American Slave Revolts in the Making of the Modern World* (Baton Rouge, La., 1974); Thomas Holt, *The Problem of Freedom: Race, Labor and Politics in Jamaica and Britain, 1832–1938* (Baltimore, 1992); Frederick Cooper, Thomas C. Holt, and Rebecca J. Scott, *Beyond Slavery: Explorations of Race, Labor, and Citizenship in Postemancipation Societies* (Chapel Hill, N.C., 2000); C.L.R. James, *The Black Jacobins: Toussaint L'Ouverture and the San Domingo Revolution* (1938; 2d rev. ed., New York, 1963).

26. See Michel-Rolph Trouillot, "An Unthinkable History: The Haitian Revolution as a Non-Event," in id., *Silencing the Past: Power and the Production of History* (Boston, 1995).

27. Gilroy, *Black Atlantic,* 276; James Clifford, "Diasporas," in *Routes: Travel and Translation in the Late Twentieth Century* (Cambridge, Mass., 1997), 268; see also Stuart Hall, "Subjects in History: Making Diasporic Identities," in *The House That Race Built,* ed. Wahneema Lubiano (New York, 1997), 289–99; Lisa Brock, "Questioning the Diaspora: Hegemony, Black Intellectuals and Doing International History from Below," *ISSUE: A Journal of Opinion* 24, 2 (1996): 10.

28. Ernest Allen Jr., "Religious Heterodoxy and Nationalist Tradition: The Continuing Evolution of the Nation of Islam," *Black Scholar* 26, 3–4 (Fall–Winter 1996): 2–34; id., "Waiting for Tojo: The Pro-Japan Vigil of Black Missourians, 1932–1943," *Gateway Heritage* 16, 2 (1995): 38–55; id., "When Japan Was 'Champion of the Darker Races': Sakota Takahashi and the Flowering of Black Messianic Nationalism," *Black Scholar* 24, 1 (Winter 1994): 23–46; Claude Clegg, *An Original Man: The Life and Times of Elijah Muhammad* (New York, 1997); Lipsitz, *Possessive Investment in Whiteness,* 184–210; Gerald Gill, "Dissent, Discontent and Disinterest: Afro-American Opposition to the United States Wars of the Twentieth Century" (ms, 1988); Marc Gallicchio, *The African American Encounter with Japan and China* (Chapel Hill, N.C., 2000).

29. Vijay Prashad, *The Karma of Brown Folk* (Minneapolis, 2000).

30. Ibid.; V.T. Rajshekar, *Dalit: The Black Untouchables of India* (Atlanta, 1995); *Untouchables: Voices of the Dalit Liberation Movement,* ed. Barbara R. Joshi (London, 1986).

31. See Wolfgang Abendroth, *A Short History of the European Working Class,* trans. Nicholas Jacobs and Brian Trench (New York, 1972), 69–76; Rod Bush, *We Are Not What We Seem: Black Nationalism and Class Struggle in the American Century* (New York, 1998), 83–112; Theodore Kornweibel, *No Crystal Stair: Black Life and the Messenger, 1917–1928* (Westport, Conn., 1975); Winston James, *Holding Aloft the Banner of Ethiopia: Caribbean Radicalism in Early Twentieth-Century America* (London, 1998); Mark Naison, *Communists in Harlem during the Depression* (Urbana, Ill., 1983), 3, 58, 17–18; Robert A. Hill, "The First England Years and After, 1912–1916," in *Marcus Garvey and the Vision of Africa,* ed. John Henrik Clarke (New York, 1974), 38–70; Tony Martin,

Race First (Westport, Conn., 1976); 237–46; Robinson, *Black Marxism,* 296–301; David Samuels, "Five Afro-Caribbean Voices in American Culture, 1917–1929: Hubert H. Harrison, Wilfred A. Domingo, Richard B. Moore, Cyril Briggs and Claude McKay" (Ph.D. diss., University of Iowa, 1977); Theman Taylor, "Cyril Briggs and the African Blood Brotherhood: Effects of Communism on Black Nationalism, 1919–1935" (Ph.D. diss., University of California, Santa Barbara, 1981); Joe Doyle, "Striking for Ireland on the New York Docks," in *The New York Irish,* ed. Ronald Bayor and Timothy J. Meagher (Baltimore, 1996), 357–74.

32. Brock, "Questioning the Diaspora," 10; Allison Blakely, *Russia and the Negro: Blacks in Russian History and Thought* (Washington, D.C., 1986); Robin D.G. Kelley, "'This Ain't Ethiopia, but It'll Do': African Americans and the Spanish Civil War," in *Race Rebels: Culture Politics, and the Black Working Class* (New York, 1994); Robin D.G. Kelley, *Hammer and Hoe: Alabama Communists during the Great Depression* (Chapel Hill, N.C., 1990); Robin D.G. Kelley, "The World the Diaspora Made: C.L.R. James and the Politics of History," in *Rethinking C.L.R James,* ed. Grant Farred (New York, 1996), 103–30; Edward T. Wilson, *Russia and Black Africa before World War II* (New York, 1974); James R. Hooker, *Black Revolutionary: George Padmore's Path from Communism to Pan-Africanism* (New York, 1967); Introduction to Albert Nzula, I.I. Potekhin, and A.Z. Zusmanovich, *Forced Labour in Colonial Africa,* ed. Robin Cohen (London, 1979); *Between Race and Empire: African-Americans and Cubans before the Cuban Revolution,* ed. Lisa Brock and Digna Castañeda Fuertes (Philadelphia, 1998); Kelley and Betsy Esch, "Black Like Mao: Red China and Black Revolution," *Souls* 1, 4 (Fall 1999): 6–41.

33. Brenda Gayle Plummer, *Rising Wind: Black Americans and U.S. Foreign Affairs, 1935–1960* (Chapel Hill, N.C., 1996); Penny Von Eschen, *Race against Empire* (Ithaca, N.Y., 1997); Timothy B. Tyson's *Radio Free Dixie: Robert Williams and the Roots of Black Power* (Chapel Hill, N.C., 1999); Van Gosse, *Where the Boys Are: Cuba, Cold War America and the Making of a New Left* (London, 1993); and "Black Power and White America" (ms); Komozi Woodard, *A Nation within a Nation: Amiri Baraka (LeRoi Jones) and Black Power Politics* (Chapel Hill, N.C., 1998); Williams Sales Jr., *From Civil Rights to Black Liberation: Malcolm X and the Organization of Afro-American Unity* (Boston, 1994); Azza Salama Layton, *International Politics and Civil Rights Policies in the United States, 1941–1960* (Cambridge, 2000), 48–58.

34. Layton, *International Politics,* 112–16, quotation from p. 116.

35. Herbert Gutman, "Work, Culture, and Society in Industrializing America," in *Work, Culture, and Society in Industrializing America: Essays in American Working-Class and Social History* (1976): 3–78. See Peter Kwong, *Chinatown, New York: Labor and Politics, 1930–1950* (New York, 1979); *The Politics of Immigrant Workers: Labor Activism and Migration in the World Economy since 1830,* ed. Camille Guerin-Gonzales and Carl Strikwerda (New York, 1993). On Mexican-American workers and "home" country politics, one could go back to pioneering texts such as Rodolfo Acuña's *Occupied America: The Chicano's Struggle toward Liberation* (San Francisco, 1972), 4th rev. ed., titled *Occupied America: A History of Chicanos* (New York, 2000); John Hart, *Anarchism and the Mexican Working Class, 1860–1931* (Austin, Tex., 1978); Juan Gomez Quiñones's essay "First Step: Chicano Labor Conflict and Organizing, 1900–1920," *Aztlan* 3 (1972). For more recent examples, see George Sanchez, *Becoming Mexican-American* (New York, 1993); Camille Guerin-Gonzales, *Mexican Workers and American Dreams* (New Brunswick, NJ., 1995); Emma Perez, "'Through Her Love and Sweetness': Women, Revolution, and Reform in Yucatan, 1910–1918" (Ph.D. diss., UCLA, 1988); Douglas Monroy, "Anarquismo y Comunismo: Mexican Radicalism and the Communist Party in Los Angeles during the 1930's," *Labor History* 24 (Winter 1983): 34–59; Mario T. Garcia, *Mexican-Americans: Leadership, Ideology, and Identity, 1930–1960* (New Haven, Conn., 1989); David Montejano, *Anglos and Mexicans in the Making of Texas, 1836–1986* (Austin, Tex., 1987).

CHAPTER 12

American Freedom in a Global Age

ERIC FONER

One hundred years ago, the United States had just emerged victorious in its "splendid little war" against Spain. It was actively engaged in the decidedly less splendid struggle to subdue the movement for independence in the Philippines. Both conflicts announced that the country was poised to take its place among the world's great powers, and writers here and abroad confidently predicted that American influence would soon span the globe. The precise nature of that influence was a matter of some dispute. In his 1902 book *The New Empire,* Brooks Adams, whose brother Charles Francis Adams served as this association's president exactly one century ago, saw America's rise to world power as essentially economic. "As the United States becomes an imperial market," he proclaimed, "she stretches out along the trade-routes which lead from foreign countries to her heart, as every empire has stretched out from the days of Sargon to our own." Within fifty years, Adams predicted, "the United States will outweigh any single empire, if not all empires combined."[1]

The year 1902 also witnessed a prediction with a somewhat different emphasis, offered by W.T. Stead in a short volume with the arresting title, *The Americanisation of the World: or, The Trend of the Twentieth Century.* Stead was a sensationalist English editor whose previous writings included an exposé of London prostitution, *Maiden Tribute to Modern Babylon.* He would later meet his death as a passenger on the Titanic. Convinced that the United States was emerging as "the greatest of world-powers," Stead proposed that it and his homeland "merge" (by which he meant both political union and individual intermarriages), so that the enervated British could have their "exhausted exchequer" revived by an infusion of America's "exuberant energies."

But what was most striking about Stead's little essay was that he located the essential source of American power less in the realm of military or economic might than in the relentless international spread of American culture—art, music, journalism, theater, even ideas about religion and gender relations. He foresaw a future in which the United States would promote its values and interests through an unending involvement in the affairs of other nations.[2]

Today, we are in many ways living in the world Adams and Stead imagined (although Britain does retain its nominal independence). At the dawn of the twenty-first century, the United States is indisputably the world's preeminent military, economic, and cultural power. Moreover, the flow of people, investment, production, culture, and communications across national boundaries that impressed both Adams and Stead continues its rapid growth. We are constantly being reminded that the world we inhabit is becoming smaller and more integrated and that formerly autonomous nations are bound ever more tightly by a complex web of economic and cultural connections. Globalization, the popular shorthand term for these processes, has been called "the concept of the 1990s." However, its novelty, extent, and consequences remain subjects of heated disagreement. Is globalization producing a homogenized and "Americanized" world, a unified global culture whose economic arrangements, social values, and political institutions are based primarily on those of the United States? Or is it transforming societies without making them identical, producing "multiple modernities" in which international images and commodities are incorporated locally in a continuing process of selection and reinterpretation?[3]

I do not plan tonight to try to answer these questions,

From *American Historical Review* 106 (February 2001): 1–16. © American Historical Association. Reprinted with permission.

which now engage the attention of some of our most prominent social scientists. But as a historian, I feel it necessary to point out that, like every other product of human activity, globalization itself has a history. The dream of global unity goes back to the days of Alexander the Great and Genghis Khan. The internationalization of commerce and culture and the reshuffling of the world's peoples have been going on for centuries. Today's globalized communications follow in the footsteps of clipper ships, the telegraph, and the telephone. Today's international movements for social change—including protests against some of the adverse consequences of globalization—have their precedents in transnational labor and socialist movements, religious revivals, and struggles against slavery and for women's rights. As for economic globalization, Karl Marx long ago pointed out that capitalism is an international system that "must nestle everywhere, settle everywhere, establish connections everywhere." This was why he and Friedrich Engels called on proletarians to unite as a global force. "All old-established national industries," they wrote, "have been destroyed or are daily being destroyed. . . . In place of the old local and national seclusion and self-sufficiency, we have intercourse in every direction, universal interdependence of nations." These words were written in 1848.[4]

Nonetheless, the dimensions and speed of globalization have certainly accelerated in the last two decades. And by remaking our present, globalization invites us to rethink our past. All history, as the saying goes, is contemporary history. Today, our heightened awareness of globalization—however the term is delimited and defined—should challenge historians to become more cognizant of how past events are embedded in an international, even a global, context. Nearly fifty years ago, Geoffrey Barraclough wondered whether histories with a "myopic concentration on individual nations" could effectively illuminate "the world in which we live."[5] For American historians, this question is even more pertinent today.

The institutions, processes, and values that have shaped American history—from capitalism to political democracy, slavery, and consumer culture—arose out of global processes and can only be understood in an international context. This, of course, is hardly a new insight. Back in the 1930s, W.E.B. DuBois insisted that it was impossible to understand the black experience in the United States without reference to "that dark and vast sea of human labor in China and India, the South Seas and all Africa . . . . that great majority of mankind, on whose bent and broken backs rest today the founding stones of modern industry." Herbert E. Bolton warned that by treating the American past in isolation, historians were helping to raise up a "nation of chauvinists."[6]

At the time, these pleas more or less fell on deaf ears. But some of the best recent works of American history have developed complex understandings of the nation's relationship to the larger world. The emerging "Atlantic" perspective on the colonial era offers the promise of seeing early American history not simply as an offshoot of Great Britain or prelude to the revolution but as part and parcel of the international expansion of European empires and the transatlantic migration of peoples. Bonnie Anderson's history of the "first international women's movement" traces the transatlantic exchange of ideas on issues ranging from suffrage to child rearing and divorce. *Barbarian Virtues,* by Matthew Jacobson, examines how a century ago Americans' real and imagined encounters with foreign peoples—as potential consumers and laborers, and as exemplars of a "lower" state of civilization—helped shape a new sense of national identity. Daniel Rodgers' *Atlantic Crossings* demonstrates that American Progressivism must be seen as part of an international discussion about "social politics." Important writings in economic history stress how world markets have shaped our agriculture, port cities, and industrial towns. Most of these works focus on relationships between the United States and Europe. But the best recent work in Asian-American studies has begun to develop what might be called a Pacific perspective that moves beyond an older paradigm based on immigration and assimilation to examine how continuing transnational cultural and economic interactions shape the experience of minority groups within the United States. Yet in nearly all areas of American history, such works remain dwarfed by those that stop at the nation's borders.[7]

A little over a decade ago, my predecessor as AHA president Akira Iriye called for historians to "internationalize" the study of history by treating the entire world as their framework of study. This is a daunting challenge, probably impossible for most historians to accomplish. Of course, as Professor Iriye well knows, international paradigms—"the West," "modernization," "the Judeo-Christian tradition"—can be every bit as obfuscating as histories that are purely national. My point is somewhat different—that even histories organized along the lines of the nation-state must be, so to speak, deprovincialized, placed in the context of international interactions. Since the birth of the modern era, the nation has constituted the principal framework for historical study. It is likely to remain so for the foreseeable future. Internationalizing history does not mean abandoning or homogenizing national histories, dissolving the experience of the United States, or any other nation, in a sea of supranational processes. International dynamics operate in different ways in different countries. Every nation, to one extent or another, thinks of itself as exceptional—a conviction, of course, rather more prominent in the United States (and among its historians) than elsewhere. But globalization does force us to think about history in somewhat different ways.[8]

Historians are fully aware of how American military might, commodities, and culture have affected the rest of the world, especially in the twentieth century. We know how the United States has exported everything from Coca-Cola to ideas about democracy and "free enterprise." Far less attention has been devoted to how our history has been affected from abroad. "Europe," Frantz Fanon wrote in *The Wretched of the Earth,* "is literally the creation of the Third World."[9] Fanon was referring not only to the wealth Europe gleaned from its colonial dependencies but to the fact that the encounters of different peoples—real encounters and those of the imagination—crystallize political ideologies and concepts of identity. They also, one might add, always seem to produce inequalities of power and of rights. Fanon's insight needs to be extended to the United States. An understanding of America cannot be obtained purely from within America. To illustrate my point, I want to refer to the most central idea in American political culture, an idea that anchors the American sense of exceptional national identity—freedom.

No idea is more fundamental to Americans' sense of themselves as individuals and as a nation than freedom. The central term in our political vocabulary, "freedom"—or "liberty," with which it is almost always used interchangeably—is deeply embedded in the record of our history and the language of everyday life. The Declaration of Independence lists liberty among mankind's inalienable rights; the Constitution announces as its purpose to secure liberty's blessings. Obviously, other peoples also cherish freedom, but the idea does seem to occupy a more prominent place in public and private discourse in the United States than elsewhere. The ubiquitous American expression, "It's a free country," invoked by disobedient children and assertive adults to explain or justify their actions, is not, I believe, familiar in other societies. "Every man in the street, white, black, red or yellow," wrote the educator and statesman Ralph Bunche in 1940, "knows that this is 'the land of the free' . . . 'the cradle of liberty.'"[10]

In *The Story of American Freedom,* published in 1998, I examined the history of the idea of freedom in the United States, viewing it as a tale of debates, disagreements, and struggles rather than a fixed category or predetermined concept.[11] While not entirely neglecting the international dimensions of American history, I emphasized how the changing meaning of freedom has been shaped and reshaped by social and political struggles within the United States—battles, for example, over the abolition of slavery, women's rights, labor organization, and freedom of speech for those outside the social mainstream. Yet America's relationship, real and imagined, with the rest of the world has also powerfully influenced the idea of freedom and its evolution. As with other central elements of our political language—independence, equality, and citizenship, for example—freedom has been defined and redefined with reference to its putative opposite. The most striking example, of course, is slavery, a stark, homegrown illustration

of the nature of unfreedom that helped define Americans' language of liberty in the colonial era and well into the nineteenth century. In the early labor movement's crusade against "wage slavery" and denunciations of "the slavery of sex" by advocates of women's rights, the condition of African Americans powerfully affected how free Americans understood their own situation.

While Americans have frequently identified threats to freedom at home, including slavery, luxury, and a too-powerful federal government, they have also looked abroad to locate dangers to freedom. The American Revolution was inspired, in part, by the conviction that Great Britain was conspiring to eradicate freedom in North America. In the twentieth century, world affairs have frequently been understood as titanic struggles between a "free world," centered in the United States, and its enemies—Nazis during World War II, communists during the Cold War, and, most recently, "terrorists," drug cartels, or Islamic fundamentalists.

Of course, the relationship between American freedom and the outside world works both ways. "America," as myth and reality, has for centuries played a part in how other peoples think about their own societies. The United States has frequently been viewed from abroad as the embodiment of one or another kind of freedom. European labor, in the nineteenth century, identified this country as a land where working men and women enjoyed freedoms not available in the Old World. In the twentieth, younger generations throughout the world selectively appropriated artifacts of American popular culture for acts of cultural rebellion. Some foreign observers, to be sure, have taken a rather jaundiced view of Americans' stress on their own liberty. The "tyranny of the majority," Alexis de Tocqueville commented, ruled the United States: "I know of no country, in which there is so little independence of mind and real freedom of discussion as in America." A century and a half later, another French writer, Jean Baudrillard, concluded his own tour of the United States with the observation that if New York and Los Angeles now stood "at the center of the world," it is a world defined not so much by freedom but by "wealth, power, senility, indifference, puritanism and mental hygiene, poverty and waste, technological futility and aimless violence."[12]

My interest [here], however, is not images of America emanating from abroad, or the global impact of the United States, but how global embeddedness has affected American history itself. At key moments in our history, America's relationship to the outside world has helped establish how freedom is understood within the United States. To a considerable degree, the self-definition of the United States as a nation-state with a special mission to bring freedom to all mankind depends on the "otherness" of the outside world, often expressed in the Manichean categories of New World versus Old or free world versus slave.

The idea of America as an embodiment of freedom in

a world overrun by tyranny goes back to well before the American Revolution. Ironically, however, this ideology must be understood not simply with reference to the unique conditions of North American settlement—available land, weak government, etc.—but as a conscious creation of European policymakers. From the earliest days of settlement, migrants from Britain and the Continent held the promise of the New World to be liberation from the social inequalities and widespread economic dependence of the Old. Many others saw America as a divinely appointed locale where mankind could, for the first time, be truly free in the sense of worshiping God in a manner impossible in Europe. But these ideas can only be understood in the context of the clash of empires that produced American settlement in the first place, and engaged the colonists in a seemingly endless series of wars involving the rival French, Spanish, and Dutch empires. British monarchs did as much as colonists themselves to create the idea of America as an asylum for "those whom bigots chase from foreign lands" by actively encouraging continental emigration to the New World in order to strengthen their colonies without depleting the population of the British Isles. As Marilyn C. Baseler writes, colonial liberty of conscience "was largely a byproduct of English policies and did not necessarily reflect a strong commitment by America's early settlers to the principles of religious freedom."[13]

The growth of the three most dynamic empires of the eighteenth century—the British, French, and Dutch—depended on the debasement of millions of people into slavery and the dispossession of millions of native inhabitants of the Americas. The yoking of freedom and domination was a global phenomenon, intrinsic to the imperial expansion of Europe, England's mainland colonies not excepted. Nonetheless, all three empires developed discourses claiming a special relationship to freedom (partly in contrast to the Spanish, who were seen as representing tyranny at home and a peculiarly inhumane form of imperialism overseas). From an international perspective, claims by Britain and its colonies to a unique relationship with liberty ring somewhat hollow. The Dutch actually had more justification in claiming to represent the principle of religious toleration, while France respected the principle of "free air"—which liberated any slave setting foot on metropolitan soil—well before Great Britain. Nonetheless, the idea that the Anglo-American world enjoyed a unique measure of freedom was widely disseminated in the colonies. Belief in freedom as the common heritage of all Britons was, Jack P. Greene writes, the "single most important element in defining a larger Imperial identity for Britain and the British Empire." It served to cast imperial wars against Catholic France and Spain as struggles between liberty and tyranny, a language in which to this day virtually every American war has been described.[14]

The coming of independence rendered the rights of "free-born Englishmen" irrelevant in America. But the revolution did more than substitute one parochial ideology of freedom for another. The struggle for independence universalized the idea of American freedom. Even before 1776, patriotic orators and pamphleteers were identifying America as a special place with a special mission, "a land of liberty, the seat of virtue, the asylum of the oppressed, a name and a praise in the whole earth," to quote Joseph Warren. This vision required a somewhat exaggerated negative image of the rest of the world. Outside British North America, proclaimed Samuel Williams in *A Discourse on the Love of Our Country* (1775), mankind was sunk in debauchery and despotism. In Asia and Africa, "the very idea of liberty" was "unknown." Even in Europe, Williams claimed, the "vital flame" of "freedom" was being extinguished. Here, and here alone, was "the country of free men."[15]

This sense of American uniqueness was pervasive in the revolutionary era, as was the view of the revolution as not simply an internal squabble within the British Empire but the opening of a new era in human history. The point was not necessarily to spark liberation movements in other countries but to highlight the alleged differences between the United States and the rest of mankind. One pamphleteer of 1776, Ebenezer Baldwin, predicted that even in the year 2000 America would remain the world's sole center of freedom. But while affirming their uniqueness, Americans from the outset were obsessed with the repute in which they were held abroad. George Washington defended the suppression of the Whiskey Rebellion, in part, because of "the impression it will make on others"—the others being European skeptics who wished to see the world-historical experiment fail because they did not believe human beings could "govern ourselves." Over half a century later, Abraham Lincoln would contend that slavery weakened the American mission by exposing the country to the charge of hypocrisy from the "enemies of free institutions" abroad.[16]

In his *History of the American Revolution* (1789), David Ramsay, the father of American historical writing, insisted that what defined the new nation was not the usual basis of nationality—a set of boundaries, a long-established polity, or a common "race" or ethnicity—but a special destiny "to enlarge the happiness of mankind." This narrative was elaborated by nineteenth-century historians such as Walter H. Prescott, Francis Parkman, and George Bancroft. In their account, the seeds of liberty, planted in Puritan New England, had reached their inevitable flowering in the American Revolution and westward expansion. These writers were fully aware of the global dimension of American history, but their conviction that the United States represented a unique embodiment of the idea of freedom inevitably fostered a certain insularity. Since territorial growth meant "extending the area of freedom," those who stood in the way—European powers with legal title to part of the North American continent, Native Americans,

Mexicans—were by definition obstacles to the progress of liberty. In the outlook of most white Americans, the West was not a battleground of peoples and governments but an "empty" space ready to be occupied as part of the divine mission of the United States.[17]

American expansion, which involved constant encounters with non-white people (or people like the Mexicans defined as non-white), greatly enhanced what might be called the exclusionary dimensions of American freedom. The nation's rapid territorial growth was widely viewed as evidence of the innate superiority of a mythical construct known as the "Anglo-Saxon race," whose special qualities made it uniquely suited to bring freedom and prosperity to the continent and the world. America may have been an empire but, in Thomas Jefferson's phrase, it was an "empire of liberty," supposedly distinct from the oppressive empires of Europe.[18]

Of course, the contradiction between the rhetoric of universal liberty and the actual limits of freedom within the United States goes back to the era of colonization. The slavery controversy was primarily a matter internal to the United States. But as an institution that existed throughout the Western hemisphere, and whose abolition was increasingly demanded by a movement transcending national boundaries, slavery's impact on American freedom had an international dimension as well. Slavery did much to determine how a nation born in revolution reacted to revolutions abroad. American culture in the antebellum period glorified the revolutionary heritage. But acceptable revolutions were by white men—like the Greeks or Hungarians—seeking their freedom from tyrannical government, not slaves rebelling against their own lack of liberty. Denmark Vesey and Nat Turner were not part of the pantheon of national heroes, nor was Toussaint L'Ouverture greeted with the same enthusiasm as Louis Kossuth. Indeed, unlike the French, whose revolution certainly had its share of violence, the carnage in Saint-Domingue was taken to demonstrate that blacks lacked the capacity for self-government—in a word, they were congenitally unfit for the enjoyment of freedom.[19]

As the nineteenth century wore on, the centrality of slavery to American life exposed the nation to the charge of willful hypocrisy, and from no quarter was the charge more severe than from blacks themselves. Black abolitionists were among the most penetrating critics of the hollowness of official pronouncements about American freedom. In calling for a redefinition of freedom as an entitlement of all mankind, not one from which certain groups defined as "races" could legitimately be excluded, black abolitionists repudiated the rhetorical division of the world into the United States, a beacon of freedom, and the Old World, a haven of oppression. "I am ashamed," declared black abolitionist William Wells Brown, "when I hear men talking about . . . the despotism of Napoleon III. . . . Before you boast of your freedom and Christianity, do your duty to your fellow man."[20]

Most strikingly, abolitionists, black and white alike, reversed the familiar dichotomy between American freedom and British tyranny. Once slavery had been abolished in the British Empire, the former mother country represented freedom more genuinely than the United States. August 1, the anniversary of emancipation in the British West Indies, became the black Fourth of July, the occasion of annual "freedom celebrations" that pointedly drew attention to the distinction between the "monarchial liberty" of a nation that had abolished slavery and "republican slavery" in the United States. With the passage in 1850 of the Fugitive Slave Act, several thousand black Americans fled to Canada, fearing reenslavement in the United States. Which country was now the asylum of the oppressed?[21]

As Linda Colley has argued, the abolition of slavery in 1833 enabled Britons to regain the earlier sense of their own nation as a paradigm of freedom. Emancipation demonstrated Britain's superior national virtue compared to the United States, and gave it, despite the sordid realities of British imperialism, an irrefutable claim to moral integrity. A similar process occurred in the United States. After decades of the slavery controversy, which had somewhat tarnished the sense of a special American mission to preserve and promote liberty, the Civil War and Emancipation reinforced the identification of the United States with the progress of freedom, linking this mission as never before with the power of the national state. By the 1880s, James Bryce was struck by the strength not only of Americans' commitment to freedom but by their conviction that they were the "only people" truly to enjoy it.[22]

If, in the nineteenth century, America's encounter with the world beyond the Western hemisphere had been more ideological, as it were, than material, the twentieth saw the country emerge as a continuous and powerful actor on a global stage. At key moments of worldwide involvement, the encounter with a foreign "other" subtly affected the meaning of freedom in the United States. One such episode was the struggle against Nazi Germany, which not only highlighted concern with aspects of American freedom that had previously been neglected but fundamentally transformed perceptions of who was entitled to enjoy the blessings of liberty in the United States. It also gave birth to a powerful rhetoric, the division of the planet into a "free world" and an unfree world that would long outlive the defeat of Adolf Hitler.

Even before the United States entered World War II, the gathering confrontation with Nazism helped to promote a broadened awareness of civil liberties as a central element of American freedom. Today, when asked to define their rights as citizens, Americans instinctively turn to the privileges enumerated in the Bill of Rights—freedom of speech, the press, and religion, for example. But for many decades, the social and legal defenses of free expression were extremely fragile in the United States. A broad rhetorical commitment to this ideal coexisted with stringent restrictions on speech deemed radical or obscene. It was only in 1939 that the Department of Justice established its Civil Liberties Unit, for the first time in American history, according to Attorney General Frank Murphy, placing "the full weight of the department . . . behind the effort to preserve in this country the blessings of liberty."[23]

There were many causes for this development, from a revulsion against the severe repression of the World War I era to a new awareness in the 1930s of restraints on free speech by opponents of labor organizing. But what Michael Kammen calls the "discovery" of the Bill of Rights on the eve of the American entry into World War II owed much to the ideological struggle against Nazism and the invocation of freedom as a shorthand way of describing the myriad differences between American and German society and politics. Once the country entered World War II, the Nazi counterexample was frequently cited by defenders of civil liberties in the United States. Freedom of speech took its place as one of the "four essential human freedoms," President Franklin D. Roosevelt's description of Allied war aims. Not only did the Four Freedoms embody the "crucial difference" between the Allies and their enemies, but, in the future, Roosevelt promised, they would be enjoyed "everywhere in the world," an updating of the centuries-old vision of America instructing the rest of mankind in the enjoyment of liberty.[24]

Talk of freedom permeated wartime America—in advertisements, films, publications of the Office of War Information, and in Roosevelt's own rhetoric. Over and over, Roosevelt described the war as a titanic battle between "freedom" and "slavery." The Free World, a term popularized in 1940–1941 by those pressing for American intervention in the European conflict, assumed a central role in wartime rhetoric. It was in a speech to the Free World Association in 1942 that Vice-President Henry Wallace outlined his vision of a global New Deal emerging from the war, in which the nation's involvement in the postwar world would universalize the Four Freedoms and ensure the promise of the American Revolution. Wallace was, in part, responding to Henry Luce's more chauvinistic call for the United States to assume the role of "dominant power in the world." But whatever their differences in outlook, both Wallace and Luce envisioned the United States as henceforth promoting freedom not merely by example or occasional international intervention but via an unending involvement in the affairs of other nations. Indeed, at the war's end, globalist language and imagery pervaded the mass media, and the idea of America having inherited a global responsibility evoked remarkably little dissent.[25]

If World War II presaged a transformation, in the name of freedom, of the country's traditional relationship with the rest of the world, it also reshaped Americans' understanding of the internal boundaries of freedom. The struggle against Nazi tyranny and its theory of a master race discredited ideas of inborn ethnic and racial inequality and gave a new impetus to the long-denied struggle for racial justice at home. A pluralist definition of American society, in which all citizens enjoyed equally the benefits of freedom, had been pioneered in the 1930s by leftists and liberals associated with the Popular Front. It became the government's official stance during the Second World War. What set the United States apart from its wartime foes was not simply dedication to the ideals of the Four Freedoms but the resolve that these should extend to persons of all races, religions, and national origins. It was during the war that a shared American Creed of freedom, equality, and ethnic and religious "brotherhood" came to be seen as the foundation of national unity. Racism was the enemy's philosophy; intolerance was a foreign import, not a homegrown product.[26]

Reading American pluralism backward into history, postwar scholars defined the United States as a nation with a purely civic identity, as opposed to the "ethnic" nationalism of other countries. The American Creed became a timeless definition of America nationality, ignoring the powerful ethnic and racial strains in the actual history of our national consciousness. At the same time, however, the rise of anticolonial movements in Africa and Asia inspired the rapid growth of what would later be called a "diasporic" consciousness among black Americans, which highlighted the deeply rooted racial inequalities in the United States and insisted they could only be understood through the prism of imperialism's long global history. Like many other products of the war years, this vision of racial inequality in the United States as part of a global system rather than a maladjustment between American ideals and behavior did not long survive the advent of the Cold War.[27]

Rhetorically, the Cold War was in many ways a continuation of the battles of World War II. The discourse of a world sharply divided into opposing camps, one representing freedom and the other slavery, was reinvigorated in the worldwide struggle against communism. Once again, the United States was the leader of a global crusade for freedom against a demonic, ideologically driven antagonist. The Cold War was a crucible in which postwar liberalism was reformulated. A revulsion against both Nazism and communism abroad, reinforced by the excesses of McCarthyism at home, propelled liberal thinkers toward a wholesale repudiation of ideological mass politics. In its place emerged a pragmatic, managerial liberalism meant to protect democratic institutions against excesses of the popular will.

The debate over communism helps explain the widespread impact, at least among liberal intellectuals, of Sir Isaiah Berlin's 1958 essay, "Two Concepts of Liberty." Berlin distinguished sharply between "negative liberty"—the absence of external obstacles to the fulfillment of one's desires—and "positive liberty," which led to the subordination of the individual to the whole by identifying the state as the arbiter of the social good. Negative liberty represented the West, with its constitutional safeguards of individual rights, positive liberty the Soviet Union. Of course, the idea of freedom as the absence of restraint had deep roots in American history, but Berlin himself was alarmed by how readily his formulation was invoked not only against communism but to discredit the welfare state and anything that smacked of economic regulation. The absorption of his essay into the mainstream of liberal thought had the effect of marginalizing a different understanding of "positive" freedom as active citizen engagement in democratic politics advanced around the same time by Hannah Arendt.[28]

With the USSR replacing Germany as freedom's antithesis, the vaguely socialistic freedom from want—central to the Four Freedoms of World War II—slipped into the background or took on a very different meaning. Whatever Moscow stood for was by definition the opposite of freedom—and not merely one-party rule, suppression of free expression and the like, but public housing, universal health insurance, full employment, and other claims that required strong and persistent governmental intervention in the economy. If freedom had an economic definition, it was no longer economic autonomy, as in the nineteenth century, "industrial democracy" (a rallying cry of the Progressive era), or economic security for the average citizen guaranteed by government, as Roosevelt had defined it, but "free enterprise" and consumer autonomy—the ability to choose from the cornucopia of goods produced by the modern American economy. A common material culture of abundance would provide the foundation for global integration—eventually including even the communist world—under American leadership. The Cold War helped secure the glorification of "free enterprise" as the most fundamental form of American freedom, an idea promoted by ubiquitous political rhetoric, advertising campaigns, school programs, and newspaper editorials. Since the Free World contained so many despotic governments (even South Africa was a member in good standing), official definitions of that geopolitical construct tended to feature anticommunism and market economics more than political liberty.[29]

Although in the late 1960s and 1970s, with the collapse of the postwar ideological consensus and a series of economic and political crises, the Cold War rhetoric of freedom eased considerably, it was reinvigorated by Ronald Reagan. The "Great Communicator" effectively united into a coherent whole the elements of Cold War freedom—negative liberty (that is, limited government), free enterprise, and anticommunism—all in the service of a renewed insistence on American's global mission. Consciously employing rhetoric that echoed back at least two centuries, Reagan proclaimed that "by some divine plan . . . a special kind of people—people who had a special love for freedom" had been chosen to settle the North American continent. This exceptional history imposed on the nation an exceptional responsibility: "we are the beacon of liberty and freedom to all the world."[30]

Today, at least in terms of political policy and discourse, Americans still live in the shadow of the Reagan revolution. "Freedom" continues to occupy as central a place as ever in our political vocabulary, but it has been largely appropriated by libertarians and conservatives of one kind or another, from advocates of unimpeded market economics to armed militia groups insisting that the right to bear arms is the centerpiece of American liberty. The dominant constellation of definitions seems to consist of a series of negations—of government, of social responsibility, of a common public culture, of restraints on individual self-definition and consumer choice. Once the rallying cry of the dispossessed, freedom is today commonly invoked by powerful economic institutions to justify many forms of authority, even as on the individual level it often seems to suggest the absence of outside authority altogether.[31]

As we enter the twenty-first century, the process of globalization itself seems to be reinforcing this prevailing understanding of freedom, at least among political leaders of both major parties and journalistic cheerleaders who equate globalization with the worldwide ascendancy of American commodities, institutions, and values. A series of presidential administrations, aided and abetted by most of the mass media, have redefined both American freedom and America's historic mission to promote it for all mankind to mean the creation of a single global free market, in which capital, natural resources, and human labor are nothing more than factors of production in an endless quest for greater productivity and profit. Meanwhile, activities with broader social aims, many of them previously understood as expressions of freedom, are criticized as burdens on international competitiveness. The prevailing ideology of the global free market assumes that the economic life of all countries can and should be refashioned in the image of the United States—the latest version of the nation's self-definition as model of freedom for the entire world. "In so many ways," writes Thomas Friedman, "globalization is us." "Us" to Friedman means the "spread of free-market capitalism to every country in the world" and the Americanization of global culture. Of course, what Friedman fails to take into account is that "us" is itself a complex and contested concept. There has always been more than one definition of America and of American freedom, and today there is more than one American vision of what globalization should be.[32]

For what one student of the subject calls "hyperglobalizers," globalization defines a new epoch in human history, in which a "global civilization" will supersede traditional cultures.[33] Having become irrelevant, the nation-state will wither away or at least surrender its economic functions. At the moment, however, rather than homogenizing the world, globalization seems to be creating all sorts of new cultural and political fissures and exacerbating old ones. The proliferation of social movements and sometimes violent conflicts based on ethnicity, religion, and local and regional cultures suggests that the arrival of a single global culture or consciousness is not yet at hand. But these developments do seem directly related to a decline in the traditional functions of the nation-state.

Politically speaking, the world is likely to remain divided into territorial states for many years to come. Nonetheless, globalization is raising profound questions about governance and accountability in the global economy and throwing into question traditional ideas about the relationship between political sovereignty, national identity, and freedom. Today, the assets of some multinational corporations exceed the gross national products of the majority of the world's nations. Decisions that affect the day-to-day lives of millions of people are daily made by institutions—the World Bank, International Monetary Fund, and transnational corporations—that operate without a semblance of democratic accountability. By expanding "individual choice" and weakening the powers of governments, declares a recent account, globalization enhances freedom.[34] This definition, however, excludes from consideration such elements of freedom, also deeply rooted in the American experience, as self-government, economic autonomy, and social justice.

The relationship between globalization and freedom may be the most pressing political and social problem of the twenty-first century. Historically, rights have been derived from membership in a nation-state, and freedom often depends on the existence of political power to enforce it. "Without authorities, no rights exist." Perhaps, in the future, freedom will accompany human beings wherever they go, and a worldwide regime of "human rights" that know no national boundaries will come into existence, complete with supranational institutions capable of enforcing these rights and international social movements bent on expanding freedom's boundaries. Thus far, however, economic globalization has occurred without a parallel internationalization of controlling democratic institutions.[35]

Like any other process rooted in history, globalization produces losers as well as winners. It creates and distributes wealth more rapidly than in the past, while simultaneously increasing inequality both within societies and in the world at large. The question for the twenty-first century is not whether globalization will continue, but globalization by whom, for whom, and under whose control. The fate of freedom is centrally involved in this question. It should not surprise us if the losers—those marginalized by globalization—adopt definitions of freedom rather different from those of the winners. It is not inevitable that globalization must take a single, neo-liberal form or that economic openness requires a state's retreat from the social protection of its citizens.[36]

At the height of the Cold War, in his brilliant and sardonic survey of American political thought, *The Liberal Tradition in America,* Louis Hartz observed that the internationalism of the postwar era seemed in some ways to go hand-in-hand with self-absorption and insularity. Despite its deepened worldwide involvement, the United States was becoming more isolated intellectually from other cultures. Prevailing ideas of freedom in the United States, Hartz noted, had become so rigid and narrow that Americans could no longer appreciate definitions of freedom, common in other countries, related to social justice and economic equality, "and hence are baffled by their use."[37]

Today, Hartz's call for Americans to listen to the rest of the world, not simply lecture it about what liberty is, seems more relevant than ever. This may be difficult for a nation that has always considered itself a city upon a hill, a beacon to mankind. Yet American independence was proclaimed by those anxious to demonstrate "a decent respect to the opinions of mankind." In the global world of the twenty-first century, it is not the role of historians to instruct our fellow citizens on how they should think about freedom. But it is our task to insist that the discussion of freedom must transcend boundaries rather than reinforcing or reproducing them. In a global age, the forever unfinished story of American freedom must become a conversation with the entire world, not a complacent monologue with ourselves.

Notes

Thanks to Professor Thomas Bender of New York University for inviting me to participate in the 1999 La Pietra Conference on Internationalizing the Study of American History, where some of the ideas in this essay were first developed, and for his extremely helpful comments on the paper I delivered there. I also wish to thank my colleague, Victoria DeGrazia, for sharing with me some of her insights on the consequences of globalization.

1. Brooks Adams, *The New Empire* (New York, 1902), 208.

2. W.T. Stead, *The Americanisation of the World: or, The Trend of the Twentieth Century* (London, 1902), 5, 59, 123.

3. David Reynolds, *One World Divisible: A Global History since 1945* (New York, 2000), 650–51; Anthony D. Smith, *Nations and Nationalism in a Global Era* (Cambridge, Mass., 1995), 1–4; David Held et al., *Global Transformations: Politics, Economics and Culture* (Stanford, Calif., 1999), 3–7; "Multiple Modernities," special issue of *Daedalus* (Winter 2000).

4. Karl Marx and Frederick Engels, *The Communist Manifesto: A Modern Edition* (New York, 1998), 39. See also Kevin H. O'Rourke and Jeffrey G. Williamson, *When Did Globalization Begin?* National Bureau of Economic Research Working Paper, 7633 (Cambridge, Mass., 2000).

5. Geoffrey Barraclough, "The Larger View of History," *Times Literary Supplement* (January 6, 1956): ii.

6. W.E.B. DuBois, *Black Reconstruction in America* (New York, 1935), 15; Herbert E. Bolton, *Wider Horizons of American History* (New York, 1939), 2.

7. J.H. Elliott, *Do the Americas Have a Common History? An Address* (Providence, R.I., 1998); Bonnie S. Anderson, *Joyous Greetings: The First International Women's Movement, 1830–1860* (New York, 2000); Matthew Frye Jacobson, *Barbarian Virtues: The United States Encounters Foreign Peoples at Home and Abroad, 1876–1917* (New York, 2000); Daniel T. Rodgers, *Atlantic Crossings: Social Politics in a Progressive Age* (Cambridge, Mass., 1998); Oscar V. Campomanes, "New Formations of Asian American Studies and the Question of U.S. Imperialism," *Positions* 5 (Fall 1997): 523–50.

8. Akira Iriye, "The Internationalization of History," *AHR* 94 (February 1989): 1–10. See also Lawrence Veysey, "The Autonomy of American History Reconsidered," *American Quarterly* 31 (Fall 1979): 455–77; Ian Tyrell, "American Exceptionalism in an Age of International History," *AHR* 96 (October 1991): 1031–55; David Thelen, "Of Audiences, Borderlands, and Comparisons: Toward the Internationalization of American History," *Journal of American History* 79 (September 1992): 432–62; Thomas Bender, *The La Pietra Report: The NYU-OAH Project on Internationalizing the Study of American History* (Bloomington, Ind., 2000). Annual reports of this project and The La Pietra Report are available on the World Wide Web at www.oah.org.

9. Frantz Fanon, *The Wretched of the Earth,* Constance Farrington, trans. (New York, 1963), 81.

10. Gunnar Myrdal, *An American Dilemma: The Negro Problem and Modern Democracy* (New York, 1944), 4.

11. Eric Foner, *The Story of American Freedom* (New York, 1998).

12. Rob Kroes, *If You've Seen One, You've Seen the Mall: European and American Mass Culture* (Urbana, Ill., 1996); David M. Potter, *Freedom and Its Limitations in American Life,* Don E. Fehrenbacher, ed. (Stanford, Calif., 1976), 2–3; Jean Baudrillard, *America,* Chris Turner, trans. (New York, 1988), 23.

13. Jack P. Greene, *The Intellectual Construction of America: Exceptionalism and Identity from 1492 to 1800* (Chapel Hill, N.C., 1993); Marilyn C. Baseler, *"Asylum for Mankind": America, 1607–1800* (Ithaca, N.Y., 1998), 4, 56.

14. Jan Lucassen, "The Netherlands, the Dutch, and Long-Distance Migration in the Late Sixteenth to Early Nineteenth Centuries," in *Europeans on the Move: Studies on European Migration 1500–1800,* Nicholas Canny, ed. (Oxford, 1994), 153; Sue Peabody, *"There Are No Slaves in France": The Political Culture of Race and Slavery in the Ancien Régime* (New York, 1996), 3–5; Jack P. Greene, "Empire and Identity from the Glorious Revolution to the American Revolution," in *The Oxford History of the British Empire,* Wm. Roger Louis, editor-in-chief, 5 vols. (New York, 1998–99), 2: 208; Linda Colley, *Britons: Forging the Nation, 1707–1837* (New Haven, Conn., 1992), 35, 53–55, 212.

15. Bernard Bailyn, *Ideological Origins of the American Revolution* (Cambridge, Mass., 1967), 119, 138–40; Theodore Draper, *A Struggle for Power: The American Revolution* (New York, 1996), 414.

16. John C. Rainbolt, "Americans' Initial View of Their Revolution's Significance for Other Peoples, 1776–1788," *The Historian* 35 (May 1973): 421–22; John C. Fitzpatrick, ed., *The Writings of George Washington,* 39 vols. (Washington, D.C., 1931–44), 34: 98; Roy P. Basler, ed., *The Collected Works of Abraham Lincoln,* 9 vols. (New Brunswick, N.J., 1953–55), 2: 255.

17. Arthur H. Shaffer, *To Be an American: David Ramsay and the Making of the American Consciousness* (Columbia, S.C., 1991), 107–12; Dorothy Ross, "Grand Narrative in American Historical Writing: From Romance to Uncertainty," *AHR* 100 (June 1995): 651–52; Joyce Appleby, Lynn Hunt, and Margaret C. Jacob, *Telling the Truth about History* (New York, 1994), 97–112.

18. Reginald Horsman, *Race and Manifest Destiny: The Origins of American Racial Anglo-Saxonism* (Cambridge, Mass., 1991), 1–4; Robert W. Tucker and David C. Hendrickson, *Empire of Liberty: The Statecraft of Thomas Jefferson* (New York, 1990).

19. Donald R. Hickey, "America's Response to the Slave Revolt in Haiti, 1791–1806," *Journal of the Early Republic* 2 (Winter 1982): 368–73; Winthrop D. Jordan, *White over Black: American Attitudes toward the Negro, 1550–1812* (Chapel Hill, N.C., 1968), 412–14.

20. C. Peter Ripley, ed., *The Black Abolitionist Papers,* 5 vols. (Chapel Hill, N.C., 1985–92), 4: 248–49.

21. John R. McKivigan and Jason H. Silverman, "Monarchial Liberty and Republican Slavery: West Indian Emancipation Celebrations in Upstate New York and Canada West," *Afro-Americans in New York Life and History* 10 (January 1986): 10–12; Paul Goodman, *Of One Blood: Abolitionism and the Origins of Racial Equality* (Berkeley, Calif., 1998), 235.

22. Colley, *Britons,* 351–59; James Bryce, *The American Commonwealth,* 2 vols. (London, 1889), 2: 635.

23. Jerold S. Auerbach, *Labor and Liberty: The La Follette Committee and the New Deal* (Indianapolis, 1966), 210–13; Michael J. Klarman, "Rethinking the Civil Rights and Civil Liberties Revolutions," *Virginia Law Review* 82 (February 1996): 43.

24. Michael Kammen, *A Machine That Would Go of Itself: The Constitution in American Culture* (New York, 1987), 336; Samuel I. Rosenman, comp., *The Public Papers and Addresses of Franklin D. Roosevelt,* 13 vols. (New York, 1938–50), 9: 672.

25. Charles D. Lloyd, "American Society and Values in World War II from the Publications of the Office of War Information" (Ph.D. dissertation, Georgetown University, 1975), 32–33; Rosenman, *Public Papers,* 10: 181, 192; 11: 287–88; 13: 32; Mark L. Chadwin, *The Hawks of World War II* (Chapel Hill, N.C., 1968), 69–70, 275; Henry A. Wallace, *The Century of the Common Man,* Russell Lord, ed. (New York, 1941), 14–19; Henry R. Luce, *The American Century* (New York, 1941), 22–27, 31–33, 37–39; John Fousek, *To Lead the Free World: American Nationalism and the Cultural Roots of the Cold War* (Chapel Hill, 2000), 73–87.

26. Wendy Wall, "'Our Enemies Within': Nazism, National Unity, and America's Wartime Discourse on Tolerance," in *Enemy Images in American History,* Ragnhild Fiebig-von Hase and Ursula Lehmkuhl, eds. (Providence, R.I., 1997), 210–23; Philip Gleason, *Speaking of Diversity: Language and Ethnicity in Twentieth-Century America* (Baltimore, Md., 1992), 190–96; Lloyd, "American Society and Values," 56.

27. Hans Kohn, *Nationalism: Its Meaning and History* (Princeton, N.J., 1955), 19–20; Penny M. Von Eschen, *Race against Empire: Black America and Anticolonialism, 1937–1957* (Ithaca, N.Y., 1997), 3.

28. Richard H. Pells, *The Liberal Mind in a Conservative Age: American Intellectuals in the 1940s and 1950s* (New York, 1985); Robert Booth Fowler, *Believing Skeptics: American Political Intellectuals, 1945–1964* (Westport, Conn., 1978); Isaiah Berlin, *Four Essays on Liberty* (New York, 1969), xliii–xlix, 118–72; Hannah Arendt, *On Revolution* (New York, 1963), 22–26, 119–21.

29. Elizabeth A. Fones-Wolf, *Selling Free Enterprise: The Business Assault on Labor and Liberalism 1945–60* (Urbana, Ill., 1994), 1–3, 44–51; Herbert McClosky and John Zaller, *The American Ethos: Public Attitudes toward Capitalism and Democracy* (Cambridge, Mass., 1984), 133; *The Public Papers of the Presidents: Harry S. Truman, 1947* (Washington, D.C., 1963), 169; David F. Schmitz, *Thank God They're on Our Side: The United States and Right-Wing Dictatorships, 1921–1965* (Chapel Hill, N.C., 1999).

30. *The Public Papers of the Presidents: Ronald Reagan, 1985* (Washington, D.C., 1988), 70; David E. Procter, *Enacting Political Culture: Rhetorical Transformations of Liberty Weekend 1986* (New York, 1991), 61–65; *The Public Papers of the Presidents: Ronald Reagan, 1986* (Washington, D.C., 1988), 1505.

31. Foner, *Story of American Freedom*, 330–32.

32. John Gray, *False Dawn: The Delusions of Global Capitalism* (New York, 1998), 216–17; Thomas L. Friedman, *The Lexus and the Olive Tree: Understanding Globalization* (New York, 1999), 309. For an alternative vision of globalization, emphasizing international social movements rather than market hegemony, see Jeremy Brecher et al., *Globalization from Below: The Power of Solidarity* (Cambridge, Mass., 2000).

33. Held, *Global Transformations,* 3–4.

34. Saskia Sassen, *Losing Control? Sovereignty in an Age of Globalization* (New York, 1996); John Micklethwait and Adrian Wooldridge, *A Future Perfect: The Challenge and Hidden Promise of Globalization* (London, 2000), 336–37.

35. Charles Tilly, "Globalization Threatens Labor's Rights," *International Labor and Working-Class History* 47 (Spring 1995): 4; Smith, *Nations and Nationalism,* 89, 97–98; Eric Hobsbawm, *On the Edge of the New Century* (New York, 2000), 31, 43; Michael Geyer and Charles Bright, "World History in a Global Age," *AHR* 100 (October 1995): 1052–57.

36. See Jonathan Michie and John Grieve Smith, eds., *Global Instability: The Political Economy of World Economic Governance* (London, 1999).

37. Louis Hartz, *The Liberal Tradition in America: An Interpretation of American Political Thought since the Revolution* (New York, 1955), 306.

PART III

TEACHING AMERICAN HISTORY IN A GLOBAL CONTEXT

After Part II's thought-provoking historical essays we turn to the practical business of developing internationalized American history courses and lessons. How can American historians' newly enlarged approaches and interpretations translate effectively into revised course designs?

In an essay reprinted here, Carl Guarneri distinguishes between "systemic" and "episodic" globalizing strategies. The first is more radical. It attempts to revamp the overall structure and periodization of U.S. history courses by using a new organizing principle. That principle may be geographic, comparative, or thematic, or perhaps a theory of historical evolution based on world history. The second strategy is more reformist. It retains the traditional periodization and sequence of survey-course topics, but it leads students to larger frames of description and analysis for each topic by working outward toward international contexts, comparisons, and connections.

The materials in Part III include suggestions for both systemic and episodic approaches. There are blueprints for adopting the longer chronology of world history; for teaching continental history, Atlantic history, or comparative Americas; and for using world-system theory to organize U.S. history courses. Systemic approaches like these may lend themselves more readily to designing honors or upper-division American history courses than the U.S. history survey, with its detailed requirements for chronology and coverage. To meet those needs we have included essays and lessons that cover specific survey-course topics and events. These can become building blocks of an episodic approach that satisfies state-mandated coverage while giving teachers the flexibility to inject comparative or transnational dimensions into the topic at hand.

Part III contains four sections. In the first section (sources 13–17), articles by Guarneri, Donald Meinig, and Maurice Godsey offer various conceptual models for globalized U.S. history courses, while essays by Peter Stearns and Mark Wallace suggest ways to integrate American history into the world history curriculum. The second section (sources 18–22) reproduces five syllabi for internationalized U.S. history courses. Four of these have been taught at the college level, and one is a detailed proposal by graduate students. Three syllabi are road maps for the survey course, two outline more advanced topics, and almost all contain extensive bibliographies. The third section (sources 23–30) gathers essays that highlight the international dimension of specific teaching topics, including the American Revolution, immigration, imperialism, the woman suffrage movement, the Cold War, and the civil rights movement. Most discuss strategies for teaching these topics. In the final section (sources 31–46), we describe or reproduce from printed sources nearly twenty lesson plans aimed at high school and beginning college students. All are based on international or cross-cultural episodes in American history, and many include related documents. They are organized in rough chronological order from the Columbian encounter to the Iraq War. For information about where to find many more such documents and lesson plans, teachers should consult the annotated resource list in Part V.

CHAPTER 13

Internationalizing the U.S. Survey Course
American History for a Global Age

CARL GUARNERI

The *La Pietra Report* of 2000, issued jointly by New York University and the Organization of American Historians (OAH), makes an eloquent appeal for a more internationalized American history. In annual conferences held over a four-year period, more than seventy-five participants reached agreement that historians must "produce a much more nuanced understanding of the place of the United States in the world in all periods in its history," and they should guide students to "look . . . beyond the official borders of the U.S. and back again."[1] Publicized widely among American historians, this document is spurring discussion at professional conventions, on history websites, and in department meetings on the topic of how U.S. history might be rethought—and retaught—in a more global context.

Actually, the *La Pietra Report* crystallizes a movement that has been forming for more than two decades. Calls to internationalize American history have appeared with growing frequency since Laurence Veysey's and Walter Hugins's seminal articles in the 1970s on global convergence and American national difference, respectively.[2] Reminders that the United States developed as part of the world rather than separate from it have emanated from conferences on introductory courses and shaped the presidential addresses of major historical associations.[3] In the 1990s the OAH and the American Studies Association undertook major initiatives to internationalize the study of America's past, including foreign-language book and article prizes, increased coverage of foreign scholarship on the United States, a newsletter series on the state of American history abroad, and special theme issues of their journals.[4] The La Pietra project was intended to provide conceptual underpinning for such initiatives and to chart future directions for scholarship and teaching. Its impact has been enhanced by endorsements from prominent

historians and especially by events in the world outside the academy. The terrorist attacks of September 11, 2001, and the issues they raised have added urgent journalistic voices to the chorus of professional ones asking Americanists to abandon isolationist narratives and stretch the boundaries of U.S. history.[5]

Taken together, these appeals and initiatives make a compelling case for enlarging the frameworks that historians use to study and teach United States history. They stress the need to test traditional ideas of American uniqueness and isolation by examining cross-national comparisons and connections. They emphasize that wider geographic and temporal contexts are required to trace the roots of globalization and to understand the trajectory of the United States' rise to global influence. The growing presence of the U.S. on the international scene, they argue, makes it crucial to study images and opinions of America held by those beyond its borders as well as the considerable impact of American economic and cultural power upon lives around the world. At the same time, looking at the United States from outside it, they assert, will help us to understand ideas, movements, economies, and environments larger than the nation that helped to shape it and those that influence it today, such as transnational migrations, religious fundamentalisms, and multinational corporations. Attitudes toward national identity vary among internationalizing advocates. Some simply acknowledge the rise of transnational identities based on race, gender, or religion, while others applaud them or seek to inculcate a sense of "global citizenship" to supplement or perhaps contest the national version. In any case, all agree that Americans are enmeshed in a world larger than their nation—indeed they always have been—and that students need a history that will help them learn how this

From *The History Teacher* 36 (November 2002): 37–64. Reprinted by author's permission.

interconnectedness came to happen and how they might act effectively within it.

These are powerful arguments, and they are being heard. There has been an unmistakably more cosmopolitan approach to American history among scholars of the past two decades. Starting with comparative studies of frontiers, slavery, and race, historians of the U.S. have expanded their reach across borders and oceans to examine international patterns of migration, working-class formation, evangelicalism, women's activism, and state development. Transnational work in such areas as biological exchange, staple-crop trade, and environmental change is steadily gaining momentum, while borderlands studies are booming.[6] In my view, the key questions concern not whether internationalization will happen—it is already transforming historical scholarship—but how it will proceed and how it should affect history teaching.

This essay is about the second question, more specifically that mainstay of the American history curriculum, the undergraduate survey course. What will happen to the U.S. survey course as American history moves toward internationalization? Is it a relic of nation-based historiography that should be discarded as historians distance themselves from the task of transmitting national myths and forming national citizens? If, on the other hand, it will continue to be with us, how should the course change to reflect a more global conception of American history? Proponents of internationalization themselves disagree about the future of the U.S. survey: some want to retain it while others propose to abolish it and absorb its American component into global or world history. The *La Pietra Report,* consistent with its careful balancing of national and transnational perspectives, suggests that the introductory survey is "properly a focal point" for creating an internationalized American history, then provides brief suggestions for reforming or reframing it.[7]

The views I present in this essay are premised on the assumption that the U.S. survey will remain for the foreseeable future a key feature of undergraduate history in the United States. Considering the many ways that the teaching of American history is embedded in political, professional, and institutional contexts that change very gradually, this seems a realistic assumption. And keeping in mind the enormously important role the American nation continues to play in students' lives and identities—and in world affairs—retaining the survey has a strong educational rationale as well.

The U.S. survey course will continue to exist, but it won't be unchanged. As new scholarship that pursues American history across national boundaries inspires college teachers, influences graduate training, and finds its way into survey textbooks, the introductory course will reflect changes to traditional frameworks in U.S. history. This trend may be accelerated by the growing number of graduate students who prepare a field in global or comparative history and by the

many teachers who teach both world history and American history. To some degree, internationalized surveys will also emerge in response to the increased diversity of American college students and to the special situation faced by those who teach U.S. history abroad.

Changes that begin to globalize U.S. history are already being introduced by individual teachers and departments, but without much publicity and coordination. For their part, proponents of internationalization have offered more exhortation than curricular strategies and examples.[8] The main intent of my essay is to provide an overview of various models and approaches for internationalizing the survey, in hopes of encouraging interested teachers and inspiring new course paradigms. A secondary aim is to address a few of the objections and obstacles that may impede this work; or, put more positively, to suggest some disciplinary connections and curricular materials that can support it.

Internationalizing Trends in the Survey Course

How will an internationalized U.S history survey look? Although it will continue to provide a factual foundation for further study of the United States, the new introductory course will also emphasize international connections, comparisons, and interpretive frameworks. Before discussing specific course models, I want to point out some general changes that internationalization may bring to the survey. Two of these—the search for new starting points and an increased attention to foreign affairs—are already well under way and can be reviewed quickly. The other four are less apparent and more prospective but potentially more revolutionary; they will require greater elaboration.

Where does American history begin? For decades the conventional starting points have been Virginia, Massachusetts Bay, and the British North American colonies, but recent U.S. history textbooks have gone back further in time and expanded their geographic reach. In tune with this trend, many survey-course teachers now take time to examine the Spanish, Portuguese, French, and Dutch empires in the New World. Some start even earlier, examining the roots of European expansion before the 1400s and the social and religious legacy of the Medieval world. Just as the latest world history textbooks have pushed back the origins of the modern world economy to the intercontinental trade routes and migrations of the period between 1000 and 1300, so too some historians report beginning their American history surveys with the rise of Eurasian trade and the spread of Islam, connecting the Silk Road to the Middle Passage.[9]

Nor is Eurasia the only site for this deeper history. When the *National Standards for United States History* (1994) labeled the period before 1620 an era when "three worlds meet," they encouraged teachers to increase their coverage of the pre-contact history of Africa and the Americas. Most textbooks now examine North American geography and portray Native American cultures, empires, and trade networks that thrived long before Europeans arrived. They also describe powerful West African kingdoms that were transformed by contacts with Arab and European traders.[10] Recast as places where Europeans, Africans, and Native Americans converged, the colonies that became the United States are now interpreted as bequeathing a complex, fascinating, and often troubled legacy of cultural collision, domination, and mixture to the new nation.

This trend of moving further back in time suggests that a more global approach offers multiple places and starting points for the narratives that create American history. Today's teachers are selecting their own emphases or even problematizing U.S. history by engaging students with the question of when and where it should begin.

Today's survey courses also feature greater consideration of America's role in world affairs. Highlighting American political, diplomatic, or military activities abroad is the most common way for teachers to inject international themes or events into survey syllabi. Concern with foreign affairs has long been a staple of survey textbooks, and although the rise of social history in the 1970s and 1980s cut into its allotted pages, especially for the nineteenth century, international relations now loom more prominently than ever in twentieth-century narratives. Two world wars, the long Cold War, the subsequent position of the United States as the world's sole superpower, and current controversies over globalization have moved the international context of recent American history into the foreground. Especially in response to the September 11 attacks and the American intervention in Afghanistan, many teachers have highlighted past events which may be analogous to the contemporary situation: Jefferson's war on the Barbary pirates, U.S. interventions in Mexico and Central America, or the Japanese surprise attack on Pearl Harbor.[11]

These two ongoing trends—toward new starting points and greater coverage of foreign affairs—reflect what I have elsewhere called the "genetic" and "foreign-relations" models of internationalization.[12] In most cases they involve the early and late stages of American history and do little to change the middle. The U.S. survey commonly opens with the genetic approach and ends with the foreign-relations paradigm. Beginning with a wide-angle, Atlantic, or hemispheric view of contact and colonialism, the course narrows to a resolutely national approach after the Revolution. Most textbooks and syllabi then concentrate almost exclusively on domestic affairs until the Spanish-American War of 1898, which is viewed as opening the era of formal imperialism and international involvement.

If the U.S. survey course is to be thoroughly internationalized, this conventional hourglass-shaped coverage will have to go. The fact is, as the *National Standards for World History* note, that between 1750 and 1914 "the history of the United States . . . was not self-contained but fully embed-

ded in the context of global change."[13] To do justice to this connectedness will require sustained attention to events and trends outside the nation, continuous engagement with the ways that American political, social, and economic developments have been implicated in world patterns and events. This is the first, and the most fundamental, of the genuinely new changes I foresee for the survey course.

From early on, events elsewhere have directed our national life. As Paul Gagnon has written, "the American history course should make it plain that the bell tolled for us when the Portuguese began African slave-trading in 1444, when the French invaded Saigon in 1859, when the Japanese humiliated Czar Nicholas in 1905, [and] when Franz Ferdinand was assassinated in 1914."[14] Conversely, from the "Columbian Exchange" onward, North American organisms, products, and political ideas have initiated important transformations around the world.[15] Simultaneous with these two-way global connections, and partly because of them, in the Americas, South Africa, and Australia there arose parallel developments that provide fruitful opportunities for cross-national comparisons. The trajectory of the United States as a European "settler society" that imported African slaves, subjugated natives, expanded along frontiers, established representative government, received immigrants, industrialized and eventually built a welfare state, suggests that the American experience is comparable to that of many other nations that were founded in the wake of European expansion.

As these broad parallels and examples of mutual influence imply, studies of the international contexts of national history tend to fall into two camps, one emphasizing episodes of connection and impact and the other examining questions of similarity and difference. It may be that in the early stages of globalizing, U.S. survey courses will replicate the dichotomy that world historians formed between "comparativists" and "interactionists," those who compare major nations, civilizations, or institutions, and those who emphasize exchanges, conquests, and migrations as the key determinants of historical change.[16] But just as world-history textbooks seem to be converging toward a mixed approach, U.S. history textbooks and teachers will probably adopt an eclectic form of internationalization. Teachers may experiment with many models, but they will probably come to realize, as scholars have discovered, that the richest versions of international history incorporate both transnational narratives and comparative analyses.[17]

A second new development I foresee is the effect that attention to larger contexts may have on the way teachers periodize U.S. history. Linking familiar American events and movements to counterparts elsewhere complicates old chronologies and may inspire new ones. A few examples suggest some of the possibilities. As colonial American history widens beyond the British thirteen colonies into the charting of a slave-based Atlantic economy, the phases of that economic system stretch into the nineteenth century and encompass the American Revolution rather than culminate in it.[18] The fact that the American Revolution itself was connected to contemporary uprisings in the Atlantic world suggests that the "Age of Revolution" continued in the United States at least into the Jacksonian era of the 1830s, perhaps (thanks to the Seneca Falls Convention) to 1848, as it did in Europe.[19] A more global perspective may indicate that two-semester survey courses should be split at points other than the ubiquitous 1877. What about 1815, when Napoleon's defeat, the end of the War of 1812, and the *Pax Britannica* finally assured the survival of the young United States? Or the 1890s, when the post–Civil War race question was finally settled, the frontier was officially closed, and the United States began its imperial phase, all of which can be seen as related developments? For the twentieth century, doesn't a transatlantic view demonstrate that Progressivism and the New Deal ought to be discussed together as the American variant of the rising Western "welfare state"?[20]

Daniel Rodgers, developing his affirmative response to this last question, has proposed that an internationalized American history be divided into five broad stages. European exploration opened an "age of outpost settlements" coexisting precariously with native societies. Then, stretching from the last quarter of the seventeenth century to the last quarter of the eighteenth, an "age of commercial Atlantic empires" tied these American settlements to European capitals, the slave coast of Africa, and the West Indian colonies in dense networks of trade. The third great phase, sparked by the American and French Revolutions and continuing beyond the American Civil War, was an "age of revolutionary nation-building." By the late nineteenth century, problems of industrialization, immigration, and urbanization challenged nations to develop the political means to curb the excesses of capitalism; thus began an "age of social politics" that encompassed American Progressivism and the New Deal and lasted into the 1940s. The most recent phase, the "age of the world hegemony of the United States," extends from World War II and the Cold War to our own time.[21]

Rodgers's internationalized schema challenges survey teachers to think in longer time spans and to cluster topics, such as the Revolution and the Civil War, that often get separated by intervening events or themes. Its "big picture" approach encourages discussion of international connections and comparisons without sacrificing the stability of a clear chronological scaffolding and without creating competing or overlapping timetables.

A more radical approach would be to highlight the varying chronologies that social and economic history introduce into historical study by adopting a heavily thematic approach: *de*periodizing rather than *re*periodizing American history. Since demographic trends, economic systems, and cultural norms change at a slower pace than political developments and have different turning points, textbooks and teachers must confront the problem of juxtaposing political events and underlying structures, the short and the long *durée*. Most U.S. history textbook writers have adjusted by organizing thematic chapters with somewhat parallel chronologies, often alternating between chapters with political narratives and those featuring social/economic description.

Internationalization promises to accelerate this trend, perhaps dramatically. One current world history textbook, *The Global Past,* divides the period between 1500 and 1900 in the Western Hemisphere into nine thematic chapters, most spanning two or more centuries: "Oceanic Explorations and Contacts, 1405–1780," "Early European Colonialism, c. 1500–c.1750," "The American Exchange, 1492–c.1750," "The African Slave Trade, 1441–1815," "Revolutions in Europe, the Americas, and Asia, 1543–1895," "The Global Industrial Revolution, c. 1770–1905," "Modern Nationalism around the Globe, 1816–1920," "Imperialism around the Globe, 1803–1949," and "Darwin, Marx, and Others Transform Our Views, 1837 Onward."[22] If American history is reorganized to address such world history topics, we can expect to see much longer, chronologically overlapping thematic units that combine the segments on colonialism, trade, slavery, revolution, nation-building, industrialization, and foreign relations that are currently scattered through several short-term chapters in conventional textbooks. Of course, teachers adopting such a strongly thematic approach must be willing to sacrifice clear decade-by-decade chronology for more intensive study of key developments and the interpretive challenge of connecting the parallel timelines of economy, society, and politics.

A third change that will probably accompany internationalization is a new, more detached stance toward the nation. It's no secret that American history as practiced and taught has been largely wedded to the project of building and preserving the nation.[23] Conventional textbooks are often framed as epics in which the nation is formed and tested: *Making a Nation, The American Journey, The Enduring Vision.* Such books, and the courses in which they are assigned, tend to assume that the national is the normative scale of the story and the nation-state is its most important protagonist. Often, too, like much of the scholarship from which they derive, such textbooks imply that the American national experience is unique—even exceptional—without subjecting such claims to careful scrutiny.

Internationalized formulations of the survey will challenge these practices. Some will start with traditional questions about national identity and development, such as what it means to be an American or what was unique about American history. But by contextualizing the United States and comparing it with other nations, they will aim to produce nuanced comparisons that break away from stereotyped dichotomies between "us" and "them," America and the rest of the world.[24] The new survey will interrogate American "exceptionalism" in its various guises, from specific claims about the importance of the frontier or the absence of socialism to the more general notion that American history has been exempt from trends and problems seen elsewhere in the world.[25] One aim of comparative analysis will be to develop a more sophisticated sense of the weave of differences and similarities that constitutes a nation's distinctiveness. Another will be to illuminate how American history has been enmeshed in networks and forces larger than the nation. As the United States takes its place among a broad spectrum of nations, the tendency will be to move "from exceptionalism to variability," to see American events as variations on global developments, and to focus as much, or nearly as much, attention on such processes and movements as on the national story.[26]

As for nation-building, it seems clear that most internationalized surveys will still include the establishment and consolidation of American political institutions and a careful consideration of the nation's founding documents—these subjects remain critical for students and citizens to understand. But in line with recent scholarship they will stress what the *La Pietra Report* calls the "historicity of nation-making."[27] This includes the sense that the United States is not a natural unit but a human creation, the study of it as an ongoing rather than a finished experiment, and the definition of it as an "imagined community" whose terms and boundaries have shifted over time.[28]

One way to impart this sense of constructedness would be to examine perennial tensions between "civic" and "ethnic" versions of American nationhood. Throughout their history Americans have argued over whether their national identity involves allegiance to a set of rules and principles that are public and color-blind, or whether "true Americans" are those who derive from white European ancestry. Placed in a global context, this tension is the American variant of the struggle between racial/ethnic inclusion and exclusion that has shaped many countries.[29] Another way to contextualize nationalism might be to examine other forms of belonging, such as allegiances to family, region, religion, race, or gender. Thus students will come to appreciate the multiple identities and solidarities, some smaller than the nation, others larger, that coexist with national identity, sometimes harmoniously but sometimes in competition or conflict. Ideally, by incorporating these diverse perspectives into its readings and discussions, the new survey will demonstrate some of the connections between domestic "multiculturalism" and global diversity.[30]

One obvious link is immigration. Studying the complex play of national and transnational identities created by migration, whether voluntary or forced, is a powerful way the survey can construct a middle position between the traditional view of the nation as subject and a global view of it as a site for larger processes that are themselves the object of inquiry. No doubt there will be many others suggested by the dialogue between American history and an emphasis on particular transnational political, social,

economic, or environmental themes. One can even imagine a future in which more aggressively globalized U.S. survey courses present the nation much more as a site than a subject, located near the midpoint between local, regional, continental, and global processes, not always the relevant unit of inquiry and only occasionally decisive as an historical intervener. Courses that center around such transnational processes as environmental change, oceanic trade, migration, and industrialization may well feature multiple focal points and several scales of historical analysis, from the local to the global.[31]

This last point is important enough to isolate as the fourth and final change on my list: a reminder that internationalized survey courses of all types will find ways to link microhistory and macrohistory, processes larger than the nation and those smaller. Just as the United States was never really separate from the world, its individuals, groups, and local communities have been enmeshed in networks of trade, migration, and culture that cross borders continually. In this age of instant communication, jet travel, global sweatshops, and "thinking globally and acting locally," the notion of interconnectedness is less abstract and foreign to American students than ever. To examine these connections in vivid and meaningful ways, an internationalized survey will trace local developments to regional, national, and transnational contexts and vice versa.[32] It will keep up a running dialogue between the ethnic and economic history of specific towns or regions and larger patterns emerging from studies of trade, industrialization, migration, and environmental change. Some survey teachers are already experimenting with a "sister cities" approach that demonstrates connections between American and overseas communities, such as the ties among Fort Ross, California, Sitka, Alaska, and St. Petersburg, Russia, in the early nineteenth century.[33] Recent books on Jews in New York and Paris, Italians in New York and Buenos Aires, and older works on Africans in Latin America and the United States, suggest that a comparative approach can be as effective as an interactionist one in connecting local with international history.[34]

Surely one benefit of stressing this micro-macro connection is to avoid the trap, familiar to world historians, of burying individuals and small groups in the discussion of large, impersonal structures or forces in history. Teachers who regularly use student autobiographies or family histories to illuminate larger historical processes have attempted to solve this problem, and no doubt future survey courses will do something similar. Through comparative biographies or representative transnational lives of indigenous peoples, colonists, migrants, slaves, sailors, missionaries, traders, reformers, entrepreneurs, political leaders and other figures powerful and small, an internationalized survey can depict people who crossed borders and transformed history. Incorporating the stories of such lives into survey courses will engage students concretely in the historical drama at the same time it raises their awareness of the many places that have informed Americans' lives and identities.

"Systemic" Models of Internationalization

How will these changes, and others that I have not foreseen, translate into new survey syllabi and course designs? Turning to this more practical concern, it may be useful to distinguish between "systemic" and "episodic" strategies for internationalizing the survey course. The former undertake a more radical or whole-cloth restructuring, the latter a more reformist or piecemeal approach that involves less drastic and uniform redesign of the course but allows for greater flexibility along the way.

Systemic approaches seek to incorporate internationalization into the overall structure of the course by using a particular theme or theory as an organizing principle. This could be done in many ways, five of which I will highlight here. One might be to reframe the course into a larger ecological or geographic unit. A survey built around North American history, as the geographer D.W. Meinig recommends, could incorporate comparisons, contacts, borderland migrations and mixings, as well as U.S. interventions and influences in Canada and Mexico.[35] Casting a wider hemispheric net, an introductory course centered on the Americas could pursue a similar strategy for the entire New World. Drawing upon scholarship that stems from Herbert Eugene Bolton's theory that North and South America share a common history, such a course could trace parallel developments in the colonial, independence, and national periods as well as analyze borderland and foreign-relations issues.[36] Alternatively, some survey courses may choose the Atlantic Basin as their primary geographic context. Because scholars of early American history have largely reframed the colonial era and American slavery as episodes in Atlantic history, there are excellent syntheses as well as case studies for teachers to draw upon.[37] For the period after 1800 there are fewer overviews due to the "hourglass effect" referred to above, but a growing monographic literature on migration, industrialization, race, class, reform, and international relations in the Atlantic Basin provides insights and readings to learn from.[38] Peering out from the other side of the continent, a Pacific Rim approach might be used to contrast or complement the Atlantic focus with its own discussion of colonialism, trade, migration, labor systems, and foreign relations. In each of these cases survey instructors will use wider geographic contexts as settings and reference points as they proceed through major events and developments in U.S. history.

A second approach, a variant of this geographic opening up of the survey, might be to use a limited number of non-U.S. societies as comparative focal points, thus incorporating a sustained binational dialogue or multinational conversation through the semester. George Fredrickson's masterly two-volume comparative study of the United States and South Africa, still the most fully-developed binational history involving the United States, provides a model and—for students up to its challenge—a text.[39] The medieval historian Marc Bloch once noted that the most illuminating comparisons are those between societies with common influences and substantial basic similarities.[40] Keeping this in mind as well as the terrain of existing comparative studies, three such reference groups seem most appropriate for comparing with the path of American history: (1) other European "white settler societies" in Latin America, Canada, Australia, and South Africa that confronted aboriginal groups and moved from colonial status to independent nationhood; (2) western European nations that forged transatlantic connections with the United States and underwent similar political, social, and industrial trends; and (3) the new political and industrial world powers of the twentieth century, Japan and Russia. There are others. The early national history of the United States, for example, suggests striking parallels with the strife-torn and dependent situation of developing nations in Asia and Africa.[41] For instructors who seek to localize such transnational comparisons, thereby linking macro- and microhistory, a survey course focusing on the United States' northern or southwestern borderlands, or the comparative cities approach mentioned above, might be attractive strategies.[42]

A third and quite different systemic strategy is to choose a facet of U.S. history that is inherently international and make it the main theme or special angle of the course. A course-long emphasis on foreign relations, war, migration, religion, trade, technology, or biological exchange would ensure that U.S. history could be studied from a sustained interactionist viewpoint that stresses America's participation in rather than isolation from the movement of peoples, goods, and ideas throughout the world.

A special emphasis upon international relations, for example, could bring foreign affairs more consistently into the survey course, especially for the often-overlooked nineteenth century. Survey teachers could situate westward expansion in a global arena by portraying such episodes as the fur trade, the Lewis and Clark expedition, the Louisiana Purchase, the Mexican War, and the Gold Rush as international phenomena. Drawing upon scholarship that explores U.S. international involvements bilaterally or even multilaterally, they can ensure that students interpret topics such as the American Revolution, the Mexican War, or the American occupation of Japan from the perspective of the various participants, not just American policymakers.[43] Examination of the ways that domestic and foreign policy have interacted can shed new light on how racial and gender thinking fostered imperialism, how labor movements influenced immigration policy, or how the Cold War gave a boost to the Civil Rights movement.[44] After the mid-nineteenth century the expanding reach of American power overseas can be demonstrated through such episodes as Commodore Perry's mission to Japan, Anglo-American relations during the Civil War, or the colonization of Hawaii, challenging the persisting myth of American isolationism.[45] And consideration of the impact of America's power abroad in the twentieth century will raise important questions about the nature of hegemony, empire, and globalization.[46]

In recent years foreign-relations historians have broadened their subject from a narrowly focused "diplomatic history" toward what Akira Iriye calls "transnational affairs," the wide spectrum of contacts between individuals and groups across national borders. Incorporating this development into the survey course entails not simply giving greater coverage to treaties and wars, but also charting international trade, technology exchange, migration, missionary activity, travel literature, or reform organizing. Like intergovernmental contacts, economic and cultural exports can be analyzed from the receiving end as well, inquiring, for example, how American sewing machines changed industry around the world or how Europeans have interpreted American movies.[47]

The issue of how outsiders see the United States, important during the nation's fragile early years, becomes equally significant during its rise to global power, as the tragic events of September 11, 2001 have reminded us. For all kinds of internationalized survey courses, whether focused on international relations or not, foreign views can provide an informative alternative to American perspectives. *Those United States,* a recently published survey-course reader, is an intriguing collection of such commentary on a wide range of topics. Those who view the United States from the outside can reveal patterns and assumptions hidden to insiders, highlight worldwide interest or indifference toward the American experiment, illuminate the motives of overseas migrants and governments, and document the effects of U.S. foreign policy abroad.[48]

Another intrinsically international subject is trade. World historians have shown the enormous impact of cross-cultural exchange in altering daily life as well as long-term patterns related to population and the global distribution of power. Rather than simply an add-on feature of American history, following the trail of commodity production and exchange could become a central strategy, providing a lens through which to view U.S. history transnationally. Beginning with the epochal exchanges following the Columbian encounter, for example, a survey course could trace the political struggles and social changes of early American history through the development of an international trade in animal products, sugar, tobacco, cod, cotton, and wheat. From there the focus could shift to industrial production in the nineteenth century or else continue with an emphasis on food: the impact of new processes of packing, canning, and freezing; immigrant foodways and their influence on American diet; the use of immigrant labor in American

agriculture; how American consumption patterns helped alter land use patterns at home and abroad; and the development and export of fast food. The theme of foodstuffs connects directly with issues related to the frontier and the environment, transportation and labor systems, the national and world economy, and foreign policy—all inherently transnational subjects. And the history of commodities offers a particularly rich model for suggesting the multiple sites and scales involved in internationalizing U.S. history. Mark Kurlansky's *Cod,* for example, artfully links the fishing industry to local life in New England, Canada, and Iceland as well as to the larger story of regional economies and international rivalries. Mark Pendergrast's *For God, Country and Coca-Cola* follows that pervasive soft drink's influence from local gas station dispensing machines to policymakers' desks at the State Department, and eventually around the globe.[49]

The same points about scale and connection apply to such survey themes as migration or race. Indeed, because they are intended as general conceptual tools, sociological categories such as migration systems, slavery, race, class, or gender deliberately slice across national boundaries. A focus on one or more of these sociological constructs—a fourth systemic strategy—can invite transnational comparisons and connections throughout the course. Running a thread on race through the survey, for example, would mean incorporating far more than slavery, the slave trade, and emancipation. It also involves introducing related comparative and international topics, such as the history of racial ideas and categories, attitudes and practices regarding racial mixture, racial claims and barriers to citizenship, theories of "split labor" and "internal colonialism," links between racism and imperialism, and the history of civil rights agitation, Pan-Africanism, and other black liberation movements.[50] As students recognize, with W.E.B. DuBois, that American racism is "but a local phase of a world problem," they will begin to appreciate the varied ways that racial categorizing has framed struggles over group identity and freedom around the globe.[51]

Finally, perhaps the most encompassing of all the systemic approaches to internationalization are those that integrate U.S. history with various stage theories or conceptual schemas employed by world historians or historical sociologists. A survey course designed with these in mind might ask students to situate American developments in such transnational interpretive constructs as Marxist theory, state-development schemas, world-system analysis, long-wave economic cycles, and other social-science models, or it might examine such meta-themes as the rise of modernity or the course of civilizations.

This is not the place for an extended discussion of such theories and their application to U.S. history. However, world-system analysis deserves additional comment because it has been so influential among world historians and is increasingly being adopted by Americanists. Introduced by Immanuel Wallerstein in the 1970s, this theory traces the development of an integrated world economy since the fifteenth century which was dominated by the rich and powerful "core" nations of western Europe and which gradually brought distant regions on its "periphery" into dependence upon its capitalist market.[52] Broadly applied to America, a world-system approach begins with North America as an outpost on the world periphery increasingly enmeshed in the web of colonization, mercantilism, and the slave trade. After independence, the United States embarks upon a course followed by other "semi-peripheral" states as it consolidates national institutions, develops export production, industrializes, urbanizes, and exerts control over its own regional hinterland. Finally, after World War I the United States emerges as the prime inheritor of the European economic might and a global power in its own right. A U.S. survey course based on this world-system scaffolding would systematically trace the United States' path from the periphery to the core of the world system, or, as world historian Michael Adas puts it, "from settler colony to global hegemon."[53]

A chronology that charts America's initially small world-significance over four centuries provides a necessary corrective to John Winthrop's endlessly repeated claim that from the outset the "eyes of all people" were trained on New England's "city upon the hill." But as the *La Pietra Report* acknowledges, using the survey course to trace the U.S. "rise to globalism" also runs the risk of "produc[ing] a form of historiographic imperialism or an ideological justification for . . . American hegemony." Historians and other critics of Francis Fukuyama's "end of history" thesis have warned against creating a triumphalist global narrative of U.S. history that feeds the dubious notion that world history has culminated in the collapse of communism and the victory of democratic, capitalist institutions.[54] Such a celebratory narrative simply flips the coin of American "exceptionalism": as Adas reminds us, while one face of exceptionalism has traditionally separated the United States from all other societies, the other has presented America as the world's "last, best hope" and promoted its global civilizing mission.[55]

It is conceivable that an internationalized survey course might simply globalize traditional American claims to moral leadership or universal principles. But the United States' growing international sway is open to many interpretations, critical as well as approving. Survey students could be encouraged to examine the notion of the United States as an imperial power, whether in the traditional sense of ancient Rome or nineteenth-century Great Britain or in some new way. By sorting out concepts such as "imperialism," "globalization," "westernization," and "Americanization," they can aim to grasp more fully the scope and limits of American power in a world in which, on the one hand, the United States is the sole remaining superpower, and on the other, its influence is constrained by competing national and transnational organizations.[56] Just as the history of empires shows that they rise and fall, the only accurate stage theories show that history does not end, but that societies and economies continue to evolve into new relationships. Analyzing these changing relations is properly the aim of an internationalized survey course, which sets out neither to praise nor criticize the United States but to understand its place in the world.

"Episodic" Approaches

Whether organized by world-system theory, large geographic units, comparative analysis, or some other principle that I have not envisioned here, systemic approaches incorporate cross-cultural study into the very fiber of the survey course. At a time when traditional national narratives are being questioned, they can provide coherent alternative frameworks, or at least unifying thematic currents, that move American history outward toward the wider world. Despite this appeal, it is certain that many historians would resist impressing these kinds of organizing frameworks onto the survey course. Some may believe that systemic internationalization will relegate U.S. history to the background too frequently; others that it will multiply the workload by requiring instructors and students to master world or other national histories in addition to that of the United States. Schemas derived from world history may also conflict with institutional requirements for the U.S. survey, which tend to emphasize events rather than structure, domestic rather than international developments. Many American public universities face requirements to cover constitutional topics, and some states have set guidelines for history instruction or teacher preparation that may discourage global approaches.

Internationalization raises its own concerns about constraining teachers' choices. An overarching schema may encourage survey instructors to impose one rigid "master narrative" on a course in which they prefer competing views, or it may compel them to omit material they consider essential because it does not fit into the course's trajectory. Further, some historians fear that these larger frameworks would inhibit Americanists from engaging in important mid-level interpretive controversies about specific events and movements: debates over the Constitution, options inside the Gilded Age labor movement, or attitudes toward the New Deal. While "the big picture" may be necessary for world historians, Americanists enjoy the relative luxury of teaching a mere 400 years of history, often over two semesters, and many want to use their time to explore events in depth as well as in their broad contexts.

There are good answers to these objections, and I anticipate that as internationalization proceeds it will spur lively debates over survey-course designs. Leaving such arguments and counter-arguments aside, for teachers who resist the systemic, whole-cloth approach there remain many possibilities for engaging an internationalized U.S. history more episodically. This would mean linking one-at-a-time or opportunistically the events and developments discussed in the survey course to a larger frame of description and analysis. The introductory survey course would still cover traditional topics, but students could be encouraged to situate many of them internationally by seeking their larger contexts and meanings.

America Compared, the collection of survey-course readings I initially developed in the mid-1990s, is based on this eclectic, episodic approach.[57] I organized it by subjecting traditional survey events to what I called the "three c's": searching for transnational *connections,* framing appropriate cross-cultural *comparisons,* and testing against social-science *concepts* such as racism or revolution. Participants at the La Pietra conferences added a fourth "c" to the list—seeking larger *contexts*—an umbrella term that reminds us that history is distinctively a contextualizing discipline.[58] With eclectic approaches such as the "four c's," the goal is to model different paths to a more broadly-framed U.S. history and to instill internationalization as a habit of mind rather than to present a new master narrative or unified interpretation of American history.

Episodic strategies of internationalizing U.S. history give survey instructors greater flexibility than committing themselves to a single transnational theme or theory. Teachers can choose the most appropriate of the "four c's" for the topic at hand. For example, they could interpret immigration as an episode in a long history of continental and transoceanic connections, present industrialization as an internationally comparative process, analyze American slavery as a site of both connection and comparison, or measure the American Revolution against various conceptual models of the nature and dynamic of revolutions. Instructors could select the most revealing supranational context for each topic without precommitting themselves to a particular comparison group or geographic frame. They could choose to work "inside out" or "outside in"; that is, to enlarge local or regional histories toward international contexts or to announce global themes whose ramifications can then be traced in local arenas.[59] Such an approach permits the Great Depression, to take one example, to be taught simultaneously as a local catastrophe, a national problem, and a world economic and political crisis with a much longer background than 1929 and with comparable effects from nation to nation.

Episodic internationalization takes advantage of the generally eclectic nature of the survey course. It enables the instructor to include world-history relevance as one of several criteria used to select course topics. It also allows certain components or "voices" in the course such as lectures, readings, visual sources, or discussions to address broad international themes while others present a more traditional, intensive look. Readings might be used to widen the perspective of lectures or vice versa. Brief segments of class time could be set aside regularly to consider internationalizing themes such as "views from abroad" or "transnational lives." Teachers could draw upon the experience of students who have come from elsewhere or have lived outside the United States to confirm or contest course generalizations or to suggest new connections and comparisons. The possibilities are virtually endless: because the U.S. survey is taught in many different places, to diverse students, and with varied pedagogical formats, there are countless ways to embed a conversation among local, national, and international history in its day-to-day operations.

Links to Diaspora Studies, Women's History, and World History

Whether an internationalized U.S history is presented in systemic or episodic form, instructors in the new survey course will engage students with an exciting but also potentially confusing history. They will give alternating or even simultaneous attention to different geographic scales, social realms, and chronologies. They will examine the coexistence (and sometimes conflict) of local, national, and transnational identities, even within the same group. In this respect it would make sense to learn from historians who have blazed similar trails. Scholars studying "diasporas," a term formerly used to describe the global scattering of Jews and Africans but now increasingly applied to Asians and other transnational migrants, can suggest ways to understand the play of multiple identities and the tensions of dual allegiances.[60] As early as 1903, W.E.B. DuBois pointed out the "double-consciousness" of being both black and American; his insight can help us to remap American history by following the international agendas as well as the national struggles of American minorities.[61] Women's history may also provide models to build upon. In the United States, it was among the first "new" histories to challenge political, event-oriented history and conventional periodization as well as to trace transnational social movements. The field's most popular reader, *Women's America,* juxtaposes the different timescales of biology, economics, family history, and politics.[62] Historians setting out to internationalize their U.S. surveys would do well to inquire about useful approaches and techniques that can be learned from our colleagues teaching introductory courses in African American, diaspora, and women's history.

As I have implied throughout this article, the experience of teaching world history is even more directly relevant. World historians have struggled with the problem of integrating different geographies, cultures, and timetables into a coherent course framework. They have debated the strengths and weaknesses of "comparativist" versus "interactionist" models for teaching global history. And they have discussed the role that U.S. history should have in the world history survey, just as Americanists have begun discussing what place "the world" should have in theirs.[63] This essay has suggested ways in which world history has already influenced how introductory U.S. history is being taught. What else might American historians learn from world historians? The American history section of the 1996 *National Standards* virtually ignored transnational themes, but the standards for World History prescribed that U.S. and world history be "interrelated in content and similar in format."[64] To what extent should the world and U.S. survey courses be synchronized with a like periodization or tied by common approaches and themes? Addressing this question could help to build bridges between Americanists and world historians, connections that might break down the rigid compartmentalization of history curricula into American history and "other" courses. This separation reinforces nationalist biases in our teaching and shortchanges students who seek to understand the world around them in all its complexity and connectedness. As the *La Pietra Report* suggests, a sustained dialogue with world history has the potential to prod teachers not simply to revitalize the U.S. survey course but to reimagine the undergraduate history curriculum more generally.[65]

Challenges and Opportunities

Teachers setting out to internationalize their U.S. history survey—and to convince others to do so—should expect to encounter difficulties, even if they choose modest "episodic" strategies. One common problem is teachers' own specialized graduate training or unfamiliarity with histories beyond American borders. While teachers cannot expect themselves to be experts in all areas, there is no avoiding the fact that internationalizing U.S. history will require additional preparation, often in unfamiliar fields. Then, too, survey students may well lack a basic knowledge of world history. This can be addressed in various ways: mini-lectures for background and chronology, guest presentations or team teaching, appointment of "area experts" among class members, or the use of library reference assignments. Such methods can allow students a meaningful entrée into transnational topics without making them feel lost or encouraging them to descend into vague generalities or national stereotypes.

Right now there is a shortage of suitably internationalized American history textbooks. New editions of existing texts have increased their pre–Columbian era and foreign-affairs coverage, and their advertisements claim that they place "U.S. History in a Global Context."[66] More thoroughly internationalized textbooks are currently in preparation. David J. Russo's *American History from a Global Perspective* is a thematic overview rather than a conventional textbook, but it could be used effectively as a survey text.[67] As for collections of readings, besides *America Compared* and *Those United States,* which I described earlier, some

teachers have developed their own coursepacks based on readings from *American Heritage* or *History Today* as well as selected book chapters and documents. As internationalization proceeds, it will produce more popular syntheses and essays that could be adopted or excerpted for survey-course students. To be sure, new course supplements will still have to compete against traditional readers using dated interpretive frameworks, some of which remain in demand after more than thirty years.

In this respect, the project of internationalizing the survey course faces the same obstacles that any revamping of the survey runs up against: institutional or faculty resistance, professional reward structures that ignore innovation in teaching surveys, and heavy teaching loads and diverse assignments. Institutional initiatives aimed at internationalizing the survey course, whether they come from professional associations or colleges themselves, will have to address this complex of resistance, overwork, and lack of incentive in addition to issues of content and pedagogy.

Still, there are encouraging trends under way that will support internationalization. Graduate history training is becoming more comparative and transnational in content; many advanced students now prepare a field in world history and are expected to teach it when hired. The growing cohort of young historians who teach both the U.S. survey and a world history course may provide a critical mass for curricular cross-fertilization and the development of new textbooks. The diversity of U.S. college students, and particularly the increasing number of those who study U.S. history in foreign universities—an important development that is beyond the scope of this essay—augment the usefulness of transnational and comparative approaches and may suggest new ways to undertake them. In short, in addition to trends in historiography, the demographics of history students and faculty may well be on the side of internationalization.

Having taught a modestly internationalized survey course for several years, I can attest that its educational benefits far outweigh its logistical difficulties or concerns about preparation or coverage. My students note that transnational and comparative approaches help them relate the United States to the rest of the world and to assess more carefully its distinctive qualities. They are quick to suggest connections between their world history and American history knowledge, and they appreciate the challenge of acquiring a global perspective on such topics as racial inequality, religious conflict, and American popular culture. Many report renewed excitement when confronted with an enlarged version of American history, whose horizons seemed to shrink as they encountered it over their school years in ever more specialized segments. I have found that embedding international themes in the introductory course is not just a workable strategy but a revitalizing one.

If internationalization is to take root in the history curriculum, as the *La Pietra Report* advocates, the U.S. survey course is an essential ground to plant the seeds. For many college students such surveys are all the American history they are going to get. For others who continue their studies, cosmopolitan habits of mind should be encouraged from the outset. Rather than waiting for students to reach upper-division or graduate work before they confront an enlarged conception of the American past, we should seize the opportunity to introduce internationalizing themes sooner. Rather than waiting for scholarship to trickle down, internationalized introductory courses can create a demand for creative textbooks and course materials. To do so will require rethinking the survey course in imaginative ways as well as overcoming a certain amount of professorial and institutional resistance. Internationalizing American history will take some effort, but it promises to bring fresh ideas and broader vistas to a traditionally insular subject that needs more than ever to connect with the wider world.

Notes

1. Organization of American Historians and New York University, *La Pietra Report: Project on Internationalizing the Study of American History* (New York: n.p, 2000), 7–8. Thomas Bender, who wrote the project's final report, is the editor of a volume of essays from the La Pietra conferences: *Rethinking American History in a Global Age* (Berkeley: University of California Press, 2002).

2. Laurence Veysey, "The Autonomy of American History Reconsidered," *American Quarterly* 31 (Fall 1979): 455–77; Walter Hugins, "American History in Comparative Perspective," *Journal of American Studies* 11 (April 1977): 27–44.

3. See, for example, Warren I. Susman, "Annapolis Conference on the Introductory Course," AHA *Perspectives* 20 (November 1982): 19; Peter N. Stearns, "U.S. History Must Be Taught as Part of a Much Broader Historical Panorama," *The Chronicle of Higher Education,* January 3, 1990, p. A44; Carl N. Degler, "In Pursuit of an American History," *American Historical Review [AHR]* 92 (February 1987): 1–12. See also Janice Radway, "What's in a Name? Presidential Address to the American Studies Association, 20 November 1998," *American Quarterly* 51 (March 1999): 1–32, esp. 18–23.

4. "Toward the Internationalization of American History: A Round Table," *Journal of American History [JAH]* 79 (September 1992): 432–542; Michael Cowan, Eric Sandeen, and Emory Elliot, "The Internationalization of American Studies," *ASA Newsletter* 17 (December 1994): 12–14. Additional "internationalization" issues of the *JAH* appeared in March, September, and December 1999.

5. See, among many such journalistic exhortations, Frank Viviano, "The High Price of Disengagement," *San Francisco Chronicle,* September 13, 2001, p. A13; and Michael Berube, "Ignorance Is a Luxury We Cannot Afford," *Chronicle of Higher Education,* October 5, 2001, pp. B5–6. For post–La Pietra endorsements of its project, see Eric Foner, "Presidential Address: American Freedom in a Global Age," *AHR* 106 (February 2001): 1–16, esp.3–4; and Linda K. Kerber, "Portraying an 'Unexceptional' American History," *Chronicle of Higher Education,* July 5, 2002, p. B14.

6. For reviews of some of these studies, see Peter Kolchin,

"Comparing American History," *Reviews in American History* 10 (December 1982): 64–81; George M. Frederickson, "From Exceptionalism to Variability: Recent Developments in Cross-National Comparative History," *JAH* 82 (September 1995): 587–604; and David Thelen, "Of Audiences, Borderlands, and Comparisons: Toward the Internationalization of American History," *JAH* 79 (September 1992): 432–51.

7. *La Pietra Report,* 12.

8. For one project, see Robert Cassanello and Daniel S. Murphree, "Implementing the La Pietra Report: Globalizing U.S. History Instruction in Birmingham, Alabama," *OAH Newsletter* 29 (November 2001): 5.

9. David Snyder, Texas A&M University, contribution to the "History Matters" E-list Forum on "U.S. History in Global Perspective," November 5, 2001. See http://historymatters.gmu.edu.

10. National Center for History in the Schools, *National Standards for United States History: Exploring the American Experience* (Los Angeles: UCLA, 1994), 39. For representative textbook coverage of the pre-contact era, see David Goldfield and others, *The American Journey: A History of the United States,* 2nd ed. (Saddle River, NJ: Prentice-Hall, 2001), Ch. 1.

11. See Nathan Williams, "How Did the United States Defeat the Barbary Pirates?" History News Network (http://historynewsnetwork.org), September 26, 2001, which provoked a two-month-long discussion on H-Net; Donald R. Shaffer, "The Grueling Campaign to Capture Pancho Villa," History News Network, September 25, 2001; and many newspaper and magazine articles comparing the September 11 attacks to Pearl Harbor, including Greg Ryan, "It's the Same, but Not," *New York Times,* December 2, 2001, Week in Review section, p. 5.

12. Carl J. Guarneri, "Out of Its Shell: Internationalizing the Teaching of United States History," AHA *Perspectives* 35 (February 1997): 1, 5–8.

13. National Center for History in the Schools, *National Standards for World History: Exploring Paths to the Present* (Los Angeles: UCLA, 1994), 203.

14. Paul Gagnon, "Why Study History?" *The Atlantic Monthly,* November 1988, p. 46.

15. Alfred W. Crosby, *The Columbian Exchange: Biological and Cultural Consequences of 1492* (Westport, Conn.: Greenwood, 1972).

16. Jerry H. Bentley, "The Quest for World-Class Standards in World History," *The History Teacher* 28 (May 1995): 450–51.

17. See Carl Guarneri, "Reflections on Comparative and Transnational Histories," paper presented at the Second La Pietra Conference on Internationalizing American History, Florence, Italy, July 5–8, 1998.

18. Nicholas Canny, "Writing Atlantic History; or, Reconfiguring the History of Colonial British America," *JAH* 86 (December 1999): 1093–1114.

19. This is the view of E.J. Hobsbawm, *The Age of Revolution, 1789–1848* (New York: New American Library, 1962), 139–40.

20. Daniel T. Rodgers, *Atlantic Crossings: Social Politics in a Progressive Age* (Cambridge, Mass.: Harvard University Press, 1998).

21. Daniel T. Rodgers, "An Age of Social Politics," in

Bender, ed., *Rethinking American History in a Global Age*, 250–52.

22. Lanny B. Fields, Russell J. Barber, and Cheryl A. Riggs, *The Global Past* (Boston: Bedford Books, 1998).

23. Joyce Appleby, Lynn Hunt, and Margaret C. Jacob, *Telling the Truth About History* (New York: W.W. Norton, 1995), 91–125; David Thelen, "Making History and Making the United States," *Journal of American Studies* 32 (December 1998): 373–97.

24. Degler, "In Pursuit of an American History," 3–4.

25. See Daniel T. Rodgers, "Exceptionalism," in Anthony Molho and Gordon S. Wood, eds., *Imagined Histories: American Historians Interpret the Past* (Princeton: Princeton University Press, 1998), 21–40; and, for a bibliographic survey, Michael Kammen, "The Problem of American Exceptionalism: A Reconsideration," *American Quarterly* 45 (1993): 1–43.

26. Frederickson, "From Exceptionalism to Variability."

27. *La Pietra Report,* 10.

28. Benedict Anderson, *Imagined Communities: Reflections on the Origin and Spread of Nationalism,* rev. ed. (London: Verso, 1991). Two excellent collections of essays on the social and cultural "construction" of the nation are Eric Hobsbawm and Terence Ranger, eds., *The Invention of Tradition* (Cambridge: Cambridge University Press, 1983); and Geoff Eley and Ronald Grigor Suny, eds., *Becoming National: A Reader* (New York: Oxford University Press, 1996), esp. Pt. II.

29. David A. Hollinger, *Postethnic America* (New York: Basic Books, 1995), 14–15, 131–63; Liah Greenfeld, *Nationalism: Five Roads to Modernity* (Cambridge, Mass.: Harvard University Press, 1992). For an account of twentieth-century America that hinges on the shifting relations between civic and racial nationhood, see Gary Gerstle, *American Crucible: Race and Nation in the Twentieth Century* (Princeton: Princeton University Press, 2001).

30. *La Pietra Report,* 6.

31. This is somewhat akin to the "international history" envisioned by Ian Tyrrell in "American Exceptionalism in an Age of International History," *AHR* 96 (October 1991): 1031–55. For the multiple scales and sites of environmental history and migration studies, respectively, see Richard White, "The Nationalization of Nature," *JAH* 86 (December 1999): 976–86; and Donna R. Gabaccia, "Is Everywhere Nowhere? Nomads, Nations, and the Immigrant Paradigm," *ibid.,* 1115–34.

32. *La Pietra Report,* 5.

33. Thomas Osborne, Santa Ana College, contribution to "History Matters" E-list Forum on "U.S. History in Global Perspective," November 6, 2001.

34. Nancy L. Green, *Ready-to-Wear and Ready-to-Work: A Century of Industry and Immigrants in Paris and New York* (Durham, N.C.: Duke University Press, 1997); Samuel L. Baily, *Immigrants in the Lands of Promise: Italians in Buenos Aires and New York City, 1870 to 1914* (Ithaca: Cornell University Press, 1999); Herbert S. Klein, *Slavery in the Americas: A Comparative Study of Virginia and Cuba* (Chicago: University of Chicago Press, 1967).

35. See Donald W. Meinig, "Continental America, 1800–1915: The View of an Historical Geographer," *The History Teacher* 22 (February 1989): 189–203. For a similar approach to current history, see Anthony DePalma, *Here: A Biography of the New American Continent* (New York: Public Affairs, 2001).

36. Lewis Hanke, ed., *Do the Americas Have a Common History? A Critique of the Bolton Theory* (New York: Knopf, 1964), reprints important contributions to this debate, including Bolton's seminal essay, "The Epic of Greater America" (1933). For a recent example of the benefits of a hemispheric approach, see Lester D. Langley, *The Americas in the Age of Revolution, 1750–1850* (New Haven: Yale University Press, 1996).

37. As representative titles, see D.W. Meinig, *Atlantic America, 1492–1800,* volume 1 of *The Shaping of America: A Geographical Perspective on 500 Years of History* (New Haven: Yale University Press, 1986); Peggy Liss, *Atlantic Empires: The Network of Trade and Revolution, 1713–1826* (Baltimore: Johns Hopkins University Press, 1983); Nicholas Canny and Anthony Pagden, eds., *Colonial Identity in the Atlantic World* (Princeton: Princeton University Press, 1987); Ira Berlin, *Many Thousands Gone: The First Two Centuries of Slavery in North America* (Cambridge, Mass.: Harvard University Press, 1998); and Peter Linebaugh and Marcus Rediker, *The Many-Headed Hydra: The Hidden History of the Revolutionary Atlantic* (Boston: Beacon Press, 2000).

38. As examples in each of these areas, see Walter Nugent, *Crossings: The Great Transatlantic Migrations, 1870–1914* (Bloomington: Indiana University Press, 1992); Colleen Dunlavy, *Politics and Industrialization: Early Railroads in the United States and Prussia* (Princeton: Princeton University Press, 1994); R.J.M. Blackett, *Building an Antislavery Wall: Black Americans in the Atlantic Abolitionist Movement, 1830–1860* (Baton Rouge: Louisiana State University Press, 1983); Jeffrey Haydu, *Between Craft and Class: Skilled Workers and Factory Politics in the United States and Britain, 1890–1922* (Berkeley: University of California Press, 1988); Bonnie S. Anderson, *Joyous Greetings: The First International Women's Movement, 1830–1860* (New York: Oxford University Press, 2000); Rodgers, *Atlantic Crossings;* and Penny M. Von Eschen, *Race Against Empire: Black Americans and Anticolonialism, 1937–1957* (Ithaca: Cornell University Press, 1997).

39. George M. Fredrickson, *White Supremacy: A Comparative Study in American and South African History* (New York: Oxford University Press, 1981), and *Black Liberation: A Comparative History of Black Ideologies in the United States and South Africa* (New York: Oxford University Press, 1995).

40. Alette Olin Hill and Boyd H. Hill, Jr., "Marc Bloch and Comparative History," *AHR* 85 (December 1980): 830.

41. Seymour Martin Lipset, *The First New Nation: The United States in Historical and Comparative Perspective,* rev. ed. (New York: W.W. Norton, 1979), Part I; Fredrickson, *White Supremacy,* Ch. IV.

42. Various borderlands topics and typologies are suggested in Meinig, "Continental America"; Jeremy Adelman and Stephen Aron, "From Borderlands to Borders: Empires, Nation-States, and the Peoples in Between in North American History," *AHR* 104 (June 1999): 814–41; and the special issue of the *JAH* on Mexico and the United States, September 1999. For a localized U.S.–Canada comparison, see Norbert MacDonald, *Distant Neighbors: A Comparative History of Seattle and Vancouver* (Lincoln: University of Nebraska Press, 1987).

43. Christopher Hibbert, *Redcoats and Rebels: The American Revolution Through British Eyes* (New York: W.W. Norton, 1990); Cecil Robinson, ed. and trans., *The View from Chapultepec: Mexican Writers on the Mexican-American War* (Tucson: University of Arizona Press, 1989); John W. Dower, *Embracing Defeat: Japan in the Wake of World War II* (New York: W.W. Norton, 1999).

44. Matthew Frye Jacobson, *Barbarian Virtues: The United States Encounters Foreign Peoples at Home and Abroad, 1876–1917* (New York: Hill and Wang, 2000); Kristen Hoganson, *Fighting for American Manhood: How Gender Politics Provoked the Spanish-American and Philippine-American Wars* (New Haven, CT: Yale University Press, 1998); Alexander Saxton, *The Indispensable Enemy: Labor and the Anti-Chinese Movement in California* (Berkeley: University of California Press, 1971); Mary L. Dudziak, *Cold War Civil Rights: Race and the Image of American Democracy* (Princeton: Princeton University Press, 2000).

45. Peter Booth Wiley, *Yankees in the Land of the Gods* (New York: Viking, 1990); Howard Jones, *Union in Peril: The Crisis Over British Intervention in the Civil War* (Chapel Hill: University of North Carolina Press, 1993); Merze Tate, *The United States and the Hawaiian Kingdom* (New Haven: Yale University Press, 1965).

46. See, as representative titles, Akira Iriye, *The Globalizing of America, 1913–1945,* vol. 3 of *The Cambridge History of American Foreign Relations* (Cambridge: Cambridge University Press, 1993); Paul Kennedy, *The Rise and Fall of the Great Powers: Economic Change and Military Conflict from 1500 to 2000* (New York: Random House, 1987); Thomas Friedman, *The Lexus and the Olive Tree: Understanding Globalization* (New York: Farrar, Straus, Giroux, 1999); Michael Hardt and Antonio Negri, *Empire* (Cambridge, Mass.: Harvard University Press, 2000); and Walter LaFeber, *Michael Jordan and the New Global Capitalism* (New York: W.W. Norton, 1999).

47. Akira Iriye, "Internationalizing International History," in Bender, ed., *Rethinking American History in a Global Age,* 51; Emily S. Rosenberg, *Spreading the American Dream: American Economic and Cultural Expansion, 1890–1945* (New York: Hill and Wang, 1982); Robert Bruce Davies, *Peacefully Working to Conquer the World: Singer Machines in Foreign Markets, 1854–1920* (New York: Arno Press, 1976); Richard Pells, *Not Like Us: How Europeans Have Loved, Hated, and Transformed American Culture Since World War II* (New York: Basic Books, 1997).

48. Gerald Michael Greenfield and John D. Buenker, eds., *Those United States: International Perspectives on American History,* 2 vols. (Belmont, CA: Wadsworth, 2000). For a useful sourcebook of foreign journalism, see Ralph E. Weber, ed., *As Others See Us: American History in the Foreign Press* (New York: Holt, Rinehart and Winston, 1972).

49. Mark Kurlansky, *Cod: A Biography of the Fish That Changed the World* (New York: Walker & Co., 1997); Mark Pendergrast, *For God, Country and Coca-Cola,* 2nd ed. (New York: Basic Books, 2000).

50. The classic essays on "split labor" and "internal colonialism," Edna Bonacich's "A Theory of Ethnic Antagonism: The Split Labor Market" (1972), and Robert Blauner's "Colonized and Immigrant Minorities" (1972), are reprinted in Ronald Takaki, ed., *From Different Shores: Perspectives on Race and Ethnicity in America,* 2nd ed. (New York: Oxford University Press, 1994), 139–60.

51. Robin D.G. Kelley, "'But a Local Phase of a World Problem': Black History's Global Vision," *JAH* 86 (December 1999): 1045–77. For a succinct transnational and comparative history of racism, see George M. Fredrickson, *Racism: A Short History* (Princeton: Princeton University Press, 2002).

52. Immanuel Wallerstein, *The Modern World-System,* 3 vols. (New York: Academic Press, 1974–89). Key excerpts have been reprinted in *The Essential Wallerstein* (New York: New Press, 2000). For a useful comparison of world-system and modernization theories, see Craig A. Lockard, "Global History, Modernization, and the World-System Approach," *The History Teacher* 14 (August 1981): 496–515.

53. Michael Adas, "From Settler Colony to Global Hegemon: Integrating the Exceptionalist Narrative of the American Experience into World History," *AHR* 106 (December 2001): 1692–1720.

54. *La Pietra Report,* 7. See Francis Fukuyama, *The End of History and the Last Man* (New York: Free Press, 1992); and Timothy Burns, ed., *After History? Francis Fukuyama and His Critics* (Lanham, Md.: Rowman and Littlefield, 1994).

55. Adas, "From Settler Colony to Global Hegemon," 1692–98. For a recent popular history that weaves both versions of exceptionalism into a narrative triumphantly predicting "yet another American century," see David Fromkin, *The Way of the World: From the Dawn of Civilizations to the Eve of the Twenty-First Century* (New York: Knopf, 1998).

56. John Tomlinson has provided two helpful conceptual guides: *Cultural Imperialism: A Critical Introduction* (Baltimore: Johns Hopkins University Press, 1991), and *Globalization and Culture* (Chicago: University of Chicago Press, 1999). See also the sources cited in note 46.

57. Carl J. Guarneri, ed., *America Compared: American History in International Perspective,* 2 vols. (Boston: Houghton Mifflin, 1997; 2nd ed., 2005).

58. Thomas Bender, Report on La Pietra Conference II (July 1998), OAH website [http:// www.indiana.edu/~oah/lapietra].

59. Robert Gregg, *Inside Out, Outside In: Essays in Comparative History* (New York: St. Martin's Press, 1999).

60. See Robin Cohen, *Global Diasporas: An Introduction* (Seattle: University of Washington Press, 1997); and Colin Palmer, "Defining and Studying the Modern African Diaspora," AHA *Perspectives* 36 (September 1998): 1, 22–25.

61. W.E.B. DuBois, *The Souls of Black Folk* (1903; reprint ed. Boston: Bedford Books, 1997), 156; Robin D.G. Kelley, "How the West Was One: The African Diaspora and the Re-mapping of U.S. History," in Bender, ed., *Rethinking American History in a Global Age,* 123–47. See also Paul Gilroy, *Black Atlantic: Modernity and Double Consciousness* (Cambridge, Mass.: Harvard University Press, 1993).

62. Linda Kerber and Jane S. DeHart, eds., *Women's America: Refocusing the Past,* 5th ed. (New York: Oxford University Press, 1999).

63. See, among many contributions, Jerry H. Bentley, "Cross-Cultural Interaction and Periodization in World History," *AHR* 101 (June 1996): 749–56; Philip D. Curtin, "The Comparative World History Approach," *The History Teacher* 18 (August 1985): 520–27; and Peter N. Stearns, "Teaching the United States in World History," AHA *Perspectives* 27 (April 1989): 12–16.

64. National Center for History in the Schools, *National Standards for History* (Los Angeles: UCLA, 1996), 44.

65. Stearns, "Teaching the United States in World History," 12; *La Pietra Report,* 11–12.

66. James A. Henretta and others, *America's History,* 4th ed. (Boston: Bedford/St. Martin's, 2000).

67. David J. Russo, *American History from a Global Perspective: An Interpretation* (Westport, Conn.: Praeger, 2000).

CHAPTER 14

Continental America, 1800–1915

The View of an Historical Geographer

DONALD W. MEINIG

I have long insisted that by their very nature geography and history are analogous and interdependent fields. And, alas, I have also had to recognize the fact that in the United States neither of our guilds has responded very effectively to that natural and logical complementarity. It is therefore especially gratifying to be invited to address this group of American historians. Some years ago I suggested that our guilds might work together in understanding the evolution of successive American wests.[1] More recently I sketched an agenda for a cooperative effort to delineate the shaping of America.[2] Currently I am at work on a multivolume historical geography, the first part of which puts America into the Atlantic context,[3] and the volume in progress which places the evolution of the United States in a continental context. It is some ideas from this current work which I wish to share with you today.

My theme is grounded on the elementary fact that the United States has neighbors. It shares the continent and adjacent seas with other states, nations, peoples. The United States not only has boundaries—precisely demarked across land and water—it has borderlands, zones of varying width, character, and complexity that overlap those boundaries on both sides and bring these areas and peoples into associations that deserve greater and more careful attention than they are usually accorded.

To reassure myself that impressions formed over many years of eclectic reading were not misleading me, I made a careful survey of a number of university-level textbooks on American history. In each case I checked for references to British North America, Quebec, Canada, Nova Scotia, Cuba, Mexico, West Indies, etc. I looked at all the maps and I read extensively in each text. What I found not only confirmed my impressions, it actually surprised me in the paucity of treatment, the rigidity of focus, the narrow internal exclusiveness of concern.

I am sure I need not review this matter in detail for the pattern is so common that most of you could recall it without effort. These bordering areas show up only episodically and with reference to a very few topics. The most prominent coverage is given to areas directly involved in the expansion of the United States and the fixing of its political boundaries in their modern form: Florida, Texas, Mexico, Oregon, and Maine; with briefer mention of Alaska, Hawaii, and Puerto Rico. A closely related topic has to do with overt military or filibuster interventions in neighboring states, such as the War of 1812, (perhaps) the Canadian rebellions and Fenian raids, and the first era of United States interventions in the West Indies and Central America. Beyond these encounters only the thinnest scattering of references appear: a sentence or two, perhaps, on the end of slavery in the British West Indies or the trouble of American investments in Mexico. Discussions of immigration often make no mention at all of Canada, nor of Mexico until the latter twentieth century. Once one makes such an assessment one has to conclude that throughout most of American history, Canada, Mexico, Cuba, and the other West Indies are of no significance whatever. If they show up on the map at all they are blank areas, without context, inert, irrelevant.

Now there are some obvious responses to such a glib critique. In any general history of the United States it is reasonable to give attention to bordering areas when there are border problems, when they have some direct bearing on the national interest and policies. Furthermore, such textbooks, after all, are shaped by many factors and are not to be taken as the measure of a professional field. There is a large specialized literature on many topics pertinent

From *The History Teacher* 22 (February 1989): 189–203. © Society for History Education. Reprinted by permission.

to these borderlands and some of it long antedates recent surges of interest in new ways of looking at our history. One thinks immediately of the work of Herbert Bolton and his students on the Spanish Borderlands, and the great Carnegie series, edited by James Shotwell, on Canadian-American Relations.

My answer to these rejoinders is as follows. First, even where Canada, Mexico, Cuba, and other adjacent areas are given attention, the common treatment of them with reference to the issues involved is seriously deficient. Second, this kind of episodic coverage has serious, insidious consequences for our common understanding of ourselves as a nation and our place in the world. The remedy is not so much a matter of adding to the list of topics covered as a matter of changing the basic context in which we view all our history. Third, textbooks are particularly pertinent to my argument because I believe that such general interpretations do—surely we must hope they do—at once reflect and shape the ways we understand ourselves. And, finally, I must emphasize that the main intent of this representation is not to find fault with historians but to bring into focus some matters that need our joint attention. There are indeed some excellent historical monographs relating to borderland topics. Viewed from my particular stance, the great need is for much more extensive and careful descriptions and analyses of the ever-changing human geography of these areas and the routine incorporation of that material at appropriate scales into our interpretations of the general course of American development. If we are to allocate blame for that kind of deficiency, the main burden must rest more on the field of geography than on history. But my main purpose is not to find fault. (I can leave that to the historians themselves, as the job James Axtell did last year on textbook treatments of the "Age of Discovery" attests.[4]) Geography and history are strategies for thinking about large and complex matters. Let us see how we might think together about this topic.

I shall begin with a parenthetical observation that one American borderland has received massive—many might think excessive—attention: the famous "frontier" of the "westward movement." Fortunately we are learning to replace the old stereotype of a borderland between "civilization and savagery" with a far more comprehensive and balanced view of a complicated encounter between cultures, with the varied peoples and interests on both sides of the "frontier" in continuous interaction and adaptation to continuously changing circumstances. In a broad historical geographic view, the Indian reservations and Indian urban ghettos of today represent the shattered fragments of a once continent-wide borderland and a continuing cultural interaction and tension. That is an enormous topic in itself, with an exciting new literature, and I shall not try to incorporate it within this paper. I do wish to mention that the removal by the United States of virtually all the Indians from east

of the Mississippi to a formal protectorate in what is now Oklahoma, Kansas, and part of Nebraska ought to be seen as an imperial program of daunting and drastic intent. It was an attempt to redesign the human geography of the nation on an almost continental scale, to create a precise, policed, and curative separation of peoples and to buy time for a systematic acculturation. The full design was a remarkable example of borderland management, an attempt at what might be called geopolitical social engineering on a grand scale. Both as a national policy and as a species of imperial response to multicultural realities I think it deserves considerably greater emphasis than it has yet received.

The idea of relocating the Indians was put forward by Thomas Jefferson in conjunction with the Louisiana Purchase. Let us begin our main consideration of borderland topics with another imperial concomitant of that Purchase, one readily acknowledged at the time but rarely featured in general histories today: the fact that with this wonderful, benign doubling of the national area the United States suddenly acquired 50,000 Louisiana Creoles, a variegated society of French and Spanish, White, Black, and all shades in between, slave and free. The Constitution and a generation of intensive political introspection had no ready solution for the problem of how to integrate and assimilate such an alien regional society into the body of the republic and nation. At the time at least some leaders of the United States suddenly saw their country as an empire in an old and uncomfortable sense of that word. Their reactions are a telling exhibit of some American cultural and political attitudes that are still very much with us and that is one reason why we should give the case more attention than it commonly receives.

The treaty declared that the inhabitants of Louisiana would be incorporated into the Union and admitted as soon as possible to the enjoyment of the rights, advantages, and immunities of citizens. But Jefferson had no intention of simply admitting Louisiana as a state. His first thought was to attach the whole settled region of lower Louisiana to Mississippi Territory so as to submerge and amalgamate these people with a large body of Anglo-Americans. He soon gave that up as impractical and set about designing a means of accomplishing the same thing in another framework. He had originally assumed that a new upriver political boundary should be drawn at the northern margins of settlement (near Pointe Coupée); he now set it much farther north so as to enclose about as much area above the French settlements as they occupied downriver with the idea of flooding all the vacant area with American soldier-colonists so as to make Louisiana "An American instead of a French state." Events did not exactly follow this plan but the intent was accomplished by American settlers and by the arbitrary addition to Louisiana of a portion of West Florida which Anglo-Americans had overrun and usurped (the "Florida Parishes").

That the American advance was by purchase rather than conquest does not alter the classic imperial characteristics of the Louisiana case. The ruling power sought to encompass, control, and reshape this "foreign body" into conformity with basic American ways. Such a policy inevitably produced resistance, which, in turn, forced compromise, such as recognition of French civil law and language. It should be made clear that Louisiana was not a relict society. It was expanding, invigorated by Creole immigrations from Santo Domingo and Cuba and the ensuing sugar boom. However much curbed and pressured and modified it became in later decades, a French Louisiana, contrary to the expectations and hopes of many nineteenth-century Americans, is still very much with us. How it has survived and adapted is a topic worth incorporating in our general histories. New Orleans, which was soon formally divided into three sectors, with the American and Spanish–West Indian on either side of the original French grid, is an important exhibit of the human geography of the case. (Comparisons with the cultural geography of Montreal would be very instructive.)

The Louisiana Purchase provided more than a seaport for Ohio and a vast opening to the West; it marked the American entry into Tropical America, with wide geopolitical ramifications. Pressures on the Florida borderlands soon followed. American statesmen and spokesmen at the time depicted Florida as a derelict piece of empire, the lair of murderous Indians, runaway slaves, renegade Whites, foreign adventurers, and that characterization has not been generally challenged in American texts. If American military interventions are no longer celebrated quite as uncritically as they long were, the idea that Spain deserved to lose a marginal province she could no longer control still comes through. That might be a considered conclusion but the case would benefit from a much clearer picture of the human geography of this borderland.

Spanish Florida was a fragile, attenuated, multiracial colony with several kinds of Europeans, Indians, and Africans living loosely together. There were Black slaves and free Blacks and these were greatly varied in origin and status: some Blacks had lived here for generations, some came as defectors during the disruptions of the American Revolution, some were left behind by British evacuees in 1784, some came from Cuba with the Spanish reoccupation, some were recent runaways from Georgia plantations, a considerable number lived as slaves or clients of Seminole households. There was turbulence and international intrigue along this frontier but Spanish Florida was not a chaotic society. For several of its peoples it was an attractive refuge from widespread disruptions and brutal conditions on the American side of the border. But Americans perceived it, or represented it, to be a "backcountry" out of control: its Black villages were a standing enticement, its Black militia (not uncommon in the Spanish system) an inflammatory exhibit, its Seminole remnants a dangerous threat. It ap-

pears that Americans seized Florida not primarily because of its larger strategic significance nor because of its land and resources but because they were determined to crush, control, or extirpate some of its peoples. This they proceeded to do, completing the task, insofar as they could, with the Seminole War by which they killed or expelled all but a small remnant that managed to disappear into the Everglades. That war became a national scandal and the fact that the Seminole lands were useless for White settlement was widely noted, but, it was argued, Florida was a "Frontier Territory" and it was best to harbor no Indians in such a place. There was the need to reshape the borderland closer to American desires.

The annexation of Florida brought Cuba prominently into the American geopolitical view. In 1821 Calhoun, Secretary of War, urged its annexation; John Quincy Adams, Secretary of State, thought bolstering the Spanish hold was the most efficacious strategy for the time, but he soon spelled out the reasons why this "natural appendage" to North America had "an importance in the sum of our national interests with which that of no other foreign territory can be compared" and why, in the larger view "it is scarcely possible to resist the conviction that the annexation of Cuba to our federal republic will be indispensable to the continuance and integrity of the Union itself."[5]

American geopolitical policy concerns with Cuba (waxing and waning at about 30-year intervals thereafter) are noted in our standard texts. But what *was* Cuba? The reader is given hardly a clue. Contrary to the common implication, Cuba was no husk of a moribund empire. In the 1820s it was a thriving, expanding economy and society. Havana was about as large as New York City; many thousands of people of talent and substance had found refuge here from the collapse of empire elsewhere. The sugar industry was booming as was the import of Africans. Cuba was the last great portal through which Africa continued to replenish and vitalize the deeply-rooted and expanding Afro-American world: over 600,000 Africans were brought in during the period following the cessation of United States imports in 1808 down to 1861.

The next flaring of American interest in Cuba was of course directly related to these very dynamic conditions. The American South and Cuba were the last flourishing sectors of the centuries-old slave-plantation economy. The planter oligarchies of the two countries had important common interests and one of the most pressing was to maintain their hold on their Black slaves. The Cuba annexation movement of the 1850s was driven more by fear than by any confident sense of American expansionist destiny. The great specter was "Africanization"—that Spain, under severe pressures from other nations, might emancipate all slaves and thereby cause a convulsion that might turn the whole island into another Haiti. The American concern (as the notorious Ostend Manifesto made clear) therefore was a more compelling version of an old theme in this sector: just as the free Blacks of Florida had made that border territory seem an intolerable threat, so the Florida Strait would be an insufficient moat from the inflammatory example of a free Cuba.

Southern interest in Cuba gets some attention in the better treatments of the complexities of the American mortal crisis, but the longer, larger significance of Cuba is never brought into focus. Cuba lies at the intersection of three great "culture worlds": the Anglo-American, the Hispanic-American, and Afro-American. Each of these was a seething world under severe stress and each would go through cataclysmic change in the latter nineteenth century. Let us give special attention to the last of these three. Of course the Afro-American "world" overlaps and is embedded within the other two in varying ways and the minute we begin to move beyond the kind of crude sketch I am offering, we encounter a really formidable set of historiographic problems lurking in these intersecting patterns: problems dealing with concepts of race, caste, and class; with characteristics of slavery and the dynamics of social formation; with dependency and autonomy within encompassing cultures; and much more. In the growing, evermore sophisticated and controversial literature on such matters a geographer finds himself especially sympathetic to Ira Berlin's insistence on the significance of time and place, that throughout their historical evolution Afro-Americans were ensconced in several distinct regional societies. He specifically confined his concern in that landmark paper to "British Mainland North America."[6] Of course everyone dealing with the general topic knows that the Afro-American world reaches far beyond the United States. My concern is not only to make that fact far more explicit but to mark off a large portion of that world as the intelligible field, the essential gross geographical framework for the full assessment of the Afro-American component in the history of the United States.

It is useful to think of that Afro-American area as having its *center* on Haiti, the one place where Blacks had violently overthrown White rule and extirpated the European planter society; a broad *heartland* extending from Baltimore to Barbados, encompassing the West Indies (including Bermuda) and the southeastern United States; a series of firm *footholds* in the Caribbean lowlands of the South and Central American mainland and in all the port cities of northeastern North America (as far as Halifax); an expanding *continental frontier* of Black migrants and laborers spreading along the canals, waterways, and railways into the urban-industrial districts of the Old Northwest; and *Atlantic outliers* in the Cape Verde Islands (from which Creole Cabo Verdeans had established footholds in the whaling ports of New England) and in the Christian Afro-American communities founded by British and American colonization societies on the West African coast. (Brazil and perhaps the Guianas can be considered another great field of activity.)

Much remains to define the parts of this vast world in terms of distinct regional variations in Afro-American life and history, as Professor Berlin has done for eastern North America. Louisiana was of course an important addition, whereas the Black society of Florida was destroyed. Cuba, Jamaica, the Bahamas, Bermuda, Barbados, Martinique are other distinct parts. How usefully we can generalize about the various Hispanic, French, British, Dutch, and Danish West Indies I am not certain, and I'm sure will always be controversial. Having identified the social geographical parts there is the need to trace and assess the connections between them. The link between the American South and Cuba we were referring to was one of common political and social interests between slave-owners rather than a vitalizing connection between Afro-American societies (it is generally agreed—but not by all—that the number of slaves smuggled across the Florida Straits was never large). Obviously, the differential timing and policies relating to emancipation and suppression of the slave trade must be taken into account.

United States military intervention and economic penetration of the American Tropics in the latter nineteenth century is a major topic in diplomatic history, but with never a hint as to what it might mean to the Afro-American world. For one thing, it multiplied the lines of connection and the ease of travel between the West Indies and North American ports, and a trickle of Blacks began to flow along those routes. The idea of migration to the United States spread through the islands, and the idea of West Indian Blacks as a labor force spread into North America. They came as field hands, factory workers, servants in hotels, resorts, and steamship lines, but they also came as artisans, shopkeepers, and professionals, and their impact on Black American society was all out of proportion to their number. (And that refers not just to those from the English-speaking islands, as the arrival of Arturo Schomburg from Puerto Rico in 1891 attests.) They formed distinct enclaves in New York and other ports and they provided leadership so critical to Black political and cultural movements that it is quite impossible to make proper sense of Afro-American history within the United States apart from this wider geographical field of activity. (Nor can one make proper sense of West Indian and Caribbean history apart from the migration of Blacks within that area in response to American activities therein, such as the Panama Canal, dockyards, plantations, etc.) Our history books and atlases commonly offer a map or two showing the distribution of Blacks (or, more usually only of slaves) in the antebellum United States. We need to see this pattern as *only one sector* of a larger Afro-American world, and we need to see that larger world as something more than simple numbers or proportions of Blacks in its many territories.[7]

Judging from my own limited reconnaissance of literature and from such recent authoritative surveys of Black history as that by Meier and Rudwick and that edited by Darlene Clark Hine,[8] I find it really amazing how narrowly national and insulated Afro-American history is in the United States. So far, we seem to have looked into this wider Afro-American world only in terms of static, model comparisons of American with Cuban or Brazilian slavery. The only external area of intrinsic interest is Africa itself. But I suppose I should not be surprised, for American history in general has yet to be cast within the appropriate context of an Atlantic World. When it is, we shall be able to see how the Afro-Americans have been a major component of a vast, dynamic pattern and process over the whole 500-year span of our history. It is interesting that the main glimmer of that sense of history today seems to come from Black politico-cultural movements such as that built around the "Africans of the Diaspora" concept.

Let us now shift our attention to the west and look at the continental stretch of the Anglo-Hispanic Borderlands. The story of Texas, from the Austin Colony to the Republic, annexation, war, and further territorial cessions, is a famous and prominent topic. But I must say that the usual presentations of Mexico in our accounts are so deficient as to be almost scandalous. The fact is that Mexico, like Cuba, is simply a coloration on the map; it is given no reality as a place. To be sure, we no longer characterize Mexican society and its leadership as utterly depraved and inept, as obviously culturally inferior, but we offer little sense of Mexico as a nation and federation and its varied regional character. Our history involves an encounter and clash between two complex systems: a westward expanding federal United States of America, energized by an aggressive, expansive population, economy, and leadership but increasingly unstable in political structure; and a northward extending United States of Mexico, not expansive in either population or economy, alarmingly unstable in its new federal system, and faced with serious problems of nation-building within an old geopolitical framework. David Weber's fine book *The Mexican Frontier*[9] offers a readily accessible view of important features of the northern border provinces, and especially of how they became increasingly linked with external areas, thereby heightening the tensions between centrifugal and centripetal pressures within the overall structure. But such basic patterns of human geography are never treated in our histories. The Texas link with Coahuila (an important factor in Texan complaints) and the utterly contrasting physical and economic geographies of these two parts are never shown. The Anglo-Americans had been lured into the wetter forested areas unattractive to Mexican colonists so that by 1835 there was a major discordance between the cultural and the political boundaries of the two peoples.

Had Mexico accepted (however reluctantly) the secession of Texas and a westward shift of that political boundary to the margins of the dry plains (as some Mexican leaders and British diplomats urged her to do) the course of history and the shape of America in this sector would surely have been drastically different. The Rio Grande boundary far overreached any Anglo-American settlements and of course the United States ultimately annexed over half of Mexico's territory and made serious efforts to obtain considerably more. One gets the impression that all this was virtually empty land—which is precisely the impression that American expansionists of the time in the White House, Congress, and newspapers wanted to give. But in fact we took in 100,000 Mexicans in those acquisitions (and there were at least 500,000 more in lands that Polk, Pierce, and Buchanan were eager to obtain), along with tens of thousands of Indians we would later conquer and subdue. New Mexico was Louisiana all over again and the way in which the central government and Anglo-Americans dealt with that captive regional society offers further important lessons about the character of imperialism, nationalism, and pluralism in America.

The human geography of these events and all subsequent history makes clear that the important feature here is not the creation of a boundary between peoples and nations but the drawing of a line *through* what has become one of the world's great cultural borderlands. We have been made very aware of that political boundary with Mexico in recent years, with much talk and considerable alarm about "losing control over our borders." It is surely our job to connect past and present, to show how the human geography of this borderland has evolved, how all the while Anglo-Americans were moving in upon their new domain and curbing and subordinating its new Hispanic societies and penetrating far south of the boundary, Hispanic-Americans were creating large urban complexes astraddle that boundary and were moving ever more deeply and extensively into the body of the United States. These are fundamental matters that surpass in importance all the ephemeral issues and programs that show up in our usual coverage of "U.S.–Latin American relations." Fortunately, this critical area is now getting intensive attention in unprecedented ways. The formation of the Association of Borderland Scholars in 1971, the publication of their basic *Sourcebook*[10] and the initiation (1986) of the *Journal of Borderlands Studies,* all with the extensive participation of bilingual scholars from many disciplines and from both sides of the border, promise to revolutionize the way we understand ourselves and our neighbors in this sector.

When we turn to our northern frontier the picture seems quite different. Americans routinely perceive and accept Canada itself as a borderland and take for granted the easy transnational movement of people, goods, money, and ideas—all the while quite blind to the fact that Canadians may have a rather different view of that boundary and what it means to live within the towering shadow of a world power. Despite the sudden creation of a New Brunswick and Upper Canada (Ontario) to harbor Loyalist refugees, for 30 years this boundary was not generally perceived on either side as a sharp line of separation in either cultural or political terms. There were already lots of Yankees in Nova Scotia and as new lands were opened Americans spread readily northward into the Eastern Townships of Quebec and westward across the Niagara River into southern Ontario. They were part of a North American movement in search of land and opportunity, and "few seemed to care whether they lived under the American or British flag."[11]

The War of 1812 marked a decisive change in such relations. This strange and controversial conflict ended in a stalemate; the Treaty of Ghent specified restoration of the *status quo antebellum* in territorial relations. But there was no way to undo historical experience. The Americans might proclaim victory and let Canada fade from view as they fixed their gaze westward, but Canadians could not forget that they had been attacked by a neighbor with whom they had had no quarrel, and not simply because they were British but because they were thought an easy prey that could be seized and incorporated into the body of a greater American Union. Having escaped that fate, they, too, might proclaim a victory, but the experience was a pivotal event for a nascent Canadian nationalism, one that could be used thereafter by those who wished to foster separatism. On the Canadian side there was now a heightened sense of two sovereignties and of the hazards of sharing a continent with a bullying neighbor, a feeling that would be reinforced by several subsequent events. The boundary itself was never a visible mark in the cultural landscape—for that one needed to look farther north to where Yankee settlers had spread up against French settlements in the seigneurial lands of the Richelieu and St. Lawrence—but was rather a line separating the allegiances and attitudes of two peoples whom visitors from abroad had a hard time telling apart.

The fixing of the political boundary in other sectors, in Maine, across the Plains, and the division of Oregon is always noted in our books but, again, rarely with any mention of the human geography, of the people most directly affected, in each case. The historical geographer James Gibson has recently offered much detail pertinent to the Oregon dispute and the reasons why he as a Canadian can regret and even resent a diplomatic settlement that is routinely presented to Americans as generous and equitable (after all, we simply extended the 49th Parallel line on west and gave them half).[12] The fact that the Webster-Ashburton line cut through the Madawaska Acadian community, the only settled district within the disputed zone, is (like the similar cleavage of the Mexican settlement along the lower Rio Grande) never mentioned. That such human geography was not of compelling concern to statesmen in distant capitals should not disqualify it from our attention.

Once our national boundaries are set, British North America essentially disappears from view; "Canada" shows up only as a name on the map across that awkward piece of Ontario that intrudes upon the rectangular frame of our country. The result is a needlessly limited and seriously warped picture of American development. I have time to mention only a few examples at various scales of topics that deserve our attention: the role of Boston as a commercial, industrial, and cultural center for seven generations of people in the Maritime Provinces and Newfoundland; the presence of the oldest indisputable European nation in North America, along the St. Lawrence; the migration of tens of thousands of those French Canadians to New England mill towns and the ties of kith and kin that have bound those two regions together ever since; the gradual shift of the cultural border zone southwards until it now lies south of the boundary where the French have become a strong presence in northern New England and New York; the role of Canada as both a source and a conduit for millions of immigrants to the United States (about 2.5 million in the period 1860–1900), and the countermovement of millions from the United States to Canada (about 1,770,000 during 1860–1900), a tide usually, but not always, running more strongly southward than northward (a significant but unknown number of those going northward were Canadian citizens returning after some years of residence in the States).[13] Thus the European peopling of the United States is a movement that can properly be told only in North American and not simply national terms.

The same holds true for the development of waterways and railroad systems together with the enormous commercial and industrial facilities and urban centers in what emerges as the great economic core of North America. To present only the United States part of those intricate networks is to cut off part of a whole and mislead as to what was in place and how it functioned. (Occasionally a textbook map will show some railroads across southern Ontario and the Canadian line to the ice-free harbor at Portland, Maine, but unaccompanied by any discussion.) And yet that international boundary was far from incidental to those developments. The United States and British North America were separate sovereignties, each with its own instruments, interests, and policies, each seeing itself in some degree competitive with, even fearful of, the other. Here we get near to the heart of the matter in this borderland: these interlocking networks and interactions developed as continental systems concomitant with vigorously maintained political separateness. How could, and why should that be? Why should there be *two* vast transcontinental dominantly English-speaking federations and societies across North America? Many respected nineteenth-century commentators on such broad geopolitical matters either failed to predict such a thing or thought it would not last.

What *is* Canada, and why is it there in its peculiar form? The creation and development of the Canadian Confederation is barely mentioned, if at all, in American history texts, yet Canada is one of the great facts of American life. The possibilities for comparison of these two structures and systems with reference to common general problems, such as European-Indian relationships, immigration and assimilation, industrialization and urbanization, and an array of questions relating to nationalism, federalism, regionalism, pluralism are unusually rich. For us the main object of such studies is not to test some social science generalization but to understand ourselves in our specific history better. To grasp what Canadians mean (and many fear) by "continentalism" will help us understand some important realities about the United States and its impact upon its neighbors.

I think Americans—students and professors, statesmen and public—ought to have a far greater understanding than they do that the American Revolution created not one country, but two, that these two are coeval and contiguous across a continent, interlocked and interdependent in myriad ways, culturally similar in profoundly "North American" ways, and yet are independent, competitive, and distinct. Canada has long been within the sphere of the American "macroculture," yet remains self-consciously separate. I think it would be salutary for Americans to ponder the fact that the bedrock of Canadian nationalism is the determination not to be American.

Thanks to the excellent work of Canadian historians and historical geographers and to thriving Canadian Studies programs in the United States, we are better poised to enlarge our focus in the north than elsewhere. But how to do it remains a challenge. Here as elsewhere, it calls for something more than an enrichment of standard topics or the addition of a few new ones. On the other hand, one cannot simply append a short overview of the full course of Canadian history. We have as yet no example to set before us. The first full coverage of the historical geography of North America, the excellent volume of commissioned essays edited by Robert Mitchell and Paul Groves[14] intentionally treats the two countries separately. (Typically, in dealing with the nineteenth century, the Canadian authors pay some attention to the United States, the American authors pay no attention whatever to Canada.) What comes through in that form of coverage is a strong sense of "parallelism" in the creation of two transcontinental entities of diverse regional parts. That is an important characteristic, but we need to see the two countries in terms of "continentalism" and "imperialism" as well.

Let me make clear that my call is not for "North American history" in place of American history, but for an American history placed in a larger North American context. That requires us to step back a bit so as to broaden our view. It means changing the scale of our standard national map so as to include the full east-west span of the main settled portions of Canada and much of Mexico and the West Indies. Think what a powerful image our common rectangular map of the 48 States is, trimmed as close as possible to our borders (the continent ends at Eastport, Maine) to get the maximum space for our internal affairs, put before us day after day in a thousand ways; over the years it becomes deeply imprinted on our minds. We should pay attention to these borderlands not as a courtesy to our neighbors (that would be a worthy corollary) but because they are there, because they are part of *our* reality and it is impossible to assess the development, character, and situation of the United States adequately without taking that larger context into account. The fact that we have long believed that once we attained our present boundaries we could ignore Canada, Mexico, and Cuba, could take them for granted as lesser, weaker states, says a good deal about the United States as a society and a force in the world, and such attitudes ought to be specified and examined in any general treatment of our history.

Calls for a "new" history have been coming in from many quarters; the need for a new "synthesis" is eagerly debated, as in the journal of this Association. Geography alone cannot provide such things but it has important potentials for the task. If we are at all concerned about preparing students for citizenship in the twenty-first century we would do well to ponder this matter of borderlands and geographic context. If anything seems certain for that century ahead it is that it is not going to be "America's century" in any way like the last 60 to 70 years. The signs become more obvious every day that Americans are going to have to share this continent and the world on rather different terms than before. To focus very directly on these borderlands and examine how we have dealt with our neighbors, what impact we have had on them and they on us, how they have reacted, adapted to us, and how we are continuously, dynamically, bound up with them will help free us from the crippling insularity of American history, the overweening "exceptionalism" of the American case, the rigidities of the assumption of the nation-state as the highest and final form in the political division of earth space. I believe historical geography is essential to any such reconstruction of our history. We have not as yet gotten very far. I hope we may be of much greater help in the future.

Notes

This paper was presented to a session of the Annual Meeting of the Organization of American Historians in Reno in 1988.

1. D.W. Meinig, "American Wests, Preface to a Geographical Interpretation," *Annals, Association of American Geographers* 62 (1972): 159–184.

2. D.W. Meinig, "The Continuous Shaping of America: A Prospectus for Geographers and Historians," *American Historical Review* 83 (1978): 1186–1217.

3. D.W. Meinig, *Atlantic America, 1492–1800,* vol. 1 of *The Shaping of America, A Geographical Perspective on 500 Years of History* (New Haven: Yale University Press, 1986).

4. James Axtell, "Europeans, Indians, and the Age of Discovery in American History Textbooks," *American Historical Review* 92 (1984): 621–632.

5. John Quincy Adams, *Writings,* edited by Worthington Chauncey Ford, vol. 7, 1820–1823. (New York: Macmillan, 1917), pp. 372–373.

6. Ira Berlin, "Time, Space, and the Evolution of Afro-American Society on British Mainland North America," *American Historical Review* 85 (1980): 44–78.

7. Numbers and simple distributions are basic of course and an interesting start was made long ago by the cultural geographer Wilbur Zelinsky, but he did not further pursue the topic. See Zelinsky, "The Historical Geography of the Negro Population of Latin America," *Journal of Negro History* 34 (1949): 153–221.

8. August Meier and Elliott Rudwick, *Black History and the Historical Profession, 1915–1980* (Urbana: University of Illinois Press, 1986), and Darlene Clark Hine, editor, *The State of Afro-American History, Past, Present, and Future* (Baton Rouge: Louisiana State University Press, 1986).

9. David J. Weber, *The Mexican Frontier, 1821–1846, The American Southwest Under Mexico* (Albuquerque: University of New Mexico Press, 1982).

10. E.R. Stoddard, R.L. Nostrand, and J.P. West, editors, *Borderlands Sourcebook: A Guide to the Literature on Northern Mexico and the American Southwest* (Norman: University of Oklahoma Press, 1983).

11. A.L. Burt, The *United States, Great Britain, and British North America* (New York: Russell & Russell, 1961).

12. James R. Gibson, *Farming the Frontier. The Agricultural Opening of the Oregon Country 1786–1846* (Vancouver: University of British Columbia Press, 1985).

13. These figures are from Randy William Widdis, "With Scarcely a Ripple: English Canadians in Northern New York State at the Beginning of the Twentieth Century," *Journal of Historical Geography* 13 (1986): 169–192.

14. Robert D. Mitchell and Paul A. Groves, editors, *North America, The Historical Geography of a Changing Continent* (Totowa, NJ: Rowman & Littlefield, 1987).

CHAPTER 15

International Baccalaureate History of the Americas
A Comparative Approach

MAURICE GODSEY

When Samuel Morse threw the switch activating the first telegraphic message, someone was purported to have remarked, "Now Maine can talk to Florida." Ralph Waldo Emerson, observing from Boston, caustically commented, "Yes, but does Maine have anything to say to Florida?"[1] Exactly my reaction when approached about taking part in this panel. What does a secondary school United States history teacher have to say to a meeting of primarily college-level historians and particularly on a panel addressing the place of United States history in world history?

The recent Bradley Commission Report suggests that we U.S. history teachers should be getting our own house in order in the secondary schools. The report concluded that history in our schools is in trouble. Executive Director of the American Historical Association Samuel Gammon was quoted in the *Cincinnati Enquirer* concerning the commission report as saying, "Our citizens are in danger of becoming amnesiacs if you maintain that history is collective memory."[2] I would not disagree with those conclusions generally, but I have been involved in several activities in recent years that give me some hope about the future for students in American history classes.

First, for the last two years I have been a reader for the Advanced Placement Testing. The number of students taking Advanced Placement courses is steadily increasing. Approximately eighty-five thousand students took the American history exam this past year [1989]. I would interpret this growth as indicating an increased seriousness about learning on the part of the student and an increased emphasis on advanced courses by the schools.

Second, my participation in a National Endowment for the Humanities Institute this past summer acquainted me with thirty Fellows selected from across the United States.

If those teachers are indicative of the history teaching going on in some of our high schools, I would say that efforts are being made to rectify the crisis in history classrooms. Admittedly, these advanced courses may not be reaching all secondary students but usually where tough, rigorous courses are offered, the entire curriculum tends to be upgraded in a trickle-down effect.

Third, as a secondary school teacher for twenty-eight years, attending local, state, and national conventions, workshops, etc., I have talked to many teachers and conclude that valuable things are happening in history classrooms. For example, I do think that many teachers are stressing "broad themes" rather than rote memorization, that many teachers are using history as a "learning process" rather than just teaching content, and that many teachers require a high degree of verbal and written expression. And although, as Paul Gagnon observed in the November 1988 issue of *Atlantic Monthly*, it has become extremely difficult with time constraints in the traditional U.S. history course to put the United States in a "global setting," some teachers do, as he urged, attempt to teach U.S. history in a global setting. He emphasizes that we must know "what has been our impact on other societies and theirs on ours." We must develop a "global consciousness."

That need to develop a "global consciousness" is the fourth area in which I have had recent experience and is primarily what brings me to this panel. I am here today to discuss a relatively new academic program called the International Baccalaureate.[3] Although new in the United States, this program, which has been in Europe since the mid-1960s, is one of the fastest growing pre-university curricula in the world. The International Baccalaureate, a two-year curriculum offered to students in the eleventh

From *The History Teacher* 23, no. 4 (August 1990): 383–394. © Society for History Education. Reprinted by permission.

and twelfth grades, is designed to prepare them for the intellectual demands of university study in nearly every country in the world. The concept of an international university entrance examination which could be taken and recognized in any country was initiated by educators in the International School in Geneva, Switzerland, in conjunction with other international schools in Wales, New York, Teheran, Copenhagen, Paris, Frankfurt, and Montevideo. Among the concerns of the founders were the unfortunate ever-increasing emphasis on education as the mere delivery of information, the related fragmentation of knowledge, the crowding out of the aesthetic and creative experience, and the need to provide for expatriate students to return to their country for university study.

Since 1971 approximately 13,000 International Baccalaureate students have been awarded diplomas and gained entrance to over 1,700 universities and colleges in nearly 70 countries. In the United States 375 leading colleges and universities have recognized International Baccalaureate diplomas for advanced placement and course credit. Presently 118 schools are offering this program in the United States, three in Ohio. From my high school, graduates of our program are currently enrolled in such national universities as the Massachusetts Institute of Technology, Harvard, Cornell, Stanford, Northwestern, Vanderbilt, Dartmouth, Georgetown, California Institute of Technology, and the University of Pennsylvania as well as many good local and regional colleges and universities. In most cases these students have received advanced placement or college credit.

The objectives in the International Baccalaureate program focus on the development of thinking skills rather than on accumulation of facts. Assessment procedures are designed to emphasize process as well as content. The syllabuses and examinations are prepared and administered under the directions of a multinational cadre of examiners and seek to incorporate the best aspects of traditions in several national secondary school systems.[4]

Now that you have a brief history of the program, its objectives, and the assessment system, let me tell you specifically about my role as an American history teacher and my efforts to integrate U.S. and world history. One of the six areas of study required by the International Baccalaureate program is called the Study of Man, with history being one of the options in the category. Schools have several regions from which to select to satisfy their history requirements: Africa; Europe, including the USSR; West and South Asia, including India and North Africa; East and South Asia and Australia; and the Americas. "Americas" in this context includes not only the United States but Canada and Latin America as well. This option was chosen at Princeton High School because it will also satisfy the Ohio state requirement for U.S. history.

Studying history with the concentration on a "region" rather than on a country forces the student to expand his/her horizons and to view his own country's history from another perspective. In the case of the Western Hemisphere history, one must not only think in terms of traditional east to west, but also north and south and constantly observe the impact of neighboring societies on each other.

In the traditional United States history course at the secondary level, students many times study U.S. history in isolation. The only mention of Canada might be as it relates to the French and Indian War, the War of 1812 and the burning of Toronto, the boundary settlements, runaway slaves seeking refuge, and maybe cooperative efforts in building the St. Lawrence Seaway. Students generally form the vague notion that we ought to like Canadians because they are like us. Canadians celebrate Christmas and Easter, speak both English and French, have an interesting group of natives living in their North called Eskimos, and often travel down Interstate 75 past Princeton High School to winter in Florida. Naturally we accept their money. Recently students may have heard something concerning a trade agreement.

About Latin America, they learn that Columbus landed somewhere in the Caribbean, that Latinos have heroes named Bolívar and San Martin, that the Monroe Doctrine protected their independence, that the Spanish-American War ended Spanish colonialism in the Western Hemisphere, that Pershing pursued Pancho Villa into Mexico, and that Wilson adopted a policy of "watchful waiting." From this study, students often infer that Latin Americans speak Spanish, are Catholic, have frequent revolutions, and want to come to the United States illegally. Thus we have border guards. Students form the vague notion that Latinos have a harder time vacationing in the United States than do the Canadians.

Concerning the rest of the world, they learn that explorers and colonizers came from Europe, that blacks came from Africa, that we fought two world wars, one in Europe and one in Europe and the Pacific, that Russia and China are communist nations, that Eastern Europe is an area of communist satellites, and sometimes at the end of the year they may hear that we fought wars in far-off Korea and Vietnam. So they conclude many times that the U.S. is like Lake Wobegon—"a place where all the women are good-looking and all the children are above average."

On the other hand, the International Baccalaureate History of the Americas course seeks to expand the students' horizons. A study of the Western Hemisphere over a two-year period, it provides students with a dual perspective: in the eleventh grade, a chronological study in depth of this region of the world and in the twelfth grade, a broad comparative analysis of many countries' responses to the forces and personalities of the twentieth century. One of the main emphases of the International Baccalaureate history course (in addition to the course content) is "how to learn." Students are expected to acquire historical skills, show an understanding of history as a distinctive form of inquiry, develop independent research skills, analyze events, and present ideas clearly and logically in written and verbal form. Students use primary and secondary sources in a critical manner, compile bibliographies, recognize and formulate significant historical questions, analyze, synthesize, and make historical judgments. On major topics, the students study divergent views held by professional historians. Texts that we chose for this course emphasize the conflicting opinions of historians. An attempt to compare and contrast the social, cultural, economic, and ideological structures of the United States, Canada, and Latin America is at the heart of the course.

In the eleventh grade, the course revolves around a group of chronological units, but begins with a unit entitled, "The Historian's Task," a title borrowed from Robert Kelley. Here the students are introduced to the tools of the historian: major guides to historical materials, documentary works, and the importance of related disciplines such as archaeology and anthropology. Students examine works for biases, differences between fact and opinion, authors' motives, and fallacies of reasoning that may occur in history. In addition, they learn the concept that history is not static but that new discoveries may lead to new interpretations about the past.

In a geography unit, the major physiographic and climatic regions of the Americas are studied. Students are encouraged to speculate on the connection between the natural environment of the Western Hemisphere and historical development. They investigate physical conditions that have contributed to international cooperation among some countries and those conditions which have led to rivalries and fragmentation among them. They learn that we share with our neighbors common geographic features.

In the pre-Columbian era a study of the origin of native Americans, their dispersal, and the evolution of distinct cultures enables students to understand the effects of the natural surroundings. Through a comparative study of selected cultures such as the Pueblos of the dry Southwest, the Iroquois of the humid eastern Woodlands, the Eskimo of the cold Canadian north, and the Arawak in the warm Caribbean, one learns that those characteristics that comprise "cultures" are many times a result of man adjusting to nature. Here is an opportunity to dispel the stereotype of American Indians—that all lived in teepees, rode horses, wore headdresses, hunted buffalo, and were warlike—and to learn that no one set of characteristics will serve to define all native Americans.

In addition, the clash of cultures upon the arrival of the European further expands the concept of "culture." The differences between native and intruder that led to an acrimonious relationship can be traced to such cultural traits as concepts of land ownership where one believed that land, like air, clouds, and rain could not be possessed while the other came from a culture where land could be owned, fenced, and jealously guarded, with property ownership being supported by civil codes. Further, in the use of land one stressed an ecological balance and the other perceived nature as a storehouse in which needs could be met by stripping without replenishing.

In the era of exploration and colonization, in addition to the traditional examination of the motive of the major colonizers, the areas colonized and the famous explorers from each, the International Baccalaureate course further seeks to view the era from a world context and to consider what world conditions led to the era of exploration. The methods of financing colonization, the theories of empire, the different administrative policies of the mother countries, and the varied political institutions that evolved in the French, Spanish, and British colonies are compared. Students, for example, compare the House of Burgesses and other units of local government in the English colonies, the Cabildo in New Spain, and the Sovereign Council of New France, and the relative constraints they might have had from the homeland. A comparison of the Royal Governor, the Intendant, and the Viceroy gives the student another dimension for analysis. The role of religion is another very important basis for comparing national policy. One can see that in both France and Spain propagation of the Catholic doctrine was important, but each went about it differently, while the diversity of religion in the English Colonies is in sharp contrast to New France and New Spain.

Studying the revolutionary eras in Latin America and the British colonies enables students to view revolutions from several comparative positions, to analyze the influence of European philosophers by reading both the Declaration of Independence and the Declaration of the Rights of Man and the Citizen, to evaluate the relative amounts of outside aid and the impact of forceful leaders. We expand this study to a world setting by attempting to apply Crane Brinton's model for revolution to see if selected twentieth-century revolutions are similar.

Concerning Canada's relation to the American Revolution one traditionally learns that there was a feeble attempt to invade Canada in the opening phase of the war and that after the war many Loyalists fled to Canada, but International Baccalaureate students learn that Ontario, New Brunswick, Prince Edward Island, and Nova Scotia became the home of so many exiles that long after the Revolution, the political leanings of that area influenced American-Canadian relations. The constant threat of the neighbors to the south did more to unify Canadians and create a sense of nationalism than did similarities in heritage which they might have possessed. In addition, our students consider the worldwide effect of the American Revolution by its precedent-setting break with a mother country that caused Great Britain to reconsider her imperialistic scheme and eventually led Canada on a march toward confederation rather than revolution. Further, the International Baccalaureate history class examines the reasons why the thirteen colonies united after independence but the Latin American colonies fragmented and developed into several autonomous states. Other comparisons in the mid-1800s relate the westward movements in both the United States and Canada, the subduing of the natives, and the binding of the people with subsidized railroad building programs.

A common theme that runs through the eleventh-grade year is the development of minority and racial conflicts. In International Baccalaureate, students are able to see that minority problems are not confined to the United States but that a comparison with Canada shows they have similar problems with the Métis and French population. The comparison with Latin America indicates that the *pureza de sangre* (purity of blood) has continued the class consciousness from the days of the *peninsulares*, *criollos*, and *mestizos* to the present. Further, the various roles of women throughout the hemisphere and the emergence of women as an intellectual force are examined. Concerning slavery, a comparison of the North American "peculiar" institution with its Latin American counterpart is an area for analysis. Why did the institution not become as rigid or harsh in South America? Several research papers of my students concluded that the view of the slave by the Catholic Church in Latin America made the difference as well as the views brought from Iberia. In comparison with Canada, students ponder why the United States had a civil war and Canada did not, even though both struggled with regional differences.

Politically, in Latin America the rise of the *caudillo*, *caudillismo*, and the cult of the personality as a generally accepted governmental system since the days of the *conquistadores* is contrasted with the constitutional systems that evolved in the U.S. and with the confederation movement in Canada, culminating with the British North American Act in 1867. Students understand the ready acceptance of strong-man rule and frequent changes in government in Latin America as compared with elections and freely elected leaders based on a document that has existed for over two hundred years. In addition, they deduce that some political problems are the same regardless of the area of the Western Hemisphere. The development of political parties based on differences of economic philosophy, states or provincial rights versus the power of the central government are common to all areas. We see that the terms "liberal" and "conservative" may have different meanings depending on where one is in the Western Hemisphere.

The rise of industrialism in the nineteenth century is another common theme of many high school history programs. However, in the International Baccalaureate we expand it to include an examination of the dissimilarities of the nations of the Western Hemisphere. One question posed is why North America became a highly industrialized area in the post–civil war era while Latin America remained primarily a supplier of raw materials and an area of devel-

oping monocultures. An emerging economy encouraged by a sympathetic central government is contrasted with a region fragmented in politics and dominated by an agrarian elite which has perpetuated its power and only recently has made an alliance with industrialists. Students discover that the expansion of technology in the United States led to a growing imperialism, to the dominance of the United States over our neighbors' economies, even to the point of being labeled "neo-colonial" and our foreign policy labeled "Dollar Diplomacy" in Latin America.

In the area of reform, comparison may also be made. The problem created by a rapidly expanding industrial society that led to the Populist and Progressive movements in the United States may be compared with similar movements in Latin America, where the aspirations of a growing middle class near the turn of the twentieth century led to a cry for removal of ruling oligarchies in many countries. Here we find an opportunity to compare some of the social and political theories arising in world thought: Marxism, Social Darwinism, Positivism, and Evolutionary Socialism.

In the twelfth grade the International Baccalaureate history course takes on two dimensions—one, a continued chronological survey of the Americas from World War I to Vietnam. The other dimension is thematic, covering some of the major world events, personalities, and forces of the twentieth century. I don't believe that this thematic approach is used in many U.S. high schools.

Five themes are emphasized as the twentieth century proceeds. First is one entitled, "Causes, Practices, and Effects of Wars." Some aspects of this topic are "total war," causes and consequences, technical developments, the difference between international and civil wars, and localized war generated by political, ideological, and economic problems of a regional nature. Wars included here are the First and Second World Wars, the Spanish Civil War, the Chinese Civil War, wars of decolonization such as in Algeria and Vietnam, the Korean War, and non-systematized war such as guerilla war. And when applicable, we look at particular effects of war on social issues such as the rights of women and minorities. Much of this topic is covered with individual student research projects and oral reporting to class on their research.

A second theme of the twentieth century is "Decolonization and the Rise of New Nations." Under this topic the student studies the many factors which provoked the changes in the former colonial empires and the different series of events which led to independence. The class examines the impact of the two world wars on the relationship between the colonial peoples and the colonial powers. Other major inquiries here are the causes of the dislocation of colonial empires, the growth of nationalism, methods of liberation, both peaceful and violent, the emergence and problems of new nation states. Ghana and India are studied in some detail as representative nations that broke with the same mother country on two continents. Students speculate on the differences here and the relationship that Great Britain had with Canada. Nkrumah and Gandhi become the focal individuals of this theme.

The third motif emphasized is the "Rise and Rule of Single-Party Dictatorships." We investigate why single-party governments usually appear in the wake of crises such as the Great Depression, and how they may vary in ideology, in social composition, in structure, and in their means of attaining goals. Also evaluated is the efficacy of the single-party state in solving the principal political, economic, and social problems of the twentieth century. Major leaders and their regimes studied here are Castro, Franco, Hitler, Mao Tse-tung, Mussolini, Stalin, and, closer to home, Perón, and Vargas. Here the question of where FDR belongs in this trend toward centralization and executive control in the 1920s and 1930s is raised. Here, also, students respond to the question, "Do the times make the man, or does the man make the times?"

A fourth theme stressed in the twentieth century is the "Establishment and Work of International Organizations." The emphasis here is on the search for collective solutions to socio-economic as well as political problems. We look at the philosophical bases as well as the historical origins of international organizations ranging from the global to the regional. The League of Nations and the United Nations are the focal points of this unit. A comparison of the evolution, structure, and relative successes of these two organizations becomes a major class project. In addition, a brief look at some other global and regional agencies such as the Organization of American States, Organization of African Unity, European Community, International Labor Organization, and the United Nations Economic and Social Council, gives students an opportunity to see international cooperation at work and speculate about the future of international organizations.

The fifth and final theme of the twentieth century is "East-West Relations after 1945." Beginning with the division of Europe after World War II, this topic seeks to explore the global implications of that division and the failure of any nation to escape the power rearrangements that evolved. Included in this is a look at the breakdown of the wartime alliances against Nazi Germany, the emergence of superpower blocs, the development of nuclear weapons, and arms control problems. In addition the students trace the course and conduct of the Cold War in Europe, including the emergence of NATO and the Warsaw Pact as well as the United States–Russian rivalry beyond Europe as seen in Korea and Cuba, and the emergence of China as an independent superpower. Although some of these themes may be studied in Advanced Placement or regular classrooms, the world view is much more emphasized in the International Baccalaureate.

Other differences include methods of presentation and evaluation. Instead of "dishing out information," the teacher encourages inquiry and critical thinking. Evaluation is rarely based on objective tests; instead the student is judged on his ability to comprehend and express the concepts studied through essays, oral presentations, panel discussions, debates, response journals on reading assignments, and written reactions to films such as "The Mission" or "Matewan." The small class size and the two-year program allow time for much that cannot be incorporated into ordinary classrooms. The textbook becomes a minor resource and there is time for Mark Lytles' *After the Fact*, Alan Bullock's biography of Hitler, cartoon analysis of the New Deal, a presentation by Congressman Mike Dewine concerning his participation in the Iran-Contra investigation, a discussion with two alumni of the Civilian Conservation Corps camps, or a talk by a Holocaust survivor.

In May of the senior year, the international assessment procedure is put into place to evaluate the students' work over the two-year period. The exam, sent under seal from the International Baccalaureate Office in Geneva, is administered over a two-day period. Part One is a "document based" exam in which the documents and major questions center around one of the five major themes of the twentieth century. Student answers must incorporate their knowledge of the topic plus interpret the documents provided for inclusion in the answer. Part Two of the exam is composed of forty questions from the major twentieth-century themes. These are broad-based, non-documentary, and somewhat open-ended in nature. Students choose two of these. The third part of the exam covers the region: the Americas. Twenty questions are set that encompass regional history from the 1750s to the present. Candidates answer three of these questions.

In addition to the two-year study and the exam session, each student must submit a "Guided Coursework Project" done in the senior year. This entails a major piece of investigative work chosen and completed under the direction of the instructor. In addition to researching and writing the paper, the candidate must prepare a twenty-minute oral presentation of his/her work to the class. The student must be able to defend major points made in the paper. This entire oral process is recorded and is sent, along with the paper, to International Baccalaureate headquarters for evaluation. Twenty percent of the candidate's grade is based on this one project.

So this is, in essence, the International Baccalaureate history of the Americas, which seeks to place the United States in a larger perspective both regionally and globally. Hopefully, the students realize the interdependency of the world community. Even as they pause during their exam, they must think of the international implications and realize that thousands of students are taking this same test in many countries of the world at the same time.

Paul Gagnon said it best in his *Atlantic Monthly* article

about how most American history courses reflect "our faith in our exceptionalism," rather than John Donne's admonition "No man is an island," which he asserts has always held true:

> Events early and elsewhere have directed our national life. The American history course should make plain that the bell tolled for us when the Portuguese began African slave trading in 1444, when the French bombarded Saigon in 1859, when the Japanese humiliated Nicholas II in 1905, when Franz Ferdinand was assassinated in 1914, when the Weimar Republic fell in 1933, when Mao took the Long March to Shensi the year after. And now it tolls for us in the investment banks of Tokyo, the sweatshops of Seoul and Hong Kong, the drug depots of Colombia and the killing grounds of the Middle East. To know and understand all this is both the birthright and the duty of citizens, but it is an enormous burden for a single textbook to bear.[5]

I would like to leave you with two thoughts today that have resulted from my connection with this approach to history. One is that we need textbooks with such an approach as I have described here. There are many "regional studies" out there but most are superficial and "cultural areas" oriented. One of my problems has been acquiring materials to fit this approach. I use a multiplicity of resources. Over the two-year period my students will be issued a dozen different texts and countless reproductions. Another is that I think you should talk to your admissions officers about their position on the International Baccalaureate Program. Most national universities have a policy in place but many smaller colleges do not. It is to your advantage to see that students that have International Baccalaureate credentials are admitted to your campus. It has been proven that they are very successful academically and make major contributions to the college community.

Notes

This paper was delivered to a session of the American Historical Association annual meeting, December 1988.

1. Alistair Cooke, *America* (New York: Alfred Knopf, 1975), p. 253.

2. *Cincinnati Enquirer*, September 30, 1988, f3.

3. Much of the information for this paper came from various pieces of promotional literature from either the International Baccalaureate of North America in New York City, or the International Baccalaureate Office in Geneva, Switzerland.

4. Judith Zinsser of the United Nations International School in New York City deserves much credit for helping to develop the curriculum guide for "History of the Americas."

5. Paul Gagnon, "Why Study History?" *Atlantic Monthly* (November 1988): 46.

CHAPTER 16

Teaching the United States in World History

PETER N. STEARNS

The dilemma is obvious, visible in most history texts and in all but the most experimental curricula: the past is divided into two parts, the United States and whatever else in the world is studied historically or, more simply and obviously, US and THEM. We can modestly rejoice of course, that there is often something beyond the national horizon, as against some teaching traditions that pay little attention to anything save the glories of one's own country and its antecedents (a narrowness true in some school systems here as well). The fact remains that the characteristic split, between purely United States courses and a world or something-else course, not only leaves bridges unbuilt but fosters in many students a truly unfortunate tendency toward historical isolationism, as the complexities and troubles of most of the world's history seem oddly unrelated to the glorious saga of our own ascent.

Students do absorb from school and from the general culture a number of myths and half-truths about America's uniqueness and its separation from most larger world processes. They can discuss these in some detail, despite their ignorance about all sorts of United States history specifics and despite considerable cynicism and intelligence in other respects. It is perpetually amazing to me how many good college freshmen know for certain that the United States has historically offered unparalleled mobility opportunities, unprecedented openness to change and progress, and unique altruism in foreign affairs (this last with specific subsets such as the fact that we "gave" the industrial revolution to Japan after World War II, a hardy perennial in my world history courses until I took firmer steps to hammer home the Meiji era).

The fact that beliefs of this sort are oversimple, verging on outright incorrect, in situating the United States in a larger world and comparative framework, suggests a serious task for world historians in helping students locate what they know or think they know about their own national past in a more general history. For students' beliefs affect not only their perceptions of the United States, but a tendency to downgrade other societies because of an implicit impulse to measure these societies against an unrealistically demanding standard. It is probably true, as Leften Stavrianos has argued, that the United States has been unusually lucky in its past, compared to other societies, though even this cannot apply to all key groups in American history, but it has obviously not exceeded world norms so blithely as many students—including students who do very well in world history per se—continue to believe.

The task of addressing these issues, of finding ways to integrate the United States to some degree into world history courses, is at least as formidable as it is compelling. World history courses almost by definition have too much to do already. At the same time the habit of assuming that students "get" their United States history in repetitious abundance, and certainly in separate courses in school and college, remains deeply ingrained. It has been undeniably convenient to let the twain not meet, given the traditions of history teaching and the burdens on those of us who foolhardily present the whole rest of the world in a semester or two. Yet the result has been to leave the task of connecting—or more commonly, of failing to connect—to students themselves. This is a conceptually demanding job, when a world history framework is juxtaposed to a usually rigorously national context presented additionally in a separate course taken in a different year. The task is complicated further, as I have suggested, by the biases many students bring to it. The result, in my firm belief, is a need to do more to provide some suggestive guidance to the process of integration, so that students do not emerge with prejudices unchallenged or simply with the sense that God decreed two different histories, one ours and one theirs.

Having said this, admittedly a fairly obvious point save for our curricular traditions, I have no magic formulas that will make the resulting integration easier. I do have some ideas that may stimulate other suggestions and actual curricular experiments, plus further knowledge of experiments already undertaken. The goal, certainly, should be clear: the need to deal with what seems to me a significant challenge in history teaching now that a world framework is increasingly envisaged.

The challenge does not add up to a need to handle a great deal of narrative detail about American history in the world history course. There is no time, and hopefully, given the possibility of cross-referencing to previous work at least in a college-level course, some limits to the necessity. The desirability of sketching key themes in the United States' past, however, and tying them into the world history framework may seem still more difficult than simply designating a few weeks' chunk to American details. It is this approach, however, that I wish particularly to address, not again with complete plans but with some thoughts on how to proceed.

The first distinction is chronological: the issue of handling American history before the 1870s differs markedly from that afterwards. While the North American colonies and the new United States were not without some economic, demographic, and symbolic significance in the wider world before 1870, these points of contact can be fairly quickly evoked and are readily outstripped by the impact of most other inhabited areas including Latin America. After about 1870 this situation changes, among other things as a result of the growing world-scale operations of American agriculture and key corporations such as the Singer sewing machine company. The familiar world political role, becoming visible by the 1890s, followed close on the heels of these earlier contacts and ushered in the overt world power impact with which we still live today, for better or worse. For a world history course that pays serious attention to the later nineteenth and twentieth centuries, then, the claim of United States history for a treatment in detail comparable to that lavished on other major societies, qualified only by a hope of greater student knowledge, is considerable. The suggestion is, then, for a chronological shifting of gears between very broad-brush treatment from the seventeenth to the later nineteenth century, and more meticulous integration over the past 100 years, based on a change in world significance that can be explicitly presented and justified to a world history class.

While detail is not required, for world history purposes, the first long period of United States–in-the-wider-world history should not be entirely neglected. It does help illustrate some themes in world history from the seventeenth century onward, as will be suggested below. It is essential as the basis for understanding later United States patterns when world significance cannot be gainsaid. Just as some sketch, albeit brief, must be offered for Russia before 1480, or Japan before and during civilization's initial advent, not for their own sake so much as in order to set some themes that persist into later periods when the societies occupy a more visible place on a world stage, so a formative United States period—if a long one—should not be entirely ignored. And this is all the more important in that student awareness and some common misconceptions begin to apply to this period, making it essential to establish some links to wider themes even before United States inclusion becomes imperative in world terms outright.

Given inherent lack of time and the need not to exaggerate American themes while paying them some heed, the first three centuries of what became United States history must obviously be inserted in a careful analytical framework, not rehearsed in a narrative for its own sake; and this analytical framework is most logically comparative. Some ingredients of North American history may of course have been developed in discussions of Amerindian societies and the European voyages of discovery; I do not mean that focus on 1600 and after has no preparation. In this treatment, however, the principal contributions of a world history framework are, first, to help students see how landmarks of what became United States history fit into larger world trends in this timespan and, second, to locate major features of this history in a comparative context.

The world history course provides an opportunity to ask students—and most of them have never really been presented with questions—what aspects of emerging United States history are truly distinctive, in a comparative framework, and whether indeed the United States was building toward becoming a "civilization" in its own right. Of course the debate about American exceptionalism needs to be framed with care, lest it escape the proper time limitations of a world history course and take on undue significance. In a course, though, that builds on a civilizational approach to some degree, and has already established the importance of careful comparison as one means of gaining intelligibility and managing data, these basic questions about early United States history follow logically. They also allow, again if only briefly, some treatment of certain of the common student misconceptions. I spend at least one session, and it is usually a lively one, talking about the American exceptionalist argument particularly as it applies before 1900. I want students to know in capsule form the latest findings about comparative mobility patterns, which indicate that American mobility culture differed from that of other frontier or early-industrial societies considerably more than the reality of mobility differed, and what this all means about the way we conceive of the United States' past in larger comparative terms. I want them to remember that key distinctive ingredients of the United States' past, such as the importance and some unusual characteristics of slavery, do not fit easily into the most conventional God-bless-America comparative framework.

And for my purposes, in a short and highly thematic world history course, I want students to see that for the most part the United States can be grasped as an extension of Western civilization. This is not, I admit to them, an incontestable choice. American exceptionalism has some valid as well as exaggerated bases in fact, even if established on carefully comparative ground rather than—as is the wont of most Americanists themselves—merely asserted. Students should acknowledge some ingredients here, as in racial and frontier issues (including proclivity to violence and relatively weak government controls), or religious and family patterns that began to take shape as early as the seventeenth century. It might be desirable, where time permits, to develop a larger civilizational category that would embrace the United States, Canada, Australia, and New Zealand, admitting close connections to Western civilization but emphasizing distinguishing experiences not all of which, however, were those of the United States alone.

But I try to defend the extension of Western civilization hypothesis, arguing indeed that there are fewer problems integrating United States history into modern Western history than there are in treating Japan as part of a Chinese-inspired East Asian civilization, a comparative civilizations problem with which my course has grappled earlier. (Indeed, an essay assignment on precisely this topic has worked rather well.) Arguments about shared cultural origins—due reminders offered about non-Western groups in the developing North American population—here blend with the startling degree of chronological parallelism around such trends as the late eighteenth/nineteenth century demographic transition; the industrial revolution; new sexual behaviors and Victorianism; more democratic politics (though here with the vital caveat that the United States was unusual, and has seen unusual results, in establishing majority male universal suffrage prior to industrialization rather than afterwards, in contrast to most other Western countries).

The exact degree of United States participation in modern Western trends, and key qualifications such as the existence of slavery and its racial aftermath or the unusual persistence of religious belief in the nineteenth and twentieth centuries, must obviously be discussed and treated as interpretive problems rather than a set of tidy historical findings; but its analytical advantages, as well as the issues left dangling, can be indicated in a fairly brief discussion. The claim of shared Western-ness can be further discussed from the vantage point of more clearly different societies in the same period of time, including in many respects Latin America, from whose angle of vision the United States as a frontier outpost of the West would

seem if anything more obvious than it does to most of us and our students.

With early United States history sketched comparatively, and its civilizational position—or lack of fully separate position—established, it is then possible to show United States participation in key world historical trends in the same three-century span. The simplest aspects involve showing United States inclusion in general Western evolution, through the industrial revolution, the growing fascination with science, and participation in political upheaval. There are, however, crosscutting currents that among other things bring early United States history into different comparative contexts without vitiating (necessarily at least) the basic Western-ness argument.

The place of the North American colonies in Wallerstein's world economy is a case in point that allows contact with some familiar facts about colonial economic dependence. North America was in some sense a peripheral economy, though outside the South a less important and therefore less closely regulated one than Latin America at the same time. Relatively weak government and coercive labor systems established in the seventeenth and eighteenth centuries certainly follow from peripheral status as Wallerstein defines it, and this can in turn (where time permits) serve as framework for more extended comparison of slave systems both in this world economy and in relation to slavery in earlier societies. It is obviously true that to the extent the North American colonies were peripheral, they managed to pull out of this status, into industrialization, unusually rapidly. This may occasion a bit of student boosterism, but it can be explained, while the lingering effects of peripheralism, in the South-North relationship or in the ongoing United States indebtedness through 1914, should also be noted.

A second crosscutting trend context, again shared with Latin America and, later, with many twentieth-century societies, involves new nation status. While students will readily see that the United States avoided some new nations problems that beset Latin America slightly later, they can also see some classic new nations issues in, for example, the Civil War. Furthermore, some ongoing effects of new nations experience, suitably glossed with an exaggerated version of the Western ideology of liberal individualism, showed in the persistent weakness of the American state. Here is a striking United States departure from Western norms until at least the 1930s, and again an interesting similarity to Latin American patterns. I have found the theme increasingly useful as a follow-up to the civilizational comparison, not because it is more important than the world economy determination but because it is more complex. It jolts students more, and usefully. American government weakness, while not a total surprise given anti-statist ideology, deserves some careful statement as against dominant Western trends and despite the tendency of conventional United States history courses to treat the state as central actor from the revolution onward. Rates of crime and vigilantism, compared to Western trends, form one useful illustration. While American political characteristics did touch base with Western (particularly British) political ideology, they also deserve assessment in the light of new nations theory and the concurrent experience of new governments in Latin America.

It is important, obviously, not to chop up the United States patterns into too many discrete fragments. Indication of basic civilizational characteristics, however, can allow crosscutting participation in certain other world patterns where the United States position differed, at least initially, from that of the Western leaders. This in turn amplifies other comparative possibilities and simultaneously shows how world patterns really apply to our own society and not simply to more remote corners of the world where the absence of full historical free will is less surprising and (to most American students) less important, less jarring. The same process, of diverse comparison and insertion in larger world trends and relationships, helps students make United States historical data, new or previously acquired, coherent and assessable in world-historical terms. And, in broad outline at least, depending on student capacity and the level of detail which time permits, it can be sketched fairly economically, precisely because it calls on skills and concepts already utilized in other segments of the world course.

Elements of the same approach obviously can continue in the amplified treatment that becomes desirable from the 1870s onward. The comparative context must be retained. As the United States matured as an industrial society, and as Western Europe shed further vestiges of traditional structures that had never taken root in North America, from peasant agriculture to monarchical government, convergence in key features of the main segments of Western society became a leading theme. Some—though by no means all—of the qualifications necessary in the earlier period, in inserting the United States as part of a large Western civilization, now declined in salience. Indeed, from the 1920s onward the United States took a leadership role in defining many key features of the Western version of advanced industrial society, particularly in the realm of consumerism and popular culture. While political differences remained (indeed widened, in comparing the United States and Britain) during the twentieth century, the "new nation" limitations on American government waned somewhat and reduced the distinction in state functions.

Obviously, world economy analysis remains useful, as the United States moved more firmly into core status along with the rest of the West (and ultimately Japan).

The principal new theme to handle is of course the United States' ascension to superpower status. This evolution, familiar enough in many ways, can organize this second of the chronological segments devoted to the United States–world interaction, centered of course on the twentieth century rather than the early-modern, industrial decades. Quite apart from the narrative material to adduce—world war roles, emergence from isolation, postwar diplomacy, the rise of multinational corporations—the theme builds on the world economy approach, in linking the more recent articulations of core status to the changing world power balance of which the United States has been a major beneficiary. There is a link too, though a more complex one, to the expanded Western civilization theme set earlier: to what extent did the United States, in gaining new military and diplomatic power, pick up distinctively Western interests and approaches? Tensions between United States–Western affiliations and the actual geography of the United States usefully inform a number of diplomatic trends in the twentieth century and shape some questions about world politics (Pacific vs. Atlantic foci) in the near future. Assessing the United States as a Western imperialist newcomer, though a distinctive one because of twentieth-century world power realities and the revolutionary heritage of the United States itself, is another useful application of earlier comparative efforts to the new world power balance. American diplomatic moralism, plus certain racist themes, obviously evoke Western impulses that were only slightly more blatant a century ago.

At the same time, the United States' world power rise complicates earlier comparisons in important respects. The United States has become, since 1945, more militarized and diplomatically conservative just as much as the West has become somewhat less so. Here, trends are at work which muddy the convergence theme. And superpower status also invites a comparison with the Soviet Union in attributes and goals beneath rhetoric; this comparison, like the new nations analysis in the previous period, may highlight complexities in the United States–as–Western model without necessarily overturning it.

The invitation, then, is to an adapted comparative approach that will build upon the obvious shift in power position over the past century while utilizing the comparative themes sketched a bit earlier in the world history course. This approach allows some extensive narrative passages where time permits. It provides students some opportunity to deal with major changes (including growing attachment to more conservative international interests—from Yankee Doodle to Great Satan in less than ten generations). It also establishes continuities with earlier features of United States society, such as the close relationship to larger Western patterns including now the movement toward a service economy and new immigration streams. It yields, finally, a chance to discuss United States world impact in something more than random fashion, by using themes from the world economy, the new superpower concept and attendant comparison, and assessment of relationships with earlier Western imperialist impulses seen not simply as thrusts toward political or economic domination but also as assertions of cultural hegemony.

Much is not covered in the scheme outlined here, given the emphasis on analytical frameworks rather than staples of the United States history game. There are surely many alternatives to the schema itself: in the whole or in part. Some instructors would doubtless find too much comparative complexity hard to handle for their student clientele and would prefer to limit the vantage points. What I do think can be widely urged, apart from some of the specifics already outlined, boils down to three main points. The first is that the United States should be discussed in the world history course for several good reasons. The second point is that this discussion can be manageable by using comparison, by dividing treatment into two basic chronological segments very simple to define in terms of world power roles, and by hooking into leading world history themes such as the unfolding of basic international economic relationships. The third point is that a variety of frameworks exist by which the inclusion of the United States can fit analytical goals and not involve an occasional somewhat random narrative stroll through episodes. Frameworks exist, in other words, that can encompass discussion of United States history within other course goals. Furthermore, these frameworks can apply to the United States a rule that I believe must be fundamental in a world history course: societies worth discussing at all must not be simply popped in and out sporadically, but given enough character that major actions, such as diplomatic initiatives, can be interpreted in terms of causation and evaluated in terms of change and continuity in light of past trajectories.

The frameworks applied to the United States may be evoked only briefly, for want of time, but a sketch at least is possible, so that students can begin to think of American history as part of a world pattern, in which some of the issues they discern in other societies can be carried over.

There is, then, a need to rethink the United States–world history relationship; the need can be manageably met, though various emphases are possible; and manageability can and should include coherence, not in terms of masses of detail but in terms of one or more analytical frameworks consistently applied.

Four final points must be made beyond these basic assertions. First, any new experiments with greater attention to the United States in world history should assume a certain amount of student obduracy. Beliefs about American separateness—a large if informal adherence to the exceptionalist school—die hard (and of course in some cases, carefully stated, they can be defended). It is easy to be disappointed about how much students can separate one framework of analysis from older habits that will crop up when a new topic or problem is addressed. Without pushing any particular conceptual agenda, it is worth noting that some points about reconceptualizing American history need to be hammered dramatically, if only to open a more questioning outlook.

Second, while good lectures and class discussions are possible around some of the points discussed above, it is obvious that some provocative reading matter that puts the United States into one or more comparative contexts would be a tremendous boon. World history books don't do this, because of their normally unanalytical approach and their particular uncertainty when it comes to United States history. Americanists tend to discourage the approach because of their normally blithe unawareness of comparative issues and possibilities (slavery and maybe why-no-socialism excepted). Some attention to relevant, and suitably brief, teaching materials would be timely, certainly feasible, and potentially a real advance in structuring history curricula.

Third, the task of relating United States and world history should be a two-way street. Without changing all their habits, Americanists should become more alert to the possibility of linking what they teach about to what students have learned or will learn in world history. This means some attention, from the more strictly United States perspective, to comparative issues and larger world trends; it means picking up systematically not only on changes in world power roles but also the impact of international influences on American life. Too much has been written of late about the problems of world history in diverting students from the values of their own society, without dealing with the total history package to which more students are exposed not only in college but in schools. While world historians can take up some responsibility for helping students to see how "our" history fits the world framework, the interchange must be mutual, as Americanists take fuller cognizance of what world history is about and how it bears on what they teach. The compartmentalization that students learn too well in history, which a world history course must attack to some degree, reflects lack of sequenced curricular relationships and, often, a real compartmentalization among historians. World historians must and can learn that their bailiwick is not "everything except the United States." American history teachers can correspondingly learn that one of their themes must be a positioning of United States development amid larger trends.

This leads to the final point, which can return us to the larger world history thrust. Until American history instructors convert to greater utilization of an international and comparative framework, world history teachers may justly fear that inclusion of United States topics will divert from their basic commitment to provide cultural breadth to a stubbornly parochial student body. Some students may indeed rivet on the United States entry into world affairs over the past century, as if this alone provided coherence in a global hodgepodge. This can be guarded against by restricting allocations of class time to reasonable proportions, and by the careful comparisons and application of larger themes already recommended. Focused discussion of the exceptional features of the United States position in the 1950s and 1960s, and the subsequent relative decline explained through a combination of American and world developments, can be a timely corrective. So can some exploration of views of the United States held by other societies, and how these link both to larger cultural diversities and to American behaviors.

Students need not emerge from a sensible presentation with a belief that the United States has become the pivot of world history, though it remains desirable if comparable attention to international influences and constraints, applied to coverage of the twentieth century in United States courses, enhances this message. While risks exist of some lack of proportion, they can be addressed. The current system, encouraging assumptions about United States–world connections to go almost entirely unexamined, is riskier still. Quite apart from its implications for properly balanced perspective on our own society, it misses opportunities for challenging analysis where students need it most, in seeing the relationships between "their" environment and the past and the wider world to which, happily, history teachers are increasingly trying to expose them.

CHAPTER 17

Integrating United States and World History
in the High School Curriculum

MARK WALLACE

This is the story of how the faculty and administration of a fairly typical suburban school district made a fundamental change in the social studies core curriculum of its schools. Located fifteen miles outside the city of Pittsburgh, Gateway School District has been considered one of the best in Pennsylvania and is designated a Blue Ribbon School of Excellence by the United States Department of Education. It is the school district from which I graduated and to which I later returned with pride as a social studies teacher. The district had a policy of reviewing each curriculum area every five years with the intent of updating and improving the respective programs. When I was asked and agreed to serve on the social studies curriculum review committee, neither I nor my social studies colleagues foresaw the need for anything more than minor changes. However, in 1995 we had a new assistant principal responsible for social studies and a new assistant superintendent who were clearly intent on carefully reviewing the entire curriculum. They had encouraged change in other subject areas and we feared that their ideas might disrupt our peaceful and effective program.

In January of 1996, in preparation for the committee's first meeting, the assistant principal distributed copies of *Charting a Course: Social Studies for the 21st Century.* We read the report carefully and agreed with several of the National Commission's recommendations. The report suggested that students be exposed to history-based social studies courses that integrated United States and world history and were organized around themes.[1] Our assistant principal, who had written a paper in graduate school that more specifically outlined a core curriculum based on *Charting a Course,* clearly had major changes in our

core curriculum in mind. As faculty, we were more than a little apprehensive about reorganizing the 9th, 10th, and 11th grade core curricula. We frankly had no intention of changing anything. In our view we had a good curriculum, one with which we were comfortable. As with most social studies teachers, major alterations in courses of study translate into lifestyle changes since new materials must be found, new ideas advanced, and new tests and activities sheets developed.

Our first official curriculum meeting was on April 30, 1996. The committee was comprised of twenty elementary and secondary teachers and administrators. We were asked to evaluate our entire curriculum, to examine its strengths and weaknesses. Those of us who were determined not to change quickly pointed out how strong the program was in United States history and government. After all, we spent all of 8th grade, 9th grade, and 11th grade on the United States. At this point however, mavericks in our group began to make some arguments against the program. Basically, they made three points that were, in essence, the reasons we decided to eventually change.

First, our curriculum left our students terribly ignorant of the world. In 7th grade we presented a basic western civilization course. After that, we offered a global studies course that was fundamentally a geography course. Thus, a graduate of Gateway High School typically knew almost nothing of world history. Despite a student body with a relatively high percentage of Asian students, our students knew very little about Asia and nothing of its history. We had to seriously ask ourselves if this was acceptable in 1996 and into the future. As people in the world were becoming more interconnected economically, socially, and even

From *The History Teacher* 33, no. 4 (August 2000): 483–494. © Society for History Education. Reprinted by permission.

politically, did we not have an obligation to educate our students differently? Could we continue to send graduates to institutions of higher learning and on into life without at least some exposure to the total human experience?

Second, our curriculum was not history-based. This was particularly true at the high school level. In 9th grade, Civics was based on the branches of government. Although the course certainly involved a fair amount of history, it was incidental to instruction on the structure, workings, and problems of government. Global Studies in 10th grade was based on geographic regions. Again, some history was taught, but the focus was on the topography, climate, and culture of various regions. Although the 11th grade course was called American Cultures, it was basically a United States history course that had almost no connection to the other two courses taught at the high school.

Third, the sequence of courses in our curriculum made little sense. Although 7th grade world history and 8th grade early United States history may have been somewhat sequential and related, students started 9th grade with Civics. The link between Civics and 8th grade United States History was weak since Civics did not build upon the 8th grade course. If anything, there was a fair amount of repetition. Moreover, 10th grade Global Studies had no relationship with Civics. Finally, the last required course in the sequence was United States History. Again, there was no relationship to the previous course of Global Studies. Basically, in the high school (9–11) we had three nonrelated courses and the five courses required on the secondary level (7–12) were only related in limited ways.

Interestingly, some members on the committee inquired about how this sequence came to be in the first place. A member with thirty-three years' service said he could not remember the sequence in any other way nor could he recall why it was configured as it was. The assistant superintendent wrote the courses in order on large paper in the front of the room. This allowed us to carefully evaluate the course sequence and we quickly determined that it made little sense. Because we had been teaching in this sequence for so long and because each individual course had many merits, nobody thought to question it. Moreover, with a little investigation, we found that most other schools followed the same sequence. In fact, most students in our country study United States history in 8th and 11th grades. Although the Bradley Commission recommends United States history in 8th and again in 11th grade,[2] it seemed fair to ask why students should wait three years before continuing a course of study. Wouldn't it be better to have a history-based curriculum that continued in some type of chronological order?

Although the logic of the arguments against the present curriculum was apparent, the committee as a whole at first resisted change. Eventually, however, after some heated debate, all high school members of the curriculum revision committee agreed to a new sequence of core courses. Ideally, what we wanted was the following:

5th Grade	United States History (Exploration to Civil War)
6th Grade	United States History (Civil War to present)
7th Grade	Civics
8th Grade	World History (ancient to about 500 C.E.)
9th Grade	World History (500 C.E. to the Columbian Exchange)
10th Grade	United States and World History (Colonization 1500 to Imperialism 1900)
11th Grade	United States and World History (Impact of Industrialization 1900 to present)

To the high school committee members, the above curriculum sequence of courses seemed perfect. On some level, all students would be exposed to United States history and government in grades 5 through 7. Then, in grade 8 they would start the study of world history and continue in 9th grade. Finally, in the 10th and 11th grades they would study integrated United States and world history. Upon completion of the required curriculum, our students would still have an understanding of United States history, but they would also have an understanding of how the United States fit into a larger global context. Although we thought it absolutely perfect, problems soon arose. Again, there were basically three issues of concern.

First, although the 5th and 6th grade teachers on the committee and in the district agreed to the proposal quickly, the 7th and 8th grade teachers basically refused to change. At first, their reasons made little sense. A common argument was that 7th graders were not intellectually prepared to learn Civics. Basically, they were contending that thirteen-year-olds could learn ancient history but not United States government. Had that been their only argument, they would have lost. However, they had more compelling reasons not to change. These involved interdisciplinary units in the 7th and 8th grade middle school. Over the past several years, the English, science, social studies, math, and reading teachers had created some common teaching units. Some of these were elaborate and involved expensive materials and field trips. They had worked hard on these units and were determined that the 7th and 8th grade curriculum would only undergo minor changes. The 7th grade teachers would still teach ancient history and would not give up their unit on the Middle Ages. However, they agreed to try to cover China, India, and Africa. The 8th grade instructors would still teach American history from colonization through the Civil War; but they would integrate more Civics-type material into their curriculum.

Second, because the 7th and 8th grade would not agree to change, and a new course was planned for the 9th grade, Civics as an independent course was gone. Most of us were convinced that most of what had been taught in Civics could be integrated into other courses in the curriculum. However, Civics was an institution. Some committee members contended that citizenship was the goal of social studies and that that goal could not be achieved without a strong Civics course in the curriculum. It was one thing to move it, but the idea of simply integrating it out of existence divided the high school staff and would later cause problems with the School Board. Although it took some time and several more meetings, all of the high school teachers finally agreed to change the 9th through 11th grade core curriculum. However, some agreed very reluctantly and would never really totally support the revisions.

Third, writing the new 10th and 11th grade courses would be a huge undertaking. To our knowledge, nobody had really ever attempted to write courses that fully integrated United States history and world history. In most places, including colleges, there were United States history courses, Western civilization courses, and world history courses. Somehow we would have to combine world and United States history into the same courses. Certainly, no materials existed that did this. Therefore, we would have to write the curriculum ourselves. Our concern was that undertaking this task would take too much time and cost too much money. Worst of all, once completed, the new courses would have to be presented to the School Board, who might simply reject the entire program. To meet this last objection, we decided we would have to present the concept to the School Board in advance of its completion. We needed to know their positions before we undertook this task.

It was October 1996 before we actually presented our ideas to the School Board. In the meantime, we had been busy researching the entire concept. We contacted professors from Carnegie Mellon University and the University of Pittsburgh. They all had praise for the idea of an integrated curriculum. In fact, almost everybody we spoke to was really very impressed with the concept. We gathered data and carefully planned our proposal to the Board. On October 7, 1996, we made a two-hour presentation. There were many questions, with the main point of contention being the loss of the Civics course. As is often the case, the Board wanted more information and time to think. Therefore, another meeting was scheduled for November. At that meeting, the Board agreed to the concept and to support our efforts financially. Although the Board went this far, we would need to meet with them at least three more times to gain complete approval for various phases of the curricula.

The task now before the entire high school social studies faculty was to write new courses of study for the grades 9 through 11. Because we knew that it would be impossible to concentrate on much of anything during the school year, the assistant principal and assistant superintendent planned a two-week summer workshop/writing session. In the meantime, we met with Dr. Peter Stearns of Carnegie Mellon University who is a nationally recognized world historian and an advocate of teaching United States history as a part of a broader historical panorama. He suggested that we begin all three core courses with an overview unit that would cover the state of the world at that time. This overview would include a survey of world geography. In Stearns' opinion, the 9th grade course should then deal with the rise of Islam (600 C.E.) and include three themes: the global impact of the rise of Islam, civilizations interacting with Islam, and the rise of Western Europe. In 10th grade he suggested we begin with the transformation of Europe and then consider the world outside of Europe. He also thought democratic revolutions, the Industrial Revolution, and Imperialism could be considered in that year. The 11th grade course, he agreed, should focus on the 20th century and include themes like reactions to industrialism, global economic changes, the two world wars, and post–World War II rise of new power centers. The course should end with a discussion on the state of the world at present. The themes, as suggested by Stearns, would connect events, people, and places. For example, the theme of democratic revolutions would connect the United States to France and to Latin America. Instead of considering these respective events in separate courses, they would be examined together under the theme of revolutions. Thus, the themes would dictate the curricula. Once we agreed on themes, decisions about what topics and ideas should or should not be included became a little easier.

After meeting with Stearns, we contacted other area professors for input. Eventually, we talked with Dr. Tim Kelly of St. Vincent College (Latrobe, Pa.), who was very excited about our idea and offered to help. In fact, Tim Kelly and his colleague from Chatham College (Pittsburgh, Pa.) Chris Michelmore directed the first week of our two-week workshop. Professor Kelly is an American historian and Michelmore is a world historian specializing in the Middle East. Together, they and a large contingent of our social studies faculty pored over textbooks and other materials. Realizing that we needed some type of text, we searched and reviewed most of the material available at that time. While one book was found for 9th grade, as expected, we found no single book or series that integrated United States and world history. For the 10th and 11th grade courses we were forced to use parts of two. We investigated removing chapters from both and rebinding. The task was made more difficult because we had to find material for three levels of difficulty for all courses. Gateway separates all social studies students into low, middle, or high tracks. As we reviewed materials, we also continued to revise the Stearns outline. We modified themes, changed projected coverage for some courses, and argued about topics that needed to be included somewhere. We were very cognizant of the fact that our School Board would be looking to make sure that "civics" was somewhere in the courses.

In addition to reviewing classroom materials and discussing the outline, Kelly and Michelmore also began introducing us to some of the literature on integrating United States and world history. We read and discussed at length an article written by Carl J. Guarneri entitled, "Out of Its Shell: Internationalizing the Teaching of United States History."[3] Guarneri basically presents four models for integration. Although we did not entirely embrace any of his approaches, his work helped us to better understand the task we were embracing. On some level Guarneri's work enhanced the intellectual justification for our curriculum changes. We were also exposed to literature on the debate over American exceptionalism. An understanding of this debate proved helpful in defending our curriculum from accusations that it marginalized the United States.

These discussions occupied the first week of our 1997 summer workshop. The second week was used for specific curriculum writing. Our assistant superintendent had a very specific and detailed format for all curriculum guides. Ultimately, it involved the establishment of what he called program standards. These would be broken down into transition standards and then further broken down into performance indicators.

Eventually, we were required to suggest strategies, materials, and evaluation methods for each unit in the course. While the finished product of such an effort was valuable, it was a cumbersome and time-consuming task. Because of the deliberate nature of the process, we agreed to phase in the new curriculum over a three-year period. The 9th grade was to be fully implemented for the 1998–99 school year, 10th was to be implemented during 1999–2000, and 11th in 2000–2001. Therefore, we knew we had at least one more school year and summer to work on this task. It is important here to note that we were compensated for all of our efforts during this and subsequent summer workshops. The first week, those in attendance received service credits that moved them along our salary scale. Those participating in the second week were paid an hourly wage.

Although most of our department members had participated in the summer workshops, some had not and we really believed that everybody should be informed about our efforts. Therefore, the department met in late August shortly before school started. All faculty members were updated and plans were made for completing the 9th grade course. All 9th grade teachers worked on the final details of the curriculum guide, and to facilitate this, substitutes were occasionally brought in and work was done during in-service days. They met formally six times between October 1997 and March of 1998.

Finally, in March of 1998, the 9th grade course of study was completed and presented to the Board for final approval. However, since the original presentation of our new approach, the make-up of the Board had changed. There were new members. They expressed concerns about the total program. Again, some members were fearful about the loss of the Civics course. However, still others were concerned about words such as "globalism" and "global citizen." By the time the 9th grade course was approved in May of 1998, the situation between some Board members and some of our department members had become tense. Unfortunately, at times the debate degenerated into questions of patriotism and ultimately the idea of American exceptionalism. Before it was over, there were letters to the editor of the local paper and even a group of citizens at a board meeting bearing red, white, and blue cupcakes. Eventually, we agreed to change some of the language in our mission statement. We eliminated some references to "global citizenship" that a few Board members found disturbing or at least not appropriate. However, we were not required to make any major changes in the actual 9th grade course of study.

In the meantime, school was out and our second summer workshop (1998) had begun. It was again under the direction of professors Kelly and Michelmore. As was true the previous summer, week one would include any faculty member wanting to attend and the second week would involve fewer people to work specifically on writing the curriculum guides. The goal of the first week was to work out topics, chapters, and pages that would be included in the 10th and 11th grade courses. In fact, this is where integrating world and United States history began. Basically, we plowed through topic after topic deciding if they fit into our themes and how they could be packaged in each course. The problem was that some areas of United States history would have to be minimized or eliminated if we were to have an integrated curriculum. For example, not as much time could be spent on the United States Civil War and it would also be considered as part of a world movement toward consolidating nation-states. The discussion was intense and minor arguments broke out at times. However, Dr. Michelmore encouraged compromise, offering many fresh ideas about how to integrate concepts. Finally, by week's end we had a detailed topic outline for both the 10th and 11th grade courses.

Moreover, these included the chapters and page numbers to be covered from both textbooks for each of the three levels for both courses. Rarely are high school teachers given the opportunity to so fundamentally design curricula. It was an extraordinary experience.

The second week of this workshop again involved specific and at times tedious curriculum writing. However, we had really accomplished the important work. It was now merely a matter of working out the details and getting the final products approved by the Board. Throughout the

1998–99 school year, some of the 10th and 11th grade teachers met to finalize the curriculum guides. At least four full school days were used. In the meantime, the 9th grade curriculum was implemented. All of the 9th grade teachers followed the guide carefully. They met informally and exchanged ideas and materials. For what might have been the first time in our department's history, a group of teachers genuinely worked together. Almost all of those involved considered the implementation a success.

By spring of 1999 we were ready to present the complete 10th and 11th grade curriculum guides to the School Board. We had also worked up some tentative plans for some senior elective courses and our goal was to gain formal Board approval for the remainder of the curricula. Because there were going to be primary School Board elections in May, we were convinced that it was in our interest to get the entire program passed as soon as possible. We met again with the Board in March. The meeting was long and there were many questions. In fact, our guides were returned to us with numerous questions and suggestions. For example, one member questioned our treatment of Stalin and the Communist Soviet Union. He implied that our curriculum needed to more strongly identify Stalin as a tyrant. We were also questioned about a statement in our curriculum guides that suggested that flaws in the United States economy in the 1920s might have led to the Great Depression. By now some in our group were becoming impatient about all the questions. We wrote a general letter back to the Assistant Superintendent thanking the Board members for their comments and suggestions. However, we made no commitment to change anything beyond what we had already done. As a result, when the final vote came on the remainder of our plan it passed with only 5 of 9 votes. Nevertheless, it did pass and we implemented the 10th grade program in the fall of 1999 and are poised to implement the 11th grade in the fall of 2000.

Looking back on our journey toward revising and improving our social studies curriculum for the 21st century, we thought it hardly worth the effort at times. However, on reflection we truly believe we have developed a model program. Our experience leads me to offer some suggestions for anybody attempting an endeavor such as ours:

- First, in order for any major curriculum change to be successful, it must be teacher-driven. These changes were not forced on our department by some administrator nor were we inspired by various national curriculum recommendations. Ultimately the changes occurred because they were intuitively attractive and we believed they would make our program better and bring vitality to our department.

- Second, consistent with the first recommendation, it is important for those pushing for change not to alienate their colleagues. There were times when some of the department members were simply told that things were changing. However, we always tried to include as many people as possible in the development of the program. We wanted everybody to feel some sense of ownership. Most of the times when we met with the Board the majority of our members were present as we tried to have all members address the Board.

- Third, expect opposition from various elements for differing reasons. Remember, to some extent curriculum revision is a political process. Therefore, be ready to compromise at times. While not every group and complaint should be accommodated, at times, minor changes may be necessary to save the program.

- Fourth, develop a detailed and well-justified rationale for the change. In other words, be ready to argue why and how a new program will significantly help the students in your district. Also, be willing to put your reputations on the line to promote your new program. In the final analysis, we were able to get our program passed because we put our reputations as teachers behind our new curriculum. Many of us had years of experience in the district and some of us were residents as well. It was difficult for our opponents to argue that these changes were inspired by outside forces. On some level, people on the Board and the community knew us and were willing to trust us.

- Finally, do it right. We spent several years working on the program. Although they questioned us at times, our Board financed our activities. They provided funds for consultants, curriculum development, and any materials we needed. Although we were passionate about our program, it was not a volunteer effort. In fact, at times being paid was the only thing that motivated us. Major curricula changes require both time and money. If the district is unwilling to support revisions financially, chances are that it will be difficult to create a quality program.

Realistically, our story is not finished. We have to implement some of our new courses and we still must deal with the problems of textbooks for integrated courses. However, we have accomplished much. Our students will be better prepared for college and generally more aware of the world around them. Most importantly, in a rapidly changing world, our students will realize that America, although important, is only a part of the total human experience. Hopefully, this understanding will make them better citizens of this country and active participants in solving global problems.

Appendix

Curriculum Themes and Topics
Gateway Senior High School Social Studies
Department

Grades Ninth through Eleventh

Grade Nine

I. Shared Characteristics of Early Civilizations (500 B.C.E. to 300 C.E.)
    A. Comparison of the geographic factors that led to the rise of early civilizations
    B. Early political and social structure of India and China
    C. Europe/Ancient Rome and the rise of Christianity
    D. Civilizations of the Americas
    E. Early civilizations of Africa
    F. Early civilizations of Japan
II. Regional Civilizations (500–1300)
    A. The rise of Europe
    B. The High European Middle Ages
    C. The Americas
III. Early Modern Times
    A. The Renaissance and Reformation
    B. Expanding networks of exchange
    C. Byzantine Empire and Russia
    D. The Muslim World
    E. Kingdoms and trading states of Africa
    F. Spread of civilization in East Asia

Grade Ten

I. The Columbian Exchange
    A. The Age of Exploration
    B. The impact of discovery of the New World on Europe, the Americas, and Africa
II. The Liberal Revolutions
    A. European political development to the 18th century
    B. The origins and outcomes of revolutions in America, France, and Latin America and the emerging political ideas of liberalism and nationalism
III. The Industrial Revolutions
    A. The origins of industrialization in Britain
    B. The impact of industrialization on economic, social, and intellectual life and the development of socialism and nationalism

    C. The spread of the Industrial Revolution
    D. Nationalism and nation-building in an industrial world (Germany, Italy, Austro-Hungarian Empire, and Japan)
    E. Civil War and Reconstruction in the United States
IV. Democratic Reforms and World Power in the Western World
    A. The growth of western democracies
    B. The new imperialism

Grade Eleven

I. Industrialism and a New Global Age
    A. Responses to economic transformations (United States and Russia)
    B. Nationalism and its growing impact in the world
II. World War I and Its Aftermath
    A. The causes and consequences of the modern global war
    B. World War I and its aftermath
    C. The United States and World War I
III. The World Between the Wars
    A. Revolution in Russia
    B. Crisis of democracy in the West
    C. Nationalism and revolution around the world
IV. World War II and Its Aftermath
    A. World War II and the beginning of the Cold War
    B. America's role in World War II and its emergence as a superpower
V. The World Since 1945
    A. Reemergence of regional culture blocs
    B. Hope and promise and disillusionment and uncertainty (focus on United States)
    C. The emergence of a new world (focus on United States foreign relations)

Notes

    1. Curriculum Task Force of the National Commission on Social Studies in the Schools, *Charting a Course: Social Studies for the 21st Century.* Washington, DC: National Commission on Social Studies in the Schools, 1989.
    2. Bradley Commission on History in the Schools. *Building a History Curriculum: Guidelines for Teaching History in Schools.* Washington, DC: Education Excellence Network, 1988.
    3. Carl J. Guarneri, "Out of Its Shell: Internationalizing the Teaching of United States History," *Perspectives: American Historical Association Newsletter,* vol. 32, no. 2 (February 1997), 1, 5–8.

CHAPTER 18

America and the World
From the Colonial Period to 1900 (History 1B03)

KEN CRUIKSHANK, MCMASTER UNIVERSITY

Purpose of the Course

What does it mean to think globally? In History 1B03, we will explore the ways in which developments in one part of the world affected developments elsewhere prior to 1900. We will focus primarily on the interaction of peoples, cultures, ideas, goods, and germs within the Atlantic world—between America, western Europe, and west Africa after 1492. The focus is on selected themes, which help to illustrate global interactions and connections. This year, we explore three major themes (each of which is associated with a courseware pack):

Unit 1: Imperial Encounters—the interaction of Europeans, their empires, and the peoples of America, particularly in the seventeenth and eighteenth centuries.

Unit 2: Atlantic World—the making of an Atlantic world, particularly in the eighteenth century, and the consequences of the movement of people, as slaves, servants, and free laborers, on both sides of the Atlantic.

Unit 3: Revolutions—the global origins and consequences of the American Revolution, and the response of the United States government to revolutions in other parts of the world in the late eighteenth and nineteenth centuries.

What does it mean to think like a historian? History 1B03 is also intended to introduce you to history as a field of study. You will have an opportunity to see how historians work, by using the kinds of documentary evidence upon which historians rely, by analyzing the way historians construct arguments, by seeing how historians relate their work to the work of other historians, and by examining differing historical viewpoints. You will have an opportunity to work like a historian, by reconstructing events and constructing historical explanations using documentary evidence and the work of other historians.

What does it mean to communicate like a historian? Historians and other university scholars share the fruits of their research by writing essays. History 1B03 is designed to enhance your academic research and essay-writing abilities. You will have an opportunity to read and apply the ideas from a "practical guide to academic essay writing." Working on these skills will enhance your performance in future history and other university courses.

Course Texts

Textbook:
Alan Taylor, *American Colonies: The Settling of North America* (New York: Penguin, 2001).

Guidebook:
Heather Avery et al., *Thinking It Through: A Practical Guide to Academic Essay Writing,* revised second edition (Peterborough: Academic Skills Centre, 1995).

Coursepacks:
Ken Cruikshank, ed., *History 1B03 Courseware Pack, Unit 1—Imperial Encounters, Unit 2—Atlantic World, Unit 3—Revolutions* (Hamilton: Titles, 2003).

Ken Cruikshank, ed., *History 1B03 Courseware Pack, Essay 1—Global Migrations, Essay 2—International Context of the U.S. Civil War OR Essay 3—Acquiring an Empire: The U.S. and the Philippines* (Hamilton: Titles, 2003).

Course Evaluation

Written Assignments: 50%
Assignment 1: Designing a Map and Writing a Thesis Statement 10%
Assignment 2: Creating a Bibliography and Doing an Outline 15%
Assignment 3: Writing a Short Essay 25%
Tutorials: 25%

Attendance, Preparation, and Participation at 6 Tutorials (6@2%) 12%

Attendance, Preparation of a Mini-Assignment, and Participation at 2 Tutorials (2@4%) 8%

Attendance, Preparation of a Mini-Assignment, and Participation at 2 Tutorials (1@5%) 5%

Final examination: 25%

Course Evaluation (Details of Written Assignments)

Assignment 1: Designing a Map and Writing a Thesis Statement

Worth 10%, due in tutorial the week of 22 September.

Details available at http://www.humanities.mcmaster.ca/~cruiksha/History1B03_AssignmentOne.htm, and in Courseware Pack, Unit 1, Chapter 2.

Assignment 2: Creating a Bibliography and Doing an Outline

Worth 15% (part 1—5%, part 2—10%), due in tutorial the week of 3 November.

The final objective of Assignments 2 and 3 is the production of a short essay on an assigned topic, 1500–2000 words (6–8 pages) in length, not including endnotes and bibliography.

1. Select one of the three essay questions below. The required readings are in the courseware packs.

Question 1: How do historians explain what motivated people from various parts of the world to migrate to the United States during the nineteenth century?

Mack Walker, *Germany and the Emigration, 1816–1885* (Cambridge: Harvard University Press, 1964), 42–69.

Dino Cinel, *From Italy to San Francisco* (Stanford: Stanford University Press, 1982), 35–70.

Yong Chen, "Internal Origins of Chinese Emigration to California Reconsidered," *Western Historical Quarterly,* 28 (1997): 520–46.

Question 2: How do historians explain why foreign powers did not intervene in the United States Civil War?

Henry Blumenthal, "Confederate Diplomacy: Popular Notions and International Realities," *Journal of Southern History,* 32 (1966): 151–71.

Howard Jones, "History and Mythology: The Crisis over British Intervention in the Civil War," in Robert E. May, *The Union, the Confederacy, and the Atlantic Rim* (West Lafayette: Purdue University Press, 1995), 29–53, 61–67.

R.J.M. Blackett, *Divided Hearts: Britain and the American Civil War* (Baton Rouge: Louisiana Sate University Press, 2001), 169–212.

Question 3: How do historians account for the decision by the United States to annex the Philippines as a result of the war of 1898?

Thomas J. McCormick, *China Market: America's Quest for Informal Empire, 1893–1901* (Chicago: Quadrangle Books, 1967), 105–25.

David F. Trask, *The War with Spain in 1898* (New York: Macmillan, 1981), 437–44, 450–56, 468–72.

Kristin L. Hoganson, *Fighting for American Manhood* (New Haven: Yale University Press, 1998), 133–55.

Assignment 2, part 1: Creating a Bibliography (5%)

1. Submit, on a single page, a formal bibliography for your essay, including a total of four sources: the three required sources from the courseware pack and one additional source. You must use proper bibliographic citation format for recording the sources (for proper bibliographic citation, consult Turabian [Chicago] Style Guide).

2. The three sources listed for your topic are required reading for your essay and must be used in the writing of your essay, and therefore must be included in the bibliography.

3. You must locate and use one additional source, which should also be included in the bibliography. It can be a scholarly article or a chapter from a scholarly book dealing with your topic.

The one additional source **must be:**

a) focused on the specific topic you are discussing
b) used in the argument you develop in your paper
c) written by a scholar different from the authors of the required readings.

The one additional source **must not be:**

a) a book review
b) a newsmagazine or newspaper article (e.g., an article from *Time* or *New York Times*)
c) a general survey textbook (e.g., Mary Beth Norton et al., *A People and a Nation*)
d) a broad survey of a historical field (e.g., Alan Taylor, *American Colonies,* or Walter LaFeber, *The American Age: US Foreign Policy at Home and Abroad*)
e) a source or document contemporary with your subject (e.g., an article on the Civil War written in 1862)
f) an encyclopedia entry
g) an internet source, unless it is an electronic online peer-reviewed article from a recognized academic journal (e.g., an electronic article from the *Journal of American History,* or the *American Historical Review* would be acceptable).

For assistance in finding an additional source, review the mini-assignment for Unit 1, Chapter 3, the material on research in *Thinking It Through,* Chapter 3, and "How to Research Your Paper" at the "United States History at McMaster" website, focusing on the pages dealing with "Journal Articles" and "Books," www.humanities.mcmaster.ca/ushistory.

The grade on the bibliography will be based on your correctly citing all four sources, and on the quality and usefulness of the additional source you have identified. In some instances, we may recommend that you find a better additional source.

Assignment 2, part 2: Doing an Outline (10%)

1. Now, use the four sources to develop your ideas on the subject. Submit, on 1–2 pages, a complete, formal outline of your answer to the essay question. Review *Thinking It Through,* 107–14, for advice on the creation of a formal outline. It should begin like this:

Thesis: In a full sentence, state your thesis. Make sure your thesis statement offers an answer to the assignment question.

1. First supporting argument, written as a complete, topic sentence. Be sure that this statement clearly supports the overall thesis of the essay, your answer to the question.

   a) a specific example you plan to use to support, clarify, and illustrate your supporting argument. (You should informally cite source for your example, e.g., Hoganson, 134.)
   b) a second specific example you plan to use to support, clarify, and illustrate your supporting argument.

For an essay of this length, you should have 3–4 supporting arguments and 2–4 reasons, examples, or illustrations for each.

Assignment 3: Writing a Short Essay
Worth 25%, Due in Tutorial the Week of 17 November.

Using the outline you submitted as assignment 2 (with any feedback suggested by your tutorial leader), write a short, formal essay. The essay should provide an answer to the question you have been asked, and should exploit your four sources effectively. The final essay should be 1500–2000 words (6–8 pages) in length, plus endnotes and a bibliography.

Use endnotes where appropriate and appropriately; do not use parenthetical citations. For proper endnote citation, consult Turabian [Chicago] Style Guide at the McMaster Libraries website.

Before submitting the essay, review and use the check-lists in *Thinking It Through,* 137–38, 158, and 172–73. They provide the basis for our evaluation of structure of the essay; we are also evaluating your ability to exploit your four sources effectively and appropriately.

Warning: If you do not use the required readings and at least one appropriate additional source, expect a grade no higher than, and probably much lower than, 55% (D).

Schedule of Lectures and Tutorials, with Readings and Assignment Due Dates

Thursday, 4 September: Introduction
"Introduction" *American Colonies,* x–xvii

Unit 1: Imperial Encounters

Monday, 8 September: Americas
"Natives, 13,000 B.C.–A.D. 1492" *American Colonies,* 4–22
8–11 September: No Tutorials

Thursday, 11 September: Invasions
"Colonizers, 1400–1800," *American Colonies,* 24–49

Monday, 15 September: Spanish Encounters
"New Spain, 1500–1600," *American Colonies,* 51–66

15–17 September: *Tutorial 1: Pueblo Revolt of 1680: Topic to Thesis*
Courseware Unit 1, Imperial Encounters, Chapter 1
Thinking It Through, 1–33

Thursday, 18 September: Spanish Borderlands
"The Spanish Frontier, 1530–1700," *American Colonies,* 68–90

Monday, 22 September: French Encounters
"Canada and Iroquoia, 1500–1650," *American Colonies,* 92–93

22–24 September: *Tutorial 2: Natchez Rebellion: Maps and Thesis Statements*
Assignment: Maps and Thesis Statements (10%)
Courseware Unit 1, Imperial Encounters, Chapter 2

Thursday, 25 September: French Borderlands
"French America, 1650–1750," *American Colonies,* 364–95

Monday, 29 September: British Encounters
"Virginia, 1570–1650," "New England, 1600–1700," *American Colonies,* 118–37, 159–186

29 September–1 October: *Tutorial 3: War and Witchcraft: Context and Chronology (4%)*
Mini-Assignment: Research

Courseware Unit 1, Imperial Encounters, Chapter 3
Thinking It Through, 34–62

Thursday, 2 October: British Borderlands
"Puritans and Indians, 1600–1700," *American Colonies,*
188–203

Unit 2: Atlantic World

Monday, 6 October: Origins of Atlantic Slave Trade
"The West Indies, 1600–1700," *American Colonies,*
205–21

6–8 October: *Tutorial 4: Historians, the Atlantic Slave*
Trade and the Development of Africa: Secondary Sources
and Critical Reading
Courseware Unit 2, Atlantic World, Chapter 4
Thinking It Through, 63–97

Thursday, 9 October: Africa and Slavery
"The Atlantic, 1700–1800," *American Colonies,* 323–37

Monday, 13 October: No Lecture—Thanksgiving

Thursday, 16 October: Peopling America: Africans
"Chesapeake Colonies, 1650–1750," *American Colonies,*
139–57

Monday, 20 October: Peopling America: Africans
"Carolina, 1670–1760," *American Colonies,* 223–44

20–22 October: *Tutorial 5: Africa to America:*
Notetaking and Numbers (4%)
Mini-Assignment: Notetaking and Numbers
Courseware Unit 2, Atlantic World, Chapter 5
Thinking It Through, 82–97

Thursday, 23 October: Peopling America: Migrations
"Middle Colonies, 1600–1700," *American Colonies,* 246–72

Monday, 27 October: Goods and Ideas on the Move:
Consumer Revolution
"The Atlantic, 1700–1800," *American Colonies,* 302–23

27–29 October: *Tutorial 6: Coming to America:*
Outlines and Arguments
Courseware Unit 2, Atlantic World, Chapter 6
Thinking It Through, 98–114

Unit 3: Revolutions

Thursday, 30 October: Revolutionary Ideas
"Revolutions, 1685–1730," "Awakenings, 1700–75,"
American Colonies, 276–300, 339–62

Monday, 3 November: Imperial Rivalries and
Revolution
"Imperial Wars and Crisis, 1739–75," *American*
Colonies, 421–37

3–5 November: *Tutorial 7: Historians Read Historians:*
Revising the Interpretation of the American Revolution
Assignment: Creating a Bibliography and an Outline (15%)
Courseware Unit 3, Revolutions, Chapter 7
Thinking It Through, 115–24

Thursday, 6 November: Explaining Revolution
"Imperial Wars and Crisis, 1739–75," *American*
Colonies, 437–43

Monday, 10 November: Revolutionary Consequences
"The Great Plains, 1680–1800," *American Colonies,*
397–419

10–12 November: *Tutorial 8: Global Consequences of*
the American Revolution: Making Connections
Courseware Unit 3, Revolutions, Chapter 8
Thinking It Through, 126–79

Thursday, 13 November: France, the Haitian
Revolution, and the U.S.

Monday, 17 November: Spanish and Mexican
Revolutions and the U.S.
"The Pacific, 1760–1820," *American Colonies,* 445–77

17–19 November: *"Tutorial 8.5"*
Assignment: Writing a Short Essay (25%)
No tutorial discussion; hand in essay.

Thursday, 20 November: Slavery, Industrial Revolution,
and the U.S.

Monday, 24 November: Slavery, the U.S., and the
Southern Revolution

24–26 November: *Tutorial 9: Colonial Revolutions and*
the American Empire: Historical Approaches and Pre-
paring for the Exam (5%)
Mini-Assignment: Preparing for the Exam
Courseware Unit 3, Revolutions, Chapter 9

Thursday, 27 November: Exam Review

Monday, 1 December: The U.S. and the Revolutions in
Cuba and the Philippines

(You can also access this course outline at http://www.
humanities.mcmaster.ca/~cruiksha/history1b03.htm)

CHAPTER 19

The United States in World History (History 230)

ALAN DAWLEY, THE COLLEGE OF NEW JERSEY

Description

An introduction to the United States in world history from the 17th century to the present. The course examines the ways internal developments unfolded within larger patterns of world history, creating a distinctly American society linked to an increasingly interdependent world. We explore links between social evolution, on the one hand, and changes in the world economy and the international state system, on the other. Throughout, there is emphasis on cultural interactions among Native Americans, Africans, Europeans, and Asians at all levels of society. America's failings are noted, along with its achievements.

The course is organized around the central theme of **capitalism and empire**. After looking briefly at 17th-century interactions between Indians and Europeans, the focus shifts to the 18th-century Atlantic economy (slave trade, mercantilism) and the evolution of American society in a world of empires. We then proceed to analysis of the relation between big business, labor, and imperialism at the end of the nineteenth century. From there we move on to look at America's extraordinary impact on the world in the 20th century, ending with observations on the relation between global capitalism and American empire.

The course is required of history majors without prerequisites and is open to students in the U.S. Studies minor and others with permission of the instructor. There are weekly readings in primary and secondary sources, regular lectures and discussions, and occasional co-curricular events. In keeping with departmental goals, students acquire basic historical knowledge of the topic, become conversant with different modes of historical thinking about the past and its relation to the present, and attain college-level skills through analysis of primary sources, critical and strategic reading of secondary works, and the writing of cogent essays on historical topics. Finally, by examining the place of the U.S.

in world history and the role of ordinary people in making history, the course is intended to foster informed citizenship at home and responsible participation in an increasingly interdependent world.

Readings

Approximately 100 pages/week in assigned texts chosen to illustrate main themes and contrasting viewpoints. It is important that you do the assigned reading prior to class and come prepared to discuss what you have read.

Gary Nash, *Red, White and Black: The Peoples of Early America*
Benjamin Franklin, *Autobiography*
Olaudah Equiano, *Interesting Narrative*
Carl Guarneri, *America Compared*, vol. II, 2d ed.
Chalmers Johnson, *Blowback: The Costs and Consequences of American Empire*
Readings packet (denoted by *) includes excerpts from John Winthrop; Bergquist, "Paradox of American Development"; Wolf, *Europe and the Peoples Without History;* Perez, *Cuba Between Reform and Revolution;* Morgan, "Cuba"; Roosevelt, *Rough Riders;* Rubens, *Liberty;* Carnegie, "Wealth"; Twain, "To the Person Sitting in Darkness"; Luce, "American Century"; Roy, "American Century"; Fishman, "Chinese Century"; Wallerstein, "America and the World" and "The Twentieth Century."

There is no required survey textbook. For those who feel a need to brush up on the basics, I would recommend reading in a good U.S. history textbook, such as John Faragher, et al., *Out of Many* (Prentice Hall); Mary Beth Norton, et al., *A People and a Nation* (Houghton Mifflin); or Alan Brinkley, et al., *American History* (McGraw-Hill).

Requirements

1. Participation   25 percent of course grade

Regular attendance and participation in class discussion; attendance at co-curricular events.

There is one formal oral presentation described under "Essay #1" below. In addition there are short response papers to readings and guest speakers graded pass/high pass/fail. Failed papers must be rewritten.

Response #1: Compare Winthrop and Franklin on wealth (1–2 pages)

Response #2: Compare Franklin and Equiano on the British empire (1–2 pages)

Responses: guest speakers

2. Essays

Essays are designed to improve the student's ability to perform in-depth analysis of primary and secondary sources, synthesize sources in a coherent argument, and write cogent, engaging compositions. Students may critique each other's papers. Criteria for evaluation are described in a handout at the beginning of the term. Assessment is by letter grade and written comment.

Essay #1 (6–7 pages)

Due: Feb. 21st   25 percent

Topic: "Capitalism and Empire in the 18th-century Atlantic World"

Using assigned readings (Franklin, Equiano, Nash, Bergquist, Wolf), discuss the relation between capitalism and empire in the 18th-century Atlantic world.

Evaluation: written feedback; letter grade.

This assignment is intended to show the importance of **framing** in painting a picture of the past. Historians do not merely sift through the sources to see what patterns emerge. They impose a frame, which determines where they will look and thus affects what they see. In older textbooks, the common frame for America in the 17th and 18th century was the thirteen British colonies that eventually became the United States. More recently, however, historians have been using the larger frame of the Atlantic world (Western Europe, West Africa, the Caribbean, and Canada) to paint their picture.

Oral presentation: the class will be divided into 5 teams representing the following: (1) Iroquois sachem; (2) British military officer; (3) African slave; (4) French merchant; (5) colonial leader. From your team's vantage point c. 1776, answer the following questions: (1) What caused the French and Indian War (7 Years' War)? (2) What were its most important consequences? Choose two persons from the team (one for each question) to make 2-minute presentations to the class.

Essay # 2 (6—7 pages)

Due: March 24   25 percent

Topic: "The Cuban-Spanish-American War"

In this exercise, we will bring different perspectives to bear in studying the struggle to free Cuba from Spanish rule. Everyone will read and discuss the same sources and will write an essay on the same topic: "Identify the main protagonists, time periods, motives, and causes of the Cuban-Spanish-American war." One half of the class will base their papers on excerpts from H. Wayne Morgan, *America's Road to Empire,* and Theodore Roosevelt, *The Rough Riders.* The other half will rely on excerpts from Louis Perez, *Cuba between Reform and Revolution,* and Horatio Rubens, *Liberty: The Story of Cuba.* One or two essays will be selected from each group for critique by the other group.

Evaluation: written feedback; letter grade.

This assignment is intended to show the importance of **vantage point** in shaping historical interpretation. Most historical accounts are written from the point of view of one nation and are, therefore, subject to cultural bias. One way to make the search for historical truth more objective is to incorporate multiple viewpoints.

3. Final Exam (6–7 pages)   25 percent

In-class essay dealing with the main theme as it pertains to the last third of the course, plus identifications of important events, facts, personalities, and patterns in the first two-thirds.

Course policies:

1) Plagiarism (see College handbook) is unacceptable.
2) Expectations: attendance at every class meeting and regular participation in discussion.
3) Grading: standards for evaluation are given in a handout at the beginning of term. Late papers will suffer a grade reduction.

Outcomes

Students will be able to demonstrate the following: knowledge at the introductory college level of the United States in world history from the 17th to the 21st century; basic methods of historical thinking; skills of analysis, synthesis, and communication necessary to reconstruct the past; appreciation of the role of ordinary people in making history; awareness of U.S. successes and failures on the world stage.

Schedule

Jan. 17 (19) Introduction: America in World History
20 Course Theme: Capitalism and Empire in American History

> *Wallerstein, "America and the World"
> Ferguson, "Imperial Denial," in Guarneri, ch. 23
> Nye, "Globalization and American Power," in Guarneri, ch. 24

PART I: Capitalism and Empire in the 18th c. Atlantic World

    24 Indians and Puritans

        Nash, *Red, White, and Black,* chs. 1, 4, 5

    27 The Protestant Reformation

        Winthrop, "Model of Christian Charity;"
"Everyday Life . . ."

    31 Capitalism and the Enlightenment

        Nash, ch. 9

        *Wolf, *Europe and the Peoples Without History*

    Feb. 3 The Spirit of Capitalism

        Franklin, "The Way to Wealth," *Autobiography*

Due: Response #1: Compare Winthrop and Franklin on wealth (1–2 pages)

    7 Slavery and Economic Development

        Nash, ch. 7

        *Bergquist, "Paradox of American Development"

    10 Slavery and Empire

        Equiano, *The Interesting Narrative,* Introduction, chs. 2–7, Map of travels

    14 Wars of Empire: French and Indian War

        Nash, chs. 10, 11

    17 Wars of Empire: The American Revolution

        Jesperson, "Imperial Responses to Revolution in Colonial America and Vietnam," in Guarneri, ch. 20

Due: Oral presentations on the causes and consequences of the French and Indian War

Due: Response #2: Compare Franklin and Equiano on the British Empire (1–2 pages)

    21 America Compared: Guest Speaker

        Time and location TBA

Due: Essay #1 Using assigned readings (Franklin, Equiano, Nash, Berquist, Wolf), discuss the relation between capitalism and empire in the 18th-century Atlantic world

PART II. Industry and Empire

    Feb. 24 The Rise of Big Business

        Blackford, "The Rise of Big Business in the U.S., Great Britain, and Japan," in Guarneri, ch. 5

    28 Labor Migration

        Nugent, "The Great Transatlantic Migrations," in Guarneri, ch. 7

    March 3 Capitalism and Socialism

        *Carnegie, "Wealth"

        Zolberg, "Why Is There No Socialism in the U.S.?" in Guarneri, ch. 6

    SPRING BREAK (March 7–11)

    March 14 Imperialism

        Winks, "American Imperialism in Comparative Perspective," in Guarneri, ch. 9

    17 Imperialism: Philippines

        Twain, "To the Person Sitting in Darkness"

        Boudreau, "America's Colonial Rule in the Philippines," in Guarneri, ch. 10

    21 Imperialism: Cuba

        *Morgan, Roosevelt, Perez, Rubens

PART III. U.S. Expansion in the American Century

    24 Americans Abroad

        *Wallerstein, "The Twentieth Century"

Due: Essay #2 Using either Morgan/Roosevelt or Perez/Rubens, identify the main protagonists, time periods, motives, and causes of the Cuban-Spanish-American War.

    28 Americans Abroad: World War I and the 1920s

        Dawley, "Woodrow Wilson at Versailles," ch. 12; R. Sklar, "Americans, Europeans, and the Movies," ch. 13; Jackson, "The Meanings of American Jazz in France," ch. 14, all in Guarneri

    31 Americans Abroad: World War II

        Dimbleby and Reynolds, "An Ocean Apart," ch. 17; Dower, "Race War," ch. 18, in Guarneri

    April 4 The Modern World Economy

        Guest Speaker (times and locations TBA)

    6 Co-curricular event: Can Globalization be Fair? (times and locations TBA)

    7 Cold War and Human Rights

        Gaddis, "American and Soviet Cold War Empires," ch. 19; Frederickson, "Resistance to White Supremacy in the U.S. and South Africa," ch. 21; Banks, "The New Feminism in America and Britain," ch. 22, all in Guarneri

    11 Global Capitalism and American Empire

        Johnson, *Blowback,* prologue, chs. 1, 3, 5

    14 Global Capitalism and American Empire

        Johnson, chs. 6, 8, 9

    18 Unintended Consequences of Empire

        Johnson, ch. 10

    21 Looking Back and Ahead

        *Luce, "American Century;" *Roy, "New American Century"; *Fishman, "Chinese Century"

    24 Review

        Review Wallerstein, "America and the World"; Ferguson; Nye

Final Exam. TBA

Supplementary Reading (selected works):

World History

Pamela Crossley, et al., *Global Society: The World Since 1900* (Boston, 2004)

Philip D. Curtin, *The World and the West: The European Challenge and the Overseas Response in the Age of Empire* (Cambridge, Eng., 2000)

Eric Hobsbawm, *The Age of Extremes: A History of the World, 1914–1991* (New York, 1994); Hobsbawm, *Age of Revolution, 1789–1848* (New York, 1963); *Age of Capital, 1848–1875* (New York, 1975); *Age of Empire, 1875–1914* (New York, 1987)

Carter Findley and John Rothney, *Twentieth Century World* (Boston, 1998)

J.A.S. Grenville, *A History of the World in the 20th Century* (Cambridge, Mass., 2000)

Barrington Moore, *Social Origins of Dictatorship and Democracy* (Boston, 1957)

Karl Polanyi, *The Great Transformation* (1944)

U.S. in World History

Carl Guarneri, *America Compared: American History in International Perspective,* 2 vols. (Boston, 1997)

Daniel Richter, *Facing East from Indian Country* (Cambridge, Mass., 2001)

Ira Berlin, *Many Thousands Gone* (Cambridge, Mass., 1998)

Peter Kolchin, *Unfree Labor: American Slavery and Russian Serfdom* (Cambridge, Mass., 1987)

James Gump, *The Dust Rose Like Smoke* (Lincoln, Neb., 1994)

David B. Davis, *The Problem of Slavery in Western Culture* (Ithaca, N.Y., 1966)

Ian Tyrrell, *Woman's World/Woman's Empire: The Women's Christian Temperance Union in International Perspective, 1880–1930* (Chapel Hill, N.C., 1991)

Leila Rupp, *Worlds of Women: The Making of an International Women's Movement* (Princeton, 1997)

Daniel Rogers, *Atlantic Crossings: Social Politics in a Progressive Age* (Cambridge, Mass., 1998)

John Dower, *Embracing Defeat: Japan in the Wake of World War II* (New York, 1999)

Richard Barnet and John Cavanaugh, *Global Dreams* (New York, 1994)

Thomas McCormick, *America's Half Century* (Baltimore, 1989)

Alan Dawley, *Changing the World* (Princeton, 2003)

James Patterson, *America in the Twentieth Century: A History* (Fort Worth, Tex., 1989)

John Bodnar, *The Transplanted* (Bloomington, Ind., 1985)

U.S. Expansion

David Healy, *U.S. Expansionism: The Imperialist Urge in the 1890s* (Madison, Wis., 1970)

Michael Hunt, *Ideology and U.S. Foreign Policy* (New Haven, 1987)

Walter Lafeber, *The American Search for Opportunity, 1865–1913* (Cambridge, 1993)

Gail Bederman, *Manliness and Civilization* (Chicago, 1995)

William Gatewood, Jr., *Black Americans and the White Man's Burden, 1898–1903* (Urbana, Ill., 1975)

Kristin Hoganson, *Fighting for American Manhood* (New Haven, 1998)

Regional: Latin America and the U.S.

Ivan Musicant, *Empire by Default* (New York, 1998)

Louis Perez, Jr., *On Becoming Cuban* (Chapel Hill, N.C., 1999)

Joseph Smith, *The Spanish-American War* (New York, 1995)

Peter Winn, *Americas: The Changing Face of Latin America and the Caribbean* (New York, 1992)

John M. Hart, *Empire and Revolution: The Americans in Mexico since the Civil War* (Berkeley, 2000)

Africa and the U.S.

Penny Von Eschen, *Race Against Empire: Black Americans and Anticolonialism, 1937–1957* (Ithaca, N.Y., 1997)

Mary Dudziak, *Cold War Civil Rights* (Princeton, 2000)

Thomas Borstlemann, *The Cold War and the Color Line* (Cambridge, Mass., 2001)

The Middle East and the U.S.

Steve Brouwer, et al., *Exporting the American Gospel: Global Christian Fundamentalism* (New York, 1996)

Burton Kaufman, *The Arab Middle East and the United States* (New York, 1996)

Said Arjomaud, *The Turban for the Crown* (New York, 1998)

Peter Kornbluh, ed., *The Iran-Contra Scandal* (New York, 1993)

Daniel Yergin, *The Prize: The Epic Quest for Oil, Money, and Power* (New York, 1991)

CHAPTER 20

The United States and the World
A Globalized U.S. History Survey

CENTER FOR WORLD HISTORY, UNIVERSITY OF CALIFORNIA, SANTA CRUZ

Between January 2005 and Spring 2007 more than a dozen UCSC graduate students of world history collaborated in developing a two-quarter model globalized U.S. history survey course. The project created an innovative lower-division curriculum for United States history reflecting new research on the impact of the world on U.S. history and the impact of the United States on world history. It attempts to align the major dates in U.S. history with world historical processes, among them the eighteenth-century Atlantic revolutions, the development of the U.S. national state, the struggle over the abolition of slavery and for women's suffrage as well as global patterns of migration.

Working under the direction of Edmund Burke III, director of the Center for World History, the students involved in the "Globalizing U.S. History" project included Sarah Doub, Urmi Engineer, Michael Jin, Eliza Layne Martin, Kevin McDonald, Michael Murphy, Anders Otterness, David Palter, Chrislaine Pamphile, Maia Ramnath, Martin Renner, Sabrina Sanchez, Peter Valceschini, and Nat Zappia.

The teacher syllabus is reprinted here. For an overview of the project, student presentations of its rationale, brief student syllabi, and an evaluative essay by Carl Guarneri, see the Center's website: http://cwh.ucsc.edu.

The United States and the World to 1850

Teacher's Syllabus

"The United States and the World, Part 1" provides an enlarged frame for U.S. history by considering world historical events and outcomes, linking local and global histories within the geographical boundaries of the modern United States, including early narratives of settlement and trade in Alaska, Hawai'i, California, and the Southwest. Based upon recent research, the course integrates the his-tory of the western United States into the larger narrative of the making of the U.S.A., connecting the region with the colonies along the East Coast and the Atlantic world. It connects the history of early encounters and relations among Native Americans, Africans, and Europeans to the broader history of the development of independent nation-states elsewhere in the Americas. Finally, the course considers the transformation of racial, gendered, and political identities in the colonial and early national United States through a world historical lens.

The purpose of this "Teacher's Syllabus" is to provide teachers interested in globalizing the history of the United States with sufficient support so that the course can become a replicable experiment. To this end we provide selected readings aimed at assisting the preparation of each lecture, together with a list of topics to be addressed.

Week 1. Introduction and Middle Earth: The Americas to 1500

Lecture I: Placing the United States in World History

- A brief historiography of American history will be given since the end of World War II: the triumphal history of the 1940s and 50s that sought consensus, the social and multicultural historians of the 60s and 70s, the biographies of the founding fathers in the 80s and 90s, and the recent trend to transnationalism in American history that has particularly manifested itself in the idea of the Atlantic world. The progression of American history will be discussed in relation to world events happening at those times, such as World War II, the Cold War, the period of upheaval in the 1960s, the Reagan administration, and the focus on terrorism after September 11, 2001.
- Students will be asked questions that historians are

attempting to answer at this time. Is globalizing American history the creation of a theoretical space to reexamine traditional ideas, or is it an increase of knowledge and methods? Is the expansion into world history just an expansion of American hegemony? What is the meaning of America?

Lecture II: The Formation of the Americas

According to Alfred Crosby, the history of the Americas began about 200 million years ago, "when a series of geological events began that brought these lands to their present locations." This lecture will discuss the environment and geological features of the Americas, as well as human populations and available resources. By framing the history of the Americas in the *longue durée,* teachers will give students a broader picture of the events that led to the modern United States.

This lecture will look at the development of complex societies in the Americas and the Pacific Islands up to the sixteenth century. There was a wide range of social structures from hunting and gathering to agricultural villages to urban societies such as the Aztecs and Incas. The ongoing discussion on how to study areas of history noted for a lack of sources and the biases inherent in the sources available will begin in this lecture.

Specific cultures that will be examined in this lecture are the Pueblo and Navajo and their settled agricultural society in the American southwest, gender and the Five Iroquois nations in the American east, and the large society of mound-building peoples in eastern North America. Also, the Toltecs, the Mexicas (or Aztecs), and the Incas and their complex empires will be discussed. Parallels with the Australian aboriginals and the development of Pacific Island society will be made in this lecture.

Lecture III: Africa and Africans

- John Thornton's *Africa and Africans in the Making of the Atlantic World* provides a summary of the history of African societies in the early modern period. From Thornton, we learn that Africans had a complex seafaring culture, adopted chiefly to trade along the West African coast. In this region, there are numerous interconnecting river systems and intercoastal waterways.
- African states were political units, usually linguistically bounded, organized around lineages and kin groups. Slavery was part of African society, as it was in other Old World societies. Africans used slaves in several contexts, including agricultural and artisanal labor. Many African states became trade and religious centers and were important in cross-cultural exchanges. The Islamic religion was spread throughout sub-

Saharan Africa, where some societies became centers of worship that were significant in the Islamic world. There was a consistent trade of mainly gold, ivory, and slaves both overland and through the seas.

Readings

Bender, Thomas. *Rethinking American History in a Global Age.* Berkeley: University of California Press, 2002.

Carney, Judith. *Black Rice: The African Origins of Rice Cultivation in the Americas.* Cambridge: Harvard University Press, 2002.

Crosby Jr., Alfred W. *Ecological Imperialism: The Biological Expansion of Europe, 900–1900.* Cambridge and New York: Cambridge University Press, 1986.

Thornton, John. *Africa and Africans in the Making of the Atlantic World, 1400–1680.* 2nd ed. Cambridge and New York: Cambridge University Press, 1998.

Week 2. The New World Forged, 1500–1700

Throughout this week, students will discuss the simultaneous transformations going on in western Europe that facilitated its global expansion. These transformations took place on mainly four fronts: religion and the Protestant Reformation, the political transformation due to new resources and institutions, economics and the ever-increasing prominence of capitalism, and new technologies and new scientific discoveries that fueled an intellectual transformation as well.

Lecture I: The South Atlantic—Silver and Spain's Global Perimeter

- This lecture reveals how Spain's silver mines in Mexico and Bolivia facilitated their attempts to settle Florida and the greater southeast. While Spain attempted to establish a defensive perimeter around the region, France and England threatened to also create military and missionary outposts on the southeastern coast. The reading by Milanich explores the impacts of the encounter between all of these groups in sixteenth-century Florida, Georgia, and South Carolina.
- Equally important, these powers (particularly Spain) ran up against indigenous "statelets" who failed to recognize the authority and legitimacy of their plans for control over the region. Cabeza de Vaca's account importantly reveals the incredibly complex interregional exchange networks existing at the time of the forging of the "New World."
- At the same time, Europeans introduced diseases that dramatically shifted the pre-contact political-economic dynamic of these powerful chiefdoms.

Lecture II: The North Atlantic and Beyond

- Lecture II attempts to dislodge the entrenched notion of the "city on a hill" in Puritan New England. While this discussion will no doubt explore the ideological tenets of European expansion into the Greater North, it will trace this back to earlier migrations of cod fisherman from both the Basque country and England.
- Equally important, students will explore the global implications of the fur trade—one of the most effective instruments forging the "New World" that involved French, Dutch, English, Russian, and indigenous participants.
- Throughout the lecture, students will also learn of the crucial role that indigenous groups played in facilitating the fur trade. Richter's reading addresses the Iroquois role, while Salisbury and Taylor explore the global and indigenous dimension of the encounter in New England.

Lecture III: Impacts of Contact—The Columbian Exchange

Finally, this lecture takes a step back and embraces a more comprehensive view of the forging of the "New World." Primarily relying on Crosby's reading (as well as parts of Richter's), students will be able to identify and understand the multilayered implications of the Columbian Exchange and its role during this period. By looking at the global diffusion of plants, animals, human populations, food crops, and disease pathogens after Columbus's voyages, students will discuss which side of the Atlantic fared better in the cross-cultural exchange. The 80 percent to 90 percent mortality within the first generation in the Americas and the Pacific Islands, the exchange of crops and animals, the forced migration of enslaved Africans, which was the largest migrant group, and the considerable migration of Europeans will be the main criteria for this evaluation. This lecture will also discuss how the biological exchanges between the Old and New Worlds permanently altered the earth's environment. It will also examine the role the Columbian Exchange had in the world population explosion that began around this time.

Readings

Crosby, Alfred. *The Columbian Exchange: Biological and Cultural Consequences of 1492.* Westport, CT: Greenwood, 2003.

Milanich, Jerald T. *Laboring in the Fields of the Lord: Spanish Missions and Southeast Indians.* Washington, DC: Smithsonian Institution Press, 1999. Pp. 150–180.

Richter, Daniel. *Facing East from Indian Country: A Native History of Early America.* Cambridge: Harvard University Press, 2003.

Taylor, Alan. *American Colonies.* New York: Viking, 2001. Chapter 8, "New England."

Week 3. Sugar, Slavery, and Society in the South, 1600–1700

Throughout this week there will be discussions about the slave trade. Direct and continuous European contact, beginning with Portuguese mariners in the fifteenth century on the west coast of Africa, brought major and rapid change to sub-Saharan societies. This lecture will look at the foundations and the brutality of the slave trade. This lecture will also discuss the political turmoil, European conquest and settlements, intertribal warfare to increase slaves, social disruption, and corruption of indigenous economies that were all consequences of the slave trade in Africa.

Lecture I: The Growth of Sugar Plantations: Production and Consumption

- This week will focus on the establishment of sugar plantations in the Caribbean Islands and the coastal plains of the South. Students will learn the geography of the islands, as well as the settlements that later become part of the United States, and the "frontier" zones in Louisiana, Tennessee, and Florida.
- Lectures will discuss sugar production in British colonies (Antigua, Barbados, Jamaica), Spanish and Portuguese colonies (Cuba, Brazil), French colonies (Saint Domingue, Martinique), Dutch colonies (Suriname), and the Danish settlement in Saint Croix.
- Sidney Mintz's *Sweetness and Power* will be a central text during this week. Lectures will explain the various processes that enabled sugar production and consumption, as well as the environmental impacts of plantation agriculture. Lectures will briefly describe other plantation crops produced in this region, including coffee, cacao, cotton, indigo, rice, and tobacco.

Lecture II: Slavery in the South

- This week's lectures will discuss the social impacts of plantation agriculture, focusing on the West African Slave Trade, African and American Resistance, and African labor in the Islands and the South.
- The variations in demography in the islands and in the mainland colonies will be discussed in relation to the variations of the different ecological zones: coastal plains, piedmont, and mountains. The lectures will compare the social and economic structures in these regions, as well as the racial and gendered categories.
- Peter Wood's text will provide students with an example of early resistance movements and demographic information regarding rice production in South Caro-

lina and the Stono Rebellion. Lectures will also discuss slavery in South Carolina, North Carolina, Virginia, and Georgia versus slavery in Florida.

Lecture III: Freedom in the South

- This lecture will focus on the liminal area of Florida, demonstrating the various meanings of freedom in this region. By studying the activity of Free Africans, Creoles, Creeks, and Seminoles in Spanish Florida, the lecture will provide an alternative view of how culture developed in this area before the Jacksonian period.
- Additionally, the lectures will discuss colonial contact with South Carolina and Georgia, and free farming in the piedmont and Appalachia, as well as Afro-Anglo-Celtic cultural hybridity in Georgia and the Carolinas. Students will view slides of vernacular architecture in the South, which will later be contrasted with industrial development in the cities.

Readings

Landers, Jane. *Black Society in Spanish Florida.* Urbana: University of Illinois Press, 1999.

Mintz, Sidney. *Sweetness and Power.* New York: Penguin Books, 1985.

Richards, John F. "Landscapes of Sugar in the Antilles." In *The Unending Frontier: An Environmental History of the Early Modern World.* Berkeley: University of California Press, 2003. Pp. 412–460.

Thornton, John. *Africa and Africans in the Making of the Atlantic World, 1400–1800.* Cambridge: Cambridge University Press, 1998.

Wood, Peter H. *Black Majority: Negroes in Colonial South Carolina from 1670 through the Stono Rebellion.* New York: W.W. Norton and Company, 1974. Pp. 13–326.

Week 4. From Rivers to Oceans: Trade on the Frontier, 1700–1800

Lecture I: Furs

- This lecture will introduce other narratives besides the traditional "westward expansion" narrative. Indeed, looked at from a world-historical perspective, western America was penetrated from the West Coast, Northern Interior, and Southern Deserts and Plains equally as much as the East. A discussion of the Russian and English competition over western furs—as well as Chinese consumption demands—reveals these other European movements.
- Equally important, the lecture will situate the powerful indigenous fur traders and chiefdoms at the heart of this story. Lightfoot's reading will importantly situate

students within the complex global network among the Russian, Chinese, English, Kwakiutl, Haida, and Spanish participants.

Lecture II: Horses

- Focusing on the adoption, spread, and ultimately explosive proliferation of horses and horse cultures throughout the Plains, Deserts, Great Basin, and Colorado Plateau, this lecture will show how the Columbian Exchange of horses created a new, hybrid cultural understanding of the "West." Importantly, the lecture will also point to the dramatic environmental and political-economic changes that horses ushered into what became known as "The West."
- As Taylor's reading will show, the evolution of borderlands and frontier slavery became intricately linked with the expansion of horse-raiding cultures adopted by both indigenous and European groups. Brooks's reading on the creation of this world provides a fascinating account of this dynamic and its relationship with the expanding world economy.

Lecture III: The Middle Ground

- Continuing with the theme of disruption introduced in lecture I, this lecture looks at the frontier exchange economy shared by French and Spanish settlers, indigenous villages, and slave communities living along the Mississippi. In many ways, this lecture most importantly reveals that the "South" was indeed once the "West."
- Students will get a sense of the shifting nature of boundaries and their relationship with the expanding world economy. As Usner's reading will demonstrate, the frontier exchange economy thrived until the late eighteenth century and helped facilitate settlement that would foreshadow the Mississippi's pivotal role in shaping the American westward expansion and its place in the global economy. Thus, the lecture will conclude—rather than begin—with Lewis and Clark's seminal journey to "map" the West.

Readings

Brooks, James. *Captives and Cousins: Slavery, Kinship, and Community in the Southwest Borderlands.* Chapel Hill: University of North Carolina Press, 2002.

Lightfoot, Kent. *Indians, Missionaries, and Merchants: The Legacy of Colonial Encounters on the California Frontier.* Berkeley: University of California Press, 2005. Chapters 2–3.

Rich, E.E. "Russia and the Colonial Fur Trade." *The Economic History Review* 7, no. 3 (1955).

Usner, Daniel. *Indians, Settlers, and Slaves in a Frontier Exchange Economy.* Chapel Hill: University of North Carolina Press, 1992.

Week 5. The Atlantic Economy Through Its Cities, 1750–1763

Lecture I: The North Atlantic—Quebec, Boston, and Philadelphia

- This week examines the cities in the colonial American world and will consider the cultural, social, and economic interactions among cities in North and South America, Europe, the Caribbean, and West Africa. Topics explored include migration (voluntary and involuntary), trade, empire building, military conquest, colonization, expansion, disease and epidemics, and trading networks. We explore the cities that became prominent through this period, considering the unique problems and opportunities that cities experienced during this time.
- The idea of colonial port cities central to the Atlantic world will be introduced in this first lecture of this week. A brief overall look at the Atlantic world's cities is also provided.
- This lecture then focuses primarily on the northern cities in the Atlantic world. Boston, Philadelphia, and Quebec will be examined in depth. These cities' backgrounds, society, and involvement in the Atlantic world, particularly its economics, will be discussed. Particular attention will be paid to the poverty in Boston, the riots in Philadelphia, and the mixing of British and French colonials in Quebec.
- The interactions between the French and English empires, as well as all settlers' interactions with the indigenous Americans, will be studied, particularly in terms of the French and Indian War: the fall of Quebec in 1758 and the Treaty of Paris of 1763 and what the change of territories meant. The different religious natures of these northern ports will also be part of this first lecture, particularly the involvement of the British colonies in the Great Awakening.

Lecture II: The Mid-Atlantic—New York and Charleston

- This lecture focuses primarily on the "middle" cities in the Atlantic world. New York and Charleston will be examined in depth. These cities' backgrounds, society, and involvement in the Atlantic world, particularly its economics, will be discussed.
- Particular attention will be paid to these cities' involvement in slavery: New York's extensive involvement in the slave trade and Charleston's involvement

in not only the slave trade, but also the selling of slaves to plantations and other slave owners. Much of both these cities' livelihood depended on slavery, and students will be introduced to what this meant to these cities.
- Other topics for this week include reaction among city dwellers to British legislation such as the Sugar Act, the Molasses Act, and the Currency Act.

Lecture III: The South Atlantic—New Orleans, Tenochtitlan, Havana, and Paramaribo

- This lecture focuses primarily on the southern cities in the Atlantic world. The cities of the Caribbean, Mexico City, and Havana will be examined in depth. These cities' backgrounds, society, and involvement in the Atlantic world, particularly its economics, will be discussed.
- Particular attention will be paid to cities' involvement in slavery. This lecture's exploration of cities involved in slavery will be compared to the "middle" cities examined in the previous lecture. The connections between these cities through slavery will also be studied.
- Interactions between the British and Spanish empires, particularly in the form of the War of the Spanish Succession, will be looked at. One focus will be on the differences in Spanish colonial urban development composed to the British, and the different purposes the city had in each empire.

Readings

Chudacoff, Howard P., and Judith E. Smith. *The Evolution of American Urban Society.* 6th ed. New York: Pearson/ Prentice-Hall, 2005.

"Early Cities of the Americas." Special issue of *Commonplace* 3, no. 4 (July 2003): www.common-place.org.

Nash, Gary. *The Urban Crucible: The Northern Seaports and the Origins of the American Revolution.* Cambridge: Harvard University Press, 1986.

Knight, Franklin W., and Peggy K. Liss. *Atlantic Port Cities: Economy, Culture, and Society in the Atlantic World, 1650–1850.* Knoxville: University of Tennessee Press, 1991.

Week 6. Atlantic Polity

Lecture I: The American Revolution (1750–1787)

- This lecture will explore the significant global influence of the Enlightenment and how the ideals of the Enlightenment affected the evolution of democratic thought, resistance, and revolution. This lecture will discuss enlightened and revolutionary ideas such as popular sovereignty, freedom, and equality and how they inspired demands for freedom of worship, expression, and political and legal equality. The ideas of Jean-Jacques Rousseau and John Locke will also be discussed.

- This lecture will also focus on the American Revolution and the tensions between the British, the North American colonies, and the French that led to the Declaration of Independence. The legacy, such as British debt and the North American tax burden, of the Seven Years' War and the protests over British goods, taxes, trade policies, and parliamentary rule will also be discussed. Other topics explored include the advantages that the British and the Americans had in the revolution, the end of the conflict, and the Constitutional Convention.

Lecture II: The Haitian Revolution (1797–1804)

- This week will explore how the French colony of Saint Domingue produced the largest and most successful slave rebellion in the Americas. The three phases of the revolution will be covered: metropolitan France and the revolution against the ancien regime, free coloreds in Saint Domingue fighting for equality with whites, and opportunity for slave uprisings in the environment of revolution.
- Students will also look at the French Revolution and discuss the maneuverings of the Estates and the formation of the National Assembly and their values. The new constitution of 1791, the Directory, and the changes in religion, dress, and women's rights will also be discussed.

Lecture III: The Impact of Revolution in the Atlantic World (1804–1813)

- This week will focus on how the revolution in Saint Domingue affected slave resistance and slavery in the newly formed United States and the Atlantic Caribbean. Latin American independence movements inspired by the Haitian and U.S. revolutions will be studied, along with the emergence of conservative and liberal ideologies.
- This week will also focus on how the limits of these revolutionary ideals were tested, specifically in the realms of slavery and women's rights. The push for the abolition of slavery and the participation of women in these new societies will be discussed.

Readings

Bailyn, Bernard. *The Ideological Origins of the American Revolution.* Cambridge: Belknap Press of Harvard University Press, 1967.

DuBois, Laurent. *Avengers of the New World: The Story of the Haitian Revolution.* Cambridge: Harvard University Press, 2004.

Geggus, David Patrick. *The Impact of the Haitian Revolution in the Atlantic World.* Columbia: University of South Carolina Press, 2001.

Week 7. Defining the Nation Against the Atlantic World, 1812–1829

Lecture I: Industry in the Atlantic World

This lecture will discuss how the immense social and economic changes of industrialization spread throughout the world. New sources of energy, new technologies, and the effects that these had on cities will be looked at.

- Topics covered will include the British monopolization of industry in the beginning, the changes Napoleon made to industry in Western Europe, and why industrialization in America was slow to start.
- This lecture will also look at the emergence of a working-class consciousness throughout the industrialized parts of the Atlantic world.

Lecture II: Religion in the Atlantic World

This lecture will center on religion and the effects that the revolutionary era had on it. The focus will be on what is called the Second Great Awakening. Students will question whether it is in fact a second awakening or if it is a continuation of the first. Allied movements in Canada and Europe will also be discussed. The ties religion had to American identity and cultural independence at this time will be examined. Students will look at the role of the frontier in religion and at the rise of religious freedom. The emerging dominance of evangelical religion will be discussed as well as the idea that to be American is to be Christian. The rise of evangelical religion contributed to women's rights by empowering leaders in the new religiously inspired institutions to purify society. African Americans and slaves also found a place in evangelical religion. We will note the role of evangelicals in attacking slavery and the slave trade in the British Empire and the United States. Religion was used to justify both slavery and abolitionism.

Other topics on religion in the Atlantic world will also be discussed, such as the dominance of Catholicism in Latin America, the rise of Transcendentalism, the rise of Zionism in response to widespread anti-Semitism, and the syncretic practices of African-American religions.

Lecture III: Wars in the Atlantic World

The War of 1812 affected banking, shipping, industry, transportation, and farming throughout the Atlantic world.

This lecture will look at these outcomes.

- This lecture examines the repercussions of the Napoleonic Wars in the Americas: for example, the United States and the War of 1812, and later, the Monroe Doctrine, the relatively peaceful transition from colony to nation for Brazil, and Simon Bolívar and the independence movements in Spanish America.
- Particular attention will be paid to class and racial transformations during these changes, such as the expansion of slavery after independence in Brazil, the class revolution and race warfare in Mexico, the renegotiation of what it means to be of mixed race in the Atlantic world, and the contradictory legacy of the Spanish American revolutions.

Readings

Butler, John. *Awash in a Sea of Faith*. Cambridge: Harvard University Press, 1992. Pp. 129–288.

Juster, Susan. "The Disorder of Women: The Feminization of Sin, 1780–1830." In *Disorderly Women: Sexual Politics and Evangelicalism in Revolutionary New England*. Ithaca, NY: Cornell University Press, 1994. Pp. 145–179.

Smedley, Audrey. *Race in North America: Origin and Evolution of a World View*. Boulder, CO: Westview Press, 1993. Pp. 201–245.

Weeks, William. *Building the Continental Empire: American Expansion from the Revolution to the Civil War*. Chicago: Ivan R. Dee, 1996. Pp. 30–58.

Westerkamp, Marilyn. *Women and Religion in Early America, 1600–1850: The Puritan and Evangelical Traditions*. London: Routledge, 1999. Pp. 104–182.

Week 8. Defining Citizenship, 1829–1837

Lecture I: People and Property

- Students will be asked how citizenship is transformed from political relationship to property ownership to race. Comparisons will be made to Great Britain and Latin American countries.
- This lecture focuses on the effects western expansion/migrations had on the people already living in areas newly settled by Europeans. All over the Americas, indigenous peoples were coming into conflict with settlers who were expanding and migrating. The United States, Canada, Argentina, and Chile all had conflicts with Native Americans that did not end well for the natives, who were generally forced onto undesirable lands. One of the more infamous removals was the Cherokee "Trail of Tears."
- Canada and Latin American countries also had ques-

tions concerning citizenship and race. This lecture will look at the concerns Canada had over the citizenship of British and French Canadians and the problems faced in Latin America over the large inequalities between the majority of landless peasants and the creole elite.

Lecture II: Industry and Agriculture

This lecture will explore the relationship between industry and agriculture. It will look at how transportation connected these, compare the lives of the workers, and look at the incorporation of the West. This lecture will also look at further economic developments in North America. The United States was experiencing a great economic expansion due to railroads, foreign capital, abundant cheap labor, free enterprise, and a stable government. Canada's economic expansion was slower, but proceeding nonetheless. Economic colonialism in Latin America will also be discussed. The majority of Latin American economies continued to export raw materials to industrial powers and did not develop. Only the wealthy prospered in these countries.

Lecture III: Slavery or Freedom?

- After 1800 and increasingly after the abolition of slavery in Great Britain in 1833, the United States was divided more and more over issues of slavery.
- In this lecture, the stories of David Walker and his invocation of the American Revolution in his attack on slavery, William Lloyd Garrison and the publishing of *The Liberator*, the American Colonization Society, the New York riot, and the cooperation of white and black women in the Antislavery Convention of American Women will all be told.
- Also in this lecture, the rebellions in the Caribbean, particularly Jamaica, and in the South, particularly the Turner Rebellion in Virginia, will be examined. The Virginia debate in the legislature over emancipation— the last feasible abolition movement from within a southern state until the Civil War—and the enactment of Great Britain's abolition in the British West Indies will be discussed as well.

Readings

Ahlstrom, Sydney. A *Religious History of the American People*. New Haven: Yale University Press, 1972.

Roediger, David R. *The Wages of Whiteness*. London: Verso, 1991. Pp. 43–92.

Schmidt-Nowara, Christopher. *Empire and Antislavery: Spain, Cuba, and Puerto Rico, 1833–1874*. Pittsburgh: University of Pittsburgh Press, 1999.

Sellers, Charles. *The Market Revolution: Jacksonian*

America, 1815–1846. New York: Oxford University Press, 1991.

Tomich, Dale. "Small Islands, Huge Comparisons: Caribbean Plantations, Historical Unevenness, and Capitalist Modernity." *Social Science History* 18, 3 (Fall 1994): 339–358.

Week 9. Migrations, 1830–1848

Lecture I: Immigration Across the Atlantic

- Ethnicity and immigration on the East Coast
- Growth of radical thought and inter-ethnic immigrant tensions
- Ethnic diversity and nativism

Millions of Europeans migrated to the United States during this time, and afterward the number increased. These immigrants contributed to U.S. industrial expansion primarily because their labor came at a low cost. The majority of European immigrants went to the United States, but others went to Canada, Argentina, Australia, South Africa, and New Zealand. Most became herders, cultivators, or unskilled laborers. This lecture will also discuss the migrants to Latin America. There, immigrants usually worked on agricultural plantations. In Cuba and the Caribbean, Asians migrated to work in the sugar fields, while Italians migrated to Argentina and Brazil.

Lecture II: Westward Expansion

- The Oregon Trail
- Mormon Settlements
- The California Gold Rush

Continual immigration and an ever-increasing population incited American and Canadian settlers to move west.

Lecture III: Immigration Across the Pacific

- Global Impacts of Gold Rush
- Large-scale immigration from across the Pacific Rim (Asia, South America, Australia) as well as overland and from Europe
- Continuing encounters in the Southwest: Texas Independence and the Mexican-American War

This lecture will discuss the migration of Chinese laborers who typically worked in mines or on railroads. Indentured labor migration was more typical from Asia, the Pacific islands, and Africa. These migrants usually worked on tropical and subtropical plantations, such as Indian laborers on Caribbean islands and Japanese laborers on Hawaiian sugar plantations. Students will explore how these large-scale migrations are a sign of the effect imperialism had on the world.

Readings

Anbinder, Tyler. *Five Points: The 19th Century New York Neighborhood That Invented Tap Dance, Stole Elections, and Became the World's Most Notorious Slum.* New York: Free Press, 2001.

Diner, Hasia. *Erin's Daughters in America: Irish Immigrant Women in the Nineteenth Century.* Baltimore: Johns Hopkins University Press, 1983.

Faragher, John Mack. *Women and Men on the Overland Trail.* New Haven: Yale University Press, 1979.

Johnson, Susan. "On the Eve of Emigration," and "Mining Gold and Making War." In *Roaring Camp: The Social World of the California Gold Rush.* New York: W.W. Norton & Company, 2000. Pp. 57–98, 185–236.

Schlissel, Lillian, Vicki L. Ruiz, and Janice Monk, eds. *Western Women: Their Land, Their Lives.* Albuquerque: University of New Mexico Press, 1988.

Starr, Kevin, and Richard Orsi, eds. *Rooted in Barbarous Soil: People, Culture, and Community in Gold Rush California.* Berkeley: University of California Press, 2000.

Week 10. The United States and the Great Divergence

Lecture I: Manifest Destiny

- The "Manifest Destiny" doctrine of the 1840s was a continuation of Euro-American territorial acquisition. Mexico was undergoing its own period of nation-building, identity creation, and political instability, with centripetal and centrifugal forces at work (i.e., Texan federalists versus centralists). Britain's role as an imperial presence in North America was also in flux, which can be seen in the peaceful compromise over the fate of Oregon Territory, as well as in the push to make Texas part of the United States rather than an independent republic under the protection of Britain.

- The Enlightenment-inspired concept of universal humanism that (inconsistently) informed the revolution-era sense of "Americanness" was increasingly replaced by an exclusive sense of nationhood informed by Anglo-Saxon (or "Caucasian") racist ideology, then gaining "scientific" credence in Britain, France, Germany. It was European Americans' close contact with "the other"—Native Americans to be displaced and African Americans to be enslaved or confined—that helped to create a pan-Atlantic racism that informed later European and American colonialist ventures in Africa and Asia.

- This racialized concept of nationhood was a deep undercurrent in the Mexican-American War and the subsequent debates over territorial acquisition and nationhood. Sectional rifts continued to grow, as anti-expansionists and some Northern antislavery advocates used racism to promote an exclusive "white-only" America (e.g., the Liberian colonization project), while expansionists and Southern slaveholders in the South used it to justify the indefinite continuation of racialized slavery and imperialism (e.g., Cuba and Nicaragua plots).
- The creation of an Atlantic-to-Pacific United States is realized at this time.

Lecture II: The "Great Divergence" in the United States—Two Responses

- Britain is the first to experience the "steam-and-coal" revolution, which allowed it to transcend the limits of the biological old regime; northeastern U.S. and some European enclaves soon follow suit. One of the first industries was cotton textiles, but then iron became important in the 1830s with proliferation of railroads, steam engines, and other machines. Politico-military power, imperialism, and rationalization for white racism became tied to new technologies such as steam-ships, railroads, metallurgy, communications, and machine parts.
- Demand from English and northeastern U.S. textile mills for cotton reinvigorated and expanded slave-based staple production; cotton became central to the economy of the South and the biggest export from the United States. The South was turning into a "colonial" agro-economy within the United States, while the North and Northwest (Midwest) increasingly industrialized and developed internally.
- With industrialization, new concepts of citizenship were required that were rooted more in the promise of social mobility, free labor, and voting rights rather than in the older "republican" concept based on the ownership of land. Although the United States demographically and politically remained strongly tied to the agricultural concept of citizenship, the system of slavery was inimical to political changes that were concomitant to steam-and-coal industrialization (strong government, infrastructure development, protectionism, etc.).

Lecture III: Political Crisis in the 1850s—Two Nationalisms, One State

- What was the future path of the United States? Was it to be a raw materials satellite, based on *herrenvolk* democracy and slavery, for a European industrial core, or a self-sufficient industrialized nation-state based on "free" wage labor? Other regions faced similar situations/threats in the nineteenth century: Germany, Italy, Russia, Japan, China, Mexico, the Ottoman Empire, Argentina, Brazil, Egypt, Ethiopia, Madagascar, etc.
- Territorial expansion of the 1840s and 1850s, in the context of the transformation going on in the North and the retrenchment of older patterns in the South, threatened to break the modus vivendi between slave and free states—the Compromise (Armistice) of 1850.
- Southern and Northern "national" identities emerged in dialectical conflict with one another, and the traditional Whig/Democrat party system began to break down. The Republican Party managed to unify Northern (exclusionary) antislavery and abolition forces, and Free Soil and industrial interests. The Southern slave states, outnumbered on the federal level, polarized toward secessionism.

Readings

Freehling, William. *The Road to Disunion (Volume 1): Secessionists at Bay, 1776–1854.* New York and Oxford: Oxford University Press, 1990.

Grant, Susan-Mary. *North over South: Northern Nationalism and American Identity in the Antebellum Era.* Lawrence: University of Kansas Press, 2000.

Holt, Michael F. *The Political Crisis of the 1850s.* New York: Wiley, 1978.

Levine, Bruce. *Half Slave and Half Free: The Roots of the Civil War.* New York: Hill and Wang, 1992.

The United States and the World, 1850 to Present

Teacher's Syllabus

"The United States and the World, Part 2," examines the history of the United States between 1850 and the present. During this period the United States came to play an increasing role on the global stage after its Civil War, notably in late-19th-century imperialism, the global depression, and two world wars and the Cold War. This course pays particular attention to world historical themes that marked the period, including industrialization, population growth, citizenship, science and technology, urbanization and suburbanization, and the exploitation of natural resources (notably the impact of the increasing reliance on petroleum after 1900). By placing America within the world, we seek to question ideas such as U.S. exceptionalism and the historical roots of U.S. hegemony, as well as more generally the utility of national histories. Finally, this course seeks to incorporate the study of culture, race, class, and gender into a new globalized U.S. history.

Week 1. The Gold Rush and Civil War

Lecture I: Looking Backward, Looking Forward

Students will be introduced to the themes and nature of the course. Among the themes addressed in this second half of our proposed course are urban growth and suburbanization, industrialization, population growth, science and technology, and the exploitation of natural resources, especially petroleum. We question ideas such as U.S. exceptionalism and the role of historically planted, deeply rooted U.S. hegemony. By breaching national boundaries and placing America within the world, students will begin to question the idea of the nation as the proper and sole container of history. Additionally, our syllabus includes culture and gender in the narrative. This syllabus, by placing world history into slightly more constrained parameters, also offers space for culture, race, class, and gender to come to the forefront.

- Opening with a review of the California gold rush immediately pulls the West Coast to the center of the narrative. On a practical level, beginning here offers a brief refresher for those who took the first half of the course and a catching up point for those joining for the first time. On a historical level, the Gold Rush is a pivotal moment of westward expansion, bringing California prominently into the national consciousness. In addition to the wealth it generated, the Gold Rush shows how the world was brought to California in a very tangible way through the immigration of miners and other entrepreneurs from Latin America, the East Coast, Australia, Europe, and Asia.
- Nations in the Americas were struggling over constitutional issues and all faced questions of citizenship during this time. The United States was conflicted over whether the federal government or the state governments would be more powerful and how slavery fit in the constitution. After independence Canada faced the problems of creating a government that appealed to both French and British citizens, and as countries in Latin America became independent they faced questions concerning reform, inequalities, and maintaining order.
- The developments that led to the Civil War include the sectional disputes over extending slavery into the western territories, the increasing differences between southerners and northerners in their views and culture and the threat of losing their lifestyle, and the breakdown of the political party system. These developments can be seen in the Compromise of 1850, the Kansas-Nebraska Act, "Bleeding Kansas," and the Dred Scott case.

Lecture II: The Civil War in Its International Context

- Covering the Civil War in the second half of the syllabus rather than assuming the traditional track of beginning with the end of Reconstruction allows for more continuity when discussing emancipation, the failure of Reconstruction, and the subsequent enduring reestablishment of unequal race relationships.
- Students will focus on the balance of resources between the North and South, the unanticipated longtime consequences of war, women and the war, wartime race relations, the reasons the North won, the implications of the first modern-ish war, and the costs of war.
- Many areas that had once had strong and vibrant cultures faced problems as they did not experience the substantial economic expansion of western Europe and the northern United States. The southern United States will be compared to areas in Latin America, Asia, and the Middle East.

Lecture III: Reconstruction: Promise and Failure to 1877

- Reform, reconstruction, and life after slavery will be looked at throughout the world. The abolition of slavery as a larger historical phenomenon will be emphasized.
- Students will examine the conflicting motivations of groups such as victorious northern Republicans, northern moderates, old southern planter aristocracy, new "other South" (yeoman farmers and unionists), and black freedmen during the Reconstruction Era. Also, the law, property titles, and federal enforcement were usually to the benefit of the original owners of the land. While northern soldiers and officials gave freedom to blacks, they did not remain in the South to guarantee that freedom. These factors made the Reconstruction era divisive.
- Special attention will be given to the reception of the Emancipation Proclamation around the world, women and the Reconstruction amendments, life after slavery, the impeachment of President Andrew Johnson and its importance to Reconstruction, and the Compromise of 1877.

Readings

Bright, Charles, and Michael Geyer. "Global Violence and Nationalizing Wars in Eurasia and America: The Geopolitics of War in the Mid-Nineteenth Century." *Comparative Studies in Society and History* 38, no. 4 (1996): 619–667.

Bright, Charles, and Michael Geyer. "Where in the World Is

America? The History of the United States in the Global Age." In *Rethinking American History in a Global Age,* ed. Thomas Bender. Berkeley: University of California Press, 2002.

Foner, Eric. *Nothing But Freedom.* Baton Rouge: Louisiana State University Press, 1983.

Stanley, Amy Dru. *From Bondage to Contract: Wage Labor, Marriage, and the Market in the Age of Slave Emancipation.* Cambridge: Cambridge University Press, 1998.

Week 2. Agriculture and Industry

Lecture I: Reconstruction in a World Perspective: Contract Society

- This lecture will focus on sharecropping in the U.S. South. It will also look at how contract laborers from India and then China replaced slave laborers when slavery was legally abolished worldwide toward the end of the century.
- Students will explore agriculture in the U.S. South and see how the California-Texas model of cotton was implemented globally.

Lecture II: Immigration from Europe, Mexico, and Asia

- This lecture will emphasize the connection between industrialization and immigration. Poor European immigrants became the new workforce as nations regulated child labor. By 1900, nearly 50 million Europeans had immigrated to new lands.
- Students will look at how these immigrants were received in their new homes and how the different gender roles, racial views, and religious practices that these immigrants brought were incorporated and changed.

Lecture III: Clearing the Land: Market-oriented Agriculture, Mining, Deforestation, Whaling

- Industrialized societies were competing for new markets, raw materials, and new territories. As an international phenomenon, the hinterlands were increasingly feeding the population in the growing cities.
- All over the world the rural way of life changed in response to the new economic and social conditions that come with industrialization. In the western United States, large-scale agriculture began and natural resources and indigenous peoples were cleared from the land. Ranching, mining, deforestation, and whaling were industrialized and many of their products became global commodities. Similar issues arose in

countries throughout Latin America, Canada, and Africa.

Readings

Beckert, Sven. "Cotton's Renaissance: A Study in Market Innovation." *Harvard Business School,* September 2005.

Cronon, William. *Nature's Metropolis: Chicago and the Great West.* New York: W.W. Norton & Company, 1991.

Fitzgerald, Debora. *Every Farm a Factory: The Industrial Ideal in American Agriculture.* New Haven and London: Yale University Press, 2003.

Goodwyn, Lawrence. *The Populist Moment: A Short History of the Agrarian Revolt in America.* New York: Oxford University Press, 1978.

Jacobson, Michael Frye. *Whiteness of a Different Color: European Immigrants and the Alchemy of Race.* Cambridge, MA: Harvard University Press, 1998.

Peiss, Kathy. *Cheap Amusements: Working Women and Leisure in Turn-of-the-Century New York.* Philadelphia: Temple University Press, 1987.

Welke, Barbara. *Recasting American Liberty: Gender, Race, Law and the American Railroad Revolution, 1865–1920.* Cambridge: Cambridge University Press, 2001.

Worster, Donald. *Rivers of Empire: Water, Aridity, and the Growth of the American West.* New York: Pantheon Books, 1985.

Week 3. The New Urbanity: Space, Society, and Politics, 1880–1914

Lecture I: Space: Physical Transformations of the City Landscape

- With the changes of industrialization came a new urbanity. People congregated in cities and were pushed into waged labor; these urban spaces offer a window for students to explore the experiences of women and the working class.
- During the Gilded Age and Progressive Era, the physical landscape of American society changed alongside developments in social patterns and political structures. This was a period of tremendous growth, development, conflict, and complexity. For example, the period saw both creative solutions for the problems of urbanity and increased racism and exclusion of Asian immigrants.
- Students will look at the exchange of ideas worldwide on technology, housing, transportation, and the City Beautiful campaigns. The Chicago Exposition as the "Model City" for both United States and the world will also be discussed.

Lecture II: Social Patterns: New Work and Amusement Opportunities for Immigrants, Women, and the Working Class

- This lecture will emphasize the global nature of women's suffrage. Also, students will see that while young working-class women found new outlets for amusement, sexuality, and labor, middle-class women expressed their class and race power in moral reform associations.
- This lecture will also look at the hostility immigrants faced.

Lecture III: Politics

- This lecture will emphasize the global elements of Progressive ideology as well as a new form of political participation—unions.
- This lecture will focus on the state regulation of industries, muckraking journalists, Tammany Hall and corruption, the enthusiasm for reform that defined the "Progressive Era," and characteristics of reformers.
- Did reform mean progress? Examples of internal strife, racism, growth of KKK, and lynching will be discussed.

Readings

Chauncey, George. *Gay New York: Gender, Urban Culture, and the Making of the Gay Male World, 1890–1940.* New York: Basic Books, 1994.

Danbom, David B. *The Resisted Revolution: Urban America and the Industrialization of Agriculture, 1900–1930.* Ames: Iowa State University Press, 1979.

Levine, Lawrence W. *Highbrow/Lowbrow: The Emergence of Cultural Hierarchy in America.* Cambridge, MA: Harvard University Press, 1988.

Montgomery, David. *Workers' Control in America: Studies in the History of Work, Technology, and Labor Struggles.* New York: Cambridge University Press, 1979.

Noble, David F. *America by Design: Science, Technology, and the Rise of Corporate Capitalism.* New York: New York: Knopf, 1977.

Rodgers, Daniel. *Atlantic Crossings: Social Politics in a Progressive Age.* Cambridge, MA: Belknap Press, 1998.

Zunz, Oliver. *Making America Corporate, 1870–1920.* Chicago: University of Chicago Press, 1990.

Week 4. Conflict Abroad, Conflict Within

Lecture I: Imperialism

- As Western Europe's industrial powers extended their control over areas of Asia and Africa, the United States, Japan, and Russia were quick to follow. These nations' new imperialism was rationalized with theories of racial and cultural superiority and implemented with new technologies of warfare; it was set up in order to supply cheap raw commodities to the imperial power and in turn to provide that power with a market for manufactured goods.
- This lecture will also examine the Spanish-American War and the U.S. possessions, including Alaska, Hawaii, Puerto Rico, the Philippines, many Pacific islands, and Cuba. Advantages and disadvantages of gaining imperial possessions will be discussed using the example of the Philippines. (The United States assisted a Filipino revolt against Spain and then purchased the colony only to fight a civil war shortly afterward that killed 200,000 Filipinos.)
- This lecture will also discuss other conflagrations, such as the Mexican Revolution and its implications for the United States, as well as the reasons for the Boxer intervention in China and the Open Door policy.

Lecture II: World War I: Domestic

- This lecture will explore how the nation was forced to make changes in its outlook, politics, and military in order to adjust to being a major world power. It will look at some of the problems, particularly in politics, that the limited national government experienced in the face of the rapid changes in the country.
- This lecture will also look at the social, gender, racial, and economic significance of the American war effort.

Lecture III: World War I: Bankers to the World

- World War I marked a change in the way the United States interacted with the rest of the globe, propelling the United States onto the world stage and marking the switch from British to U.S. global hegemony—a metaphorical passing of the baton of empire. At the end of the war it appeared that colonial empires were the same, but they were funded by U.S. money. In this way, colonialism was reinvented. At the same time, freedom movements began in places such as India and China.
- Students will focus on the unexpected aspects of this war for everyone involved: the new technologies that changed the experience of war and led to heavy casualties; the concept of total war and its impact on civilian populations; government control of factories; propaganda; women's labor; civilian deaths; the Russian Revolution; and the harsh terms of the Paris Peace Conference.

Readings

Hoganson, Kristen. *Fighting for American Manhood: How Gender Politics Provoked the Spanish-American and Philippine-American Wars.* New Haven: Yale University Press, 1998.

Iriye, Akira. *From Nationalism to Internationalism: U.S. Foreign Policy to 1914.* Boston: Routledge & Kegan Paul, 1977.

Jacobson, Matthew Frye. *Barbarian Virtues: The United States Encounters Foreign Peoples at Home and Abroad, 1876–1917.* New York: Hill and Wang, 2000.

Offer, Avner. *The First World War: An Agrarian Interpretation.* New York: Oxford University Press, 1989.

Renda, Mary. *Taking Haiti: Military Occupation and the Culture of U.S. Imperialism, 1915–1940.* Chapel Hill: University of North Carolina Press, 2000.

Saul, S.B. *The Myth of the Great Depression, 1873–1896.* London: Macmillan, 1985 [1969].

Skowronek, Stephen. *Building a New American State: The Expansion of National Administrative Capacities, 1877–1920.* New York: Cambridge University Press, 1982.

Wexler, Laura. *Tender Violence: Domestic Visions in an Age of U.S. Imperialism.* Chapel Hill: University of North Carolina Press, 2000.

Week 5. A New America, a New World?

Lecture I: Limits of Citizenship and Democracy

- Looking at the Pan-African movement of the 1920s and 1930s highlights the cultural and political interrelationships between Harlem, the Caribbean, Africa, and Europe. Other global overviews include the advent of immigration restrictions, including the creation of the U.S. border patrol in 1924, and battles over women's suffrage culminating in the passage of the nineteenth amendment in 1920.
- Throughout the world, people were feeling disillusioned—the cruel realities of trench warfare shook the liberal ideals of the Enlightenment and the 1920s were marked by uncertainty and questioning of science, art, and religion. People turned to extreme leaders and nationalism. With its limited involvement in World War I, the United States did not suffer as distinct a shock as other nations.
- For this era, we touch on U.S. experiences such as Mexican repatriation and other internal migrations. We also focus on changes in American lifestyle and values in terms of communications and religion, and women and consumerism, and their reflection in literature and art.

Lecture II: Global Depression and Disorder

- Our lectures on the 1930s stress the Great Depression as a global depression, not just a U.S. phenomenon. Global depression deepened political and social anxiety. This lecture will explain the cycles of war reparations and debt payment that were largely responsible for the disintegration of the post–World War I global economy.
- Students will look at how various strata of society were affected by the depression. This lecture will discuss the Poor People's March, suicides, Hoovervilles, and rural migration.

Lecture III: Reactions to Depression

- This lecture will focus on government responses globally and the New Deal. Students will look at the New Deal as one manifestation of an increased role of the state in managing the economy. Comparisons can be made to National Socialism in Germany, the planned economy in the USSR, and other fascist or authoritarian regimes (Portugal, Spain, Japan, Italy, etc.). Most nations, including the United States, would not substantially recover from the Depression until re-armament and war demand revived industrial production.
- Students will look at how economic nationalism was favored over international cooperation: with the collapse of the international gold standard, nations and empires turned inward by raising tariffs, extending subsidies, and creating "currency blocs" (i.e., the dollar, pound sterling, yen, reichsmark, franc).

Readings

Cohen, Lizabeth. *Making a New Deal: Industrial Workers in Chicago, 1919–1939.* New York and Cambridge: Cambridge University Press, 1990.

Gomez, Michael A. *Reversing Sail: A History of the African Diaspora.* Cambridge: Cambridge University Press, 2005. Esp. Chapters 6–8 and Epilogue.

Hurt, Douglas. *The Dust Bowl: An Agricultural and Social History.* Chicago: Nelson Hall, 1981.

James, Winston. *Holding Aloft the Banner of Ethiopia: Caribbean Radicalism in Early Twentieth-Century America.* London: Verso Press, 1998.

Kessler-Harris, Alice. "In the Nation's Image: The Gendered Limits of Social Citizenship in the Depression Era." *Journal of American History* 86, 3 (1999): 1251–1279.

Kindleberger, Charles. *The World in Depression, 1929–1939.* Berkeley: University of California Press, 1986 [1973].

Pells, Richard H. *Radical Visions and American Dreams:*

Culture and Social Thought in the Depression Years. New York: Harper & Row, 1973.

Rothermund, Dietmar. *The Global Impact of the Great Depression, 1929–1939.* London and New York: Routledge, 1996.

Sanchez, George. *Becoming Mexican American: Ethnicity and Acculturation in Chicano Los Angeles, 1900–1943.* New York: Oxford University Press, 1993.

Worster, Donald. *Dust Bowl: The Southern Plains in the 1930s.* New York: Oxford University Press, 1979.

Week 6. World War II and the Postwar Order

Lecture I: World War II and the Homefront

- This lecture will look at the isolationism of the United States in the context of growing geopolitical conflict elsewhere. British and French policymakers did not want to fight another war and sought to appease Nazi Germany's aggression to create a bulwark against Bolshevism. But Hitler sought nothing less than hemispheric hegemony and pulled all of Europe into total war. Similarly, Japan descended into military dictatorship and strove to create its own global sphere of dominance, which came into conflict with, among other powers, the United States in the Pacific.

- Mobilization for war had large ramifications domestically. Women worldwide performed industrial work and joined auxiliary forces; they also participated as prostitutes and, involuntarily, as "comfort women." There was a promise of an integrated army for blacks in the United States. Mass mobilization and the imperative for national unity disciplined organized labor, but also created an expectation of economic and political betterment for services rendered in wartime (higher wages and labor unions, the G.I. Bill, homeownership, etc.). World War II was another total war and civilians were targets for blockades, internment, and aerial attacks.

Lecture II: The Bomb

- The Second World War was unprecedented in the scale of deaths and devastation. It began with millions of deaths when the Japanese invaded China and ended with more death when the atomic bombs were dropped on Hiroshima and Nagasaki. Many soldiers and civilians died in Siberian and German death camps, and Nazi genocidal policies were responsible for the deaths of millions of Jews and Slavs, as well as Roma, political dissidents, and persons otherwise deemed unfit.

- This lecture will set the stage for the beginning of the Cold War. Most of the human costs of World War II were borne by the Soviet Union, but its victory against the brunt of Nazi aggression and subsequent seizure of most of Eastern and Central Europe assured its superpower status. In the context of such incredible destruction, and despite the loss of over 400,000 combatants, the United States was exceptional among all the belligerents in that its economic base was not destroyed, and in fact thrived. The projection of the United States's industrial, technical, and financial power was crucial in the Allied victory and assured its leadership role in the capitalist world.

- This lecture will use the development and deployment of the atomic bomb as a potent symbol of total war: on the one hand, it required a complex educational system, government support, and the most advanced industrial techniques; on the other, its express purpose was to terrorize civilian populations into surrender.

Lecture III: U.S. Hegemony in the Petroleum Age

- The industrial and technological prowess of the triumphant United States created domestic consensus and externally set the framework for postwar reconstruction in the West.

- This lecture will look at the measures—economic, financial, military, and political—that the United States undertook at the end of the war and in the immediate postwar years to rebuild the global order to its advantage. Topics to explore are the Bretton Woods system, the IMF and World Bank, the Marshall Plan, the Truman Doctrine, British bankruptcy, postwar Japan, and "brushfire" conflicts in Greece, China, and Korea. Another important shift was the restructuring, with U.S. policy guidance, of the West's economies around petroleum. (This also brought with it significant strategic implications for the Middle East.)

Readings

Campbell, D'Ann. "Women in Combat: The World War II Experience in the United States, Great Britain, Germany, and the Soviet Union." *Journal of Military History* 57, no. 2 (1993): 301–323.

Escobar, Arturo. *Encountering Development: The Making and Unmaking of the Third World.* Princeton: Princeton University Press, 1995.

Graebner, William. *The Age of Doubt: American Thought and Culture in the 1940s.* Boston: Twayne, 1991.

Heardon, Patrick. *Architects of Globalism: Building a New World Order During World War II.* Fayetteville: University of Arkansas Press, 2002.

Hein, Laura, and Mark Selden, eds. *Living with the Bomb: American and Japanese Cultural Conflicts in the Nuclear Age.* Armonk, NY: M.E. Sharpe, 1997.

Heinberg, Richard. *The Party's Over: Oil, War, and the*

Fate of Industrial Societies. Gabriola, BC: New Society Publishers, 2003. Esp. Chapters 1 and 2.

McMichael, Philip. *Development and Social Change: A Global Perspective.* Thousand Oaks, CA: Pine Forge Press, 2004.

Painter, David S. *The Cold War: An International History.* London and New York: Routledge, 1999.

Sherwin, Martin, and Kai Bird. *American Prometheus: The Triumph and Tragedy of J. Robert Oppenheimer.* New York: Vintage, 2006.

Week 7. Suburban Nation

Lecture I: Fueling the American Dream

- This lecture will focus on the domestic ramifications of the economic and social changes in the postwar United States. The economic boom, the increased corporate impact on everyday American life, unions and Keynesianism, changing work patterns, and the continued plight of agriculture and rural society will be discussed.

- This lecture will approach the postwar boom by looking at the explosive increase in petroleum use in concert with new technologies. This can include car culture, commercial jets, plastics, industrialization of agriculture and the food system, the kitchen debates between Nixon and Khrushchev, and the competition in science and technology between the U.S. and the Soviet Union as exemplified by the space race.

Lecture II: Nuclear Family, Nuclear Holocaust

- This lecture will look at the culture of the postwar decade. U.S. leaders held families up as domestic containment and the best defense against communism. Women were encouraged to stay at home to raise children and not work. Students will discuss the Red Scare and Senator Joseph McCarthy; rampant poverty, racism, and segregation; the increasing pressure to conform and the retreat to family and home; the flight to the suburbs; and the G.I. Bill.

- Students will also discuss the social norms so important at this time and the conformity in school and religious life, as well as the early counters to this culture such as the beat generation, popular music, American artists, Alfred Kinsey, *MAD Magazine*, and *Playboy.*

Lecture III: Production and Reproduction

- This lecture will examine the "baby boom" and massive population increase on a worldwide scale, which produced a dramatic demographic bump. Faster and cheaper transportation, the Green Revolution, and the end of the power of European empires led to mass population movements and growth worldwide. Immigration from Latin America to the United States transformed American culture. This lecture will also discuss the population shift to the Sunbelt states, "white flight" into the suburbs, and the "urban crisis."

- This lecture will deal with the global spread of prosperity and "Americanization" in the West, and the concurrent efforts by Eastern Bloc and Third World countries to modernize and improve standards of living.

Readings

Duany, Andres, et al. *Suburban Nation: The Rise of Sprawl and the Decline of the American Dream.* New York: North Point Press, 2000.

Flink, James J. *The Car Culture.* Cambridge, MA: MIT Press, 1975.

Kelman, Ari. *The River and Its City: The Nature of Landscape in New Orleans.* Berkeley: University of California Press, 2003. Esp. "Epilogue: The Simple Needs of Automobiles."

May, Elaine Tyler. *Homeward Bound: American Families in the Cold War Era.* New York: Basic Books, 1998.

McShane, Clay. *Down the Asphalt Path: The Car and the American City.* New York: Columbia University Press, 1994.

Sugrue, Thomas. *The Origins of the Urban Crisis: Race and Inequality in Postwar Detroit.* Princeton: Princeton University Press, 1996.

Vonnegut, Kurt. *Player Piano.* New York: Dell, 1952. (Fiction)

Week 8. The Effects of the Demographic Bump

Lecture I: Dilemmas of Managing the World

- This lecture will draw on Bright and Geyer's work to set the stage for the external and internal challenges to the postwar U.S. regime of global order in the 1960s and 1970s. It will focus on the macroeconomic problems and geopolitical conflicts that were part of this process, including: the quagmire of the Vietnam War, the collapse of the Bretton Woods system, stagflation, the OPEC oil embargo, the Non-Aligned movement, and the continuing challenge of the Soviet Union and China.

- Topics discussed in this lecture include: the Cuban Missile Crisis, assassination of JFK, Great Society, Mao vs. USSR, independence movements in the world (including Vietnam), continuation of the

Cold War, nationalism and religious movements (Catholics, India, Iran, Iraq, Islam, Palestine, missionaries, Third Great Awakening), Geneva Accords, SEATO.

Lecture II: Freedom Dreams?

- This lecture will explore how the global economic, demographic, and political challenges to U.S. hegemony influenced and were influenced by domestic upheavals, and forced a rethinking of the postwar social contract.
- Topics discussed in this lecture look at domestic social struggles through a comparative lens. In the United States: Civil Rights, MLK, César Chavez, ethnic studies movement, black universities, Wounded Knee, desegregation, affirmative action, repeal of Exclusion Act, Mississippi Summer, Malcolm X, Watts Riots, Fair Housing Act, feminism. Worldwide, there were also severe strains on social reproduction caused by an exploding youth population and conflicts over the terms of the social contract ("global" 1968 in Japan, Mexico, France, Czechoslovakia).

Lecture III: Delusions of Revolution

This lecture will emphasize a more cultural approach, utilizing visual and music media. Topics touched on in this lecture include: Hippies, drugs, student revolution, global youth culture, university tumult and rejection of the "multiversity" (the original conception of UCSC), '68 Revolution, music, Vietnam, how Third World liberation became sexy, Earth Day (picture of "Spaceship Earth"), the Port Huron Statement. Events and movements in the United States will be placed in comparison with similar movements around the world, from Mexico City to Prague to Tokyo and Paris.

Readings

Betts, Raymond. *Decolonization.* New York: Routledge, 2004.

Bright, Charles, and Michael Geyer. "Where in the World Is America? The History of the United States in the Global Age." In *Rethinking American History in a Global Age,* ed. Thomas Bender. Berkeley: University of California Press, 2002.

Dudziak, Mary L. *Cold War Civil Rights: Race and the Image of American Democracy.* Princeton: Princeton University Press, 2002.

Ferrall, James J. *The Spirit of the Sixties: The Making of Postwar Radicalism.* New York: Routledge, 1997.

Kelley, Robin D.G. *Freedom Dreams: The Black Radical Imagination.* Boston: Beacon Press, 2002.

Kurlansky, Mark. *1968: The Year That Rocked the World.* New York: Random House Trade Paperbacks, 2005.

Morris, Charles. *A Time of Passion: America, 1960–1980.* New York: Harper & Row, 1984.

Rosen, Ruth. *The World Split Open: How the Modern Women's Movement Changed America.* New York: Penguin, 2000.

Stone, Robert. *Dog Soldiers.* New York: Houghton Mifflin, 1973. (Fiction)

Taibo, Paco Ignacio II. *'68.* New York: Seven Stories Press, 2004.

Film: *Berkeley in the Sixties.* Directed by Mark Kitchell, 1990.

Week 9. Paradox of Peace

Lecture I: Cold Realities

This lecture will discuss the shape of the Cold War through the 1970s and 1980s. The economic downturn of the 1970s challenged the "development consensus," leading to a challenge to the legitimacy of both the U.S. and Soviet blocs, and the immiseration of much of the postcolonial Third World and nationalist movements. Connected to these phenomena are: awareness of the failings of the Green Revolution, collapse of Keynesian policy dominance, Third World debt and the IMF/World Bank, "opening" of China under Deng Xiaoping, and continuation of high energy prices (second embargo in 1979).

Lecture II: Hippies to Yuppies

This lecture will track the shift of culture in a more conservative direction. It examines intellectuals, cynical youth culture, the bureaucratization of the environmentalist movement, decline of unions and the rise of the Rust Belt, *Roe v. Wade* and the entry of women into the workforce and professions, libertarianism, Cold War, and the U.S. Drug War.

Lecture III: End of the Cold War

This lecture will discuss the end of détente and the rise of the Reagan adminstration's more aggressive political and military policies. It will also cover the political and economic implosion of the Soviet regime of order: failure of *glasnost* and *perestroika,* Chernobyl, Afghanistan, the grinding-down of the planned economy and the failure to adopt Third Wave technologies, loss of Eastern Bloc. In the United States, with the sudden end of the Cold War came changes in foreign policy: the United States as the sole superpower muddles through its role as the global and humanitarian policeman; continuation of the Drug War and ongoing investment in military-industrial-Congress complex.

Readings

Butler, Jon. "Jack-in-the-Box Faith: The Religion Problem in Modern American History." *Journal of American History* 90, 4 (March 2004): 1357–1378.

Carroll, Peter. *It Seemed Like Nothing Happened: The Tragedy and Promise of America in the 1970s.* New York: Holt, Rinehart, and Winston, 1982.

Hodgson, Godfrey. *The World Turned Right Side Up: A History of the Conservative Ascendancy in America.* Boston: Houghton Mifflin, 1996.

Kling, Rob, Spencer Olin, and Mark Poster, eds. *Post-Suburban California: The Transformation of Orange County Since World War II.* Berkeley: University of California Press, 1991.

Leffler, Melvyn. "The Cold War: What Do 'We Now Know'?" *American Historical Review* 104, 2 (April 1999): 501–524.

Putnam, Robert D. *Bowling Alone: The Collapse and Revival of American Community.* New York: Simon & Schuster, 2000.

Week 10. A Global Nation

Lecture I: Neoliberalism and the Electronics Revolution

This lecture will focus on technological and macroeconomic change and how it altered everyday life and the structure of society. This includes (economically) the Washington Consensus and the predominance of neoliberalism, and (technologically) the electronics and communications revolution. Information and capital flows became global and nearly instantaneous, but this "postindustrial" "iPod" economy was made possible by lower fossil energy costs following the end of the oil embargoes of the 1970s. Developed nations' policymakers and multinational corporations favored eliminating barriers to free trade, which accentuated the movement of manufacturing and industrial centers to platforms in the "developing" world and promoted service and information sectors in the "developed" world. This increases intra-national economic polarization and disrupts notions of geographically discrete First and Third Worlds.

Lecture II: Globalization and Its Discontents

- This lecture will juxtapose the trends outlined in the first lecture with domestic and global reactions and responses. Transnational institutions are increasingly shaping the world and are often not restricted by any one legal system or government. In the case of corporations this often means that they go wherever goods and services can be found most cheaply, but in the case of nongovernmental organizations (NGOs) this means they can address international problems without being constrained by the policies of one country.

- Millions of workers have moved to new industrial centers. For example, Indians migrated to South Africa, Egyptians to the Gulf States, Turks to Germany, Mexicans to the United States, and Chinese to Canada. These new industrial centers often create unprecedented human and environmental problems due to rapid urbanization. Some migrants are unwillingly trafficked or sold into slavery. Many international migrants can send money back to their families or return to their homes after working.

- Consumers all over the world are increasingly using the products and images of the global economy and entertainment complex to define themselves. World cultures are influenced by and modeled on the styles of dress, entertainment, and music of the United States, but also are increasingly set within regional and local identities. Many resist globalization and see it as a threat to their culture, values, and livelihoods. Nations with access to new technologies and capital are favored in the global economy, while poorer nations find it hard to not be economically dependent.

Lecture III: The Price of Prosperity

- Students will question the price of preserving the American way of life, and its survival into a uncertain future. This lecture will tie together U.S. support of autocratic regimes in the Middle East, increasing dependence on foreign oil in these regions, the rise of militant Islam, 9/11, and the spectacular rise of China in the early 2000s. The goal of this lecture is to reiterate to students that the United States has always been a part of the world, but that they should start to see "globalization" with the United States in a dominant role as an historical artifact.

- Economies in many parts of the world are booming, as are populations, but many of the world's peoples live in poverty. The demands of the global market have environmental consequences such as global climate change, deforestation, extinction of species, and the imminent coming of Peak Oil.

Readings

Bender, Daniel E., and Richard A. Greenwald. *Sweatshop USA: The American Sweatshop in Historical and Global Perspective.* New York and London: Routledge, 2003.

Bender, Thomas, ed. *Rethinking American History in a Global Age.* Berkeley: University of California Press, 2002.

Brown, Kate. "Gridded Lives: Why Kazakhstan and Montana Are Nearly the Same Place." *AHR* 106, no. 1 (February 2001): 17–48.

Davis, Mike. *Planet of Slums.* New York: Verso, 2001.

Hondagneu-Sotelo, Pierrette. *Doméstic: Immigrant Workers Cleaning and Caring in the Shadows of Affluence.* Berkeley: University of California Press, 2001.

Kunstler, James Howard. *The Long Emergency: Surviving the Converging Catastrophes of the Twenty-First Century.* New York: Atlantic Monthly Press, 2005.

Parreñas, Rachel Salazar. *Servants of Globalization: Women, Migration and Domestic Work.* Stanford: Stanford University Press, 2001.

Film: *Crude Impact.* Vista Clara Films, 2006.

CHAPTER 21

The North and South Atlantic Core (History 506)

Erik Seeman, State University of New York at Buffalo

Goals

This course will introduce students to the historiography of the rapidly growing field of the Atlantic World. Within the historical profession, the term "Atlantic World" is usually applied to the North Atlantic in the early modern period. This course will engage with that material while also expanding the concept to include the South Atlantic and the post-colonial era. Students will gain an understanding of how the field has been defined, how the field has changed over time, and how the field might evolve in the future. This course is required for those History Ph.D. students who wish to offer the "North and South Atlantic" for the major field of their oral examinations. It is highly recommended for those who wish to offer a minor oral examination field in the Atlantic World, and for anyone who wishes to employ transnational or comparative perspectives on the past.

Assignments

This course requires several two- to three-page papers and a final historiographical essay.

Short Papers

This is an enormous field and it will be impossible for students to sample more than a small fraction of the relevant literature. To help remedy this problem, students will work together to create a portfolio of summaries that will be useful both in preparing for exams and in grasping this field. Every student will read the required text(s) each week. In addition, each student will be assigned to a group: A, B, C, or D. Every week, one member of each group will read an additional text and write a two- to three-page summary for other students to read. The papers must be completed and sent by e-mail attachment to all class members by noon of the Tuesday before class. Students are expected to print their classmates' papers, read them, and compile them in a three-ring binder. By the end of the semester, students will have a collection of summaries of the major works on the North and South Atlantic. Each student will thus be responsible for a number of short papers equal to the total number of weeks divided by the number of people in his or her group.

Historiographical Essay

Each student will choose a topic for an in-depth review of the recent literature in 12 to 15 pages, due by noon Thursday, May 4. Students should consult with me during office hours no later than April 6 about an appropriate topic. Students may use the lists of Further Reading to get started, though other subjects not covered by the lists can also be studied. The additional reading for the paper should amount to about four books and two articles (though these are not hard and fast figures). This paper may be used as a prospectus for a later research project or as the first step toward a dissertation topic.

Grading

Class discussion will constitute the majority of the final grade, with the written assignments making up the balance.

Readings

The following books are required reading and may be purchased at the University Bookstore. You may also wish to check online booksellers like amazon.com and half.com for used books.

Inga Clendinnen, *Ambivalent Conquests: Maya and Spaniard in Yucatan, 1517–1570,* 2d ed. (New York, 2003). The first edition is also fine.

Frederick Cooper, Thomas C. Holt, and Rebecca J. Scott, *Beyond Slavery: Explorations of Race, Labor, and Citizenship in Postemancipation Societies* (Chapel Hill, 2000).

Victoria de Grazia, *Irresistible Empire: America's Advance Through Twentieth-Century Europe* (Cambridge, Mass., 2005).

Jean de Léry, *History of a Voyage to the Land of Brazil,* edited by Janet Whatley (Berkeley, 1993).

Laurent Dubois, *Avengers of the New World: The Story of the Haitian Revolution* (Cambridge, Mass., 2004).

Paul Gilroy, *The Black Atlantic: Modernity and Double Consciousness* (Cambridge, Mass., 1993).

Anthony Grafton, *New Worlds, Ancient Texts: The Power of Tradition and the Shock of Discovery* (Cambridge, Mass., 1992).

Catherine Hall, *Civilising Subjects: Metropole and Colony in the English Imagination, 1830–1867* (Chicago, 2002).

David Hancock, *Citizens of the World: London Merchants and the Integration of the British Atlantic Community, 1735–1785* (New York, 1995).

Daniel R. Rodgers, *Atlantic Crossings: Social Politics in a Progressive Age* (Cambridge, Mass., 1998).

Christopher Schmidt-Nowara, *Empire and Antislavery: Spain, Cuba, and Puerto Rico, 1833–1874* (Pittsburgh, 1999).

January 19: Introduction

January 26: Overviews

Required Texts

David Armitage, "Three Concepts of Atlantic History," in David Armitage and Michael J. Braddick, eds., *The British Atlantic World, 1500–1800* (New York, 2002), 11–27.

Bernard Bailyn, "The Idea of Atlantic History," *Itinerario* 20 (1996): 19–44.

Joyce E. Chaplin, "Expansion and Exceptionalism in Early American History," *Journal of American History* 89 (March 2003): 1431–55.

Jack P. Greene, "Beyond Power: Paradigm Subversion and Reformulation and the Re-Creation of the Early Modern Atlantic World," in Greene, ed., *Interpreting Early America: Historiographical Essays* (Charlottesville, Va., 1996), 17–42.

Shared Texts

A: Nicholas Canny, "Writing Atlantic History; or, Reconfiguring the History of Colonial British America," *Journal of American History* 86 (December 1999): 1093–1114.

B: David Hancock, "The British Atlantic World: Coordination, Complexity, and the Emergence of an Atlantic Market Economy, 1651–1815," *Itinerario* 23 (1999): 107–26.

C: Silvia Marzagalli, "The French Atlantic," *Itinerario* 23 (1999): 70–83.

D: Carla Rahn Phillips, "The Iberian Atlantic," *Itinerario* 23 (1999): 84–106.

For Further Reading

David Armitage and Michael J. Braddick, eds., *The British Atlantic World, 1500–1800* (New York, 2002).

Bernard Bailyn, *Atlantic History: Concept and Contours* (Cambridge, Mass., 2005).

Wim Klooster and Alfred Padula, eds., *The Atlantic World: Essays on Slavery, Migration, and Imagination* (Upper Saddle River, N.J., 2005).

D.W. Meinig, *The Shaping of America, Volume I: Atlantic America, 1492–1800* (New Haven, 1986).

Ian K. Steele, *The English Atlantic, 1675–1740: An Exploration of Communication and Community* (New York, 1986).

Alan Taylor, *American Colonies* (New York, 2001).

Deborah Gray White, "'Yes,' There Is a Black Atlantic," *Itinerario: European Journal of Overseas History* 23 (1999): 127–40.

February 2: Narratives of Discovery and Conquest

Required Texts

Jean de Léry, *History of a Voyage to the Land of Brazil,* edited by Janet Whatley (Berkeley, 1993).

"Digest of Columbus's Log Book," in J.M. Cohen, ed., *Christopher Columbus: The Four Voyages* (London, 1969), 51–73.

Shared Texts

A: Alvar Núñez Cabeza de Vaca, *Castaways,* edited by Enrique Pupo-Walker (Berkeley, 1993).

B: Ramsay Cook, ed., *The Voyages of Jacques Cartier* (Toronto, 1993), ix–xli, 3–89.

C: Second Letter of Hernando Cortés to the Emperor, in *Five Letters of Cortés to the Emperor,* edited by J. Bayard Morris (New York, 1969), 31–133.

D: Luciano Formisano, ed., *Letters from a New World: Amerigo Vespucci's Discovery of America* (New York, 1992).

For Further Reading

Allan Greer, ed., *The Jesuit Relations: Natives and Missionaries in Seventeenth-Century North America* (Boston, 2000).

Peter C. Mancall, ed., *Envisioning America: English Plans for the Colonization of North America, 1580–1640* (Boston, 1995).

Stuart B. Schwartz, ed., *Victors and Vanquished: Spanish and Nahua Views of the Conquest of Mexico* (Boston, 2000).

February 9: The Black Atlantic (Prof. Jason Young, guest faculty)

Required Text

Paul Gilroy, *The Black Atlantic: Modernity and Double Consciousness* (Cambridge, Mass., 1993).

Optional Media Supplement

Black Atlantic CD—click for list of songs and artists

Shared Texts

A: Ira Berlin, *Many Thousands Gone: The First Two Centuries of Slavery in North America* (Cambridge, Mass., 2000).

B: Michael Gomez, *Exchanging Our Country Marks: The Transformation of African Identities in the Colonial and Antebellum South* (Chapel Hill, 1998).

C: Melville Herskovits, *The Myth of the Negro Past* (Boston, 1958 [1941]).

D: Richard Price and Sally Price, *Maroon Arts: Cultural Vitality in the African Diaspora* (Boston, 1999).

For Further Reading

Trevor G. Burnard, *Mastery, Tyranny, and Desire: Thomas Thistlewood and His Slaves in the Anglo-Jamaican World* (Chapel Hill, 2004).

Grey Gundaker, *Signs of Diaspora, Diaspora Signs: Literacies, Creolization, and Vernacular Practice in African America* (New York, 1998).

Gwendolyn Midlo Hall, *Africans in Colonial Louisiana: The Development of Afro-Creole Culture in the Eighteenth Century* (Baton Rouge, 1992).

Darlene Clark Hine and Jacqueline McLeod, eds., *Crossing Boundaries: Comparative History of Black People in Diaspora* (Bloomington, Ind., 1999).

Charles Johnson, *Middle Passage* (New York, 1990).

Jane Landers, *Black Society in Spanish Florida* (Urbana, Ill., 1999).

Jennifer L. Morgan, *Laboring Women: Reproduction and Gender in New World Slavery* (Philadelphia, 2004).

Philip D. Morgan, *Slave Counterpoint: Black Culture in the Eighteenth-Century Chesapeake and Lowcountry* (Chapel Hill, 1998).

Caryl Phillips, *Cambridge* (New York, 1992).

Joseph Roach, *Cities of the Dead: Circum-Atlantic Performance* (New York, 1996).

Jon Sensbach, *Rebecca's Revival: Creating Black Christianity in the Atlantic World* (Cambridge, Mass., 2005).

Mechal Sobel, *The World They Made Together: Black and White Values in Eighteenth-Century Virginia* (Princeton, 1987).

Sterling Stuckey, *Slave Culture: Nationalist Theory and the Foundations of Black America* (New York, 1987).

Robert Farris Thompson, *Flash of the Spirit: African and Afro-American Art and Philosophy* (New York, 1983).

John Thornton, *Africa and Africans in the Making of the Atlantic World, 1400–1680,* 2d ed. (New York, 1998).

February 16: European-Indian Interactions

Required Text

Inga Clendinnen, *Ambivalent Conquests: Maya and Spaniard in Yucatan, 1517–1570,* 2d ed. (New York, 2003).

Shared Texts

A: James Axtell, *The Invasion Within: The Contest of Cultures in Colonial North America* (New York, 1985).

B: James Lockhart, *The Nahuas After the Conquest: A Social and Cultural History of the Indians of Central Mexico, Sixteenth through Eighteenth Centuries* (Stanford, 1992).

C: Neal Salisbury, *Manitou and Providence: Indians, Europeans, and the Making of New England, 1500–1643* (New York, 1982).

D: Ian K. Steele, *Warpaths: Invasions of North America* (New York, 1994).

For Further Reading

Eric Hinderaker, *Elusive Empires: Constructing Colonialism in the Ohio Valley, 1673–1800* (New York, 1997).

Francis Jennings, *The Invasion of America: Indians, Colonialism, and the Cant of Conquest* (New York, 1975).

James H. Merrell, "The Indians' New World: The Catawba Experience," *William and Mary Quarterly* 41 (October 1984): 537–65.

Susan Elizabeth Ramírez, *The World Upside Down: Cross-Cultural Contact and Conflict in Sixteenth-Century Peru* (Stanford, 1996).

Daniel K. Richter, *The Ordeal of the Longhouse: The Peoples of the Iroquois League in the Era of European Colonization* (Chapel Hill, 1992).

Daniel K. Richter, *Facing East from Indian Country: A Native History of Early America* (Cambridge, Mass., 2001).

Erik R. Seeman, "Reading Indians' Deathbed Scenes: Ethnohistorical and Representational Approaches," *Journal of American History* 88 (June 2001): 17–47.

Tzvetan Todorov, *The Conquest of America* (New York, 1984).

Richard White, *The Middle Ground: Indians, Empires, and Republics in the Great Lakes Region, 1650–1815* (New York, 1991).

February 23: The Circulation of Ideas

Required Texts

Anthony Grafton, *New Worlds, Ancient Texts: The Power of Tradition and the Shock of Discovery* (Cambridge, Mass., 1992).

Shared Texts

    A: Jorge Cañizares-Esguerra, *How to Write the History of the New World: Histories, Epistemologies, and Identities in the Atlantic World* (Stanford, 2001).

    B: J.H. Elliott, *The Old World and the New, 1492–1650* (Cambridge, Eng., 1970).

    C: Anthony Pagden, *The Fall of Natural Man: The American Indian and the Origins of Comparative Ethnology* (New York, 1982).

    D: Benjamin Schmidt, *Innocence Abroad: The Dutch Imagination and the New World, 1570–1670* (New York, 2001).

For Further Reading

D.A. Brading, *The First America: The Spanish Monarchy, Creole Patriots, and the Liberal State, 1492–1867* (New York, 1991).

Joyce E. Chaplin, *Subject Matter: Technology, the Body, and Science on the Anglo-American Frontier, 1500–1676* (Cambridge, Mass., 2001).

Stephen Greenblatt, *Marvelous Possessions: The Wonder of the New World* (Chicago, 1991).

Karen Ordahl Kupperman, ed., *America in European Consciousness, 1493–1750* (Chapel Hill, 1995).

Walter Mignolo, *The Darker Side of the Renaissance: Literacy, Territoriality, and Colonization* (Ann Arbor, 1995).

Anthony Pagden, *European Encounters with the New World: From Renaissance to Romanticism* (New Haven, 1993).

Anthony Pagden, *Lords of All the Worlds: Ideologies of Empire in Spain, Britain and France c.1500–c.1850* (New Haven, 1995).

Stuart B. Schwartz, ed., *Implicit Understandings: Observing, Reporting, and Reflecting on the Encounters Between Europeans and Other Peoples in the Early Modern Era* (New York, 1994).

March 2: Trade, Economics, Migration

Required Text

David Hancock, *Citizens of the World: London Merchants and the Integration of the British Atlantic Community, 1735–1785* (New York, 1995).

Shared Texts

    A: Aaron Spencer Fogleman, *Hopeful Journeys: German Immigration, Settlement, and Political Culture in Colonial America, 1717–1775* (Philadelphia, 1996).

    B: Alison Games, *Migration and the Origins of the English Atlantic World* (Cambridge, Mass., 1999).

    C: Joseph E. Inikori, *Africans and the Industrial Revolution in England: A Study in International Trade and Economic Development* (New York, 2002).

    D: Sidney W. Mintz, *Sweetness and Power: The Place of Sugar in Modern History* (New York, 1985).

For Further Reading

Bernard Bailyn, *Voyagers to the West: A Passage in the Peopling of America on the Eve of the Revolution* (New York, 1986).

David Birmingham, *Trade and Empire in the Atlantic, 1400–1600* (London, 2000).

David Cressy, *Coming Over: Migration and Communication Between England and New England in the Seventeenth Century* (New York, 1987).

Philip D. Curtin, *The Rise and Fall of the Plantation Complex: Essays in Atlantic History* (Cambridge, 1992).

Denys Delâge, *Bitter Feast: Amerindians and Europeans in Northeastern North America, 1600–64* (Vancouver, 1993).

Patrick Griffin, *The People with No Name: Ireland's Ulster Scots, America's Scots Irish, and the Creation of a British Atlantic World, 1689–1764* (Princeton, 2001).

John J. McCusker, *Essays in the Economic History of the Atlantic World* (London, 1997).

John J. McCusker and Russell R. Menard, *The Economy of British North America, 1607–1789,* 2d ed. (Chapel Hill, 1991).

John J. McCusker and Kenneth Morgan, eds., *The Early Modern Atlantic Economy* (New York, 2000).

March 9: Wars of Independence

Required Text

Laurent Dubois, *Avengers of the New World: The Story of the Haitian Revolution* (Cambridge, Mass., 2004).

Shared Texts

A: Susan Dunn, *Sister Revolutions: French Lightning, American Light* (New York, 2000).

B: Eliga H. Gould, *The Persistence of Empire: British Political Culture in the Age of the American Revolution* (Chapel Hill, 2000).

C: Andrew Jackson O'Shaughnessy, *An Empire Divided: The American Revolution and the British Caribbean* (Philadelphia, 2000).

D: Jaime E. Rodriguez O., *The Independence of Spanish America* (Cambridge University Press, 1998).

For Further Reading

Colin G. Calloway, *The American Revolution in Indian Country: Crisis and Diversity in Native American Communities* (New York, 1995).

Laurent Dubois, *A Colony of Citizens: Revolution and Slave Emancipation in the French Caribbean, 1787–1804* (Chapel Hill, 2004).

David P. Geggus, ed., *The Impact of the Haitian Revolution in the Atlantic World* (Columbia, S.C., 2001).

Eliga H. Gould and Peter S. Onuf, eds., *Empire and Nation: The American Revolution in the Atlantic World* (Baltimore, 2005).

C.L.R. James, *The Black Jacobins: Toussaint L'Ouverture and the San Domingo Revolution,* 2d ed. (New York, 1963).

Lester D. Langley, *The Americas in the Age of Revolution 1750–1850* (New Haven, 1996).

Peter Linebaugh and Marcus Rediker, *The Many-Headed Hydra: Sailors, Slaves, Commoners, and the Hidden History of the Revolutionary Atlantic* (Boston, 2000).

R.R. Palmer, *The Age of the Democratic Revolution: A Political History of Europe and America, 1760–1800,* vol. 1, *The Challenge* (Princeton, 1959).

John K. Thornton, "'I Am the Subject of the King of Congo': African Political Ideology and the Haitian Revolution," *Journal of World History* 4 (1993): 181–214.

March 23: Britain and the Caribbean, Metropole and Empire (Prof. Patrick McDevitt, guest faculty).

Required Text

Catherine Hall, *Civilising Subjects: Metropole and Colony in the English Imagination, 1830–1867* (Chicago, 2002).

Shared Texts

A: Simon Gikandi, *Maps of Englishness: Writing Identity in the Culture of Colonialism* (New York, 1996).

B: Paul Gilroy, *"There Ain't No Black in the Union Jack": The Cultural Politics of Race and Nation* (London, 1987).

C: Laura Tabili, *"We Ask for British Justice": Black Workers and the Construction of Racial Difference in Late Imperial Britain* (Ithaca, 1994).

D: Chris Waters, "'Dark Strangers in Our Midst': The Discourse of Race Relations," *Journal of British Studies* 36 (April 1997): 207–38.

March 30: Abolition

Required Text

Christopher Schmidt-Nowara, *Empire and Antislavery: Spain, Cuba, and Puerto Rico, 1833–1874* (Pittsburgh, 1999).

Shared Texts

A: Robin Blackburn, *The Overthrow of Colonial Slavery, 1776–1848* (London, 1988).

B: David Brion Davis, *The Problem of Slavery in the Age of Revolution, 1770–1823* (Ithaca, 1975).

C: Seymour Drescher, *Capitalism and Antislavery: British Mobilization in Comparative Perspective* (London, 1986).

D: Eric Williams, *Capitalism and Slavery* (Chapel Hill, 1944).

For Further Reading

Leslie Bethell, *The Abolition of the Brazilian Slave Trade* (Cambridge, 1970).

David Brion Davis, *The Problem of Slavery in Western Culture,* 2d ed. (Oxford, 1988).

David Eltis, *Economic Growth and the Ending of the Transatlantic Slave Trade* (New York, 1987).

David Murray, *Odious Commerce: Britain, Spain, and the Abolition of the Cuban Slave Trade* (Cambridge, 1980).

Richard S. Newman, *The Transformation of American Abolitionism: Fighting Slavery in the Early Republic* (Chapel Hill, 2002).

Howard Temperley, *British Antislavery, 1833–1870* (London, 1972).

April 6: Comparative Post-Emancipation

Required Texts

Frederick Cooper, Thomas C. Holt, and Rebecca J. Scott, *Beyond Slavery: Explorations of Race, Labor, and Citizenship in Postemancipation Societies* (Chapel Hill, 2000).

Leslie A. Schwalm, "'In Their Own Way': Women and Work in the Postbellum South," in *A Hard Fight for We: Women's Transition from Slavery to Freedom in South Carolina* (Urbana, 1997), 187–233.

Shared Texts

A: Eric Foner, *Nothing But Freedom: Emancipation and Its Legacy* (Baton Rouge, 1983).

B: Thomas C. Holt, *The Problem of Freedom: Race, Labor, and Politics in Jamaica and Britain, 1832–1938* (Baltimore, 1992).

C: Rebecca J. Scott, *The Abolition of Slavery and the Aftermath of Emancipation in Brazil* (Durham, N.C., 1988).

D: Rebecca J. Scott, *Slave Emancipation in Cuba: The Transition to Free Labor, 1860–1899* (Princeton, 1985).

For Further Reading

Kathleen Mary Butler, *The Economics of Emancipation: Jamaica and Barbados, 1823–1843* (Chapel Hill, 1995)

Kim D. Butler, *Freedoms Given, Freedoms Won: Afro-Brazilians in Post-Abolition São Paulo and Salvador* (New Brunswick, N.J., 1998).

Barbara Jeanne Fields, *Slavery and Freedom on the Middle Ground: Maryland During the Nineteenth Century* (New Haven, 1985).

Eric Foner, *A Short History of Reconstruction, 1863–1877* (New York, 1990).

W.A. Green, *British Slave Emancipation: The Sugar Colonies and the Great Experiment, 1830–1865* (Oxford, 1976).

Leon F. Litwack, *Been in the Storm So Long: The Aftermath of Slavery* (New York, 1979).

Julie Saville, *The Work of Reconstruction: From Slave to Wage Laborer in South Carolina, 1860–1870* (New York, 1994).

Amy Dru Stanley, *From Bondage to Contract: Wage Labor, Marriage, and the Market in the Age of Slave Emancipation* (New York, 1998).

April 13: Transatlantic Transfer in the 19th and 20th Centuries (Prof. Dorothee Brantz, guest faculty)

Required Text

Daniel R. Rodgers, *Atlantic Crossings: Social Politics in a Progressive Age* (Cambridge, Mass., 1998), read all, but focus on the prologue and chs. 2, 3, and 9.

Shared Texts

A: Arnold Lewis, *An Early Encounter with Tomorrow: Europeans, Chicago's Loop, and the World's Columbian Exposition* (Urbana, 1997).

B: Jacques Portes, *Fascination and Misgivings: The United States in French Opinion, 1870–1914* (New York, 2000).

C: William W. Stowe, *Going Abroad: European Travel in Nineteenth-Century American Culture* (Princeton, 1994).

D: Frank Trommler and Elliott Shore, eds., *The German-American Encounter: Conflict and Cooperation Between Two Cultures, 1800–2000* (New York, 2001).

For Further Reading

Frank Costigliola, *Awkward Dominion: American Political, Economic, and Cultural Relations with Europe, 1919–1933* (Ithaca, 1984).

Stefan Kühl, *The Nazi Connection: Eugenics, American Racism, and German National Socialism* (New York, 1994).

Charles S. Maier, "Between Taylorism and Technocracy: European Ideologies and the Vision of Industrial Productivity in the 1920s," *Journal of Contemporary History* 2 (1970): 27–61.

Kiran Klaus Patel, "The Power of Perception: The Impact of Nazi Social Policy on the New Deal," in *Americanization, Globalization, Education,* ed. Gerhard Bach, Sabine Bröck-Sallah, and Ulf Schulenberg (Heidelberg, 2003), 97–112.

Anthony Sutcliffe, *Towards the Planned City: Germany, Britain, the United States, and France, 1780–1914* (New York, 1981).

April 20: No class—work on final papers

April 27: America and Europe in the 20th Century (Prof. Andreas Daum, guest faculty)

Required Texts

Victoria de Grazia, *Irresistible Empire: America's Advance Through Twentieth-Century Europe* (Cambridge, Mass., 2005).

"Introduction: Americanization Reconsidered," in *Transactions, Transgressions, Transformations: American Culture in Western Europe and Japan,* ed. Heide Fehrenbach and Uta G. Poiger (New York, 2000), xiii–xl.

Shared Texts

A: Volker R. Berghahn, *America and the Intellectual Cold Wars in Europe: Shepard Stone Between Philanthropy, Academy, and Diplomacy* (Princeton, 2001).

B: Richard F. Kuisel, *Seducing the French: The Dilemma of Americanization* (Berkeley, 1993).

C: Uta Poiger, *Jazz, Rock, and Rebels: Cold War Politics and American Culture in a Divided Germany* (Berkeley, 2000).

D: Thomas Risse-Kappen, *Cooperation Among Democracies: The European Influence on U.S. Foreign Policy* (Princeton, 1995).

For Further Reading

Philipp Gassert, "Atlantic Alliances: Cross-Cultural Communication and the 1960s Student Revolution," in *Culture and International History,* ed. Jessica C.E. Gienow-Hecht and Frank Schumacher (New York, 2003), 135–56.

Petra Goedde, *GIs and Germans: Culture, Gender and Foreign Relations, 1945–1949* (New Haven, 2003).

Ian C. Jarvie, *Hollywood's Overseas Campaign: The North Atlantic Movie Trade, 1920–1950* (New York, 1992).

Geir Lundestad, *'Empire' by Integration: The United States and European Integration, 1956–1997* (Oxford, 1998).

Mary Nolan, *Visions of Modernity: American Business and the Modernization of Germany* (New York, 1994).

Richard Pells, *Not Like Us: How Europeans Have Loved, Hated, and Transformed American Culture Since World War II* (New York, 1997).

Reinhold Wagnleitner, *Coca-Colonization and the Cold War: The Cultural Mission of the United States in Austria After the Second World War* (Chapel Hill, 1994).

CHAPTER 22

Teaching Comparative United States and South Africa Race Relations

DEREK CATSAM

Robert Kennedy in South Africa: An Introduction

On June 6, 1966, after much diplomatic wrangling and a good deal of gnashing of teeth on the part of South Africa's apartheid leadership, Robert Kennedy gave a speech at the University of Cape Town. In recent years the former Attorney General had made a transformation from ardent Cold Warrior to staunch defender of human rights. The man who had once done his best to forestall civil rights advances by asking the Freedom Riders to engage in a "cooling off period" had within a few years become a crusader for racial and economic justice both at home and abroad. The speech was part of a larger visit to the country that had been opposed by most white South Africans and not a small number of Americans.

The National Union of South African Students (NUSAS) had invited Kennedy to give the Day of Affirmation address on a chilly winter day at the university that had come to be known as "Moscow on the Hill" because of the left-liberal politics that pervaded campus, much to the displeasure and discomfort of some of the most powerful men (and they were overwhelmingly men, with their positions in the *Broederbond* and seats in parliament) in South Africa. Fifteen thousand people gathered to hear Kennedy's words.

Many of these gathered around the outside of the packed auditorium, hoping to hear the speech on loudspeakers set up to deal with the expected overflow. Members of the security forces sabotaged this plan by snipping the speaker wires. His speech, like his visit as a whole, was electrifying for many South Africans, frightening for some, and representative of a man and politician who in five short years had transformed himself remarkably.[1]

Kennedy's visit to South Africa is significant for a number of reasons, and it is worthy of a study all its own.[2] But one aspect that is easy to overlook is the explicit comparisons between the United States and South Africa that Kennedy evoked. These comparisons were intended mostly to draw in his audience, and Kennedy's main concerns were the links between America's policies and South Africa's increasingly isolated regime as well as the nature of that regime on its own terms. But his opening remarks are worth considering:

> I come here this evening because of my deep interest and affection for a land settled by the Dutch in the mid-seventeenth century, then taken over by the British, and at last independent; a land in which the native inhabitants were at first subdued, but relations with whom remain a problem to this day; a land which defined itself on a hostile frontier; a land which has tamed rich natural resources through the energetic application of modern technology; a land which was once the importer of slaves, and now must struggle to wipe out the last traces of that former bondage. I refer, of course, to the United States of America.[3]

One imagines that this little intellectual sleight of hand went over well among an audience that was accustomed at least by reputation to the legendary Kennedy family wit. This introduction was sly, ironic, unexpected, and yet spoke larger truths: the United States and South Africa share a great deal in common, despite the transoms of time, space, history, geography, politics, and culture that separate them. That Robert Kennedy was able to capture the intriguing linkages between Apartheid South Africa and an America still coming to grips with its own racial realities has not of course

From Derek Catsam, "Brave New World: Teaching Comparative United States and South Africa Race Relations," *Safundi: The Journal of South African and American Comparative Studies,* no. 16 (October 2004). Reprinted by permission of the publisher Taylor & Francis Ltd.

been lost on historians—this journal exists for just such a purpose. For a quarter century or so, since the publication of the keystone works by John D. Cell and George Fredrickson, scholars, however tentatively, however suggestively, have been working on developing a scholarly, intellectual, and narrative framework through which to compare the histories of two nation states that on matters racial have not lived up to their creed. Far less common have been efforts to bring these comparisons into the classroom.

The reasons for this are obvious, but nonetheless worth reiterating: students have a difficult time with comparison; most do not even know much about civil rights in the United States, never mind South Africa; works written accessibly enough for undergraduates can be hard to find; there are not a whole lot of professors who can teach such a class; some departments might look askance at such an effort, especially where department politics have created fiefdoms in which an Africanist might not be comfortable with someone they perceive as an Americanist encroaching on their turf, and vice versa; and, perhaps most important, for student and teacher alike, such a course is simply not very easy.

As uncomfortable as I am both using the first person and telling others how to teach—I am generally not patient with those who come bearing pedagogical theory or methodological advice—I have taught a course on comparative race relations in the United States and South Africa in the past to undergraduates, and at my new institution I will be reshaping the course into a graduate seminar. The positive response the course received from my students in the past, and the fact that I do not stake any claims that there is a right or wrong way to teach anything, never mind something so complex and exciting as comparative history, coupled with the fact that I research, write, and publish in both the United States and South Africa, have driven me to write this essay, which includes a copy of a syllabus that is in the midst of being reshaped but that will share the same contours as its predecessor.

The Syllabus

Here is a sample, truncated copy of a syllabus based on one I have used in the past (and which will look a good deal like the one I plan to use in the future):

Civil Rights in the United States and South Africa

Syllabus—Fall 2003

Required Textbooks

C. Vann Woodward, *The Strange Career of Jim Crow*
Steven F. Lawson and Charles Payne, *Debating the Civil Rights Movement*
Nigel Worden, *The Making of Modern South Africa*

Lewis Baldwin, *Toward the Beloved Community*
Francis Njubi Nesbitt, *Race for Sanctions*
George Fredrickson, *The Comparative Imagination*

Overview of the Course

W.E.B. DuBois asserted in 1903 that the "problem of the Twentieth Century" is "the problem of the color line." In his most famous work the sociologist Gunnar Myrdal labeled race the "American Dilemma." The struggle for racial justice has arguably been the preeminent domestic story in American history, particularly in the twentieth century and especially the quarter century or more after World War II. The same can surely be said for South Africa. In this course we will examine the black struggles for civil rights, broadly defined, from the late 1880s and focusing in particular on the decades after 1945 in both the United States and South Africa. We will explore how Americans of African descent and the majority of South Africans fought against the onerous restrictions of white supremacy and how they mobilized to assert their fundamental rights. We will also examine white resistance to civil rights, political mobilization for and against racial justice, and we will get to know many of the individuals and events on both sides of the color line that has so defined and stratified the people of these two troubled countries. Finally, we will spend a great deal of time drawing comparisons between the Jim Crow South and Apartheid South Africa in hopes of developing an understanding of how Jim Crow and apartheid could have endured for so long and what it took to make them fall.

Course Schedule

Week One (August 25–27):
Reading: Woodward v–xvii, 221–232, 3–10.
Week Two (September 1–3):
Reading: Woodward, 11–147. Fredrickson, 1–19.
Week Three (September 8–10):
Reading: Woodward, 149–220. Fredrickson, 23–36.
First Paper Due: September 10 in class.
Week Four (September 15–17):
Reading: Lawson & Payne, 3–149. Fredrickson, 37–46.
Week Five (September 22–24):
Reading: TBA
Second Paper Due: September 24, in class.
Week Six (September 29–October 1):
Reading: Worden, vii–xi, 1–73. Fredrickson, 77–97.
Week Seven (October 6–8):
Reading: Worden, 74–169. Fredrickson, 117–131.
Third Paper Due October 8, in class.
Week Eight (October 13–15):
Reading: Baldwin, 1–92. Fredrickson, 135–148.
Week Nine (October 20–22):

Reading: Baldwin, 93–185. Fredrickson, 149–172.
Fourth Paper Due October 22, in class.
Week Ten (October 27–29):
Reading: Nesbitt, vii–56. Fredrickson, 173–188.
Week Eleven (November 3–5):
Reading: Nesbitt, 57–96. Fredrickson, 189–212.
Week Twelve (November 10–12):
Reading: Nesbitt, 97–172.
Fifth Paper Due November 12, in class.
Week Thirteen (November 17–19):
Reading: TBA.
Week Fourteen (November 24–26):
Reading: None. Have a Great Thanksgiving Break!
Week Fifteen (December 1–3):
Reading: Class presentations.
Final project: There will be a final paper in this class with details to be announced.

The Rationale

In putting together a good course, content is (or at least should be) the *sine qua non* of the whole endeavor. Many people will not or do not acknowledge it, but some students do not just take history because they need to, but also because they are genuinely interested in it. This is particularly so in a course on South Africa and the United States. They think it sounds like a pretty cool idea, and they are right. But most professors teach at places where we would feel lucky if our students had a firm grounding in either the Civil Rights Movement or the apartheid era. In most cases, we will find that they are sketchy on both, if they are conversant with either at all. This raises more than a bit of a dilemma for the professor whose first goal is to engage students in content. The most logical way to address this is through the selection of readings, which for most of us is the foundation of every course that we teach. When introducing students to the new concepts of comparative history, the first steps nonetheless are not comparative. To ensure that students have the rudiments, I choose readable basic books that will give them some foundation for understanding the histories of the two countries in question.

Woodward's classic may be in many ways dated, but it introduces students to the history of the Jim Crow South and exposes them to a classic in the field. These are both good things, and Woodward dates a whole lot better than most historians. Lawson and Payne's book, which is part of a nice little Rowman and Littlefield series, "Debating 20th Century America," brings students up to speed on contemporary debates about civil rights historiography, and begins to get them thinking critically about this material.

On the South African side, I have considered a number of possibilities, including William Beinart's book on twentieth century South Africa. My preference would generally be for Alister Sparks' *The Mind of South Africa* for its general readability, but it is out of print. I have used Worden's book with some success, but this is a space on the syllabus that is far from set. For a more advanced group, or for graduate students, I might well use Dan O'Meara's flawed but vital *Forty Lost Years,* and I have entertained adding one of the books on the "New South Africa," depending again on the caliber of students in the course.

It is from here that we enter the realm of comparison, albeit from a pretty broadly defined parameter that many might accuse of being American-centric. I am sensitive to this criticism. But I am teaching American students with a limited background on Africa. The easiest way for them to grasp this material and to make the necessary comparisons is to do so through the lens of what they should know best, which is the American context. To demand more of them in an already challenging course seems to be unfair to them simply to placate a criticism that may be fair from a scholarly vantage point, but not especially legitimate when we are trying to excite and challenge students. The first book I use is Lewis Baldwin's book on Martin Luther King and his influence on South Africa, *Toward the Beloved Community.* In addition to giving them an inroad by a figure with whom they are already familiar, it makes comparisons that they can begin to connect based on their other readings, on our discussions, and on my lectures, which pepper the class, especially in the first few weeks. Nesbitt's book is a new addition which allows the students to think about connections between South Africa and the United States, and also to think about the ways in which understanding foreign policy and diplomacy, as well as protest movements, requires a comparative framework. The sanctions debate requires them to synthesize a great deal of what they have encountered before it, and helps to culminate the class.

Tying all of this together is George Fredrickson's elegant collection of essays, *The Comparative Imagination.* One of our foremost historians, Fredrickson has become the doyen of comparative South African–United States scholarship, with two profoundly important books and many essays, most of which are gathered in this collection. I pepper the class with essays, some of which work, some of which flop, but all of which work toward getting students to think comparatively. Further, the brightest students will take to Fredrickson, and they will use his ideas to push the class forward even if many of their peers struggle with ideas that most of us who write in these areas find humbling. By the halfway point of the term the course changes from one in which the students face an even mix of lectures on the various contexts and pretty tightly focused discussions, to discussions that are more student centered, by which I mean, the burden shifts to them to carry the ideas, to determine our direction. I'll nudge them as necessary, and I keep the discussion going, but as we progress they find that they have ideas that have begun to percolate, and if things are working out well, the class has become theirs by the time most survey classes are taking their midterms.

Assignments in the class come in the form of five four-to-five-page papers plus a final project that usually involves synthetic work of eight to ten pages. The shorter papers focus primarily on ideas from the reading. My tendency is to keep the paper topics as broad as possible, but to give them direction, especially early in the semester, while still giving them room to see what they can concoct. They sometimes surprise themselves. They often surprise me—and usually for the better. The longer papers are trickier, which is why they tend to be shorter than what I might ask from an upper level seminar class in a different topic in which I'd assign a more traditional twelve- to fifteen-page paper or other research assignment. But again, many of them usually rise to the challenge, which is exciting and gratifying.

Marching Toward Freedom: Conclusion

In his Cape Town speech, Robert Kennedy spoke of problems overcome and those that remained in the United States and linked them to those that continued to prevail elsewhere. "We recognize," he argued, "that there are problems and obstacles before the fulfillment of . . . ideals in the United States as we recognize that other nations, in Latin America and in Asia and in Africa have their own political, economic, and social problems, their unique barriers to the elimination of injustices."[4] One can debate whether or not as historians and teachers it is our job to try to instill a sense of a usable past in our students. However, whether we try to do so or not we certainly can and should show how across transoms of time and space different peoples and different nation-states have both built and confronted barriers. We must seek points of confluence in our pasts. But as Robert Kennedy noted, we also must be willing to acknowledge difference, to recognize that even where we see analogies and points of comparison we must accept disjunction and points of contrast:

All do not develop in the same manner and at the same pace. Nations, like men, often march to the beat of different drummers, and the precise solutions of the United States can neither be dictated nor transplanted to others, and that is not our intention. What is important, however, is that all nations must march toward increasing freedom; toward justice for all; toward a society strong and flexible enough to meet the demands of all of its people, whatever their race, and the demands of a world of immense and dizzying change[s] that face us all.[5]

The world our students confront is no less dizzying even if it may seem slightly less immense than in Robert Kennedy's time. In a comparative history course, we can teach them commonality, but we can also help them to appreciate and respect difference. We can blow up myths of exceptionalism while still revealing to them the exceptional, and we can help them understand the United States while also shedding light on at least one other part of the rest of the world. All in all, not a bad way to spend a semester.

Notes

1. On the Kennedy speech see Arthur Schlesinger, *Robert Kennedy and His Times* (Boston: Houghton Mifflin, 1978), pp. 743–750, and Evan Thomas, *Robert Kennedy: His Life* (New York: Touchstone, 2000), pp. 320–323.

2. Larry Shore, guest editor of this special pedagogy issue, has in fact assembled an impressive collection of archives—photographs, transcripts, political cartoons, and video and audio recordings—detailing Kennedy's activities in South Africa in 1966. See Larry Shore, "Ripple of Hope in the Land of Apartheid: Robert F. Kennedy in South Africa, June 4th–9th, 1966," *Safundi: The Journal of South African and American Comparative Studies* 9 (May 2002).

3. Senator Robert F. Kennedy, "Day of Affirmation Address," University of Cape Town, Cape Town, South Africa, June 6, 1966. There are two versions of this address—the text as delivered and the news release copy. Both are available in Robert Kennedy's papers at the JFK Library in Boston, but they are also accessible through the library's website. I have used the text as delivered, which is available at http://www.jfklibrary.org/r060666a.htm.

4. Ibid.

5. Ibid.

CHAPTER 23

Internationalizing Three Topics in the U.S. History Survey Course

THOMAS J. OSBORNE

Across the spectrum of academic disciplines, history is one of the few to be organized largely on the basis of the nation-state. With a few notable exceptions, only since the 1960s have American historians begun to see the limitations that this nation-bounded approach has imposed on our field. Since then a movement to internationalize the study and teaching of United States history, by de-provincializing and recentering the field, has been gaining momentum.[1] Significantly, this movement is not aimed at supplanting the nation-state as a major unit of historical inquiry; rather it aims at supplementing that unit of inquiry with others that are smaller or larger spatially, which in some cases requires enlarging temporal parameters as well. The Organization of American Historians has been playing a leading role in this movement, in part by its involvement in the recently completed La Pietra Project.[2] Drawing on the work and results of that Project, this article offers history instructors three examples, each of which relates to a specific episode in America's past, of how we can internationalize our college-level United States history survey courses. . . .

The *La Pietra Report,* after laying out the reasons for reconceptualizing American history along global, comparative lines, addresses the issues and challenges involved in restructuring the history curricula at both the undergraduate and graduate levels. Most importantly for purposes of this article, the Report specifically addresses "The U.S. History Survey Course," stating: "The United States history survey course is properly a focal point for the creation of an internationalized American history. If in the survey course one embraces the simple advice to follow the people, the money, the knowledges [ideas and information], and the things, one would quite easily—on the basis of pure empiricism—find

oneself internationalizing the study of American history. One might reasonably anticipate that constructing and teaching such survey courses would stimulate new research and interpretations, as has happened with world history."[3] In the remainder of this essay, I will apply the statement just quoted to three topics ordinarily covered in our United States history survey courses, showing and suggesting how an internationalized treatment of the subject matter might work. In each instance, I followed the people, the money, and the ideas. I picked topical areas that lend themselves fairly easily to transnational coverage and recommend that those just starting down this road do likewise. Here I will look at the American Revolution, Romanticism and Reform in the Antebellum Era, and American Imperialism in the 1890s. My comments are based on my teaching and on work that I am doing in conjunction with three other historians on a college-level survey textbook that situates American history in a global context.

Internationalizing United States History: My Method

In both my teaching and writing I have developed a method for internationalizing my American history survey courses, an endeavor that is still in progress. With variations, I follow four basic steps for each topic that I am internationalizing. First, I prepare and distribute global and national chronologies for the topic about to be covered. Second, I usually open each new topic with a vignette that lifts the subject matter out of its traditional context and situates it in a broader, spatially and temporally expanded, international framework. Third, I search out links or connections between

From Thomas Osborne, "Implementing the *La Pietra Report:* Internationalizing Three Topics in the U.S. History Survey Course," *The History Teacher* 36, no. 2 (Feb. 2003): 163–176. © Society for History Education. Reprinted by permission.

happenings in the United States and developments—sometimes parallels—beyond America's borders. Fourth, when bringing my material on a given theme to a close, I consider the question of American exceptionalism by exploring historical features that may be unique or merely distinctive, defining, or unusual regarding the United States.

The term "exceptionalism" requires a brief explanation.[4] I use it in the sense that a given feature of American history is unique only in some limited and specific way because I cannot imagine using the term to suggest that our nation somehow stands outside the sweep of global history, exempt from its encounters and tribulations. From its inception, America has been connected to the international milieu, be it the continent it straddles, the Caribbean Basin, or the Atlantic and Pacific worlds. In short, exceptionalism should be viewed within the larger context of international connections in order to avoid enshrining United States history in narratives remarkable only for their provincialism. So viewed, I employ the term "exceptionalism" to mean unique or virtually one of a kind, but (again) only in a limited, and appropriately nuanced sense. To communicate the idea of important though lesser degrees of difference than exceptionalism implies, I utilize such terms as "distinctive," "defining," or "unusual." As a result of interrogating exceptionalism in this fashion, students gain a clearer understanding of how the United States is both similar to and different from other nations. Only against such a backdrop of connections and comparisons can students gauge the meaning of episodes and developments in America's past.

Applying this or virtually any other methodology to internationalize our United States history survey courses raises the issue of what gets left out of our course in order to make room for the new transnational coverage. However, new course content and perspectives have been a perennial challenge for history teachers, especially since the 1960s when gender and multicultural considerations and, more recently, environmental issues began to be factored into survey textbooks. They have managed somehow, and when our survey textbooks are sufficiently internationalized the problem of what classroom material to retain and what to discard will be greatly minimized, particularly for those instructors who adhere closely to the textbook. Until then, teachers will be on their own to determine how far and how fast to internationalize their courses. While awaiting the publication of more fully internationalized survey textbooks, teachers might want to consider using an abridged textbook, which allows for adding new internationalized content to lectures and handouts without putting the students on information overload, and possibly assigning a supplemental internationalized reader. Two such readers, both of which are useful, are Carl J. Guarneri's two-volume edited work, *America Compared: American History in International Perspective* (1997), and Gerald M. Greenfield and

John D. Buenker's two-volume edited work, *Those United States: International Perspectives on American History* (2000). Guarneri's reader features secondary accounts written by current scholars, while Greenfield and Buenker's reader is comprised of primary documents. Brief and incisive essays written by the editors introduce the chapters in both of these works.

The American Revolution

This is the first example I offer showing how to implement the recommendations of the *La Pietra Report* in a college-level survey course in United States history. Because the global and national chronologies noted as my first step seem self-explanatory, I will not discuss them further, and will instead devote the remainder of this article to the other steps already mentioned. I turn to the second step, the International Framework. After first covering the background causes of the American Revolution, I mention the "shot heard round the world" in mid-April 1775, near the Concord Bridge, noting the tactics and heroism of the Minutemen. This event, I add, is seen by many as the defining one during the opening stages of the American Revolution. But a more determinative event, I assure classes, took place a year later in Paris, where a fictitious trading firm—Roderigue Hortalez and Company—began the illegal funneling of arms to the American rebels. In fact, without French arms (France supplied ninety percent of the gunpowder used by Continental troops in the first two years of the war), money, and troops and Dutch loans along with Spanish military aid, the Revolution most likely would not have begun successfully.[5] The French weapons and munitions were shipped across the Atlantic to Portsmouth, New Hampshire, from where they were transported inland to the forces of American General Horatio Gates. This foreign aid was far more critical, I tell students, than the heroics portrayed in the recent movie "The Patriot," starring Mel Gibson, who plays a Rambo-like one-man-army guerrilla commando. In fact, that movie simply perpetuates the self-aggrandizing and provincial view that the Revolution was won primarily, if not solely, by the courageous exploits of highly individualistic American militia leaders. So following the flow of armaments and money from Europe to the American colonies in an opening vignette easily situates the American Revolution in an international framework.

For the next step, Connections to Developments Beyond America's Borders, I can point to numerous links between the American Revolution and the wider world. Besides the indispensable foreign aid that has just been noted, I can show how the Declaration of Independence was translated and viewed in Europe, and/or treat 1776 as the harbinger of "the age of democratic revolution" that extended from the last quarter of the eighteenth century through the first half of the nineteenth century.

Students in my classes have been interested in how the various European countries translated and responded to the Declaration of Independence. Borrowing heavily from the March 1999 issue of the *Journal of American History* (particularly articles by Willi Paul Adams and other foreign scholars), I prepared a handout on this matter for students. For example, I note that French translations of Jefferson's "pursuit of happiness" stressed a more precise social right to a life of modest comfort and health. French translations replaced "happiness" (*bonheur*) with "well-being" (*bienêtre*).[6] This rendering of the Declaration de-emphasizes the role of individual effort in the expectation of enjoying a materially based contentment. (Having conducted a comparative study of several modern European social welfare systems in 1996 under a travel grant from the State Chancellor's Office, I tell my students that this French interpretation of "pursuit of happiness" accords with the premises on which France's current social welfare system is based.) This use of translated documents illustrates how, in accordance with the *La Pietra Report*'s recommendations, we can internationalize our courses by following the flow of ideas across national borders.

Additionally, students in my survey courses consider 1776 as a harbinger of "the age of democratic revolution," comparing and contrasting the American Revolution with other upheavals of the late eighteenth and early nineteenth centuries. In doing so, students trace the diffusion of revolutionary ideas throughout the Western World. While intellectuals in France saw in the American Revolution the embodiment of their own radical creed, they often failed to see major differences between the cataclysms of 1776 and 1789. For example, the French sought a total break with their past and opted to experiment in a wholesale fashion with republican governance. The Americans, on the other hand, I tell students, remained intent on preserving many aspects of their English heritage and pursued republicanism with greater caution and moderation than did the French. Also, while the French attached great value to public order and cohesion, Americans stressed individual freedom.[7] This difference in values goes far, I explain to classes, toward helping us understand why even today the French champion social solidarity (as evidenced in the nationwide strike of 1996), while Americans are much less apt to think and act collectively (a partial explanation for the defeat of former President Bill Clinton's health care plan).

The revolution in Saint Domingue (today's Haiti) in 1791 affords another connective link between 1776 and the wider world. Like Britain's Thirteen Colonies, Saint Domingue waged a war for independence against a European imperial power (in this case France), espousing ideals of freedom and equality that were prominent in both the American and French Revolutions. Yet only the Haitians were successful in ending slavery in their revolution.[8] One of the many ironies regarding Thomas Jefferson that I share with

students is embedded in a letter that he wrote to his friend James Madison in 1799, expressing alarm that the freeing of blacks in Saint Domingue could ignite an international slave rebellion. "If this combustion can be introduced among us [Southern slave owners] under any veil whatever, we have to fear it."[9] That the author of the Declaration of Independence should have penned those words invariably leads to a lively discussion in my classes about how revolutionary Jefferson was, and how America's planter aristocracy interpreted the Declaration's claim that "all men are created equal." In this case the Haitian revolutionaries provide my students with an international standard for gauging the disparities between the Declaration's revolutionary credo and the reality of human bondage throughout the American South in the late eighteenth century. To present a balanced view, I also tell students that though the revolution in Saint Domingue abolished slavery, it brought to power the dictator Toussaint L'Ouverture.

Next I consider American exceptionalism. After noting similarities between the American Revolution and other "democratic" revolutions of the time, I discuss with students the exceptionalistic view of Seymour Martin Lipset that 1776 marked the first major successful anti-colonial war in modern world history.[10] The resulting ascendancy of the civilian over the military branch of government in the aftermath, I note, was a distinctive and perhaps exceptional feature of the American Revolution. Moreover, our Revolution was distinctive, I point out, in that proportionately it led to the highest level of emigration following it among all of the upheavals of the period. For example, the American Revolution produced over six times as many émigrés per 1000 of population as in France after the Revolution of 1789.[11] The migration of 80,000 or more Loyalists to Canada, the West Indies, and Europe points students to an important international consequence of the American Revolution. So here is another instance of where simply following the flow of people, as the *La Pietra Report* urged, facilitates the internationalization of the subject matter.

Romanticism and Reform in Antebellum America

In introducing the International Framework in my second example, I do not begin with the standard textbook account of how New England Transcendentalists, influenced by European "Romantics," undertook the establishment of an American literary tradition. Rather, I start with a vignette about Margaret Fuller's extensive travels in Europe between 1846 and 1850. I note how, serving as a correspondent for the New York *Tribune,* Fuller went down into a coalmine in Newcastle, England, to observe the dismal working conditions of laborers. She was further appalled by the abject poverty she encountered in Glasgow, Liverpool, London, and Paris. The plight of poor women disturbed her most. In one of numerous letters she wrote to the New

York *Tribune,* Fuller said: "I saw here in Glasgow persons, especially women, dressed in dirty, wretched tatters, worse than none, and with an expression of listless, unexpecting woe upon their faces."[12] As a result of this and other similar experiences abroad, Fuller, a feminist before departing for Europe, moved more and more toward being an outspoken paladin for women. I relate her meetings with Quakers and socialists, as well as her sexual awakening and political radicalization—in short, how her life was changed and her writing empowered by gritty and poignant experiences in a wider world. Fuller's odyssey, in effect, becomes my class's window into the Euro-American social ferment that infused reform movements in the United States during the second quarter of the nineteenth century.

In exploring Connections to Developments Beyond America's Borders regarding American Transcendentalism, I show how Ralph Waldo Emerson, Henry David Thoreau, and others were influenced by Plato's idealism as well as by ideas found in Hindu texts such as the Bhagavad-Gita, Immanuel Kant's stress on intuition and universal ethics (Categorical Imperative), Samuel Taylor Coleridge's distinction between "reason" and "understanding," and Emanuel Swedenborg's mysticism.[13] Similarly, a handout I share with students notes how New Englander Albert Brisbane studied in Paris under utopian socialist Charles Fourier and afterward persuaded George Ripley to adopt the new form of political economy at Brook Farm, which, in turn, was visited by a number of European reformers, including Scottish manufacturer Robert Owen.[14] Also, I mention Frances Wright's utopian socialist venture in Nashoba, Tennessee, where the fiery Scotswoman also embarked on efforts to end slavery and advance the causes of interracial marriage and women's liberation.

In addition to Fuller and Brisbane, a number of other American writers also traveled to Europe for artistic inspiration and insight. Emerson, an oracle of Transcendentalism, traveled to Europe in 1832–33, meeting and befriending writers Thomas Carlyle, William Wordsworth, and Samuel Taylor Coleridge, all three of whom dazzled Emerson with their discourses on German idealism.[15] Similarly, I tell students, Nathaniel Hawthorne spent several years in the early 1850s in Liverpool, England, serving as American consul, after which he lived in Italy for two more years gathering experiences that would become grist for his *Passages from the French and Italian Notebooks* (1871) and other writings. In Florence he was an occasional guest at the palazzo of English poets Robert and Elizabeth Browning.[16] These transatlantic interactions in which American intellectuals were influenced by the ideas of leading thinkers in Europe help students see United States history in a broader spatial and thematic context. Again, following the flow of people and ideas enables us as instructors to more easily internationalize course content.

In looking for American exceptionalism with respect to this topic, I point out that throughout the antebellum period a number of American characteristics stand out and in a few instances could be considered exceptional, as some European visitors and commentators testified. First, individualism was far more pervasive in the United States than anywhere else in the world and for that reason could be considered exceptional. The writings of Thoreau, Emerson, Melville, and Whitman along with the opinions of numerous Europeans attested to the power of the solitary American directing his own fate. Second, religiosity seemed much stronger in the United States than elsewhere, noted Alexis de Tocqueville. Third, and related to the religiosity, Americans moralized in public discourse—often invoking Biblical language—to a far greater extent than people in other countries. Fourth, Americans were unusual and possibly singular in their propensity for "voluntary association," as is seen in the abolitionist, peace, temperance, and other movements for societal reform in the antebellum period. Fifth, Thoreau's philosophy of nonviolent resistance to unjust laws and governments constituted a highly original and arguably exceptional contribution to global politics.

American Imperialism in the 1890s

For the International Framework for this topic, the World's Fair held in Omaha in the summer of 1898 has served as a broad backdrop.[17] Among the numerous international exhibits at this fair was a Chinese Village, organized by a Chicago merchant and an agent of the Union Pacific Railroad. The aim of that exhibit was to excite the public's imagination about the fabled markets of China and entice prospective investors into the trade with Asia and the Pacific. The Chinese market seemed critical in 1898, I explain to students, as government and business leaders feared a relapse into economic depression if America's surplus manufactures were not marketed in Asia. Coaling stations and naval bases in the Pacific and Caribbean, along with a canal across the isthmus of Central America, were thought necessary to tap that trade.[18] While America's Pacific commerce was promoted at the exposition, crowds were also drawn to the usual complement of exotic displays. For example, at the Philippine Village fairgoers were treated to the spectacle of Filipino warriors, some of whom reportedly had "cannibalistic proclivities."[19] In this case, instead of taking my students to some foreign locale to stage the opening scenes of American imperialism, the World's Fair brought foreign locales to the United States, providing a useful international venue for introducing the subject of overseas empire.

In accordance with the *La Pietra Report,* I show my students Connections to Developments Beyond America's Borders in the case of American imperialism in the 1890s by tracing the flow of people and ideas back and forth between the United States and nations in the Pacific and Asia. For example, I treat the New England Congregational missionaries who began arriving in Hawai'i in 1820 and their more business-minded descendants as agents of American empire because most of them strongly supported annexation to the United States. In fact, these transplanted Americans in Hawai'i overthrew the monarchy in 1893 with help from United States Marines for the purpose, in part, of handing over the archipelago to Uncle Sam.[20] Similarly, American ties to China were strengthened by missionaries and particularly by Department of State Sinologist W.W. Rockhill. Fluent in Mandarin and Tibetan (and French as well), Rockhill traveled extensively throughout China and other parts of Asia with guides in the latter half of the nineteenth century. Later he was instrumental in the drafting of the Open Door Notes of 1899 and 1900.[21] So America's global reach at the turn-of-the-century is explained, in part, by its people's connections or ties to distant lands. Following those connections during the decades leading up to the 1890s, as has been shown, helps internationalize the imperial episode.

Did American imperialism show American exceptionalism? The United States was unusual, I emphasize in class, in the sense that it was the most reluctant of the Great Powers to acquire an overseas empire. This reluctance was due in part to the anti-imperialist ideology on which the country was founded. Significantly, no other imperial nation in the late nineteenth century had to confront an anti-imperialist movement as determined as the one launched in the United States, which was comprised of former presidents, heads of universities, labor leaders, and eminent intellectuals and publicists.[22] (Interestingly, a transnational, comparative study of late nineteenth century anti-imperialism has yet to be written.) In the years since the turn-of-the-century, the American public has remained ambivalent at best about our nation's global sway and involvements, and before the mid-twentieth century, historians often shied away from even using the terms "empire" and "imperialism" in reference to United States foreign policy. Instead, the term "expansion" seemed preferable. America's style of reluctant imperialism, then, was distinctive among the Great Powers.

Conclusion

In this age of globalization, the *La Pietra Report* should command the attention of all scholars and teachers of United States history. While challenging the history profession to widen the lens through which our nation's past is studied, the report does not go beyond limning a few trajectories to help educators reframe their courses. This is as it should be. When we educators begin following the people, the money, the ideas, and the things, we will discover all sorts of creative ways to internationalize our courses. This article is offered in that spirit; that is, in the hope that it may trigger some ideas about additional ways to explore and teach the transnational and related spatial and temporal contexts of American history. Students are looking for a history that speaks to the globalized present; thanks to the ground breaking internationalized studies of the past forty years or so, we are in a good position to offer our classes a rescaled and more inclusive narrative that is bound to stimulate thinking and learning about our nation's journey through time.

Notes

An earlier version of this article, under a slightly different title, was presented at the Organization of American Historians Annual Conference in 2002 in Washington, D.C.

1. One of the first major steps in the direction of internationalizing America's past was taken by C. Vann Woodward, who edited a seminal work in the late 1960s, *The Comparative Approach to American History* (New York: Basic Books, 1968). At that time and in that work, historians teaching at institutions in the United States focused on comparing such international phenomena as frontier advances, revolutions, institutions of government, experiences with slavery and its abolition, reform movements, imperialisms, and economic development. Scholars took the next major step toward internationalization in the 1990s by ushering in what they called "transnational" history. Generally, this term referred to phenomena—such as popular culture, politics, and migrations—that passed through a nation, both transforming it and being transformed by the process itself. Since the 1990s, if not before, the number of historians in foreign countries studying America's past has increased dramatically, and throughout the world there has developed a fresh appreciation for the importance of geographic and cultural perspectives on the study of United States history. See, especially, David Thelen, "The Nation and Beyond: Transnational Perspectives on United States History," *Journal of American History* 86 (December, 1999), 965–975. While the conceptual work of internationalizing the study of American history continues, a third step toward extending the spatial boundaries of United States history has been the more recent focus on the classroom applications of the newly globalized historical thinking. The most authoritative and suggestive work on this matter is Carl J. Guarneri's "Out of Its Shell: Internationalizing the Teaching of United States History," *AHA Perspectives* 35 (February 1997), 1, 5–8.

2. *La Pietra Report: Project on Internationalizing the Study of American History* (New York: The Organization of American Historians and New York University, 2000).

3. *La Pietra Report,* p. 12.

4. I wish to acknowledge my debt to Professor Carl J. Guarneri of St. Mary's College of California, who read a preliminary draft of this paper and encouraged me to infuse more conceptual rigor into my use of the term "American exceptionalism." We met as participants in the La Pietra Project.

5. Robert H. Ferrell, *American Diplomacy: A History* (New York: W.W. Norton, 1969), p. 34. Figures for the extent of economic aid provided the American revolutionaries by France, Spain, and the Netherlands can be found in Curtis P. Nettels, *The Emergence of a National Economy, 1775–1815* (New York: Harper Torchbooks, 1969), pp. 20–21.

6. Elise Marienstras and Naomi Wulf, "French Translations and Reception of the Declaration of Independence," *Journal of American History* 85 (March 1999), 1314–1315.

7. Susan Dunn, *Sister Revolutions: French Lightning,*

American Light (New York: Faber and Faber, Inc., 1999), pp. 152–153.

8. Lester D. Langley, *The Americas in the Age of Revolution, 1750–1850* (New Haven: Yale University Press, 1996), p. 102.

9. Langley, *The Americas in the Age of Revolution,* p. 129.

10. Seymour Martin Lipset, *The First New Nation: The United States in Historical and Comparative Perspective* (New York: Doubleday & Co., 1963), p. 17; and more recently by the same author, *American Exceptionalism: A Double-Edged Sword* (New York: W.W. Norton & Co., 1997), p. 18. In the latter work Lipset acknowledges that Iceland was technically the first colony of a European power to gain its independence.

11. Gordon S. Wood, *The Radicalism of the American Revolution* (New York: Vintage Books, 1993), p. 176.

12. Quoted in Eve Kornfeld, *Margaret Fuller: A Brief Biography with Documents* (Boston: Bedford Books, 1997), p. 57. For a critical analysis of Fuller's letters from Europe to the New York *Tribune* and her other writings while overseas, see William W. Stowe, *Going Abroad: European Travel in Nineteenth Century American Culture* (Princeton, N.J.: Princeton University Press, 1994), pp. 102–124.

13. Charles Capper and Conrad Edick Wright, eds., *Transient and Permanent: The Transcendentalist Movement and Its Contexts* (Boston: Massachusetts Historical Society, 1999), pp. 121–226; Paul F. Boller, *American Transcendentalism, 1830–1860: An Intellectual Inquiry* (New York: G.P. Putnam's Sons, 1974), pp. 34–98.

14. Carl J. Guarneri, *The Utopian Alternative: Fourierism in Nineteenth Century America* (Ithaca, N.Y.: Cornell University Press, 1991), p. 2. Interestingly, Brisbane was dismissive of G.W.F. Hegel, whom he had also studied under in Berlin, because the latter's vision of a better society did not extend beyond European civilization. Fourier, by contrast, envisioned a better future for human beings around the world through the adoption of utopian socialism. See Robert D. Richardson, *Emerson: The Mind on Fire* (Berkeley: University of California Press, 1995), p. 365.

15. Richardson, *Emerson,* pp. 127–152.

16. Shortly after attending the La Pietra Conference in 2000, I visited the Browning Institute at Casa Guidi, the mid-nineteenth century Florence residence of English poets Robert and Elizabeth Browning. Their palazzo served as a gathering place for writers and artists, particularly but not exclusively from the British Isles and the United States. The décor of the library remains faithful to that of a mid-nineteenth century Florentine palace. Stepping across the threshold into that room, with its richly upholstered chairs and well-stocked bookcases, immediately transported me back in time. Like Hawthorne, Fuller was also a guest of the Brownings, who were emotionally devastated when they learned of Fuller's death by drowning, along with the loss of her Italian husband and son, in a shipwreck on her return voyage to the United States in the summer of 1850. Afterward, Mrs. Browning wrote that Margaret Fuller's "death shook me to the very roots of my heart." Kornfeld, *Margaret Fuller,* pp. 236–237.

17. Robert W. Rydell, *All the World's a Fair: Visions of Empire at American International Expositions, 1876–1916* (Chicago: University of Chicago Press, 1984), pp. 105–125.

18. Thomas J. Osborne, "Trade or War? America's Annexation of Hawaii Reconsidered," *Pacific Historical Review* 50 (August 1981), 298–302.

19. Rydell, *All the World's a Fair,* p. 120.

20. Thomas J. Osborne, *"Empire Can Wait": American Opposition to Hawaiian Annexation, 1893–1898* (Kent, Ohio: The Kent State University Press, 1981), p. xii.

21. *American National Biography,* s.v. "Rockhill, William Woodville," by Noel Pugach.

22. Robert L. Beisner, *Twelve Against Empire: The Anti-Imperialists, 1898–1900* (New York: McGraw-Hill Book Co., 1968), pp. xi–xii.

CHAPTER 24

America on the World Stage
OAH Magazine of History

This essay series is conceived and overseen by the OAH–Advanced Placement Joint Advisory Board on Teaching the U.S. History Survey. Aimed at helping secondary and college-level instructors in the design and substance of the U.S. history course, the essays in this series take up the challenge posed by the OAH's *La Pietra Report*: that it is time for "rethinking American History in a global age." Internationalizing the teaching of U.S. history, the authors of the *Report* argue, will help students "better understand the emergence of the United States in the world and the significance of its power and presence." The survey course seems to be the best place to begin such a reframing.

The essays treat significant topics and events in United States history, emphasizing both the importance and the distinctiveness of the American national experience in the context of world history. Treatment of subjects and themes is both comparative and "interactive" (i.e., showing how American events actually interrelated with events elsewhere). Perhaps most important, topics are presented in a way that will allow their smooth placement into the "traditional" syllabus of the survey course. . . .

—Gary. W. Reichard
Chair, OAH–AP Joint Advisory Board on Teaching the U.S. History Survey, and Series Editor

Essays in the series:

1. David Armitage, "The Declaration of Independence in World Context," *OAH Magazine of History* 18, no. 3 (April 2004): 61–66.

2. Leila J. Rupp, "From Rosie the Riveter to the Global Assembly Line: American Women on the World Stage," *OAH Magazine of History* 18, no. 4 (July 2004): 53–57.

3. Patrick Wolfe, "Race and Citizenship," *OAH Magazine of History* 18, no. 5 (October 2004): 66–71.

4. Carole Shammas, "America, the Atlantic, and Global Consumer Demand, 1500–1800," *OAH Magazine of History* 19, no. 1 (January 2005): 59–64.

5. Melvyn P. Leffler, "Cold War and Global Hegemony, 1945–1991," *OAH Magazine of History* 19, no. 2 (March 2005): 65–72.

6. Suzanne M. Sinke, "Crossing National Borders: Locating the United States in Migration History," *OAH Magazine of History* 19, no. 3 (May 2005): 58–63.

7. Philip D. Morgan, "Origins of American Slavery," *OAH Magazine of History* 19, no. 4 (July 2005): 51–56.

8. Ted Steinberg, "Lawn and Landscape in World Context, 1945–2000," *OAH Magazine of History* 19, no. 6 (November 2005): 62–68.

9. Edward L. Ayers, "The American Civil War, Emancipation, and Reconstruction on the World Stage," *OAH Magazine of History* 20, no. 1 (January 2006): 54–59.

10. Stephen Aron, "Returning the West to the World," *OAH Magazine of History* 20, no. 2 (March 2006): 53–60.

11. Stuart M. Blumin, "Driven to the City: Urbaniza-

tion and Industrialization in the Nineteenth Century," *OAH Magazine of History* 20, no. 3 (May 2006): 47–53.

12. Penny M. Von Eschen, "Globalizing Popular Culture in the 'American Century' and Beyond," *OAH Magazine of History* 20, no. 4 (July 2004): 56–63.

13. Daniel T. Rodgers, "Worlds of Reform," *OAH Magazine of History* 20, no. 5 (October 2006): 49–54.

14. Kevin Gaines, "The Civil Rights Movement in World Perspective," *OAH Magazine of History* 21, no. 1 (January 2007): 57–64.

15. Mark A. Noll, "Nineteenth-Century Religion in World Context," *OAH Magazine of History* 21, no. 3 (July 2007): 51–56.

[**Editor's note**: All of these essays, except no. 8, have been reprinted in *America on the World Stage: A Global Approach to U.S. History*, Gary Reichard and Ted Dixon, eds., (Urbana: University of Illinois Press, 2008), accompanied by essays on teaching strategies.]

CHAPTER 25

AP Central Articles on Internationalized U.S. History
The College Board

The College Board's AP Central website (http://apcentral. collegeboard.com/apc/Controller.jpf) contains feature articles on the state of the field and on teaching the AP U.S. history course. Several of these are articles from the "America on the World Stage" series in the *OAH Magazine of History* (see Chapter 24). Among other articles related to internationalizing American history are the following:

1. Thomas Bender, "Rethinking American History in a Global Context"

Summarizing the theme of his book *A Nation Among Nations* (2006), a leading "globalizing" U.S. historian shows how, contrary to the myth of American "exceptionalism," American history has been embedded in global developments since 1500.

2. Richard White, "Imagine There Is No Country"

Focusing on the American West, a prominent practitioner of the "New Western History" uses Native American history, railroads, and environmental history to demonstrate that "the nation state cannot contain all the histories that flow through it."

3. Mike Henry, "Teaching About the Atlantic World in the AP U.S. History Classroom"

This essay suggests that AP teachers reorganize the early part of the course from 1450 to about 1750 around the concept of the Atlantic world. Instead of examining the age of exploration, colonial settlement, and development through the lens of nationality, teachers might approach this epoch with a broader, transnational view. The essay is accompanied by a sample outline, a lesson plan on slavery, and a bibliography.

4. Marc Aronson, "Why Tea? The Global Story of the American Revolution"

The author of *The Real American Revolution* turns 1776 into a global narrative by beginning with financial maneuverings in London and the shifting fortunes of the British East India Company in India, both of which help to precipitate the Boston Tea Party.

5. David Brion Davis, "Looking at Slavery from Broader Perspectives"

An eminent historian of American slavery suggests that U.S. history teachers show their students the "big picture": the transnational relationships that constituted an Atlantic slave system as well as the place of racial slavery in the evolution of the Western and modern worlds.

6. Kevin Gaines, "Incorporating African American History into the U.S. History Survey Course"

Rather than separating African American history from "mainstream" U.S. history, this essay proposes an approach that connects black history to America's changing relationship to the world and global struggles over racial justice. It illustrates the point by contrasting constructions of race among nations and by linking America's wars of imperialism to racial segregation at home.

7. Scott Kaufman, "Incorporating Diplomatic History into the American History Survey"

This brief essay suggests themes that can thread U.S. foreign relations through the survey course and link them to basic American traditions: U.S. support for free trade, American ambivalence about revolution and imperialism, Americans' reluctance to join formal international alliances, and their desire to spread their institutions abroad.

8. Scott Kaufman, "Guide to Korean War Resources"

This article suggests primary and secondary sources, multimedia resources, and teaching strategies. The author stresses that "anyone teaching the Korean War in detail must emphasize is that it was a case of the Cold War superimposed upon a civil war."

9. Scott Kaufman, "Guide to Vietnam War Resources"

This article selects historical works, primary sources, and multimedia materials on the U.S. war in Vietnam that can assist AP teachers, and it suggests appropriate assignments for students.

CHAPTER 26

Teaching Gender Relations in Settler Societies
The United States and Australia

M. ALISON KIBLER

Transnational and comparative approaches to women's history have started to influence the way instructors teach the United States women's history survey course. Ellen Carol DuBois and Vicki Ruiz, for example, introduce "transnationalism" as a theme of the third edition of *Unequal Sisters: A Multicultural Reader in U.S. Women's History.*[1] Emphasizing the global context of the United States and the movement of people and ideas across national borders, the editors include articles about gender relations across North American frontiers, the international connections and tensions among female reformers, and the lives of immigrant women in the United States.[2] To build on developments like these, women's historians need to discuss further the challenges of integrating transnational approaches into the teaching of United States women's history and to exchange teaching ideas that develop overlapping American and global contexts.[3] With these goals in mind, this article offers a strategy for using Australian women's history in a United States women's history survey course.

Mixing some Australian women's history into a United States women's history survey can be a provocative way to explore gender relations in settler societies. As historian Carl Guarneri and others have noted, settler societies, including Canada, Australia, South Africa, and the United States, have already been mined for their rich comparative resources.[4] Feminist scholars working within a variety of disciplines and national histories have discussed the centrality of gender relations to the establishment and growth of settler societies.[5] Historians have explored white women's participation in empire-building through their work as missionaries, anthropologists, reformers, and tourists.[6] They

have debated the extent to which colonial governments undermined the power of indigenous women but have also questioned the characterization of indigenous women as passive victims of white settlement by emphasizing their collective efforts to sustain their cultures.[7] Throughout these accounts historians often emphasize the ways that social constructions of sex differences—notions of masculinity and femininity—shape the conflicts and mediations of settlement. As historian Nancy Shoemaker explains, "cultural constructions of gender had as much influence on the contact experience as economic, political and social interactions."[8]

To develop the theme of gender relations in settler societies, I recommend using transnational categories, such as gender frontier and settler colonialism, direct comparisons between Australian and American women's history, and a discussion of feminist ideology in international women's organizations.[9] Three topics for lecture and discussion develop these concepts and comparisons: the encounter between European and indigenous gender systems, feminist imperialism, and "settler anxiety" in Australian and American suffrage campaigns. These topics emphasize the centrality of gender relations to the history of settler societies, connect gender and race relations, and suggest the Pacific region as a focus of women's history. These three topics build on each other to make transnational gender frontiers a significant theme of a United States women's history survey course.

In this essay I hope to show that a series of small changes—refocusing existing lectures, adding a few key readings—can create a significant new transnational theme

From M. Alison Kibler, "Settling Accounts with Settler Societies: Strategies for Using Australian Women's History in United States Women's History Classes," *The History Teacher* 37 (February 2004): 155–170. © Society for History Education. Reprinted with permission.

in a United States women's history survey class. This article offers some of the necessary contextual information for developing this theme, including the histories of Australia and the United States as settler societies, and suggests key readings, discussion themes, and in-class exercises. Taken together, these techniques can achieve some of the advantages of a comparative women's history course. They draw students' attention to transnational trends and events that shaped American history and challenge assumptions of American exceptionalism.

American and Australian Settler Societies: Similarities and Differences

Australian and American history are part of a broad pattern of Western European colonization dating from the fifteenth century.[10] Australia and sections of the United States began as settler colonies, as opposed to "colonies of exploitation." In colonies of exploitation, the more common form of colonization, a small group of male administrators did not settle permanently, but focused on extracting resources and labor for the colonial power. In settler societies, on the other hand, European migrants gained dominance over indigenous peoples as they established permanent, mixed-sex societies. This interaction between migrant and indigenous populations created heterogeneous populations. Although settler colonies gained political independence from the metropolis, they remained dependent on the mother country as well.

Describing three types of settler societies along a continuum, D.K. Fieldhouse defined mixed, plantation, and pure settlements. In mixed colonies white migrants encountered a large native population that was somewhat weakened by population loss because of disease or political fragmentation in relation to settlers. Whites did not devastate the native population in mixed settlements to the same extent that they did in pure settlements, but they did succeed in establishing economic and political superiority. A landlord–peasant form of labor relations usually sustained these colonies. Plantation colonies, in contrast, relied on imported workers, usually some type of slave labor, to produce agricultural staples for the international market. In pure settlement colonies, white settlers annihilated or cordoned off the indigenous population, used a white workforce, and established a firm European cultural identity.[11]

Historians have argued that Australia and parts of North America fit the model of a pure settler society. The New England colonies of North America resembled the pure settlement type but southern colonies such as South Carolina and Virginia were plantation colonies, with few European settlers and a large number of African slaves involved in growing crops for export to Europe.[12] In pure settler colonies, indigenous populations were decimated and isolated, and European migrants and their offspring (not slaves or

other imported labor) were responsible for the population growth and workforce of the society.

Along with understanding the basic definitions of settler societies, students in a United States women's history survey course will need some of the broad outlines of Australian history before delving into the gender relations at the core of American and Australian settlement. While Spanish settlement of the Rio Grande Valley began in the late sixteenth century and the British arrived in Jamestown in the early seventeenth century, European settlement of Australia commenced only in the late eighteenth century. In 1787 the "First Fleet" of convicts and their keepers left Britain for Australia and arrived in 1788.[13] British settlers, convicts, and later immigrants encountered communities of Aborigines who had inhabited the land for approximately 40,000 years. Various groups spoke different languages and had both peaceful and antagonistic relationships with each other. They lived in small, mobile communities across the continent and sustained themselves with hunting and gathering. Increasing numbers of British settlers, with superior weapons, wrested land from the Aborigines for pastoralism. Though Aborigines resisted with guerrilla tactics, Europeans occupied most usable land by 1850, leaving many thousands of Aborigines dead from disease or violence. By the mid-nineteenth century colonial administrators and missionaries worked to place Aborigines on reserves, where they were coerced into European lifestyles.[14] Despite their differences, the settler societies of Australia and North America share a basic similarity: they are racially and ethnically heterogeneous populations in which European settlers gained dominance over the indigenous inhabitants.[15]

The Gender Frontier of Settler Societies

A useful starting point for an American women's history survey is the concept of the "gender frontier." Originally developed by historian Kathleen Brown, a gender frontier is a clash of different gender systems, in which "cultural differences in gender divisions of labor, sexual practices and other signifiers of gender identity such as clothing or hair significantly influenced how European and indigenous peoples perceived each other."[16] The gender frontier was a site of misunderstanding, a source of struggle and, in some cases, a common touchstone. The concept of the gender frontier helps students understand the multiple meanings of gender for historical analysis. Gender is the social construction of sex difference which, as comparative women's history demonstrates so well, varies cross-culturally and historically. But gender is also a "primary way of signifying relationships of power," according to Joan Scott.[17] For example, gender metaphors underpin other power relations across frontiers. The gender frontier, in Brown's account, created religious, linguistic, and economic exchanges and struggles within colonialism.

The idea of the gender frontier can be introduced by

pairing an article about European settlement in New South Wales with an essay on the Anglo-Algonquian frontier: Ann McGrath's essay, "The White Man's Looking Glass: Aboriginal-Colonial Gender Relations at Port Jackson," and Kathleen Brown's "The Anglo-Algonquian Gender Frontier."[18] Students can locate and compare each author's definition of a gender frontier. Brown describes a gender frontier as the "site of creative and destructive processes resulting from the confrontations of culturally-specific manhoods and womanhoods."[19] And McGrath similarly explains how two gender systems, "each novel to the other," shaped the interactions between the English and the indigenous people.[20]

Once the definition of gender frontier is well established, class discussion can then focus on Australian and American encounters. First, the perception of gender differences was used by the colonizers to justify their claims to land and "civilization." In the confrontation between two gender systems, European settlers interpreted indigenous gender relations as backward. British migrants in Australia, for example, criticized Aboriginal marriage customs, including marriage by capture, and saw their own courtship rituals as proof of their superiority. The British in the Chesapeake region also saw gender relations among the Indians as a sign of their inferiority. Indian men were seen as poor providers because women did most of the agricultural production. "Anglo-Indian gender differences," concludes Brown, "similarly provided the English with cultural grist for the mill of conquest."[21]

Second, sexual encounters across cultural boundaries were both expressions of colonial power and indigenous resistance. In assessing the sexual relationships across the gender frontier, I ask students to consider the agency of indigenous women. Would they describe these women as victims of male settlers? Sexual relationships certainly bolstered colonial masculinity and helped subjugate the indigenous population. Sexual access to native women was assumed to be one of the benefits of colonial exploration and settlement; and colonial standards condoned relations between white men and indigenous women but condemned relations between white women and indigenous men. McGrath shows, for example, that male migrants' sexual relations with indigenous women were accepted while white women who became involved with Aboriginal men were ostracized. But this characterization of sexual relationships is not yet complete. Both Aboriginal and American Indian women may have pursued sexual relationships with white men with the hope of integrating the English into their society or the intention of undermining their power. Brown notes, for example, that Indian women often lured white men to their deaths with the promise of sexual intimacy.

The Cult of Domesticity and Colonialism

When, later in the syllabus, I cover the "cult of domesticity" of the mid-nineteenth century—the idea that a woman's primary contributions were piety, purity, submissiveness, and domesticity—I show how the development of this ideal in American religious, political, and economic life had transnational implications. It justified women's roles as colonizers and it was the basis of conflict across "gender frontiers" when reformers upheld it as a standard for indigenous women to copy. To address these themes, I ask students to read an article by Patricia Grimshaw, "Colonialism, Gender and Representations of Race," which compares Western impressions of indigenous culture in Australia and Hawaii in the middle of the nineteenth century. Grimshaw chooses this comparison because the Polynesians in Hawaii resemble other native Pacific populations, particularly the Maori of New Zealand, and because Captain James Cook arrived in Hawaii in 1778, only eight years after he had explored Australia, whose native people were very different.

This pairing is useful for drawing distinctions between different types of settler societies.[22] For most of the nineteenth century, Hawaii is best characterized as a mixed settler society in which a large indigenous population with complex social organization confronted a small group of settlers. Prior to 1820, only a small number of foreigners lived in Hawaii, and they were not allowed to own land.[23] By the middle of the nineteenth century, however, private land holdings, including sugar plantations, were in the hands of American settlers. Three quarters of the arable land was under white control by 1888.[24] As in other mixed settler societies, the strong indigenous population of Hawaii was weakened in relation to Europeans by disease and subsequent population loss but was not subjugated to the same extent as native peoples in "pure" settler societies. Native Hawaiians had a greater role in local and national politics than their counterparts on the American mainland.

As part of my introduction of the cult of domesticity in class, I discuss the roles of missionary wives in Hawaii. Along with providing an important context for understanding Grimshaw's essay, this material raises two important questions: To what extent did the wives of missionaries disrupt the cult of domesticity in their own work? Did women play a distinct role in the attempts to assimilate native populations? The cult of domesticity paved the way for missionary wives' public roles. These women were often ambitious and unconventional, pursuing "unusual careers as Christian teachers on a distant, non-Christian frontier."[25] But with piety as the basis of their public roles, women could pursue travel and adventure and still find general acceptance for their extension of women's duty in this era. The cult of domesticity also circumscribed their activities as missionaries. Their primary responsibility was housekeeping and child rearing but they also were assigned to instruct Hawaiian women and provide native women with shining examples of domestic virtue.

With this background in mind, students can then discuss

Grimshaw's essay—a comparison of colonialism and the "woman question" in Hawaii and Australia. These discussions reinforce the concept of gender frontiers, since missionaries in each setting confronted an unfamiliar gender division of labor among the indigenous population. The depiction of gender differences, in each case, defended the colonial enterprise.[26]

American missionaries expected to find the harsh oppression of women in Hawaii based on their knowledge that Hawaiian religion defined women as unclean, thus requiring their separation from men. But men cooked for themselves and shared in childcare, and women could dissolve marriages easily and often. Non-elite women held a comparable position to men of their class in relation to production and reproduction.[27] Elite men and women dominated ordinary men, and female chiefs were not submissive to men. Missionaries were troubled by the extended family network on which mothers often relied to care for their children, and by the promiscuity of single and married women. Reformers responded to these trends by trying to build up and isolate the nuclear family and to domesticate Hawaiian women within that family structure. They urged them to give up traditional pastimes such as surfing and smoking and to undertake domestic production such as spinning instead; and they advised women to surrender to their husband's authority but advocated a Christian marriage of companionship and mutual respect as well.[28]

How did missionaries' impression of gender relations among Kooris in Australia compare with the Hawaiian case study? Grimshaw details the white missionaries' depiction of Kooris in the region that became Victoria after 1851. These missionaries were working to segregate the Koori from white settlers, and thus facilitate white expansion, but also to assimilate Kooris into western society. Many missionaries believed that Aboriginal women were degraded by male polygamy, excessive Aboriginal male sexuality, and violence. As one white male observed, "The Women . . . are generally a most miserable and truly pitiable race of beings, over whom the men exercise a cruel and tyrannical despotism."[29] Seeing Aboriginal women only as sexual victims, colonial observers did not understand the planning involved in Aboriginal marriage relationships. In addition, white men usually believed Koori men were not good providers, because women performed much of the labor to feed and sustain families by gathering food and medicinal plants every day with other women.[30] These observers did not see that Aboriginal women were also valued for their central role in clan survival. Missionaries in the Australian colonies in the nineteenth century provided some education for Aboriginal children, usually in gender specific tasks, and also attempted to curtail traditional indigenous practices, such as "wandering" to gather food and visit family in favor of a western sedentary lifestyle and work ethic.[31]

To draw these two examples together, a small group

activity can ask students to assess the ways that the "cult of domesticity" shaped two different gender frontiers—in Hawaii and southern Australia. Relying on Grimshaw's article as well as lecture material related to the missionary wives in Hawaii, half of the small groups must imagine that they are Protestant missionaries in southern Australia and the other half wives of Protestant missionaries in Hawaii in 1830. Both are setting up schools for indigenous girls. The questions to be discussed are: What curriculum would they establish and why? What kind of obstacles would they face? After answering these questions the Australian and Hawaiian groups should exchange their findings and write at least two links between the "cult of domesticity" and colonialism. Group leaders should then share these with the whole class for discussion.

Women's Rights and Empire

My lectures on the campaign for woman suffrage now look outside of the United States to develop two themes: feminist imperialism in international organizations and "settler anxiety," which Pat Grimshaw defines as the fears about the racial composition of the new nation or territory. The feminist imperialism of the Woman's Christian Temperance Union (WCTU) and settler anxiety shaped the early suffrage victories in the Pacific region, including the American West, Australia, and New Zealand.[32] The Anglo-American leaders of the WCTU espoused feminist imperialism, though they were often ambivalent about it, and the WCTU also played a leading role in the early suffrage victories in the American West and outside of the United States.

The importance of the WCTU for the American suffrage campaign is well known. The largest American women's group in the late nineteenth century, the WCTU developed a wide reform agenda, including woman suffrage, to reach its primary goal—curbing men's excessive drinking. Their arguments combined moral expediency (the notion that women's votes would clean up politics) with claims of social justice, and their grassroots organizing helped them reach many more women than purely suffrage groups, which were usually based in larger towns.[33] The WCTU believed women would be united in a worldwide sisterhood when they recognized their common oppression as women. Their search for "sisterly solidarity" led to pioneering cross-cultural efforts but also stalled in the face of American racism and empire.[34]

The influence of this organization reached well beyond American borders. Frances Willard established the World's WCTU (WWCTU) in 1883 with Lady Henry Somerset of the British Woman's Temperance Association. Willard had been interested in international work since 1875 when she planned the Woman's International Temperance Convention. The Methodist focus on foreign missionary work also contributed to her international commitment. The WWCTU sent missionaries to Australia and New Zealand in the 1880s, and by 1920 there were forty national affiliates.[35] Thirty-four women were commissioned between 1888 and 1925 as round-the-world missionaries; another thirty-four American women traveled to other countries as missionaries and organizers from 1876 to 1928.[36]

By looking at how the WCTU worked inside and outside of the United States, students can get a strong impression of the fragile unity of women in the WCTU. Ruth Bordin and Glenda Gilmore have shown that the WCTU both upheld and challenged racism in its structure and rhetoric. For example, in the late nineteenth century, North Carolina's WCTU was, according to Gilmore, pioneering in its interracial cooperation. "Under the heat of temperance fever, racial boundaries softened ever so slightly."[37] Although the WCTU organized white and black women in segregated local unions at approximately the same rate in the South, the segregated local unions were integrated into the same state and national WCTU organizations through the 1880s. Willard, whose abolitionist parents had participated in the Underground Railroad, spoke to white and black audiences when she toured the South.[38] Nevertheless, with inconsistent support from the WCTU, the organization of northern black women, often undertaken by African American women, proceeded unevenly and there were only a few examples of racial integration in the administration of the overwhelmingly white northern unions. The WCTU was, therefore, an overwhelmingly segregated organization, in which black activists were "junior partners" who reported to white women.[39] Willard, for example, made inflammatory remarks about the importance of protecting Southern womanhood, which supported the traditional justification for lynching.[40]

Just as racism ultimately overshadowed the WCTU's efforts to create interracial bonds among women within the United States, imperialism also deterred its search for an international sisterhood. WWCTU missionaries tried to liberate women from other cultures along with themselves. They sought the excitement of travel and careers and often criticized practices that they believed harmed women, such as foot binding in Asia.[41] But the WWCTU's international work focused on the Anglo-American world and its colonial extensions, including Australia, New Zealand, and South Africa. WWCTU missionaries largely believed that Anglo-American women were the most advanced, while nonwestern women suffered on the lower rungs of civilization. Clara Parrish, a WCTU organizer who had spent many years in Asia, expressed this sense of superiority well when she said, "Japan is not a civilized country yet, although it may have put on some of the outward forms of civilization. . . . Only Christianity and Christian Temperance can ever make it such."[42]

Historian Ian Tyrrell has shown, however, that the WWCTU's cultural imperialism was mitigated by several factors. Drawing on their cross-cultural experiences, many missionaries realized that Europeans had brought liquor to other cultures, and that other religions already upheld temperance principles. Sara Crafts, a WWCTU officer, remarked, "The one great virtue of the Mohammedan religion is prohibition."[43] Some also proclaimed the respect due to all people, regardless of race or religion, and denounced Chinese exclusion from the United States. As Mary Leavitt remarked after a trip around the world, "I have conversed with persons of every colored race on earth who were as well fitted by native ability, by education, by manners, by elevation of character and purity of life to take the title of gentleman or lady as any white person in the United States."[44]

Group work in class can reinforce the connections between domestic racism and feminist imperialism. For this purpose I have adapted an assignment from the Binghamton University's "Women and Social Movements" web site: "The Willard-Wells Controversy" <http://womhist. Binghamton.edu/teacher/wctu2.htm>. I have small groups in class read one of four documents (available at this web site) related to the debate between Ida B. Wells and Frances Willard about lynching.[45] Each group must present a summary of its assigned article to the class, paying attention to the identity and political persuasion of the publication. Then the whole class addresses several questions suggested on the web site, including: "What was Willard's view of African Americans?" and "Why was Ida B. Wells critical of Willard's position?" I also ask students to compare Willard's position on race relations in the United States to her missionary work with women in other countries. The documents related to the Wells-Willard controversy expose both Willard's racism and her pioneering work organizing African American women. My lectures on Willard's international work reveal a similar mixed legacy: women in the WWCTU sometimes supported, and sometimes questioned, feminist imperialism.

An investigation of the WCTU also brings the Pacific region into focus as a site of early victories for woman suffrage. In all the sites of early woman suffrage victories, the WCTU was the largest voice for woman suffrage, and in some cases, it was the only voice.[46] For historians of American women, early suffrage victories in the western states usually do not receive much attention in a survey class, and the concurrent victories in the Australian colonies, the Commonwealth of Australia, and New Zealand might warrant only a curious footnote, at best. But the suffrage victories in the Pacific region can become a powerful focal point for a discussion of race, gender, and politics in these outposts of settler societies. In turn, a consideration of victories in Australia and New Zealand can add new clues to the ongoing puzzle of western women's suffrage in the United States.

Can we define a regional pattern for victories, or is each

achievement of suffrage for women a result of unique local circumstances? When Wyoming and Utah achieved statehood in 1890 and 1896 respectively, woman suffrage was already part of their state constitutions after it had been legalized by the territorial legislatures. Political leaders in Wyoming hoped that becoming the first territory or state to pass woman suffrage would bring positive publicity to counter the reputation of violence associated with Wyoming. The territory believed it had recruited more families to the area because of woman suffrage, and retained this right for women when it became a state in 1890. In Utah the complex issue of polygamy played a major role in passage of woman suffrage, as Mormons hoped that women's votes would show outsiders that they actually supported polygamy. When Utah's women received the vote in 1870, they did uphold polygamy.[47]

The British colonies of South Australia and Western Australia, both with semi-independent governments, also ratified woman suffrage in response to the urging of temperance advocates in 1894 and 1899 respectively. The new Commonwealth government of Australia faced a problem because women in some states already were exercising their right to vote, while women of other states were barred. To resolve this quandary the Commonwealth granted all women the right to vote, but also excluded Aboriginal men and women from citizenship rights.

Although these areas have diverse histories and each suffrage win was, in itself, complicated, it is useful to draw out some of the similarities of the locations of early suffrage victories. Three elements of frontier life in these settler societies may have contributed to the passage of woman suffrage. First, the message of the WCTU may have resonated more on the frontier than in urban areas because the dangers of male drinking were perhaps heightened on these "male dominated frontiers of white settlement."[48] In addition, the relationship between these frontier settlements and the metropolitan centers created two strains of political thought that helped support women's voting rights. On the one hand, the remote areas attempted to set themselves apart from elites of the East Coast, or their colonial homelands, by supporting social reform movements.[49] Political liberalism, or support for democratic reforms, enunciated by the labor movement in Australia and the Populist party in Idaho and Colorado, contributed to women's suffrage achievements.[50] This liberalism and the absence of a strong conservative elite, in contrast to metropolitan centers, helped these communities carve out an identity. On the other hand, an alternative strain of settler identity contributed to women's suffrage as well—settler anxiety about white power over the indigenous populations. White settlers had recently subjugated native populations, and claims for white women's voting rights often emerged as a defense of "mothers of the white race, which would populate and dominate these new lands."[51]

These examples reveal how different phases in the development of settler societies framed key moments in women's history: frontier expansion, cross-cultural contact, and suffrage campaigns. The "woman question" was bound up with the comparison between settler and indigenous women and with the establishment of a hierarchy of nations. The broad outline of settler societies thus provides a framework for the local intersections of Australian and American women's history in colonial contact, missionary projects, and suffrage campaigns. The transnational and comparative approach that I have outlined points students to the common gender frontiers in these societies, while raising questions about particular national and local developments as well.

Notes

Part of the impetus for this article comes from my experience as an American women's historian who lived in Canberra, Australia, from 1997 to 2002. During this time I began to look for ways to connect American women's history to the Australian context.

1. Vicki L. Ruiz and Ellen Carol DuBois, eds., *Unequal Sisters: A Multicultural Reader in U.S. Women's History.* 3rd ed. (New York: Routledge, 2000). The articles addressing transnationalism include: James F. Brooks, "'This Evil Extends Especially to the Feminine Sex': Captivity and Identity in New Mexico, 1700–1846"; Antonia I. Castañeda, "Gender, Race and Culture: Spanish Mexican Women in the Historiography of Frontier California;" Alice Yang Murray, "Ilse Women and the Early Korean American Community: Redefining the Origins of Feminist Empowerment"; and Ellen Carol DuBois, "Woman Suffrage around the World: Three Phases of Suffrage Internationalism."

2. For examples of comparative research, see: Mary Jo Maynes, Ann Waltner, Birgitte Soland, and Ulrike Strasser, eds., *Gender, Kinship, Power: A Comparative and Interdisciplinary History* (New York: Routledge, 1996); Ulla Wikander, Alice Kessler-Harris, and Jane Lewis, eds., *Protecting Women: Labor Legislation in Europe, the United States and Australia, 1880–1920* (Urbana: University of Illinois Press, 1995); and Desley Deacon, "Politicizing Gender," *Genders* 6 (Fall 1989): 1–19.

3. For an excellent example of these efforts see Carl J. Guarneri, *America Compared: American History in International Perspective* vol. 1 (Boston and New York: Houghton Mifflin Co., 1997), viii; and Guarneri, "Out of Its Shell: Internationalizing the Teaching of United States History," *AHA Perspectives* 35.2 (February 1997): 1, 5–7.

4. See, for example, George Fredrickson, *White Supremacy: A Comparative Study of American and South African History* (New York: Oxford University Press, 1981); Fredrickson, *The Comparative Imagination: On the History of Racism, Nationalism and Social Movements* (Berkeley: University of California Press, 1997); and Ian Tyrrell, *True Gardens of the Gods: California and Australian Environmental Reform, 1860–1930* (Berkeley: University of California Press, 1999). Dolores Janiewski writes that "[a]lthough an emphasis upon 'American exceptionalism' has led many American scholars to avoid consideration of the United States as a 'settler society,'

it can, nonetheless, be usefully compared to other examples of settler colonialism" (132). Dolores Janiewski, "Gendering, Racializing, Classifying: Settler Colonization in the United States, 1590–1990," *Unsettling Settler Societies: Articulations of Gender, Race, Ethnicity and Class,* edited by Daiva Stasiulis and Nira Yuval-Davis (London: Sage, 1995), 132–160.

5. Stasiulis and Yuval-Davis, "Introduction: Beyond Dichotomies—Gender, Race, Ethnicity and Class in Settler Societies," *Unsettling Settler Societies,* 13–16.

6. See, for example, Nupur Chaudhuri and Margaret Strobel, eds., *Western Women and Imperialism: Complicity and Resistance* (Bloomington: Indiana University Press, 1992); Angela Woollacott, *To Try Her Fortune in London: Australian Women, Colonialism and Modernity* (New York: Oxford University Press, 2001); and Patricia Grimshaw, *Paths of Duty: American Missionary Wives in Nineteenth-Century Hawaii* (Honolulu: University of Hawaii Press, 1989).

7. See, for example, Theda Perdue, "Cherokee Women and the Trail of Tears," *Journal of Women's History* 1 (1989): 14–30; and Katherine Osburn, "'Dear Friend and ex-Husband': Marriage, Divorce and Women's Property Rights on the Southern Ute Reservation, 1887–1930," *Negotiators of Change: Historical Perspectives on Native American Women,* edited by Nancy Shoemaker (New York: Routledge, 1995), 157–175.

8. Nancy Shoemaker, "Introduction," *Negotiators of Change,* 20.

9. In this way I follow Carl J. Guarneri's proposal that "international connections, transnational categories as well as direct comparisons between nations" need to be interwoven into the U.S. history survey. Guarneri, *America Compared* I:viii.

10. Patrick Wolfe, *Settler Colonialism and the Transformation of Anthropology: The Politics and Poetics of an Ethnographic Event* (London and New York: Cassell, 1999), 25–26.

11. D.K. Fieldhouse, *The Colonial Empires from the Eighteenth Century* (New York, 1965), 11–12.

12. George Fredrickson, "Colonialism and Racism," *The Arrogance of Race: Historical Perspectives on Slavery, Racism, and Social Inequality* (Middletown, CT: Wesleyan University Press, 1988), 221, 224–225. See also Janiewski, "Gendering, Racializing and Classifying," 133.

13. Captain James Cook is remembered as the father of Australia because of his 1770 exploration of the southern coast of the continent. But prior to Cook's expedition, Spanish and Dutch sailors had also landed briefly in Australia.

14. Patricia Grimshaw, "Maori Agriculturalists and Aboriginal Hunter-Gatherers: Women and Colonial Displacement in Nineteenth-Century Aotearoa/New Zealand and Southeastern Australia," *Nation, Empire, Colony: Historicizing Gender and Race,* edited by Ruth Roach Pierson and Nupur Chaudhuri (Bloomington: Indiana University Press, 1998), 23–26; and Jackie Huggins and Thom Blake, "Protection or Persecution: Gender Relations in the Era of Racial Segregation," *Gender Relations in Australia: Domination and Negotiation,* edited by Kay Saunders and Raymond Evans (Sydney: Harcourt, Brace Jovanovich, 1992), 4. These two settler societies are also intertwined historically. The American colonies' break from Britain spurred the settlement of the first Australian colony, New South Wales. The first fleet of British convicts and their keepers was commissioned after the American colonies had won their independence from Britain, thus shutting off one stream of convict settlement.

15. Stasiulis and Yuval-Davis, "Introduction: Beyond Dichotomies—Gender, Race, Ethnicity and Class in Settler Societies," *Unsettling Settler Societies,* 2–3.

16. Kathleen Brown, "Brave New Worlds: Women's and Gender History," *William and Mary Quarterly* 3rd series, vol. 50, no. 2 (April 1993): 318.

17. Joan W. Scott, *Gender and the Politics of History* (New York: Columbia University Press, 1988), 42.

18. Ann McGrath, "The White Man's Looking Glass: Aboriginal-Colonial Gender Relations at Port Jackson," *Australian Historical Studies* 24.95 (October 1990): 189–206. Kathleen Brown, "The Anglo-Algonquian Gender Frontier," *Negotiators of Change,* 26–48. Brown's essay is the first article in Dublin and Sklar's textbook, *Women and Power in American History.* For more Australian background, see Patricia Grimshaw, Marilyn Lake, Ann McGrath and Marian Quartly, *Creating a Nation: 1788–1990* (McPhee Gribble, 1994), especially chapter 8, "Gendered Settlements," and Donald Denoon and Philippa Mein Smith, with Marivic Wyndham, *A History of Australia, New Zealand and the Pacific* (Oxford and New York: Blackwell Publishers, 2000).

19. Brown, "The Anglo-Algonquian Frontier," 27.

20. McGrath, "The White Man's Looking Glass," 189.

21. Brown, "The Anglo-Algonquian Frontier," 36.

22. Modern Hawaii, according to Haunani-Kay Trask, is a settler society, "like its colonial parent, the United States." Trask, "Settlers of Color and Immigrant Hegemony: Locals in Hawaii," *Amerasia Journal* 26.2 (2000): 2.

23. John Whitehead, "Hawaii: The First and Last Far West," *Western Historical Quarterly* 23 (1992): 158.

24. Haunani-Kay Trask, *From a Native Daughter: Colonialism and Sovereignty in Hawaii* (Monroe, ME: Common Courage Press, 1993), 8.

25. Patricia Grimshaw, *Paths of Duty: American Mission Wives in Nineteenth-Century Hawaii* (Honolulu: University of Hawaii Press, 1989), 5.

26. Patricia Grimshaw and Andrew May, "'Inducements to the Strong to be Cruel to the Weak': Authoritative White Colonial Male Voices and the Construction of Gender in Koori Society," *Australian Women: Contemporary Feminist Thought,* edited by Norma Grieves and Aisla Burns (Sydney: Allen and Unwin, 1994), 102–116. See also Grimshaw, *Paths of Duty.*

27. Grimshaw, *Paths of Duty,* xvii.

28. Grimshaw, *Paths of Duty,* 161–178.

29. As quoted in Grimshaw and May, "Inducements to the Strong," 101; originally, J.C. Symons, *Life of the Rev. Daniel James Draper* (Melbourne, 1870), 356. Grimshaw and May include other passages as well: "The Government of the Aborigines is strictly Patriarchal" (W. Thomas, "Brief Remarks on the Aborigines of Victoria, 1838–9," La Trobe Library, Victoria, MS 7838, 10), and "As regards the females, they must obediently serve their masters in every season and under all circumstances" (R.B. Smyth, *The Aborigines of Victoria,* 2 vols., Melbourne and London, 1878, 46). For a brief summary of missionary influence in Australia, see Jackie Huggins and Thom Blake, "Protection or Persecution? Gender Relations in the Era of Racial Segregation," in *Gender Relations in Australia,* 3–58. Huggins and Blake note early missionary outposts in Parramatta in 1815 and Lake Macquarie in 1825.

New South Wales, on the other hand, did not encourage missionary developments (43).

30. Nancy Williams and Leslie Jolly, "From Time Immemorial? Aboriginal Societies Before White Contact," *Gender Relations in Australia,* 15–17. See also Annette Hamilton, "A Complex Strategical Situation: Gender and Power in Aboriginal Australia," *Australian Women: Feminist Perspectives,* edited by Norma Grieve and Patricia Grimshaw (Melbourne and New York: Oxford University Press, 1981), 69–85.

31. Grimshaw, et al., *Creating a Nation,* 140–143.

32. Ian Tyrrell explains that WCTU activists were feminists "attempting to expand the area of opportunities for women, however complicated and compromised that process might have been." Tyrrell, *Woman's World, Woman's Empire: The Woman's Christian Temperance Union in International Perspective, 1880–1930* (Chapel Hill: University of North Carolina Press, 1991), 9. Leila Rupp uses the term "feminist orientalism" instead of feminist imperialism to convey the hierarchical relationship that feminist internationalists set up between the backward East, in which women were degraded, and the civilized West. See Rupp, *Worlds of Women: The Making of an International Women's Movement* (Princeton: Princeton University Press, 1997).

33. Tyrrell, *Woman's World, Woman's Empire,* 222–224.

34. Tyrrell, *Woman's World, Woman's Empire,* 6.

35. Tyrrell, *Woman's World, Woman's Empire,* 2.

36. Tyrrell, *Woman's World, Woman's Empire,* 83.

37. Glenda Gilmore, *Gender and Jim Crow: Women and the Politics of White Supremacy in North Carolina, 1896–1920* (Chapel Hill: University of North Carolina Press, 1996), 49.

38. Ruth Bordin, *Woman and Temperance: The Quest for Power and Liberty, 1873–1900* (Philadelphia: Temple University Press, 1981), 82–84; and Bordin, *Frances Willard: A Biography* (Chapel Hill: University of North Carolina Press, 1986), 216–218. Gilmore also notes Willard's abolitionist parents (*Gender and Jim Crow,* 49).

39. Gilmore, *Gender and Jim Crow,* 49.

40. Angela Scheuerer, "Why Did African-American Women Join the Woman's Christian Temperance Union between 1880–1900?" <http://womhist.Binghamton.edu/wctu2/intro.htm>. For other discussions of the connections between domestic racism and imperialism, see Kristin Hoganson, "'As Badly Off as the Filipinos': U.S. Women's Suffragists and the Imperial Issue at the Turn of the Twentieth Century," *Journal of Women's History* 13.2 (Summer 2001): 9–33; and Rosalyn Terborg Penn, "Enfranchising Women of Color: Woman Suffragists as Agents of Imperialism," *Nation, Empire, Colony,* 41–56.

41. Tyrrell, *Woman's World, Woman's Empire,* 82.

42. Tyrrell, *Woman's World, Woman's Empire,* 103; originally in WWCTU, 6th cov., 1903, p. 72.

43. Tyrrell, *Woman's World, Woman's Empire,* 100.

44. Tyrrell, *Woman's World, Woman's Empire,* 101.

45. The selections on this website are: Interview with Frances Willard, "The Race Problem," *The Voice,* 28 October 1890, p. 8; Ida B. Wells, "Mr. Moody and Miss Willard," *Fraternity,* May 1894, pp. 16–17; "Frances: A Temporizer," *Cleveland Gazette,* 24 November 1894, p. 2; and "Words with Christian Women," 20 October 1895.

46. Grimshaw, "Women's Suffrage in New Zealand Revisited: Writing from the Margins," *Suffrage and Beyond: International Feminist Perspectives,* edited by Caroline Daley and Melanie Nolan (New York: New York University Press, 1994), 34.

47. Gayle Gullett, "Women's Suffrage," *Encyclopedia of the American West,* edited by Charles Phillips and Alan Axelrod (New York: Macmillan Reference USA, 1996), 1771–1772. See also Richard White, *"It's Your Misfortune and None of My Own": A History of the American West* (Norman and London: University of Oklahoma Press, 1991), 355–359; John Putnam, "A Test of Chiffon Politics: Gender Politics in Seattle, 1897–1917," *Pacific Historical Review* 69.4 (November 2000): 595–616; Sarah Barringer Gordon, "'The Liberty of Self-Degradation': Polygamy, Woman Suffrage and Consent in Nineteenth-Century America," *Journal of American History* 83.3 (December 1996): 815–847.

48. Patricia Grimshaw, "Settler Anxieties, Indigenous Peoples, and Women's Suffrage in the Colonies of Australia, New Zealand, and Hawaii, 1888 to 1902," *Pacific Historical Review* 69.4 (November 2000): 558.

49. Gullett distinguishes between the significance of these social movements and the widely discredited argument that "Western culture . . . was more democratic than Eastern culture" (1771).

50. Gullett, "Women's Suffrage," 1772.

51. Grimshaw, "Settler Anxieties," 556.

CHAPTER 27

Sisters of Suffrage

British and American Women Fight for the Vote

BARBARA WINSLOW

A transatlantic view of the entire women's suffrage movement highlights ties between the United States and Britain. Hundreds of thousands of women petitioned, canvassed, lobbied, demonstrated, engaged in mass civil disobedience, went to jail, and engaged in hunger strikes in a seventy-five-year ongoing political and social struggle for the right to vote. In the United States, the organized movement for women's suffrage began in 1848, when 300 people showed up in the small bustling town of Seneca Falls, New York, to attend the first women's rights convention, which was organized by Elizabeth Cady Stanton, Lucretia Mott, and three other women's rights reformers. Stanton drafted a Declaration of Sentiments for the convention, which called for, among many things, "right [of women] to the elective franchise." Organizing for women's suffrage was temporarily suspended as a result of the Civil War (1861–65). After Reconstruction ended in 1876, most women's rights energies were channeled into the struggle for suffrage. From 1876 until the beginning of the twentieth century, most suffrage organizing consisted of countless local and state campaigns, involvement in referendums, and convincing politicians to support women's suffrage. And during those years, women won the right to vote in Wyoming, Colorado, Idaho, and Utah. The growth of urbanization and industrialization in the late nineteenth century, combined with a more restive organized labor and social reform movement, intensified the struggle for women's suffrage. In the early years of the twentieth century, more and more states granted women's suffrage, and the National Women's Suffrage Association (NWSA), having just united rival suffrage organizations,

pressed its claim for state and federal women's suffrage amendments. In 1920, the Nineteenth Amendment granted women the right to vote.

In England, the organized suffrage movement began in 1866, when a number of prominent women's rights reformers gathered some 1,500 signatures on a petition to Parliament requesting the right to vote. Signers included John Stuart Mill, who had successfully run for Parliament on a platform that included votes for women. From 1870 to 1905, a period often referred to as "the doldrums," suffragists did not make significant headway in mobilizing either widespread support or popular enthusiasm for extending the suffrage. But with the explosion of "militancy," beginning in 1905, hundreds of thousands of women pushed women's suffrage to center stage, challenged conventional notions of women's roles, and confronted the government in never-before-dreamed-of acts of mass militancy and civil disobedience. English women won limited suffrage in 1918, and then in 1928, the majority of English women won the right to vote.

There are many commonalities and links between these histories of suffrage. English and American suffragists had a long history of relationships and organizational connections with each other. The idea of a woman's rights convention was first formulated by Elizabeth Cady Stanton and Lucretia Mott while they attended the World Anti-Slavery Conference in London in 1840. Stanton and other U.S. women's rights reformers remained in contact with their English sisters. In the twentieth century the links continued. Emmeline, Christabel, and Sylvia Pankhurst, leaders of the militant wing of the English suffragette movement, made

From *History Now,* no. 7 (March 2006). Reprinted courtesy of the Gilder Lehrman Institute of American History. To read other articles from the Institute's *History Now* online journal, visit www.historynow.org.

a number of visits to the United States. American women, including Harriot Stanton Blatch, Alice Paul, and Lucy Burns, worked with the Pankhursts and the Women's Social and Political Union (WSPU), and introduced the WSPU's ideas of militancy and pageantry to the U.S. women's suffrage movement.

Along with the long-standing political and social relationships between the British and U.S. movements, there were similarities both in the circumstances that these movements faced and in their styles and approaches. One similarity was that in both countries suffrage was based on gender. In the period before the American Revolution, propertied women in a few colonies could vote, but when the U.S. Constitution was ratified, states specifically gave men the vote. (New Jersey briefly granted property-owning women the vote but rescinded it soon afterwards.) In England the reform bills of 1832 and 1867 respectively excluded women.

In both countries, to be sure, suffrage was based on class, race, nation, and religion as well as on gender. Another similarity is that suffragists in both countries were outside the political establishment. They had to campaign alone, without support from national leaders—presidents and prime ministers—or from the major political parties—the Democrats and Republicans in the United States, and in Britain, the Liberal, Conservative, and Labour parties. Suffragists in both countries (and overwhelmingly in the United States) were white and middle-class, and their arguments for women's suffrage reflected their class position. In the first phase of the two campaigns, the arguments for suffrage focused on equality; in the latter part of the nineteenth century and first two decades of the twentieth century, women's unique contribution to nation- and empire-building was put forward as an argument for suffrage. Both suffrage movements sought the vote for privileged women, ignoring at best, opposing at worst, suffrage for working-class and colonized women—and in the United States, for African American women. Another common thread was the impact of World War I on women and the struggle for suffrage. Many historians have noted that women's war work convinced a number of men (who were voters) that women's enthusiastic participation in the war effort had earned them the right to vote.

Thus, the U.S. and British women's suffrage movements clearly shared many features. But there were also several important differences. First, in England, unlike the United States, suffrage was by 1866 based on property as well as gender. The Liberal and Conservative parties were not interested in expanding suffrage at all; the radical and labor movements, which did argue for expanding adult suffrage, ignored women. To these groups, "adult suffrage" was the code word for "adult male suffrage." However, the political argument for women's suffrage, Votes for Women, meant voting rights on the same basis as men. Thus, given the

exclusion of non-propertied working-class men from the electorate, Votes for Women in England meant votes for propertied women.

In the United States, where race was more divisive than class, the franchise had been extended to almost all white male citizens by 1836. The struggle to extend the franchise to African Americans was a central demand of African American abolitionists. The Fourteenth and Fifteenth Amendments guaranteed the franchise to African American men, but specifically excluded women. After 1870, issues of race and racism shaped the U.S. women's suffrage movement. While African American women supported and organized for suffrage, they were denied admission into the major suffrage organizations and meetings; meanwhile, suffragists used arguments of white racial supremacy as a rationale for giving women the vote.

Second, England had a parliamentary government, and therefore, the strategy and tactics of the suffragists were based on convincing the party in power to introduce and pass legislation. The militant wing of the suffrage movement, led by the WSPU, vowed to campaign against all parliamentary candidates of the political party in power if women's suffrage legislation was not enacted. In the United States, a representative republic, there were no national elections that would simultaneously determine the ruling party of both the executive and the legislature—and thus suffragists did not have the same kind of centralized power base to which they could appeal. In addition, each state was responsible for determining its own suffrage status. So suffragists had to adopt two strategies: One was to ignore the federal government and campaign on a state-by-state basis. This appealed in part to conservative and Southern women, who could maintain racially exclusionary suffrage laws in their particular states. The other approach was to campaign for an amendment to the Constitution—a federal approach. This entailed convincing Congress as well as campaigning on a state-by-state basis. In the end, it took a federal amendment to enact women's suffrage in the United States.

A final difference was the degree of militancy in the two movements. The history of the twentieth-century English suffrage movement is dominated by the militant leadership of the WSPU. Hundreds of thousands of women took to the streets, demonstrated, heckled politicians, chained themselves to Parliament, blew up buildings, smashed windows, went to jail, and endured the torture of forced feeding; in short they disrupted Edwardian England in a way not seen in the country since the days of the Chartist agitation. The mass militancy of women no doubt was a major factor in forcing the Liberal government to grant women's suffrage in 1918.

There was no equivalent to this level of militancy in the United States. This is not to say that there weren't mass demonstrations, picketing, and pageantry. Alice

Paul's Congressional Union continued the struggle for suffrage during World War I, with members demonstrating and chaining themselves to the White House, and suffering arrest, prison, and forced feedings. However, this militancy and disruption were not on the same scale as English militancy.

For all the commonalities and differences, in both countries the hope for social peace was an overriding factor in winning women's suffrage. Both countries had experienced growing social unrest before World War I, and it was thought that enfranchising women just might placate a significant section of the population and bring it into the workings of the state. Finally, in both the United States and Britain, the struggle for women's suffrage was, in the words of leading suffrage historian Ellen DuBois, "a concrete reform and a symbol of women's freedom, widely appreciated as such by supporters and opponents alike."[1]

Note

1. DuBois, *Woman Suffrage and Women's Rights* (New York: New York University Press, 1998), p. 4.

Selected Bibliography

Women in American History: General Works

Balser, Diane. *Sisterhood and Solidarity: Feminism and Labor in Modern Times.* Boston: South End Press, 1987. A lively collection of essays studying women as activists in America from the 18th century to the present.

Berkin, Carol Ruth, and Mary Beth Norton. *Women of America: A History.* Boston: Houghton Mifflin Co., 1979.

Cott, Nancy F., ed. *No Small Courage: A History of Women in the United States.* New York: Oxford University Press, 2000. With chapters provided by several distinguished scholars.

Evans, Sara M. *Born For Liberty: A History of Women in America.* New York: Free Press; Toronto: Collier Macmillan, 1991.

Flexner, Eleanor. *Century of Struggle: The Woman's Rights Movement in the United States.* Cambridge, MA: The Belknap Press of Harvard University Press, 1975. This pioneering work is now available in a Belknap paperback (1996).

Kerber, Linda K., and Jane Sherron De Hart. *Women's America: Refocusing the Past.* Ithaca: Cornell University Press, 2003. This is now in its 6th edition (originally published in 1995)—a rewarding compendium of essays, source documents, and illustrations.

Lucey, Donna M. *I Dwell in Possibility: Women Build a Nation, 1600–1920.* Washington, DC: National Geographic, 2001. A good pictorial work.

Scott, Anne Firor. *Natural Allies: Women's Associations in American History.* Urbana: University of Illinois Press, 1991.

_____ and Andrew MacKay Scott. *One Half the People: The Fight for Woman Suffrage.* Urbana: University of Illinois Press, 1982.

Stanton, Elizabeth Cady, Susan B. Anthony, and Matilda Joslyn Gage. *History of Woman Suffrage.* 6 vols. Salem, NH: Ayer, 1985. A reprint of the monumental work begun by Stanton and Anthony, with the first volume published in 1887. Ida Harper prepared the last two volumes, which bring the series through events in 1920.

Wald, Carol. *Myth America: Picturing Women, 1865–1945.* New York: Pantheon Books, 1975.

Printed Collections of Documents and Documentary Histories

Beer, Janet, Anne-Marie Ford, and Katherine Joslin. *American Feminism: Key Source Documents, 1848–1920.* London; New York: Routledge, 2003.

Cott, Nancy F., ed. *Root of Bitterness : Documents of the Social History of American Women.* Boston: Northeastern University Press, 1996.

Cullen-DuPont, Kathryn. *American Women Activists' Writings: An Anthology, 1637–2002.* New York: Cooper Square Press, 2002.

Frost-Knappman, Elizabeth, and Kathryn Cullen-DuPont, eds. *Women's Suffrage in America: An Eyewitness History.* New York: Facts on File, 1992.

Keetley, Dawn, and John Pettegrew, eds. *Public Women, Public Words: A Documentary History of American Feminism.* Madison, WI: Madison House, 1997–2002.

Langley, Winston E., and Vivian C. Fox. *Women's Rights in the United States: A Documentary History.* Westport, CT: Praeger, 1998. Good source book of documents and commentaries spanning three centuries.

Moynihan, Ruth Barnes, Cynthia Russett, and Laurie Crumpacker. *Second to None: A Documentary History of American Women.* Lincoln: University of Nebraska Press, 1993.

Norton, Mary Beth, and Ruth M. Major. *Problems in American Women's History: Documents and Essays.* Lexington, MA: D.C. Heath, 1996.

Skinner, Ellen, ed. *Women and the National Experience: Primary Sources in American History.* New York: Longman, 2003.

Woloch, Nancy, comp. *Early American Women: A Documentary History, 1600–1900.* Boston: McGraw-Hill, 2002.

Printed Reference Works

Encyclopedia of Women in American History. Armonk, NY: Sharpe Reference, 2002.

Hewitt, Nancy A., ed. *A Companion to American Women's History.* Oxford, UK; Malden, MA: Blackwell, 2002.

Notable American Women, 1607–1950: A Biographical Dictionary. Cambridge, MA: Belknap Press of Harvard University Press, 5 vols. 1971–2004. This wonderful series began publication in 1981 with three volumes edited by Edward and Janet Wilson. Since then, there have been two supplementary volumes, *Notable American Women: The Modern Period* (1980) and *Notable American Women: A Biographical Dictionary Completing the Twentieth Century* (2004).

Opdycke, Sandra. *The Routledge Historical Atlas of Women in America.* New York: Routledge, 2000.

Strom, Sharon Hartman. *Women's Rights.* Westport, CT: Greenwood Press, 2003. A good guide with historical introductions, documents, and bibliographies.

The Women's Suffrage Movement in Britain

Bartley, Paula. *Emmeline Pankhurst.* London; New York: Routledge, 2002.

Bouchier, David. *The Feminist Challenge: The Movement for Women's Liberation in Britain and the USA.* New York: Schocken Books, 1984. This study looks at women's activism in the two nations after World War II.

Davis, Mary. *Sylvia Pankhurst: A Life in Radical Politics.* London; Sterling, VA: Pluto Press, 1999.

Harrison, Patricia Greenwood. *Connecting Links: The British and American Woman Suffrage Movements, 1900–1914.* Westport, CT: Greenwood Press, 2000.

Holton, Sandra Stanley. *Feminism and Democracy: Women's Suffrage and Reform Politics in Britain, 1900–1918.* Cambridge: Cambridge University Press, 1986.

Larsen, Timothy. *Christabel Pankhurst: Fundamentalism and Feminism in Coalition.* Rochester, NY: Boydell Press, 2002.

Pugh, Martin. *Women's Suffrage in Britain, 1867–1928.* London: Historical Association, 1980.

van Wingerden, Sophia A. *The Women's Suffrage Movement in Britain, 1866–1928.* New York: Macmillan Press, 1999.

Winslow, Barbara. *Sylvia Pankhurst: Sexual Politics and Political Activism.* New York: St. Martin's Press, 1996.

CHAPTER 28

From Immigration to Migration Systems
New Concepts in Migration History

DIRK HOERDER

Traditionally, the United States, like Canada, has been considered a country of immigrants. From a European perspective, the very same men and women were emigrants. From Asia, again according to traditional notions, Chinese and others came as sojourners and would later return to their true "homes." Men and women from Africa suffered through the Middle Passage and subsequently were bound as slaves. Mexicans came as *braceros.* Such views imply that Europeans made decisions and came as immigrants, while Asians moved about and settled temporarily, Africans arrived under force, and Mexicans came with their arms (*brazos*) ready for labor—hearts and minds did not count. From all three continents and from South America, migrants came in multiple trajectories.

Yet terminological inaccuracies belie these well-known assumptions. "Europeans," "slaves," and "Orientals" mix different frames of reference: geographic origin, legal and labor status after migration, and ascription of culture. Asia—viewed from the North American Pacific coast—is located not in the orient where the sun rises, but far to the west. More Europeans came as temporarily bound indentured servants during the colonial period than as free or self-paying migrants. And the first newcomers from Asia were self-paying migrants who established communities; bound contract laborers, called "coolies," came later. In a hemispheric perspective, before the 1830s more Africans than Europeans came to the Americas. From Halifax, Canada, via the U.S. South to the Caribbean and Brazil, they always included a free segment, if a very small one. Of the European "immigrants" in the decades after 1885, one-third were sojourning migrant laborers.

In order to shift from Eurocentric immigration and ethnic history to new paradigms, scholars are beginning to study the complex trajectories of migrants and their patterns of mobility, or "migration systems." This essay summarizes recent research trends by describing the various characteristics of migration systems, detailing the specific systems that have contributed to North American immigration, and reviewing both contemporary historiography and primary sources for this topic.

Complex Trajectories: How Men and Women Migrated

The terms "immigration" and "emigration" denote a mono-directional and permanent move into or out of a country. "Migration," a less specific term, allows for many possible trajectories. Migration is also flexible with regards to time span. It can be seasonal, temporary for months or years (sojourning), unintentionally or involuntarily permanent, or permanent. Sojourners who intended to return but died at their destination became unintentionally permanent migrants; exiles who could not return became involuntarily permanent ones.

As to directions and destinations, migration occurs in stages or in circular movements; it may be mono- or multi-directional. Men and women may migrate in stages from a village to a mid-sized town, earn money and acquire urban skills, then decide on a further move into a different culture. On the other hand, individuals or families distant from the pull of nearby towns and cities—people from central Sweden, for example—moved directly to a transoceanic destination because migration in stages would only have increased costs. Multidirectional migrations brought Italian

From *OAH Magazine of History* 14, no. 1 (Fall 1999): 5–11. © Organization of American Historians. Reprinted with permission.

men and women to France, northern Africa, Argentina, or North America, some reaching each continent in their lifetime. Chinese men selected destinations within the Chinese diaspora across Southeast Asia, the European-ruled colonial world, or the independent states of the Americas. Mental maps of migrants differed from geographical ones. Places as far as a continent off, but with relatives and jobs, were emotionally and materially nearby, while neighboring social spaces may have seemed very distant.

From among the many available destinations, potential migrants could choose only from those about which they had information. They preferred letters or oral accounts by earlier migrants whom they trusted. Most men and women invested all they owned into their move, and a miscalculation would spell disaster. As a result, recruiting brochures, such as those from midwestern states seeking settlers, were met with skepticism, since their promises could not be verified. If reliable information about several destinations was available, migrants preferred those where relatives or friends lived. They would provide shelter for the first nights after arrival and help gain access to jobs commensurate with the newcomers' skills or to agricultural land commensurate with their means. This moral economy of mutual aid militated against letters to kin and acquaintances bragging of material success. Recipients who decided to migrate on the basis of the misinformation would expect substantial help from the letter-writer.

Often families negotiated which of several siblings could leave, with young women occupying the weakest bargaining position. They might be prevented from making their own choice by social norms against women traveling alone, or in times of need they might be sent off into domestic work. On the other hand, women did establish their own migration patterns once "pioneers" among them had established access to a segment of the labor market, whether domestic or factory work. Among most ethnocultural groups in the past, men migrated first and either divided chores among themselves or hired one woman to do the domestic work for several men. Hardly anywhere did "unlimited opportunities" permit a one-to-one relationship of waged work and non-waged family labor.

Migration Systems and Agency

According to Leslie Moch and James Jackson, a migration "system" connects two or more societies, each composed of various hierarchical social groups with differing interests, economic positions, and political systems.[1] It involves clustered moves between a region of origin and a receiving region, continues over a period of time, and is distinct from non-clustered multidirectional moves. Immigrant letters and return migrants provide the information links. Potential migrants, rightly or wrongly, perceive comparatively fewer constraints and increased opportunities at the destination.

Gold rush migrants excepted, they did not expect unlimited opportunities but made their decisions because they preferred "unknown possibilities to known impossibilities."[2] The family or village-centered information flow to men and women in the societies of origin about perceived achievements or failures made systems self-regulating. Each and every individual's change in his or her migration trajectory influenced the volume and impact of the system as a whole. When in the 1880s western and northern European men and women found more jobs in the growing industries at home and decided not to leave, eastern and southern Europeans began to migrate in larger numbers and U.S. industrialists changed production methods from skilled to unskilled labor to tap this reservoir. Thus "system" and "agency" conditioned each other.

Agency is best analyzed on three levels: a macro-level of global economy and whole societies, a meso-level of regional economies and cultures, and a micro-level of neighborhoods and families.[3] Whereas Fernand Braudel distinguished the world of finance, the market economy, and material life, the emotional, intellectual, and spiritual considerations of actors and interest groups need to be made explicit as well.[4]

On each level, actors are born into families with cultural traditions and develop cultural practices. Migrants, including slaves, carried a plethora of their rich cultural norms and practices with them. In contrast, the vast majority carried few material possessions. Survival thus demanded immediate labor for subsistence or subsidies from resident peoples. Pilgrims and Puritans received corn from Native Peoples; the famine-era Irish on Canada's Grosse Isle obtained medical aid; and labor migrants in Montreal, New York, and San Francisco accepted the shelter offered by friends and kin. While many free migrants increased their material security within a relatively short time, enslaved migrants could only reconstruct their human and social capital under the weight of rigorous constraints.

The macro-level of agency analyzes patterns of capital transfer and power relationships between civilizations. Theoretical approaches include analyses of world systems, the emergence of the Atlantic World, and the investment patterns of European financiers in the New World sugar and cotton economies in competition with production in other regions of the world. Developments are not attributable only to capital, the British Empire, or American Imperialism; settler and labor migrants influence macro-level policies with day-to-day resistance or strikes, or by struggling for inclusion in the world market.

Economic relationships help determine migration patterns. Growing economies that provide job opportunities are attractive to migrants. Stagnating economies lose human capital. Since the cost of raising children and providing education is borne by the society of origin and since the elderly are left behind, migrants transfer social investments from a society of origin to the receiving society and reduce their "dependency cost," the transfer of resources to the generations outside the prime working age.

Political relationships determine whether migration is free or unfree. Slaves to the Americas or forced laborers to Nazi Germany were transported under unequal global power relations. Like free migrants, to survive they had to come to terms with the new world into which they were cast. Unlike free migrants, their options were extremely limited.

In addition, potential migrants evaluate options on a meso-level where decisions are based on regional cultures and economies, which may diverge substantially from national patterns. Likewise, assimilation into a new society takes place on the meso-level of particular regional settings, which affect access to education, land, and the labor market.

Finally, the micro-level of individual human capital analyzes the propensity to migrate in terms of personal psychology and capability. In most cases, migrants make decisions in the context of family economies, at the most productive stage of their life-cycle, and in gendered spheres. Kinship patterns, neighborhood relations, access to information, and regional job and income opportunities provide the framework for these decisions. Family economies, emotional relationships, and age influence who departs, when they depart, and what if any material support the travelers receive.

Family decisions within gender and intergenerational hierarchies involve free migrants as well as self-bound laborers.[5] "Free" assumes a voluntaristic decision without reference to societal limitations. For example, the differentiation of Asian migrants into passengers and indentured laborers better reflects the difference between self-paying (free) migrants and those who mortgaged their labor power for a number of years to defray the cost of migration.

Reconceptualizations

Four major migration systems populated North America. Most common is the *dual Euro-Atlantic* system, in which Mediterranean Europeans moved primarily to Central and South America, and Europeans north of the Alps traveled mainly to North America. Italians integrated the dual system into one whole by migrating first between Italy and Argentina, and then, after the 1880s, to North America. Transoceanic migrations were related to intra-European moves to agricultural frontiers in the eighteenth century and to industrialized centers since the second half of the nineteenth century.

The *Afro-Atlantic* system involved West Africa and subsequently the Congo and Angola regions, as well as the Portuguese-dominated segments of East Africa. All were regions of origin for the migration of free sailors, merchants, and slaves. Those who settled in the Caribbean created in-

dependent Afro-Caribbean societies during the nineteenth century. Slaves reaching the United States often had suffered through a period of acculturation ("seasoning") on Caribbean plantations and faced a second adaptation to yet another society and labor system. On the large Caribbean and South American plantations, African ethnocultural groups could reestablish their belief and kinship systems; in contrast, cultural mixing in the United States resulted in a generic Afro-American (or, more correctly, Afro-U.S.) society. Though the slave trade was outlawed in the U.S. and British colonies by 1808 and slavery was illegal in the British Empire after 1834, in reality the trade lasted to the 1870s.

The *transpacific* system began in the 1570s and was originally directed to the Spanish colonies. After the 1840s it assumed new importance with both free and "coolie" migrations to the Pacific coast of the Americas and the Caribbean islands. Racist exclusion reduced this system to a trickle from the 1930s to the 1950s, though it never completely ended. A third phase began in the 1960s with the end of traditional patterns of migration in Asia caused by the retreat of the British Empire and the destruction wrought by Japan's imperialism. In the 1980s the transpacific system surpassed the stagnating Atlantic one.

Originally, *intra-American* migrants moved mainly in the bicultural Hispanic-Anglo region between Texas and California. Only in the 1920s did a small migration from the Caribbean to the cities of the East Coast begin. Refugee-generating U.S. policies in several Central and South American countries, educational prospects in the United States, and economic opportunities in the United States and Canada have led to a growth in volume since the 1950s, as well as to an expansion of the region of origin, which now encompasses the whole of Latin America.

Internal migration in the United States involved western settlement and eastward rural-urban migrations, Anglo-Hispanic intermingling across the Southwest, the south-north migration of Afro-Americans, and the dustbowl flight of the 1930s. More recently, retirement and Sunbelt migration, as well as rustbelt emigration have become common.

A Review of the Literature

Thomas Archdeacon provides an overview of research on migration to the United States before the 1880s, while John Bodnar does the same with labor migrants since the 1870s. Both studies reflect the theoretical sophistication of migration history, but remain within the Euro-Atlantic and non-gendered tradition. In contrast, Roger Daniels, Ronald Takaki, and Sucheng Chan have contributed surveys of migration from Asia, while David Reimers studies the country's most recent migrants. Donna Gabaccia concentrates on women immigrants and achieves global coverage. The collection of essays by Silvia Pedraza and Ruben Rumbaut goes one step further by integrating slaves, post-emancipation Afro-Americans, and First Peoples into the narrative. The history of the United States has thus changed from a national story of Anglo hegemony to one of many-cultured interaction. It might be said that the gates of Ellis and Angel Islands admitted people into the population long before historians, as gatekeepers of national lore, admitted the newcomers—and resident Others—into national memory.

Recently historians have reconceptualized migration into a framework of Atlantic economies (Hoerder) and incorporated slave exports into our understanding of the African diaspora (Bonnett and Watson, Conniff and Davis, Gilroy, Thompson, and Thornton). Yet gaps remain: no survey of the Chinese diaspora has been written, and Hugh Tinker's 1974 study continues to be the most important reference on migration from India under British rule.

In different ways, Stephen Castles and Mark Miller, Lydia Potts, and Saskia Sassen-Koob interpret labor migration within a context of capitalist labor demands worldwide, while Paul Lovejoy and Nicholas Rogers, as well as David Northrup, take on the broad spectrum of unfree labor.

The outdated concept of assimilation—unconditional acceptance of the values of the allegedly superior receiving culture—is also undergoing revision. In its place, Dirk Hoerder offers research on interactive acculturation while Christiane Harzig and Ewa Morawska study the complex processes of cultural interaction. Kathleen Conzen and others explore ethnicity as a construct of the receiving society. Nina Glick-Schiller and her co-authors argue that with increased mobility, acculturation is being replaced by migrants' ability to function in several cultures—the direct opposite of older concepts of uprootedness and social disorganization.

Similarly, historians have discarded the simple push-pull model of migration in favor of complex analyses of migrants' motivations, their life strategies, and family economies. Douglas Massey, et al., provide the best summary of recent economic and sociological approaches in their study of Mexican migration to the United States. Finally, several collections of essays present the results of the new approaches (Yans-McLaughlin, Vecoli and Sinke, Hoerder and Moch).

The traditional immigration and ethnic history has thus become an interdisciplinary field that links society of origin and receiving culture through socio-geographical and transitional processes. Personal human resources and social capital permit easy transcultural passages. Like unfree labor migrants of the past, modern refugees leave societies of origin because of circumstances beyond their control and face more problems of adjustment than self-willed migrants.

Global Villages in the Past: Case Studies

Migrants' mental maps spanned continents. We can learn about them from the many autobiographical accounts pub-

lished as monographs or in anthologies.[6] Migrants mediated between cultures, living transcultural lives with multiple identities. Forced migrants had to preserve or reconstruct identities after violent disruptions; men and women of diasporas moved without ever seeming to leave the orbit of their original culture. An example of the latter is the Sardinian migrant who worked in Panama, Pennsylvania, and New York, but always stayed with Sardinians: *Tutto il mondo è paese*—the whole world is a village/the whole world is in the village.[7]

Rosa Cavalleri, from a small Italian town near Milan, began as a child migrant to silk factories a day's trip away. Women from her town migrated to textile factories (short-distance, semi-skilled migration), while men traveled to perform roadwork in southern France (medium-distance, unskilled work). Some men, Rosa's husband among them, left for iron mines in Missouri (long-distance, on-the-job training). The men called for women as wives (migration into unpaid labor) or boardinghouse keepers (entrepreneurial tasks). From the small Italian town three women were called to silk factories in Japan to teach their skills.

When Rosa joined her husband in the 1880s to run his boardinghouse, she had less than twenty-four hours to adjust: She had to boil coffee, unfamiliar to her so far, because it had been restricted to the rich in Italy; she had to change her Lombardo style of cooking to generic Italian since men from the South were among the boarders; she had to buy food from German-speaking farmers and pick up the mail from an English-speaking postmaster. She also did the accounting for the men. She became self-confident, leaving her abusive husband, fleeing to friends in Chicago, and getting a divorce in an American court. During a visit to her small hometown, she talked back to the high and mighty, and she became the guide for others crossing the ocean.[8]

To live transcultural lives and still function emotionally required flexibility and assessment of both roots and destinations. A woman from Transylvania, the descendant of German immigrants, crossed the Atlantic in 1910. After living with her husband in the United States for ten years, she returned to bring over their two daughters, whom she had left in the care of her sister. She traveled in her best Transylvanian dress, which she probably had not worn since arriving in America. She wanted to appear to neighbors as the same woman who had left a decade ago, not as a foreigner. For her daughters she had brought modern urban dresses from America to spare them the ridicule of looking like country bumpkins. Although she spoke the Transylvania German dialect mixed with American words, her daughters spoke Hungarian. In this family's economy, childcare, emotions, wage labor, and cultural retention and change connected an urban American neighborhood with a small town in the Balkans.[9]

Olaudah Equiano's life story describes the uprooting, violent Middle Passage, and difficult adjustment of slaves.

Numerous oral histories and autobiographical writings of immigrants from Asia have been published in the last decade. The easy cooperation of the German-Polish Wicks/Boyki family on the Canadian Pacific coast with First Peoples, Japanese-Canadian fishing families, and Chinese cannery workers reflects a mutual respect in everyday life quite different from the racial and ethnic boundaries constructed by gatekeepers.[10] Most students in North America have their own family's migration stories to tell. I have found in my own classes that many students in Europe have them as well.[11]

Notes

1. See also Mary M. Kritz, Lin L. Lim, and Hania Zlotnik, eds., *International Migration Systems: A Global Approach* (New York: Oxford University Press, 1992), 1–16; Robert J. Kleiner, et al., "International Migration and Internal Migration: A Comprehensive Theoretical Approach," in *Migration across Time and Nations: Population Mobility in Historical Context,* ed. Ira Glazier and Luigi de Rosa (New York: Holmes and Meier, 1986), 305–17; James T. Fawcett and Fred Arnold, "Explaining Diversity: Asian and Pacific Immigration Systems," in *Pacific Bridges: The New Immigration from Asia and the Pacific Islands,* ed. James T. Fawcett and Benjamin V. Carino (Staten Island: Center for Migration Studies, 1987), 453–73; Ronald Skeldon, *Population Mobility in Developing Countries: A Reinterpretation* (New York: Belhaven Press, 1990), 27–46; and Mike Parnwell, *Population Movements and the Third World* (New York: Routledge, 1993).

2. Walter T.K. Nugent, *Crossings: The Great Transatlantic Migrations, 1870–1914* (Bloomington: Indiana University Press, 1992), 96.

3. Nancy L. Green, "The Comparative Method and Poststructural Structuralism: New Perspectives for Migration Studies," in *Migrations, Migration History, History: Old Paradigms and New Perspectives,* ed. Jan Lucassen and Leo Lucassen (New York: Lang, 1997), 57–72; and Dirk Hoerder, "Segmented Macrosystems and Networking Individuals: The Balancing Functions of Migration Processes," ibid., 73–84.

4. Fernand Braudel, *Civilization and Capitalism: 15th to 18th Century,* trans. Sian Reynolds, 3 vols. (New York: Harper and Row, 1981–1984), 1:23–24.

5. Louise A. Tilly and Joan W. Scott, *Women, Work, and Family* (New York: Holt, Rinehart, and Winston, 1978).

6. See Paul Lauter, "Teaching History through Immigration Stories," *OAH Magazine of History* 13, no. 2 (Winter 1999): 10–13.

7. "John D. Chessa," in *The Immigrants Speak: Italian Americans Tell Their Story,* ed. Salvatore J. LaGumina, 2nd ed. (New York: Center for Migration Studies, 1981), 25–27.

8. Marie Hall Ets, ed., *Rosa: The Life of an Italian Immigrant* (Minneapolis: University of Minnesota Press, 1970).

9. Dirk Hoerder, ed., *Josef N. Jodlbauer: Dreizehn Jahre in Amerika, 1910–1923* (Wien: Boehlau, 1996), 28–29.

10. Olaudah Equiano, *The Interesting Narrative of the Life of Olaudah Equiano,* ed. Robert J. Allison (Boston: St. Martin's Press, 1995); Joann Faung Jean Lee, ed., *Asian Americans:*

Oral Histories of First Generation Americans from China, the Philippines, Japan, India, the Pacific Islands, Vietnam, and Cambodia (New York: New Press, 1992); Elaine H. Kim and Eui-Young Yu, eds., *East to America: Korean American Life Stories* (New York: New Press, 1996); and Walter Wicks, *Memories of the Skeena* (Seattle: Hancock, 1976).

11. Thomas Dublin, ed., *Becoming American, Becoming Ethnic: College Students Explore Their Roots* (Philadelphia: Temple University Press, 1996).

Bibliography

Archdeacon, Thomas J. *Becoming American: An Ethnic History.* New York: The Free Press, 1983.

Bodnar, John. *The Transplanted: A History of Immigrants in Urban America.* Bloomington: Indiana University Press, 1985.

Bonnett, Aubrey W., and C. Llewellyn Watson, eds. *Emerging Perspectives on the Black Diaspora.* Lanham, MD: University Press of America, 1990.

Castles, Stephen, and Mark J. Miller. *The Age of Migration: International Population Movements in the Modern World.* New York: Guilford Press, 1993.

Chan, Sucheng. *Asian Americans: An Interpretative History.* Boston: Twayne, 1991.

Conniff, Michael L., and Thomas J. Davis. *Africans in the Americas: A History of the Black Diaspora.* New York: St. Martin's Press, 1994.

Conzen, Kathleen N., et al. "The Invention of Ethnicity: A Perspective from the U.S.A." *Journal of American Ethnic History* 12 (1992): 3–41.

Daniels, Roger. *Asian America: Chinese and Japanese in the United States since 1850.* Seattle: University of Washington Press, 1988.

———. *Coming to America: A History of Immigration and Ethnicity in American Life.* New York: HarperCollins, 1990.

Gabaccia, Donna. *From the Other Side: Women, Gender and Immigrant Life in the U.S., 1820–1990.* Bloomington: Indiana University Press, 1994.

Gilroy, Paul. *The Black Atlantic: Modernity and Double Consciousness.* Cambridge: Harvard University Press, 1993.

Glick-Schiller, Nina, Linda Basch, and Cristina Blanc-Szanton. *Towards a Transnational Perspective on Migration: Race, Class, Ethnicity, and Nationalism Reconsidered.* New York: New York Academy of Sciences, 1992.

Harzig, Christiane, ed. *Peasant Maids, City Women: From the European Countryside to Urban America.* Ithaca: Cornell University Press, 1997.

Hoerder, Dirk, ed. *Labor Migration in the Atlantic Economies: The European and North American Working Classes during the Period of Industrialization.* Westport, CT: Greenwood Press, 1985.

Hoerder, Dirk, and Leslie Page Moch, eds. *European Migrants: Global and Local Perspectives.* Boston: Northeastern University Press, 1996, especially "From Migrants to Ethnics: Acculturation in a Societal Framework," 211–62.

Jackson, James H., Jr., and Leslie Page Moch. "Migration and the Social History of Modern Europe." *Historical Methods* 22 (1989): 27–36. Reprinted in Hoerder and Moch, *European Migrants,* 52–69.

Lovejoy, Paul E., and Nicholas Rogers, eds. *Unfree Labour in the Development of the Atlantic World.* London: Frank Cass, 1994.

———. "International Migration Theory: The North American

Case." *Population and Development Review* 20 (December 1994): 699–752.

Massey, Douglas S., et al. "Theories of International Migration: Review and Appraisal." *Population and Development Review* 19 (September 1993): 431–66.

Morawska, Ewa. *For Bread with Butter: The Life-Worlds of East Central Europeans in Johnstown, Pennsylvania, 1890–1940.* Cambridge: Harvard University Press, 1985.

Northrup, David. *Indentured Labor in the Age of Imperialism, 1834–1922.* New York: Cambridge University Press, 1995.

Nugent, Walter T.K. *Crossings: The Great Transatlantic Migrations, 1870–1914.* Bloomington: Indiana University Press, 1992.

Pedraza, Silvia, and Ruben G. Rumbaut, eds. *Origins and Destinies: Immigration, Race, and Ethnicity in America.* Belmont, CA: Wadsworth, 1996.

Potts, Lydia. *The World Labour Market: A History of Migration.* Translated from the German by Terry Bond. London: Zed Books, 1990.

Reimers, David M. *Still the Golden Door: The Third World Comes to America.* 2nd ed. New York: Columbia University Press, 1992.

Sassen-Koob, Saskia. *The Mobility of Labour and Capital: A Study in International Investment and Labor Flow.* New York: Cambridge University Press, 1988.

Segal, Aaron. *An Atlas of International Migration.* London: Hans Zen, 1993.

———. *A Different Mirror: A History of Multicultural America.* Boston: Little, Brown, 1993.

Takaki, Ronald. *Strangers from a Different Shore: A History of Asian Americans.* Revised ed. Boston: Little, Brown, 1998.

Tanner, Helen Hornbeck, et al., eds. *The Settling of North America: The Atlas of the Great Migrations into North America from the Ice Age to Present.* New York: Macmillan, 1995.

Thompson, Vincent Bakpetu. *The Making of the African Diaspora in the Americas, 1441–1900.* New York: Longman, 1987.

Thornton, John. *Africa and Africans in the Making of the Atlantic World, 1400–1680.* New York: Cambridge University Press, 1992.

Tinker, Hugh. *A New System of Slavery: The Export of Indian Labour Overseas, 1830–1920.* New York: Oxford University Press, 1974.

Vecoli, Rudolph J., and Suzanne M. Sinke, eds. *A Century of European Migrations, 1830–1930.* Urbana: Illinois University Press, 1991.

Yans-McLaughlin, Virginia, ed. *Immigration Reconsidered: History, Sociology, and Politics.* New York: Oxford University Press, 1990.

CHAPTER 29

Rethinking Themes for Teaching the Era of the Cold War

NORMAN L. AND EMILY S. ROSENBERG

The tried-and-true strategies for teaching the early Cold War period focus almost exclusively on several important, but increasingly conventional, themes. Beginning with wartime and immediate post–World War II tensions, there is the familiar story of "responses" by the United States to Soviet-Communist "expansion." Highlighting events such as the Truman Doctrine, the Marshall Plan, the Berlin Blockade, NATO, and the Korean War, this narrative about the origins and elaboration of "containment" policies inevitably revolves around political events in Washington. Even if teachers take a "revisionist" approach, throwing into question the cold warriors' images of a ruthlessly expansionist U.S.S.R. and a reluctantly-internationalist United States, the focus on a bi-partisan, anti-communist foreign policy remains essentially the same.

In addition, units on the Cold War traditionally consider anti-communism at home. Seemingly the obvious counterpart to the primary foreign-policy theme, this story has its own familiar events and cast of characters, such as Harry Truman's loyalty programs and Senator Joe McCarthy.

Although these two narratives will likely remain part of any teaching unit on the early Cold War, there are good reasons to consider supplementing them and refocusing attention on other important themes that characterize the period from 1945 to about 1963.

I. Debates over Mass Culture and Youth Culture

Normally associated with foreign affairs, the theme of "containment" applies to other areas of Cold War history, including the lengthy debates over mass, commercial culture. In much the same way that defenders of anti-communist

policies talked about safeguarding the nation from policies and ideas attributed to an expansive communism, many of the same people also spoke about protecting the population, particularly young people, from the expansion of products and images disseminated by publishers (especially of comic books), Hollywood, and the fledgling television networks.

In fact, the coalition supporting containment of mass culture proved even broader than that urging restraint of the U.S.S.R. Although only the most myopic anti-communists identified commercial culture with communism, a wide spectrum of people—progressives, middle-of-the-road liberals, and conservatives—could all identify mass culture with the kind of regimented, totalitarian society of the political right or left. Consequently, agreement on the banal, antisocial impact of television and comic books often cut across political alignments and united unlikely allies during the Cold War era.

Students of the MTV generation, familiar with contemporary debates over the impact of violence on television or rap music lyrics, may find it relatively easy—and highly enlightening—to sample analogous debates from 1940s and 1950s over questions such as TV or violent comic books. Why, they might consider, do cultural products so often become the flash point for multidimensional social issues?

The great comic book debate, which is perceptively analyzed in James Gilbert's *A Cycle of Outrage* (1986), provides an important point at which concerns about mass culture and the emerging youth culture coincided. Moreover, this theme, as with many others of the Cold War era, can be traced back to the World War II period, providing a

From *OAH Magazine of History* 8, no. 2 (Winter 1994): 5–9. © Organization of American Historians. Reprinted by permission.

concrete example of the ways in which postwar history was not *simply* a reaction to the U.S.–U.S.S.R. conflict.

Wartime social changes, especially those that seemed to be fragmenting family life, gave new importance to cultural forms specifically aimed at young people. At a basic demographic level, the boom in babies that accompanied the early Cold War period began during World War II. Similarly, *Seventeen* magazine and the popular *Archie* comic book series (which itself focused upon the specific problems of a group of affluent teenagers) were just two of the youth-oriented products that emerged, alongside a growing fear of "juvenile delinquency," during World War II. (*Seventeen* magazine is available on microfilm, while there are numerous reprints of *Archie* and other comics from the 1940s.) Another excellent primary source for exploring the connections between wartime and postwar developments is *Rebel Without a Cause,* which appeared as a book in 1944 and was finally adapted for Hollywood in 1955. The film, which posthumously confirmed James Dean's superstardom, can prompt discussions about the symbolic dimensions of youth politics, including family and gender roles.

As Gilbert's book notes, concerns about the effects of such cultural products, particularly on young people, stemmed in part from the discovery of affluent teenagers as a specific marketing segment. Even before baby boomers became teenagers during the mid-1950s, businesses had already begun to target certain products, such as comic books and 45 rpm records, at a burgeoning youth audience, a development that seemed, in the context of the unsettled Cold War climate, almost subversive. Indeed, the anti-comic crusader Frederic Wertham, a "liberal" on many other Cold War issues, entitled his jeremiad about the evils of comics, *The Seduction of the Innocent.* One could easily imagine the same title being given to a study of the dangers of communist propaganda.

The mass and youth culture themes, with their echoes in contemporary debates, also provide an interesting way to approach broader cultural questions, especially those related to the complex dynamics of censorship. Despite a broad-based critique, for example, regulation of commercial culture often took place outside of the formal legal system: in efforts of self-regulation, such as the comic book code or the blacklist within the entertainment industry. *The Front* (1976), a motion picture produced by many people who had been "blacklisted" during the Cold War era, raises questions about censorship and its limitations. Students might consider what countervailing cultural forces prevented Congress from enacting a Truman Doctrine or a Marshall Plan to meet the purported mass-culture menace.

Finally, consideration of commercial and youth cultures can help to suggest the complexity of the Cold War years. Controversies in these areas cannot mechanistically be linked to familiar Cold War themes, such as anti-commu-nism; but as the common imagery of "subversion" and "seduction" suggest, they are not entirely unconnected. More broadly, consideration of cultural issues may allow teachers to locate the desire to contain postwar changes with something deeper, and more complex, than a simple, reflexive fear of communism.

II. Gender and Sexuality

The complex interrelationships between anti-communism and other issues of the 1940s and 1950s also appear in controversies related to gender and sexuality. Conflicts in these areas often overlapped with concerns specifically related to developments in mass and youth cultures. The 1940s and 1950s, in this sense, offer numerous works of mass culture, such as *Catcher in the Rye,* that became identified as the "causes" for a general breakdown of "traditional" gender and sexual mores. More broadly (and much more subtly), the Cold War period saw efforts to "contain" certain changes in everyday life, especially those associated with women's roles and with issues of sexuality.

The steady expansion of the postwar labor market and new opportunities in higher education provided women with alternatives to early marriages (and family life) *and,* simultaneously, created important social and cultural anxi-eties. Similarly, despite the images suggested in popular fare such as *Leave It to Beaver,* even the "traditional" family of the Cold War period—one in which Dad worked in the marketplace while mother labored at home—created, as well as salved, social and cultural tensions.

In tracking debates over the role of "mom" during the Cold War period, for example, historians such as Elaine Tyler May (*Homeward Bound*) and Stephanie Coontz (*The Way We Never Were*) show the extent to which rhetoric from the anti-communist crusade coincided with that used on the domestic gender front. Women who were considered "too sexy" were "bombshells," while the abbreviated swimsuits, the bikinis, took their name from the nuclear tests conducted on a South Pacific atoll. And in a famous pamphlet prepared by civil defense officials to prepare citizens for Cold War conflict, deadly nuclear materials were represented as scantily-dressed, sexually-alluring women who seemed on the verge of going out of control.

In contrast, stress on a mother's "traditional" family role seemed a means by which to "contain" women within the confines of marriage and home. As mainstream TV shows like *Leave It to Beaver* graphically preached, the ideal moth-er avoided both "dangerous" attire and unorthodox ideas. She took an active interest in child-rearing, though remained wary of being too "motherly," thus smothering her children with a deadly malady that psychologists called "momism." Moreover, women who did not want to play such a differ-ent role, or played it badly, found themselves castigated for being mentally unbalanced; *Life* magazine once labeled women who worked outside the home as a "disease," while *Esquire* called working wives a "menace."

It might be interesting for students to consider how anxieties and changes related to gender roles, like those revealed in debates over mass culture, may (or may not) relate to Soviet-American tensions.

III. The Civil Rights Era

In looking at the complex interweaving of themes, it is also possible to refocus the period from the mid-1940s to about 1963 in more radical ways than those earlier suggested. Looking at this period in terms of race, one might entitle it the Civil Rights, rather than the Cold War, Era.

As with mass culture and gender roles, World War II also brought significant changes in the area of race. African-American leaders immediately pressed for guarantees that discriminatory hiring practices would not deny black workers jobs in the burgeoning defense industries. In order to dramatize the need for this goal, A. Philip Randolph, an African-American union leader, announced plans for a massive march on Washington on behalf of jobs. Anxious to head off the demonstration, President Franklin Roosevelt created an executive agency, the Fair Employment Practice Commission, that was charged to investigate jobs issues and to press for non-discriminatory hiring practices. In response, Randolph canceled the proposed march, though later developments proved this cancellation merely a postponement.

World War II exerted a powerful effect on racial developments. Responding to the federal initiative set in motion by Randolph and other civil rights activists, nearly two million African-Americans left the South in search of jobs in the northern and western states during the 1940s. Similarly, nearly as many new immigrants from Mexico, who arrived under the national government's *bracero* program, settled in California and the Southwest. Seeking wartime jobs, they joined an already significant Mexican-American population in finding discrimination. In the short run, these demographic changes brought tensions, including violent confrontations in Los Angeles, the "Zoot Suit" Clash of 1943, and in Detroit, where there was serious racial conflict in 1944. At the same time, of course, the Roosevelt administration forcibly removed more than one hundred thousand people of Japanese ancestry—citizen and non-citizen alike—from their West Coast homes to "Relocation Centers."

In the longer run, however, the 1940s saw the beginnings of aggressive campaigns for greater national protection of civil rights. Even during the war itself, for instance, a federal court, under prodding from a citizen's review panel, held that the Mexican-Americans arrested during Zoot Suit clashes had been denied their civil rights. And in an ironic way, the wartime internment camps and the postwar tensions associated with the Cold War aided a broader civil rights campaign. Following the war, for example, the Supreme Court decision legitimating the relocation camps, *Korematsu v. U.S.*, seemed the kind of acute constitutional embarrassment that only new legal decisions, which were more favorable to civil rights claims, could undo. Similarly, the nation's worldwide crusade against communist tyranny and on behalf of American-inspired freedom appeared to demand more aggressive efforts to address civil rights issues at home. In this sense, the anti-discrimination decisions of the United States Supreme Court, such as *Brown v. Board of Education* (1954), seem (in the words of one legal historian) almost "inevitable." (The video documentary *The Road to Brown* explains legal developments in a clear, non-technical manner.)

Yet, if World War II and postwar international conditions weighed toward some measures to protect civil rights, nothing in this structural backdrop predetermined either the timing or form of the steps actually taken. Here, students should understand how the commitment of civil rights activists—in actions such as the Montgomery bus boycott—translated the possibilities for civil rights activities into positive legislation and programs. Using 1963 to mark one end point in the "civil rights era," of course, allows the March on Washington, the old dream of A. Philip Randolph, to serve as an important focal point for discussing how ideas from the past reappear in new situations. Similarly, ending a unit with the August 1963 March on Washington, and with Kennedy's November assassination, may allow students to prepare for a post-1963 unit by speculating on what type of civil rights legislation might be expected during Lyndon Johnson's presidency.

In short, shifting the focus from the Cold War to civil rights helps to suggest how the Cold War, while not irrelevant to a wide variety of issues, should not be seen as the only story of the period from the 1940s to about 1963.

IV. Rethinking the Cold War World Itself

As U.S.-Russian relations cease to dominate international relations in this post–Cold War era, frameworks other than simple bipolar rivalry may increasingly emerge as more relevant to Cold War events as well. One possible historical framework is the rise of the national security state; another would focus on issues of state-building and anti-colonialism abroad.

What many scholars, such as Daniel Yergin and Athan Theoharis, have called the "national security state" grew up in the context of the Soviet threat. The National Security Act of 1947 constituted a massive reordering of governmental power by its creation of the National Security Council and the Central Intelligence Agency. By the end of the Korean War, a sprawling federal bureaucracy, dominated by military spending and increasingly concerned with surveillance at home and covert action abroad, had transformed the relationship of the national government to everyday life. Although these transformations cannot be abstracted from the perceptions of Cold War dangers, like many cultural issues of the era, they can also be seen as part of a continuum that reached back to World War II, the New Deal, and before. The growth of executive branch power and of bureaucratic secrecy constitute long-term trends that helped create the Cold War even as they were also strengthened by it.

Other long-range trends in the political economy of the postwar years may also prove to have more lasting repercussions than the international Cold War itself. Some candidates to become central themes of the postwar era include: spending on the military sector as a means of stabilizing the economy and promoting growth (military Keynsianism); the shifts in regional power associated with the rise of the sun/gunbelt in the South and West and the relative decline of the North and East; and the environmental and health implications of the nuclear arms race together with the assorted chemical pollutants piled up at governmental military sites. Even when the international Cold War is a badly faded memory, Americans will still be grappling with its domestic consequences.

Some scholars are now also refocusing the story of the international politics of the Cold War. Rather than examining how U.S.–U.S.S.R. rivalries shaped politics in client and allied states, they show how political dynamics in these other states helped to create the global bipolar division between the two superpowers. This recasting edges U.S.-Soviet relations away from center stage and brings forward other issues, such as ethnic/regional rivalries in some states and disputes over anti-colonial strategies in the so-called "third world."

For years, the implicit or explicit interpretations of the Cold War suggested that during the 1950s and 1960s the superpowers increasingly targeted the "third world" as an arena of conflict. Countries in Africa, Latin America, and Asia came into the story of the Cold War more as pawns in superpower chess games than as players themselves. As scholars have looked more closely at what once seemed to be "the periphery" of the Cold War, however, the question

of who manipulated whom seems ever more ambiguous. As societies tried to reestablish themselves after World War II or to move out of colonial status, for example, rival political factions often appealed for superpower support to enhance their domestic positions. (Korea and Vietnam might be illustrations.) Superpower rivalry was thus often enhanced by the internal dynamics of many emerging nations.

In another example, superpowers could find that their "credibility" became so beholden to certain allies that they could often feel manipulated by them. The Soviet Union was saddled with Cuba's Fidel Castro and his demands; the United States had Ferdinand Marcos and his embarrassingly corrupt regime in the Philippines. The more carefully one looks at Cold War crises, in other words, the less one sees dominant superpowers grabbing for client states and the more one sees a complex world in which internal rivalries and postcolonial politics fed a bipolar split. As with earlier social and cultural themes, such a framework, acknowledging the extraordinary complexity of ethnic/regional rivalries and the active, rather than passive, role of many states, has greater relevance to the post–Cold War order in which students now live.

Obviously, most teachers will not want to drop entirely the familiar Cold War themes of bipolar rivalry and the anti-communist crusade at home. But to students living in a decade in which both the U.S.S.R. and "world communism" have disappeared, any of these other topics may seem much more salient and provoke more penetrating discussions.

Bibliography

Coontz, Stephanie. *The Way We Never Were: American Families and the Nostalgia Trap.* New York: Basic Books, 1992.

Gilbert, James B. *A Cycle of Outrage: America's Reaction to the Juvenile Delinquent in the 1950s.* New York: Oxford University Press, 1986.

Lindner, Robert M. *Rebel Without a Cause: The Hypnoanalysis of a Criminal Psychopath.* New York: Grune & Stratton, 1944.

May, Elaine Tyler. *Homeward Bound: American Families in the Cold War Era.* New York: Basic Books, 1988.

Salinger, J.D. *The Catcher in the Rye.* Boston: Little, Brown, 1951.

Wertham, Frederick. *Seduction of the Innocent.* New York: Rinehart, 1954.

CHAPTER 30

A World to Win

The International Dimension of the Black Freedom Movement

KEVIN GAINES

In 1957, while attending the independence festivities in the new West African nation of Ghana, formerly Britain's Gold Coast colony, Martin Luther King, Jr. achieved the high-level contact with the Eisenhower administration that had eluded him back in the United States. Greeting Vice President Richard Nixon, the head of the American delegation, King said he was glad their paths had finally crossed, "but I want you to come to visit us down in Alabama where we are seeking the same kind of freedom that the Gold Coast is celebrating." The new nation's leaders had invited King along with several African American civil rights leaders as a gesture of solidarity. For his part, Nixon was there as part of a fact-finding tour of Africa that would highlight the continent's strategic importance as a potential Cold War battleground.

Upon his return, King regaled his congregation at Dexter Avenue Baptist Church in Montgomery, Alabama, with a euphoric account of the moment at which the Union Jack was replaced by the flag of the new nation of Ghana. Recalling his emotional response to the Ghanaian crowd's shouts of "Freedom!," King launched into a now familiar peroration: "And I could hear that old Negro spiritual once more crying out: Free at last, free at last, Great God almighty, I'm free at last . . . And everywhere we turned, we could hear it ringing out from the housetops . . . Freedom! Freedom!" King told his congregation that Kwame Nkrumah, Ghana's U.S.-educated prime minister, had issued a standing invitation for African Americans to move to Ghana, contributing their skills and resources to building the new nation.[1]

King's presence at Ghana's independence celebration underlines the importance of the decolonization of Africa for the civil rights movement in the United States. That insight is a product of recent scholarship that has reframed the study of U.S. race relations and the civil rights movement within an international setting. In addition, scholarship on transnational black politics and radicalism has helped uncover the significance of Ghana and other African independence movements for African American struggles for equality in the United States. Such scholarship poses an important counter to the domestic emphasis that has informed most previous scholarly and popular understandings of the struggle for racial equality.

There are good reasons why most Americans have tended to view the movement through a national prism. Indeed, popular memory of the civil rights movement limited by a domestic U.S. perspective is better than no memory at all. What is more, anniversaries of the movement's historical milestones, or the passing of civil rights icons, have become occasions for collective remembrance. The recent deaths of Rosa Parks—widely credited with launching the Montgomery bus boycott—and Coretta Scott King and observances of the fifty years since the boycott in 1955 and the Supreme Court's 1954 *Brown v. Board of Education* decision, all summoned forth media narratives of the nation's triumph over Jim Crow.

But academic historians working at the intersection of civil rights and foreign relations have taken up the challenge of moving beyond a resolutely U.S.-bound perspective on the civil rights movement. A growing number of writers are dismantling the boundary between domestic and foreign policy and portraying the civil rights movement as a matter of fundamental international concern. Their work demonstrates that, at the height of the Cold War, U.S. officials were acutely concerned with managing perceptions

From *OAH Magazine of History* 20, no. 5 (October 2006): 14–18. © Organization of American Historians. Reprinted by permission.

of domestic racial turmoil among "uncommitted" new and emerging Asian, African, and Middle Eastern nations.[2] Such scholarship reveals that policymakers viewed civil rights reforms as crucial for maintaining the image of the United States as leader of the "Free World."

These new works, similar to those which foreground local dimensions of the freedom movement and focus on the movement's unheralded grassroots leaders, offer a more complex and critical portrayal of U.S. liberalism and a more multilayered depiction of African American activism.[3] Following the work of Clayborne Carson, Taylor Branch, and David Garrow, recent scholarship has focused on tensions within the liberal state that prevented those in charge from acting forcefully on their rhetorical support for desegregation and decolonization. These new appraisals of the movement also examine the movement's internal tensions, analyzing differences of gender, ideology, and tactics as aspects of the larger tension between national civil rights leaders and grassroots activists. An international framework also challenges conventional narratives about how the movement began. In the new scholarship, the emphasis on the *Brown* case and the Montgomery boycott as catalysts for the modern civil rights movement gives way to portrayals of "the long civil rights movement." These studies explore organizational links between civil rights and labor organizations that dated back to the New Deal and to World War II, as well as the intersection between black activism, the interracial pacifist movement, and African and Asian anticolonialism.[4]

For example, the historian Mary Dudziak points out that briefs for *Brown* placed international criticism of U.S. race relations at the center of their arguments for desegregation. Indeed, the sense that racial inequality was the Achilles heel of America's image as leader of the Free World persuaded the Eisenhower administration to send abroad such African American cultural productions as *Porgy and Bess* and such jazz musicians as Louis Armstrong and Duke Ellington. Moreover, the landmark 1963 March on Washington was assiduously promoted overseas by the U.S. Information Agency, in part to repair the damage done by the scenes of chaos and repression in Birmingham just a few months earlier.

As several scholars have shown, worldwide news coverage of desegregation crises in such cities as Little Rock and Birmingham helped forge unexpected and often tension-filled alliances between movement leaders and a foreign policy establishment that influenced both the character and limitations of civil rights reforms. Jazz musicians, for instance, brought their own agendas on their State Department tours, asserting a far more egalitarian view of democracy than that promoted by their government. In 1963, members of the Duke Ellington Orchestra touring the Middle East questioned the extent to which they performed exclusively for elite audiences already familiar with jazz,

when they had originally expected to play "for the people," introducing jazz to the masses. A lively debate then ensued among officials and musicians over who counted most as target audiences.[5]

In a different way, John D'Emilio's biography of Bayard Rustin exemplifies how a global perspective on the movement can reveal symbiotic connections between domestic and international activism over the course of the long civil rights movement. Rustin, who as a top advisor to Martin Luther King persuaded him to embrace nonviolence and almost single-handedly organized the March on Washington in 1963, had come of age politically in left-wing organizations and the interracial pacifist movement of the 1940s. Inspired by the success of nonviolence in the struggle for Indian independence, Rustin and others applied Gandhian methods of direct action in desegregation campaigns in the urban North during the 1940s. Working with the civil rights and labor activist A. Philip Randolph, Rustin also opposed discrimination in wartime industrial production. In response to the Red Scare of the 1950s, Rustin and other pacifists then decided to internationalize the peace movement, aligning themselves with African nationalists. He forged alliances with African leaders during the early 1950s and lectured widely on peace and nonviolence. In 1959, after prodding King to incorporate labor issues into his civil rights agenda, Rustin joined other pacifists in a direct action protest in Africa against plans by France to conduct nuclear testing in the Sahara desert. France exploded a nuclear weapon, but the Sahara protest lent momentum to an international movement for nuclear disarmament. Rustin remained, as King would eventually become, a forceful advocate for economic democracy and redistributive justice as central to the struggle for equality.

Rustin's peripatetic career reflected his wide-ranging commitments to social justice in the United States and Africa, and to pacifism, labor, and human rights causes. But as D'Emilio shows, for all his achievements and his importance as a strategist for King and the movement, Rustin's homosexuality made him a problematic figure to his ostensible allies in the movement. In 1960, Rustin was devastated when King, capitulating to the threat of scandal, temporarily banished Rustin from his circle of advisors.

Another key work that reframes civil rights as an international concern is Brenda Gayle Plummer's encyclopedic study of the sustained engagement with foreign affairs by black leaders and their organizations from the 1930s onward. During World War II, black spokespersons waged the Double V campaign, linking their support for and military participation in the global struggle to defeat fascism with their demand for an end to the homegrown fascism of Jim Crow in the South.

But Plummer reminds us that African Americans did not demand equal rights solely for themselves. They insisted that the principles of self-determination advanced in the

Atlantic Charter be extended to colonized African peoples. In 1942, the black scholar Lawrence D. Reddick convened a meeting in New York City about Africa and the war. There, in the spirit of Double V, Africans from Senegal, Nigeria, the Gold Coast, and Ethiopia insisted that they be guaranteed their liberation at war's end.

Reddick had met these and other future African nationalist leaders in Harlem, and he would later accompany King to Ghana and write *Crusader for Nonviolence* (1959), a book about the Montgomery movement and its young leader. Reddick thus exemplified the vibrant wartime coalition of black American journalists and civil rights leaders who linked demands for freedom in the United States with anticolonial struggles in Africa. During World War II, as Penny Von Eschen has written, the Council on African Affairs, led by W.E.B. DuBois and Paul Robeson, made the case for African freedom in the black press and built alliances with nationalist movements in India and both South and West Africa. During the early Cold War, the U.S. government targeted black Americans who energetically supported the cause of anticolonialism in Africa. The State Department took away the passports of DuBois and Robeson, and even prominent black liberals—including Ralph J. Bunche, a top United Nations official, and civil rights attorney Pauli Murray—were subjected to federal investigations. When the Justice Department prosecuted DuBois, at the age of eighty-three, for his involvement with an international pacifist organization, he immediately became an object lesson for black intellectuals, although he was eventually acquitted. Meanwhile, NAACP director Walter White jettisoned his own militant anticolonialism and began to argue that civil rights reforms in the United States were essential if America were to triumph in the struggle with the Soviet Union.

Emphasizing global influences on the civil rights movement necessarily involves paying more attention to the relationship of northern blacks both to the movement and to the American nation itself. For African Americans in the North—who were mostly a generation or less removed from Jim Crow terror—the independence of Ghana in 1957 and the Cuban revolution two years later, offered hope for the imminent demise of the South's egregious form of white supremacy. The status of Harlem as a cosmopolitan site of black modernity was reinforced by its proximity to the United Nations and diplomatic representatives of African nations, whose dignified presence on the world stage provided affirming symbols of black power.

In September 1960, Cuba's Fidel Castro and his delegation stayed in Harlem during the meeting of the United Nations General Assembly. Cheering crowds flocked to the Hotel Theresa, reveling in Harlem's sudden transformation from neglected ghetto to a geopolitical forum that also attracted Egypt's President Gamal Abdel Nasser, Ghana's Nkrumah, and Soviet Premier Nikita Khrushchev. Nation of Islam minister Malcolm X—a scathing critic of both the federal government and civil rights leaders—conferred with Castro and hailed decolonization in Africa and Asia as a sign that the tide of history was also turning in favor of the freedom struggle of African Americans.

In the U.S. press, 1960 was widely heralded as "the year of Africa." It was anticipated that over thirty new African nations would gain independence. One of these nations was the Congo, which had been colonized by Belgium. Castro's visit to New York thus occurred as many Harlemites and residents of northern black communities were closely following the political crisis in the Congo. Belgian officials had subverted the new nation's sovereignty, engineering the secession of the mineral-rich Katanga region. Prime Minister Patrice Lumumba had appealed to the United Nations to oppose secession and came to the General Assembly to ask its support. Eisenhower administration officials bluntly rejected Lumumba's appeal for assistance. Worldwide condemnation greeted the announcement of his death in February 1961. Lumumba, who was executed while in the custody of Belgian troops, had been widely portrayed in the Western press as a pro-communist upstart, as if to offer justification for his removal.

For many black Americans, Lumumba's murder fueled a mistrust already kindled by numerous incidents of racial discrimination against African diplomats stationed in the United States. In Harlem, Lumumba's death was the last straw for a group of African Americans who decided to mount a demonstration at the U.N. Security Council. In 1961, writers LeRoi Jones and Maya Angelou and members of several black nationalist and cultural organizations vented their fury with an angry protest in the gallery, replete with shouted denunciations of the crime and skirmishes with U.N. guards.

Lumumba's death and the U.N. protest against it were defining moments for a generation of young African American and African intellectuals and activists. The celebrated author James Baldwin and the Pulitzer-Prize-winning playwright Lorraine Hansberry both defended the U.N. demonstrators against charges that they were inspired by communists. Three years later, Malcolm X invoked Lumumba's killing when he declared, provocatively, that John F. Kennedy's assassination represented "chickens coming home to roost"—an indictment of JFK's tolerance of violence to achieve his objectives abroad. The U.N. protest signaled the advent of a new, uncompromising African American nationalism, skeptical of the benefits of integration in the South and highly critical of U.S. policy toward Africa, particularly its appeasement of the apartheid regime in South Africa, which was lethally suppressing nonviolent demonstrators. Advocates of this emerging ideology increasingly identified with Malcolm X. Like Malcolm, they were articulating an adversarial vision of African American citizenship, a sense of nationhood and civic engagement that would be realized through identification with the black diaspora, even as American liberals insisted that African Americans were nothing if not American.[6]

Hoping to prevent future outbreaks of the disruptive nationalism exhibited at the U.N. protest, State Department officials sought to cultivate closer ties with black civil rights leaders. In the spring of 1963, a perilous juncture marked by the repression of civil rights demonstrators in Birmingham, the American Negro Leadership Committee on Africa (ANLCA) was born of an alliance between foreign policy makers and prominent black leaders—including King, A. Philip Randolph, Roy Wilkins, James Farmer, and Dorothy Height. The group provided a supportive forum for Secretary of State Dean Rusk's appeal for desegregation as an imperative necessity for national security. But the ANLCA fared badly when it lobbied the Johnson administration to change its policy toward the Congo. U.S. military air support of Belgium's bloody suppression of Congolese nationalists toward the end of 1964 had aroused nearly universal condemnation among black leaders. That action had prompted the intervention of the ANLCA, which Johnson and his national security team soundly rejected, maintaining that African American civil rights leaders were not entitled to their own critique of U.S. foreign policy.

The challenges to U.S. power mounted by revolutions in Africa and elsewhere in the Third World also preoccupied Malcolm X during the last eleven months of his life—when he had left the Nation of Islam (NOI). Deprived of the resources and publicity infrastructure of the organization he helped build and stalked by NOI members intent on silencing him for his apostasy, Malcolm tried to reinvent himself by traveling throughout the Middle East, Africa, and Europe. Early in 1964, with a group composed of secular black activists and Muslims who followed him out of the NOI, Malcolm founded the Organization of Afro-American Unity (OAAU) in Harlem. The group was inspired by the Organization of African Unity, whose summit meeting Malcolm would later address in Cairo in July. There, he asked African leaders to support his plan to go to the U.N. to charge the United States with violating the human rights of African Americans. He did not get the chance to campaign at the U.N., and the OAAU languished, partly due to internal conflicts over the leadership roles it entrusted to women. But Malcolm, a mesmerizing speaker and peerless debater, impressed numerous audiences of students he addressed in both Africa and Europe. Appearing before Oxford University's Debate Union late in 1964, Malcolm condemned the Western media's contempt for African liberation and advocated self-defense as a necessary counterforce to the organized violence of Western neocolonial powers. Back in the United States, Malcolm sought to mend fences with civil rights leaders and found a receptive audience among the young activists of the Student Nonviolent Coordinating Committee.

Before his murder in February 1965, Malcolm advised "Afro-Americans" to return spiritually, culturally, and philosophically to Africa. That was Malcolm's contribution to the ongoing struggle over the terms of African American identity. Malcolm and his followers insisted that a black and African heritage was a legitimate basis for full participation in American life. The defiant act of renaming a people was, at the same time, the grounds for belonging to the nation, for international affiliation, and ultimately for a radical democratic politics that might transform the entire world. At the end of his life, Malcolm no longer restricted his larger vision to black people. Still, in speaking of the "Afro-American," Malcolm had signaled anew the importance of being both black and American, with no contradiction between the two. In eulogizing Malcolm, the actor and activist Ossie Davis stressed this theme: "Malcolm had stopped being a Negro years ago . . . Malcolm had become an Afro-American, and he wanted—so desperately—that we, that all his people, would become Afro-Americans too."

An emphasis on the international dimension of the civil rights movement also foregrounds issues of gender, specifically women's status within the movement. As Brenda Plummer has noted, during the 1950s the State Department employed several black women among the many public figures who were recruited to defend the image of America against the nation's overseas critics. In my own study of the African American community in Ghana, I found that many expatriate men engaged in the kind of casual sexual liaisons that are routinely available to tourists in an impoverished society. At the same time, African American women's expectations of an autonomous life clashed with the gender hierarchies of African societies. Among expatriate women activists whose demand for gender equality was central to their politics, sexism loomed large in their analysis of why the movements for black and African liberation both failed to realize their goals. If racism was the Achilles heel of U.S. foreign policy in the postwar era, male dominance functioned similarly as a liability for revolutionary and radical movements.[7]

Reframing the African American struggle for equality and full citizenship within the context of the decolonization of Africa throws into sharp relief a conflict over the larger meaning of U.S. citizenship. What kind of American citizens would black Americans be permitted to become after the passage of landmark civil rights bills during the 1960s? As Ossie Davis understood, Malcolm X's use of "Afro-American" challenged U.S. officials who wanted to confine black claims to legal equality and an allegiance to the nation. It has become almost a cliché that Malcolm "internationalized the struggle" after his break with the Nation of Islam at the end of 1963. But, by then, the struggle for civil rights was already deeply international in character. It was a major objective of U.S. officials to ensure that the objectives of the civil rights movement and the political aims and affiliations of black Americans stayed within the bounds of Cold War liberalism.

When leaving Ghana in 1964, Malcolm X had a demoralizing encounter with his former protégé, the boxer Muhammad Ali. Ali had sided with Malcolm's antagonist, Elijah Muhammad, and dumped Malcolm soon after he won the heavyweight championship. Ali, who became the most famous athlete in the world, soon grew to regret his betrayal. But in 1966, when he refused to join the U.S. Army in protest against the war in Vietnam, Ali both epitomized and vindicated the expansive vision of African American citizenship espoused by his former mentor. In taking that stand, the boxer was standing on the shoulders of Malcolm X and of those unsung black activists in the United States and Africa who still have much to teach us about the global dimensions and responsibilities of Americans and the role of U.S. power in the world.

Notes

1. Kevin Gaines, *American Africans in Ghana: Black Expatriates and the Civil Rights Era* (Chapel Hill: University of North Carolina Press, 2006).

2. Gerald Horne, *Black and Red: W.E.B. DuBois and the Afro-American Response to the Cold War, 1944–1963* (Albany: State University of New York Press, 1985); Brenda Gayle Plummer, *Rising Wind: Black Americans and U.S. Foreign Affairs, 1935–1960* (Chapel Hill: University of North Carolina Press, 1996); Penny Von Eschen, *Race Against Empire: Black Americans and Anticolonialism, 1937–1957* (Ithaca: Cornell University Press, 1997); Mary Dudziak, *Cold War Civil Rights: Race and the Image of American Democracy* (Princeton: Princeton University Press, 2000); Thomas Borstelmann, *The Cold War and the Color Line: American Race Relations in the Global Arena* (Cambridge: Harvard University Press, 2002); Carol Anderson, *Eyes Off the Prize: The United Nations and the African American Struggle for Human Rights, 1944–1955* (Cambridge: Cambridge University Press, 2003); Azza Salama Layton, *International Politics and Civil Rights in the United States* (New York: Cambridge University Press, 2000); Nikhil Pal Singh, *Black Is a Country: Race and the Unfinished Struggle for Democracy* (Cambridge University Press, 2004); David Levering Lewis, *W.E.B. DuBois: The Fight for Equality and the American Century, 1919–1963* (New York: Henry Holt, 2000); Kenneth Janken, *White: The Biography of Walter White, Mr. NAACP* (New York: New Press, 2003); John D'Emilio, *Lost Prophet: The Life and Times of Bayard Rustin* (New York: Free Press, 2003).

3. On the local aspects of the movement, see John Dittmer, *Local People: The Struggle for Civil Rights in Mississippi* (Urbana: University of Illinois Press, 1994); Charles Payne, *I've Got the Light of Freedom: The Organizing Tradition and Mississippi Freedom Struggle* (Berkeley: University of California Press, 1995); for accounts of previously unsung African American leadership see Chana Kai Lee, *For Freedom's Sake: The Life of Fannie Lou Hamer* (Urbana: University of Illinois Press, 1999); Timothy B. Tyson, *Radio Free Dixie: Robert F. Williams and the Roots of Black Power* (Chapel Hill: University of North Carolina Press, 1999); Barbara Ransby, *Ella Baker and the Black Freedom Movement: A Radical Democratic Vision* (Chapel Hill: University of North Carolina Press, 2002).

4. Clayborne Carson, *In Struggle: SNCC and the Black Awakening of the 1960s* (Cambridge, Mass.: Harvard University Press, 1981); Taylor Branch, *Pillar of Fire: America in the King Years, 1963–1965* (New York: Simon & Schuster, 1998); David Garrow, *Bearing the Cross: Martin Luther King and the Southern Christian Leadership Conference* (New York: William Morrow, 1986); Robert Korstad and Nelson Lichtenstein, "Opportunities Found and Lost: Labor, Radicals and the Early Civil Rights Movement," *Journal of American History,* 75 (December 1988): 786–811; Robert Korstad, *Civil Rights Unionism* (Chapel Hill: University of North Carolina Press, 2004); Von Eschen, *Race Against Empire;* D'Emilio, *Lost Prophet.*

5. Penny Von Eschen, *Satchmo Blows Up the World: Jazz Ambassadors Play the Cold War* (Cambridge, Mass.: Harvard University Press, 2004).

6. Gaines, *American Africans in Ghana.*

7. Gaines, *American Africans in Ghana.* Also see Toni Cade Bambara, ed., *The Black Woman: An Anthology* (New York: New American Library, 1970).

CHAPTER 31

EDSITEment Lesson Plans

National Endowment for the Humanities

EDSITEment (http://edsitement.neh.gov/) is a sponsored project of the National Endowment for the Humanities in partnership with the Thinkfinity project, funded by the Verizon Foundation. The EDSITEment website includes dozens of online lesson plans in American and world history, which integrate web resources to promote active learning. All EDSITEment resources have been reviewed for content, design, and educational impact in the classroom. They have been judged by humanities specialists to be of high intellectual quality.

EDSITEment lesson plans in history include the following elements: an introduction and guiding questions, learning objectives, background information, suggested activities, extensive links to primary source documents, and ideas for extending the lesson. A complete list of lesson plans, which is constantly updated, is available at http://edsitement.neh.gov/lesson_index.asp.

Below are listed eight lesson plans that are especially relevant to U.S. history teachers who are looking for international themes and frameworks. All are for Grades 9–12.

1. Images of the New World

(http://edsitement.neh.gov/view_lesson_plan.asp?id=714)

Richard Miller
Beacon High School
New York, NY

David Jaffee
City College of New York, CUNY
New York, NY

Pennee Bender
American Social History Project, CUNY
New York, NY

Introduction

How did the English picture the native peoples of America during the early phases of colonization of North America? Where did these conceptions come from and how accurate were they? How much influence did they have on the subsequent development of relations between the two groups?

In addition, how do you get people to move to a faraway, largely unknown, and potentially dangerous locale? What are the instruments of encouragement and motivation that one might provide? This was the challenge facing the supporters of the English effort to colonize Virginia at the start of the 17th century.

In this lesson, students will analyze visual and literary portraits of the New World that were created in England at this time, and the impact they had on the development of the patterns of colonization that dominated the early 17th century.

This lesson will enable students to interact with written and visual accounts of this critical formative period at the end of the 16th century, when the English view of the New World was being formulated, with consequences that we are still seeing today.

2. Choosing Sides: The Native Americans' Role in the American Revolution

(http://edsitement.neh.gov/view_lesson plan.asp?id=718)

Megan Mehr
Brooklyn International High School
New York, NY

David Jaffee
City College of New York, CUNY
New York, NY

Introduction

At the outbreak of the Revolutionary crisis in the 1760s, Native Americans faced a familiar task of navigating among competing European imperial powers on the continent of North America. At the close of the era in the 1780s, Native Americans faced a "New World" with the creation of the new United States of America.

During the years of conflict, Native American groups, like many other residents of North America, had to choose the loyalist or patriot cause—or somehow maintain a neutral stance. But the Native Americans had distinctive issues all their own in trying to hold on to their homelands as well as maintain access to trade and supplies as war engulfed their lands. Some allied with the British, while others fought alongside the American colonists.

In this lesson, students will analyze maps, treaties, congressional records, first-hand accounts, and correspondence to determine the different roles assumed by Native Americans in the American Revolution and understand why the various groups formed the alliances they did.

3. The Monroe Doctrine: Origins and Early American Foreign Policy

(http://edsitement.neh.gov/view_lesson_plan.asp?id=574)

Introduction

James Monroe spent most of his life in public office, devoting a significant portion of his career to foreign affairs. He served as George Washington's Minister to France, but was eventually recalled by the President. Thomas Jefferson appointed Monroe as a special envoy for negotiating the purchase of New Orleans and West Florida. He and principal negotiator Robert Livingston exceeded their authority and all expectations by acquiring the entire Louisiana Territory as well as a claim to all of Florida. Next, Monroe became Minister to Great Britain. Under James Madison, he served as Secretary of State and Secretary of War.

Monroe brought a vision of an expanded America to his presidency—a vision that helped facilitate the formulation of what has become known as the Monroe Doctrine. Because this Doctrine bears his name, the general public is not inclined to recognize the significant contributions made by Secretary of State John Quincy Adams and unofficial presidential advisor Thomas Jefferson.

In this unit, students will review the Monroe Doctrine against a background of U.S. foreign relations in the early years of the republic. In particular, they will examine Monroe's involvement in American diplomacy while serving in a variety of positions before he was elected president. They will become familiar with Monroe's beliefs in an expanded United States as well as an expanded role for the United States in the Americas. Students will also read primary source material reflecting the independence movement in South America, which served as the direct impetus for the Monroe Doctrine. Finally, small groups will analyze some documentary evidence of Adams's role and Jefferson's advice regarding the Monroe Doctrine. The class will debate how credit for the Doctrine should be "allocated."

This unit of study prepares students to reflect on the Doctrine. What were its most significant goals? In what ways, if any, was it intended to provide peace and safety for the United States, protect the newly independent Latin American states, and/or promote expansionist goals of the United States in the Western Hemisphere?

4. The Debate in the United States over the League of Nations

(http://edsitement.neh.gov/view_lesson_plan.asp?id=475)

Introduction

American foreign policy continues to resonate with the issues surrounding the debate over U.S. entry into the League of Nations—collective security versus national sovereignty, idealism versus pragmatism, the responsibilities of powerful nations, the use of force to accomplish idealistic goals, the idea of America. Understanding the debate over the League and the consequences of its ultimate failure provides insight into international affairs in the years since the end of the Great War and beyond.

In this lesson, students read the words and listen to the voices of some central participants in the debate over the League of Nations.

Note: This lesson may be taught either as a stand-alone lesson or as a sequel to the complementary EDSITEment lesson U.S. Entry into World War I: A Documentary Chronology.

5. Jazz and World War II: A Rally to Resistance, A Catalyst for Victory

(http://edsitement.neh.gov/view_lesson_plan.asp?id=379)

Introduction

The Second World War had an enormous effect on the development of jazz music, which, in turn, had a role to play in the American war effort. Jazz and jazz-influenced popular music were a rallying cry for U.S. servicemen, and helped as well to boost the morale of loved ones at home, who by listening to patriotic and romantic songs on the radio and on their phonographs were encouraged to wage war on the home front. The U.S.O. helped lift the spirits of U.S. servicemen at home and abroad as it brought popular Hollywood and musical celebrities together to perform for the troops. Jazz musicians also worked throughout the war on patriotic films. There is an unintended tribute to the broad influence of jazz music (and of the many prominent African American and Jewish American jazz musicians) in Hitler's ban, in 1939, on jazz and swing music in Germany.

This lesson will help students to understand the effects that the Second World War had on jazz music and the contributions that jazz musicians made to the war effort. The activities below help students explore the role of jazz in American society and the ways that jazz functioned as an export of American culture and a means of resistance to the Nazis. Gathering together excerpts of important works by both jazz historians and jazz musicians, the culminating activity helps students develop a broader historical perspective on the effects that World War II had on the course of jazz music.

6. American Diplomacy in World War II

(http://edsitement.neh.gov/view_lesson_plan.asp?id=702)

Alonzo L. Hamby
Ohio University
Athens, Ohio

Ben S. Trotter
Bexley High School
Bexley, Ohio

Introduction

The most terrible war in human history, World War II was fought by the United States to achieve objectives that would not only protect the American nation from aggression but also would permanently better the lot of humankind. Sixty years after its end, the world still lives with the unfolding of its consequences—the rise and decline of the Soviet Union, the end of German aspirations to European dominance, the demise of Western colonialism, a 45-year East-West Cold War and its aftermath, the rebirth of Imperial Japan as a bastion of liberal capitalism, the rise of China as East Asia's dominant power. Whether in the continued tension between Japan and China or in the turbulence of the Middle East, the war's legacies loom large in all our lives.

This four-lesson curriculum unit will examine the nature of what Winston Churchill called the "Grand Alliance" between the United States, Great Britain, and the Soviet Union in opposition to the aggression of Nazi Germany and Imperial Japan.

The first lesson deals with the formation of the alliance, surveying the breakdown of the German-Soviet pact and the developing accord between the Soviet Union (Union of Soviet Socialist Republics) and the emerging alliance between the United States (officially neutral until December 1941) and Great Britain (at war with Germany since September 1939). It effectively culminates with the "Declaration of the United Nations" (January 1, 1942) and subsequent aid agreements in the emergent allied front against the German-Italian-Japanese axis.

The second lesson covers the uncertain period from early 1942 through much of 1943. During much of this period the Grand Alliance was on the defensive. Even after the Soviet Union began to advance after its victory at Stalingrad, the Western powers were unable to establish a major second front in Western Europe. Whether the alliance could hold together, or whether the Soviet Union might make a separate peace, was uncertain. This lesson plan examines the tensions and the sources of ultimate cohesion within the Grand Alliance during the period that eventual victory seemed uncertain.

Lesson three covers issues concerning the future of Europe during the final phase of the wartime alliance. Among the salient questions were those regarding the fate of the Eastern European nations, the future of Germany, and the establishment of a new international organization to replace the League of Nations. Behind them all was the problem of whether the liberal, democratic West and the Marxist, totalitarian Soviet Union could continue to coexist as allies.

Lesson four focuses on two major postwar issues in Asia. The first was the American hope of establishing China as a great power despite its grave internal divisions and the insistence of the Soviet Union on dominance in Manchuria. The second was the American policy of ending Western imperialism in Southeast Asia. In both cases, American diplomacy had to grapple with the differing objectives of other important partners in the Grand Alliance. Teachers with limited time may wish to select only one of these problems for class exercises and discussions. The documents relating to each have been grouped together in order to facilitate such an option.

Throughout modern history, former Grand Alliances—including the ones that defeated Germany in World War I, Napoleon's France in the early nineteenth century, and Britain in the age of the American Revolution—had come apart once they had served their purpose. President Roosevelt and large numbers of the American people believed that the World War II Grand Alliance would have a different future. This unit invites students to think in general terms about the nature of military and diplomatic alliances. Are they generally matters of convenience and historical circumstance, or more lasting arrangements based on common basic principles?

Documents from the Yale Avalon project, Teaching American History.com, and other online resources will serve as primary sources for this lesson.

7. The Origins of the Cold War, 1945–1949

(http://edsitement.neh.gov/view_lesson_plan.asp?id=688)

John Moser
Ashland University
Ashland, Ohio

Lori Hahn
West Branch High School
Morrisdale, Pennsylvania

Introduction

Although the alliance between the United States and the Soviet Union had brought victory in World War II, wartime cooperation meant glossing over many serious differences between the two. Since the Bolshevik Revolution of 1917, Soviet leaders had been claiming that communism and capitalism could never peacefully coexist. Beginning in the 1930s Josef Stalin had tried to reach some sort of understanding with the West, but only because he viewed Nazi Germany as the greater threat. Indeed, after concluding that the West was not interested in working with him, he made his own agreement with Hitler in 1939. That agreement, of course, was quickly forgotten after the German invasion of the Soviet Union two years later.

After the United States entered the war in December 1941 the administration began encouraging Americans to view the Soviet Union not as a threat, but rather as a partner both for victory over the Axis and for maintaining peace in the postwar world. In newspaper and magazine articles, speeches and Hollywood films, Americans were told again and again that although the Russian people had a different economic system, they were equally committed to democratic values and to a peaceful, stable world order.

This message, hammered home from 1942 to 1945, meant that after the war Americans would be in for a rude shock. Agreements regarding the postwar world were reached at Yalta and Potsdam, but the Soviets wasted no time in violating them. After driving German forces out of Eastern Europe they set about creating communist puppet states throughout the region, apparently ignoring their promises to allow democratic elections there. Having just won a world war, they seemed intent on setting the stage for another.

To the new administration of Harry Truman, this behavior was reminiscent of Hitler's in the 1930s. Like many of the statesmen of his age, he believed that the proper means of responding to an international bully was a credible threat of force; "appeasement" was a dirty word, as it would only lead to new demands. Thus Truman decided on a strategy known as "containment," in which the Soviets would be prevented—militarily if necessary—from using force to export their ideology abroad. Containment would, in fact, remain the cornerstone of U.S. foreign policy for the next fifty years.

Containment assumed many different forms. Under the Truman Doctrine the president pledged to defend "free peoples" everywhere through economic and military aid. The Marshall Plan provided billions of dollars for economic recovery to Western Europe, lest misery in France, Germany, and Italy lead to communist electoral victories in those countries. The North Atlantic Treaty Organization was a formal military alliance, and a clear message to Moscow—the United States would fight to defend Western Europe. Ultimately it would lead to actual war in Korea.

Containment was not without its critics, and among the most perceptive was journalist Walter Lippman. Lippman believed that the result would be an ongoing "cold war" that might never involve actual combat, but would continue to drain American resources as the United States was committed to resist communism everywhere it might appear. And indeed, "Cold War" is exactly the term that has come to define the entire period from 1945 to 1989. In this curriculum unit students will learn how the Cold War began, from the agreements reached at Yalta and Potsdam in 1945 through the formation of NATO in 1949.

8. "The Missiles of October": The Cuban Missile Crisis, 1962

(http://edsitement.neh.gov/view_lesson_plan.asp?id=683)

John Moser
Ashland University
Ashland, Ohio

Lori Hahn
West Branch High School
Morrisdale, Pennsylvania

Introduction

Most historians agree that the world has never come closer to nuclear war than it did during a thirteen-day period in October 1962, after the revelation that the Soviet Union had stationed several medium-range ballistic missiles in Cuba. This lesson will examine how this crisis developed, how the Kennedy administration chose to respond, and how the situation was ultimately resolved. By examining both government documents and photographs, students will put themselves into the role of President Kennedy during this crucial period, considering the advice of key administration figures and deciding on a course of action.

Additional Resource

The EDSITEment Reference Shelf, currently under development, includes guidelines for evaluating online resources, links to websites listing national and state educational standards, and a curriculum planner. See: http://edsitement. neh.gov/reference_shelf.asp.

CHAPTER 32

Spanish Colonization of New Spain

Benevolent? Malevolent? Indifferent?

MELINDA K. BLADE

The impact of the Age of Exploration has led some historians to consider this period as a "turning point" in history. Students learning aspects of the Age of Exploration need to be aware of the myriad motives that drove the European countries to explore, conquer, and settle the New World. Those reasons varied from desiring to trade and thus obtain new products, to finding the Northwest Passage and discovering new lands. Europeans also wanted adventure and to Christianize those not baptized in the "One and True Faith."

Exploration led to a dramatic increase in the size of European state treasuries. It allowed for the exchange of cultural ideas, the introduction of different foodstuffs, the study of flora and fauna in various parts of the world, and the intellectual expansion of knowledge. As New World colonization efforts succeeded, the colonies added to the wealth of the mother countries and provided Europeans greater prosperity than they had known before.

European colonization, however, was not without shortcomings. As the colonies became the source of wealth for the mother countries, the lives of the indigenous population were molded to fit the desires of the conquerors. However colonizers did not agree among themselves about the way that Indians should be treated. In the case of New Spain (a viceroyalty that laid claim to today's Central America north of Panama, all of Mexico, and much of the southwestern United States) Spanish ranchers, farmers, and miners wanted easy access to free Indian labor and found ways to obtain it. Other Spaniards, especially missionaries, wanted the native populations treated with compassion, with the goal of converting them to Christianity. Bureaucrats were often torn between their obligation to enforce their sov-

ereign's orders to treat Indians kindly and to promote the conversion of Indians, and their desire to enrich themselves and their cronies at the expense of Indians.

This lesson plan will enable students in both high school and the introductory college course in United States history to have a better grasp of the contradictions inherent in the colonization and missionization of New Spain—ongoing processes that lasted through the eighteenth century. To allow students to obtain an understanding of the people responsible for colonization, the accompanying activities encourage them to visualize the experience through the eyes of the different social and economic groups affected by colonization and the ensuing missionary and political actions of the Spanish. Different types of projects are offered so that students can enter the experience though various learning modalities.

History is often an imprecise discipline. It allows students to gain an appreciation of the past, but challenges them to refrain from letting modern-day ethical issues color their perception of past events. Contemporary ethics and values are of no consequence when ascertaining the ethics and values of Spaniards of the 1500s, 1600s, and 1700s, but a consideration of Spanish policies and the practices of individual Spaniards reveals a mix of benevolence, malevolence, and indifference when seen through the eyes of contemporaries.

Objectives

1. To clarify the reasons why European countries began exploration and colonization efforts in the New World.

From *OAH Magazine of History* 14, no. 4 (Summer 2000): 54–58. © Organization of American Historians. Reprinted with permission.

2. To articulate the primary characteristics of mercantilism and its impact on the domestic and foreign policy of Spain.

3. To explain Spain's political atmosphere during the sixteenth and seventeenth centuries.

4. To discuss the religious fervor that led to the Christianization efforts of the Spanish missionaries.

5. To identify the significant advances in science and technology that enabled the Europeans to explore the rest of the world.

6. To explain the impact of the conquistadores and the missionaries on the indigenous population of New Spain.

7. To analyze the cultural and economic patterns of interaction between the Spaniards and the indigenous population.

8. To interpret accurately specific primary sources related to the colonization efforts.

9. To delineate the goals that Spain had for New Spain.

10. To prepare a cogent essay regarding the Spanish treatment of the indigenous population by Spanish conquistadores, bureaucrats, and missionaries.

Activities

I. Film

Use of film in the history curriculum needs to be approached with an awareness of the potential for distortion of historical information and the need for the filmmakers to convey a certain, preconceived perspective. With that caveat in mind, the 1986 movie *The Mission* provides an introduction to the eighteenth-century Spanish Jesuit missionary presence among the Guaraní in South America.

The movie, approximately 125 minutes long, provides students with different perceptions of the same circumstances and thus presents them with the moral consequences of decisions made by political and religious leaders. The movie also enables students to visualize the difficulty of governing an empire thousands of miles away without the benefit of modern instantaneous communication. Articles by Barbara Ganson and James Schofield Saeger (see Sources for Further Study) can provide further perspective on the film.

Before showing the film, distribute the following Reflection Questions. Ask students to keep these questions in mind as they watch the movie. After the viewing, either discuss the questions as a class or have students complete them individually as homework.

Reflection Questions for The Mission

1. Which historical events does the film depict? Does it portray them accurately?

2. What interpretation of the era does the film present?

3. In the film, those who hold political power feel compromised by the presence of the Jesuit mission and call upon church leadership, as representatives of divine power, to intervene, judge, and arbitrate the transfer of power. What is the political significance of the Church's hierarchy becoming involved in the political issues? How does the film portray the leaders of the Church? How does it portray the political leaders?

4. The indigenous people clearly are cultured, as evidenced by their musical ability and their excellent artisanship. They have also become Christian. However, both the Spanish and the Portuguese continue to dehumanize them, spout fears about them, and ultimately claim a need to subjugate them. Each of these actions seems to justify slavery as a common good. What underlies these efforts by those who wish to oppress the Indians? How are similar rationalizations utilized in contemporary culture? Who are the oppressed of today?

5. Rodrigo Mendoza murders his protégé and the lover of his betrothed. As penance and in an effort to earn his redemption, he carries an unbearably heavy load of his former weapons and armor. These items represent his arrogance and egoism, which has led him to justify killing. At the end of his pilgrimage, he finally accepts the release of his burden. He then weeps copiously. Why?

6. As Mendoza is accepted into the Indian community, they paint his body; he is given a Bible to read, and he later expresses a desire to join the Jesuits. His former life is transformed by these experiences. What is different and what is the same as Mendoza enters his "new life"?

7. After an outburst before the political leaders of Spain and Portugal, Mendoza apologizes, even though he had spoken the truth. At this point, all Jesuits are suspected of holding political leaders in contempt, and thus, the Jesuits represent a major threat to the status quo. How did the Jesuits gain such "power"?

8. To preserve the Church in Europe, the Jesuit missions in Latin America were destroyed. Explain the relationship between the two, and identify what was really at stake.

9. The Indians decide to fight for their home at the mission, and the Jesuits stay. Three of the four Jesuits choose to fight alongside the Indians, while one refuses to fight. He claims, "You promised your life to God, and God is love. You cannot die with blood on your hands." Who is right, those who fight or the one who refrains from fighting?

10. How does the martyrdom of the eighteenth-century Jesuits compare to that of the twentieth-century Jesuit martyrs of El Salvador (16 November 1989), or that of Archbishop Oscar Romero (24 March 1980)?

11. Contemporary liberation theology claims to enunciate the Gospel values of Jesus as being in solidarity with the poor. This ideology has gained supporters, particularly in Latin America, among those who strive to assist the marginalized who suffer political and economic oppression. Liberation theologians insist that the poor be accorded the dignity and power that Jesus preached in the Gospels. How do the actions of the Jesuit missionaries relate to the theology of modern-day liberation theologians?

II. Timeline

Ask students to prepare a timeline of the Spanish explorers and their places of exploration. Have them indicate the outcome of the exploration (i.e., colonization, establishment of a mission, abandonment of the site, settlement, etc.) on the timeline. For comparison, students should add key dates relating to French and English exploration and colonization.

III. Propaganda

Discuss with students the various types of propaganda available to the Jesuit or Franciscan missionaries. Break the class into groups and assign a specific Indian group to each. Then have students devise a list of appropriate strategies the missionaries may have used to entice Native Americans to attend Catholic religious ceremonies.

IV. Maps

Have students prepare maps indicating their awareness of the expansiveness of the Spanish Empire. These maps should identify areas and the dates of their conquest, as well as indicating the exploration routes of the Spanish explorers. Have students use overlay maps of sixteenth-century exploration with contemporary maps in order to correlate New Spain with its contemporary counterparts.

V. Identification of Important People

Ask students to provide a one-to-two-paragraph identification of important people involved in the exploration, colonization, and missionary work of New Spain, particularly its northern frontiers. Include the following:

A. Hernán Cortes
B. Montezuma/Aztecs
C. Bernal Díaz del Castillo
D. Bartolomé de las Casas, O.P.
E. Juan de Oñate
F. Viceroy Luis de Velasco
G. Diego de Vargas
H. Eusebio Kino, S.J.
I. Juan María Salvatierra, S.J.
J. Cuerno Verde
K. Juan Bautista de Anza
L. Salvador Palma
M. José de Galvez
N. Junípero Serra, O.F.M.
O. Father Fermín Francisco de Lasuén, O.F.M.
P. Carlos III

VI. Technology of the Period

Have students research the technology present at the time of colonization. How were adobe bricks made? How were cattle used in the hide and tallow industry? How was water diverted for village use? Allow the students to present the information orally so that the entire class will benefit from their work.

Use this information to encourage group cooperation by having the class prepare a diorama of a typical village of some native group. This diorama should illustrate the technology of the time and include changes brought about through contact with Spaniards. Reinforce for the students the central presence of the Catholic Church within the villages of some Indian peoples. What are the limitations and biases of the sources from which we reconstruct Indian life?

VII. Mercantilism

Mercantilism, defined simply, is an economic and political theory that gained prominence during the Age of Exploration. It maintained that countries should accumulate bullion (gold and silver), establish colonies to provide a ready-made source of goods for the Mother Country, and develop a favorable balance of trade through the establishment of industry.

Assign a research project where students explore the main tenets of mercantilism, drawing conclusions about its effects on present-day economics. Questions that might assist them in this effort are:

1. How does a developed country establish its economic policy? What decision-making processes do the leaders of the country institute to establish economic viability in a global economy?

2. How might countries rich in natural resources improve their balance of trade?

3. How does the fluctuation of gold prices impact a country's economy?

4. Are gold and silver the desired acquisitions of countries today?

5. Do countries today view their political power as being economically based, as was true in the Age of Exploration?

6. In what ways do developing countries struggle to maintain a favorable balance of trade?

7. What international movement has arisen in the past few years to assist developing countries in their economic struggle? (A call to eradicate debts owed to developed countries.)

VIII. Religious Orders

Have students research the prominent religious orders present in New Spain. Background on the Franciscans, Dominicans, and Jesuits will enable students to better understand the political power wielded by these orders and the ensuing political differences that led to the expulsion of the Jesuits from New Spain and the resulting takeover of the missions by the Franciscans and Dominicans.

IX. Role-playing

Assign students identities from the following list and have them write a diary from this perspective. Teachers need to determine the time period and length of the diary entry. Those details might depend upon significant historical events that occurred and how the imaginary diarist might respond to that information. Students should be reminded that some of the imaginary respondents might be illiterate (such as the Native American man and woman). Thus, their entries might then be recorded via an (imaginary) oral history response.

A. Native American living under the *encomienda* system, a system of forced labor or tithe
B. Spanish nobleman
C. Queen of Spain
D. Jesuit or Franciscan priest
E. Native American woman
F. Native American man
G. Spanish noblewoman living in New Spain
H. Spanish viceroy
I. Bureaucrat for the Council of the Indies, which formulated policy for New Spain

X. Bureaucracy of New Spain

Have students develop a chart indicating the governmental structure present in New Spain. Include the *audiencias,* local magistrates, *alcaldes mayores, corregidores,* and town council (*cabildos* or *ayuntamientos*).

XI. Primary Sources

Use the following primary sources to allow students to draw their own conclusions regarding the mind-set of Spaniards as they colonized and Christianized the native population of New Spain.

Unless otherwise stated, these documents can be found in Charles Gibson, *The Spanish Tradition in America* (New York: Harper and Row, 1968). Page numbers are given in parentheses.

A. Letters of Father Junípero Serra (Antonine Tibesar, ed. and trans., *Writings of Junipero Serra,* 4 vols. Washington, DC: American Academy of Franciscan History, 1955–1966.)
B. Sections from Bernal Díaz's *The Conquest of New Spain* (translated by John M. Cohen, Baltimore: Penguin Books, 1963.)
C. Royal Order for New Discoveries of 1573 (Dora P. Crouch, et al., *Spanish City Planning in North America* [Cambridge: MIT Press, 1982].)
D. Account of the Pueblo Revolt of 1680 (Gibson, 183–93)
E. Laws of Burgos, 1512–1513 (Gibson, 61–82)
F. *Sublimis Deus,* papal Bull, 1537 (Gibson, 104–5)
G. New Laws of the Indies, 1542 (Gibson, 109–12)
H. Treaty of Tordesillas, 1494 (Gibson, 42–51)

XII. Debates

After students have studied the primary sources sufficiently, divide the class into debate teams. Assign each team specific positions and specific "people" and stage a debate regarding Spanish policy in the New World.

Conclusion

The above activities, while not exhaustive, are designed to foster deeper awareness within the students of the reasons for colonization, the methods used to colonize, and the ensuing missionary efforts in New Spain. The students should, at the conclusion of the unit, be able to explain the rationale for Spain's foreign policy toward New Spain and the rationale for the procedures used to Christianize the indigenous population.

Further, the students should be able to articulate, both orally and in writing, the debate that has ensued among historians as to the Spanish attitudes and actions toward Native Americans: were they benevolent, malevolent, or indifferent?

Primary Sources

Bolton, Herbert E., ed. *Spanish Exploration in the Southwest, 1542–1706.* 1908. Reprint, New York: Barnes and Noble, 1967.

Díaz del Castillo, Bernal. *The Conquest of New Spain.* Translated with an introduction by John M. Cohen. Baltimore: Penguin Books, 1963.

Gibson, Charles, comp. *The Spanish Tradition in America.* New York: Harper and Row, 1968.

Mozifio, José Mariano. *Noticias de Nutka: An Account of Nootka Sound in 1792.* Ed. and trans. Iris H.W. Engstrand. Seattle: University of Washington Press, 1991.

Tibesar, Antonine, ed. and trans. *Writings of Junipero Serra.* 4 vols. Washington, DC: American Academy of Franciscan History, 1955–1966.

Sources for Further Study

Brading, D.A. *The First America: The Spanish Monarchy, Creole Patriots, and the Liberal State, 1492–1867.* New York: Cambridge University Press, 1991.

Cooke, Jacob Ernest. *Encyclopedia of the North American Colonies.* 3 vols. New York: Charles Scribner's Sons, 1993.

Crouch, Dora P., Daniel J. Garr, and Axel I. Mundigo. *Spanish City Planning in North America.* Cambridge: MIT Press, 1982.

Cutter, Charles R. *The Protector de Indios in Colonial New Mexico, 1659–1821.* Albuquerque: University of New Mexico Press, 1986.

Cutter, Donald, and Iris Engstrand. *Quest for Empire: Spanish Settlement in the Southwest.* Golden, CO: Fulcrum Publishing, 1996.

Cutter, Donald C. *California in 1792: A Spanish Naval Visit.* Norman: University of Oklahoma Press, 1990.

Engstrand, Iris H.W. "The Eighteenth Century Enlightenment Comes to Spanish California." *Southern California Quarterly* 80 (Spring 1998): 3–30.

———— "The Enlightenment in Spain: Influence upon New World Policy." *The Americas* 41 (April 1985): 436–44.

Dunne, Peter Masten. *Black Robes in Lower California.* Berkeley: University of California Press, 1952.

Ganson, Barbara. "'Like Children under Wise Parental Sway': Passive Portrayals of the Guaraní Indians in European Literature and *The Mission.*" *Colonial Latin American Historical Review* 3 (Fall 1994): 399–422.

Greenleaf, Richard E. *The Roman Catholic Church in Colonial Latin America.* New York: Knopf, 1971.

Guest, Francis F. *Fermín Francisco de Lasuén: A Biography.* Washington, DC: Academy of American Franciscan History, 1973.

Gutierrez, Ramon A. *When Jesus Came, the Corn Mothers Went Away: Marriage, Sexuality, and Power in New Mexico, 1500–1846.* Stanford: Stanford University Press, 1991.

Haring, Clarence H. *The Spanish Empire in America.* 1947. Reprint, New York: Harcourt, Brace and World, 1963.

Ives, Ronald L. *José Velásquez: Saga of a Borderland Soldier.* Tucson: Southwestern Mission Research Center, 1984.

Kanellos, Nicolas. *Thirty Million Strong: Reclaiming the Hispanic Image in American Culture.* Golden, CO: Fulcrum Publishing, 1998.

Maclachlan, Colin M., and Jaime E. Rodriguez O. *The Forging of the Cosmic Race: A Reinterpretation of Colonial Mexico.* Expanded edition. Berkeley: University of California Press, 1980.

Meigs, Peveril. *The Dominican Mission Frontier of Lower California.* Berkeley: University of California Press, 1935.

Meyer, Michael C., William Sherman, and Susan M. Deeds. *The Course of Mexican History.* New York: Oxford University Press, 1999.

O'Malley, John W. *The First Jesuits.* Cambridge: Harvard University Press, 1993.

Powell, Philip Wayne. *Tree of Hate: Propaganda and Prejudices Affecting United States Relations with the Hispanic World.* New York: Basic Books, 1971.

Saeger, James Schofield. "*The Mission* and Historical Missions: Film and the Writing of History." *The Americas* 51 (January 1995): 393–415.

Sale, Kirkpatrick. *Conquest of Paradise.* New York: Knopf, 1990.

Wagner, Henry Raup, and Helen Rand Parish. *The Life and Writings of Bartolomé de las Casas.* Albuquerque: University of New Mexico Press, 1967.

————. *The Spanish Frontier in North America.* New Haven: Yale University Press, 1992.

Weber, David J., ed. *What Caused the Pueblo Revolt of 1680?* Boston: Bedford/St. Martin's, 1999.

Internet Resources

Web sites spring up with great frequency. Numerous university sites contain information regarding specific periods of history. The following are given as possible sources for information concerning the Age of Exploration and the Spanish presence in the New World. The accuracy and timeliness of the sites are not guaranteed.

Age of Exploration: <http://www2.sunysuffolk.edu/westn/explor.html>.

Age of Exploration Timeline: <http://www.mariner.org/age/histexp.html>.

Aztec Account of the Conquest of Mexico: <http://www.fordham.edu/halsall/mod/aztecs1.html>.

Cultural Readings: Colonization and Print in the Americas: <http://www.library.upenn.edu/ special/ gallery/kislak/ promotion/ diaz.html>.

European Voyages of Exploration: <http://www.acs.ucalgary.ca/ HIST/tutor/ eurvoya/ aztec.html>.

North American Wilderness Trail Educational Resources: <http://www.therapure.com/anza-trail/education.htm>.

Resources for Spain: <http://www.ukans.edu/-iberia/ssphs/ spain-resources.html>.

Spanish Missions of California: <http://library.thinkquest.org/3615>.

CHAPTER 33

Disease in the Atlantic World, 1492–1900

KAREN E. CARTER

Before Columbus made his infamous voyage to the New World in 1492, the Americas existed in complete isolation from the rest of the major landmasses of the globe. As Europeans—and later Africans—began to trickle across the Atlantic, they brought with them a whole host of organisms that indigenous Americans had never seen before, from horses, cattle, and chickens to food crops and even weeds. The newcomers also inadvertently brought diseases caused by tiny pathogens that found an entire population without immunity. Epidemics of smallpox, measles, mumps, malaria, typhus, influenza, and yellow fever proceeded to ravage the American Indian population generation after generation. This demographic catastrophe is essential to an understanding of the creation of the Atlantic World, since so many of the European activities in the New World might have been curtailed if the Indians had maintained their numbers and been able to better defend themselves against European encroachment.

This lesson plan will give students a broad understanding of how such a widespread demographic collapse happened and what general effects it had. Then students will study the effects of one specific disease, smallpox, on a specific population: the Huron and Algonquin of New France in the seventeenth century. Finally, students will return to a broader perspective once again by researching the effects of epidemic disease in other parts of the world in the early modern period.

National Standards

Era 1: Standard 2B—Demonstrate understanding of the Spanish Conquest of the Americas

Era 2: Standard 1C—Demonstrate understanding of the European struggle for control of North America

Student Objectives

Students will be able to:

1. Understand how the history of the opening of the Atlantic World in 1492 and the history of disease are related.

2. Understand the effects of disease on populations in the Atlantic World, including American Indians, Europeans, and Africans.

3. Understand the difference between epidemic and endemic diseases.

4. Recognize how differences in culture and religion can affect reactions to epidemic disease.

5. Understand the limitations early modern peoples had in dealing with epidemic disease and how modern science overcame many of those limitations in the twentieth century.

6. Read and analyze primary documents.

7. Conduct research on a given epidemic in the early modern world and write creatively about it.

Time

This lesson plan requires two forty-five minute class periods, in addition to any in-class research time you are inclined to allow.

From *OAH Magazine of History* 18, no. 3 (April 2004): 27–32. © Organization of American Historians. Reprinted by permission.

Background

This lesson should be given in conjunction with material on the Age of Exploration and the discovery of the Americas. Students should ideally have some background on the Spanish conquests in Central and South America, as well as early European settlements in North America.

Procedure

A. Introductory Activity

Use the game, "Tricky True or False" (see Appendix, below) to introduce some of the basic ideas about the effects of disease in the early modern Atlantic World. After allowing approximately five minutes for the students to answer the following twelve true or false questions on their own, explain that the purpose of the game is for the students to see if they can "beat" the teacher by answering the most questions correctly. Read each question aloud, and then ask how many answered true and how many answered false. If the majority of the class answers correctly, then the class gets a point. If not, the teacher gets a point. At the end of the game, if the students have more points than the teacher, then they win some sort of reward. I usually give extra credit points, equivalent to the number of points by which they won.

These questions are introductory questions for students who have had little or no previous exposure to material about diseases in the Atlantic World. Students should understand that they will not be penalized for incorrect answers.

Most of the questions are also designed for discussion. After revealing the correct answer, ask the students how they arrived at their answers. Have students correct their own papers and make notes in the space provided after each question.

1. The most devastating disease that Europeans brought with them to the New World was smallpox.

Answer: True. Because smallpox is so easy to catch, has such high mortality rates, and has no animal carrier or vector, it was the most effective killer in the New World. Smallpox can be transferred through direct contact with an infected person, by inhaling infectious droplets in the air, or even by contact with the dried-out scabs of an infectious person. The virus that causes smallpox can survive for several weeks outside the human body, so a person could catch it just by handling infected clothing. The sick person is also contagious for a long period of time: beginning fourteen days after the first exposure to the virus, an infected person is contagious for sixteen days.[1]

Ask students if they know of other diseases brought to the New World from either Europe or Africa. The list should include measles, mumps, malaria, yellow fever, influenza, typhus, and plague.

2. Because of outbreaks of diseases, the native population of Hispaniola (today Haiti and the Dominican Republic) was reduced by one-half—from 750,000 to 375,000—in the first fifty years after Columbus landed there in 1492.

Answer: False. Estimates of the pre-Columbian population of Hispaniola range from 60,000 to nearly 8 million, and the native population stood at 33,523 in 1510, 26,334 in 1514, and 2,000 in 1542, or a 97 percent loss, using the lowest estimate for the initial population. For many of the islands in the Caribbean, this kind of devastation was typical. For the Americas as a whole, approximately 90 percent of the native population, estimated at 100 million in 1492, was destroyed as a result of the European invaders and the diseases they inadvertently brought with them.[2]

3. The native peoples of the Americas died so easily from disease because their immune systems were weakened by warfare and famine caused by European invaders.

Answer: False. Although warfare and famine can make diseases worse, the most important factor is how often people had been exposed to the various disease-causing pathogens. Diseases like smallpox, malaria, yellow fever, and measles had never been seen before in the New World, so none of the natives had any immunity against them. Remind students that these diseases did not just affect people in the Americas: disease was a major limiting factor for all human populations in the Atlantic World. For example, even in the eighteenth century, smallpox accounted for 10 to 15 percent of all deaths in Europe; 80 percent of those victims were under ten years of age. Children who survived, then, had lifelong immunity. Thus in any given outbreak in the Americas, only a small percentage of Europeans who had not been exposed previously would get the disease, while 100 percent of the native population was at risk.[3]

4. Chicken pox is a disease that is endemic in the United States today.

Answer: True. Explain the difference between an "epidemic" and an "endemic" disease. Endemic disease is always present in a population, usually in the form of a childhood disease. Often, a milder form confers immunity with a smaller percentage of deaths than an epidemic disease. For example, most children get chicken pox and easily survive it. Then they are immune from it for life. An epidemic disease is usually a stronger strain, with higher rates of mortality, and is found in populations that have had little or no previous exposure. Severe Acute Respiratory Syndrome (SARS) is a new, global epidemic disease in the world today and monkeypox is a new epidemic in the United States. Smallpox, measles, and yellow fever were epidemic diseases in the Americas in the early modern period. It took about five or six generations for these diseases to become endemic in the New World.

5. The people in the Americas did not have chicken pox because they did not have any chickens.

Answer: False. The term chicken pox has nothing to do with chickens—it comes from the Latin word *cicer,* or chickpeas, because the Romans apparently thought the spots looked like chickpeas. Still, it is true that diseases and animals are closely related. Most of the Old World diseases came originally from animals. This is true today as well: SARS, for example, probably jumped from a cat-like animal called a civet, to the humans who ate it. Because Europeans had a large number of domesticated animals that they had been in close contact with for thousands of years, pathogens made the jump from animal hosts to human hosts, creating diseases like smallpox. Native American populations had only two large domesticated animals, the alpaca and the llama, both found only in some regions of the Andes, so the likelihood of contracting mutated diseases from animals was much smaller. Make sure that students understand that the form of the disease that the vast majority of people in the early modern world contracted did not come directly from contact with animals: the human form of smallpox had mutated thousands of years earlier and was transferred only from human to human. Yellow fever, similarly, probably originally came from monkeys and was transferred to humans when mosquitoes bit infected monkeys and then carried the virus to human hosts. Then a human form of the disease was created and transferred by mosquitoes from human to human.

6. Native Americans got their revenge on European invaders by giving them syphilis, a disease that Europeans had never seen before.

Answer: False. Some historians now believe that syphilis was present in Europe before 1492. The strain that resulted from sexual contact between Europeans and Native Americans, however, was much stronger than the nonvenereal version that a few isolated European regions had experienced. This new version was carried back to Europe and spread among the population there.[4]

7. Although there was an outbreak of smallpox during the Revolutionary War, George Washington had been vaccinated so he was able to continue to lead the American army.

Answer: False. There are two things wrong with this statement. First, Washington was not affected by the smallpox outbreak during the Revolutionary War because he had had the disease when he was nineteen years old. In 1751, he traveled with his half-brother Lawrence to Barbados. At some point during this trip, Washington contracted a case of smallpox which was virulent enough to keep him from writing in his diary for twenty-four days in November and December of 1751. He returned to Virginia in 1752 with lifelong immunity.

The second problem with this statement is with the term "vaccination." No one was vaccinated for smallpox in the eighteenth century, but some were beginning to be inoculated. Vaccination involves an injection of material that will keep a person from acquiring a disease and confer lifelong immunity. Inoculation involves purposely exposing a person to the virus so that he or she will get a mild form of the disease and then have immunity. In George Washington's day, this meant taking matter from the pustules of a person with smallpox and scratching it into the skin of a healthy person. After a few days, the person would get a mild form of smallpox that was usually survivable. Exposure by injection almost always results in a mild form of the disease: even today, no one is sure why this is the case.[5]

8. Europeans thought that climate was the primary cause of diseases like yellow fever and malaria because they were usually only found in hot and moist environments.

Answer: True. The English word "malaria" actually comes from the Italian word, *mal'aria,* or bad air. No one knew that yellow fever and malaria were spread by mosquitoes until the late nineteenth century, and so the belief that warm, moist air or putrid smells could cause changes in body chemistry that would then produce disease persisted. In fact, it is the mosquitoes that thrive in this environment, meaning people are more likely to be bitten by a mosquito carrying the virus that causes malaria or yellow fever. Both of these diseases arrived in the Americas in the blood of a sick person who was then bitten by mosquitoes. The mosquitoes carried the virus and passed it along to any other people they might bite. In addition, female mosquitoes also handed down the virus to their offspring, meaning that it could exist in mosquito populations even in areas where human populations were not very large. By the mid-seventeenth century, yellow fever was endemic in the European, native, and African populations of the islands of the Caribbean. The constant presence actually prevented foreign powers from conquering the islands because any foreign troops arriving from Europe usually got sick before they could effectively wage war.[6]

9. When Europeans arrived in the Americas, they needed a lot of laborers to work on sugar plantations. They chose to use African laborers rather than Indians because Africans were already immune to European diseases.

Answer: False. Early modern Europeans did believe that Africans were less susceptible to tropical diseases, but unless African slaves had had previous exposure, they were no more likely to be immune to smallpox, malaria, or yellow fever than any of the Indian or European populations. Although all of the major diseases were present in Africa, they could not be found in all parts of Africa. Thus, an African slave might be immune to malaria and yellow fever, but not smallpox, or vice versa. An African slave brought from a village far from the Atlantic coast most likely had no immunity to these diseases at all. Mortality on slave ships was often close to 25 percent; many of these deaths were likely from disease, although we have no way of discovering even approximate percentages. The one exception is those Africans born with the sickle-cell trait: a genetic mutation that brings immunity to malaria from birth but can also lead to high childhood mortality due to anemia. Probably only a very tiny percentage of Africans taken to the Americas aboard slave ships actually had this gene.

10. Europeans were not able to colonize Africa in the early modern period because half of the Europeans who tried to travel beyond the Atlantic coast of Africa died from malaria.

Answer: True. Records of the British army for the years 1817–1836 show that 77 percent of the European soldiers sent to West Africa died from disease. Europeans were able to colonize Africa only in the late nineteenth century, after discovering that daily doses of quinine prevented the virus from doing any damage.[7]

11. Because of modern medical technology, today both malaria and smallpox have been eradicated.

Answer: False. Although smallpox now exists only in laboratories—the last known death from smallpox was in 1978 when a woman contracted the disease in a lab, not from any naturally occurring source—malaria continues to be a major problem in Africa today. Malaria infects 500 million people a year; of those, 2.7 million die. Half of these are children—enough that one child dies every thirty seconds. Before AIDS, malaria was still the number one killer in Africa.

Malaria has not been eradicated for several reasons. First, a person who gets malaria is only immune to future attacks for three or four years, so the number of possible hosts for the virus is always very large. Second, there is no vaccine for malaria, as there is for smallpox. The virus that causes malaria is much more complex than the one that causes smallpox, so it is more difficult to tame. It also develops drug-resistant strains quickly, so new drugs have to be found. Third, malaria is most prevalent in some of the poorest regions of the world where there is simply not enough money for drugs and for mosquito-control programs.[8]

12. Disease was the most important reason why Europeans were able to conquer the New World.

Answer: True. The answer to this question is actually debatable and designed to lead to a class discussion to conclude the exercise. Ask students to give reasons why this statement could be false. In the end, emphasize that while other European advantages—metal weaponry, horses, and internal divisions among the native peoples—might have been important in individual circumstances, in the long run it was the devastating effects of disease that allowed Europeans to dominate the Americas so completely.

B. Primary Source Analysis

In this section of the lesson, students will read and compare two primary source documents, each describing how French colonists and American Indians in New France dealt with the constant presence of smallpox in the first half of the seventeenth century. These descriptions are part of a set of documents known as the *Jesuit Relations*—seventeenth-century letters written to Jesuit superiors detailing the successes and difficulties of Catholic missions in New France. They are available online at <http://puffin.creighton.edu/jesuit/relations/>. Volume 15, document XXX, chapter I is a letter written by François Joseph Le Mercier in 1638. It describes tension between the missionaries and the Indians because the latter believed that the newcomers were deliberately making them sick. Volume 19, document XLI, chapter XI provides the opposite perspective. Written by Paul Le Jeune in 1640, the letter describes the work of nuns at a hospital and shows that some American Indians readily accepted the help of the missionaries and actually converted to Catholicism because of the disease. The web site provides these documents for free and is searchable, and texts can be downloaded easily.

Divide the students into groups of four or five. After they read the documents, have them answer the following questions as a group. Then discuss the documents as a class.

Discussion questions

1. What do the American Indians in document XXX (Le Mercier) believe to be the cause of the sickness that is killing so many people? Several causes are given: list as many as you can.
2. How do the missionaries react to the sickness of the natives? What do they believe is the cause of the disease?
3. What does Le Mercier's account tell us about the religious beliefs of the Indians? How do these beliefs affect their understanding of the smallpox epidemic?
4. In document XLI, Le Jeune recognizes that people who were born in New France were susceptible to smallpox, while those born in France were not. How does modern medicine explain this? How does Le Jeune explain it?
5. What do these documents tell us about the symptoms of smallpox? What kind of treatments did the hospital nuns give to their patients?
6. Describe how the Indians reacted to the missionaries and to smallpox in Father Le Jeune's account.

How are their reactions different from those found in Le Mercier's text? Can you speculate as to why there were such different feelings about the presence of missionaries?

7. Both of these accounts show that a great many Indians became infected with smallpox, and a large number of those died. What kind of effects would this have on a society?

8. Think about what would happen if over half of your own family members and friends died from an unknown disease. What would change about your life? What if you did not know what the cause of the disease was? Whom would you blame?

9. Do you think an outbreak of epidemic disease could have such a drastic effect on American society today? What tools do we have in the twenty-first century that can help minimize the effects of epidemic diseases? Think about how some modern epidemics, like AIDS, SARS, West Nile Virus, and monkeypox, have been dealt with by authorities in the United States.

C. Research Project

Return the students to their groups and assign each group to research a major early modern epidemic. Using the materials they find, each group should then write a newspaper article from the perspective of the society experiencing the disease. Students should feel free to be creative, while being as historically accurate as possible. The article should include the following:

- description of the disease and its effects on people
- theories about the origin of the disease, keeping in mind the limitations of scientific knowledge of the infected society
- suggestions on what should be done about the epidemic, again considering the limitations of knowledge and resources in the early modern period

After the groups have finished their articles, assign new groups, each containing one member of the original group. Each individual should then share the article with the other members of the new group.

Suggested Research Topics

- The black plague in fourteenth-century Europe
- The smallpox epidemic of 1518–1519 in Central Mexico that helped Cortés in his conquest of the Aztecs
- The smallpox epidemic of 1775–1782 that took place in the American colonies and affected the Revolutionary War
- Cholera epidemics in the United States and Europe in the nineteenth century

- European influenza outbreaks in the eighteenth century
- The Hawaiian smallpox epidemic of 1853.

Notes

1. Elizabeth A. Fenn, *Pox Americana: The Great Smallpox Epidemic of 1775–82* (New York: Hill and Wang, 2001), 15–20.

2. These population estimates can be found in Noble David Cook, *Born to Die: Disease and New World Conquest, 1492–1650* (Cambridge, UK: Cambridge University Press, 1998), 23–4; and William H. McNeill, *Plagues and Peoples* (Garden City, NY: Anchor Press, 1976), 203–4.

3. Peter C. English, "Smallpox," in *The Cambridge World History of Human Disease*, Kenneth F. Kiple, ed. (Cambridge, UK: Cambridge University Press, 1993), 1010.

4. Jon Arrizabalaga, "Syphilis," in *The Cambridge World History of Human Disease*, Kenneth F. Kible, ed. (Cambridge, UK: Cambridge University Press, 1993), 1025–33.

5. Elizabeth A. Fenn's *Pox Americana*, 13–5, 31–3, gives information on Washington's bout with smallpox and inoculation procedures in the late eighteenth-century colonies.

6. See the essay by J.R. McNeill in this issue of the *OAH Magazine of History*, 9–13.

7. Daniel R. Headrick, *The Tools of Empire: Technology and European Imperialism in the Nineteenth Century* (New York: Oxford University Press, 1981), 62–3.

8. Donovan Webster, "Malaria Kills One Child Every 30 Seconds," *Journal of Public Health Policy* 22 (2001): 23–33.

Bibliography

Bazin, Hervé. *The Eradication of Smallpox: Edward Jenner and the First and Only Eradication of a Human Infectious Disease*. Andrew and Glenise Morgan, trans. San Diego, CA: Academic Press, 2000.

Bushnell, O.A. *The Gifts of Civilization: Germs and Genocide in Hawaii*. Honolulu: University of Hawaii Press, 1993.

Cohn, Samuel K. *The Black Death Transformed: Disease and Culture in Early Renaissance Europe*. New York: Oxford University Press, 2002.

Cook, Noble David. *Born to Die: Disease and New World Conquest, 1492–1650*. Cambridge, UK: Cambridge University Press, 1998.

Crosby, Alfred. *The Columbian Exchange: Biological and Cultural Consequences of 1492*. Westport, CT: Greenwood Publishing Company, 1972.

———. *Ecological Imperialism: The Biological Expansion of Europe, 900–1900*. Cambridge, UK: Cambridge University Press, 1986.

Diamond, Jared. *Guns, Germs, and Steel: The Fates of Human Societies*. New York: W.W. Norton & Co., 1997.

Fenn, Elizabeth A. *Pox Americana: The Great Smallpox Epidemic of 1775–82*. New York: Hill and Wang, 2001.

Hays, J.N. *The Burdens of Disease: Epidemics and Human Response in Western History*. New Brunswick, NJ: Rutgers University Press, 1998.

Headrick, Daniel R. *The Tools of Empire: Technology and European Imperialism in the Nineteenth Century*. New York: Oxford University Press, 1981.

————, ed. *The Cambridge World History of Human Disease.* Cambridge, UK: Cambridge University Press, 1993.

Kiple, Kenneth F., and Stephen V. Beck. *Biological Consequences of European Expansion, 1450–1800.* Brookfield, VT: Ashgate, 1997.

Kohn, George Childs, ed. *Encyclopedia of Plague and Pestilence: From Ancient Times to the Present.* New York: Facts on File, 2001.

McNeill, William H. *Plagues and Peoples.* Garden City, NY: Anchor Press, 1976.

Patterson, K. David. *Pandemic Influenza, 1700–1900: A Study in Historical Epidemiology.* Totowa, NJ: Rowman and Littlefield, 1986.

Rosenberg, Charles E. *The Cholera Years: The United States in 1832, 1849, and 1866.* Chicago: University of Chicago Press, 1987.

Watts, Sheldon. *Epidemics and History: Disease, Power, and Imperialism.* New Haven, CT: Yale University Press, 1997.

Ziegler, Philip. *The Black Death.* London: Collins, 1969.

Appendix

Disease in Early Modern Atlantic World: A Tricky True or False Game

This game will introduce some of the basic ideas about the effects of disease in the early modern Atlantic World. The purpose of the game is for the students to see if they can "beat" the teacher by answering the most questions correctly.

Procedure—Circle "True" or "False" to each of the following twelve questions. After approximately five minutes, read each question aloud, and then ask how many answered true and how many answered false. If the majority of the class answers correctly, then the class gets a point. If not, the teacher gets a point.

1. The most devastating disease that Europeans brought with them to the New World was smallpox. True or False?

2. Because of outbreaks of diseases, the native population of Hispaniola (today Haiti and the Dominican Republic), was reduced by one-half—from 750,000 to only 375,000—in the first 50 years after Columbus landed there in 1492. True or False?

3. The native peoples of the Americas died so easily from disease because their immune systems were weakened by warfare and famine caused by European invaders. True or False?

4. Chicken pox is a disease that is endemic in the United States today. True or False?

5. The people in the Americas did not have chicken pox because they did not have any chickens. True or False?

6. Native Americans got their revenge on European invaders by giving them syphilis, a disease that Europeans had never seen before. True or False?

7. Although there was an outbreak of smallpox during the Revolutionary War, George Washington had been vaccinated so he was able to continue to lead the American army. True or False?

8. Europeans thought that climate was the primary cause of diseases like yellow fever and malaria because they were usually only found in hot and moist environments. True or False?

9. When Europeans arrived in the Americas, they needed a lot of laborers to work on sugar plantations. They chose to use African laborers rather than Indians because Africans were already immune to European diseases. True or False?

10. Europeans were not able to colonize Africa in the early modern period because half of the Europeans who tried to travel beyond the Atlantic coast of Africa died from malaria. True or False?

11. Because of modern medical technology, today both malaria and smallpox have been eradicated. True or False?

12. Disease was the most important reason why Europeans were able to conquer the New World. True or False?

CHAPTER 34

Witches in the Atlantic World

ELAINE BRESLAW

This topic examines the beliefs about witchcraft and the nature of witch-hunts in a variety of cultures that rim the Atlantic Ocean. The focus is on areas that participated, either passively or actively, in the European westward expansion from the fifteenth to the eighteenth century. Those areas include western Europe, England and Scotland, parts of West Africa, and American Indian groups, all of whom felt the impact of this expansion and were brought into close contact because of it. The reading material noted under "Suggested Strategies" is available in my text, *Witches of the Atlantic World: A Historical Reader and Primary Sourcebook* (New York University Press, 2000). The lesson plan is adapted from my college-level course on the same subject.

It is important that teachers make some assumptions about the subject and convey these as givens or "facts" to the students. Students have to understand that before the eighteenth century, people everywhere lived in a world populated by invisible supernatural forces, their presence sensed in even the most mundane aspects of life. Witchcraft was one way to explain the presence of evil, to establish a cause for misfortune and disease, to justify natural occurrences like storms and earthquakes, to give meaning to mysterious events, and to provide answers to problems that seemingly defied reasonable explanations. Magic both caused those events and could be used to undo the harmful effects.

The nature and extent of the power of those forces varied from culture to culture. In some, it came from a variety of gods or spiritual entities capable of doing both good and evil deeds. When the gods inflicted harm it was sometimes in retaliation for human behavior that violated a sacred practice. Or misfortune could be caused by people thought to be manipulating a spiritual power through magic to cause harm. Calamities, if not due to divine providence, could be traced to an evil human agent, a witch, working through that invisible spiritual realm. It was necessary in the first case to appease the gods through some socially acceptable magical rituals and in the second to control, banish, or even destroy those people with malicious intent.

Christianity, on the other hand, associated magical practice solely with evil doings. The witch was one who received his or her power from an evil force called Satan, a devil, a ruler of darkness who was determined to overthrow the true deity by subverting his kingdom on earth. Although the notion of an evil force was transcultural, the devil idea—a separate and single spiritual malevolency—is a unique part of the Judeo-Christian (and the Islamic) tradition that distinguishes European witchcraft beliefs and witch-hunts from many other societies.

Anthropologists make a distinction between witches and sorcerers. Witches are those whose power is inborn, part of their very nature, and possibly due to some physiological abnormality. Sorcerers differ in that their skill requires the use of artifacts, is learned rather than inherited, and is a deliberately directed magic usually for harmful purposes. Historians generally ignored these distinctions and lump both groups in one category of occult practitioners called witches or use the two terms interchangeably.

The scholars who study these witchcraft beliefs and rituals generally do not believe that the practices have any concrete reality beyond the psychological. The discussion in the classroom should not focus on the magical practices themselves. The teacher's emphasis should be on the social, emotional, and religious context of occurrences attributed to

From *OAH Magazine of History* 17, no. 4 (July 2003): 43–47. © Organization of American Historians. Reprinted by permission.

witchcraft and the role of witches and witch-hunts in these communities rather than the magical rituals themselves.

Objectives and National Standards

1. To interpret primary documents, as suggested by Standard Three of the National Standards for History, under "Historical Thinking."
2. To broaden the students' understanding of other cultures and their religious beliefs.
3. To establish who are the most likely people to be accused of witchcraft and why some people are more likely to be persecuted as witches than others.
4. To learn why witch-hunts occur at particular moments in history, what sets them off, and what effects they have on their social environments.
5. To understand that there are a variety of beliefs about witchcraft as well as universal assumptions.
6. To put what happened in Salem, Massachusetts, in 1692 into an historical context.

Procedures

Each topic should begin with the posing of a provocative question or the reading of a primary source that is analyzed and discussed in class.

Topical Outline

Part I: Definitions of terms followed by discussion of folk traditions:

1. Ancient folk traditions of the European continent
2. American Indian spiritual traditions
3. Spiritual focus of West African societies along the Atlantic coast and African American derivations

Part II: European attitudes toward witches from different religious perspectives:

1. The Roman Catholic Church
2. The newer Reformation churches
3. The English Protestant world
4. Why women were most often accused of witchcraft

Part III: Anglo-American (English colonies) events

1. Magical folk traditions in America
2. Puritan reaction to witchcraft
3. Witches in New England before the Salem events

Part IV: Salem, Massachusetts, 1692

1. The events
2. The trials and executions
3. How it ended

Suggested Strategies and Reading

As an introduction during the first class, pose the question of whether witchcraft really exists. Define witchcraft as the belief in the power to change the course of events using some magical ritual—a charm, a curse, a spell—or an emanation from the eye. Emphasize that the causal connection is psychological and depends on the power of suggestion. Only believers will respond to magical rituals. Nature, of course, is immune. On the other hand, if an earthquake follows a magical incantation, it can be reassuring to be able to blame it on a human agent.

Pose a secondary question of who is a witch? Students may refer to movies, TV depictions, Harry Potter, or other literary sources. These are all modern ideas and may not be related to the historical notions. Some may refer to the Christian definition of Satanic pacts and servants of the devil. A good working definition is that witches are people who think they can influence spiritual forces directly in order to affect material existence. Not all people agree on whether this power to manipulate occult forces is a natural or acquired ability. Nor is there agreement as to the nature of the spiritual forces or how to appeal to them. Magical rituals differ radically in different parts of the world and the effectiveness of any ritual or belief depends largely on cultural conditioning. What seems to work in one culture does not necessarily have any influence on those who are unfamiliar with that practice.

Content for Topics

Part I: Definitions of terms followed by discussion of folk traditions

1. Ancient folk traditions of the European continent
There is a witchcraft lore in Europe that is much older than Christianity and has little connection to those religious beliefs. Astrologers in Europe consulted the stars to foretell the future. Cunning folk on the continent and England carried on an oral tradition of healing with herbs invested with magical powers. Ordinary people in Europe were not concerned about Satan's involvement with their magical practices unless provoked to think along those lines by church officials.[1] Among the lay people in Europe witches were not always a menace to society. They had much to offer. Only after contact with Christianity did the distinction between those witches who were evil and those who were socially useful become blurred.

Who were the people most likely to be accused of witchcraft?

Some may have been "cunning folk," known to be skilled in the use of magic. More likely they were people who stood out because of odd or antisocial behavior. Folk in the Atlantic world shared the view that evil witches were deviant people who threatened to disrupt the harmony of the community and could not get along with their neighbors.[2] Labeled a witch or sorcerer, such a person became a visible, physical presence that could be blamed for calamities that beset the community.

2. American Indian spiritual traditions

Among the Indians, the shaman acted much as the cunning folk in Europe—curing illness, divining the future, resolving interpersonal conflicts. Preventing evil doings was more a matter of avoidance—not wanting to offend the spirits because that would disrupt a cosmic balance. The notion of a totally good God was an absurdity since their experience taught that all gods were capable of doing good or causing harm.[3] Misfortune then was not so much the result of evil acts as of broken taboos, of human failings. Ritual magic was essential to restore the balance in the cosmic order by appealing to the good will of the spirits. The shaman, the magical practitioner, was a respected person in Indian communities. These religious practices were demonized by Europeans.

It is possible that the belief in evil witchcraft and the occurrence of witch-hunts among New England Indians were the result of contact with European ideas and European cruelty and not part of an indigenous belief system.[4] North American Indians may have had no concept of a separate evil power among their own gods, but they did associate the acts of their adversaries, especially the Europeans, and the diseases brought with them, with malevolent forces.

3. Africans and African Americans

Africans, like their other sixteenth- and seventeenth-century Atlantic counterparts, lived in a world inhabited by spirits that continually acted on the destiny of human beings. Basic to the cosmos of many Africans were the twin beliefs that the spirits of the dead continue to reside in the village among the living and that all human suffering and adversity have a spiritual cause.[5] The harmful effects of these spirits, sometimes due to ancestors who have been offended, could be relieved only by appropriate rituals performed by the witch doctor or Obeah as a healer. Like the shaman, the witch doctor's skill in magical healing was especially respected.

A strong belief in the spiritual basis of disease and death, along with the sensitivity to witchcraft and sorcery, was carried over to America by Africans brought as slaves.[6] But for Africans in the English colonies the experience of cultural exchange was very different from that of the native American peoples. The weak physical position of the African as a slave cultivated more contempt than fear and thus the African worldview was ignored. The English made little attempt to convert Africans to their Christian beliefs. The result was the retention of many shared African ideas about the spiritual realm and the imaginative merging of magical practices taken from a variety of cultures but often hidden from the eyes of Europeans. Various types of sorcery, called Obeah and condemned as conjuring or witchcraft by the English, predominated in the English colonies.[7]

There is no doubt that the strong spiritual component of traditional African religions contributed to the continuing belief in witchcraft and the fear of ghosts, those spirits of the dead who might return to haunt the living who had offended them in life. Because of this idea that the spirits of the dead continue to reside among the living and can cause harm (or protect the family if adequately venerated), it was essential to show respect toward those who had died. Funerals, then, are an important source of information on attitudes toward witchcraft and sorcery among Africans and African Americans.[8]

Part II: European attitudes toward witches from different religious perspectives

Within Christian churches, mystical rituals were considered part of the worship of God and, therefore, by definition a valid exercise of religious expression. Outside the church similar rituals, said the theologians, appealed to the devil, the anti-Christ. Such practices were Satanic in origin. Most importantly, all magic of the folk or of other religious traditions, by their very nature non-Christian, were associated with devil worship and had to be destroyed. Witch-hunts became moral crusades intent on clearing the world of some category of people identified as evil agents, servants of Satan, and called witches.[9] It was assumed that witches were bent on corrupting the particular church, whether of Protestant or Roman Catholic.

These notions regarding the source of the witch's power partially explain the ferocious and sporadic witch-hunts of the sixteenth and seventeenth centuries in the European world. Witch-hunts became a way to assure a conformity of religious practices in Europe and America, in moral terms to institute a communal spiritual cleansing. Destruction of other belief systems was supported by a mandate to wipe out the forces opposing the true God, thus justifying large-scale witch-hunts.

1. The Roman Catholic Church

The Roman Catholic stereotype of the witch is described vividly in the fifteenth-century publication called *Malleus Maleficarum*.[10] Also known as the "Hammer of Witches," it was compiled by two Dominican priests and inquisitors in Germany: the Inquisitor General, Father James Sprenger, and Father Heinrich Kramer, called by his Latinized name,

Institoris, who was the main author. The work became the most important source of information on witches and witchcraft for both Protestants and Catholics and was consulted by theologians as late as the eighteenth century. According to the *Malleus,* the witch was one who, through an agreement with the devil, acquired special powers to do both harm and solve problems or cure sickness. The theory about the demonic focus of magical practices lingers on in the mythology of witchcraft.

2. The Newer Reformation churches

Witch-hunters became even more zealous as the Reformation heated up on the continent. The leaders of newly created non-Catholic churches (Protestants) were anxious to impose their ideas on the uninitiated and the partially Christianized folk who continued to practice older occult rituals and to force their ideas on Catholics within their communities. Protestantism had to secure its place by requiring conformity. Political leaders may have found witch trials useful means of getting rid of their secular opposition, but the religious justification, the urge to combat the devil, provided the moral force.

Courts in Protestant countries on the continent also followed the inquisitional procedures that had been used in Catholic countries to stamp out witchcraft. Torture remained the most effective means of eliciting confessions of diabolical collusion. Once found guilty, the accused, usually after confessing, were executed by burning at the stake (more likely garroted first). Such admissions of guilt and the public executions that followed, in turn, confirmed the morality and legitimacy of the new Protestant regimes.[11]

3. The English Protestant world

In England, although confessions to witchcraft were desired, the procedures and definition of the crime differed. Witchcraft, according to the English civil authorities, was a crime against society and, even though it might be heresy in the eyes of the church, the accused were subject to secular and not ecclesiastical law. The civil authorities were prohibited from using torture as a method of eliciting confessions. For a definition of the crime of witchcraft and how it was treated in the courts, Michael Dalton's seventeenth-century handbook is especially useful as a source.[12]

4. Why women were most often accused of witchcraft

Witchcraft, in the European experience, had also come to be a peculiarly female act.[13] It was one of the few crimes in the Anglo-American world in which the husband was not held accountable for his wife's illegal actions. Christian theologians, both Catholic and Protestant, set out extensive evidence to explain why women were more vulnerable to Satan's appeal than men were, justifying the greater persecution of women during witch-hunts. In most places the stereotype of the witch was of an old woman, widowed or never married, poor and dependent on others for sustenance, with an unpleasant and abrasive personality, who was often at odds with others.[14] Such disagreeable people became useful scapegoats in times of adversity.

Part III: Anglo-American events

The work in this section is on the New England experience. There were very few witchcraft trials in the more southerly colonies and only one execution.[15] In contrast, sixty-one people were tried for witchcraft in Connecticut and Massachusetts between 1647 and 1691 (before Salem) and fifteen or sixteen of them were executed.[16] Additionally, thirty people were convicted in the Salem court in 1692 and of those nineteen were executed.

1. Magical folk traditions

In America, where few people were persecuted for witchcraft before the 1660s, belief in magical powers was still part of the mental baggage the Puritans brought from old England.[17] Although such practices were condemned by the clergy, they continued to be used when orthodox methods of healing failed. Many of these beliefs and practices were exposed during the witch trial testimonies and can also be found in the writings of theologians, especially Increase and Cotton Mather. Of particular interest is Cotton Mather's 1689 *Memorable Providences.*[18] Here he describes what he thought was evidence of the devil's work in the Puritan community. In the process he provides a concise outline of his beliefs about witches, their powers, and why they appeared in Massachusetts. His stories may well have contributed to popular fears by confirming folk tales of miraculous happenings and paving the way for the more vigorous prosecution of witches in New England.

2. Puritan reaction to witchcraft

While playing up the reality of the devil, Puritans may have actually encouraged dependence on sorcerers and charmers to do what was forbidden. The Puritan clergy put their followers in the intolerable position of asserting the reality of witchcraft while denying any effective and legitimate cure of its evil effects.[19] It is no accident that cases of religious possession, sometimes interpreted as bewitchment, usually occurred in situations of intense religious experience. The strengthened belief in witchcraft may have been an essential element of the peculiar Puritanism developing in America.

3. Witches in New England before the Salem events

Of the many incidences of witchcraft in colonial New England, the most dramatic events were connected with cases of demonic possession. Two cases that have left detailed first-hand accounts provided opportunities to focus in on the fears and beliefs widespread in the English colonies:

the Goodwin children's bizarre behavior reported by Samuel Willard, and Elizabeth Knapp's experiences reported by Cotton Mather.[20] Students can read those reports and use them as a basis for discussion.

Part IV: Salem, Massachusetts, 1692

There is something about the Salem experience that takes it beyond the ordinary in a world that routinely executed witches.

The events of 1692 continue to both repel and fascinate the public after more than three hundred years. The drama of the persecutions has captured the literary imagination worldwide as it has repeatedly over the years intrigued American scholars. The events have not only led to a continuing controversy over the causes of such a horror, but also to the question of whether Salem was somehow outside the tradition of European witch-hunting. As the last of the witch-hunts to occur in the English-speaking world, Salem represents a culmination and useful ending for a study of witchcraft and witch-hunts at the end of the seventeenth century.

1. The events
Some time should be devoted to a description of the political problems of Massachusetts in the 1680s, the continuation of Indian warfare, the factionalism in Salem Village because of the desire for independence from the Salem Town, and the dispute between Samuel Parris and his opponents.[21] With that as a background, describe the events in the Parris household that led the girls to accuse three women of witchcraft and the peculiar role played by Tituba through her confession.[22]

2. The trials and executions
Choose one of the accused witches and have the students read the testimony out loud in the class to dramatize the incident.[23] Bring their attention to the use of spectral evidence and hearsay, neither of which had been used to convict people in earlier New England trials.

3. How it ended
In October, the Governor dissolved the court of Oyer and Terminer, effectively ending the use of spectral evidence. There were no further executions for witchcraft in Salem. The trials continued in January under the aegis of a different set of rules that forbade the use of spectral evidence and with a less emotionally charged judicial body. Thirty-three more trials were conducted in several locations but only three people were convicted under the new rules. These three were also reprieved by the Governor, who decided that they were not responsible for their actions.

In the aftermath there was a great deal of remorse in the colony. On 17 December 1696 the General Court of Mas-

sachusetts tried to make amends by declaring a day of fast and prayer. The day of prayer was to be held throughout the province on 14 January 1697. That proclamation led to a series of individual apologies for participation in the Salem trials. A good example of this remorse is the apology of a group of jurymen that was first published in 1700.[24]

Notes

1. Richard Godbeer, *The Devil's Dominion: Magic and Religion in Early New England* (Cambridge, UK: Cambridge University Press, 1992), 30–46.

2. Geoffrey Parrinder, *Witchcraft: European and African* (London: Faber and Faber, 1963), 192–97.

3. Fernando Cervantes, *The Devil in the New World: The Impact of Diabolism in New Spain* (New Haven, CT: Yale University Press, 1994), 40–46.

4. Alfred Cave, "Indian Shamans and English Witches," *Essex Institute Historical Collections* 128 (1992): 241–54.

5. John S. Mbiti, *African Religions and Philosophy* (New York: Praeger, 1969), 107–18; Eugene D. Genovese, *Roll, Jordan, Roll: The World the Slaves Made* (New York: Random House, 1974), 210–12.

6. Philip D. Morgan, *Slave Counterpoint: Black Culture in the Eighteenth-Century Chesapeake Lowcountry* (Chapel Hill, NC: University of North Carolina Press, 1998), 612–25.

7. William D. Piersen, *Black Yankees: The Development of an Afro-American Subculture in Eighteenth-Century New England* (Amherst, MA: University of Massachusetts Press, 1988), 80–86.

8. Morgan, 640–42.

9. Brian P. Levack, *The Witch-Hunt in Early Modern Europe,* 2d ed. (New York: Longman, 1995), 27–67.

10. Sections from this work are reprinted in *Witches of the Atlantic World,* Elaine G. Breslaw, ed. (New York: New York University Press, 2000), 21–27, 289–95.

11. Levack, *Witch-Hunt,* 100–119.

12. Reprinted in *Witchcraft in the Atlantic World,* 365–68.

13. John Putnam Demos, *Entertaining Satan: Witchcraft and the Culture of Early New England* (New York: Oxford University Press, 1982), 57–64, 86–94.

14. There are many works that focus on this misogyny, but see especially Christina Larner, *Enemies of God: The Witch-Hunt in Scotland* (Baltimore, MD: Johns Hopkins University Press, 1981), 94–102; Joseph Klaits, *Servants of Satan: The Age of Witch Hunts* (Bloomington: Indiana University Press, 1985), 65–74; Carol F. Karlsen, *The Devil in the Shape of a Woman: Witchcraft in Colonial New England* (New York: Norton, 1987), 117–52.

15. Richard Beale Davis, *Intellectual Life in the Colonial South 1585–1763,* 3 vols. (Knoxville: University of Tennessee Press, 1978), II: 653–62.

16. Demos, *Entertaining Satan,* 401–8; Godbeer, *Devil's Dominion,* 238–42.

17. David Hall, *Worlds of Wonder, Days of Judgment: Popular Religious Beliefs in Early England* (New York: Knopf, 1989), 71–110.

18. A section of this work is in *Witches of the Atlantic World,* 42–46.

19. Richard Weisman, *Witchcraft, Magic, and Religion in Seventeenth-Century Massachusetts* (Amherst, MA: University of Massachusetts Press, 1984), 23–29.

20. These reports are reprinted in *Witches of the Atlantic World,* 235–55.

21. On this factional conflict see especially Paul Boyer and Stephen Nissenbaum, *Salem Possessed: The Social Origins of Witchcraft* (Cambridge, MA: Harvard University Press, 1974).

22. Elaine G. Breslaw, *Tituba, Reluctant Witch of Salem: Devilish Indians and Puritan Fantasies* (New York: New York University Press, 1996).

23. Some of these testimonies are reprinted in *Witches of the Atlantic World.* The most complete collection of legal records relating to the Salem court cases is *The Salem Witchcraft Papers: Verbatim Transcripts of the Legal Documents,* 3 vols., ed. Paul Boyer and Stephen Nissenbaum (New York: Da Capo Press, 1977).

24. In *Witches of the Atlantic World,* 420–21.

Suggested Reading for Students

Readable popularized versions of the Salem episodes include Bryan F. Le Beau, *The Story of the Salem Witch Trials* (Saddle River, NJ: Prentice Hall, 1998), and Frances Hill, *A Delusion of Satan: The Full Story of the Salem Witch Trials* (New York: Doubleday, 1995). Marion Starkey's highly dramatized *The Devil in Massachusetts: A Modern Enquiry into the Salem Witch Trials* (New York: Doubleday, 1949) tells a fascinating story, but many of the details have been disputed by scholars. Arthur Miller's play, *The Crucible* (1953), is well worth reading for its depiction of the generalized fear in Salem that was at the root of the witch-hunt even though the love interest angle is pure fiction. The movie, which is very faithful to the play, is available on video.

Suggested Reading

Cohn, Norman. *Europe's Inner Demons: An Enquiry Inspired by the Great Witch-Hunt.* New York: Basic Books, Inc., 1975.

Erikson, Kai. *Wayward Puritans: A Study in the Sociology of Deviance.* New York: John Wiley & Sons, 1966.

Flint, Valerie I.J. *Rise of Magic in Early Medieval Europe.* Princeton, NJ: Princeton University Press, 1990.

Gildrie, Richard P. *The Profane, the Civil, and the Godly: The Reformation of Manners in Orthodox New England, 1679–1749.* University Park: Pennsylvania State University Press, 1994.

Ginzburg, Carlo. *The Night Battles: Witchcraft and Agrarian Cults in the Sixteenth and Seventeenth Centuries.* Baltimore, MD: Johns Hopkins University Press, 1983.

Hansen, Chadwick. *Witchcraft at Salem.* New York: George Braziller, 1969.

Klaits, Joseph. *Servants of Satan: The Age of Witch Hunts.* Bloomington: Indiana University Press, 1985.

Métraux, Alfred. *Voodoo in Haiti.* New York: Schocken Books, 1972.

Parrinder, Geoffrey. *Witchcraft: European and African.* London: Faber and Faber, 1963.

Sidky, H. *Witchcraft, Lycanthropy, Drugs, and Disease: An Anthropological Study of the European Witch-Hunts.* New York: Peter Lang, 1997.

Thomas, Keith. *Religion and the Decline of Magic.* New York: Charles Scribner's Sons, 1971.

CHAPTER 35

New York Was Always a Global City

The Impact of World Trade on Seventeenth-Century New Amsterdam

DENNIS J. MAIKA

New York has always been a "global" city, if we employ that adjective the way it is presently being used. "Global" suggests a connection to a wider world; "globalization" is offered to characterize our current "interconnected system."[1] But the world's interconnectedness is not a new phenomenon. The "world that trade created" has existed for centuries.[2] An awareness of a unique type or degree of globalization before the post–Cold War era opens up new opportunities for teaching American history, and offers to teachers and students new ways to consider current issues using the historical past.[3]

This new view is especially relevant to the colonial period in American history and to the history of New York in particular.[4] From its earliest beginnings as Dutch New Amsterdam, New York's involvement in global commerce had an impact on the people who lived and worked in the city. The underlying purpose of this lesson is to consider some of the issues that were raised by the citizens of New Amsterdam and how their political institutions sought to resolve them. To guide the lesson, the essential question to keep in mind is: How effective were New Amsterdam's political institutions in offering solutions to trade-related issues?

The Dutch experience in the New World, especially in North America, has often been neglected in American history courses. Most courses of study overlook the fact that in the seventeenth century the Netherlands was Europe's leading commercial power. This was the "Golden Age" of Dutch commerce and culture, when merchants from the Netherlands traded with all parts of the world and Dutch artists like Rembrandt and Vermeer reflected their country's prosperity. Needless to say, Dutch success led to international rivalries, especially with France and England. Although the Dutch experience in New Netherland and New Amsterdam represented only a small part of their global interests, it offers an especially revealing case study about the ways a unique group of individuals negotiated the practical realities of trade, made sense of the world of commerce, and prospered from it.

National Standards

This lesson plan conforms to the following National History Standards:

> Era 2, Colonial Settlement (1585–1762)
> Historical Thinking Standards:
> Standards 3 and 4—Historical Analysis and Interpretation.
> Standard 5—Historical Issues-Analysis and Decision-Making.

Student Objectives

1. To understand significant issues and problems that relate to commerce in seventeenth-century New Amsterdam and appreciate the complexity of these issues.
2. To consider the effectiveness of political institutions in offering solutions to issues raised by regional and international commerce.
3. To analyze primary source documents.
4. To develop an appreciation for the Dutch experience in the seventeenth-century Atlantic World.

From *OAH Magazine of History* 18, no. 1 (April 2004): 43–49. © Organization of American Historians. Reprinted by permission.

Time

At most, this lesson plan will take three forty-minute classes. The lesson could easily be shortened or condensed. This lesson would fit before a discussion of the English Navigation Acts and mercantilism. It could also be a useful stimulus to current events discussion on one or several aspects of globalization today.

Background

Very soon after Henry Hudson's voyage of exploration in 1609, Dutch investors energetically participated in trade for furs and other commodities in New Netherland, an area stretching from the South River (now the Delaware River), to the North River (now the Hudson River) and the Fresh River (now the Connecticut River). After several years of private investment activity, the States General, the governing body of the Netherlands, created the West India Company (WIC) in 1621. The company was a state-sponsored monopoly that limited private entrepreneurship and held broad powers over a wide geographic area that included possessions in North and South America and the West Indies. In what would become the colony of New York, the WIC maintained two important trading centers: at Fort Orange/Beverwijck, now Albany, and at New Amsterdam, now New York City. After experimenting with various ways to encourage Settlement—the well-known "patroonship" plan, for example—and turn a profit, the WIC decided in 1640 that the best way to encourage trade and growth in New Netherland was to give up its monopoly on the fur trade. Once again, Dutch private investors speculated on New Netherland trade, many of them employing local residents as their "factors" to help exchange Dutch manu-factured goods for furs and tobacco. At the same time, a lively trade in foodstuffs and slaves developed between New Amsterdam and the West Indies. After a troubling decade of domestic Indian wars and the First Anglo-Dutch War (1652–1654), the strategy had begun to work—New Amsterdam, the "capital" of New Netherland, had begun to experience a trading boom by the 1650s. The lesson tries to capture this period, placing students into that unique mo-ment in time when people of New Amsterdam anxiously anticipated an increase in trade but were well aware of the attending difficulties.

Some of the important concerns for New Amsterdam traders are included in this lesson. Searching for order and stability in the world of commerce, the people of New Amsterdam turned to several different political institutions: the States General and the Directors of the West India Company in Holland; the Director General and Council, the governing arm of the WIC in New Netherland, led by Petrus Stuyvesant from 1647–1664; and the Court of Burgomasters and Schepens, the government of New

Amsterdam after it became a chartered city in 1653. Their concerns were articulated in various ways to these different governing bodies and are summarized and rephrased for the purpose of this lesson.

Procedure

The various steps could be divided over several days, de-pending on student ability level, class size, and access to the Internet.

1. Introduce students to the lesson's essential ques-tion: How effective were New Amsterdam's institutions in offering solutions to trade-related issues?
2. Have students brainstorm possible trade-related issues and share their thoughts in a brief class discussion.
3. Have students develop some historical context and awareness of New Netherland history. Since most textbooks offer either limited or inaccurate infor-mation, an important corrective would be to spend time with the "Virtual Tour of New Netherland," a feature prepared by the New Netherland Project <http://www.nnp.org/newvtour/>. Students can use the site as a way to gather relevant, accurate data; a broad view of New Netherland would be useful and informative, but an understanding of the material in the "Manhattan" section would be immediately relevant to this lesson. Be sure students are familiar with the political institutions at work in New Amsterdam: the Dutch West India Company, Director General Petrus Stuyvesant and his Council, and the Court of Burgomasters and Schepens, New Amsterdam's city government. If the Internet is not readily available, teachers can easily extract or print information from the web site.
4. The teacher will divide the class into five teams. Each team should first receive a copy of one of the five "Issues" and "Descriptions"; "Solution" documents should be distributed later. Teams will read and discuss the Issue and Description, check for understanding, then develop specula-tions with rationale on the best ways to resolve the issue.
5. After speculations have been completed, team members should read the "Solution" documents. Teams should then discuss the solutions offered in the document and compare and contrast them with their earlier speculations. Team members will then develop their analysis of the solutions offered in the document and answer the essential question.

6. Once the team work has been done, teams should share their conclusions with the other members of the class. Presentations should include a brief explanation of the issue, the solution offered in the document, and an analysis.

7. As students listen to the presentations, they should collect data that they could use to write their own final reflections on the essential question.

8. When all teams have presented their conclusions, each individual student should prepare a written "Final Reflection" (length to be determined by the instructor). In addition to answering the essential question, students should be encouraged to consider broader applications, for example, to what extent should government be involved in regulating trade? Does government involvement in commerce inhibit free trade or encourage it?

9. The teacher should lead a concluding full-class discussion on the essential question and the broader implications raised by the issues.

Suggestions for Further Reading

On trade in New Netherland, New Amsterdam, and early New York: Oliver A. Rink, *Holland on the Hudson: An Economic and Social History of Dutch New York* (Ithaca, NY: Cornell University Press, 1986); Dennis J. Maika, "Commerce and Community: Manhattan Merchants in the Seventeenth Century" (Ph.D. dissertation, New York University, 1995); Cathy Matson, *Merchants and Empire: Trading in Colonial New York* (Baltimore: Johns Hopkins University Press, 1998).

On Dutch New York: Donna Merwick, *Possessing Albany, 1630–1710: The Dutch and English Experiences* (New York: Cambridge University Press, 1990) and *Death of a Notary: Conquest and Change in Colonial New York* (Ithaca, NY: Cornell University Press, 2002); Edwin Burrows and Mike Wallace, *Gotham: A History of New York City to 1898* (New York: Oxford University Press, 1999), early chapters; Joyce Goodfriend, *Before the Melting Pot: Society and Culture in Colonial New York City, 1664–1730* (Princeton: Princeton University Press, 1994); Firth Haring Fabend, *A Dutch Family in the Middle Colonies, 1660–1800* (New Brunswick, NJ: Rutgers University Press, 1991); and Russell Shorto, *The Island at the Center of the World: The Epic Story of Dutch Manhattan and the Forgotten Colony That Shaped America* (New York: Doubleday, 2004).

Other valuable sources: *De Halve Maen: Magazine of the Dutch Colonial Period,* published by the Holland Society of New York; *Cultures, Commerce, and Community: A Teacher's Resource Guide for the Study of the 17th Century City of New Amsterdam* (New York: The New-York Historical Society, 2002).

Notes (Lesson Plan)

1. Thomas L. Friedman, *The Lexus and the Olive Tree* (New York: Anchor Books, 2000), xvi.

2. See, for example, Kenneth Pomeranz and Steven Topik, *The World That Trade Created: Society, Culture, and the World Economy, 1400 to the Present* (Armonk, NY: M.E. Sharpe, 1999).

3. Thoughtful essays on the subject are offered in Thomas Bender, ed., *Rethinking American History in a Global Age* (Berkeley: University of California Press, 2002).

4. Interesting interpretive ideas are offered in Karen Ordahl Kupperman, "International at the Creation: Early Modern American History," and Ian Tyrrell, "Beyond the View from Euro-America: Environment, Settler Societies, and the Internationalization of American in History," in Bender, *Rethinking American History in a Global Age,* 103–22, 168–91.

Handout

Issue #1: To what extent should New Amsterdam residents have special privileges over non-residents?

Description: New Amsterdam's city magistrates, themselves merchants, complained about "peddlers" ("*schotsman*" in Dutch) who sailed from the Netherlands to the North River (Hudson River), then bypassed Manhattan and went to Fort Orange (modern-day Albany). These peddlers usually refused to sell their goods in Manhattan, preventing local residents from getting much-needed supplies, and violating the trading monopoly the WIC had guaranteed to New Amsterdam when it made it the capital of New Netherland (this privilege was called the Staple Right). When some peddlers actually did stop to sell goods at Manhattan, they often undersold local merchants and accepted cash instead of credit for their sales. New Amsterdam merchants were also upset by the fact that non-resident traders like the peddlers were not contributing anything to the community either in taxes to support the city, or by agreeing to serve in the local militia (the *Burgher Guard*) in times of danger. In their 1657 petition to Director General Stuyvesant and his Council, the city magistrates requested that local residents be granted the *burgher right*—the exclusive right reserved only to local residents to buy, sell, and set up shop within the city of New Amsterdam. As Stuyvesant considered this request, he had to follow orders from the WIC directors in Amsterdam who, three years earlier, had refused to force all traders to own houses or land in New Amsterdam, believing such a restriction would actually interfere with free trade. Nevertheless, the WIC did recognize that some privileges should be given to local residents, and thus required that all peddlers at least keep an "open store" in New Amsterdam in which to sell their goods, and pay some of the same taxes borne by the local residents. This was not enough for New Amsterdam magistrates, who, in 1657 still felt that peddlers were undermining the position of local residents. As you consider the Issue, think about what alternatives Stuyvesant had and what his course of action should be.[1]

The Solution: Excerpts from Petrus Stuyvesant, "In Council at Fort Amsterdam, January 23, 1657":[2]

" . . . it seems proper that this community and the inhabitants of this City should be favored with some privileges and encouraged to continue, considering what they have done in the English and Indian troubles and what they may have to do at some future time, as this place, being the principal capital and frontier place, will always have to bear the brunt of the first and most frequent attacks, and is therefore liable to be subjected to a great deal of labor, troubles and expenses. . . ."

As to the Burgher Right, "it is . . . my opinion, that we keep as close as possible to the advice and letter of (the WIC officials) . . . that henceforth, no newly arriving traders, let them be skippers, sailors or peddlers, or whatever they may be called, shall be allowed to sell, transport or export into the country their merchandise, unless they have first keep (an open) shop in this City, either in their own or a leased house or room, as the trader may find more convenient. . . ."

(But) "all arriving traders shall henceforth, before they are allowed to keep an open shop, request from the (City Government) the Burgher Right, on condition of duly paying for it (50 guilders for the Great Burgher Right, 20 guilders for the Small Burgher Right), (and) taking the oath of fidelity to the supreme government of Director General and Council of New Netherland . . . this done, they shall be allowed to open shop either in a purchased or rented house, . . . and they shall not be prevented or forbidden to trade and traffic like other burghers, freemen and inhabitants of this province. . . ."

"Because no Burgher . . . right binds a man . . . for longer than his convenience requires, it is therefore my advice that even though they may have acquired the Burgher Right for the time of their sojourn here, they shall lose (it) upon returning to the Fatherland (but can ask and pay for it again if they return, unless they continued to rent or own property in Manhattan)."

Issue #2: How could smuggling be stopped?

Description: "Smuggling" is generally defined as "trading illegally," that is, trying to avoid a country's laws that regulate trade. In America today, U.S. Customs Service officials try to prevent smuggling at airports and seaports. In seventeenth-century New Netherland, trading regulations were made by the WIC; smuggling was one of the WIC's most important concerns because the company made money by collecting duties (taxes or tariffs) on imported and exported goods. There were various ways that individuals (merchants, skippers, sailors) tried to smuggle:[3]

- Unloading cargo at places where there were no WIC officials to collect duties, i.e., finding coves or inlets along the coast rather than unload at New Amsterdam.
- Unloading cargo at night when it would difficult for officials to see what was going on.
- Lying or misleading WIC inspectors about what cargo was on board a ship by falsifying official cargo lists.
- Bribing WIC inspectors.
- Leaving port quickly without giving inspectors time to check the cargo. It is important to remember that any trader, even a resident of New Amsterdam, could be involved in smuggling. Obviously, a merchant could realize more of a profit if he/she did not have to pay duties or tariffs.

The Solution: Excerpts from "Ordinance Renewing and Amending the Prohibition Against Smuggling, and the Establishment of Shipping Regulations to Prevent Smuggling," by the Director General and Council, August 11, 1656:[4]

1. "That all private ships, yachts, barks, ketches, sloops and vessels, whether of Dutch, English, French, Swedish or any other nationality, desiring to anchor at this island of Manhattans and this city" (be required to anchor at the specified location) "and at no other place; on pain of paying 25 guilders for the first time, 50 guilders for the second time, to be forfeited after they have been warned."

2. "All ships . . . shall, before discharging and loading any goods or merchandise, be obliged to present a manifest or invoice of their cargo to the director general or his deputy the fiscal, and submit themselves to his inspection both on their arrival and departure, and if he should find any more goods than appear on the submitted inventory, manifest or invoice, such goods, according to customary procedure, shall be declared confiscated . . . and five times the value of the imported concealed contraband shall be exacted. . . ."

3. "The receipt or delivery of all goods and merchandise, which are delivered on shore or received on board, shall be made and take place, without any exception or deceit of persons within the limits of this city and in no way beyond the same, and that during daylight hours' forfeiting one quarter part of the discovered goods for the first offense; and, in addition to this, forfeiting the scow, boat or vessel used to unload them for the second offense."

Issue #3: How could New Amsterdamers guarantee the accuracy of "weights and measures"?

Description: Today, we take for granted that the gallon of milk we buy is really a full gallon, that the pint of ice cream is really a full pint. In 1657, however, many questions arose concerning the accuracy of the various units of weight and measurement in use. Imagine buying what you think is a gallon of milk and getting only three and ½ quarts because the milk container didn't really hold a full gallon. Or think about going to a butcher to buy a pound of meat, but his scale was off (either deliberately or not) and he sold you only ¾ of a pound but you paid for a full pound. Similar questions were raised by the people in New Amsterdam in 1657 who wanted to be sure, when they were buying or selling goods, either wholesale or retail, that they were getting the quantity they were paying for.

For reference, here are some of the common weights and measures used in old Amsterdam in the seventeenth century:[5]

A can = 1 quart
A schepel = 0.764 bushel of wheat, or 1.2 bushels of salt
A voet = 11.143 inches
An ell = 27 inches
A vadem (fathom) = 6 feet
An ons = 1 ounce
A pond = 1 pound

The Solution: Excerpts from the Meeting of the Court of Schout, Burgomasters and Schepens, New Amsterdam, January 13, 1657:[6]

"Whereas the Schout, Burgomasters and Schepens of the City of Amsterdam in New Netherland have considered it highly necessary, that agreeably to the laudable customs of our Fatherland, rules be made for the stamping of casks, cans, weights, ells, and schepels, to prevent all questions and differences, arising therefrom, and that everybody may have just measure,—Therefore, their Honors have appointed (a) Surveyor and Gauger . . . who is to measure and stamp at the request of the receiver or deliverer . . . all (containers) . . . in accordance with the customs of Old Amsterdam. For (this) gauging and stamping, the Surveyor and Gauger shall receive (specific fees from whoever requested the measurement)."

"(To prevent the) many frauds and abuses . . . nobody, be it of what position, condition, or nation he may be, shall be allowed to use within the jurisdiction of this City any other ell, weight or measure than those used in the renowned City of Amsterdam in the Netherlands, and that this order may be carried out, all who sell goods here . . . are commanded to come with their weights and measures, used for delivery or receipt, once a year . . . to the City hall, and then to have them measured in the presence of two members of the Court, for which they are to pay (specific fees) into the treasury of the City."

"And if . . . anybody is found who still uses not measured weights and measures in delivering of receiving goods, he shall pay a fine of 10 fl. the first time, 20 fl. the second time and double as much the third time with closing of his shop."

Issue #4: How to prevent the export of poor quality tobacco?

Description: The fur trade was essential to the growth and development of New Netherland, but by the 1650s, New Amsterdam had also become a leading exporter of tobacco, sending large shipments of packed leaf to Holland. Although some of the exported tobacco was grown in New Netherland, an increasingly large amount came from the English Chesapeake colonies of Virginia and Maryland; this Chesapeake tobacco was sent to Manhattan and reloaded on ships bound for Holland. As the volume of the tobacco trade increased, so did complaints about the quality of tobacco—what was described as "poor, bad, rotten or mouldy tobacco" was being sent to merchants in Holland who very unhappy with both the product and their partners. Some of this "unmerchantable" tobacco was actually being hidden deep inside the large tobacco barrels (called "hogsheads" containing hundreds of pounds) where it could not be easily detected. Protecting the reputation of tobacco shipped from New Amsterdam was essential because who in Europe would want to buy poor quality tobacco? As early as 1638, the WIC had appointed Tobacco Inspectors, but by the 1650s, their job had become more difficult.

The Solution: Excerpts from "Renewal of the Ordinance Regulating Tobacco," February 18, 1653:[7]

"Those who have tobacco to inspect, shall see to it that it is brought before the inspectors in barrels and casks, which tobacco after inspection shall remain in the barrels and casks at a designated place until the same shall be shipped from here."

"All tobacco which is offered to the inspectors for inspection and judged by them under oath to be unmerchantable tobacco, the inspectors, in order to prevent fraud, shall without connivance or regard to person, immediately burn the same. . . ."

"All the barrels and hogsheads coming here with tobacco from Virginia and offered for inspection, the inspectors shall be allowed to unhoop at their discretion so that they may see into the middle of the tobacco (where commonly deception is concealed). . . ."

Excerpts from Ordinance Regulating the Inspection of Tobacco, March 30, 1657:[8]

"It is . . . thought best and most proper . . . that three sorts or distinctions of tobacco be made by the inspector, and inspected and marked in this manner, namely:

The best sorts or hogsheads: V.G. which shall signify Virginia Good; or N.G. New Netherland Good.

The next sorts: V.M. or N.M. and shall signify Virginia or New Netherland Merchantable tobacco.

The third sort: V.S. or N.S. and shall signify Virginia or New Netherland Poor (*slecht* is the Dutch word for poor) tobacco.

The last sort, which may not even be considered poor, shall be marked with an O. . . ."

"Meanwhile, are all persons forewarned and cautioned not to ship any Virginia, or New Netherland tobacco before and until the same be examined, inspected and marked or branded, in accordance with the tenor hereof, by the inspector to be appointed and sworn for that purpose, on pain of forfeiting one pound Flemish (6 guilders) for every hogshead, to be paid as well by the merchant who shipped it, as by the skipper who received it."

Issue #5: How could New Amsterdam's money system be made more reliable?

Description: Today, the idea of "money" seems easy enough to grasp. Americans earn, spend, and save money measured in "dollars" and "cents." And, as we rely on the dollars and coins that the United States government makes for our use, we accept the paper and metal currency as our "medium of exchange." In New Amsterdam, as in other colonies, the system of money and currency was much more complicated primarily because most of the metal currency used in Europe never made the journey across the Atlantic Ocean. So what was a New Amsterdamer to do? Although the Dutch system of currency was well known (1 guilder = 20 stivers; 1 Carolus guilder = 1 ½ guilders = 1 daalder), there were very few actual coins available in Manhattan. New Amsterdamers were forced to rely on available "commodities" for their medium of exchange; beaver pelts, pounds of tobacco, and sewant (Indian wampum) became local "commodity money" whose value was calculated in Dutch guilders. By far, the most commonly used currency was sewant—belts of carefully strung, tubular beads made from sea shells by Long Island Indians. Dark purple (black) beads were more valuable than white beads, both about a quarter-inch long, carefully drilled and polished before being strung together in belts. The value of sewant, like other forms of commodity money, could change given the laws of supply and demand—the more sewant there was, the less valuable it became, and the less it could buy. Thus, the problem for New Amsterdamers in 1657 was that sewant was becoming unreliable as a medium of exchange—it was being counterfeited, beads not strung together properly, and a great quantity of it was being "dumped" into New Amsterdam by New Englanders, making it worth less and upsetting the prices of goods that were purchased every day.

The Solution: Excerpts from "Ordinance Regulating The Currency," from a session of the Director General and Council held in Fort Amsterdam in New Netherland, January 3, 1657:[9]

" . . . Inasmuch as, for want of silver and gold coin or other pay, sewant must, in smaller quantities, serve as the currency between man and man, buyer and seller, . . . (we) hereby resolve and ordain to rate sewant . . . at the value of beaver (pelt), the beaver (pelt) being still reckoned, until further order and advice from patria (the Netherlands), at 8 guilders and no higher."

"And in order to prevent in future the complaints of miscounting the sewant, . . . (we) further ordain and command that, from this time forward, . . . sewant shall . . . be paid out or received . . . only by a stamped measure, authorized to be made and stamped for that purpose, . . . the smallest of which measures shall be 5 stivers; the whole 10, and the double 20 stivers."

Excerpts from Petition from the Burgomasters and Schepens of the City of New Amsterdam to the Director General and Councilors of New Netherland, September 19, 1658:[10]

"(We) respectfully request (that you) provisionally fix the sewant at 8 white and 4 black beads per stiver."

Excerpts from Petition from the Burgomasters and Schepens of the City of New Amsterdam to the Directors of the West India Company, September 19, 1658:[11]

"We . . . request your Honors in a friendly manner, that you would be pleased to send to the Director General, . . . silver coin of an unusual stamp or mint, and having received that, better order can be introduced than by the (Director) General and Council in Seawant and beavers. . . ."

Notes (Handout)

1. The description is based on several documents: "In Council at Fort Amsterdam, the 18th of September 1648"; "Directors of the West India Company to Director General and Council, Amsterdam, March 12, 1654"; and "Petition of the Burgomasters and Schepens to the Director General and Council of New Netherland," January 22, 1657, in *Collections of the New-York Historical Society for the Year 1885* (New York, 1886), 1–4.

2. *Collections of the New-York Historical Society for the Year 1885* (New York, 1886), 5–7.

3. Adapted from "Ordinance Concerning Vessels and Smuggling," (July 4, 1647), Charles T. Gehring, ed., *Laws and Writs of Appeal, 1647–1663* (Syracuse, 1991), 1011; "Ordinance Against Boarding Ships Arrived at New Amsterdam Before they are Registered," (27 June 1652), Ibid., 28–9.

4. Gehring, *Laws and Writs of Appeal, 1647–1663,* 62–3.

5. Charles T. Gehring, ed., *The Curacao Papers* (Syracuse, 1986), xxx–i.

6. Berthold Fernow, ed., *The Records of New Amsterdam from 1653 To 1674 Anno Domini,* 7 Vols. (Baltimore, 1976). I: 29–30.

7. Gehring, *Laws and Writs of Appeal,* 49–50.

8. Ibid., 81–3.

9. Ibid., 75–6.

10. Fernow, *Records of New Amsterdam,* III: 16; see also "Letter from the Directors at Amsterdam to the Director General and Council," April 7, 1657, in Charles T. Gehring, ed., *Correspondence, 1654–1658* (Syracuse, 2002), 126.

11. Fernow, *Records of New Amsterdam,* III: 17. There is no evidence that this action was ever taken.

CHAPTER 36

The *Code Noir*

North American Slavery in Comparative Perspective

KEVIN ARLYCK

One of the great contradictions in the history of slavery is its growth and entrenchment at a time when the ideals of liberty and equality were being promoted in the United States as basic tenets of the new Republic. This fundamental paradox cannot be emphasized enough with students, and exploring it in depth is a wonderful means of introducing them to the intricate legacy of slavery in this country and to help them develop the critical faculties they need in order to better understand the many complexities of United States history. The following document complements students' factual knowledge about slavery by encouraging them to interpret the past.

The institution of slavery in the United States is best understood in an international context, as part of an Atlantic slave system that developed across four continents and several centuries. To better grasp the similarities and differences between the various national and regional variants that evolved, and appreciate the ways in which the United States system was both a typical and "peculiar" institution, it is important that students be exposed to documentary evidence regarding slavery outside the United States.

The *Code Noir* provides an excellent opportunity for students to explore this issue of similarity and difference. Conceived and written largely by Jean-Baptiste Colbert, King Louis XIV's finance minister, in 1685, it was a coherent and comprehensive body of law establishing the status and standing of slaves in all French American colonies. While individual colonies and states in English North America enacted a wide range of statutes addressing a variety of questions in the slave society, no national or comprehensive slave code emerges. By looking at the *Code Noir* after a study of slavery in the British colonies and United States, students will be able to notice aspects of slavery (in their legal form, at least) that differ between the two systems. I have edited the *Code* rather extensively, for two main reasons. First, students should focus their attention on certain key areas of the code, primarily religion, marriage, and commerce. My second concern is readability: many students read below their grade level, and I sought to boil each article down to its essential provisions, for the sake of clarity. I believe that my editing and translations of Articles 38, 43, and 47 have preserved the original meaning. The questions that follow are intended to frame a discussion with students that will allow them to delve, in a preliminary way, into some of the deeper complexities of slavery as it was constructed in the Atlantic world.

Coordinating with the National Standards for History

This lesson plan complements the objectives outlined in Era 2: Colonization and Settlement of the National Standards of History. Particularly, this lesson plan fulfills Standard 3, by which students should understand how the values and institutions of European economic life took root in the colonies and how slavery reshaped European and African life in the Americas.

Time:

This lesson should require one or two class periods.

From *OAH Magazine of History* 17, no. 3 (April 2003): 37–40. © Organization of American Historians. Reprinted by permission.

Procedure:

1. Start by asking students: *Why would King Louis want a code of laws for all of the slaves in the French colonies?* Students can respond orally or in writing, and then share responses.
2. Introduce the background and purpose of the *Code*. A short reading from an encyclopedia or website might be helpful.
3. Read Articles II, III, V, VI aloud, and ask students to respond to this question: *How did the French feel about slaves and religion?* One option is to model a written response for students, with which they can practice independent work.
4. Allow students time to read the rest of the document (or selections), and then respond to these or similar questions independently: *What was life like for slaves who wanted to get married? What were some things they had to consider when getting married? Why do you think slaves were not allowed to sell things? If you were a slave in a French colony, how would you feel about this Code? What would you like and what would you dislike? What if you were a slave owner?* This final question can also be offered as an in-class reflection or homework.
5. Ask students to compare British and French colonial slavery policies for further study. For example: *The British colonies in America had a lot of different laws about slaves, but never made a comprehensive code like this one for all slaves in all places. Why do you think the British and Americans never made one?*

Sources:

"The Code Noir" (1685). John Garrigus, trans., available at <http://www.vancouver.wsu.edu/fac/peabody/codenoir.htm>.

Articles 38, 43, and 47 "Ordonnance du Roi." Available at: <http://julienas.ipt.univ-paris8.fr/~aceme/codes.html>.

Document: The *Code Noir*

Edict of the King concerning the enforcement of order in the French American islands from the month of March 1685.

Louis, King of France . . . Since we owe our attention to all the peoples that God has put under our obedience . . . to regulate the status and condition of the slaves in our said islands, and desiring to provide for this . . . we have said, ruled, and ordered . . . that which follows.

Article II.

All the slaves who will be in our Islands will be baptized and instructed in the Catholic religion.

Article III.

We forbid any public exercise of any religion other than the Catholic.

Article V.

We forbid our subjects . . . to disturb or prevent our other subjects, even their slaves, from the free exercise of the Catholic religion.

Article VI.

We charge all our subjects . . . to observe Sundays and holidays that are kept by . . . the Catholic religion. We forbid them to . . . make their slaves work on these days.

Article IX.

The free men who will have . . . children from their concubinage with their slaves [will] be deprived of the slave and the children.

Article X.

[M]arriages will be observed both for free persons and for slaves . . . without the consent of the father and the mother of the slave being necessary, but that of the master alone.

Article XI.

We . . . forbid masters to . . . constrain their slaves to marry against their will.

Article XII.

The children who will be born of marriage between slaves will be slaves and will belong to the master of the women slaves.

Article XIII.

[I]f a slave husband has married a free woman, the children, both male and girls, will . . . be free like her . . . and that if the father is free and the mother enslaved, the children will be slaves.

Article XV.

~~We forbid slaves to carry any weapon, or large sticks.~~

Article XVI.

[W]e forbid slaves belonging to different masters to gather in the day or night.

Article XVIII.

We forbid slaves to sell sugar cane for whatever reason.

Article XIX.

We forbid them also to [sell] at the market.

Article XXVI.

The slaves who are not fed, clothed and supported by the masters . . . will notify our attorney [and] the masters will be prosecuted by him.

Article XXXIII.

The slave who will have struck his master . . . in the face, will be punished with death.

Article XXXVIII.

~~An escaped slave gone for one month . . . will have his~~ ears cut off. [For] the third offense he will be punished by death.

Article XLIII.

We direct our officers to prosecute masters or commanders who kill a slave under their ownership or direction.

Article XLVII.

Married slaves, and their young children, if they are owned by the same master, may not be sold separately.

Article LIX.

We grant to manumitted slaves the same rights, privileges and liberties enjoyed by persons born free.

CHAPTER 37

Indian Removal

Manifest Destiny or Hypocrisy?

DAVID L. GHERE

The U.S. government policy of Indian Removal in the 1830s provides a focus for the exploration of a variety of related issues in cross-cultural relations during our nation's first half-century of existence. American expansion in general, and the Indian Removal policy in particular, were so devastating to the Indians that they prompted spirited opposition from [Native Americans] and necessitated justification by governmental officials. This lesson plan uses quotations from both U.S. government officials and Indian leaders over a half-century to convey the attitudes and assumptions that guided both sides in their interaction.

Objectives for the Students

1. To examine the various ethnocentric assumptions and attitudes that enabled U.S. government officials to justify their policies toward Native Americans.
2. To understand the variety of Native-American responses to the encroachments on their land and to the threats to their culture.
3. To experience the imagery and use of metaphor and simile which was so prominent in Native-American oratory.

Teaching Materials

Handout #1—"Justifications for Conquest" containing quotes from Tennessee Governor John Sevier in 1798, John Quincy Adams in 1802, Secretary of War John C. Calhoun in 1818, and Georgia Governor George Gilmer around 1830.

Handout #2—"Native American Responses to Expansion" containing single statements by Red Jacket, a Seneca chief in 1792, and by Pushmataha, a Choctaw leader in 1812, as well as two by Tecumseh, a Shawnee chief, in 1795 and 1812.

Handout #3—"Indian Removal Policy" containing excerpts from speeches by President Andrew Jackson in 1835 and Indian Commissioner William Medill in 1848.

Handout #4—"Native American Responses to Indian Removal" containing quotes from Black Hawk, a chief of the Sauk and Fox in 1833, Speckled Snake, a Creek elder in 1829, and George Harkins, a chief of the Choctaws in 1832.

Conduct of Class

The first portion of the class should be devoted to frontier relations during the early nineteenth century, which were characterized by numerous examples of both confrontation and accommodation. This part of the class can be concluded in about twenty-five minutes or expanded to fifty minutes if the instructor chooses to promote an in-depth analytical discussion of government attitudes and justifications and Native American responses.

One option would be to begin class by distributing Handout #1: "Justifications for Conquest" and Handout #2: "Native American Responses to Expansion." Students could then be asked to identify and explain the justifications for conquest in Handout #1 and the solutions to frontier problems proposed in Handout #2. This could be

From *OAH Magazine of History* 9, no. 4 (Summer 1995): 32–37. © Organization of American Historians. Reprinted with permission.

a homework assignment to prepare for class the next day or an in-class group activity. The instructor could ask how these views relate to the wars, treaties, and land cessions from 1780 to 1815.

A second option would be to start out by discussing the three U.S. policy options: destroy the Indians, assimilate the Indians, or respect Indian rights and sovereignty. Student ideas could be elicited concerning the extent to which the first two alternatives were pursued and why the third choice was not seriously considered. As the discussion develops, the instructor can read each quotation on Handouts #1 and #2 separately whenever that specific quote seems most appropriate to the discussion. Students could then discuss which views would logically lead to policies of confrontation or assimilation and how they relate to the wars, treaties, and land cessions from 1780 to 1815.

The second portion of the class should focus on the policy of Indian Removal and Native-American reaction to that policy. This could be concluded in twenty-five minutes if discussion is limited and the class is primarily conducted in a lecture format. A full fifty-minute period would enable much more discussion and greater analysis of the situation. Also, conducting the first and second portions of the class on consecutive days (even if each is limited to only twenty-five minutes of class time) allows for homework assignments to prepare for the second portion of the class.

The instructor could distribute Handout #3 and ask students in what ways these quotes portray the Indian Removal policy as beneficial to the Indians. What assumptions about the adaptability of the Indians lend support to the removal policy? (They can hunt buffalo; plenty of room so other Indians will not object to the newcomers.) Which statements in these documents are distortions of the truth? (At the expense of the U.S. government; adopt agriculture in an area then known as "The Great American Desert"; this land forever guaranteed to them.) Compare the favorable options and autonomy for Indians depicted in Jackson's statement with Medill's vision of the inevitable changes that circumstances will force on the Indians. What other contradictions are there between the two documents? Additional questions could include: Do these two officials believe the Indians can ever be assimilated into society? Is the removal policy based on the assumption that the Indians cannot assimilate or that removal gives them more time so that they can assimilate?

Another option (or an additional area for discussion) could be pursued by the instructor posing the question: What aspects of white culture were the Indians expected to adopt so as to assimilate into society? Students could use the Jackson and Medill quotes or their textbook, or they could engage in a brainstorming activity to determine what changes were thought to be necessary for Indians to assimilate. This could be a question for a homework

assignment or an in-class group project. The lists could then be discussed and evaluated by exchanging them between the groups or reading them to the whole class. The instructor then could relate the story of the Cherokees who did everything that was demanded (adopted Christianity, representative government, legal system, individual land ownership, and written language as well as white methods of agriculture, education, dress, and mode of living) and still had their land taken and were forced to move to Oklahoma.

The class would conclude with an examination of Native-American responses to Indian Removal. The quotes from Black Hawk, Speckled Snake, and George Harkins could be distributed, and discussion could focus on the similarities and differences between these three responses to Indian Removal. What kind of arguments does each use in criticizing the removal policy? What attitudes are revealed about frontier relations in the past and what are the authors' expectations for the future? All six Native-American quotations can be discussed concerning the imagery and the use of metaphor and simile in Native-American orations. The class could conclude with some examples of the tragedies that occurred in the "Trail of Tears."

Further Reading

The most useful work for government documents is Francis Paul Prucha, ed., *Documents of United States Indian Policy* (Lincoln: University of Nebraska Press, 1975). Numerous examples of Indian oratory are contained in Peter Nabokov, ed., *Native American Testimony: An Anthology of Indian and White Relations: First Encounter to Dispossession* (New York: Harper and Row, 1978); and T.C. McLuhan, *Touch the Earth: A Self-Portrait of Indian Existence* (New York: Promontory Press, 1971). Jerry R. Baydo, *Readings in American Indian History* (Wheaton, Ill.: Gregory Publishing Company, 1992), contains quotations from both sides.

Students or the instructor desiring more background information about frontier relations during this period could consult three brief books: Jerry R. Baydo, *The History of the American Indian* (Wheaton, Ill.: Gregory Publishing Company, 1992); Theda Perdue and Michael Green, *The Cherokee Removal: A Brief History with Documents* (New York: St. Martin's Press, 1995); and Philip Weeks, *Farewell, My Nation: The American Indian and the United States, 1820–1890* (Arlington Heights, Ill.: Harlan Davidson, 1990).

Handout #1—Justifications For Conquest and Indian Removal

Governor John Sevier of Tennessee in 1798:
"By the law of nations, it is agreed that no people shall

be entitled to more land than they can cultivate. Of course no people will sit and starve for want of land to work, when a neighboring nation has much more than they can make use of."

John Quincy Adams in 1802:

"What is the right of the huntsman to the forest of a thousand miles over which he has accidentally ranged in quest of prey? Shall the fields and valleys, which God has formed to teem with life of innumerable multitudes, be condemned to everlasting barrenness?"

Secretary of War John C. Calhoun in 1818:

The Indians "neither are, in fact, nor ought to be, considered as independent nations. Our views on their interests, and not their own, ought to govern them. By a proper combination of force and persuasion, of punishments and rewards, they ought to be brought within the pales of law and civilization. Left to themselves, they will never reach that desirable condition. Before the slow operation of reason and experience can convince them of its superior advantages, they must be overwhelmed by the mighty torrent of our population."

Governor George Gilmer of Georgia (ca. 1830):

"Treaties were expedients by which ignorant, intractable, and savage people were induced without bloodshed to yield up what civilized people had the right to possess by virtue of that command of the Creator delivered to man upon his formation—be fruitful, multiply, and replenish the earth, and subdue it."

NOTE: The Calhoun quote is from Francis Paul Prucha, ed., *Documents of United States Indian Policy* (Lincoln: University of Nebraska Press, 1975), 32. The other three quotes are taken from my teaching notes, and I have been unable to determine the original sources.

Handout #2—Native Americans Responses to Expansion and Indian Removal

Red Jacket, a Seneca chief, in 1792:

"We first knew you as a feeble plant which wanted a little earth whereon to grow. We gave it to you; and afterward, when we could have trod you under our feet, we watered and protected you; and now you have grown to be a mighty tree, whose top reaches the clouds, and whose branches overspread the whole land, whilst we, who were the tall pine of the forest, have become a feeble plant and need your protection.

"When you first came here, you clung around our knee and called us father; we took you by the hand and called you brothers. You have grown greater than we, so that we can no longer reach your hand; but we wish to cling around your knee and be called your children."

Tecumseh, a Shawnee chief, in 1795:

"My heart is a stone: heavy with sadness for my people; cold with the knowledge that no treaty will keep whites out of our lands; hard with the determination to resist as long as I live and breathe. Now we are weak and many of our people are afraid. But hear me: a single twig breaks, but the bundle of twigs is strong. Someday I will embrace our brother tribes and draw them into a bundle and together we will win our country back from the whites."

Tecumseh, a Shawnee chief, in 1811:

"Every year our white intruders become more greedy, exacting, oppressive, and overbearing. . . . Wants and oppression are our lot. . . . Are we not being stripped day by day of the little that remains of our ancient liberty? . . . Unless every tribe unanimously combines to give a check to the ambition and avarice of the whites, they will soon conquer us apart and disunited, and we will be driven away from our native country and scattered as autumnal leaves before the wind."

Pushmataha, a Choctaw leader, in 1811:

"If Tecumseh's words be true, and we doubt them not, then the Shawnee's experience with the whites has not been the same as that of the Choctaws. These white Americans buy our skins, our corn, our cotton, our surplus game, our baskets, and other wares, and they give us in fair exchange their cloth, their guns, their tools, implements, and other things which the Choctaws need but do not make. . . . You all remember the dreadful epidemic visited upon us last winter. During its darkest hours these neighbors whom we are now urged to attack responded generously to our needs. They doctored our sick; they clothed our suffering; they fed our hungry; . . . So, in marked contrast with the experiences of the Shawnees, it will be seen that the whites and Indians in this section are living in friendly and mutually beneficial terms."

NOTE: Quotes from T.C. McLuhan, *Touch the Earth: A Self-Portrait of Indian Existence* (New York: Promontary Press, 1971), 69, 116–7; and Jerry R. Baydo, *Readings in American Indian History* (Wheaton, Ill.: Gregory Publishing, 1992), 52.

Handout #3—Indian Removal Policy

President Andrew Jackson in his annual message to Congress in 1835:

"All preceding experiments for the improvement of the Indians have failed. It seems now to be an established fact that they can not live in contact with a civilized community and prosper. . . .

"The plan for their removal and re-establishment is founded upon the knowledge we have gained of their character and habits, and has been dictated by a spirit of enlarged liberality. A territory exceeding in extent that relinquished has been granted to each tribe. . . . The Indians are removed at the expense of the United States, and with certain supplies of clothing, arms, ammunition, and other indispensable articles; they are also furnished gratuitously with provisions for the period of a year after their arrival at their new homes. In that time, from the nature of the country and by the products raised by them, they can subsist themselves by agricultural labor, if they choose to resort to that mode of life; if they do not they are upon the skirts of the great prairies, where countless herds of buffalo roam, and a short time suffices to adapt their own habits. . . .

"The pledge of the United States has been given by Congress that the country destined for the residence of this people shall be forever 'secured and guaranteed to them.' A country west of Missouri and Arkansas has been assigned to them, into which the white settlements are not to be pushed. No political communities can be formed in that extensive region, except those established by the Indians themselves or by the United States for them and with their concurrence."

Indian Commissioner William Medill in 1848:

"Apathy, barbarism and heathenism must give way to energy, civilization and Christianity; and so the Indian of this continent has been displaced by the European. . . .

"The policy already begun and relied on to accomplish objects so momentous and desirable to every Christian and philanthropist is, as rapidly as it can safely and judiciously be done, to colonize our Indian tribes beyond the reach, for some years, of our white population; confining each within a small district of country, so that as the game decreases and becomes scarce, the adults will gradually be compelled to resort to agriculture and other kinds of labor to obtain a subsistence. . . .

"The strongest propensities of an Indian's nature are his desire for war and his love of the chase. . . . But anything like labor is distasteful and utterly repugnant to his feelings and natural prejudices. He considers it a degradation. . . . Nothing can induce him to resort to labor, unless compelled to do so by stern necessity; and it is only then that there is any ground to work upon for civilizing and Christianizing him. But little, if any, good impression can be made upon him in these respects, so long as he is able to roam at large."

NOTE: The quotes are from Francis Paul Prucha, ed., *Documents of United States Indian Policy* (Lincoln: University of Nebraska Press, 1975), 71–2, 77–8.

Handout #4—Responses to Indian Removal

Black Hawk, Chief of the Sauk and Fox, 1833:

"We always had plenty; our children never cried from hunger, neither were our people in want. . . . The rapids of Rock River furnished us with an abundance of excellent fish, and the land being very fertile, never failed to produce good crops of corn, beans, pumpkins, and squashes. . . . Our village was healthy and there was no place in the country possessing such advantages, nor hunting grounds better than those we had in our possession. If a prophet had come to our village in those days and told us that the things were to take place which have since come to pass, none of our people would have believed him."

Speckled Snake, Creek elder (aged 100+), 1829:

"Brothers! I have listened to many talks from our Great Father. When he first came over the wide waters, he was but a little man. . . . His legs were cramped by sitting long in his big boat, and he begged for a little land to light his fire. . . . But when the white man had warmed himself before the Indians' fire and filled himself with their hominy, he became very large. With a step he bestrode the mountains and his feet covered the plains and the valleys. His hand grasped the eastern and the western sea, and his head rested on the moon. Then he became our Great Father. He loved his red children, and he said, 'Get a little further, lest I tread on thee. . . .' Brother I have listened to a great many talks from our great father. But they always began and ended in this—'Get a little further; you are too near me.'"

George W. Harkins, district chief of the Choctaw Nation, 1832:

"We were hedged in by two evils, and we chose that which we thought least. Yet we could not recognize the right that the state of Mississippi had assumed to legislate for us. Although the legislators of the state were qualified to make laws for their own citizens, that did not qualify them to become law makers to a people who were so dissimilar in manners and customs as the Choctaws are to the Mississippians. Admitting that they understood the people, could they remove that mountain of prejudice that has ever obstructed the streams of justice, and prevented their salutary influence from reaching my devoted countrymen? We as Choctaws rather chose to suffer and be free, than live under the degrading influence of laws where our voice could not be heard in their formation.

"I could cheerfully hope that those of another age and generation may not feel the effects of those oppressive measures that have been so illiberally dealt out to us. . . . I ask you in the name of justice for repose, for myself and my injured people. Let us alone—we will not harm you, we want rest. We hope, in the name of justice that another outrage may never be committed against us."

NOTE: The quotes are from T.C. McLuhan, *Touch the Earth: A Self-Portrait of Indian Existence* (New York: Promontory Press, 1971), 3, 73, 139.

CHAPTER 38

Mexico's Loss of Land

Perspectives from Mexico and the United States

RESOURCE CENTER OF THE AMERICAS

This lesson examines an important time in both U.S. and Mexican history. In the early–mid-1800s, the U.S. acquired vast new territories while Mexico lost almost half of its territory. How did this happen? How did people in the United States and Mexico feel about the critical decisions that changed their borders? The period of time that includes the annexation of Texas and the Mexican-American War is often given little coverage in U.S. history courses, but merits much greater attention. The history of these conflicts is crucial for understanding U.S.–Mexico relations today. In particular, it allows us to reconsider the argument made by many in the current immigration debate that Mexicans entering California, Arizona, New Mexico, and Texas are "illegals."

The lesson begins by exploring the attempts of U.S. citizens living in Texas to secede from Mexico, and the U.S. government's later acquisition of Mexican territory. Students learn about the Mexican-American War and the concept of Manifest Destiny using a number of primary sources representing different perspectives. These documents will help students to examine their own and others' interpretations of and biases about important ideas and historical events. This period of history is important for understanding contemporary U.S.–Mexico relations, the use of ideology to justify expansion, and an individual's responsibility to society.

Learner Objectives

- To explain the economic and racial roots of Manifest Destiny and analyze how the concept influenced the westward expansion of the country.

- To explain the causes of the Mexican-American War, the sequence of events leading to the outbreak of war, and the consequences of the Treaty of Guadalupe Hidalgo.
- To analyze the Mexican-American War from different perspectives.

Concepts

- Annexation
- Manifest Destiny

Major Questions to Be Addressed

- What arguments were used to justify U.S. expansion and to oppose Mexico's loss of land?
- How did the Mexican–U.S. relationship change in the mid-nineteenth century?

Exploring the Connections

- In Mexico the conflict with the United States is known as the American Intervention, while in the United States it is referred to as the Mexican-American War or the Mexican War. The war of 1846 was a conflict between two countries over land on which many Mexican people lived and whose descendants continue to live today.

Teaching Strategies

- Reading, writing, group discussion, and image analysis

From *OAH Magazine of History* 10, no. 2 (Winter 1996): 24–34. © Organization of American Historians. Reprinted by permission. This lesson plan originally appeared in Octavio Madigan Ruiz, Amy Sander, and Meredith Sommers, *Many Faces of Mexico* (Minneapolis: Resource Center of the Americas, 1995).

Materials Provided

- Mexico After Independence (Handout 1)
- Examining Perspectives (Handouts 2a, b & c)
- Examining Perspectives Question Sheet (Handout 3)
- Map of Mexican Territory Acquired by United States (Image)

Time Required

- 1 class session

Preparation for Lesson

- Make one copy of each Handout for each student.
- Ask students to read Handout 1 before coming to class.
- Students should think about their responses to the reflection questions raised in the text and write their responses in their journals.
- Make an overhead of the map.

Sequence of Lesson

Anticipatory Set, 5 minutes

1. Introduce the day's lesson by asking provocative questions about the reading, such as, "Was the Mexican-American War really nothing more than a border skirmish?" and "What was at stake for both Mexico and the United States?"

Body of Lesson, 45 minutes

2. Ask students if they have any questions about the reading and try to clarify any questions. Place the overhead of the map showing Mexico's loss of land to the United States on the projector. Ask students to briefly summarize the various conflicts which led to Mexico's loss of land (the fight over Texas and the Mexican-American War).

    For a more dramatic display of the vast amount of territory Mexico lost, make a photocopy of the map and cut apart the Texas annexations, the land acquired under the Treaty of Guadalupe Hidalgo, and the contemporary map of Mexico. Then, place the pieces of territory lost over the contemporary map of Mexico and compare the size of the territories.

3. Distribute one copy of Handouts 2a–2c to each student to read individually during class.

4. Divide students into pairs or small groups. Students should reflect upon what they read in the handouts and discuss their responses to the questions on Handout 3. Students may write one group response or individual responses to the questions on Handout 3. (Students should finish as homework any questions not answered.) Alternatively, the instructor may wish to use the questions on the handout as discussion questions for a discussion with the entire class.

Closure

5. Ask students to imagine how they might have felt about Mexico's loss of land if they had lived in that era. Do a quick straw poll of those in support of, or in opposition to, the war. Ask students to briefly share their reasons for supporting their position.

Evaluation

Evaluate student responses on the Question Sheet (Handout 3).

Assignment

Think about the arguments both in support of, and in opposition to, U.S. expansion. Write about how you think those arguments pertain to U.S. foreign policy today (e.g., U.S. actions in Panama, Iraq, Somalia, and Haiti).

Extension Lesson

A painting by John Gast expressed many Americans' feelings about westward expansion in the early to middle 1800s. The painting entitled "American Progress," which depicts Manifest Destiny as a woman, helped to shape people's vision of a modern empire filling a continent. Obtain a reproduction or enlarged photocopy of the painting (included in many social studies textbooks, or in history books at the library). Ask students to analyze the painting and to answer the following:

- What images does John Gast use to depict the concept of Manifest Destiny?
- Does Gast's depiction of East and West reveal his biases?
- Based on this painting, how do you think Gast and others who believed in Manifest Destiny felt about Indians?

(This extension lesson is adapted from "Opposition to the Mexican War of 1846," *OAH Magazine of History,* Spring 1994.)

Handout 1: Mexico After Independence

In 1824, the Estados Unidos Mexicanos (United States of Mexico) was formed. The new country was a federal republic, consisting of 19 states and 4 territories. It had a constitution which called for the separation of legislative, judicial and executive powers, and which established both a senate and a chamber of deputies.

After the war of independence from Spain (1810–1821), the process of creating a new nation was difficult. People disagreed about which type of government to create. Some favored a centralist model with a strong national government, while others favored a federalist model with more independence for the regions. All were concerned that the model chosen should restore order and be respected by people both within and outside of Mexico. Mexicans had a long history of foreign domination, and wanted to establish a governmental system that would protect their land and people from domination by the United States and European countries.

The early years of the republic were turbulent ones. The leadership of the country changed hands several times. General Santa Anna, who had been a prominent military officer in the war with Spain, was President eleven different times between 1832 and 1855. While the Mexican people were focused on resolving internal issues, a new problem was developing in Mexico's northern territories from Texas to the Pacific Ocean.

The Texas Territory

The U.S. government's purchase of the Louisiana Territory from France in 1803 nearly doubled the size of the United States. By 1819, the U.S. had added eight new states in addition to the Missouri and Arkansas territories, which bordered Mexico. U.S. citizens began to move into these territories, and from there, they began to enter the Mexican territories of California, New Mexico, and Texas. Although officials from Spain and Mexico gave some U.S. citizens permission to settle on land in Texas, the majority of people settled on the land illegally, in part because the land in Texas cost only one-tenth as much as land in the United States.

Increasing numbers of U.S. citizens entered the Texas territory and ignored Mexican laws and customs. For instance, slavery was illegal in Mexico—it had been outlawed since 1829. Mexican officials objected to settlers who brought slaves from the United States. Many settlers ignored the decree and kept their slaves. Mexico also required those settling in Texas to convert to Catholicism, which many people resisted. Mexican leaders became increasingly frustrated by the people living in Texas, but the unstable government could do little to enforce its laws in the distant Texas territory.

[Pause for Reflection: Why did people want to settle in the Texas territory?]

The Alamo

As the Mexican Republic became more established after gaining independence from Spain, Mexican leaders paid more attention to what was happening in Texas.

The Mexican government was concerned the U.S. government would use the settlements in Texas as an excuse to claim that territory. General Santa Anna came to power in 1832, reinforced the Mexican army in Texas, and ordered more strict law enforcement in the region. The Texans rebelled, and Santa Anna mobilized troops in Texas to put down the rebellion. His troops arrived outside of San Antonio in 1836, and the rebels abandoned the city and barricaded themselves in a mission fort called the Alamo outside of the town. Santa Anna was determined to crush the rebellion, and killed all but a few women.

What Santa Anna did not know was that other resisters met and declared Texas an independent state on March 2, 1836. The Texans organized reinforcements and eventually defeated Santa Anna's forces. Mexico continued to view Texas as a rebellious state, but its attempt to crush the rebellion failed.

[Pause for Reflection: Why was Mexico concerned about settlements in Texas?]

Texas' Bid to United States for Statehood

The U.S. government recognized Texas as an independent government, nicknamed the Lone Star Republic. However, the U.S. government refused its petition for admission as a state into the United States. From 1836 to 1845, the possible annexation of Texas was a controversial political issue in the United States. At stake was Texas' admittance as a free or slave state. Many Northerners in the United States objected to admitting another slave state, whereas many Southerners favored admitting a slave state. If Texas had been admitted as a slave state, it would have changed the balance of power between slave and nonslave states.

The 1844 presidential election was pivotal in determining Texas' future. Henry Clay, who opposed Texas' annexation, ran against James Polk, an expansionist who favored annexing Texas. Polk won the election, and Congress passed the proposal for Texas' annexation on March 1, 1845. From the perspective of the U.S. government, Texas had achieved statehood. The Mexicans, however, maintained the United States had illegally acquired Mexican territory. Although Mexican leaders wanted to stop the U.S. government from taking Texas, they did not want to enter into a costly and damaging war with the United States.

Polk sent a negotiator to Mexico with orders to offer the Mexicans $5 million for New Mexico and $25 million for California. In return, Mexico would agree to recognize the Rio Grande as the official border between the two countries. Polk hoped to almost double the size of the United States. He especially wanted California, because its ports would give the United States access to the Pacific Ocean and valuable trade routes to Asia. The Mexicans refused to even meet with Polk's negotiator, which made Polk furious. In retaliation, he began looking for a way to provoke the Mexicans into war. Polk knew that war with Mexico would be controversial, but he also believed many U.S. citizens were eager to expand to the Pacific coast even if it meant war.

[Pause for Reflection: Why did the United States originally refuse to admit Texas as a state? What do you think U.S. officials' motives were for annexing Texas? What was Mexico's response?]

Manifest Destiny

Although many U.S. citizens rejected expansionism, a majority embraced the idea. In the summer of 1845, John O'Sullivan, editor of the newspaper *Democratic Review,* wrote that it was "Our manifest destiny to overspread the continent allotted by Providence for the free development of our yearly multiplying millions." In other words, it was the "manifest destiny," or God-given right and ultimate fate, of the United States to gain control of the entire North American continent. The ideology of Manifest Destiny suggested that since God intended the United States to control the continent, there must be something special about the white people who populated the country. Manifest Destiny provided the justification for invading lands already being used by Indians and Mexicans, whom many Whites considered to be lazy, inferior, and unworthy.

[Pause for Reflection: Using your own words, how would you explain the concept of Manifest Destiny to someone who didn't know what the term meant?]

War with Mexico

General Zachary Taylor led U.S. troops to a piece of land between the Nueces and Rio Grande rivers, territory claimed by both Mexico and the United States. Although it is unclear who fired first, there were casualties on both sides. Taylor sent a message to Polk, telling him that the Mexicans had caused American blood to be shed on American soil. Polk drafted a declaration of war on May 11, 1846, which the House of Representatives passed 173 to 14. The Senate passed it the following day.

During the next two years, the United States and Mexican armies battled one another. The U.S. army, however, had superior firepower and advanced quickly toward the Mexican interior. The U.S. army captured Mexico City in the autumn of 1847, leaving the countryside in disarray and the government in shambles. Some members of the Mexican Congress wanted to stop the bloody war with the United States, while others argued that Mexico should resist the U.S. occupation.

Polk and other U.S. leaders were reluctant to make Mexico a part of the United States, in part because it would be difficult to control a group of people who spoke a different language and had a different culture. In 1848, U.S. and Mexican officials signed the Treaty of Guadalupe Hidalgo.

It established the Rio Grande as the southern border of Texas and allowed the U.S. to purchase the California and New Mexico territories for $15 million. This vast territory included all or parts of the future states of Colorado, Wyoming, Utah, Arizona, New Mexico, Nevada, and California. This vast region contained bountiful natural resources and strategic ports, which allowed the U.S. government and businesses to acquire important resources. The land acquisition was not complete, however. The U.S. government also wanted the Mesilla Valley (today Southern New Mexico and Arizona) because it offered the best location for building a railroad to newly acquired California. In 1853, the U.S. government purchased a strip of land in the Gadsden Purchase. The United States defeat of Mexico and the acquisition of Mexican territory was an important factor in the rise of the United States to a world superpower.

[Pause for Reflection: How do you think the Mexicans living in Arizona, California, Colorado, New Mexico, Texas, and Utah felt about living in U.S.-controlled territories after the war with Mexico? What do you think some of the advantages and disadvantages were?]

Handout 2a: Examining Perspectives: Mexican Perspective

(The following selection is excerpted from a Mexican textbook on the annexation of Texas and the U.S. Intervention in Mexico, as presented in a book titled *As Others See Us.* This book gives students and teachers the opportunity to understand U.S. history from a different perspective. Note: this is not the only perspective which Mexican people hold about the war.)

Texas was annexed to the United States by the treaty of April 12, 1844, despite the protests of our [the Mexican] government and even though the treaty was rejected by the American Congress. Thereupon the annexation of the territory [Texas] was proposed in the House and approved on March 1, 1845, which forced our Minister in Washington to withdraw. The Texans, backed by the American government, claimed that its boundaries extended to the Rio Bravo del Norte [Rio Grande], whereas in fact the true limits had never passed the Nueces River. From this [boundary dispute] a long controversy developed [during which negotiations were carried on] in bad faith by the Americans.

They ordered troops to invade places within our territory, operating with the greatest treachery, and pretended that it was Mexico which had invaded their territory, making [Mexico] appear as the aggressor. What they were really seeking was to provoke a war, a war in which the southern states of the Union were greatly interested, in order to acquire new territories which they could convert into states dominated by the slavery interests. But since the majority of the people of the United States were not pro-slavery nor in favor of a war of conquest, President Polk tried to give a defensive character to his first military moves, foreseeing the opposition which he would otherwise encounter. Once he obtained a declaration of war, Polk made it appear that he wanted nothing more than peaceful possession of the annexed territory. When at last the city of Mexico was captured, he made his fellow countrymen understand that they would receive no other indemnity for the expenses of war and the blood spilled than a cession of territory. Thus Polk would achieve the goal he sought from the outset. . . .

The Mexican War was a brilliant move astutely planned by the United States. The magnificent lands of Texas and California with their ports on both oceans, the gold deposits soon to be discovered in the latter state, and the increase in territory which made possible the growth of slave states compensated [the United States] many times over the costs in men and money of the unjust acquisition. . . .

Handout 2b: Examining Perspectives: Support for War

In 1845, the Washington *Union,* a newspaper that supported the position of President Polk, insisted that westward expansion into Mexican lands was inevitable. An editorial in the paper asked: "Let the great measure of annexation be accomplished, and with it the questions of boundary and claims. For who can arrest the torrent that will pour onward to the West? The road to California will be open to us. Who will stay the march of our western people?"

The influential *American Review* said that Mexico should bow before "a superior population, insensibly oozing into her territories, changing her customs, and out-living, out-trading, exterminating her weaker blood."

The New York *Herald* said in 1847, "The universal Yankee nation can regenerate and disenthrall the people of Mexico in a few years; and we believe it is a part of our destiny to civilize that beautiful country."

The Reverend Theodore Parker of Boston criticized war with Mexico, arguing that the United States should expand not by war but by the power of ideas. He referred to the Mexicans as "a wretched people; wretched in their origin, history and character." He viewed U.S. expansion as the "steady advance of a superior race, with superior ideas and a better civilization."

An editorial in the *Congressional Globe* echoed this sentiment, stating, "We must march from Texas straight to the Pacific Ocean. . . . It is the destiny of the white race." Many leaders shared these attitudes. Ohio Congressman Delano described Mexicans as an inferior people who "embrace all shades of color . . . a sad compound of Spanish, English, Indian and Negro bloods . . . and resulting, it is said, in the production of a slothful, ignorant race of beings."

On May 9, even before Polk had received news of any battles between U.S. and Mexican troops, Polk held a cabinet meeting. He recorded in his diary what he said at the meeting.

"I stated . . . that up to this time, as we knew, we had heard of no open act of aggression by the Mexican army, but that the danger was imminent that such acts would be committed. I said that in my opinion we had ample cause of war, and that it was impossible . . . that I could remain silent much longer . . . that the country was excited and impatient on the subject. . . ."

When Polk heard the news of U.S. casualties, he and his cabinet decided to declare war. The declaration of war contained the following text:

> After reiterated menaces, Mexico has passed the boundary of the United States, has invaded our territory and shed American blood upon the American soil. . . . The cup of forbearance has been exhausted, even before the recent information from the frontier of the [Rio Grande]. But now, after reiterated menaces, Mexico has passed the boundary of the United States, has invaded our territory, and shed American blood upon American soil. She has proclaimed that hostilities have commenced, and that the two nations are now at war.
>
> As war exists, and, notwithstanding all our efforts to avoid it, exists by the act of Mexico herself, we are called upon by every consideration of duty and patriotism to vindicate with decision and honor, the rights, and the interests of our country.

The U.S. House passed the war resolution by a vote of 174 to 14. Senators debated the measure, which was limited to one day, and approved the measure by a vote of 40 to 2. The poet Walt Whitman reacted to the declaration of war against Mexico by writing in the *Brooklyn Eagle,* "Yes: Mexico must be thoroughly chastised! . . . Let our arms now be carried with a spirit which shall teach the world that, while we are not forward for a quarrel, America knows how to crush, as well as how to expand!"

Handout 2c: Examining Perspectives: Opposition to War

Colonel Ethan Allen Hitchcock, an aide to General Taylor, wrote the following in his diary:

"I have said from the first that the United States are the aggressors. . . . We have not one particle of right to be here. . . . It looks as if the government sent a small force on purpose to bring on a war, so as to have a pretext for taking California and as much of this country as it chooses, for, whatever becomes of this army, there is no doubt of a war between the United States and Mexico. . . . My heart is not in this business . . . but, as a military man, I am bound to execute orders."

Some newspapers protested the war from the very beginning. Horace Greeley wrote in the New York *Tribune* on May 12, 1846:

"We can easily defeat the armies of Mexico, slaughter them by the thousands, and pursue them perhaps to their capital; we can conquer and 'annex' their territory; but what then? Who believes that a score of victories over Mexico . . . will give us more liberty, a purer Morality?"

Congressman Joshua Giddings, one of a small number of war dissenters in Washington, wrote:

"In the murder of Mexicans upon their own soil, or in robbing them of their country, I can take no part either now or hereafter. The guilt of these crimes must rest on others—I will not participate in them."

Other political leaders shared Giddings' views. *A Massachusetts Protest of the Mexican War,* written in 1847, made the following claim:

> Resolved, That the present war with Mexico has its primary origin in the unconstitutional annexation to the United States of the foreign state of Texas while the same was still at war with Mexico; that it was unconstitutionally commenced by the order of the President, to General Taylor, to take military possession of territory in dispute between the United States and Mexico, and in the occupation of Mexico; and that it is now waged ingloriously—by a powerful nation against a weak neighbor—unnecessarily and without just cause, at the immense cost of treasure and life, for the dismemberment of Mexico, and for the conquest, of a portion of her territory, from which slavery has already been excluded . . .

Abraham Lincoln was a first term member of the U.S. House of Representatives elected in 1846. On January 12, 1848, he delivered one of the few speeches he made while in Congress. He challenged President Polk's war against Mexico:

> The President sent the army into the midst of a settlement of Mexican people who had never submitted, by consent or by force, to the authority of Texas or of the United States, and . . . thereby the first blood of the war was shed. . . .
>
> [If] he can show that the soil was ours where the first blood of war was shed—that it was not within an inhabited country, or, if within such, that the inhabitants had submitted themselves to the civil authority of Texas or of the United States . . . then I am with him. . . . But if he can not or will not do this . . . then I shall be fully convinced of what I more than suspect already—that he is deeply conscious of being in the wrong; that he feels the blood of this war. . . . As I have before said, he knows not where he is. He is a bewildered, confounded, and miserably perplexed man.

The war had just begun when a writer named Henry David Thoreau refused to pay taxes to support the war. While he was in jail, his friend Ralph Waldo Emerson visited him. Emerson agreed with Thoreau's position against the war, but thought his protest was in vain. When Emerson visited Thoreau, he asked, "Henry David, what are you doing in there?" Thoreau reportedly replied, "Ralph Waldo, what are you doing out there?" Two years later, Thoreau gave a lecture entitled "Resistance to Civil Government," later printed in an essay, "Civil Disobedience":

"It is not desirable to cultivate a respect for the law, so much as for the right. The only obligation which I have a right to assume is to do at any time what I think is right. . . . Law never made men a whit more just; and, by means of their respect for it, even the well-disposed are daily made the agents of injustice."

Handout 3: Examining Perspectives: Question Sheet

1. What perspective did the Mexican textbook authors have on the war with the United States?
2. What are some of the arguments that political leaders, journalists, and others made supporting U.S. expansion?
3. What are some of the reasons that President Polk gave for asking Congress for a Declaration of War? Do you think he had the support of the majority of U.S. citizens? Why or why not?
4. What are some of the arguments that political leaders, journalists, and others made opposing U.S. expansion and the Mexican-American War?
5. Why do you think there was so much opposition to the Mexican-American War?
6. Think about how Hitchcock, Lincoln, Thoreau, and Emerson responded to government policies. How did their approaches differ? What role do you think individuals have in taking responsibility for government policies with which they disagree?
7. Do you think the war against Mexico was a "just" war? Explain.

Map: Mexican Territory Acquired by the United States, 1848

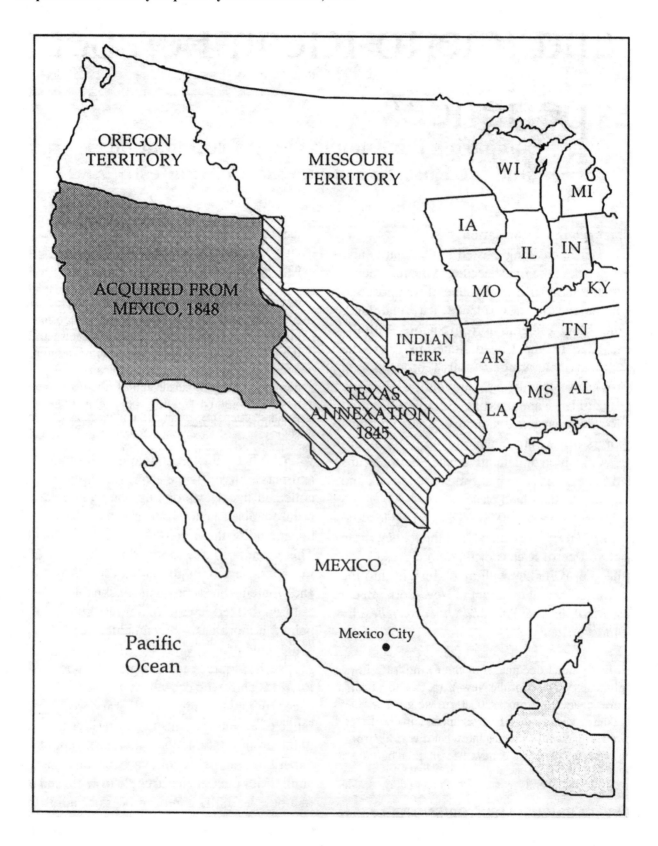

CHAPTER 39

Comparing the Emancipation Proclamation and the Russian Emancipation Manifesto

CLAIR W. KELLER

Purpose

The purpose of this lesson is to compare the ideas and context of the Emancipation Proclamation issued by President Abraham Lincoln on September 22, 1862, and the Emancipation Manifesto issued on March 3, 1861, by Tsar Alexander II of Russia.

Objective

At the conclusion of the lesson the student should be able to:

1. identify the essential points of each document;
2. compare the essential points of each document;
3. explain the circumstances that led to the issuing of each document;
4. compare the impact of each document; and
5. read for details.

Background Information on the Emancipation Manifesto

Russia's defeat in the Crimean War (1853–1856) at the hand of English, French, and Turkish forces, and the humiliating peace terms that the victors imposed injured Russia's prestige. The defeat showed Russia's military weakness, the country's backwardness, and exposed the economic, administrative, and social ineptness of Russia's autocratic regime. As a result, Emperor Alexander II and some of his advisors became convinced that reforms, long sought by the liberals in Russia and opposed by the con-servative elements, were long overdue. The emancipation of the serfs, the first of these reforms, shattered the entire structure of Russian society and forced the government to introduce educational, legal, municipal, military, and other reforms, thus laying the foundation for a vast transformation of Russian society.

In order to "avoid all misunderstanding and to protect public and private interest," the government established a special "Office of Peasant Affairs" that was entrusted with the affairs of the peasant communes established on the estates of the nobility. Justices of the peace were appointed in every district to solve disputes. Each village commune wrote a charter which enumerated the amount of land allotted to the peasants for permanent use and outlined the scope of the peasants' obligations to the nobles. During the two-year period in which the charters were to go into effect, the peasants were to remain obedient to the nobles and fulfill their obligations. Eventually courts and police would be established on each estate. The manifesto urged the "freed serfs, on the eve of a new future" which was opening to them, to appreciate and recognize the considerable sacrifices the nobility had made on their behalf. It also pointed out that "abundance is acquired only through hard work, wise use of strength and resources, strict economy, and above all, through an honest God-fearing life."

Terms of the Emancipation Manifesto were implemented as follows:

1. Serfs became legally free.
2. Between one-third and one-half of private estate land was transferred to the newly freed peasants.

From *OAH Magazine of History* 4, no. 1 (Winter 1989): 56–59. © Organization of American Historians. Reprinted by permission.

3. Government audit commissions determined the value of the land.

4. The peasants receiving land paid for it by: (a) giving one-fourth of the price to the original owner on installments; and (b) three-fourths of the price to the government over a forty-nine-year period.

5. The government in turn reimbursed the original owners for this three-fourths amount, using long-term interest-bearing bonds.

6. The land that the freed serfs received actually was assigned to peasant communes, which then allotted portions of the land to families belonging to the commune for the use of the family (that is, the commune owned the land, and the individual family had tenure for their portion of the land).

Preparation

On the previous day, students should be assigned text material concerning Lincoln's decision to issue the Emancipation Proclamation. They should be instructed to look for reasons why the Emancipation Proclamation was issued in September 1862, what it accomplished, and identify its impact on the war. Students should also be assigned to read a world history textbook (you could use several different textbooks or provide a short handout) describing the circumstances related to issuing the Emancipation Manifesto. Ask students to answer the same questions listed above. Point out that the purpose of the lesson is to compare these two emancipation documents.

[Note: Some students might be assigned to read the circumstances surrounding other such emancipation actions (e.g., Brazil, Belgian Congo, etc.).]

Lesson Procedures

Introduction. Review the background of the Emancipation Proclamation. Discuss with students the question of whether Lincoln's decision to issue the Emancipation Proclamation can be considered an act of desperation, an act of military necessity, or an act of humanitarianism. Suggest possible reasons for each position, but do not attempt to reach closure at this time.

Transition to the Lesson. Point out that the same question could also be asked of Emperor Alexander II.

Developing the Lesson

1. Review the circumstances for issuing each document. [See the background information above on the Emancipation Manifesto.]

2. Have students read the following excerpts from the Emancipation Proclamation. Make certain they understand vocabulary, i.e., what is meant by emancipation?

That on the 1st day of January, A.D. 1863, all persons held as slaves within any State or designated part of a State the people thereof shall then be in rebellion against the United States shall be then henceforward, and forever free; and the executive government of the United States, including the military and naval authority thereof, will recognize and maintain the freedom of such persons and will do no act or acts to repress such persons, or any of them in any efforts they may make for their actual freedom.

. . . I do order and declare that all persons held as slaves within said designated States and parts of States are and henceforward shall be free, and that the executive government of the United States, including the military and naval authorities thereof, will recognize and maintain the freedom of said persons.

And I hereby enjoin upon the people so declared to be free to abstain from all violence, unless in necessary self-defense; and I recommend to them that, in all cases when allowed, they labor faithfully for reasonable wages.

And I further declare and make known that such persons of suitable condition will be received into the armed service of the United States to garrison forts, positions, stations, and other places, and to man vessels of all sorts in said services.

Discussion Questions

What does the first paragraph imply was taking place in some southern states? Which slaves were freed? (Use a map to show what areas were affected.) What role was the military to play? What is suggested by the directive to the military? Were freed slaves given any rights? Are opportunities for employment suggested? Will freed slaves be able to fight against southern soldiers? Why were freed slaves given such a limited role in the armed forces?

3. Have students read the following excerpts from The Emancipation Manifesto:

By the Grace of God We, Alexander II, Emperor and Autocrat of All Russia, King of Poland, Grand Duke of Finland, etc., make known to all Our faithful subjects: Examining the condition of the classes and professions comprising the state, We became convinced that the present state legislation favors the upper and middle classes, defines their obligations, rights, and privileges, but does not equally favor the serfs, so designated because in part from old laws and in part from custom they have been hereditarily subject to the authority of landowners, who in turn were obligated to provide for their wellbeing. [Although some nobles have kept their obligations to the serfs, others have not]. . . . Because of the decline of the simplicity of morals, because of an increase in the diversity of relations, because of the weakening of the direct paternal attitude of nobles toward the peasants, and because noble rights fell sometimes into the hands of people exclusively concerned with their personal interests, good relations weakened. The way was opened for an arbitrariness burdensome for the peasants and detrimental to their welfare, causing them to be indifferent to the improvement of their own existence. . . .

We have left to the nobles themselves, in accordance with their own wishes, the task of preparing new proposals for the new organization of peasant life—proposals which would limit their rights over the peasants, and the realization of which would inflict on them [the nobles] some material losses. Our confidence was justified. . . . These committees, after collecting the necessary data, have formulated proposals on a new arrangement for serfs and their relationship with the nobles.

On the basis of the above mentioned new arrangements, the serfs will receive in time the full rights of free rural inhabitants.

The nobles, while retaining their property rights on all the lands belonging to them, grant the peasants perpetual use of their [dwellings] in return for a specified obligation; and, to assure their livelihood as well as to guarantee fulfillment of their obligations toward the government, [the nobles] grant them a portion of arable land fixed by the said arrangements as other property.

While enjoying these land allotments, the peasants are obliged, in return, to fulfill obligations to the noblemen fixed by the same arrangements. In this state, which is temporary, the peasants are temporarily bound.

At the same time, they [the peasants] are granted the right to purchase their [dwellings], and, with the consent of the nobles, they may acquire in full ownership the arable lands and other properties which are allotted them for personal use. Following such acquisition of full ownership of land, the peasants will be freed from their obligations to the nobles for the land thus purchased and will become free peasant landowners.

This new arrangement, because of its complexity, cannot be put into effect immediately. A time of not less than two years is necessary. During this period . . . the order now actually existing on the estates should be maintained.

Discussion Questions

Why does Alexander think it is necessary to issue the manifesto? How was the manifesto developed? What did the freed serfs receive? What were their obligations? How long would it take before the process of freedom was completed?

4.   After discussing the documents, create a comparison chart on the chalkboard or on an overhead projection. Have students, either in groups or as a class, complete the chart. The three-column chart, whose headings are: "Items for Comparison," "Emancipation Proclamation," and the "Emancipation Manifesto," should pose the following questions under the heading "Items for Comparison": Who issued the document? What position did each leader hold? Who was affected by each of the documents? Who gained or who lost under the documents? What freedoms and rights were granted? What new problems were created? What motivated those who issued each document? What other comparisons can be made between the two documents?

5.   After completing the chart, discuss the following: What are the similarities and differences between the two documents? Which action provided greater opportunity? How do you account for the differences in the documents? Which document had the greater significance? Can the Emancipation Proclamation be viewed as a "racist" document? How did these emancipations differ from others? [This is to be used if students have been assigned to investigate other emancipations.] Were motivations similar? Were motives other than humanitarian at work in issuing these documents? Is there a difference between the rhetoric of emancipation and the reality of emancipation?

Conclusion

Why has the Emancipation Proclamation been considered important? Is this justified? In comparison with other emancipations, can the Emancipation Proclamation be viewed as a significant humanitarian event?
[Note: You might also use the terms of emancipation listed in the teacher background information for a comparison with the reconstruction plans proposed by Lincoln, Johnson, and the radicals in Congress.]

CHAPTER 40

Italians Around the World

Teaching Italian Migration from a Transnational Perspective

DENNIS J. TOWNSEND

The Age of Immigration, 1870 to 1920, is usually a major unit for United States history classes. More often than not, the exodus of European and Asian immigrants to the United States for economic and political freedom forms the core focus. Within the unit teachers stress the effects of settlement on the immigrants and their contributions to their newfound homes.

Unfortunately, such an approach to immigration is not without problems. Students are led to believe that immigration took place in one giant wave and then basically stopped. Furthermore, instructors too often ignore the fact that a fair number of these immigrants were seasonal workers who returned to their homelands. Likewise, many classes fail to discuss the networking that took place among the immigrants and the impact such a network had on economic and geographic decisions. Finally, students hardly ever learn that there were destinations other than the United States for migrants.

I believe that teaching a unit based on the migratory experience of one particular group of immigrants gives a better understanding of the entire immigration experience. Thus, in this lesson, I have focused on Italian immigrants as they moved throughout the world during this era. Likewise, by studying the events taking place in the United States and the newly-born nation of Italy during the Age of Immigration, students see a connection between United States history and world history. The following lesson plan, divided into three sections, provides a comparative global perspective of the Italian diaspora and thus will enhance the teaching of the immigration experience.

Overall Time Frame

The three sections of the lesson require a total of four class periods.

Section I

This part of the lesson uses group work to introduce the economic factors that influenced migration.

Time Frame

This section takes two class periods to complete.

Objectives

1. To understand the concept of a diaspora.
2. To gain an introductory knowledge of the economic needs of the United States and other world regions during this period.

Materials Needed

- U.S. history textbooks
- World history textbooks
- Related books and magazines
- Internet connection (if possible)

Procedure

1. Open with a student discussion on "What is a diaspora?" Allow the students to give examples of their understanding of the term. Guide the

From *OAH Magazine of History* 14, no. 1 (Fall 1999): 40–43. © Organization of American Historians. Reprinted by permission.

class to an understanding that diasporas are not always politically motivated but can also be driven by economic decisions.

2. Divide the class into four equal groups. Have each group research and answer one of the following four questions, using the materials listed above. Emphasize that each group should focus on the economic factors involved in their area of research.

a. How did the emancipation of slaves affect the plantation and extraction industries of the American South?

b. How did the spread of industrial capitalism affect the northeastern United States?

c. How did the spreading of capitalism in Great Britain and northern Europe affect the African and Asian world?

d. What did the nations of South America offer as an incentive for immigrating there and why?

3. Have the students present their findings to the entire class.

Section II

Using maps, this part of the lesson connects economic circumstances to the geographic movement of people.

Time Frame

Section II can be completed in one class period.

Objective

To develop an understanding of Italian migration during the Age of Immigration.

Materials Needed

- Map of Italy, photocopied for each student
- Map of the world, photocopied for each student

Procedure

1. Hand out copies of a map of Italy and have the students study its topographic features. Ask the students where industrial and agricultural development would be likely to take place and why.

2. Lead a class discussion of possible parallels between the United States and Italy during the late nineteenth century.

3. After the students have developed their hypotheses, provide a brief overview of Italy in the nineteenth century, using the lecture format given below.

4. Divide the students into small groups and have them consider where people with the following occupations would migrate to.

a. Mason
b. Day laborer
c. Miner
d. Farmer
e. Merchant

5. Hand out copies of a world map and have the students:

a. chart the passage of each group;

b. explain on the back of the map why they chose the destination they did; and

c. explain on the back of the map how the migrants traveled and how they obtained the means to do so.

Lecture Format

A. Italian Unification

1. The Congress of Vienna (1814–1815) had serious consequences in Italy.

a. Prince Klemens von Metternich of Austria sought to strengthen the countries around France in order to stop French aggression, restore a balance of power, and restore royal families to thrones lost during the reign of Napoleon.

b. Italy was divided and placed under foreign control: Austria ruled northern Italy; Spain ruled southern Italy.

2. During 1848 revolts took place in eight separate states on the Italian Peninsula.

a. Giuseppe Mazzini, an early leader of Italian nationalism, briefly headed a republican government in Rome.

b. As the revolts failed, the former rulers returned.

c. Italian nationalists looked toward the Kingdom of Sardinia for leadership. Made up of Piedmont, Nice, Savoy, and the island of Sardinia, it was the only Italian state ruled by an Italian dynasty.

3. In 1852 King Victor Emmanuel II named Count Camillo di Cavour prime minister.

a. Cavour was a moderate nationalist who made the unification of Italy his highest priority.

b. Cavour used an alliance with Napoleon III to annex all of northern Italy, except Venetia, by 1860.

c. Cavour secretly aided nationalist rebels in the southern half of Italy.

4. In May 1860 Giuseppe Garibaldi led his "Red Shirts" into battle in Sicily.
   a. Garibaldi was victorious and marched north to liberate Italy, gaining volunteers along the way.
   b. Count Cavour arranged a meeting between Garibaldi and King Victor Emmanuel II in Naples.
   c. Garibaldi willingly gave the king ruling power over southern Italy.
5. In March 1861 the Italian parliament met in Turin and declared Victor Emmanuel II king of Italy.
   a. The new nation had a government led by a constitutional monarch and elected parliament.
   b. In 1866 Venetia became part of Italy.
   c. In 1871 Italy took over the papal states and Rome became the capital city.
B. Italian development
   1. Northern Italy industrialized.
      a. The parliament saw this as a necessary step in the development of the Italian nation.
      b. Parliament passed laws favoring northern industrialization at the expense of southern Italy. (Southern Italy was seen as backward—too agrarian to modernize.)
      c. Northern cities attracted workers from across Italy and other parts of the world. A poor industrial proletariat developed in the North.
      d. Northern cities wanted cheap food and raw materials from the southern half of Italy.
   2. Southern Italy developed a plantation system.
      a. Poor farmers lost their land due to indebtedness.
      b. Rich landowners and northern investors bought the cheap land.
      c. Southern farmers either became tenant farmers or migrant farm hands.
   3. Low wages and poor working conditions became the impetus for immigrating.

Section III

This section adds a comparative perspective to the lesson by focusing on Italians and Russian Jews.

Time Frame

One class period is necessary for the completion of this lesson.

Objectives

1. To comprehend the migratory experience of Italians during the Age of Immigration.
2. To gain a comparative perspective by studying the experience of Russian Jewish immigrants.

Procedure

1. Open the class with the following statement: "You are a poor farm laborer and have received a letter from your brother telling you about job opportunities in the United States. He encourages you to join him. What should you do?"
   a. As the students respond, add that they are married with children. Then continue asking them what they would do.
   b. Encourage the students to consider all of the problems and possibilities involved with migrating to the United States.
2. Using the lecture format given below, provide an overview of the experience of Italians and Russian Jews who immigrated.
3. Have the students write an essay from the perspective of a wife whose husband has migrated to the United States and requested that she join him there.

Lecture Format

A. Between 1870 and 1920 two-thirds of Italian immigrants were men.
   1. Prior to 1896 over 50 percent were peasants.
   2. From 1896 to 1920 the majority were *braccianti* (landless, wage earning laborers), and the rest were either artisans or industrial workers.
B. The oppression of Russian Jews during the pogroms sanctioned by the Czar encouraged many Jews to leave Russia.
   1. The majority of Jewish emigrants from Russia were of the Orthodox tradition in Judaism.
   2. Many of these immigrants took jobs in U.S. cities in either the garment industry or the diamond industry. Banned from rural areas in Russia, they had lived in Jewish ghettoes in Russian cities.
   3. This group struggled with the settled German Jewish community, the majority of which were of the Reform tradition.
      a. The Reform Jewish tradition favored cultural assimilation whereas the Orthodox tradition preferred to be a separate people, culturally.

b. German Jews looked upon the Russian Jews as being backward due to their dress and religious practices, which continued to reflect their former way of life in Russia.

4. Because they fled religious persecution, few Jews returned to Russia after arriving in the United States.

C. "Networking" had a profound impact on the immigration experience.

1. Italian men who worked abroad periodically returned to Italy.

a. Some of these men had earned enough money to buy a piece of land in Italy and retire there.

b. Others visited their old homes and told of job opportunities.

c. The returning workers provided names and references to Italian men who had trade skills so they could obtain employment abroad.

2. Industries in the United States hired skilled Italian men as labor recruiters who returned to their hometowns to hire skilled laborers.

a. These labor recruiters hired skilled workers for designated jobs in specific corporations.

b. The recruiters promised a better life for the workers in the United States.

3. Family members, friends, and former neighbors wrote letters telling of the job opportunities abroad.

a. The established immigrants sent photographs of life in their newfound homes to entice immigration.

b. Family members mailed money to help their kin afford emigration.

c. Family members that were established in the new country temporarily housed relatives and helped them find jobs, usually in the same place of employment.

D. Migrants faced cultural and economic obstacles when traveling to a new location.

Resources

Archdeacon, Thomas J. *Becoming American: An Ethnic History.* New York: The Free Press, 1983.

Bodnar, John. *The Transplanted: A History of Immigrants in Urban America.* Bloomington: Indiana University Press, 1985.

Gabaccia, Donna. *From Sicily to Elizabeth Street: Housing and Social Change Among Italian Immigrants, 1880–1930.* Albany: State University of New York Press, 1984.

Hammond Historical Atlas of the World. Revised edition. Maplewood, NJ: Hammond, 1989.

Howe, Irving. *World of Our Fathers.* New York: Schocken Books, 1989.

Kessner, Thomas. *The Golden Door: Italian and Jewish Mobility in New York City, 1880–1915.* New York: Oxford University Press, 1977.

Taylor, Philip. *The Distant Magnet: European Emigration to the U.S.A.* New York: Harper and Row, 1971.

The World in My Hand: Italian Emigration in the World, 1860–1960. Roma: Centro Studi Emigrazione, 1997.

CHAPTER 41

Eleanor Roosevelt and the Declaration of Human Rights
A Simulation Activity

SALLY GILBERT AND KATHY SCHOLLENBERGER

When the United Nations established its Human Rights Commission in 1946 out of concern for victims of World War II, Eleanor Roosevelt (ER) was chosen to chair its effort to draft a Declaration of Human Rights (DHR). Her choice as leader of this endeavor was particularly appropriate because of her commitment to refugee issues as well as her long history of social justice efforts during her tenure as First Lady. In her public role, she wrote a newspaper column for many years called "My Day" where she took forward-looking stands on Communism, civil rights, the status of women, and loyalty oaths, to name a few. She also privately lobbied her husband, Franklin D. Roosevelt, whenever she recognized injustice: for example, internment of Japanese Americans in camps and the widespread lynching of black men. The commission's mission was to create a document that might help prevent another world war and serve as a model for how human beings and nations should treat each other. The General Assembly of the United Nations adopted the resulting declaration on 10 December 1948. The following activity gives students the opportunity to simulate this undertaking.

Time Frame

This lesson requires three class periods, with some student preparation ahead of time.

Objectives

1. To understand the importance of documents in history.
2. To learn about the postwar era through documents.
3. To realize the complexity of the creation of an international document such as the DHR.
4. To consider the leadership skills of ER.

Handouts

1. Declaration of Human Rights.
2. "The Promise of Human Rights," *Foreign Affairs* (April 1948).

Both of these handouts are available at <http://www.udhr.org/>, a site in honor of the fiftieth anniversary of the declaration. This site also includes a brief biography of ER and photos that provide useful background.

Set-up

Date: 27 January 1947

Place: Lake Success, New York

Event: Initial meeting of the Human Rights Commission, created by the Economic and Social Council of the United Nations

People present: Seventeen members of the commission, each chosen by his/her government. The representatives are from the following countries: Australia, Belgium, Belorussia, China, Chile, Egypt, France, India, Lebanon, Panama, the Philippines, Ukraine, the U.S.S.R, Yugoslavia, Uruguay, the United Kingdom, and the United States. (This plan is based on a class of seventeen; teachers can make adjustments by

From *OAH Magazine of History* 15, no. 3 (Spring 2001): 35–36. © Organization of American Historians. Reprinted by permission.

doubling the number of representatives per country.) Eleanor Roosevelt is the U.S. representative and permanent chairman. Dr. Peng-Chun Chang, representing China, is vice-chairman, and Dr. Charles Malik of Lebanon is serving as recorder.

Goal: To come to some initial agreement about the articles to be included in the DHR

Plan

Before the first class

1. Assign each student a role as country representative.
2. Allow students time to do some research about their country, its status in 1947, and the world at that time. Students might use these questions as guidelines: What are the major issues of concern to your country's citizens? Which of these seems most pressing? What effect did the recent war have on your country? How stable is your government? What kind of government does your country have? Are there specific issues of concern involving children, elderly people, women, minorities?
3. Ask students to come to class with a list of five articles for consideration in the initial draft of the DHR. (Only the officers will have read the actual declaration; it is essential that the other delegates not see the DHR before the second class.)

During the first class

1. Divide students into three groups.
2. Have those three groups meet in character for twenty-five minutes to compare notes, argue for inclusion or omission of certain matters based on their countries' interests, and attempt to agree on a list of ten articles for inclusion.
3. Instruct the three officers (who will have read the actual document and "The Promise of Human Rights" so that they know what ER thought was most important) to move from group to group filling their roles as go-betweens and mediators.
4. During the last twenty minutes of class, have ER and Dr. Chang run a discussion about the commonalities in countries' suggestions for inclusion. Instruct Dr. Malik to record the suggestions for a memo to the drafting committee. Have ER and

Dr. Chang remind the delegates to focus on the concepts, not the language, since that will be the work of the drafting committee.

During the second class

1. In order to move the activity along, explain that, since the last gathering of the Human Rights Commission, a drafting committee has met and written a draft of the declaration. Have ER and Dr. Chang distribute that document (the actual DHR) to the original groups for their perusal. In those groups, have representatives read the articles and look at what has been included and omitted. They should prepare to explain their reservations as well as the basis for their endorsement of the declaration.
2. During the last fifteen minutes of class, have ER and Dr. Chang call the full commission to order. They should allow each representative the opportunity to briefly voice the compromises his or her country will be making for the greater good in signing this document.

During the third class

1. Have students consider and discuss these questions:
   a. What would make countries agree to such a principled document?
   b. What do you think happened to this document? What effect do you think it had? (After students have speculated about this, the teacher can talk about what actually happened. The "Recommended Web Sites" below provide information about the creation and impact of the DHR.)
   c. What challenges do you think ER faced as chairman of the Human Rights Commission?
   d. What did you learn from this simulation?

Recommended Web Sites

The Eleanor Roosevelt and Human Rights Project: <http://www.gwu.edu/-erpapers/>

The Franklin and Eleanor Roosevelt Institute: <http://www.feri.org/>

In Your Hands: The Universal Declaration of Human Rights at 50: <http://www.undr50.0rg/>

The United Nations: <http://www.un.org/>

CHAPTER 42

Martin Luther King, Jr.'s "Beyond Vietnam"

Erin Cook and Stan Pesick

On April 4, 1967, Martin Luther King, Jr., made his most public and comprehensive statement against the Vietnam War. Addressing a crowd of 3,000 people in Riverside Church in New York City, King delivered a speech entitled "Beyond Vietnam." He pointed out that the war effort was "taking the young black men who have been crippled by our society and sending them 13,000 miles away to guarantee liberties in Southeast Asia which they had not found in southwest Georgia and East Harlem." Although some activists and newspapers supported King's statement, most responded with criticism. King's civil rights colleagues began to disassociate themselves from his radical stance, as the NAACP issued a statement against merging the civil rights movement and peace movement. King remained undeterred, stating that he was not fusing the civil rights and peace movements, as many had suggested. Two weeks after delivering his speech, King led thousands of demonstrators on an antiwar march to the United Nations.

Overview

The goal of this unit is to have students analyze, within the context of a particular historical period, Dr. King's decision to speak out against the war in Vietnam. Why did he make his choice? What risks were involved? How was his speech received? Ultimately, this unit asks students to connect this speech to the present by having them consider which of Dr. King's ideas about America's role in the world are relevant to us today. In addition to encouraging active learning and the development of critical thinking skills, this lesson will help students see King as more than a civil rights leader as

they explore the political and social implications of King's position against the war and his call for economic justice.

In addition to King's "Beyond Vietnam" speech, this lesson includes a number of primary source documents that will help students respond thoughtfully to the questions raised above. Without the appropriate historical context, however, students may have difficulty making sense of the complex issues that connect the war and domestic policy. Therefore, it is essential that students have a basic understanding of the history of the war in Vietnam and the public debate that was taking place in the U.S. at that time. This unit also supports students as they grapple with the ideas and questions raised in the documents themselves.

King's "Beyond Vietnam" speech includes a great deal of information, and we encourage teachers to break the document into at least two parts to make the material more manageable. The speech can be accessed in its entirety on the King Papers Project's web site at <http://www.kingpapers.org>. For this particular unit, we have chosen to use a newspaper editorial, two letters to the editor, and letters written to and by King to help students explore both sides of the issue as well as give them a broader historical context. For some useful information on teaching with primary sources, see Joan Musbach's "Using Primary Sources in the Secondary Classroom," *OAH Magazine of History* 16 (Fall 2001), 30–32.

National Standards

While most of us are accustomed to learning and teaching about King in the context of the civil rights movement,

From *OAH Magazine of History* 19, no. 1 (January 2005): 41–50. © Organization of American Historians. Reprinted by permission.

this lesson quite purposefully positions King in a different historical realm. Although King's role as a civil rights leader is still very relevant, we believe teaching about King in the context of the Vietnam War can help students deepen their knowledge of both King and the U.S. involvement in Vietnam. This lesson plan will fulfill the following standards in the *National Standards for United States History*:

Era 9: Postwar United States (1945–1970)

Standard 3C: Demonstrate understanding of the foreign and domestic consequences of U.S. involvement in Vietnam by:

- Assessing the shifts of public opinion about the war.
- Evaluating how Vietnamese and Americans experienced the war and how the war continued to affect postwar politics and culture.
- Analyzing the constitutional issues involved in the war and exploring the war's legacy.

Standard 3 of the Standards in Historical Thinking: Historical Analysis and Interpretation.

Time

This unit is designed for three to five class periods, depending on whether students read the materials and write their reflective journal entries in or out of class.

Objectives

- To use primary sources to analyze the reasons Dr. King spoke out against the war in Vietnam and how this action was received.
- To place King's "Beyond Vietnam" speech into historical, social, and political context.
- To improve analytical and critical thinking skills.
- To develop strong arguments based on primary source materials.
- To broaden students' perception of King beyond that of a civil rights leader.

Preparation and Resources

The questions that guided the development of this lesson are: Why did King choose to speak out against the war in Vietnam? What can this decision teach us about King? What can the response to this speech teach us about the social and political climate during this period? And finally, how are King's words applicable today? In addition to King's "Beyond Vietnam" speech, students will work with documents that reflect both the support and criticism that followed King's speech.

This lesson utilizes a number of materials that can be found on the Martin Luther King, Jr. Papers Project web site at <http://www.kingpapers.org>, including primary documents, the King Encyclopedia, and a King chronology. The web site can be used by teachers in preparation for the lesson and may also be used by students to supplement an activity. Teachers may also join the Liberation Community, which provides access to a searchable database of documents, a discussion group, and printable King-related documents. We also suggest reading Chapter 30 of *The Autobiography of Martin Luther King, Jr.* (1998), edited by Clayborne Carson. This chapter provides detailed background regarding King's decision to speak out against U.S. involvement in Vietnam.

Procedure

Part 1: Establishing the Historical Context for "Beyond Vietnam"

- For this "anticipatory set" give students two minutes to write down names and references that come to mind when they think of the Vietnam War. Next, have them do the same thing for Martin Luther King, Jr. Have students break into pairs and share their answers. Ask students if any of them included Dr. King in their Vietnam list or if anyone referred to Vietnam when writing about Dr. King. In addition to establishing the historical context for the lesson, this activity will highlight the fact that Martin Luther King, Jr., and the Vietnam War are taught in isolation from one another, even though each had a profound impact on the other.
- Introduce King's "Beyond Vietnam" speech by showing the first ten minutes of episode 4, "The Promised Land," of the PBS documentary *Eyes on the Prize II* (1992), if available. Follow with a discussion of the documentary.
- Have students read the first section of "Beyond Vietnam," available on the King Papers web site (http://www. kingpapers.org → King Resources → Documentary Inventory → 1967), or at least the excerpt reprinted in Clayborne Carson's article "King's Path to Antiwar Dissent" in this issue of the *OAH Magazine of History,* pages 27–28.

Part 2: Why did King speak out and how was his speech received?

Have students form two groups: one that supports King's decision to speak out against the war and one that feels he made an error. Give each group a packet that you have assembled beforehand, consisting of documents reprinted at the end of this lesson: the *New York Times* editorial "Dr.

King's Error," two letters to the editor of the *Times,* a letter written to King, and a three-page letter authored by King. You might supplement these documents with historical materials from local papers, if available. Instruct each group to use the documents that support and refute their position to develop as strong an argument as possible. You may have students write an editorial to present to the class or have a less formal presentation where students field questions from the opposing group.

Some questions to consider for the activity are:

1. Was King's decision to speak out against the war a departure from his stated philosophical, political, and/or social commitments?
2. What relevance does his role as a clergyman have for King's position? What about as a Nobel Peace Prize recipient? What about his role as a civil rights leader?
3. Do you believe there was a relationship between the war in Vietnam and the civil rights struggle at home? Why or why not?
4. Were there any inconsistencies with King's stated position on the war in Vietnam and his stated position as a civil rights leader? Consider the role of nonviolence.
5. What were some of the main criticisms King's opponents made regarding his statement on the war in Vietnam? What were some of the main arguments made by those defending King's position?
6. What if King had not taken a position on the war in Vietnam? Would it likely have undermined his stated commitment to nonviolence and social justice, or would it have merely highlighted his commitment to the civil rights movement?
7. What role, if any, might King's race have had to do with how his statement was received?
8. Do you believe that moral, religious, and political considerations should be separated if it serves a tactical goal?
9. In his letter to the editor of the *New York Times,* "Dr. King Backed," James Bevel states, "Logically, the welfare of non-white peoples in this nation is inextricably linked with the welfare of nonwhite peoples around the world." Do you agree? Why or why not?
10. What sort of impact do you believe King's decision to speak out against the war had on the civil rights movement? If you believe it harmed the movement, was it worth it?
11. Finally, how are these issues relevant today? How might this relate to our current situation in Iraq? Could the case be made that our current foreign policy has implications for domestic policy? How?

Have students read the remainder of "Beyond Vietnam" and complete the primary source evaluation included at the end of this lesson plan. Have students share their responses with the class.

Part 3: What new information have we learned about Martin Luther King, Jr., and Vietnam?

In small groups, have students look in their textbooks for an entry on King and Vietnam. If one exists, have them expand upon it based on what they have learned in this lesson. If one does not exist, have them write an original entry. Have students share answers with the class.

Part 4: Essay

Using information gathered in parts 1–3 of this unit, students should write an essay that responds to King's call for a "revolution of values" and discuss how his words are relevant today.

Bibliography

Carson, Clayborne, ed. *Autobiography of Martin Luther King, Jr.* New York: Warner Books, 1998.

Garrow, David. *Bearing the Cross: Martin Luther King, Jr., and the Southern Christian Leadership Conference.* New York: W. Morrow, 1986.

King, Martin Luther, Jr. "Address on Selma March, March 9, 1965."

_____. "Draft, Address delivered at Mass Rally at the Ninth Annual Convention of the Southern Christian Leadership Conference." August 12, 1965.

_____. "Why Are You Here?" Address delivered at the Summer Community Organization and Political Education (SCOPE) orientation. June 15, 1965.

Radical Times: The Antiwar Movement of the 1960s. <http://www.library.thinkquest.org/27942/index.htm>.

Handout 1: Primary Source Evaluation

Title of primary source document:

_____

Author: _____

Date: _____

1. Use one sentence to state the author's thesis.
2. What is the author's intent in creating this document? Provide examples from the document to support your answer.
3. What does this document tell us about the values and beliefs of the person or persons that produced it?
4. What does this document tell us about the social

and political climate of the particular period when it was produced?

5. Briefly explain your response to this document. How do the issues addressed in this document relate to our current social/political environment?

6. Write a question to the author that is left unanswered by the document.

Document 1

"Dr. King's Error," *New York Times,* April 7, 1967, 36. Copyright © 1967, The New York Times Co. Reprinted with permission.

In recent speeches and statements the Rev. Dr. Martin Luther King Jr. has linked his personal opposition to the war in Vietnam with the cause of Negro equality in the United States. The war, he argues, should be stopped not only because it is a futile war waged for the wrong ends but also because it is a barrier to social progress in this country and therefore prevents Negroes from achieving their just place in American life.

This is a fusing of two public problems that are distinct and separate. By drawing them together, Dr. King has done a disservice to both. The moral issues in Vietnam are less clear cut than he suggests; the political strategy of uniting the peace movement and the civil rights movement could very well be disastrous for both causes.

Because American Negroes are a minority and have to overcome unique handicaps of racial antipathy and prolonged deprivation, they have a hard time in gaining their objectives even when their grievances are self-evident and their claims are indisputably just. As Dr. King knows from the Montgomery bus boycott and other civil rights struggles of the past dozen years, it takes almost infinite patience, persistence and courage to achieve the relatively simple aims that ought to be theirs by right.

The movement toward racial equality is now in the more advanced and more difficult stage of fulfilling basic rights by finding more jobs, changing patterns of housing and upgrading education. The battlegrounds in this struggle are Chicago and Harlem and Watts. The Negroes on these fronts need all the leadership, dedication and moral inspiration that they can summon; and under these circumstances to divert the energies of the civil rights movement to the Vietnam issue is both wasteful and self-defeating.

Dr. King makes too facile a connection between the speeding up of the war in Vietnam and the slowing down of the war against poverty. The eradication of poverty is at best the task of a generation. This "war" inevitably meets diverse resistance such as the hostility of local political machines, the skepticism of conservatives in Congress and intractability of slum mores and habits. The nation could afford to make more funds available to combat poverty even while the war in Vietnam continues, but there is no certainly [*sic*] that the coming of peace would automatically lead to a sharp increase in funds.

Furthermore, Dr. King can only antagonize opinion in this country instead of winning recruits to the peace movement by recklessly comparing American military methods to those of the Nazis testing "new medicine and new tortures in the concentration camps of Europe." The facts are harsh, but they do not justify such slander. Furthermore, it is possible to disagree with many aspects of United States policy in Vietnam without whitewashing Hanoi.

As an individual, Dr. King has the right and even the moral obligation to explore the ethical implications of the war in Vietnam, but as one of the most respected leaders of the civil rights movement he has an equally weighty obligation to direct that movement's efforts in the most constructive and relevant way.

There are no simple or easy answers to the war in Vietnam or to racial injustice in this country. Linking these hard, complex problems will lead not to solutions but to deeper confusion.

Document 2

Transcriptions
"Letters to the Editor of *The Times,*" *New York Times,* April 12, 1967, 46.

Dr. King Backed

To the Editor:

The New York Times has rendered a great disservice to the peace and civil rights movements in this country by making a futile attempt to dissociate the two.

In an April 7 editorial *The Times* severely criticized the Rev. Dr. Martin Luther King Jr., president of the Southern Christian Leadership Conference, for "fusing" the peace and civil rights issues into a single concern.

Logically, the welfare of nonwhite peoples in this nation is inextricably linked with the welfare of nonwhite peoples around the world. American Negroes, Puerto Ricans, Indians and Mexicans all have an exceedingly direct stake in the Administration's posture in Vietnam. They have experienced first hand the Government's disrespect for humanity and dignity at home and are compelled to voice their outrage at the calculated destruction abroad of their Vietnamese brothers.

The American Government seems, in fact, to be embarked upon a program of systematic genocide in Vietnam and it is for this reason, perhaps more than any other, that colored peoples everywhere must speak out and act courageously.

Those Americans opposing the war cannot any longer be

guilty of silence while American nonwhites who have been deprived of their full citizenship are sent to their death in President Johnson's illegal, immoral and unjust war.

In order to dramatize the growing opposition to the war, thousands of Americans of all races, creeds, religions and national origins will gather together in San Francisco and in New York City on April 15 for the Spring Mobilization protest march and rally.

Before the eyes of the world the Spring Mobilization will launch a sustained, serious movement which will begin to put an end to the senseless slaughter that is taking place in the name of democracy.

[Rev.] JAMES BEVELL
National Director
Spring Mobilization Committee To End the War
   in Vietnam
New York, April 8, 1967

War Stand Rejected

To the Editor:

I consider that my support of the Urban League and membership in the N.A.A.C.P., to say nothing of my contributions to various liberal causes, entitle me to consider myself a white person of goodwill as that term was used by Dr. Martin Luther King in *The Times* of April 5.

Far from being willing personally to boycott the Vietnam war, however, or even to have my son claim status as a conscientious objector, I assert that it is necessary to support the war in Vietnam.

Dr. King's simplistic assertion that our Government is the "greatest purveyor of violence in the world today" and his analogy between the use of new weapons by our forces in Vietnam and the use of strange medicines and torture by Hitler's murderers in the concentration camps of Nazi Germany raise grave doubts in my mind as to his ability to think clearly.

Dr. King and his ilk do not speak for me and mine.

JOSEPH LEWIS SIMON
New York, April 5, 1967

Document 3

1321 Ordway St., N.W.
Washington, D.C. 80016
April 2, 1967

Rev. Martin Luther King
332 Auburn Avenue, N.E.
Atlanta, Georgia 30303   *PERSONAL*

Dear Dr. King:

Your recent pronouncements which now go so far as to suggest the possibility of encouraging civil disobedience over Vietnam, cause me a great personal dilemma.

You will see enclosed my annual SCJC Sustaining Contributors Card. I never thought I would find myself in a position whereby it might seem morally indefensible to contribute to SCLC. But that, sir, is my awful problem.

I belong to a school of thought which I hope is large. To wit: I find it totally consistent to be willing to die, if necessary, for the cause of civil rights in the United States and, equally, to die, if necessary, to defend the rights of those to whom we have pledged our aid in Vietnam.

I do not mean to argue the issue. You undoubtedly know my position and I know yours. Vietnam is one of the most complex issues in our national history. I am a man who can respect your point of view and I do. And I know enough about you to know that you can at once respect and disagree with me. But if I see my contributions going increasingly to support a campaign against Vietnam, where am I left? That is not my purpose in supporting SCLC.

And yet, would it not be a vicious way to show my objection if I withdrew my support from SCLC? There is my dilemma. I expect that I will resolve it by continuing, as in the past, to give all I can to the negro scholarship fund, the legal defense fund, the ACLU, etc. But I deeply regret that I can no longer in good conscience help pay the overhead of the extremely important SCLC.

I have pondered this deeply. I *know* that the civil rights movement relates closely to Vietnam. I *know* the national treasure being expended in Vietnam detracts from the civil rights programs. I *know* that a deprived negro family in an overcrowded tenement finds scarce comfort in the thought that his welfare may be subordinated to the progress of a war on the other side of the world. And yet I feel so strongly that this is one of the many times in US history where domestic priorities must be temporarily re-arranged in order to secure the survival necessary to fight the domestic causes that I simply cannot support any agency which uses its power to oppose a foreign policy in which I deeply believe. I believe I am right and that is all there is to say. If we are not successful in our foreign policies, the grandchildren of the deprived tenement dwellers of today will not be members of tomorrow's American middle classes.

Respectfully yours,
Jay H. Cerf

Document 4

334 Auburn Ave., N.E.
Atlanta, Georgia 30303
Telephone 522·1420

Southern Christian Leadership Conference
Martin Luther King, Jr., *President*
Ralph Abernathy, *Treasurer*
Andrew J. Young, *Executive Director*

Thank you for your recent letter to me.

I am sorry that my recent speeches on Vietnam has [*sic*] cost us your support. However, I feel that war is no longer, if it ever was, a valid way to solve international problems.

Even the negative good served by a war against an evil force such as Hitler can no longer be considered worth the costly risk to mankind, for the ultimate weapons of today mean only the destruction of mankind. Man can no longer afford war. We must find a non-violent way to settle the problems of the world.

It has been my consistent belief and position that non-violence is the only true solution to the social problems of the world and of this country. The principle of love which has motivated so many to strike out against the evils of racism here in America must motivate us to protest the brutal destruction of the Vietnamese people. It would be false for those of us who have protested against the continuation of American oppressiveness of its black minority, to not also protest against the attempted continuation of colonialism in Vietnam. For the Vietnamese have been struggling for 30 years against massive Japanese, French and American occupation forces.

After participating in the defeat of Japanese militarism, the Vietnamese proclaimed their independence under the leadership of their war time commander against the Japanese—Ho Chi Minh. They likened their own course to that of the American patriots who fought in the Revolutionary War, quoting in their own historic documents from our own Declaration of Independence. They did not seek alliances with Moscow or Peking but petitioned to be made a member of the French Commonwealth. Their petition was refused. Their right to choose their own destiny was denied. They were thrown onto their own resources, and those of whoever might help them, while France waged a senseless and wasteful war of colonial suppression.

If North Vietnam is communist today, we have ourselves to blame. If they are alienated from America and American ideals we have ourselves to blame. For we rejected their appeal for friendship and understanding.

I do not intend to link the Civil Rights Movement organizationally to the Peace Movement. The Vietnam Summer Program and the Southern Christian Leadership Conference are in no way linked organizationally. I feel, however, that it is not possible for men of good will to segregate their principles for matters of expediency, tactics or any other reason. The presence of two evils requires us to speak out against the two evils.

I am not claiming for the Negro people special privileges to choose which war they wish to fight in, although this construction has unfortunately been placed on some of my remarks. I am, rather, stating general principles, which I believe that all men of good will can follow and adapt to their personal lives. However, I do feel that the Negro people, because of their peculiar experiences with oppression through the use of physical violence, have a particular responsibility to not participate in inflicting oppressive violence on another people. This is not a privilege but an exceptional moral responsibility, the weight of which is far from a happy burden.

I fear that much of America has failed to understand the full meaning of the non-violent method. Too many Americans support non-violence here within the United States of America for Negroes, but do not see in it, any such restrictions to the U.S. Government in its conduct of foreign policy. Such people who hold this contradictory position are not true believers in non-violence. So I say that it is wrong for anyone to praise me for my non-violent stand on Civil Rights and condemn me for being non-violent on Vietnam.

Finally, let me say that I have taken a stand against the war in Vietnam because my conscience leaves me with no other choice. I have been strongly influenced by the prophets of old and those who place the search for truth above expediency. I would like to hope that I am not a concensus [*sic*] leader, constantly determining what is right and wrong by taking a sort of Gallup poll of the majority opinion. Ultimately, a genuine leader is not a searcher of consensus, but a molder of consensus. On some positions, cowardice asks the question, is it politic? Vanity asks the question, is it right? There comes a time when one must take a stand that is neither safe nor politic, nor popular, but he must take it because it is right. This is where I find myself today.

Sincerely yours,
Martin Luther King, Jr.

CHAPTER 43

Comparing U.S. and Vietnamese Textbooks on the Vietnam War

JOHN J. DEROSE

Throughout my twelve years of teaching history, my students have frequently expressed curiosity about the way past events involving the United States were viewed by other nations. For instance, my students have often wondered how World War II is presented to students in Germany, or what students in Japan learn about the dropping of the atomic bombs. I have often used the Internet to find primary sources from other countries—such as wartime propaganda posters—to help students analyze events from different points of view. Secondary sources from the perspectives of other countries are also available in print or online. I have even been fortunate enough to have foreign exchange students who are willing to talk about what they were taught of the past and the teaching materials used in their nations.

During the past year, I have also used a book called *History Lessons: How Textbooks from around the World Portray U.S. History,* by Dana Lindaman and Kyle Ward, to help my students look at events from a global perspective.[1] The book includes passages about significant events in American history translated into English from textbooks around the world and can be used to help students make comparisons with their own textbook's version of events. I taught the following lesson on the Vietnam War using excerpts from this book and from our own textbooks to compare how American and Vietnamese texts described the war.

The Vietnam War Textbook Lesson

Overview

Students will compare and contrast passages about the Vietnam War from excerpts of a Vietnamese textbook with

passages from their own U.S. history textbook. (The author used excerpts from *History Lessons.*)

Suggested Time

1–2 class periods

NCSS Standards Addressed

II. Time, Continuity and Change
IX. Global Connections

Objectives

Students will:

1. Compare and contrast their textbook's account of the Vietnam War with a Vietnamese textbook account of the same event or period, to consider disparate historical perspectives.
2. Interpret the biases and limited perspectives present in textbook accounts.
3. Evaluate the quality of historical sources of information.

Exercise

Students should read their own textbook's account of the Vietnam War. Since many U.S. history textbooks devote an entire chapter to this event, this comparison activity might work best at the end of the unit, when students have almost finished reading the chapter and have also viewed other

John J. DeRose, "Comparing International Textbooks to Develop Historical Thinking," *Social Education* 71, no. 1 (January/February 2007): 36–39. © National Council for the Social Studies. Reprinted by permission.

sources of information. My students use McDougal Littell's *The Americans: Reconstruction to the 21st Century,* which covers the Vietnam War in Chapter 22.[2] Students should also read about the Vietnam War from a Vietnamese textbook, excerpted in *History Lessons: How Textbooks from around the World Portray U.S. History* (pp. 311–315).

After students finish reading both textbook accounts, they answer the following questions on a separate sheet of paper:

1. How are the accounts similar?
2. How are the accounts different?
3. What possible biases or limited perspectives exist in our textbook's account of this event?
4. What possible biases or limited perspectives exist in the Vietnamese textbook's account of this event?
5. Explain why you think, or do not think, that one of these textbook accounts is more accurate than the other.

The teacher should start the lesson by telling students that they must all offer a verbal response to these questions to receive full credit for this assignment. To make sure that all students comment on the passages, they should each write their names on slips of paper and be allowed to place them in a small box when they have offered a substantial response for the day. The teacher will then lead students in a discussion of the questions.

The similarities and differences between the Vietnamese textbook passage and the account from my students' textbook (listed in Table 1) can serve as a teacher's guide, student handout, or overhead notes after the class has discussed the first two questions. This information will vary with the textbook that the teacher uses in his or her classroom.

Class Discussion of Vietnamese and American Textbooks

The classroom discussion with my students, after comparing the textbook accounts of the Vietnam War, was extremely insightful. Many students readily noticed major similarities between the accounts. In particular, students observed that both passages cited March 1965 as the beginning of U.S. troop involvement and March 29, 1973, as the date when American forces left Vietnam; and both textbooks also claimed that the United States dropped about 8 million tons of bombs during the war. Students noted that both texts cited the fall of the French at Dien Bien Phu as the event that increased American involvement. According to our textbook, "In the wake of France's retreat, the United States took a more active role in halting the spread of communism in Vietnam."[3] The Vietnamese textbook states, "After the failure of the French Army at Dien Bien

Phu . . . America, under Eisenhower, 'filled the vacancy' in southern Vietnam."[4] At the same time, students recognized vast differences between the texts. One student pointed out that our textbook said President Kennedy "sent thousands of military advisors to help train South Vietnamese troops."[5] In contrast, the Vietnamese textbook described this same action by stating that Kennedy sent Special Forces to carry out a "special war." It went on to say:

> "Special war" was a new form of war, carried out by a puppet army, directed by the American army, and dependent on American artillery, equipment, technology, and transportation. The basic ploy of the "Special War" was to "use Vietnamese people to fight Vietnamese people."[6]

A few students also observed that their U.S. history textbook consistently maintained that American presidents involved in the war were seeking to contain communism. For example, as if to justify Eisenhower's actions in Vietnam, our textbook said, "During a news conference in 1954, Eisenhower explained the domino theory, in which he likened the countries on the brink of communism to a row of dominoes waiting to fall one after the other."[7] Our textbook also claimed that Johnson "spoke determinedly about containing communism" in Vietnam.[8] Students discussed the manner in which the Vietnamese textbook offered a different motivation for U.S. involvement in that country. It said, "Five generations of American presidents, with their legs bound together, oversaw four different American plans of imperialist attack and invasion."[9] Many students also noticed that the war is always referred to as "The Vietnam War" in their textbook. However, the Vietnamese textbook refers to the conflict as "The American War."[10] Student recognition of the differences between the two accounts led to an interesting discussion about biases in textbooks. One student pointed out that the United States has a legacy of imperialism, and that student defended the perspective of the Vietnamese people, who believed that American troops were in their country simply to serve America's interest in expanding and maintaining power around the world. Consequently, this student, and others who agreed with him, observed that from this point of view, it made sense to view the war (as the Vietnamese textbook did) as America's war and as a fight against imperialism.

At the same time, a few students observed that there were some Vietnamese people who were opposed to communist rule and who welcomed U.S. assistance in fighting the formation of a unified communist nation. To these students, it seemed equally accurate for their textbook to describe the war as a Vietnamese war and as an effort to halt the spread of communism.

Students' differing perspectives of the textbook accounts created a perfect opportunity for me to help them see the complexity involved in writing and studying history. I explained to my students that even if historians come to some agreement on dates or other details, factors like the purposes or consequences of an event are often contested and debated. To emphasize this further, I pointed out that the Vietnamese textbook passage concluded by stating, "Our victory is a source of inspiration to all revolutionary movements in the world."[11] However, I challenged my students to consider if the war could fully be considered "inspirational" and "victorious" for Vietnam when, as our textbook points out, "North and South Vietnamese deaths topped 2 million."[12] Consequently, I reiterated that it is crucial for historians and students of history to consider multiple perspectives when studying the past.

The most engaging part of the class discussion occurred when students began to debate which textbook provided a more accurate account of the event. Many students argued that their textbook's account was more valid and reliable because it, at least, recognized the internal division in the United States during this time, with a whole section of the chapter entitled "A Nation Divided," and it also highlighted U.S. misdeeds or abuses such as the My Lai Massacre.[13] In the students' estimation, sentences from the Vietnamese text stating, "It was a great patriotic war, a war of national liberation to protect our nation," oversimplified the war, presenting it as a case of a unified nation fighting against a brutal oppressor.[14] These students suggested that the Vietnamese textbook account was likely communist propaganda censored by the government.

At the same time, other students contended that the texts were both biased since each described significant aspects of the war from its own country's perspective and ignored, or minimized, the perspective of the other nation. These students suggested that, in spite of including U.S. wrongdoings, their own textbook's focus on the "strong support for containment" of communism downplayed the perspective of many Vietnamese people that the United States was using Vietnam for its own self-interest.[15] Similarly, these students also said the Vietnamese textbook was biased, completely ignoring abuses committed by the communists against their people and some Vietnamese efforts to resist living under communism.

I concluded the discussion by highlighting that it is impossible to avoid some degree of bias when writing about the past.[16] However, the quality of all historical accounts is not necessarily the same. Skilled historians examine as many points of view as possible when studying an event. In the process of reading and writing about history, they also attempt to determine the consistency of the evidence presented and examine the limited perspectives in the viewpoints that they study. Therefore, I told my class, students who study history must work equally hard to examine how well accounts about the past include multiple, and even opposing, perspectives and cite significant evidence to maintain accuracy.

Table 1. Similarities and differences between the U.S. and Vietnamese textbook accounts

Similarities

- Both texts explain that the United States dropped about 8 million tons of bombs on Vietnam, which was more tonnage than any previous war.
- Both texts explain that the last American troops left Vietnam on March 29, 1973.
- Both texts agree on the general course and dates of American involvement. They delineate between Americans sending advisors in 1961 significant increases in actual combat troops in 1965, and the gradual withdrawal of combat troops and "Vietnamization" of the war beginning in 1969.
- Both texts explain that the United States' main entrance into the war occurred when the French left after their defeat at Dien Bien Phu.

Differences

- The textbook from the United States calls the war "The Vietnam War." The Vietnamese textbook calls the war "The American War."
- The textbook from the United States defines the end of the war as South Vietnam surrendering to North Vietnam. The Vietnamese textbook defines the end of the war as the last American troops leaving Vietnam.
- The textbook from the United States says that, under President Kennedy, in 1961 military advisors were sent "to help train South Vietnamese troops." The Vietnamese textbook describes this same American effort in 1961 as an attempt to "use Vietnamese people to fight Vietnamese people."
- The textbook from the United States indicates that America's plan in Vietnam was to halt the spread of communism. The Vietnamese textbook defines America's plan as an "imperialist attack and invasion."

Extended Teaching and Assessment Activities

The following activities could also be used by teachers for further discussion, enrichment, and assessment:

1. The teacher may want to simply check students' written answers to the five previously mentioned discussion questions and assess their thoughts and analysis. It might be helpful to give students an opportunity to revise their answers after the discussion.
2. *History Lessons* also includes Canadian and French textbook accounts of the Vietnam War. Students could read either or both of these passages

and answer the same five discussion questions. Then students should be divided into four different groups and assigned either the Vietnamese, American, French, or Canadian passage. Students could engage in a classroom debate over the passages' biases and accuracy and should be prepared to defend their positions.

3. Students could write a textbook account about the Vietnam War from the perspective of a different country they have studied during this time period (a country for which they do not have a textbook excerpt available). Students might be graded on their ability to include details related to that nation's possible perspective and interpretation of this event during this time. For instance, my students spend a significant amount of time studying Russia and China during the Cold War and would write a textbook passage about the Vietnam War from the perspective of one of these countries.

4. Students could do research outside of the textbook on individuals or groups involved in the Vietnam War. For instance, students could gather information about people and groups like Ho Chi Minh, Ngo Dinh Diem, the Vietcong, Lyndon Johnson, William Westmoreland, the Green Berets, antiwar protestors, etc. After students complete their research, they could write a position paper discussing how these people or groups felt about the different textbook accounts of the Vietnam War. They could then represent or role play these individuals or groups in a classroom panel discussion about their views on the different textbook passages.

Students should pay particular attention to differing perspectives of the textbook accounts and the support provided by individuals in the panel discussion to defend their positions.

Notes

1. Dana Lindaman and Kyle Ward, *History Lessons: How Textbooks from around the World Portray U.S. History* (New York: The New Press, 2004).

2. Gerald A. Danzer, J. Jorge Klor de Alva, Larry S. Krieger, Louis E. Wilson, and Nancy Woloch, *The Americans: Reconstruction to the 21st Century* (Evanston, IL: McDougal Littell, 2005).

3. Danzer, Klor de Alva, Krieger, Wilson, and Woloch, 732.

4. Lindaman and Ward, 312.

5. Danzer, Klor de Alva, Krieger, Wilson, and Woloch, 732.

6. Lindaman and Ward, 313.

7. Danzer, Klor de Alva, Krieger, Wilson, and Woloch, 731.

8. Ibid., 737.

9. Lindaman and Ward, 315.

10. Ibid., 313.

11. Ibid., 315.

12. Danzer, Klor de Alva, Krieger, Wilson, and Woloch, 759.

13. Ibid., 742.

14. Lindaman and Ward, 314.

15. Danzer, Klor de Alva, Krieger, Wilson, and Woloch, 737.

16. See Howard Zinn, *You Can't Be Neutral on a Moving Train: A Personal History of Our Times* (Boston: Beacon Press, 1995).

CHAPTER 44

Borderlands, Diasporas, and Transnational Crossings
Teaching LGBT Latina and Latino Histories

HORACIO N. ROCQUE RAMÍREZ

I loved María, I adored María. María was my savior. . . . I was young and impressionable and I stopped going to work. My mother was really counting on that money because things were really bad and my stepfather was going to school. I was lying to her, telling her I was going to work. When payday came my mother couldn't find me. I was up in my girlfriend's house with María. My mother went looking for me and found me in this room with María. She dragged me out and pulled me downstairs. As she dragged me through the streets, I was screaming, "María, I love you! I'm going to go with you, María!" So that is how I came out. I had no choice but to come out![1]

At age fourteen, feeling depressed and not fitting into her English language–dominant neighborhood as a dark-skinned Puerto Rican, Julia Pérez found love briefly with María in 1950s New York. Julia, her three siblings, and her mother had moved from Puerto Rico in the postwar period into an old, mostly Jewish neighborhood in the Bronx. Eventually learning to speak English on her own, she became a black-identified Puerto Rican lesbian. Like hundreds of thousands of other Puerto Ricans building a new community in the city, Julia survived the poverty and discrimination surrounding her family; she recalls whites' insults of her being just one more of the many "Goddamn Spics." But Julia also survived the confusion, isolation, and challenges that came alongside the exciting new knowledge of her desires for other women at a time when she was a target both as a Puerto Rican and a lesbian.

What can students glean from the oral history excerpt above? What are some of the key words they can identify

in Julia's memory of her life as a young, Spanish-speaking teenager in New York City? What is the relationship that they can see, for example, between love and work? Lastly, how could they describe Julia's "process" for "coming out" as a Puerto Rican lesbian?

To appreciate both LGBT (lesbian, gay, bisexual, and transgender) and Latino history in the United States simultaneously, several essays, anthologies, and independent videos provide historical context of this largest "minority" population. These documents are key entries into this mostly unwritten history. Like Julia's narrative, these are bottom-up stories of everyday, mostly unknown women and men. In their stories, they trace their childhood, their migrations, their family life, their encounters with racism, and their erotic lives through memory. Oral histories in particular provide an excellent opportunity to teach both the stories and the creation of these primary sources for both Latino and LGBT history.

Using these testimonies of struggle and survival, this teaching strategy introduces students to three important concepts: the borderlands, the diaspora, and the "transnation." Five goals in this integration of LGBT and Latino history appear below.

Student Objectives

1. To become familiar with how ordinary Latino-American experiences both reflect and interrupt dominant American cultural norms about race, ethnicity, sexuality, gender, class, culture, and nationality.

From *OAH Magazine of History* 20, no. 2 (March 2006): 39–42. © Organization of American Historians. Reprinted by permission.

2. To become familiar with the context for understanding the multiracial, multilingual, and multinational population of Latino/Latina Americans.[2]

3. To analyze how "race" and "culture" are defined and to reconsider the dominant black/white binary that frames narratives concerning civil rights struggles in post–World War II America.

4. To analyze the importance of individual and collective struggles for social justice simultaneously along multiple experiences—sexuality, ethnicity, gender, race, and class—in the context of, but also in opposition to, dominant historical narratives of such struggles emphasizing one single axis.

5. To become familiar with three analytic approaches for studying Latino/a history: "borderlands," "diaspora," and "the transnation."

The "Borderlands"—Multiple Identities

Students are used to thinking of easily mapped, discretely bounded borders between nation states. The late Chicana lesbian author Gloria E. Anzaldúa (1942–2004) instead argued for the "borderlands," a site for political, historical, and sexual consciousness for appreciating the coming together of different cultures. In a consciousness of the borderlands or an in-between state, Anzaldúa argued, there is a tolerance for ambiguity and seeming contradictions. What may some of these contradictions be? Students' cultural knowledge of Latinos in the United States likely will revolve around traditional notions of the family and of conservative Catholicism. Related to these two notions is the expectation that families and the Church will be homophobic and thus shun their LGBT members. These are indeed some of the contradictions of which Anzaldúa spoke, the "borderland" between being gay or lesbian and a Chicana or Latino. But she saw this condition as a source of strength and creativity. She refused to privilege a single, "core" identity, either as lesbian or Chicana. She confronted homophobia and sexism in Latino community life, and racism and xenophobia in mainstream Anglo culture, drawing upon these forms of exclusion to develop a hybrid sense of self: a woman of the borderlands. In reading her essay "La Conciencia de la Mestiza: Towards a New Consciousness," students can appreciate the idea of plural identities: not from a single source, but from many historical sources at the same time.[3] Using the literal borderlands of the U.S.-Mexico divide as a metaphor, she privileged a mestiza or mixed-race consciousness.

While Anzaldúa interpreted the borderlands as a site of strength for her mestiza self, experiencing in-between cultural spaces can be challenging. Because homophobia continues to be a lived risk for LGBT Latinas and Latinos, students can consider what the implications of this discrimination can be. They can benefit from a close examination of one of the few gay Chicano testimonials about the painful negotiation between family and desire in the age of AIDS. Before considering the following excerpt, they can ask themselves: what is the place of emotions or loneliness in LGBT history? What do everyday forms of discrimination cause on the bodies of those targeted?

> These high-power street lamps can't burn out the gang-infested walls. Black spray paint letters fuse into unlit alleys. Parked cars are tombstones. The air is sewer-scented. I've been here before, time after time, told my mother where our old house would be buried, near the call box, under the fast lane. She knows when I ramble it's the virus. She questions me about what my doctor has said, ignores my response when I say, I'm just lonely.[4]

In his courageous words as a gay Chicano living with AIDS, the late Gil Cuadros, who died from the disease in 1998, ventures into the negotiation of home, family, and death. As students can appreciate in his writings, he was making visible at least two forms of denial in his community: that of being gay as a Chicano, and the reality of AIDS. Laying bare both the postindustrial urban decay of Los Angeles with the equally destructive forces of gay loneliness in the age of AIDS, Cuadros narrates his Aztlán, his sense of a Chicano homeland. In this homeland, he describes the need he felt to leave blood family, and the need to try to return to it in the final years of his life. Through his prose, students can begin to understand the historical place of AIDS in the United States in the last two decades of the twentieth century.

Cuadros's *City of God* offers an excellent and accessible opportunity for students to appreciate gay history from an offspring of the Chicano Movement. Alongside Cherríe L. Moraga's essay "Queer Aztlán," Cuadros's Chicano memory tackles nationalist politics, ethnic community destruction, and gay belonging. Especially for recent generations of students unaware of the violent history of AIDS, *City of God* is an ideal, deeply felt primary document.

Latino "Diasporas" and Liberation Struggles since the 1960s

However insightful, the metaphor and reality of the borderlands are not sufficient to account for all Latina and Latino experiences. For those not crossing (just) Mexican-U.S. national and ethnic boundaries, the distances are not of a boundary dividing two nation states, but of other passages. Introducing students to the notion of "diaspora"—a people's historical, often ongoing dispersal from their original homeland—offers them the opportunity to consider how particular racial and ethnic groups continue to have historical, affective ties that extend beyond national borders. For diasporic Puerto Rican history, for example, "*el charco*"—the Atlantic waterway separating the island from the U.S. mainland—is a different form of crossing. As island citizens tied to the United States through colonial relations, LGBT Puerto Rican migrants, as we saw in Julia's excerpt, have a diasporic relation to the island. As Frances Negrón-Muntaner argues in her video, *Brincando el Charco: Portrait of a Puerto Rican,* to be simultaneously gay and Puerto Rican does not allow for "suspending" one identity—sexual consciousness—over another—racial or ethnic (black, Latina). Through her autobiographical video, students can consider her provocative question: what is the language of liberation—English, Spanish, "Spanglish"—for those experiencing immigrant histories, sexual politics, and national aspirations at the same time?

One of the goals for integrating LGBT and Latino histories is to allow students to enter stories where there does not have to be a separation between these two areas. Indeed, we can teach the Chicano movement through the life-story of Chicana lesbian participants, and, similarly, gay liberation through the life stories of Latinos active in that struggle. The 1969 Stonewall Inn riots in New York have yet to be placed in the context of the desires for racial justice of the LGBT rioters of color during those nights of reaction against the actions of the police. Stonewall and its June commemoration have become the symbols and annual reminders of the need to celebrate new freedoms and the right to public lives as gay, lesbian, bisexual, and transgender peoples. But the dominant images in today's mainstreaming of the event remain overwhelmingly white, male, and masculine. This is an ironic, misleading historical rendition, given the growing knowledge that LGBTs of color, especially the nongender conformers, were central actors in the riots. Using Martin Duberman's writing on the late male-to-female transgender Stonewall rioter Silvia Ray Rivera, students can use the episode to consider gay liberation and how it is rendered historically.[5] Such a simultaneous consideration of racial and sexual liberation speaks to Chicana lesbian playwright Cherríe L. Moraga's prophetic warning against the ranking of oppressions. "The danger lies," Moraga explained in her essay, "La Güera," "in failing to acknowledge the specificity of the oppression": to fail to see the racial dimensions of LGBT struggles, and the sexual specificities of civil rights.[6] Students can be asked to consider: what were the types of "ranking of oppression" in the 1960s and 1970s, and, how may some of these same rankings be at work today? How have they changed?

The Latino Transnation and New LGBT Bodies in the 1990s and Beyond

When I was growing [up] in El Salvador, it was either you were a man, or you were a woman. If you were a man, you have to be with women. If you were a woman, you have to be with men. And I was a *lesbian,* the day I was born. I was, you know, baby butch. And I didn't wanna be with men. All my friends at age 14 wanted to be with guys and I didn't. I wanted to be with a woman. So therefore, I needed to be a man. So I considered the idea of changing my sex so I could finally be a man, so I could have the *right* to be with a woman. When I came to this country [the U.S.] that changed. It gave me another notion. It educated me in a way that, "I *have* choices." I don't have to be a man, because I can still stay in a woman's body, be a woman, and be with a woman.[7]

How do their nations of origin figure in the lives of LGBT Latina and Latino immigrants establishing new possible genders and sexualities in the United States? Does a narrator like Ana above, as a butch-identified lesbian living in a new country, ever stop identifying as a Salvadoran? With increased discussion of globalization and cross-border movements of peoples, students can appreciate the lived reality of the "transnation" for millions of Latinos in the United States, including the LGBT. This transnation speaks to the constant relations and ties between at least two different nation states bridged through the migrations of its citizens. Certainly, Cuban, Mexican, and Salvadoran migrants—among many others from Latin America—experience this reality in the United States. Importantly, their experience challenges earlier models of linear assimilation: from a status of recent immigrant to one of eventual full enfranchisement.

The 2004 groundbreaking video documentary *Mind if I Call You Sir?* offers this and other lessons for students to consider in LGBT Latino histories. The oral history–based video follows the lives of several narrators and their relationships to their families, their genders, and their bodies; it was a response to 1990s debates among Latina lesbians about the transformation of some in their ranks from lesbian-identified women to female-to-male transgender men. Like Salvadoran Ana above, the women and men speak about personal histories of attraction, cultural and national expectations, and feelings about the bodies they occupy or feel they must change. Like Ana and tens of thousands of others continuing to cross into the United States—Guatemalans, Colombians, Brazilians—joining other Latin American migrants, refugees, and exiles, they maintain active affective and economic relations with their homelands. These cross-border relations shape "a transnation," not a cleanly defined single national space but a mediated transnational one where LGBT identity is also part of finding a new ground.

As *Mind if I Call You Sir?* and other documents explored here show, migrant LGBT oral histories shed light on larger questions informing Latino histories: How do historical processes of migration for LGBT women and men impact their sense of gender and sexuality? How is a butch Chicana able to relate to the exclusionary tactics of male leadership in the Chicano Movement? How do these experiences of gender or sex for these historical actors relate to families and community? What is beautifully obvious in these oral histories and body narratives of self is that to speak of LGBT histories is to take the body seriously as its own record of change and continuity. Students should be able to see how, despite changes in sexual or gender identification, these women and men usually remain tied to their ethnic communities.

Finally, to appreciate LGBT Latina and Latino histories can require a challenging though rewarding move for students: to leave the classroom and go into the community where some of the "old timers" still socialize; to the surviving leaders of the first lesbian and gay organizations; or to the former leadership of the various Latino movements to ask for the LGBT presence in their ranks. They are usually there, if one gets to look.

These are amazing opportunities for students to think about the usually hidden dimensions of LGBT genders and sexualities. Indeed, the "new" LGBT bodies and genders students begin to understand through Latino history may be those who still survive today but require student initiative to identify. Depending on geography, access, and commitment, students across the United States can thus begin to appreciate new LGBT borderlands, diasporas, and transnational passages.

Notes

1. Julia Pérez, "I'm from Humacao (Oral History)," in Juanita Ramos, ed., *Compañeras: Latina Lesbians: An Anthology* (New York: Routledge, 1994), 20.

2. Readers should also consult the overviews of Latina and Latino history, including lesson plans, in the Winter 1996 issue of the *OAH Magazine of History,* volume 10.

3. Gloria Anzaldúa, "La Conciencia de la Mestiza: Towards a New Consciousness," in *Borderlands, La Frontera: The New Mestiza* (San Francisco: Aunt Lute Books, 1987), 77–91.

4. Gil Cuadros, "My Aztlán: White Place," in *City of God* (San Francisco: City Lights Books, 1994), 54.

5. Martin Duberman, *Stonewall,* reprint (New York: Plume, 1994, 1993).

6. Cherríe Moraga, "La Güera," in *Loving in the War Years: lo que nunca pasó por sus labios,* rev. ed. (Cambridge, MA: South End Press, 2000), 44.

7. Ana, in *Mind if I Call You Sir? A Discussion between Latina Butches and Female-to-Male Transgendered Latinos,* VHS, produced by Karla E. Rosales, directed by Mary Guzmán (San Francisco: StickyGirl Productions, 2004), emphases in original.

Recommended Videos

Brincando el Charco: Portrait of a Puerto Rican. Produced, written, and directed by Frances Negrón-Muntaner. VHS. New York: Hipspic Productions, 1994.

Mind If I Call You Sir? A Discussion between Latina Butches and Female-to-Male Transgendered Latinos. VHS. Produced by Karla E. Rosales, directed by Mary Guzmán. San Francisco: StickyGirl Productions, 2004.

Recommended Fiction

Trujillo, Carla. *What Night Brings: A Novel.* Willimantic, CT: Curbstone Press, 2003.

Recommended Non-Fiction

Anzaldúa, Gloria. "La Conciencia de la Mestiza: Towards a New Consciousness." In *Borderlands, La Frontera: The New Mestiza.* San Francisco Francisco: Aunt Lute Books, 1987, 77–98.

Aponte-Pares, Luis, and Jorge B. Merced, "*Páginas Omitidas:* The Gay and Lesbian Presence." In Andres Torres and Jose E. Velasquez, eds., *The Puerto Rican Movement: Voices from the Diaspora.* Philadelphia: Temple University Press, 1998, 296–315.

Cantú, Lionel. "A Place Called Home: A Queer Political Economy of Mexican Immigrant Men's Family Experiences." In Mary Bernstein and Renate Reimann, eds., *Queer Families, Queer Politics: Challenging Culture and the State.* New York: Columbia University Press, 2001, 112–36.

Chavez-Leyva, Yolanda. "Listening to the Silences in Latina/Chicana Lesbian History." In Carla Trujillo, ed., *Living Chicana Theory.* Berkeley, CA: Third Woman Press, 1998, 429–34.

Cortez, Jaime, ed. *Virgins, Guerrillas & Locas: Gay Latinos Writing About Love.* San Francisco: Cleis Press, 1999.

Cuadros, Gil. *City of God.* San Francisco: City Lights, 1994.

Duberman, Martin. *Stonewall.* Reprint. New York: Plume, 1994, 1993.

Gilmartin, Katie. "The Culture of Lesbianism: Intersections of Gender, Ethnicity, and Sexuality in the Life of a Chicana Lesbian." In Toni Lester, ed., *Gender Nonconformity, Race, and Sexuality: Charting the Connections.* Madison: The University of Wisconsin Press, 2002, 160–79.

La Fountain-Stokes, Larry. "1898 and the History of a Queer Puerto Rican Century: Gay Lives, Island Debates, and Diasporic Experience." *Centro Journal [Centro de Estudios Puertorriqueños]* ii (Fall 1998): 91–109.

Moraga, Cherríe. "La Güera." In *Loving in the War Years: lo que nunca pasó por sus labios.* Rev. ed. Cambridge, MA: South End Press, 2000, 42–51.

———. *The Last Generation: Prose and Poetry.* Boston: South End Press, 1993.

Peña, Susana. "Visibility and Silence: Mariel and Cuban American Gay Male Experience and Representation." In Eithne Luibhéid and Lionel Cantú Jr., eds., *Queer Migrations: Sexuality, U.S. Citizenship, and Border Crossings.* Minneapolis: University of Minnesota Press, 2005, 125–45.

Perez, Emma. "Queering the Borderlands: The Challenges of Excavating the Invisible and Unheard." *Frontiers: A Journal of Women Studies* 24 (2003): 122–31.

Perez, Laura M. "Go Ahead: Make My Movement." In Naomi Tucker, ed., with Liz Highleyman and Rebecca Kaplan. *Bisexual Politics: Theories, Queries & Visions.* New York: Haworth Press, 1995, 109–14.

Ramos, Juanita, ed. *Compañeras: Latina Lesbians. An Anthology.* New York: Routledge, 1994.

Roque Ramírez, Horacio N. "'That's My Place': Negotiating Racial, Sexual, and Gender Politics in San Francisco's Gay Latino Alliance, 1975–1983." *Journal of the History of Sexuality* 12 (April 2003): 224–58.

CHAPTER 45

America Held Hostage

The Iran Hostage Crisis of 1979–1981 and U.S.-Iranian Relations

LAWRENCE A. WOLF

On November 4, 1979, a mob overran the U.S. Embassy in Tehran, Iran, and seized the American diplomats and soldiers stationed there. That event shocked the American people and has had a lasting impact on U.S.-Iranian diplomatic relations. More than twenty-five years after that fateful November day, students might well wonder why and how the U.S. relationship with Iran grew so cold and what it will take to achieve a thaw leading to a normalization of relations.

In order to understand how this single event traumatized relations between the two countries, students will need to understand the historical events leading up to the Iranian Revolution of 1978–79 and the way in which prior and subsequent actions by the U.S. government made many Iranians contemptuous of America. Students must note that while the Iran Hostage Crisis—involving both the takeover of the U.S. Embassy in Tehran and the subsequent holding of 52 hostages for 444 days—was a significant event, it was but one episode in a long line of developments that caused the deterioration of relations between Iran and the United States.

The Crisis must be positioned in a larger context. It must be viewed as part of a socioeconomic and religious revolt that swept through Iran in the late 1970s. The causes of the revolution were deeply rooted in the practices of a repressive government that, in its attempts to reform, actually united the working class with the downtrodden masses. Fervor among religious people to protect the "old ways" from the forces of modernism, together with the rise of the modern media with its zeal for information, contributed to a mounting tide of revolution with the means to market its ideas widely. Ultimately, the taking

of American hostages provided a unifying symbol of the Iranian revolution and a rallying cry for the people of Iran to vent their anger at the United States. The Iran Hostage Crisis generated anger against the West that has persisted to the present day.

This lesson plan will focus on two distinct time frames in Iran: 1907–79 and 1979–81. It is important for students of history to understand clearly the forces at work that drive a people to revolt against their government. These forces are sometimes aided by unintended consequences of actions taken by foreign governments acting on their own behalf. Students will explore American and British actions in Iran during the first half of the twentieth century and their subsequent effects on Iran. Students will then proceed to that fateful day in November when Americans sat in stunned disbelief as their nation was held hostage by a group of Iranian students.

National Standards

This lesson plan will help students master the following standards in the *National Standards for United States History:*

Era 9:	Postwar United States (1945 to early 1970s)
Standard 2B:	The student understands U.S. foreign policy in Africa, Asia, the Middle East, and Latin America.
Era 10:	Contemporary United States (1968 to the present)
Standard 1C:	The student understands major foreign policy initiatives.

From *OAH Magazine of History* 20, no. 3 (May 2006): 27–30. © Organization of American Historians. Reprinted by permission.

Time

This lesson plan is designed for a high school audience and will take either two or three class periods. Class size should be 20–30 students, but the size is not critical to the project.

Objectives

1. Students will understand that a nation's foreign and domestic policies are developed around its own self-interest.
2. Students will learn that past events often have unintended consequences in the future.
3. Students will discover that Iran and the United States were once allies and they will probe the reasons why the two countries became bitter enemies.
4. Students will realize that successful revolutions have either mass appeal to a large number of people or overwhelming support from the military, or both.
5. Students will analyze American policies toward the Iranian Revolution.
6. Students will examine the role of the United States in the political struggles of Iran.

Procedures

The teacher will begin the lesson by asking the following questions:

- Why did the Iran Hostage Crisis happen?
- What could or should the United States have done to prevent it from happening?

Step 1: Divide the class into two groups, assigning each group one of the time frames (1907–79 or 1979–81). The groups will work separately and simultaneously to achieve their goals. Provide a list of questions to each group to help it in its research and to serve as a guideline for its oral presentation at the end. See Appendix A for a list of essential questions.

Step 2: Give both groups a list of pertinent vocabulary words with the appropriate definitions. The purpose is to give students a similar baseline from which to work and to reduce the variables in their research. See Appendix B for appropriate vocabulary words.

Step 3: Distribute to each student two pages containing only web-like diagrams, which they can fill in as they acquire information. One page will have the word "Who?" at its center, with four to six lines emanating outward. The other will have the word "What?" at the center, with four to six lines also extending outward. Subdivide each large group into three smaller groups, two that correspond to the

individual web-like pages and a third assigned to prepare a final timeline/oral presentation.

Step 4: Hand out a list of key Web sites that students can use as they conduct their research. (Hopefully, your school has the resources to provide laptop computers for the classroom; if not, you should reserve the computer lab for two days. Every student does not need a computer, although such an arrangement would be ideal.) See Appendix C for a sample list of appropriate Web sites.

Step 5: When the students have completed the diagrams, each group will create its own timeline of critical events. This page can be either computer-generated or created from a model provided by the teacher.

Step 6: On the second or third day of the lesson, students from group one will begin an oral presentation of the facts, as they know them. The oral presentations must answer the essential questions the students received at the beginning of the exercise. After group one has finished (allow 10–15 minutes), group two will follow the same procedure. The teacher should direct the presentation by asking essential questions at appropriate times to facilitate the presentation.

Step 7 (optional): Ask students (either individually or in two collaborative groups) to write an essay on a major research topic. See Appendix D for suggested essay assignments.

Appendix A

Essential Questions: Group One

1. How did Muhammad Reza Pahlavi become the Shah of Iran? Why was his father deposed in 1941?
2. Why was Iran thought to be so important to the Allies during World War II?
3. After Muhammad Mosaddeq became Prime Minister in 1951, what action did he take with respect to the Anglo-Iranian Oil Company? What was the British response?
4. What was "Operation Ajax"? How was Britain able to convince the United States to participate in a coup to oust Mosaddeq?
5. What kind of ruler was Shah Muhammad Reza Pahlavi? What was the "White Revolution" and who led the opposition to it in Iran? How did the Shah use the SAVAK to put down opposition?
6. How did the increases in oil revenues actually create an economic problem for the masses of the people of Iran? (Hint: consider distribution of wealth.)
7. How were social and religious mores fractured by the Shah's government?
8. What were the events of the so-called "Black Friday" and why did they eventually lead to the exile of Shah Muhammad Reza Pahlavi in 1979?

9. Who was President of the United States during the final years of the Shah's reign, and what actions did the U.S. government undertake to keep the Shah in power?

Essential Questions: Group Two

1. Why and how did the Ayatollah Khomeini first attempt to oppose the "White Revolution"?
2. What happened to the Ayatollah as a result of his opposition to the Shah?
3. What or who was the base of support for the Ayatollah in Iran?
4. What events led to the return of the Ayatollah to Iran in 1979?
5. What specific action by the United States led Iranian students to attack the American Embassy and take the staff as hostages?
6. What were the demands of the students who seized the hostages? What was President Carter's immediate response to this deed?
7. When diplomatic efforts to free the hostages stalled, President Carter authorized a rescue mission. What happened?
8. How did the combination of an American presidential election, a failed rescue attempt, and a war with Iraq actually help bring the hostage crisis to an end?

Appendix B

Group One Vocabulary

SAVAK: Iranian secret police under the rule of the Shah.

Coup d'etat: A swift and usually violent overthrow of a government, often using military force.

Exile: The forced expulsion of someone from his/her native land by official decree.

Shah: The official title of Muhammad Reza Pahlavi, leader of Iran from 1941 to 1979.

Political asylum: Protection for a person in a country from another country that the person departed. (For example, the United States provided asylum to the Shah after he left Iran.)

Anglo-Iranian Oil Company: A major British company that dominated Iran's oil industry for much of the early twentieth century.

Nationalization: The seizure of a private company by a national government. Muhammad Mosaddeq (as prime minister of Iran) nationalized the Anglo-Iranian Oil Company in 1951.

Imperialism: The practice of building an empire by taking colonies or by exerting political or economic dominance over other nations.

Tehran Conference of 1943: A conference at which the United States, Great Britain, and the Soviet Union agreed to ensure Iran's independence after World War II.

Group Two Vocabulary

Ayatollah Ruhollah Khomeini: Islamic clergyman of Iran who voiced opposition to the Shah's pro-Western policies and led the Iranian people in a 1978–79 revolution.

Hostage: A person seized and held against his or her will for political, financial, or other gain to the hostage-taker. Iranians held 52 Americans as hostages and demanded the return of the Shah to Iran in 1979–1981.

Revolution: A sudden change in the status of a country caused by political, economic, or religious factors. The Iranian Revolution of 1978–79 involved civil unrest causing the deposing of the Shah.

Operation Eagle Claw: A failed U.S. military operation to rescue the hostages in 1980.

Freezing assets: Prohibiting the transfer of assets (money) for political or legal reasons. The United States froze Iranian assets in U.S. banks until the hostages were released.

Embargo: A prohibition against the import or export of goods or services to another country. The United States, joined by other countries, imposed an embargo on the shipment of goods to Iran until the hostages were released.

Fatwa: An official Islamic edict calling for a specific action to be taken by Muslims.

Economic Boycott: Collective action by one or more states to abstain from economic dealings with another state for political reasons. The United States organized an economic boycott against Iran while the hostages remained in captivity.

Theocracy: A form of government which recognizes God as the supreme authority in matters of the state. Iran became a theocracy under the rule of Ayatollah Khomeini.

Nightline: A late-night television show on the ABC network that began during the hostage crisis as a nightly update of the situation.

Appendix C

Iran Chamber Society. "History of Iran: Islamic Revolution, 1979." <http://www.iranchamber.com/history/islamic_revolution/islamic_revolution.php>.

Khorrani, Mohammad Mehdi. "The Islamic Revolution." <http://www.internews.org/visavis/btvpagestxt/theislamicrevolution.html>.

mbeaw.org. "Iran: Islamic Revolution, 1979–1981." <http://www.mbeaw.org/resources/countries/iranrevolution.html>.

Milani, Abbas. "Iran: A Revolution Betrayed." *Hoover Digest* 4 (Fall 2003). <http://www.hooverdigest.org/034/milani.html>.

Search for "Iranian Revolution 1978–1979" on <http://www.google.com>.

Appendix D

Essay question / Research topic number 1.

How did Western diplomacy in Iran from 1907 to 1978 actually help to destabilize the situation there and lead to the rise of a revolutionary atmosphere? This essay should examine colonial efforts early in the century as well as political and international intelligence operations in the post–World War II era.

Essay question / Research topic number 2.

Examine the causes, the level of participation by the people, the "tipping point" events, and the consequences of the Iranian Revolution of 1978–79 and compare that revolution with one of the following:

1. American Revolution of 1776;
2. French Revolution of 1789;
3. Russian Revolution of 1917; or
4. Chinese Revolution of 1949.

CHAPTER 46

Cultural Aspects of American Relations with the Middle East

PAUL R. FRAZIER

Given that the Middle East and the religion of Islam have been featured in the news on a regular basis since the attacks of September 11, 2001, students and teachers would do well to know as much as possible about the two topics, and especially about how the United States interacts with and relates to the people of the Middle East. It is relatively easy to work such information into a U.S. history lesson, and students may appreciate learning about a topic that is both history and current events.

Of course, relations between East and West go back many centuries, beginning with the conflicts between the Greeks and the Persian Empire. From that moment on, East and West have interacted in many ways. Three books provide especially helpful information on the subject. The relationship the West has had with the Middle East is well documented in *What Went Wrong* (2002) by Bernard Lewis. Edward Said's widely-read book *Covering Islam* (1981) discusses how the West has viewed the East for many centuries. And *American Orientalism* (2002) by Douglas Little presents excellent coverage of how the United States has viewed the Middle East since 1945.

Students usually read about and discuss the Middle East in the context of U.S. foreign policy and formal state-to-state relationships. However, nations also interact on cultural grounds, and cultural relations can have an impact on foreign policy. Cultural interaction can encompass many strands, including religion, trade, pop culture, and the media. Given that we live in a society highly driven by the media, this lesson plan focuses on the role the media has played in shaping perceptions about the Middle East and its varied and diverse peoples.

National Standards

This lesson plan will help students master the following standards in the *National Standards for United States History:*

Era 10: Contemporary United States (1968 to the present)

Standard 1C: The student understands major foreign policy initiatives.

Standard 2C: The student understands changing religious diversity and its impact on American institutions and values.

Standard 2D: The student understands contemporary American culture, particularly the influence of the media on contemporary American culture.

Time

Two 40-minute class periods.

Student Objectives

1. To define and recognize stereotypes and how they are formed.
2. To compare stereotypes about Islam to the actual tenets of the religion (the Five Pillars).
3. To understand cultural interaction and the role of the media.
4. To examine primary sources for cultural bias.
5. To fit this cultural interaction into the larger historical context.

From *OAH Magazine of History* 20, no. 3 (May 2006): 31–33. © Organization of American Historians. Reprinted by permission.

Background and Preparation

This lesson plan will fit readily into a U.S. history survey course, shortly after students learn about the 1973 oil embargo, the Carter Administration, and the Iran Hostage Crisis. It was during these key moments that Americans became painfully aware of the Middle East and its relevance. Not surprisingly, the same period also gave rise to many modern stereotypes concerning the Middle East and its people. During and after the oil embargo and the Iran Hostage Crisis, American newspapers were filled with political cartoons of Arabs and Muslims. Hollywood also got into the act by creating stereotypes that have persisted to this day. If time is an issue at the end of the school year, this lesson can be easily shortened to one period.

Teachers will be well prepared if they read the following books: *What Went Wrong* by Bernard Lewis, *The U.S. Media and the Middle East* (1995) by Yahya Kamalipour, *Epic Encounters* (2001) by Melani McAlister, and *American Orientalism* by Douglas Little. Of course, one need not read these books cover to cover. I suggest reading selected chapters dealing with the media. These sources will provide more than enough preparation for teaching this lesson plan.

Procedure

1. For homework, one week before the lesson is to begin, tell students to clip an article or political cartoon relevant to the Middle East from any major newspaper or news magazine. They may also view a movie or nightly newscasts about the Middle East or Islam. They should be ready to summarize their findings for the class on the day the lesson begins. If a student elects to view a movie it need not be about Islam, but should at least include some Islamic characters. Any number of made-for-television movies or Hollywood productions will be a good place to start.

2. Day One of the Lesson
   A. Have the students share their articles, cartoons, newscasts, and movies with the class and discuss the similarities of their findings.
   B. Ask the class what a stereotype is. This question may generate quite a bit of conversation as students volunteer examples. With the teacher's guidance the class should come up with the definition of the term.
   C. You may want to ask students to give examples of stereotypes of Americans or how Americans are perceived overseas. Do not be surprised if students are totally unaware of the negative image Americans have among many people abroad. Students may be able to name the characteristics of what we popularly refer to

as the "ugly American": i.e., overfed, lazy, stupid, loud, and violent. We know that not all Americans fit such a description. The key question, however, is why other people see Americans that way. You may need to help students pinpoint the reasons. A good place to start is with the media. Hollywood exports movies and television shows, non-Americans read glossy American magazines, and American music and video games are popular around the world. In many ways these bits of U.S. culture are all some people know of America and its people. Students will be acutely aware that all the mentioned products produced by American media are full of graphic language, sex, and violence, and are anti-intellectual.

   D. Next, ask the students to identify stereotypes of Arabs or Muslims. They may have an easier time with this exercise. Possible answers will include: terrorists, fanatics, backwards, uncivilized, camel thieves, oil barons, sheiks, and belly dancers. Ask why they see the diverse people of the Middle East in such a way. They may have no idea why they hold these perceptions. Again, the issue comes back to how the media shape perceptions.
   E. Examples can show students how the U.S. media portray Middle Easterners. Political cartoons are abundant and students usually like trying to de-code their meaning. The daily newspaper is a good place to start and the major news magazines such as *Time* and *Newsweek* have political cartoons as well. An extensive collection of cartoons is posted online at <http://dmoz.org/Society/Politics/News_and_Media/Cartoons/>. Also check out the book *Split Vision: The Portrayal of Arabs in the American Media* (1977), edited by Edmund Ghareeb. *The U.S. Media and the Middle East* by Yahya Kamalipour studies Arabs in political cartoons and students' perceptions of them. Unfortunately, the book includes no actual cartoons, but the statistics are enlightening. You may also visit the Arab American Institute Web site at <http://www.aaiusa.org> for general education needs regarding the Middle East.
   F. While viewing selected cartoons, help students identify the stereotypical characteristics and ask why the artists put them there. What is the point each cartoon is making? Political cartoons are not very subtle, but other media-driven stereotypes are. For example, ask the class if any of them have seen the Disney movie *Aladdin* (1992). Does anyone remember

overt racial and ethnic stereotyping from that movie? Probably not.

G. Show the first ten to twenty minutes of *Aladdin* and ask the students to look for stereotypes. If needed, you can point out that the main characters—with whom the audience is supposed to identify and like—are basically white people with a tan while other characters, especially the evil Jafar, are truly stereotyped. You can also mention that by the end of the movie Aladdin becomes more and more Western/American in outlook and less and less Middle Eastern as he defeats Jafar.[1] Students likely will be struck that something as seemingly innocent as a Disney movie could be so powerful in shaping perceptions.

3. Homework for Day Two

A. Read "Hollywood Holding Us Hostage: Or, Why Are Terrorists in the Movies Middle Easterners?" by Linda Fuller. The essay appears in Kamalipour's *The U.S. Media and the Middle East,* recommended earlier. The reading is short and will reinforce the discussion about *Aladdin.*

4. Day Two of the Lesson

A. Now that the stereotypes have been established, find out what the students actually know about Islam. Being a suicide bomber, for example, is not one of the basic tenets of Islam; this point should be made very clear to students.

B. These basic tenets, called the Five Pillars, include:

The Creed: "There is no god but God and Muhammad is his Prophet."

Fasting: This is done during the month of Ramadan.

Almsgiving: Muslims must give charitably to the poor.

Pilgrimage: Every believer is supposed to go to Mecca at least once.

Prayer: Muslims pray five times per day while facing Mecca. It may be helpful to point out some of the similarities to Christianity and Judaism, namely praying, fasting, and giving to the poor. Students may be surprised to see more similarities than differences.

C. So if there are similarities to focus on, how did the stereotypes originate? There have been stereotypes surrounding Middle Easterners for centuries, but the stereotypes we are currently facing developed recently. Hopefully at this point students will cite their reading from the previous night. If not, you can steer them

in that direction. You may want to focus on "Cinematic Stereotyping as Propaganda," an interesting part of the reading assignment. Be sure students understand this concept exactly and how it is a part of the various movies discussed in the essay.

D. The question of "why?" is sure to come up. Why did Hollywood make these types of movies beginning in the 1970s? Why was there a perceived need for anti-Arab propaganda? Here is where all of this discussion can fit into the historical context of the class. Prior to the oil embargo and the Iran Hostage Crisis, the Middle East did not even register on the radar screens of most Americans. Then suddenly it was there, inescapable and frustrating. Hollywood capitalized on the frustration and anger of Americans and made those feelings worse. It should be noted that Hollywood has a long history of this kind of behavior. For decades Hollywood turned out numerous anti-Soviet Cold War movies for the same reason, namely to capitalize on the fears and frustrations of the American public.

E. At this juncture it will be helpful to point out the nature of the media. Ask the students why the media covers what it does on the nightly news and why Hollywood makes the types of movies that it makes. One answer is that the media are in the business of making money and that the sensational or unusual sells; typical daily life, comparisons of religions, and commonalities do not.

F. Cultures and states interact in numerous ways. In this case, they are interacting through a very powerful and influential mediator, the U.S. media. Students spend more time with the media each day than they do in the classroom. It stands to reason that many of their opinions are going to be formed outside the classroom and much of their knowledge base will depend on those who control the media, not on their teachers and parents. Much the same can be said about adults and where they get their information. If voting constituents want a "get tough" approach to the Middle East, then politicians are forced to comply if they want to keep their jobs; thus the link between foreign policy and cultural interaction.

Alternate Plans

If you wish, you can substitute the following video for part of Day Two's lesson after you cover the Five Pillars: "Young

Voices from the Arab World: The Lives and Times of Five Teenagers." The video runs about 30 minutes and can be found at <http://www.amideast.org>.

As a substitute or additional activity, you can give your students an interesting quiz about Arab Americans to test their knowledge and challenge their assumptions. The quiz is found at: <http://www.aaiusa.org/quiz.htm>.

Note

1. Yahya R. Kamalipour, ed., *The U.S. Media and the Middle East: Image and Perception* (Westport, CT: Greenwood Press, 1995), 217.

Bibliography and Suggestions for Further Reading

Primary Sources

Selected Documentation Pertaining to U.S.-Arab Relations. Rev. and expanded ed., 3rd ed. Washington, DC: American-Arab Affairs Council, 1990.

Secondary Sources

Godfried, Nathan. *Bridging the Gap Between Rich and Poor: American Economic Development Policy Toward the Arab East, 1942–1949.* Westport, CT: Greenwood Press, 1987.
Kamalipour, Yahya R., ed. *The U.S. Media and the Middle East: Image and Perception.* Westport, CT: Greenwood Press, 1995.
Lewis, Bernard. *What Went Wrong? The Clash Between Islam and Modernity in the Middle East.* London: Weidenfield & Nicolson, 2002.
Little, Douglas. *American Orientalism: The United States and the Middle East Since 1945.* Chapel Hill: University of North Carolina Press, 2002.
McAlister, Melani. *Epic Encounters: Culture, Media, and U.S. Interests in the Middle East, 1945–2000.* Berkeley: University of California Press, 2001.

PART IV

VIEWS FROM ABROAD

One crucial component of a globalized American history—paying greater attention to how foreign scholars, teachers, and students view U.S. history—is the subject of Part IV. As more and more Americans travel around the world and their nation pursues economic and military involvements overseas, foreign views of the United States take on heightened importance. Serious discussion of U.S. foreign policy demands knowledge of its reception and impact abroad. Our American students will enter a global arena where anti-Americanism has surged in recent years, according to public opinion polls. Understanding "why America fascinates and infuriates the world"—the subtitle of a recent bestselling book—will be essential for forming educated and responsible citizens.

Views from abroad can also help us to see American history anew. How others see us is not always accurate—striking insights alternate with stark misinterpretations, and prior allegiances can inhibit genuine attempts at cross-cultural understanding. But foreign observers are natural comparativists. They can offer revealing reminders of things Americans overlook or take for granted about American society, such as its guarantees of free expression or its high incidence of violent crime. They can suggest a larger frame of reference for developments normally seen only in domestic terms; for example, by relating the rise of Protestant fundamentalism in the United States to global religious trends. They can highlight areas of commonality between societies that Americans usually contrast with their own. And they can chip away at Americans' prejudices and stereotypes about foreign groups or nations.

There is another benefit when history teachers pay attention to foreign views: they can help us to address the difficulties that non-native students face in confronting U.S. history. How can teachers present American history effectively to non-Americans? The number of students outside the United States who are learning English and taking courses in American history and culture has risen dramatically. These gains are paralleled by growing numbers of non-native-born students inside the United States. Thanks to the large-scale global immigration of recent decades, "America in the World" has its mirror image in "The World in America." Whether teaching abroad or facing international and immigrant students in American classrooms, U.S. history instructors confront common problems: finding appropriate points of entry where American ideas and institutions can be introduced, translating American practices in terms understandable to outsiders, bridging gaps of cultural prejudice, and resisting the tendency to simplify and stereotype the American past—or to sanitize it.

Three episodes of cross-cultural teaching are covered in the following selections. Brett Berliner's review of *History Lessons* directs teachers to a wonderful teaching tool: an anthology that shows how U.S. history is portrayed in textbooks around the world. James Tagg provides a thoughtful and detailed analysis of how (and why) Canadian students interpret American history and culture comparatively and selectively. Finally, Maureen Flanagan takes us to Egypt on her Fulbright professorship to experience the triumphs, frustrations, and lessons learned from presenting U.S. history—and representing the United States—to Arab student audiences.

CHAPTER 47

American History Lessons Around the World

BRETT BERLINER

Perhaps the most current banal cliché in American politics is the claim that 9-11 changed everything. Rather, little has changed in the world, save the introduction of emotive fodder for political agendas. Nowhere has this more impacted secondary schools than in history classes, where teachers are asked to explain some people's contempt of America—or at least the American government. One attempt to show how others view us is in Lindaman and Ward's timely *History Lessons,* an anthology of excerpts from secondary school history textbooks from around the world. Although Lindaman, a Harvard graduate student in Romance Philology, and Ward, an Assistant Professor of History and Political Science at Vincennes University, offer virtually no analysis (their thoughts are almost solely expressed in the excerpts they selected), the implications of their work raises profound questions about the larger utility of our test-driven curricula in an epoch when culture wars lead to bloody geo-strategic wars.

The secondary school United States History survey course provides many functions; most notably, it transmits national myths, develops a national identity, and forms a national citizenry. It has done this for years through the construction and perpetuation of a master narrative: the rise, development, and flourishing of democratic values, institutions and American power. But for some four decades, the U.S. narrative has been under siege: social historians and so-called revisionists have not only exploded the grand narrative, but greatly expanded the American story. The experiences of women, minorities, and excluded or marginalized populations can no longer be overlooked, though often they are only acknowledged in a blurb set alongside, but outside, the grand narrative in a textbook. Nevertheless, our history is now more nuanced, richer, and longer, as evidence by the heft of textbooks today.

Still, though, the master narrative is a limited or, as Lindaman and Ward suggest, an "isolationist" national story (p. xviii). Our national history texts parsimoniously account for other societies or perspectives. This has not gone unnoticed in the profession. Indeed, in 2000 the Organization of American Historians in its "La Pietra Report," edited by Thomas Bender, published a call to internationalize the American history survey. The La Pietra Report suggested that the American experience should be placed in the widest possible context. Our story would no longer be about our exceptionalism but our connections and comparisons to global forces, events, and ideas. The consequences of this are potentially profound: U.S. periodization may be altered and the viewing of American history from other angles will not just widen the lens on our history and refine our ideas, but even call into question our national myths and identity. At a minimum, this project will teach us that others do not see us as we see ourselves.

History Lessons proves this maxim. Lindaman and Ward judiciously assume that all national textbooks assert a particularistic national identity and grand narrative. Moreover, by virtue of their adoption in state supported or recognized schools, "textbooks are a quasi-official story, a sort of state-sanctioned version of history" (p. xviii). Studying foreign texts, then, will provide us with "foreign perspectives on U.S. history" (p. xx) and an indication of the identity, if not counter-identity, of our global neighbors. In this the authors succeed quite well. Although they articulate no unifying themes in their anthology, one does emerge: foreign nations have no choice but to acknowledge and wrestle with both

From *History Lessons: How Textbooks from Around the World Portray U.S. History,* by Dana Lindaman and Kyle Ward. *Education Review,* August 18, 2004. http://edrev.asu.edu/reviews/rev295.htm. Reprinted by permission.

the rise of American power and the relative or real weakness of their own nation's power.

History Lessons demonstrates this by organizing the excerpts much like a U.S. survey textbook, from the first explorations of North America by Vikings and later Columbus to the American Revolution to westward expansion to world power and contemporary history. Excerpts have been selected from secondary school texts from our ostensible allies in Europe, Canada, and Israel, to our Latin and South American neighbors, to countries with which we have more problematic relationships, such as Russia, North Korea, Iran, and Saudi Arabia. Surprisingly, texts from such powers as China, India, and Pakistan are not represented in the book. Each excerpt is preceded by the briefest of introductions, and selections generally, but not exclusively, address issues covered in American history that impact other countries.

Some of what we learn from foreign countries is unexceptional. A Caribbean text, for example, presents Columbus as a flawed and equivocal figure. He is not a heroic figure but one enmeshed in royal politics and subject to royal whims. Caribbean students learn that he forcibly taxed the indigenous Arawaks, and when they did not pay, he enslaved them. Later, his activities in the New World led to his ultimate arrest. There is much that is accurate, though not new, in this rendition of Columbus. The larger question that we must ask, however, is if we expand our narrative to include this information, how will it affect our founding myths? Perhaps by knocking down mythic straw men, we as a people could become more democratic and honest, rather than less.

More problematic and much more interesting is the wary eye Canadian texts cast on American expansionist desires and power. The War of 1812, texts inform Canadian students, was not so much about trade disputes, security, and lingering power struggles with Britain; rather, "most of all, the Americans coveted Canada" (p. 53). Canadians further learn that the U.S. invasion of their land led to heightened nationalism, but their texts emphasize the danger of an expansionist America. In discussing the Civil War, for example, Canadian texts state that the North was considering annexing Canada to make up for lost Southern states. Finally, Canadians are taught to accept their subordinate status to the U.S. In the wake of World War II and British weakness, "Canadian foreign policy began to mirror that of the Americans. In this respect, Canada was in step with the major European industrial powers, which depended on American aid . . . and rarely questioned American foreign policy" (p. 248). This lack of challenging the U.S. does not, however, suggest Canada agrees with us; rather, despite Canadians believing our foreign policy intentions to have been exaggerated in the past, "publicly . . . Canada supported American views" (p. 248). Students thus learn what it means to be subordinate—and duplicitous.

Furthermore, foreign students learn that interests and *realpolitik,* not moral imperatives or special relations, govern world politics. Indeed, British texts explain that despite their instrumental history against the slave trade, Britain was sympathetic to the Southern cause because of economic ties. Like its former colony Canada, Britain too articulates its weakness relative to the U.S. The Suez Crisis, not a major topic in the U.S. survey, was of crucial world significance, especially because American and Soviet actions halted the invasion. The consequences of this are made clear to all British school children: "the Suez Crisis underscored the real limits to Britain's freedom of action on the international stage" (p. 288). French texts are more strident in their analysis of the crisis: "Thus the two Great Powers demonstrated their desire to control the planet. . . . The crisis also marked the decline of both France and the [*sic*] Great Britain which were no longer able to act without the agreement of the two Great Powers" (p. 289).

Countries south of our border are no less wary of American power. Mexico, which lost significant territory to the United States, sees in the Monroe Doctrine only U.S. ambitions: "The political and military events of the American continent demonstrated how such a declaration could be manipulated in order to justify the imperialistic comportment of the United States, itself" (p. 62). Brazil's critique of U.S. interventions go further: "the US aimed to serve its own political and economic interests and as such guaranteed itself the right to use military force to intervene in the countries of the continent, claiming for itself the title of America" (p. 134).

The Great Depression, which began in America, had profound effects around the globe. Post-communist Russian texts still suggest ambivalence toward capitalism: "the victorious slogans about crisis-free economic development and optimistic predictions of an upcoming time of prosperity turned out to be no more than an empty bluff" (p. 193). While American texts discuss those out of work and the coming of the New Deal, French texts cast a slightly teleological eye to the horrors of the subsequent years: "Democracy suffered the most because it had taken root in the wealthy countries, those most affected by the depression. . . . On the European continent, the social crisis led to a radicalization of the extremes . . . [and] a renaissance of racism and anti-Semitism" (pp. 189–199).

The American use of atomic weapons to end World War II is a topic that lends itself to moral, political, and strategic debates. American texts raise some of these issues and often suggest the bomb was necessary to save American lives. Japanese texts, by contrast, not only question its necessity, but put it in a broader geo-strategic context: "[the U.S.] had succeeded in experiments to create the world's first atomic bomb and motivated also by the desire to come out of the war more powerful than the Soviet Union, dropped an atomic bomb . . . making this the worst tragedy in the history of mankind" (pp. 239–240). Thus contemporary Japanese students are taught that the U.S. will sacrifice anything for its strategic ends, a sobering thought in today's world.

Most pressing today is our ability to understand Islamic nations and their beliefs about the U.S. Perhaps we need only examine Saudi Arabian texts to shed light on our standing in the Islamic Middle East. In discussing Israeli wars, one Saudi text claimed, "the forces of Imperialism, Crusadism and Zionism cooperated in pouring their hidden malice on the Arabs and the Muslims" (p. 352). One could only imagine what is taught in the madrassas.

If one has the patience to slug through many excerpts from foreign textbooks, most as poorly written as American texts, one will find that Lindaman and Ward have provided us with a rich, even entertaining, but limited source for understanding the U.S. from non-American perspectives. Indeed, its very structure limits its utility. Excerpts are typically brief and devoid of any context or analysis, and the professional will find little new "factual" information here. In addition, this book begs for further studies: we know some of what is taught, but what foreign students actually learn from their texts should be addressed. Furthermore, one would wish the authors investigated or at least speculated on the instrumentality of the ideas presented in these texts.

These reservations really are asking the authors to write a different and more sophisticated book, admittedly an unfair criticism. What the authors did is a very yeoman job of collecting and organizing interesting selections, and their book is useful not only for the classroom teacher, but also for challenging our educational policies. First and most obviously, *History Lessons* is a useful complement and corrective to any American history textbook, and it takes a small step toward internationalizing our national history. In addition, it allows us to problematize our identity and investigate the national identity of others. Most dramatically, it demonstrates that history is subjective, not a startling point but one that must be addressed, especially for its significant policy implications. Indeed, if one accepts that good history is an expansive view of history that incorporates the widest array of sources and viewpoints, we should include the type of examples Lindaman and Ward excerpt in our courses. But how compatible, for example, is either the Saudi view of Middle Eastern history or the Japanese view of Hiroshima with our view of history? Clearly, "objective" high-stakes testing is antithetical to multiple perspectives of history, and open-ended essay exams that give credit to many foreign views, though conceivable, is as unlikely today as it was during the Cold War, World War II, or any other epoch in our history. Given our current testing mania and political climate, *History Lessons* notwithstanding, our teaching of history is impoverished and our national myths and identity continue to be reified. The costs of this national project may be high, as one French text warns: "The Cold War is finished but it still remains to construct a new international order. . . . [T]he law of the jungle prevails" (p. 377). Never has a text been so accurate and never has the broadening of our national history been more needed.

CHAPTER 48

American History, Canadian Undergraduates, and Nationalism

JAMES TAGG

It often happens this way. I am having coffee with a colleague when a couple of his or her students come over to say hello. During introductions, it comes out that I teach history. This receives a good enough response until I am compelled or my colleague goes on to declare that I am an American historian. Embarrassed silence often follows, at least until one of us manages to change the subject. Although I sometimes perversely imagine that such telling silence is more *mis-en-scène* than honest reaction, real emotions are at work here. Good manners and false protests of ignorance about American history cloak underlying anti-American sentiments among our students. Behind the façade, a jumbled set of emotions inform their discomforted imaginations. They are offended by the patronizing and condescending attitudes of Americans when the latter comment on, or intrude into, the outer world. They dislike the vulgar materialism of American society; scorn dumbed-down American culture; and are uncomfortable with the too familiar, too upbeat, too in-your-face candor of many Americans. A plethora of negatively perceived elements of the American past always linger on their historical horizons, especially modern and contemporary matters like Vietnam, the recurring ironies of so-called "free trade," and the two wars on Iraq. American arrogance and self-righteousness; American ignorance of, and uninterest in, Canada; and American political, economic, and cultural "imperialism" frame these sometimes guarded feelings. But in public conversation around an American (as anyone who teaches American history is assumed to be), words are measured, opinions are guarded, sentiments are sometimes suppressed.[1]

Complicating these "anti" emotions is a still more profound yet not always well articulated fear that Canadian culture, and likely Canadian sovereignty, will be overwhelmed by a United States too ignorant and too uninterested to even notice the consequences of their actions. Some Canadians combine this with a guilt-ridden corollary and irony—that Canadians individually and collectively are the too-willing or at least too-passive accomplices in this process. This not so subtle "American takeover" irony is therefore as important in defining Canadian attitudes about Canada as it is in defining Canadian attitudes about the United States.

It is for these reasons that many students approach my classes and my subject with an apprehension not found in British, Russian, and French history courses. No reflective Canadian comes to American history either unengaged or *tabula rasa;* American history is not "just academic." Students carry the heavy baggage of Canadian nationalist emotions and assumed knowledge of the United States, and a powerful interplay between these emotions and this knowledge in their approach to American history is inevitable.

Those unfamiliar with issues of Canadian identity and nationalism might be discomforted about the tone and thrust of what they have read thus far. That discomfort can be mitigated in part by understanding that Canadians accept and sometimes even celebrate many of the imperatives derived by living next to the United States. Canadians enthusiastically embrace good trade relations with the United States, and they have a seemingly endless appetite for American popular culture. They admire American energy and most of the principles of civic governance and civil rights promoted in American nationalism. In addition, the near

From James Tagg, "'And, We Burned Down the White House, Too': American History, Canadian Undergraduates, and Nationalism," *The History Teacher* 37, no. 3 (May 2004). Reprinted by permission.

hegemonic victory of social history—with its focus on the lived experiences of ordinary people as well as elites, its emphasis on group interaction, and its inclusion of minorities and formerly marginalized groups in the shared cultural experience of society at large—ameliorates somewhat the troubled vision students and others hold of a dangerous and rapacious American nation-state.

None of these "positive" attitudes and directions, however, can override the necessity most Canadians feel for upholding their own cultural and national identity. Critics of nationalism in general often offer up what might be termed a "strong" definition of nationalism that emphasizes the ideological, patriotic, chauvinistic, and culturally homogeneous character of most nationalisms.[2] To some extent my Canadian students seem to identify American nationalism with these "strong" terms even though they intellectually know some of the social, racial, and cultural facts that place limitations on that definition for the United States, and even though the United States has been and remains racially and ethnically diverse, often experiencing a Canadian-like confusion among its own regional and national identities.[3]

If Canadian students are apt to envision in the United States a powerful Euro-American style of nationalism and the centralized nation-state solidarity that appears to go with it, they and Canadians at large are less certain about Canadian nationalism. Some, especially in the 1960s and early 1970s, accepted as normative and desirable this "strong" definition of nationalism; others opposed it, favoring a "weak," benign nationalism in which diversity, pluralism, and internationalism were encouraged under the transparent umbrellas of good provincial and federal governments, individual equality, and a loose sense of being Canadian.

This latter "weak" nationalism has predominated in Canada. . . . Despite Québecois' "strong" regional-ethnic nationalism, both they and other Canadians hold a special relationship to nature, to history, and to nation building, that has allowed most of Canada to stitch together a truly modern, or even "post-modern" nationalism.[4] As Canadian journalist Richard Gwyn observes, Canadian nationalism has emerged from the "state-nation," and it is the Canadian state that "has formed up and has shaped our character in a way that is true for no other people in the world."[5] At the same time Gwyn observes a light quality to this nationalism. "We are strongly attached to our weak attachments to each other," Gwyn quotes one observer.[6] A bemused sense of fragility and necessity for accommodation generally dominate the Canadian nationalist imagination. Combined with the always looming threat of "continentalism,"[7] a quiet appreciation of Canada's vulnerability and a low-level anxiety for the nation's future mark Canadian nationalism, not jingoism and chauvinism. It is therefore this "weak" yet real and complex nationalism that collides in American history classrooms in Canada with the imagined clarity of "strong" American nationalism and with the threat of American

absorption or "continentalism." This essay is largely about the interplay of these nationalisms in the context of the shifting fortunes and opportunities for American history in Canada as I have experienced them locally over the past thirty-odd years.

American History in Canada

The popularity of American history in Canada has remained fundamentally strong over the years I have taught in Alberta. Cursory examination shows that Canadian universities proportionately hire more American historians than are hired in any other country except the United States, and any slog through Canadian calendars and other non-American university course listings would similarly show that Canadian students encounter more opportunities to take American history than do Asian, Latin American, or even European students.[8] No other English-speaking country compares with Canada when it comes to the number of undergraduate students who encounter American history.[9] The burgeoning of Canadian universities in the 1960s and the availability of American history courses in those universities were obviously fundamental contributors to its popularity. Concomitantly, Canadian history and Canadian studies, and American history and American studies were being promoted as subjects necessary and worthy of encouragement.[10]

Within this educational-expansionist context, however, international affairs, high politics, cultural drift, and local events shaped the uneven fortunes of American history at my university from the beginning of my teaching career onward. The 1960s set the tone with buoyant optimism in both the United States and Canada as high politics began to shed its dowdy image, as "Ike" gave way to JFK, and "Dief" gave way to Trudeau; as the "Quiet Revolution" promised a latter-day liberation in Quebec, and the Civil Rights movement promised a new participatory democracy in the United States; and, as Canadian universities prospered, and their students faced the happy prospect of securing employment in the career of their choosing. . . .

Then came the political fallout from the 1960s that, even in our remote corner of the continent, had profound and immediate effects. The assassinations of Martin Luther King, Jr., and Bobby Kennedy, and Richard Nixon's election to the presidency in 1968 slowly came to be perceived here as the end of liberalism, the end of civil rights, and the end of the liberal ethic for the United States. Watergate added the exclamation mark. Meanwhile, students at my university encountered two reality shocks from which they took a long time to recover. One involved our Student Council's invitation to the Black Panthers to speak on campus. It could not be accepted because the Royal Canadian Mounted Police stopped the Panthers at the border. The other occurred when the student newspaper was shut down and its editors threatened with prosecution for publishing the manifesto of the FLQ [*Front de libération du Québec*, a Marxist separatist movement] in October 1970. However innocent, it was treated as a serious contravention of the Trudeau government's War Measures Act. Civil Rights, free speech, and a free press, all hallmarks of the American heritage, appeared in disarray beginning in the early 1970s. Across the border, Vietnam increasingly loomed as the ugly antithesis of social progress.

As contemporary events soured the youthful passions of my students and me, old style "strong" nationalism asserted itself in Canada. The "Committee for an Independent Canada," including a local chapter, promoted the nationalist cause with passion, castigating American interlopers (presumably including me) who came north and took Canadian jobs, and who presumably instilled American values and threatened Canadian autonomy. Behind the dramatic rhetoric, they naively proposed a vigorous Canadian nationalism and patriotism that they claimed would inevitably be kinder and gentler than the jingoism of the United States.[11] Nationally, Prime Minister Pierre Trudeau shed his boyish light-heartedness. The new Trudeau was tough and anti-American, disdainful of the vulgarities of American culture while exploiting the lessons it taught in image politics. Trudeau and Nixon mixed like oil and water.[12]

American history enrollments dipped at my university, partly as a consequence of these factors, partly from the growth of new subject fields in our department of history, and perhaps partly (as the astute reader will be thinking by now) from ineffective teaching on my part. National and local trends alike, laced with ideological frustration and anti-American rhetoric, boded poorly for the teaching of American history. Some teachers simply accommodated themselves to the temper of those times by incorporating anti-American styles in their pedagogies.[13]

The political and public blandness of the 1980s and 1990s—decades devoid of reform but not of rhetoric, decades of war as television programming, and of radical capitalist rhetoric that stirred few souls—permitted students a kind of non-engaged opportunity to poke at the American giant from the safe haven of our larger and increasingly democratized university classrooms. Only a few hard-boiled conservatives took American history as a consequence of the American turn to the right, and even they refused to embrace the deception that it was "morning in America again." Anti-American hostility toward what the young identified as American rapacity and endlessly worsening corrupt American public morality continued to be the primary chorus of vocal students.

Students born between the late 1960s and the early 1980s were, however, more besotted with American cultural representations, events, and icons than those who had come before. On the one hand, they embraced American "fashions," thought in Americanized images, and had been at least partly schooled by American television. On the other hand, and not insignificantly, from the 1970s on, they had been lectured in their classrooms and through the media on their need to find and promote Canadian identity and to preserve Canadian culture. In an interesting blend, cultural familiarity with the United States coupled with curiosity born from a homegrown Canadian identity crisis conspired by the 1980s to fashion more student interest in American history. . . .

The maturation of social history from the 1980s on also made American history more a subject of Canadian empathy than of nationalist anger. It made all history more diverse and more interesting, and enrollments in all of our history courses improved substantially. By happy coincidence, then, our survey courses encouraged perspective and synthesis at a time when historical writing was losing much of that advantage. Our advanced courses gave us room to incorporate the brighter and more varied palette of modern social and popular culture history. . . .

But despite all of the things that enhanced the popularity of American history after the early 1980s, a perceivable undertow of student hostility and frustration toward the United States remained the most constant and unique element in teaching American history.

A Survey of Student Attitudes

Over the years, term papers, examinations, and personal discussions with students have given me more than a few ideas about Canadian undergraduate attitudes toward the United States and American history. To further test my understanding of those opinions, an anonymous opinion survey was administered in the 2002 spring semester to my senior level early American history course and to my survey level "Main Themes" course.

I was not really surprised either by the personal backgrounds of those who returned my long survey,[14] or by their answers to a broad range of opinion questions about the United States. Every one of them listed "patriotism" and "nationalism" (or terms that equaled the same thing) as the American quality most worthy of admiration and praise. The image of national solidarity, "love of country," "pride," and "togetherness" constituted the patriotism they admired. No particular trait or characteristic of being American—not, for example, constitutional freedoms (except for one respondent), civil rights, generosity, the ideal of equality—was suggested as the central prop beneath "patriotism" and "nationalism." It was just the sheer sense of emotional bondedness of Americans that they admired. As one student mentioned, the 4th of July "supersedes our weak little July 1st celebrations."[15] Canadian students deeply feel the fragmentation of a Canada born with geographic, historic, and linguistic separation. Because of this, and perhaps because many of them understand that the United States is a country of deep regional divisions as well, they are in genuine awe of American patriotism and nationalism.[16] In teaching American history, the "patriotism" lessons remain clear: first, the ideological foundations of different societies in history, no matter how seemingly familiar, require persistent definition and re-definition; and secondly, although twenty-first-century disgust with "nationalism" and the nation-state may express fashionable and current utopian hopes for the future, the differing nation-states and nationalisms are elements fundamental to understanding American history in Canada.[17]

Of course, the paradoxes of patriotism were not lost on these students when they answered my question on the most objectionable national quality of Americans. Indeed, a couple of them simply used their response on the first question as their response to this one. Here the ramifications of patriotism and nationalism—"ignorance" of other countries and societies, and "arrogance" built of self-satisfaction and self-congratulation—were mentioned by almost all of the respondents. Slavery, racism, segregation, economic inequality, materialism, and gun culture made brief secondary appearances on their lists. Arrogance, the product of "unchecked patriotism" constructed on the premise that "anything that is American is better," was easily twinned by these students (and most students I have taught over the years) with American ignorance of other cultures and countries (especially Canada). This was further joined with Americans' assuming that they were "guardians of the Free World" or taking "on a role of referee even if they do not understand the subject matter."[18] American unilateralism and uncooperativeness with other countries—undoubtedly exacerbated by the recent so-called "war on terrorism" and the then impending war on Iraq—made stronger appearances in this survey than I have sensed in previous years. The existence of these sentiments all indicate an urgent need for us to teach more American foreign affairs and foreign policy history. But there is more to it. Many undergraduates read American diplomatic history textbooks as if they were courtroom testimony in the prosecution of the United States. To some extent, American diplomatic and foreign affairs history has come to define its boundaries broadly in recent decades, incorporating the complexities and contexts of world affairs, of republican ideology, of democratic pluralism, and of a variety of ethnic, religious, and regional conditions. However, diplomatic history must continue to widen its contexts if Americans hope to avoid stoking the sentiment of anti-Americanism.[19]

Subsequent opinion questions on the best and worst characteristics of "American government and constitutionalism" produced more mixed results. While some students noted the capacity of the American government to "rally" the public and to "act" when called upon, more of them saluted the checks and balances of the American system, including federalism, division of powers in general, restric-

tion of terms for presidents and other officeholders, frequent elections, and an "effective Senate." On the negative side, a majority mentioned corruption and immorality in American politics, while others raised "horse trading," the ideological limits of the two-party system, too little care for the poor and the oppressed, and, again, the uninformed involvement of the United States in other countries' affairs. Several sentiments drive these Alberta undergraduate views: their desire, as Canadians, to have governments responsive to the variety of Canadian interests; their wish, as western Canadians, for a federal government that can be checked by an elected and effective Senate; and their desire to keep the advantages of parliamentary initiative and the integrity of "responsible government" in Canada while gaining frequent elections, rotation in office, and the more frequent accountability of the American system. But in my experience, the virtues and failures of both the Canadian and American political systems are frequently lost on all but the most sophisticated political science or history students. Students confuse the two systems in gross ways, and fail to understand their ideological underpinnings, to say nothing of their functions. Sorting out these matters in teaching American history in Canada is essential, and when any of my courses hit the snag of the United States Constitution, we have to stop and review the fundamental structure and function of that constitutional system before we can move on.

The positive and negative aspects of "American culture" are far less difficult for them to sort out, or so they assume. Almost all cite one or another aspect of popular culture as the great American contribution to the world, although scattering acknowledgments were given to the Bill of Rights, the invention and furtherance of modern capitalism, "devotion to education," and even American humanitarian aid. The negatives followed the same channels, with the excesses of individualism, consumerism, and materialism held up for condemnation, along with passing critical references to the right to bear arms, the American "melting pot" myth, and the falsity of the "American Dream." One wag offered the old quip: "what culture?"

Popular culture, employed frequently by non-Americans as an accessible mode of interpreting the United States, presents special challenges for teaching undergraduates. Canadian youth come to the university unschooled in American history, including fundamental understanding about American ethnic and racial history, American social discourses and religious typologies, class systems and class relations, and "master narrative" mythologies. To be sure, as conspicuous and conscious consumers of American popular culture even young Canadians understand much about modern American capitalism and marketing, and movies inform them about some values (and fears) of Americans over time. Most also share with their American contemporaries the language and culture of popular music. But students often apply the apparent universalist significances of current popular culture backward in time, creating a fictional American past filled with easy homilies about American individualism and hedonism. At the same time, it is difficult for them to understand the roots and meaning of music like blues and jazz because they have not yet learned enough about slave cultures, African-American and other ethnic cultures and religions, regional societies, and various dynamic influences specific to the United States in the nineteenth and twentieth centuries. In short, it is often ironic that while we expect popular culture and its metaphors to explain fundamental things about the American past to a general population, popular culture as an analytical subject may be better suited to advanced students and scholars already familiar with some of the elusive social underpinnings of American culture.

Opinions about the greatest "American contribution to world civilization" produced reluctant and diffuse answers, including American initiatives in World War I, Edisonian-type inventions, human and civil rights. On the other hand, several respondents predictably identified American deployment (not necessarily development) of the atomic bomb in World War II as the greatest "assault on world civilization." Despite my attempts to encourage debate on the necessity and/or justice of the A-bomb's use in August 1945, it is usually only young men with militarily-inclined interests who defend Truman's decision.[20] Others persist in condemning the United States, however, at least in part in order to allow themselves to judge negatively American policies and practices during and after the Cold War. Unfortunately, a non-complex view of the A-bomb decision also suppresses their capacity to accept the role of contingency in American history after 1945.

Finally, among the broad opinion questions, students were asked to rank the "five greatest and five worst Americans" over time. Most of the replies were predictable; they lacked range in a way that demonstrates the drubbing good biography has received over the past twenty years. Martin Luther King, Jr., Abraham Lincoln, Benjamin Franklin, FDR, JFK, and George Washington—in that order—make up their "greats." Only two women—Susan B. Anthony and Marilyn Monroe—made the list, along with a few modern and popular figures like Walt Disney, Neil Armstrong, and Michael Jordan. Only one student mentioned any literary figure, while the worlds of cultural reform, business and commerce, and science received little acknowledgement. "Great" Americans, as defined here, are national icons, monuments rather than persons, emblems of some more generalized condition such as forthrightness, steadfastness, virtue, or reform.

The "worst" Americans list was filled by persons all too grotesque in their memorability, including badly damaged individuals like Charles Manson, Timothy McVeigh, David Koresh, Jeffrey Dalmer, and O.J. Simpson. Bill Clinton, George W. Bush, and Ronald Reagan appeared on behalf

of the politicos, along with a few Confederate Civil War officers. Oprah Winfrey and a small group of what they defined as "irritating" popular icons also appear. Aside from the Confederate officers, the villains' list is all from the late twentieth century. History softens or ameliorates the memory of a Jeffrey Amherst, Nathan Bedford Forrest, George Armstrong Custer, cruel nineteenth-century industrialists, and even 1920s and 1990s Wall Street swindlers. Richard Nixon, now a distant figure to most students, got only one vote. The relationship between the narratives of individual human lives and the nature of an historic era is weakly comprehended here. Without a better understanding of real people—not just the icons, celebrities, and infamous—American history moves from human history to a general set of ideologies, faceless postures, and flawed typologies, thus encouraging the pre-existing tendency of Canadian students to pillory the character of Americans and confuse American history with a static set of essences.

More specific questions about events and eras in American history yielded some modestly interesting results. Opinions on the writing and history of the United States Constitution and Bill of Rights—"civil religion" for many Americans—received a ho-hum response; many acknowledged its political significance in the eighteenth century but most found it just another frame of government today. As one said, it was now no better and perhaps not as good as the republican constitutions of France and Germany or even the constitutional monarchies of Great Britain and Canada. Teaching American constitutional history in Canada, even to advanced students, is problematic, with the origins, impact, scope, and complexities of the "supremacy clause" (Article VI), and the rise of "judicial review" the hardest aspects of American constitutionalism to explain. English and Canadian common law traditions are well planted, even in the minds of twenty-year-olds born near or after adoption of the Canadian Charter of Rights and Freedoms.

Unlike their American counterparts, Canadian undergraduates celebrate the War of 1812 as an important and pivotal event. For them, it was a war won by Canada and, as they gratuitously gloat, their side burned down the White House as well.[21] They realize, of course, that the Treaty of Ghent gave them no territory and no dominion over the United States but the fact that they avoided absorption by the United States provides their main source of interest in that war. The United States Civil War, by contrast, is not always felt in its full dimension of ferocity and tragedy. They admit it was a just and noble cause to end slavery but also note that Americans were latecomers in ending slavery. The era of industrial development that followed the Civil War is passively approved by most students (in examinations they often applaud Andrew Carnegie for his views on welfare capitalism). They too seamlessly identify this "root, hog, or die" era with that of the late-twentieth-century American thrust for dynamic capitalist expansion. As Albertans generally unfamiliar with labor unions, they are puzzled by the emerging labor movement of the late 1800s and early 1900s. And, when I use Robert Wiebe's now old but still brilliant *Search for Order* to discuss the profound social transformation of late nineteenth- and early twentieth-century America, they seem bewildered by the massive ideational and material forces at work in the period.[22] The late nineteenth century increasingly emerges as a "world we have lost," especially with the collapse of working-class consciousness in the academy and culture at large.

In the twentieth century, almost all salute the American effort in World War II as among the high points of American altruism (despite the "bomb"). But this only makes their caustic criticism of American involvement in the Cold War that followed more severe. In straw polls over the years, and in my recent survey, students by large majorities blame the beginnings of the Cold War primarily on the United States, and by even larger majorities blame the deepening of the Cold War on the United States. With the exception of a few tough minded, anti-communist "Cold Warriors," most students take a leftist line that is not dissimilar from that of Joyce and Gabriel Kolko in the 1960s and 1970s. The more middle-ground judgments of John Lewis Gaddis and others do not seem to move them.[23] The reasons for this are both simple and subtle. If pushed, students will admit they expect better out of a democratic United States than the McCarthy era and the assemblage of ill-advised policies and hysterical reactions that have marked American foreign affairs for a half century. They also know, but are loath to admit, that while United States policies and actions have largely become known, the severest policies and actions of Stalin and his successors, even with the recent release of historical documents, have been under-publicized and too lightly considered.[24] While they embrace the self-criticisms many Americans have made of Cold War policies and actions, most Canadian undergraduates also dismiss the 1950s and 1960s as a time of fraudulent banality. They choose to ignore the good news aspects and domestic buoyancy in that period in favor of identifying only its vacuity and materialism.

The Civil Rights movement, long a popular and positive topic among students, has lost its urgency and luster; many now shrug and say it was long overdue by the 1960s; others question its durability and long-term consequences in a culture that they often claim is still racist. Some of this is avoidance, of course, as Canadian "separate worlds" relations with their native populations strongly suggests. A feel-good Canadian multiculturalism, heavily sponsored by the federal government but with real roots in popular sentiment as well, often salves the consciences of Canadians, even those of us who live near insular Indian reservations. Furthermore, twenty years ago, Canadian students clamored to get presentation and term paper assignments on civil rights and the women's movement; now both are a

hard sell. Radicalism in the 1960s continues to be popular, primarily because of student familiarity with the music and the celebrities of the era. But from the 1990s on, intense interest in the reform eras and hot-topic controversies of the twentieth-century, such as the abortion debate, has either declined or become more diffuse.

As for economic affairs, globalism-on-American-terms-only is the theme as they read history backwards, identifying everything from the nineteenth century onward with American capitalist rapacity. Yet, most see Americans in general as simple victims of the Great Depression of the 1930s, and about half of them salute American leadership in global economic matters, while the other half condemn things like the IMF and World Bank as tools of American imperialism.

Problems Teaching the American Revolution

Some of the Canadian undergraduate student opinions cited above will be familiar to American historians who have heard the same views or variants thereof in the United States. In order to suggest subtle nuances that are less often encountered by United States–based American historians, it may be instructive to look at one specific example—the American Revolution—to illustrate how problematic and different teaching in Canada can be.

My Canadian undergraduate students do not find the American Revolution a dull subject. They enjoy reading older works, especially those with some narrative structure, like Benjamin Labaree's *The Boston Tea Party,* Hiller Zobel's *The Boston Massacre,* Robert Gross's *Minute Men and their World,* Alfred Young's *George Twelves Hewes,* and David Hackett Fischer's *Paul Revere's Ride.* They determinedly work through Bernard Bailyn's *Ideological Origins* and Gary Nash's *Urban Crucible,* and, they give favorable reviews to Gordon Wood's *The Radicalism of the American Revolution,* which I use as a comprehensive text in my advanced early American course.[25]

They do not necessarily believe or accept what these works have to say, however, nor do most of them find the American Revolution revolutionary. It is not just a matter of the old line that the American Revolution does not meet the standards of violence and destruction apparent in the French and Russian Revolutions. In opposing the idea that the American Revolution was revolutionary, they are in the company of many Americanists, of course, from old imperial school scholars like Charles M. Andrews and Lawrence Henry Gipson to neoimperialists like T.H. Breen and the Seven Years' War expert Fred Anderson. All of these historians see the Revolution set in a longer time frame than the 1760s and 1770s and against a much broader landscape of place than the Atlantic seaboard.[26] In fact, the first challenge many of my undergraduates face when taking up the Revolution is the need to adopt an interpretive playing field both wider (geographically) and longer (chronologically). Comprehending the American Revolution as "merely" another of Robert R. Palmer's Atlantic revolutions used to be a interpretive tack taken by some.[27] Insisting on an exclusively imperialist view is still another approach.

My Canadian students also seem unable, in many instances, to overcome a kind of inborn Burkean conservatism, a social prejudice in favor of gradualist history carried forward glacially by habit, history, and ancient institutions. After the *Annales* school re-emerged in classrooms in the 1970s, new force and language was appropriated to this prejudice. Either the Revolution was the mere flotsam and jetsam of superficial events, or it was just part of the larger, more profound, deep currents of European history. Given the English origins of the American colonies, the backing of imperial school ideas, and what they selectively choose to accept from the neo-conservative, opposition Whig school, shorn of its most dynamic ideological and emotional elements, "no real revolution" must be the right answer to my examination questions on the subject. History is a slow, meandering stream when it runs its truest course, they imply, and the American Revolution is not seen to deviate much from that course. For a few, the chance to squelch the exceptionalist view of American history is redolent throughout their essays on the American Revolution.

For many students also, human nature, especially that of Americans, is *ipso facto* self-interest at a petty level. American self-interest in the 1760s, therefore, just got mixed up with a few irritating taxes. Reading modern American avarice and love of low taxes back to the eighteenth century, some students are content to believe that a pure-and-simple desire to avoid taxes was at the heart of the Revolution. Others understand the tax crisis as just a symbol of larger issues of representation but then get confused when the proposals of Governor Bernard and Joseph Galloway and others for representation fell on deaf ears. They are not much better off with issues of class or interest conflict as elucidated best by Gary Nash and Woody Holton.[28] In the end, they believe that the Americans perceived an economic advantage for themselves in independence. Many agree with one of my survey respondents who argued that with a slight change in policies, the British could have held onto their troublesome colonies.

Coming from a non-revolutionary history of their own, one that made only slow, evolutionary gains in acquiring ultimate national autonomy, Canadian students are skeptical about any other historical model of national development.[29] They are dubious about the explosive emotional potential contained in the ideological arguments of Bailyn and Wood, and they latch on to any slight criticism I might offer of those arguments in order to dismiss ideology as a motive factor in revolutionary America. Although they accept the autonomous qualities of New England Puritan culture and Virginia planter culture that preceded the revolution, they

do not easily absorb or acknowledge Opposition Whig or Country vs. Court tendencies or classical republican antecedents to the American Revolution.[30] Virtue over corruption and liberty over power are seen as slogans, not deeply ingrained elements of ideology. Gordon Wood's article on conspiracy and the paranoid style is frequently distorted into a psycho-historical interpretation whereby paranoid Americans revolted merely as a consequence of foolish fears, or collective mental illness.[31]

Students often suggest that ideas were employed mendaciously as excuses for some underlying, selfish motive of the colonists, and the most frequent rationale offered for the Revolution is that Americans felt they could succeed better commercially without the mother country. Even when we turn to Joyce Appleby's work, students embrace her ideas on material self-interest but do not readily comprehend her larger arguments on affective liberty.[32] Much the same fate befalls Wood's *Radicalism,* which many, if not most, students—confronting history backward from the comfort of well-established modern ideas about liberty, democracy, and equality—claim contains few truly radical consequences of the Revolution. They do not recognize such things as the end of deference and elite control as the powerful transformation it really was.

The American Revolution suggests how difficult it can be for students to accept ideological and nationalist differences. Some students, as mentioned earlier, still see "nationalism" as coterminous with the nationalism of language, blood, or ethnicity, and are even loath to accept what Michael Ignatieff describes as a "civic nationalism" based on ideology not birth, a nationalism that was first introduced by the American experience.[33] Their opinions show the difficulty of teaching a subject in which *a priori* assumptions about American national character (e.g., modern materialism) are read back into the past. The failure of the ideological argument to find acceptance by my students in this course demonstrates the profound need for more courses in European, British, and American intellectual history. Altogether, teaching the American Revolution is an interesting challenge in getting students to abandon large mindsets and to think in terms of different cultures, times, and contingent possibilities.

Closing Observations

American readers may find that this essay gratuitously exaggerates stubborn anti-Americanism among Canadian undergraduates. It does not. On the other hand, it should be acknowledged that most of these students share with American students presentist deceptions and generalized clichés about American history. Canadians are also deeply curious about American history, and many recognize that they occupy a unique perch above the 49th parallel to view and interpret the American past. Most intelligent students assume (probably erroneously) that they know as much or more about the American past as do their American counterparts. But for all Canadian students, knowledge and perception are double-sided. They must penetrate the veneer of their Canadian prejudices about American character and must understand American-held prejudices as well. They must juggle two mythologies, ignoring neither but understanding how each mythology interplays with historical realities. . . .

Inevitable comparison lies at the heart of learning American history in Canada. Even implicit rather than explicit comparisons of the evolution of British North American colony into the country of Canada set against the American revolutionary experience and the subsequent nation-founding of the United States allow students to ask important questions about material and ideological elements too easily assumed as natural givens by more insular American students and their professors.

The virtues of comparative history have long been touted and do not need repeating. It is worth noting, however, that Canadian undergraduates, however much they study the subject, are not likely to lose the advantage—an advantage more culturally than geographically derived—that they hold over American undergraduates in the sphere of comparison. One would like to think that American colleges and universities, by increasing Canadian and Mexican studies in the United States, would improve their capacity to understand Canada and Mexico as well as themselves in the process. There is no evidence, however, that these national comparisons will be made by Americans. Although no American would like to say it, the populations are either too small (Canada) or the economic and cultural impacts perceived to be too weak (both Canada and Mexico) or the social origins too "foreign" (Mexico) for Americans to perceive either country or culture as anything but marginal and peripheral. Furthermore, the "new Rome," as a consequence of its singular military power and economic dominance in the world, magnanimously imagines it can bring other cultures and societies into its tent. It is a tent where the terms of reference and the diction of values are pre-determined in an American way and, consequently, those who choose, or must remain, outside the tent are automatically and tautologically marginalized.[34]

Most of the literature written over the past thirty years on the teaching of American history has suggested that American history can best be taught by including formerly disadvantaged groups—African-Americans, Hispanics, and Native Americans, for example—in the historical landscape.[35] But while no one would dispute this as a necessary and desirable goal, inclusion of them under the American axiom of "strong" nationalism leads to a history of diversity within America alone, a history whose progress winds inevitably toward further inwardness, to an ever more generalized yet exceptionalist definition of what it is to be American and

to "share" American values. The comparative impulse for Americans is thereby satisfied by keeping it geographically "in-house," a circumstance which shelters comparative elements under the pantheon of American values and identity markers. Ideas like "freedom," "democracy," and "equality" not only become co-opted and forced into the service of one nationalism, but it is also more difficult to compare the American past with others because of their self-referential and singular American definitions.

This American variant to inclusion, which compromises comparative history built on using concepts that, if not familiar and shared, are at least reasonable starting points for understanding, also makes problematic the other major recommendation found in the teaching-of-history literature—the need for world history. If world history is simply a collage of national and regional events—"this" happened here while "that" happened there, and "meanwhile" "this" was happening somewhere else—it is obviously meaningless, with every national and regional history sharing nothing more than temporality. If world history is to be built around large ideas—democracy, modernization, the rule of law, even self-actualization—centripetal forces of American nationalism will narrow the definition of these terms and the focus of such world history, largely rendering it useless. If world history is truly comparative and blended national or regional history, Canadians and many others may be keen but the attraction will be lost on most Americans (if not American historians).[36]

For now, we are left with national history as the unfashionably still dominant unit of historical understanding. Outside of Europe—where national, comparative, and pan-European history might have better potential to co-exist—Canadian undergraduate students at least have a greater opportunity than those from most other nations to interpret the past of their most powerful neighbor. Proximity and dependence are part of this equation; experience, and the history of historical study in Canada, is another part. But being different from Americans, and comprehending the utility and human need to understand that difference better, is the best part.

When I became a Canadian citizen in the mid-1980s, I had to be examined by a citizenship judge. When she asked what I did for an occupation, I told her I taught history at the University of Lethbridge. Pressed for my field, I had to reply, "American history." Without losing a beat, she said, "That's too bad. What we need is more Canadian History." It was not the warmest of welcomes to Canada. She was also ill informed if she thought American history was taking time and energy that should have gone into Canadian history. Canadian history and Canadian studies have grown enormously in Canadian universities during the past half century. American history has also grown. The growth may have been coincidental in part, but these subjects also need each other. American history will thrive if Canadian history is healthy and prospering; Canadian history will prosper if American history maintains a healthy presence. Perspective, knowledge, and identity—even of the workings of history in general—will improve as a result. Knowing ourselves in a nationalist sense and knowing our neighbors need not remain mutually exclusive endeavors.

Notes

The author wishes to thank June Tagg, Maren Wood, and the journal's reviewers for their especially helpful criticisms.

1. Dale Carter, an Englishman teaching in Denmark, notes that Danish students assume that "any American professor teaching them (usually a visitor) has as part of their agenda a defense of the United States. They are perceived as part teacher, part advocate." See John Ingham *et al.*, "Teaching American Studies Abroad: A Symposium at the University of Toronto, 23 April 1999," *Canadian Review of American Studies,* 29: 3 (1999), 97.

2. An example of this definition may be found in Anthony H. Birch, *Nationalism and National Integration* (London: Unwin Hyman, 1989), 4.

3. Recognition of this shared confusion over identities is made in Ramsay Cook, *Canada, Québec and the Uses of Nationalism,* second ed. (Toronto: McClelland & Stewart, 1995), 222–23.

4. For a brief description of some elements of Canadian distinct identity see Cook, *Canada, Québec and the Uses of Nationalism,* 196–209; On "post-modern" nationalism see Richard Gwyn, *Nationalism with Walls: The Unbearable Lightness of Being Canadian* (Toronto: McClelland & Stewart, 1995), 243–54.

5. *Ibid.,* 17–18.

6. *Ibid.,* 182.

7. Denis Stairs, "North American Continentalism: Perspectives and Policies in Canada," in David Cameron, ed., *Regionalism and Supranationalism: Challenges and Alternatives to the Nation-State in Canada and Europe* (Montreal: The Institute for Research on Public Policy and Policy Studies Institute, 1981), 83–109, identifies five areas in which "American penetration of Canadian society" perceivably exists—diplomatic, economic, cultural, informational, and philosophical intrusion. In short, almost all meaningful areas of national existence are affected by "continentalism," and Stairs demonstrates some of the peculiar ways in which Canada as a nation has reacted to those penetrations or threats of penetration.

8. The meager presence of American history in some foreign universities is surprising. Linda K. Salvucci, "Did NAFTA Rewrite History? Recent Mexican Views of the United States Past," *Journal of American History,* 82: 2 (September, 1995), 646–47, notes that only 50 of the 50,000 students at the National University in Mexico City enrolled in the year-long American history survey.

9. In an older article, David H. Burton, "Teaching American History at British Universities: The Continuing Challenge," *History Teacher,* Vol. 6, No. 2 (1973), 267–280, lists 38 universities and 108 faculty teaching some aspect of American history in the United Kingdom, numbers that are surely larger now. Burton lists a number of things that retard American history in universities, however: early specialization by students matriculating into university, the limited availability of U.S. History in optional subject matter for A-level exams, a tendency to blend American history into a broader western or world history, and a lack of proximity to and interest in the United States. See also Marcus Cunliffe, "Teaching United States History Abroad: Great Britain," *The History Teacher,* Vol. 18, No. 1 (November, 1984), 69–74; and, Marcus Cunliffe, "American Studies in Europe," *American Studies,* Vol. 9, No. 3 (1971), 22. Others testify that American history is often taught extensively in survey mode but less so in advanced courses or that American history is taught topically at best to serve the limited purpose of comparing and contrasting cultures. See, for example, Leopold S. Launtiz-Schürer and Joseph M. Siracusa, "Some Recent Trends in the Study of United States History in Australia: A Bicentennial Note," *American Studies International,* Vol. 16, No. 2 (1977), 22–33; and, Basil A. Le Cordeur, "American History for South Africa: Perceptions and Objectives," *American Studies International,* Vol. 32, No. 1 (1994), 96–102. By contrast, Canadians seem to enroll broadly in American history survey courses, and many students go on to take further American history courses, some even pursuing it as a major subject in graduate school. Stephen J. Randall and Albert Desbiens, "A Guide to the Study of United States History in Canada, 1945–1980," *American Studies International,* Vol. 23, No. 2 (1985), 67–68, claims that in 1958, only 10 or 20 Canadian universities offered more than one specific course in U.S. history, and the largest offered anywhere was four. By 1980–81, however, a survey of English Canadian universities revealed "some 331 courses devoted exclusively to United States history were offered, plus 78 others which dealt at least in part with an aspect of American history, such as slavery, women's studies, business history, and diplomatic history." Of 38 universities surveyed, 25 had master's level work and 17 doctoral level work in American history. Even in Québec, seven of nine departments of history in 1980 taught American history. By 1985, over a twenty-year period, there had been approximately 140 master's theses and doctoral dissertations written on American history in Canada. Limited library resources and press outlets for scholarship in U.S. History alone restrained growth in the field, Randall and Desbiens noted.

10. An early appeal by a prominent Canadian university figure for more American studies in Canada can be found in Claude Bissell, "American Studies in Canadian Universities," *Queen's Quarterly,* 66: 3 (Autumn, 1959), 384–87. Peter Buitenhuis, "American Studies in Canada," *American Studies,* Vol. 10, No. 1 (1971), 19–24, lamented how Canadian nationalism had frustrated the rise of American studies in the 1960s but offers evidence as well that Canadian studies and American studies were in fact growing apace.

11. On the "nationalism" challenge see, for example, Buitenhuis, "American Studies in Canada," 19–24.

12. Walter LaFeber, *The American Age: United States Foreign Policy at Home and Abroad,* 2nd ed. (New York: W.W. Norton & Co., 1994), 662, claims that new American taxes on imports from Canada (1971), extreme differences over Vietnam, and a weakening Canadian military involvement with the U.S., meant that Canadian-American "relations approached a twentieth-century low" by 1976.

13. The "flag-waving patriotism and self-congratulation" of Americans has pushed some Canadian teachers of American history to adopt anti-American extremes in response. See

Paul W. Bennett, "'Beneath the Gloss and Floss': Teaching American History in 'The Great White North,'" *The History Teacher,* 23:4 (August, 1990), 449–453.

14. Twenty-three students (only four from my senior class) responded to this survey out of a possible fifty-seven. They were evenly divided by gender; all but two were in their twenties or younger. They were also evenly divided between those in their first two years of university and those in the last two years. Half had already taken at least six courses in history. All claimed Canadian citizenship; two claimed dual Canadian/American citizenship. Almost all were from Alberta and all were from the West. Most had traveled fairly widely and often to the American West and Midwest. Most claimed to have read at least one article or book on American history. Even with already clearly developed views about the United States, most were surprisingly reluctant to claim that they had more than modest knowledge about history. Newspapers and television, they claimed, were the most important sources of their knowledge.

15. A poll reported in Toronto's *The Globe and Mail,* June 29, 2002, A9, summarizes Canadian ambivalence. Some 74% claimed Americans did "a better job of celebrating their accomplishments than Canadians"; on the other hand, 71% disagreed with the proposition that "Americans have more important people and accomplishments to celebrate than Canadians."

16. William Lyon Mackenzie King, Canada's long-serving prime minister of the depression and World War II eras, was at least partly right when, while lamenting Italy's invasion of Ethiopia, he famously declared that " . . . if some countries have too much history, we [Canada] have too much geography." See Dominion of Canada, *Official Report of Debates, House of Commons,* First Session; Eighteenth Parliament. Vol. IV, (June 18, 1936), 38–68. King acknowledged in this speech the advantages Canada shared with its good neighbor, the U.S., in not suffering all of the historical baggage of Europe. At the same time he noted the problem of establishing and retaining Canadian sovereignty over Canada's vast and thinly populated territory.

17. For example, Birch, *Nationalism and National Integration,* 223–24, notes that "there is no evidence at all of public loyalties being transferred from national governments to supranational organizations. . . . Possessive nationalism is very much stronger than incipient internationalism."

18. Marcus Cunliffe, the friend, promoter, and teacher of American studies in Great Britain, rightly answered Americans who found foreign students too anti-American: "The history of nation states is *per se* in large part a record of jingoism, aggression and prevarication—and this is true of new nations no less than old ones. Americans have often adopted a tone of moral superiority in analyzing other national societies. Why be surprised that the tone is resented, or its justice challenged?" See Cunliffe, "Teaching United States History Abroad," 71. Le Cordeur further notes that, "What is especially fascinating for South Africans about American history is the irony of that peculiar mixture of extreme idealism and its all-too-frequent violation or non-realization which has been a hallmark of 'the American experiment.'" See "American History for South Africa," 97.

19. Paul Gagnon has observed that, "To study foreign affairs without putting ourselves [meaning Americans] into others' shoes is to deal in illusion and to prepare students for a lifelong misunderstanding of our place in the world," *The Atlantic Monthly,* 262 (November, 1988), 63.

20. The critical arguments usually offered can be found in Gar Alperovitz, *Atomic Diplomacy: Hiroshima and Potsdam* (New York: Penguin, 1985) and *The Decision to Use the Atomic Bomb and the Architecture of an American Myth* (New York: Knopf, 1995). For a middle ground see Barton J. Bernstein, "Roosevelt, Truman, and the Atomic Bomb, 1941–1945," *Political Science Quarterly,* 90 (Spring, 1975), 23–24, 30–32, 34–43, 44–54, 57–69. Plausible defenders of the bomb's use are Herbert Feis, *The Atomic Bomb and the End of World War II* (Princeton, N.J.: Princeton University Press, 1966), and Robert James Maddox, "Why We Had to Drop the Atomic Bomb," *American Heritage,* 46 (May/June, 1995).

21. This popular observation is frequently made by students. Listen to "The White House Burned (The War of 1812)," by "Three Dead Trolls in a Baggie" from their album "Steaming Pile of Skit."

22. Robert H. Wiebe, *The Search for Order, 1877–1920* (New York: Hill and Wang, 1967).

23. See Joyce and Gabriel Kolko, *The Limits of Power: The World and United States Foreign Policy, 1945–1954* (New York: Harper & Row, 1972). More conservative arguments are offered in John Lewis Gaddis, *The United States and the Origins of the Cold War, 1941–1947* (New York: Columbia University Press, 1972), *Russia, the Soviet Union, and the United States* (New York: McGraw-Hill, 1978), and *The Long Peace: Inquiries into the History of the Cold War* (New York: Oxford University Press, 1987); Michael S. Sherry, *In the Shadow of War: The United States Since the 1930s* (New Haven, Conn.: Yale University Press, 1995); and, Walter La Feber, *America, Russia, and the Cold War* (New York: McGraw-Hill, 1993).

24. See John Lewis Gaddis, *We Now Know: Rethinking Cold War History* (New York: Oxford University Press, 1997).

25. See respectively Benjamin Labaree, *The Boston Tea Party* (New York: Oxford University Press, 1964); Hiller Zobel, *The Boston Massacre* (New York: W.W. Norton and Co., 1970); Robert Gross, *The Minute Men and Their World* (New York: Hill and Wang, 1983); Alfred Young, *The Shoemaker and the Tea Party: Memory and the American Revolution* (Boston: Beacon Press, 1999); David Hackett Fischer, *Paul Revere's Ride* (New York: Oxford University Press, 1994); Bernard Bailyn, *The Ideological Origins of the American Revolution* (Cambridge, Mass.: Belknap Press of Harvard University Press, 1967); Gary Nash, *The Urban Crucible: Social Change, Political Consciousness, and the Origins of the American Revolution* (Cambridge, Mass.: Harvard University Press, 1979); and Gordon S. Wood, *The Radicalism of the American Revolution* (New York: A.A. Knopf, 1991).

26. Although their arguments vary widely see, for example, Charles M. Andrews, *The Colonial Background to the American Revolution* (New Haven, Conn.: Yale University Press, 1931); Lawrence Henry Gipson, *The Coming of the American Revolution* (New York: Harper, 1964); T.H. Breen, "'Baubles of Britain': The American Consumer Revolutions of the Eighteenth Century," *Past & Present,* 119 (May 1988), 73–104; and Fred Anderson, *Crucible of War: The Seven Years' War and the Fate of Empire in British North America, 1754–1766* (New York: Vintage Books, 2000).

27. Robert R. Palmer, *The Age of Democratic Revolutions,* 2 vols. (Princeton, N.J.: Princeton University Press, 1959).

28. Nash, *Urban Crucible*. Woody Holton, *Forced Founders: Indians, Debtors, Slaves, and the Making of the American Revolution in Virginia* (Chapel Hill, N.C.: Published for the Omohundro Institute of Early American History and Culture by the University of North Carolina Press, 1999).

29. On the other hand, Seymour Martin Lipset is too strong in proclaiming that the "basic organizing principles" of Canada differ from the United States in that Canada represented and continues to represent "counterrevolution" and thus "is a more class-aware, elitist, law-abiding, statist, collectivity-oriented, and particularistic (group-oriented) society than the United States." See *Continental Divide: The Values and Institutions of the United States and Canada* (New York: Routledge, 1990), 8 and *passim*.

30. At least until recently, some American teachers and scholars had also apparently found it difficult to promote the ideological origins of the American Revolution instead of the older theory of Lockean liberalism. See, for example, Earl Sheridan, "The 'Republican Revision' and the Teaching of American Government," *PS: Political Science and Politics,* 20:3 (1987), 689–91.

31. Gordon S. Wood, "Conspiracy and the Paranoid Style: Causality and Deceit in the Eighteenth Century," *William & Mary Quarterly,* 39:3 (July, 1982), 401–41. Students are amused to find themselves on the opposite side from Dr. Benjamin Rush who believed that adherents to Great Britain and Americans who did not support the revolution suffered a derangement he called "Revolutiana." See Charles Royster, *A Revolutionary People at War: The Continental Army and American Character, 1775–1783* (Chapel Hill, N.C.: Published for the Institute of Early American History and Culture by the University of North Carolina Press, 1979), 286–88.

32. See especially Joyce Appleby, *Capitalism and a New Social Order: The Republican Vision of the 1790s* (New York and London: New York University Press, 1984), 15–23.

33. For a brief discussion of this definition of nationalism see Michael Ignatieff, *Blood and Belonging: Journeys into the New Nationalism* (London and Toronto: Penguin Books, 1994), 5–9.

34. R.G. Collingwood puts it bluntly. Identifying the rise of national history with the rise of Rome, he states that a new idea of history arose, "a history in which the hero of the story is the continuing and corporate spirit of a people and in which the plot of the story is the unification of the world under that people's leadership." See *The Idea of History* (New York: Oxford University Press, 1956), 34.

35. This is based on a review of the bibliographic guide, *America: History & Life,* from its beginnings in the 1960s to the present.

36. George M. Fredrickson protests that attempts to compare whole nations will, in the case of the United States, lead to the trumpeting of American "exceptionalism" in an "oversimplified" and "idealized" way. He warns that such whole comparisons will result in placing the "nation as the foreground" while "creating a generalized image of others as background." See "From Exceptionalism to Variability: Recent Developments in Cross-National Comparative History," *Journal of American History,* 82:2 (September, 1995), 587–604. Foreground and background are much closer for Canadians, and comparative nationalisms more able to share the foreground.

CHAPTER 49

Being the "Other"

Teaching U.S. History as a Fulbright Professor in Egypt

MAUREEN A. FLANAGAN

If for Russell Johnson the experience of teaching the Gilded Age and Progressive Era in Turkey was that of being in a "not so strange land," my four months as a Fulbright professor at the University of Alexandria in Egypt were often quite the opposite. There I was truly a stranger in a strange land. But it is important to note right from the start that by strange I mean foreign in the sense that American history of any sort is not part of the Egyptian university curriculum. So much so that before I arrived in Egypt I had been given only a hazy idea of what I might be teaching. Once there I quickly found that I had to jettison the proposal that I had submitted for the Fulbright competition—to teach about the processes and ideas of democracy in U.S. history, most especially in the Gilded Age and Progressive Era. The reasons for my inability to teach what I had proposed help explain much about the place of U.S. history, indeed all of "western" history, in Egyptian universities, and how the situation differs enormously from those described for Canada, Mexico, and Turkey. In these "post–eleventh September" days, it seems to me especially important to understand that while in the U.S. we seek to expand our university history curricula into a world vision, in Egypt exactly the opposite has been happening. Why this should be so in the age of globalization, and what lessons it has for U.S. historians, I think are among the valuable insights that can be gained from a Fulbright teaching fellowship in the Arab world.

The University of Alexandria is the second oldest public university in Egypt. The faculty of arts, to which I was attached, has approximately 15,000 students in history, philosophy, sociology, anthropology, political science, and foreign languages. With the exception of those enrolled in the English curriculum, the majority of the students speak little or no English. Language was thus the first hurdle that I encountered upon my arrival. The request for an American Fulbright professor to teach at the university had originated with one of the senior professors in the history department whose career in U.S. history had included time spent in the U.S. He was concerned with the diminished position of U.S. history in the department curriculum. There was a single required one-term course, taught now by a professor not trained in the U.S. whose command of English was very shaky. But since the majority of history students speak little English, and I do not speak Arabic, once I arrived in Alexandria, but not before, it registered on all involved that I could not teach in the history department because of the language barrier.

But there were other barriers that also could not be surmounted. The history department, for example, did not particularly want to have me there. The reasons for this explain some of the current attitude in much of Egyptian academia toward U.S. history. I was perceived as the outsider who was there to propagandize in favor of the U.S. My first realization of this came in a two-hour meeting with the Dean of Faculty and the heads of departments conducted in Arabic, English, and French where several of those attending made it clear that they did not want me teaching their students. Between English and French I grasped the gist of this situation and the sympathetic faculty in the English Department—where I ended up teaching—later confirmed this for me. An element of this problem—and something that I encountered in every part of my Egyptian experience—was that many of the faculty had already decided for themselves what U.S. history was.

From *Journal of the Gilded Age and Progressive Era* 1, no. 4 (October 2002): 347–363. Reprinted by permission.

So, the course in U.S. history was taught by a professor whose publications were all dedicated to showing the U.S. as a racist, anti-immigrant, and imperialist nation. I want to make it clear that this professor was not herself hostile to me, or professionally hostile to the U.S. But her English language skills were not extensive, and she had been trained in Egypt within a context of viewing all U.S. history as first and foremost the history of imperialism. That being the case, history students at the University of Alexandria were taught only this perspective on U.S. history.

The final obstacle to teaching in the history department was that I was a western woman. I received the distinct impression that in a department that was all Egyptian and primarily male, the response to having me in the department ranged with few exceptions from disinterest, to discomfort, to hostility. The hostility, it seemed to me, was a minority sentiment, yet, the department was clearly not enthusiastic about accommodating a westerner, and especially not a western woman. This situation was only one of many in which I experienced the differences in ideas of gender roles between the U.S. and Egypt. So, I ended up teaching U.S. culture, broadly defined through history and literature, in the English department. Here, too, the make-up of the department was undoubtedly responsible for how I was accepted. The overwhelming majority of both the faculty and graduate and undergraduate students were female and most of the senior faculty had earned their doctorates in England, Ireland, or the U.S. They welcomed me with enthusiasm and great kindness. Many of the graduate students—who really were junior faculty members—were especially concerned to help me and most anxious that my experience at the University would be one from which I would develop a positive impression of Egypt.

The English department had two tracks for undergraduate students: those in English literature and those in English language training. I was assigned to teach three classes, one primarily to literature students, a second to language students, and a third course that was required of all students in the department—Western Civilization. This latter course touched only peripherally on the U.S. so I will focus in this essay on the other two courses, but will return to the Western Civilization course later because my experiences teaching it give additional context to some of the issues and problems that I encountered throughout my time in Egypt.

My two other courses were seminar-style reading courses that were required for all second-year and fourth-year students. As reading courses they had no set theme, so I was able to select readings that focused on the Gilded Age and Progressive Era [GAPE]. My first obstacle in these courses was that the students had no books and the professors had to furnish all the readings. On the one hand, this situation rather perversely worked to my advantage as it left me free to choose my own material. But it also meant that I could only require the students to read small amounts of materi-als that they could afford to xerox and I was constantly scrambling to find appropriate material. Thus, despite these being labeled reading courses, only a limited amount of reading could be assigned. Fortunately, I was able to use many of the same materials in both classes. Overall, I found that presenting my students with readings that contained universal themes of human existence worked best when trying to get them to grasp U.S. culture. In setting up the readings in this way, I then could move from the universal to the particulars of U.S. history.

As a historian, I was somewhat frustrated that the situation meant that for the most part I had to assign literature rather than history. To deal with this, I sought out readings whose subject matters lent themselves to explaining GAPE history: immigration and Americanization, urbanization, technological and industrial development, faith in progress, cultural dislocation, and even some gender analysis, were the themes that appeared constantly in my chosen readings. An additional challenge to teaching history through literature, especially to students with no background in the material, was that I could not make linear presentations. Every class, instead, was structured around themes as they arose in the readings. So even though the readings were historically situated, my typical approach had to be to emphasize themes while moving back and forth in time and filling in the history details.

A selection of some of these readings serves to illustrate the approaches that I used. I had brought with me a copy of Edgar Lee Masters' *Spoon River Anthology* (1914) from which I assigned several prose poems. I quickly learned that a work such as this was invaluable for it allowed me to assign short passages that the students could afford to xerox and circulate among themselves. Masters' meditations on death, disappointment, and the unfairness of small-town American life in the post–Civil War era opened a discussion on the transition in the U.S. from rural, small-town agricultural life into a growing urban, industrial society. I was then able to reinforce their sense of such a historical transition by comparing it to the social upheavals in post–World War Egypt when massive numbers of the poor left the countryside and crowded into Cairo, Alexandria, and their outskirts. Moreover, many Egyptian students in the almost tuition-free government universities are the first literate generation in their families, so the themes of dissatisfaction and dislocation resonated with them.

The majority of my students were women and they were struck by the poems titled "Tom Merritt," "Mrs. Merritt," and "Elmer Karr." These matter-of-factly recount a triangle in which a woman's lover kills her husband, despite her attempts to end the affair. The students readily grasped the universal sexist attitudes embodied in these pieces. The men have first names; the woman is identified only by her marital status. The woman is legally punished far more severely than the man even though he had committed the actual murder. She is sentenced to thirty years in prison where she dies. He receives fourteen years and then returns to the community, which embraces him again. From these same poems, I was then able to move on to discuss the growth in the late-nineteenth-century woman's movement for legal reform as well as the suffrage movement in the GAPE.

Using Carl Sandburg's *Chicago* (1916) I followed up on the aspects of urbanization that I had raised in the discussions from the *Spoon River Anthology*. What was it that cities had to offer to all those people pouring into them in the early twentieth century, what was it like to live in them, and why did these conditions spark the reforms of the Progressive Era were all issues that arose in discussing this poem. As a historian of Chicago, of course, I was happy to be able to focus more on this city in particular and then to move on to describing other large American cities of the time. This reading also alerted me to something that American historians take for granted but that was a rather alien idea to my Egyptian students as I explained progressive reform. The fact that individuals could organize and have an effect on government, that is, could achieve several of their objectives, is virtually unknown in Egyptian society where the concept of a civil society is very weak. This became clear to me not just in these classes but in another context at another university, as I will explain later. Thus, beyond them grasping the specific changes that took place then across American society—consumer protections, workers' organizations, increased government regulation of the economy—and imagining the problems that cities were confronting, most of the students remained unable to see why the changes were enacted or what was important about them.

To teach about immigration I used with some success the "Introduction" to Henry Roth's *Call It Sleep* (1934), which describes the main character's arrival in New York as a little boy with his mother to meet his father who had immigrated earlier. The father was already assimilating himself to the U.S. and was very angry to see them arrive dressed as "foreigners," even though they were wearing what, in their home country, were their finest clothes. The father wanted only to speak English, which of course neither the mother nor little boy understood. In the father's mind the clothing and lack of English stamped his family as peasants tied to a land and a way of life that he not only rejected but to which he was trying to pretend he had never belonged. This relatively short reading raised again for the students the issues of dislocation experienced by immigrants as they move from a known culture to an unknown one, the problems of acculturation and assimilation, and one generation's or individual's rejection of the older culture. The father's mania to be accepted as an American allowed me to explain about the making of an American identity, but also to discuss the reasons for native-born reaction against immigrants, especially the poor, unskilled, and possibly

illiterate ones that came in such great waves into the U.S. early in the century, and thereby the surge in anti-immigrant sentiments that resulted in the imposition of legal barriers to immigration. By fortunate circumstance, I had brought with me some notes on immigration so that I could reinforce the literary depiction with totals of immigrants from 1900–1914 and their places of origin, and to explain how the origins and cultural backgrounds of late-nineteenth-century and early-twentieth-century immigrants differed from those of earlier immigrants.

I did try one piece with the fourth-year literature students that did not work well. That was T.S. Eliot's *Lovesong of J. Alfred Prufrock* (1917). The language was simply too obscure for them to make their way through. Yet, as we went through it line by line, I was able to introduce the concept of modernization and convey to them some of the problems facing U.S. society by the second decade of the century: the new affluence being experienced by a segment of the population, the growth of a culture of consumption, the imbalance of wealth between rich and poor, the focus on material success, and the alienation felt by some members of American society in the face of this increasing affluence. I was then able to contrast the themes of the poem with what was happening to immigrants, the workers, and to women across the first two decades of the new century and to push on into explaining the 1920s. One thing that I learned from discussing the 1920s through this poem, however, was how open my students were to thinking the worst of American society. They especially wanted to blame the American emphasis on individualism to the exclusion of the family for the ills of its society. They noted the lack of any attention to family in *Prufrock* and one student ultimately expressed the opinion that an important difference between Egyptians and Americans was that while the former valued and found purpose and comfort in family, the latter went to psychiatrists. Since virtually none of my students had any background in western history, the finer nuances of democratic individualism and where the individual fit into U.S. society remained a mystery. More than once in talking to Egyptian students and professors I was bluntly told that Americans had no sense of family. In response, I always stressed that difference of ideas might indicate just that—difference, but not lack of or inattention to some concept—but, this was not an idea that they were very willing to accept when I offered it. It did not help, of course, that much of their "knowledge" of the United States had come through American television shows and movies, which despite a growing backlash within Egypt against them, were widely disseminated and avidly watched.

When *Prufrock* did not work easily, I found another way to get across the GAPE, including the concepts of faith in progress, and certain American "myths" about equality and opportunity. We discussed the movie *Titanic*, which they had all seen. For whatever its flaws in historical accuracy as we historians debate them, for students with little background in U.S. history this movie works marvelously well. They were able to see in the character of Rose the boredom with modern life for an upper-class woman, thus picking up on a theme from *Prufrock*. The characters of Rose's mother and fiancé reflected the class snobbery, insensitivity, conspicuous consumption, and dilettantism of the upper classes of the time. The ship's architect and the steamship company executive embodied the period's characteristic faith in technology and belief that nature could be conquered by western expertise and superiority. Yet the doubts that the architect had about the "unsinkability" of the ship, and the free-spirited, artistic character of Jack, the working class young man attracted to Rose, also raised questions about the faith in technology and its superiority to nature. Jack's character also served to illustrate the pervasive American ideas that class is no impediment to advancement in the U.S. and that "regular" or "working" people are "heroic." The movie reinforced this latter idea by juxtaposing the callous disregard for the safety and lives of the lower classes in the failure to provide enough lifeboats, and the loading of first class passengers into the available ones while the steerage passengers were locked below deck, against Jack and Rose's "selfless" and "heroic" attempts to get those same people to safety. (At the time, of course, I had no way of knowing how this latter idea would become such a significant part of the discourse of the events of September 11, 2001.) The expectation of a better life expressed by the steerage class passengers before the ship hits the iceberg additionally served to illustrate the lure of the "American dream," the promise of opportunity, for Europe's lower classes who were flooding across the Atlantic at the time.

Perhaps it is merely a sign that students everywhere find pop culture more accessible than high culture that they were more willing to engage more dispassionately the ideas of American culture depicted in *Titanic* rather than the presentation of essentially similar ones in *Prufrock*. But I came to feel also that teaching U.S. history in Egypt meant giving the students a "balanced" portrait of American culture—that is good and bad together, even if both sides were exaggerated, possibly pandering to American "myths," or even verging on the fictitious. So, I found myself . . . raising the specter of "myths" but without undertaking the critical examination of them that I would do with U.S. students.

As I worked my way through the Gilded Age and Progressive Era, I also used some of Eric Foner's *The History of American Freedom*. I felt that it was important for my students to see how the concept of individual freedom has shaped all of U.S. history. As my classes were progressing, I came to realize how deeply rooted this idea is in American society and that lacking experience with and understanding of this concept, my students might be able to grasp the "facts" of the GAPE but could not easily move beyond them to grapple with the reasons and contradictions of the

events and personalities of this era. A few examples from my third class, Western Civilization, illustrate the difficulty of this task. This course is required for all the students in the English department, whose professors believe that their students must understand something about western culture in order to comprehend and then teach English literature and language. . . .

As with my other classes, the western civilization students had no text. The professor has one Xerox copy of it and a second copy circulates among the students, who xerox the assigned pages and share the copies among themselves. With 140 students it goes without saying that many of them never read a word of it. In this class, I introduced the students to a more American method of teaching than the Egyptian one that they were used to, which takes the text and goes through it paragraph by paragraph in class. I, on the other hand, focused on the main ideas, summarizing and elaborating on them. Some of the students were intrigued by this method, while some of them were clearly unsettled by it. I had always to keep in mind, however, that at the end of the term I had to give them an exam, on the basis of which they passed or failed the course. Thus I needed to present the material in ways that could then be given back on exams that were meant to test more the acquisition of facts than the understanding of ideas. The exam results showed that some of the students had worked on and grasped the concepts; others were clearly just confused or had not bothered. . . .

Even for the majority who passed the exam, however, many ideas of western culture remained hazy at best. In this regard, the unfamiliarity with the concept of the free individual in U.S. society was matched by the unfamiliarity with the Lockean idea of the consent of the governed, which I had to teach as part of the textbook chapter on the Enlightenment. In one of my first classes on this chapter I thought that I had given a fairly clear and simple explanation of this concept, complete with examples. Yet, several students approached me after class to ask for clarification. They did not understand, they explained, what was meant by the "consent of the govern*ment*." That was the first time that I confronted the challenge of teaching ideas that would be readily understood by a U.S. university student, even one who had never heard of Locke or been presented academically with the phrase "consent of the governed." My discussions with my Egyptian students underlined for me how alien this concept was to them as they did not have a grasp of what role the "governed" possibly had to play in government beyond voting. From that point on in my western civilization course I was even more careful of what I presented and how I explained it. And this experience of being confronted directly with cultural difference—as opposed to imagining something intellectually—was one of the most enlightening moments of my time as a Fulbright.

The last piece that I used that I want to discuss here

was the introduction to John Steinbeck's *Grapes of Wrath.* Although a reading on the early stages of the Great Depression usually falls outside the purview of the GAPE, Steinbeck's vivid picture of the effects of the arrival of the dust storms on both the people and the land helped me to close off some of the issues that we had already discussed. The students were struck first by the universality of human suffering. They could imagine how the people felt. And for Egyptian students it was particularly poignant as they live in a country where only 5 percent of the land is cultivatable non-desert. The universal struggle of people against a hostile environment was one they could easily imagine and we were able to discuss the dislocations and hardships facing Americans in the 1930s, no matter the apparent affluence of the country. I also then could return to the reform ideas of the Progressive Era, the sense of social responsibility and social justice that had motivated some of these reforms, and discuss how the economic depression of the 1930s resulted in more acceptance in the U.S. that government had a responsibility to care for its people. That experiences of hardship and suffering, of economic failures, could result in societal changes seemed more accessible ideas to them than those of freedom and consent.

Beyond classroom teaching, as a Fulbright professor I was expected to give a series of lectures both at Alexandria and at other universities. I took advantage of the overwhelmingly female population of the English department to present my one large lecture there on the topic of the U.S. women's and suffrage movements as part of the GAPE. In all my other lectures, I emphasized the themes of immigration, identity, and diversity—which I had quickly learned interested Egyptian students—in the Progressive Era through the 1920s. These lectures broadened my experiences in the Egyptian university system, gave me access to more students and professors, and provided additional opportunities to teach about the Gilded Age and Progressive Era. They became more successful as I gathered experience and understanding of the Egyptian context, but how successful always depended on the specific audience.

I gave my first lecture outside of Alexandria to the fourth-year English literature students at the University of Cairo. The flexibility that I had learned after spending two months in Egypt came in handy in this instance. As I arrived in Cairo the day before the lecture I received a phone call from the professor who was arranging the lecture. Could I, she asked, work into my talk explanations of F. Scott Fitzgerald's *The Great Gatsby?* Suppressing a brief surge of panic, I said certainly, and a hasty trip to the bookstore of the American University of Cairo secured a copy of a book that I had not read since I was an undergraduate. I spent the evening reading it and writing references to Gatsby into my already prepared talk on "Immigrants, Hyphenated-Americans, and Americans."

By this point in my tenure in Egypt I had not only learned more about flexibility, but now understood how fundamental concepts of American culture and identity that we as Americans simply take for granted can be utterly foreign to many Egyptians. So, I began my lecture by relating an anecdote from a conversation I had had upon my arrival in Alexandria with the Dean of Faculty. He told me that he had recently been to New York City and when walking around was startled by all the different languages he heard being spoken. His question to me was "Are there any Americans in New York City?" The answer I gave to him, and to the students in Cairo, is that most of those people he heard speaking everything but English were probably either Americans or on the way to becoming Americans. Arriving from somewhere else with different languages, religions, and cultural habits is our shared experience (except for Native Americans), an experience that in turn has shaped what it means to be an American. I was able to use *Gatsby* to illustrate the realities and tensions of this immigration experience as well as the processes of "becoming" American in the GAPE. The desire to be identified as "American"; the consumer culture with acquisition of property as a symbol of having "made it"; the striving for success which in the book was illustrated by name changing—Gatz became Gatsby—and geographic mobility; the absence of any mention of religion; the focus on the individual and individual achievement, all emerge in *Gatsby* as defining characteristics of American culture and identity. But, Fitzgerald was also in this book questioning what all of this meant and whether American culture and individualism contained tragic flaws. From this last issue I was able to discuss how Americans, especially in the Progressive Era, have often believed that democracy requires the freedom to discuss and critique openly the flaws of American society.

This lecture may well have been the most successful one that I gave in Egypt. The students followed it carefully and asked many good questions. In fact, they were so enthusiastic about having the opportunity to talk about American culture that they asked one of the sponsoring faculty members if I could come speak to their class that followed my lecture, which I gladly did.

The Fulbright office in Cairo then asked me to participate as a co-keynote speaker at a daylong conference it was sponsoring at Suez Canal University for the 50th anniversary of the Bilateral Egypt–United States Fulbright Commission. The theme of the conference was Multiculturalism: Dialogues Across Cultures. This was obviously aimed to address the contemporary context, but being a historian I was able to use this theme to tie together past and present. To do this, I returned to the context of the massive immigration into the U.S. in the late nineteenth and early twentieth centuries and how it brought to the U.S. people from almost all over the world. One of the things that I did in this and in almost every lecture that I gave in Egypt was to rattle off a list of the diverse ethnic and religious groups in the U.S. . . . . I always felt that it was absolutely necessary to impress upon Egyptians just how diverse the U.S. is and has been, because what we Americans take for granted, for others is only the haziest of notions. My audiences were always fascinated with my lists, to the point of actually starting to exclaim aloud their astonishment as I got into it. Having raised so clearly the context of diversity in the U.S., I then went on to address the question of how people of such diverse ethnicities, cultures, and religions learn to live together. To explore this question, I centered the remainder of the talk around three early-twentieth-century issues: the growth of a civic culture, the social settlement movement, and particularly Jane Addams, and the development of the social justice and women's peace movements. For the growth of civic culture, I discussed the ways in which the Progressives—very broadly defined—used nongovernmental organizations, public meetings and fora, ethnic and worker associations, and women's groups as venues for discussing social problems, constructing agendas for reform and change, and for lobbying government for change. I also discussed the promotion of free public education as an integral part of creating a democratic civic culture, the hallmarks of which include open, public debate, a willingness to allow controversy, dissent, and disagreement and to listen to contrary opinions, and to try and appreciate and understand the perspective of another person or group. In regard to the settlement house movement, I explained how the settlement house workers moved into poor, immigrant neighborhoods believing that an immigrant society could only work if there were dialogues across cultures; that only when people from different cultures learned about each other and learned to talk to one another could they understand each other. As an aspect of this movement, I was able to explain the evolution in the Progressive Era of the concept of social justice.

Although as historians we would argue about the "progressive" nature of many of these ideas, for instance debating whether public education was more about creating good, obedient citizens than about creating a democratic civic culture, my experience of teaching in another culture taught me that those kinds of professional, intellectual debates had to remain very much in the background. My audiences in Egypt did not have any factual foundation from which to enter into such debates. Thus, I found myself always tending, as I came to think of it, to "accentuate the positive." And since my mission in this talk was to promote the ideals of dialogues across cultures, focusing on the open and democratic aspects of the Progressive Era was the natural thing to do. After explaining some about American ideas of creating a national civic culture, constructing dialogues among different groups within a culture, and promoting ideals of social justice for all groups within society, I turned to Jane Addams and the women's peace movement as a hook for moving from the national to the international context. I

discussed how Addams first led a peace movement to keep the U.S. out of World War I, and then in the aftermath of that terrible war called for international dialogue that would increase mutual understanding so that war could be avoided in the future. I explained how an important element of her work for international peace was her insistence in the development of a kind of international civic culture. As so much of the interwar peace movement headed by Addams was composed of women, I was able to discuss the importance of gender for the growth of any international civic culture. Underlying that earlier peace movement was a belief by many women that if women across the world could talk to each other first and foremost as women who suffered the common grief of losing loved ones in war, then they could learn that they had more in common as human beings than they had differences in coming from different cultures. As ideas about gender form an important part of my own work, I used every opportunity that I could to broach the subject of gender, although always very carefully as this was not an idea that was talked about very openly in the Egyptian curriculum.

Finally, this conference afforded the opportunity to talk more directly to a group of students and faculty from Suez Canal and other universities who were participating. After the formal presentations we broke down into small discussion groups, with each group having one or two Americans—Fulbright professors, graduate students, or staff. In my group, the Egyptian participants were quite interested to discuss the idea of a civic culture. They readily admitted that nothing along the lines that I had described existed in their society. As an example they discussed how a program that non-governmental organizations managed to start—to immunize school-aged children—foundered once the NGO could no longer support it. What they described was the absence of any process for translating a private effort into a public program, to develop a sense that there might be a public good in government providing social services, and they were interested to figure out what it might take to change this circumstance.

My last lecture outside of Alexandria was probably my least satisfying experience as a Fulbright professor. The reasons for this serve to illustrate the somewhat tricky position in which a Fulbright lecturer might find her/himself in Egypt. First, this was at a provincial university, which meant that the students there were less cosmopolitan certainly than those in Cairo but also than many in Alexandria. Second, this lecture was done at the behest of the American Cultural Center in Alexandria, which is a branch of the U.S. Embassy. How much contact any Fulbright professor has with the State Department varies according to country. My sense in Egypt was that being seen as a representative of the U.S. government had its problems.

The students and professors attending this lecture were again from the English department, so I designed a lecture that I hoped could appeal to their interests, titled "Historical Aspects of American Literature." While the lecture itself was rather well received—the head of the department even expressed his pleasure (and surprise) that a historian could give a presentation so relevant to literature—sharing the podium with the head of the American Center seemed to generate fewer questions about U.S. history and literature as discussed in my lecture and more hostile questions attacking contemporary U.S. culture. So, for example, the points that I had made about how the diversity of religions in the U.S. meant that there could be no state religion—an idea with which my audiences readily agreed when I pointed out to them that if there were a state religion, American Muslims might have less freedom of religious worship and practice—in this context elicited negative comments about "blasphemy" and about Americans not having religion. These, I think, were comments that emanated from preconceptions that a non-religious state must be one without religion, but were also a reaction against the presence of a representative of the U.S. government. My fairly frank discussion of slavery and the aftermath of racial segregation and discrimination—which in other contexts had worked rather well—at this university seemed merely to reinforce a notion of the U.S. as an unreconstructed racist society. Similarly, my explanations of American individualism were taken as confirmation, as one student expressed it, that the U.S. had no family values. Beyond what they see on dreadful American TV and movies, this insistence seemed also to come from the fact that many of the attending students were currently reading an Edward Albee play about a totally dysfunctional American family. They were taking this play as representative of all American families, a notion that their Yale-trained professor had apparently not disabused them of. In this instance, I was struck forcefully by how the freedom that Americans usually enjoy to critique their society, often by presenting a worst-case scenario or by engaging in fairly vicious satire, can be accepted by another culture as simply a true portrait of the entire society.

While my experience of teaching U.S. history in Egypt fits somewhat into the concept of the "other" as Georg Leidenberger describes, in Egypt it seems to me there is an important difference. Many of the salient ideas and themes of U.S. history, such as individualism, lack of a state religion, a constitution that guarantees freedom of speech, a functioning civil society that allows competing interests to address government, for example, have no precise counterpart in Egyptian history. It is not merely a matter of different ideas, or different enforcement mechanisms; it is a true cultural difference in the perception of how a country and its culture work. This cultural dissonance creates two problems for any American teaching U.S. history there. The first is how to explain that history in ways that won't play too easily into preconceived notions about the U.S., and the second problem is how to formulate a balanced presentation so that one does not sound like a self-promoting American. . . . [I]n Egypt, in every presentation one had to negotiate a tricky path through the minefields of cultural differences and pride, to avoid as much as possible sounding like the "other" and implying that U.S. history and culture were more advanced than Egyptian.

All that said, the question remains, was my time in Egypt worth the difficulties of living and teaching in a very different country and culture, and one in which being a western woman presented additional daily and professional trials? My answer is yes. It was a salient experience to live and teach as the "other," which was surely how I was perceived in Egypt, and to learn directly how the U.S. and its history are seen by a society whose history and culture are so profoundly different from my own. . . .

Egyptian students and professors are curious about the U.S., but the deep-rooted historical and cultural chasms between them and Americans are very difficult to bridge. I found myself constantly thinking about how to explain the GAPE period in U.S. history as a product of its historical context, of the world as it was then, and not simply the product of U.S. arrogance, racism, and imperialism; to teach without covering up the flaws of that history or the failures to live up to the exquisite rhetoric of the country's founding documents, but also without neglecting to emphasize the strengths of American history and culture.

After living and teaching in Egypt for four months, listening to Egyptian students and professors, making acquaintances there, nothing about the events and aftermath of September 11, 2001, has surprised me. I do not want to dwell on this in this essay, except to use this observation to return to a point in my opening paragraph. As history departments in U.S. universities seek to construct a global curriculum, . . . in Egypt the opposite is happening. That is not simply the fault of U.S. historians, of course. . . . But we might well benefit from looking for ways to reach out to academics in countries such as Egypt either by applying for Fulbright teaching positions or by participating in Fulbright summer programs that bring foreign scholars to the U.S. to study U.S. history. As Russell Johnson points out, despite great cultural differences, societies around the globe undergo many similar, if not exact, experiences and problems. There may well be ways in which the GAPE experience of the U.S. of the processes of industrialization, urbanization, political and economic reform, constructing a civic culture, and agitating for women's rights, to name a few areas, can open dialogues across cultures that will help us confront contemporary global problems and increase mutual understanding.

PART V

ADDITIONAL RESOURCES

This section contains a directory of printed and Internet resources where teachers can find relevant materials beyond those included in this book. We have tried to make this list as useful as possible to instructors interested in internationalizing their treatment of U.S. history. It is not a general bibliography of American history; instead, it is focused specifically on materials that enlarge the scope of U.S. history, including books, historical journals, documents, syllabi, lesson plans, websites, and videos. Each entry is annotated to describe its contents in detail and to direct teachers to its most relevant features. Note that the list includes not only U.S. history materials, but also many world history sources that American history teachers can mine for information, course readings, and lesson plans.

Teaching American history in global perspective requires teachers to stretch their expertise beyond familiar subjects and to explore ideas that challenge conventional frameworks. We hope that the materials gathered in this book make these tasks more compelling and at the same time less daunting. Speaking from our own experiences and those of colleagues around the country, we believe that the benefits of this approach far outweigh the efforts involved in adopting it. Many teachers report renewed excitement for American history when they reframe it as part of the global story. Those who value integrative learning relish the opportunity to make connections between their American and world history courses. Students appreciate an approach that helps them relate the United States to the world and assess more carefully its distinctive qualities. They welcome the challenge of an American history that enlarges and synthesizes their knowledge rather than repeats what they have learned before or buries itself in details without context. Our students need a national history that makes sense of the multicultural and globalized world they live in and that prepares them to be effective actors and responsible citizens in it. Rethinking our nation's history and reshaping its teaching for a global age requires us to study the United States in contexts beyond itself.

CHAPTER 50

Additional Resources to Support Teaching U.S. History in a Global Context

CARL GUARNERI AND JAMES DAVIS

Note: For further research, see also the notes, bibliographies, and syllabus reading lists contained in the selections in this book. The following list includes some of the books they mention, but it supplements them with many additional sources.

Textbooks, Overviews, and Readers

World History Textbooks

Teachers of American history should consult world history textbooks for suggestions on how to link American and world history. These texts vary greatly in the amount of coverage they give the United States and in how they situate the American experience in global developments. In some textbooks, native societies of the Americas before 1500 are integrated into the timelines of societies in Africa and Oceania, but more often they are covered in a chapter of their own. Of special note is the comparative environmental focus of Felipe Fernández-Armesto, *The World: A History* (Upper Saddle River, NJ: Pearson/Prentice Hall, 2006), which begins with the geography and initial peopling of the New World and continues through the origins of cultivation, centralized empires, ecological exchanges, and the global economy. Almost all of the leading world history textbooks entwine the stories of European expansion after 1450, the African slave trade, and colonization in the Americas. Most also cover the American Revolution as part of an age of revolutions that included the French and Haitian Revolutions and Latin American independence movements.

The following textbooks offer a useful hemispheric (comparative North/South America) perspective on nation building in the nineteenth century:

Bentley, Jerry, and Herbert Ziegler. *Traditions and Encounters: A Global Perspective on the Past.* 3rd edition. New York: McGraw-Hill, 2005.

Bulliet, Richard, and others. *The Earth and Its Peoples: A Global History.* 4th edition. Boston: Houghton Mifflin, 2008.

McKay, John P., and others. *A History of World Societies.* 7th edition. Boston: Houghton Mifflin, 2007.

Tignor, Robert, and others. *Worlds Together, Worlds Apart: A History of the Modern World from the Mongol Empire to the Present.* 2nd edition. New York: W.W. Norton, 2008.

Peter Stearns, Michael Adas, and others, *World Civilizations: The Global* Experience, 5th ed. (Upper Saddle River, NJ: Pearson Prentice Hall, 2007), Howard Spodek, *The World's History,* 3rd ed. (Upper Saddle River, NJ: Pearson Prentice Hall, 2005), and Felipe Fernández-Armesto's *The World* do a good job of integrating American industrialization and urbanization into global trends. Most world history textbooks consider U.S. imperialism in the context of Europe's "New Imperialism" of the 1885–1914 era, and most blend American developments during the 1920s and the Great Depression into a more global narrative. Suggestively internationalized views of the Cold War are presented in Craig A. Lockard, *Societies, Networks, and Transitions: A Global History* (Boston: Houghton Mifflin, 2008), and Tignor, *Worlds Together, Worlds Apart.* Contemporary globalization is covered well in Bentley/Ziegler, Fernández-Armesto, and Tignor. Overall, the textbooks by Bulliet, Lockard, McKay, and Robert W. Strayer's *The Making of the Modern World,* 2nd ed. (New York: St. Martin's, 1995) offer the most substantial treatment of the United States prior to 1945, but at the price of juxtaposing its history with trends elsewhere rather than integrating it into a global framework. For settler-society approaches to the United States, see Stearns/Adas, *World Civilizations,* and Stearns, *World History in Brief,* 6th ed. (New York:

Longman, 2006). The Stearns/Adas text also contains a concise and very teachable feature essay entitled "The United States in World History."

Non-Textbook World Histories

In this category of books, the series by Eric Hobsbawm, *The Age of Revolution, 1789–1848* (1962), *The Age of Capital, 1848–1875* (1975), *The Age of Empire, 1875–1914* (1987), and *The Age of Extremes, 1914–1991* (1994)—republished by Vintage in 1996—stands out for its influence, its incisive interpretations, and its suggestive comments that place the United States in the big picture. A more recent influential synthesis, C.A. Bayly, *The Birth of the Modern World, 1780–1914* (London: Wiley-Blackwell, 2004), emphasizes the complexities of globalization and offers globally informed treatments of U.S. imperialism, white–Indian relations, and the American Civil War. Among recent books with a longer time span, Felipe Fernández-Armesto, *Millennium: A History of the Last Thousand Years* (New York: Free Press, 1996), features a strong Atlantic focus, witty prose, and many provocative insights about how the Americas fit in. J.R. McNeill and William H. McNeill, *The Human Web: A Bird's Eye View of World History* (New York: W.W. Norton, 2003), organizes human history around "webs" of power and exchange, providing a shorthand prehistory of today's globalization.

See also the following titles:

Abernethy, David B. *The Dynamics of Global Dominance: European Overseas Empires 1415–1980.* New Haven: Yale University Press, 2000. Contains frequent references to the role of the United States in European global expansion from the American War of Independence to the Cold War.

Christian, David. *Maps of Time: An Introduction to Big History.* Berkeley: University of California Press, 2004. A valuable introduction to the emerging field of "Big History," with consideration of how industrialization, technological change, and other developments in the United States contributed to larger global trends.

Cocker, Mark. *Rivers of Blood, Rivers of Gold: Europe's Conquest of Indigenous Peoples.* New York: Grove Press, 1998. Places frontier wars with Native American peoples into a global context.

Curtin, Philip D. *Cross-Cultural Trade in World History.* London: Cambridge University Press, 1984. Influential study of the cultural implications of world trade, with an interesting section on the North American fur trade.

Curtin, Philip D. *The World and the West: The European Challenge and the Overseas Response in the Age of Empire.* London: Cambridge University Press, 2000. Thoughtful discussion on the interaction of the West with rest of the world, with consideration of the United States in the Pacific, the Vietnam War, and the popularity of the Ghost Dance among Native Americans.

Diamond, Jared. *Collapse: How Societies Choose to Fail or Succeed.* New York: Penguin, 2005. A geographer examines the success or failure of various societies, with interesting sections on Montana and the Anasazi in the Southwest.

Greenfeld, Liah. *Nationalism: Five Roads to Modernity.* Cambridge, MA: Harvard University Press, 1992. An influential work of historical sociology that examines England, France, Russia, Germany, and the United States.

Hobsbawm, Eric. *Nations and Nationalism Since 1780: Programme, Myth, Reality.* London: Cambridge University Press, 1990. An overview of nationalism in world history with discussions of the English language and immigration in the United States.

Hugill, Peter J. *Geography, Technology, and Capitalism: World Trade Since 1431.* Baltimore: Johns Hopkins University Press, 1993. Contains an important section on the emergence of the United States as a world trading power.

Landes, David S. *The Wealth and Poverty of Nations: Why Some Are So Rich and Some So Poor.* New York: W.W. Norton, 1999. This provocative and highly readable overview of the rise of the West analyzes the successful industrialization of the United States.

Manning, Patrick. *Migration in World History.* London: Routledge, 2004. This concise overview incorporates the Native American crossings, the Atlantic slave trade, colonial migrations, and the industrial migration of 1870–1914 to North America into world-historical patterns.

Matossian, Mary Kilbourne. *Shaping World History: Breakthroughs in Ecology, Technology, Science, and Politics.* Armonk, NY: M.E. Sharpe, 1997. Fascinating discussion of Native American technologies and agriculture.

McNeill, J.R. *Something New Under the Sun: An Environmental History of the Twentieth-Century World.* New York: W.W. Norton, 2000. Influential overview of twentieth-century environmental history with extensive considerations of how technological and economic developments in the United States have affected the world environment.

Moore, Barrington, Jr. *Social Origins of Dictatorship and Democracy: Lord and Peasant in the Making of the Modern World.* Boston: Beacon Press, 1967. This classic comparative study of different roads to modernity analyzes the American Civil War as "the last capitalist revolution."

Pacey, Arnold. *Technology in World Civilization.* Cambridge, MA: MIT Press, 1991. Vast overview of basic trends in world technological development from the ancient world to the present period, with a comparative section on nineteenth-century technology in the United States.

Richards, John F. *The Unending Frontier: An Environmental History of the Early Modern World.* Berkeley: University of California Press, 2003. Interesting sections on fishing, hunting, and the fur trade in the United States.

Smil, Vaclav. *Energy in World History.* Boulder, CO:

Westview Press, 1994. A survey of energy uses and sources from the ancient world to the present, with discussion of energy developments in the United States.

Stavrianos, L.S. *Global Rift: The Third World Comes of Age.* New York: William Morrow and Company, 1981. Using a very dynamic definition of the Third World, Stavrianos develops a comprehensive survey of the impact of the United States and other Western nations on the non-European world.

Stearns, Peter N. *The Industrial Revolution in World History.* Boulder, CO: Westview Press, 1993. Comparative study of industrialization in different national contexts, including the United States.

Weaver, John C. *The Great Land Rush and the Making of the Modern World, 1650–1900.* Montreal: McGill-Queen's University Press, 2003. Compares natives' dispossession and the redistribution of their land in North America, Australia, New Zealand, and South Africa.

Wills, John E. *1688: A Global History.* New York: W.W. Norton, 2001. An original glance at world history in a single year, 1688, including colonial New England.

Wolf, Eric R. *Europe and the People Without History.* Berkeley: University of California Press, 1982. An anthropologist offers a path-breaking study of European expansion, with extensive materials on the Americas.

Yergin, Daniel. *The Prize: The Epic Quest for Oil, Money and Power.* New York: Simon and Schuster, 1991. Timely study of the impact of oil and the search for oil on international wars and diplomacy, emphasizing the expanding role of the United States.

World History Readers

Among several such books on the market, the following document collections contain sets of primary sources that juxtapose and/or compare American developments with those elsewhere:

Andrea, Alfred J., and James H. Overfield. *The Human Record: Sources of Global History.* 6th edition. Boston: Houghton Mifflin, 2008.

Reilly, Kevin. *Worlds of History: A Comparative Reader.* 3rd edition. New York: Bedford/St. Martin's, 2007.

Stearns, Peter, and others. *Documents in World History.* 5th edition. New York: Longman, 2008.

Wiesner, Merry E., and others. *Discovering the Global Past: A Look at the Evidence.* 3rd edition. Boston: Houghton Mifflin, 2007.

Full-Scale U.S. History Textbooks

As of yet, no full-scale American history textbook integrates world and transnational developments into its story. Such books are being developed. Meanwhile, several textbooks have added documents and feature essays that attempt to expand the national frame of their narrative. Teachers looking for global material should consult these features for lively vignettes and broadened context. For examples, see the following:

Boyer, Paul S., and others. *The Enduring Vision: A History of the American People.* 6th edition. Boston: Houghton Mifflin, 2008: "Beyond America—Global Interactions."

Brinkley, Alan. *American History: A Survey.* 12th edition. New York: McGraw-Hill, 2007: "America in the World."

Henretta, James A., and others. *America's History.* 8th edition. New York: Bedford/St. Martin's, 2008: "Voices from Abroad."

Nash, Gary B., and others. *The American People: Creating a Nation and a Society.* 7th edition. Upper Saddle River, NJ: Pearson Prentice Hall, 2005: "How Others See Us."

Norton, Mary Beth, and others. *A People and A Nation.* 8th edition. Boston: Houghton Mifflin, 2008: "Links to the World."

Roark, James L., and others. *The American Promise: A History of the United States.* 4th edition. New York: Bedford/St. Martin's, 2009: "Beyond America's Borders" and "Global Comparisons."

American History Textbooks, Overviews, and Readers

Bender, Thomas. *A Nation Among Nations: America's Place in World History.* New York: Hill & Wang, 2006. Revisits five episodes in American history to demonstrate how a global view can change historians' interpretations.

Bender, Thomas, ed. *Rethinking American History in a Global Age.* Berkeley: University of California Press, 2002. A wide-ranging and sophisticated collection of essays in which scholars discuss methods and implications of internationalizing U.S. history.

Benjamin, Thomas, Timothy Hall, and David Rutherford, eds. *The Atlantic World in the Age of Empire.* Boston: Houghton Mifflin, 2001. Part of the "Problems in World History" series, this paperback includes excerpts from important historical works covering the period from the Columbian encounter to the Atlantic Revolutions of 1776–1826.

Breen, T.H., and Timothy Hall. *Colonial America in an Atlantic World.* New York: Pearson Longman, 2004. This textbook centers on the development of the North American region that became the United States, but places its history from the eve of contact to 1763 in the context of cultural interaction and commercial rivalries.

Davies, Edward J. *The United States in World History.* London: Routledge, 2006. A concise treatment that concentrates on the modern period, especially the impact of American industrialism and mass culture.

Egerton, Douglas R., Alison Games, Jane G. Landers, Kris Lane, and Donald R. Wright. *The Atlantic World: A*

History, 1400–1888. Wheeling, IL: Harlan Davidson, 2007. A pioneering text that integrates European, North American, South American, and (to a lesser extent) African history into an Atlantic framework.

Fernández-Armesto, Felipe. *The Americas: A Hemispheric History.* New York: Modern Library, 2003. A succinct and opinionated comparative overview of North and South America from the pre-contact era to the present.

Greenfield, Gerald Michael, and John D. Buenker, eds. *Those United States: International Perspectives on American History.* 2 vols. Fort Worth, TX: Harcourt Brace College Publishers, 2000. A collection of foreign commentary on American culture and events, intended as a survey-course supplement.

Guarneri, Carl J., ed. *America Compared: American History in International Perspective.* 2 vols. 2nd ed. Boston: Houghton Mifflin, 2005. A course reader with historians' essays that place major survey-course topics in U.S. history in an international context.

Guarneri, Carl. *America in the World: United States History in Global Context.* New York: McGraw-Hill, 2007. A brief narrative text/supplement that examines issues from the contact era to contemporary globalization, situating America's role as frontier, colony, nation, and empire in global terms.

Lindaman, Dana, and Kyle Ward. *History Lessons: How Textbooks from Around the World Portray U.S. History.* New York: The New Press, 2004. Revealing excerpts from foreign secondary school textbooks covering major events in U.S. history.

Lipset, Seymour Martin. *American Exceptionalism: A Double-Edged Sword.* New York: W.W. Norton, 1996. Affirms American uniqueness by examining Americans' ideas and values comparatively.

Meinig, D.W. *The Shaping of America.* 4 vols. New Haven: Yale University Press, 1986–2005. An innovative look at North American development by a historical geographer, this series keeps regional and global trends in view and features excellent maps and diagrams. The first volume, *Atlantic America, 1492–1800,* is especially framed transnationally.

Nash, Gary. *Red, White, and Black: The Peoples of Early North America.* 5th ed. Upper Saddle River, NJ: Prentice-Hall, 2005. This fine synthesis incorporates recent scholarship and views early American history in Atlantic terms as the collision of Native American, European, and African peoples.

Reichard, Gary, and Ted Dixon, eds. *America on the World Stage: A Global Approach to U.S. History.* Urbana: University of Illinois Press, 2008. This collection gathers essays from the series on "America on the World Stage" in the *OAH Magazine of History* (see Chapter 24), and includes accompanying essays with teaching strategies.

Russo, David J. *American History from a Global Perspective: An Interpretation.* Westport, CT: Praeger, 2000. Relates selected features of U.S. history such as government, agriculture, religion, and social structure to larger world patterns.

Shannon, Timothy J. *Atlantic Lives: A Comparative Approach to Early America.* New York: Pearson Longman, 2004. This primary-source reader features first-person testimonies that place colonial American history in a comparative context with the wider Atlantic world.

Stearns, Peter N., and Noralee Frankel, eds. *Globalizing American History: The AHA Guide to Re-Imagining the U.S. Survey Course.* Washington, DC: American Historical Association, 2008. This pamphlet reprints the AHA report on "Internationalizing Student Learning Outcomes in History" (see Chapter 4) and includes four essays that discuss how to implement it in the U.S. survey.

Taylor, Alan. *American Colonies.* New York: Viking Penguin, 2001. A panoramic history of the world inside North America before 1763 that covers a wide range of groups and includes environmental considerations.

Tyrrell, Ian. *Transnational Nation: United States History in Global Perspective Since 1789.* New York: Palgrave Macmillan, 2007. This concise overview by a leading "offshore" historian of America offers a comparative perspective on the relationship between events and movements in the United States and the wider world.

Webber, Ralph E., ed. *As Others See Us: American History in the Foreign Press.* New York: Holt, Rinehart, and Winston, 1972. A useful collection of foreign commentary on American historical events.

Woodward, C. Vann, ed. *The Comparative Approach to American History.* Reprint ed. New York: Oxford University Press, 1997. Originally published in 1968, this collection includes classic essays on such topics as the Revolution, frontier, immigration, socialism, imperialism, and reform, analyzed in internationally comparative terms.

Books on Special Topics

Anderson, Bonnie. *Joyous Greetings: The First International Woman's Movement, 1830–1860.* New York: Oxford University Press, 2000. Joins American feminism to transatlantic currents in the era surrounding the 1848 European revolutions.

Anderson, Fred. *Crucible of War: The Seven Years' War and the Fate of Empire in British North America, 1754–1766.* New York: Vintage, 2000. A panoramic history that shows the global reach and historical importance of what the colonists called the French and Indian War.

Armitage, David. *The Declaration of Independence: A Global History.* Cambridge, MA: Harvard University Press, 2007. Discusses how the Declaration of Independence was interpreted outside the United States and how it influenced later nationalist and revolutionary movements.

Aronson, Marc. *The Real Revolution: The Global Story of American Independence.* New York: Clarion Books, 2005. Aimed at young readers, this lively narrative uses the latest scholarship to link the Revolution to imperial rivalries and the fortunes of the East India Company.

Axtell, James. *The Invasion Within: The Contest of Cultures in Colonial North America.* New York: Oxford University Press, 1985. A sensitive look at attempts by the French, English, and Native Americans to convert and transform each other.

Baily, Samuel L. *Immigrants in the Land of Promise: Italians in Buenos Aires and New York City, 1870–1914.* Ithaca, NY: Cornell University Press, 1999. Compares the background and adjustment of Italian immigrants to two prime New World urban destinations.

Bailyn, Bernard. *Atlantic History: Concepts and Contours.* Cambridge, MA: Harvard University Press, 2005. Sketches the rise of the concept of Atlantic history and the main features of the approach.

Berlin, Ira. *Many Thousands Gone: The First Two Centuries of Slavery in North America.* Cambridge, MA: Harvard University Press, 2000. A sweeping history that places early American slavery in regional, Caribbean, and Atlantic contexts.

Blackford, Mansel G. *The Rise of Modern Business in Great Britain, the United States, and Japan.* Chapel Hill: University of North Carolina Press, 1988. A comparative survey that stresses America's lead in corporate size and structure and attempts to explain it.

Bolt, Christine. *The Women's Movements in the United States and Britain from the 1790s to the 1920s.* Amherst: University of Massachusetts Press, 1993. Compares and demonstrates connections between the long struggles for women's rights in America and Great Britain.

Calloway, Colin G. *The American Revolution in Indian Country.* Cambridge: Cambridge University Press, 1995. Presents the American Revolution as a multisided conflict in which Native Americans were involved but which by and large diminished their lands and power.

Calloway, Colin G. *New Worlds for All: Indians, Europeans, and the Remaking of Early America.* Baltimore, MD: Johns Hopkins University Press, 1998. An innovative synthesis that recasts colonial North America as the story of cross-cultural encounters and exchanges.

Carwardine, Richard. *Transatlantic Revivalism: Popular Evangelicalism in Britain and America, 1790–1865.* Westport, CT: Greenwood, 1973. Interprets the Second Great Awakening in light of the Anglo-American Protestant revival movement.

Crosby, Alfred. *The Columbian Exchange: Biological and Cultural Consequences of 1492.* Westport, CT: Greenwood, 2003. A pioneering study of the transfer of plants, animals, and diseases between the Old and New Worlds, originally published in 1972.

Crosby, Alfred. *Ecological Imperialism: The Biological Expansion of Europe, 900–1900.* Westport, CT: Greenwood, 2004. Describes Europe's makeover of the flora and fauna in the "Neo-Europes" of the temperate New World.

Davis, David Brion. *Inhuman Bondage: The Rise and Fall of Slavery in the New World.* New York: Oxford University Press, 2006. Situates New World slavery in a global context and illuminates important historical debates over its rise, features, and decline.

Dawley, Alan. *Changing the World: American Progressives in War and Revolution.* Princeton: Princeton University Press, 2003. Places Woodrow Wilson's World War I crusade and more radical variants in a global setting that includes Bolshevism, imperialism, and international social movements.

Degler, Carl N. *Neither Black Nor White: Slavery and Race Relations in Brazil and the United States.* Madison: University of Wisconsin Press, 1986. Compares life in and under slavery in the two largest New World slave societies.

deGrazia, Victoria. *Irresistible Empire: America's Advance Through 20th-Century Europe.* Cambridge, MA: Harvard University Press, 2005. How American consumer culture transformed traditional Europe and thwarted Nazi and Soviet alternatives.

Doyle, Don H., and Marco Antonio Pamplona, eds. *Nationalism in the New World.* Athens: University of Georgia Press, 2006. Sophisticated essays that "Americanize" debates on nationalism by analyzing the various forms of nationhood in the United States, Canada, and Latin America.

Dubois, Laurent. *Avengers of the New World: The Story of the Haitian Revolution.* Cambridge, MA: Harvard University Press, 2004. A vivid narrative history that suggests the Haitian Revolution's radicalism and importance in hemispheric and world-history terms.

Dudziak, Mary L. *Cold War Civil Rights: Race and the Image of American Democracy.* Princeton: Princeton University Press, 2000. Demonstrates how Cold War considerations moved U.S. policymakers toward supporting racial equality under the law.

Dunn, Susan. *Sister Revolutions: French Lightning, American Light.* New York: Faber and Faber, 1999. An engaging comparative analysis of the two revolutions that emphasizes their differences, including provocative final chapters on their legacies.

Egnal, Marc. *Divergent Paths: How Culture and Institutions Have Shaped North American Growth.* New York: Oxford University Press, 1996. Focusing on the northern and southern United States and French Canada, this book sorts out the factors that shaped different paths of economic development in these regions.

Elliott, J.H. *The Old World and the New, 1492–1650.* Cambridge: Cambridge University Press, 1970. A concise study of the impact of discovery and conquest on Old World society, economy, and culture.

Elliot, John H. *Empires of the Atlantic World: Britain and Spain in America, 1492–1830.* New Haven: Yale University Press, 2006. A grand synthesis that compares the empires constructed by Spain and England in the Americas.

Fredrickson, George M. *Black Liberation: A Comparative History of Black Ideologies in the United States and South Africa.* New York: Oxford University Press, 1995. Traces parallels and shared influences between American and South African black activists.

Fredrickson, George M. *White Supremacy: A Comparative Study of American and South African History.* New York: Oxford University Press, 1981. A sweeping comparative history of two settler societies, with many insights about race, frontiers, and nation building.

Garraty, John A. *The Great Depression.* New York: Anchor Books, 1987. Enlarges analysis of the Depression to include connections and comparisons among the United States, Europe, and Latin America.

Gump, James O. *The Dust Rose Like Smoke: The Subjugation of the Zulu and the Sioux.* Lincoln: University of Nebraska Press, 1994. Parallels America's reservation wars with Britain's campaigns against South African natives in the era of imperialism.

Hanke, Lewis, ed. *Do the Americas Have a Common History?* New York: Knopf, 1964. Brings classic and modern essays into dialogue on the "Bolton thesis," the idea of a shared Western Hemispheric history.

Harrison, John F.C. *Quest for the New Moral World: Robert Owen and the Owenites in Britain and America.* New York: Scribner's, 1969. A pioneering study of utopian socialism and labor reform that offers a model for transatlantic social history.

Heffer, Jean. *The United States and the Pacific: History of a Frontier.* Notre Dame, IN: University of Notre Dame Press, 2002. Traces the long history of American exploration, trade, and colonizing in the Pacific basin.

Hoerder, Dirk. *Cultures in Contact: World Migrations in the Second Millennium.* Durham, NC: Duke University Press, 2002. A sweeping overview that relates colonial settlement, the slave trade, and later European and Asian migrations to the New World to developments in world history.

Hogan, Michael J., and Thomas G. Paterson, eds. *Explaining the History of American Foreign Relations.* 2nd ed. Cambridge: Cambridge University Press, 2004. Helpful essays that review topics and trends in recent scholarship on U.S. foreign relations.

Jacobson, Matthew Frye. *Barbarian Virtues: The United States Encounters Foreign Peoples at Home and Abroad, 1876–1917.* New York: Hill and Wang, 2000. An examination of American contact with the world from 1876 until World War I, arguing for a close relationship between immigration and American foreign policy.

Johnson, Paul. *The Birth of the Modern: World Society, 1815–1830.* New York: HarperCollins, 1991. One of the few books that sees Jacksonian democracy as part of a transatlantic movement in the age of reform.

Klein, Herbert S. *The Atlantic Slave Trade.* Cambridge: Cambridge University Press, 1999. A concise and reliable overview of how the trade operated and its impact on the Americas.

Kolchin, Peter. *Unfree Labor: American Slavery and Russian Freedom.* Cambridge, MA: Harvard University Press, 1987. This detailed comparison of coerced labor in distant lands yields revealing similarities and differences.

Kramer, Paul A. *The Blood of Government: Race, Empire, the United States, and the Philippines.* Chapel Hill: University of North Carolina Press, 2006. This analysis of American colonialism traces U.S. participation in the global construction of race and empire.

Lafeber, Walter. *The American Search for Opportunity, 1865–1913.* Cambridge: Cambridge University Press, 1995. Argues that the U.S. rise to world power disrupted international relations.

Lafeber, Walter. *The New Empire: An Interpretation of American Expansion, 1860–1898.* Ithaca: Cornell University Press, 1963. An essay on American expansion in the late nineteenth century that emphasizes economic motives.

Langley, Lester D. *The Americas in the Age of Revolution, 1750–1850.* New Haven: Yale University Press, 1996. Compares North American and Latin American independence movements and the contrasting societies that emerged.

Langley, Lester D. *The Americas in the Modern Age.* New Haven: Yale University Press, 2003. Continues the story of North-South interactions and comparisons after 1850.

Linebaugh, Peter, and Marcus Rediker. *The Many-Headed Hydra: Sailors, Slaves, Commoners, and the Hidden History of the Revolutionary Atlantic.* Boston: Beacon Press, 2000. A pioneering work of transnational history, this book finds a revolutionary counterculture among exploited workers on the Atlantic's waters.

Lipset, Seymour Martin. *Continental Divide: The Values and Institutions of the United States and Canada.* New York: Routledge, 1990. Charts cultural and political differences between neighboring nations, and suggests the historical reasons they arose.

Lipset, Seymour Martin. *The First New Nation: The United States in Historical and Comparative Perspective.* New York: W.W. Norton, 1979. Considers the young United States as a new nation comparable to emerging twentieth-century nations in Africa and Asia.

Lipset, Seymour Martin, and Gary Marks. *It Didn't Hap-*

pen Here: Why Socialism Failed in the United States. New York and London: W.W. Norton, 2000. An analysis of the "problem" of American socialism that stresses the nation's distinctive cultural attitudes and political institutions.

Longley, Kyle. *In the Eagle's Shadow: The United States and Latin America.* Wheeling, IL: Harlan Davidson, 2002. A readable and reliable survey of U.S.-Latin American relations since independence.

Macmillan, Margaret. *Paris 1919: Six Months That Changed the World.* New York: Random House, 2002. A dramatic history of the Versailles treaty, the U.S. role in it, and the consequences of the World War I settlement.

Mann, Charles. *1491: New Revelations of the Americas Before Columbus.* New York: Knopf, 2005. Uses recent archaeological and anthropological evidence to portray Native Americans as more numerous and technologically advanced than previously thought.

Montejano, David. *Anglos and Mexicans in the Making of Texas, 1836–1986.* Austin: University of Texas Press, 1987. A model borderland study that charts changing ethnic and racial relations.

Nichols, Roger L. *Indians in the United States and Canada: A Comparative History.* Lincoln: University of Nebraska Press, 1998. Integrates the history of government policies and Indian life on both sides of the border.

Nugent, Walter. *Crossings: The Great Transatlantic Migrations, 1870–1914.* Bloomington: Indiana University Press, 1992. An informative analysis of European immigration to the United States compared to Argentina, Brazil, and Canada.

O'Shaughnessy, Andrew Jackson. *An Empire Divided: The American Revolution and the British Caribbean.* Philadelphia: University of Pennsylvania Press, 2000. Shows the reverberations of the American Revolution in the British West Indies, and suggests why the colonies there did not rebel.

Palmer, R.R. *The Age of the Democratic Revolution: A Political History of Europe and America, 1760–1800.* 2 vols. Princeton: Princeton University Press, 1959. The classic account that locates the American Revolution in a transatlantic era of revolution.

Pells, Richard. *Not Like Us: How Europeans Have Loved, Hated, and Transformed American Culture Since World War II.* New York: Basic Books, 1997. Surveys the reception of American mass culture in Europe, arguing that Europeans have not become "Americanized."

Plummer, Brenda Gayle. *Rising Wind: Black Americans and U.S. Foreign Affairs, 1935–1960.* Chapel Hill: University of North Carolina Press, 1996. Details American blacks' interest in Pan-Africanism and other racial struggles abroad.

Rauchway, Eric. *Blessed Among Nations: How the World Made America.* New York: Hill and Wang, 2006. Argues that America's openness to flows of labor, capital, and technology helped the United States to become a world power and, paradoxically, an "exceptional" nation.

Rodgers, Daniel T. *Atlantic Crossings: Social Politics in a Progressive Age.* Cambridge, MA: Harvard University Press, 1998. Shows how Americans borrowed many welfare-state measures from Europeans from the 1890s to the 1940s.

Rosenberg, Emily S. *Spreading the American Dream: American Economic and Cultural Expansion, 1890–1945.* New York: Hill and Wang, 1982. How American colonialism and aggressive trade policies promoted U.S. business and mass culture abroad.

Rupp, Leila J. *Worlds of Women: The Making of an International Women's Movement.* Princeton: Princeton University Press, 1997. A path-breaking comparative and transnational history of transatlantic women's organizations from the 1880s to 1945.

Rydell, Robert W. *All the World's a Fair: Visions of Empire at American International Expositions, 1876–1916.* Chicago: University of Chicago Press, 1984. Interesting examination of American efforts at self-representation through world fairs.

Schivelbusch, Wolfgang. *Three New Deals: Reflections on Roosevelt's America, Mussolini's Italy, and Hitler's Germany, 1933–1939.* New York: Macmillan, 2006. Investigates the shared elements of populism and paternalism in New Deal and fascist responses to the crisis of the Great Depression.

Silbey, David J. *A War of Frontier and Empire: The Philippine-American War, 1899–1902.* New York: Hill and Wang, 2007. A multifaceted reconsideration of the American war in the Philippines with discussion of emerging Philippine nationalism, American domestic politics, and American foreign policy.

Slatta, Richard N. *Cowboys in the Americas.* New Haven: Yale University Press, 1990. A colorful survey of shared cowboy practice and lore on the North and South American frontiers.

Suri, Jeremi, ed. *The Global Revolutions of 1968.* New York: W.W. Norton, 2007. A collection of primary sources and historians' essays that situates American protest movements of the 1960s globally.

Takaki, Ronald. *Strangers from a Different Shore: A History of Asian Americans.* New York: Little, Brown, 1989. A colorful survey notable for its use of oral testimony and its inclusion of Hawaii.

Tucker, Richard P. *Insatiable Appetite: The United States and the Ecological Degradation of the Tropical World.* Berkeley: University of California Press, 2000. Analyzes the workings of "corporate imperialism" in Latin American "banana republics" and elsewhere.

Turner, Frederick Jackson. *Frontier and Section: Selected Essays.* Englewood Cliffs, NJ: Prentice-Hall, 1961. Includes Turner's classic essay on the significance of the frontier in American history.

Tyrrell, Ian. *True Gardens of the Gods: Californian-Australian Environmental Reform, 1860–1930*. Berkeley: University of California Press, 1999. This pioneering transnational history analyzes environmental exchanges between two similar nations on the Pacific rim.

Weber, David J. *The Spanish Frontier in North America*. New Haven: Yale University Press, 1992. Examines Spanish explorations, missions, and policies in the land that later became the U.S. Southwest.

Weinberg, Gerhard L. *A World at Arms: A Global History of World War II*. Cambridge: Cambridge University Press, 1994. A superb one-volume history that places U.S. participation in perspective.

Westad, Odd. *The Global Cold War: Third World Interventions and the Making of Our Times*. Cambridge: Cambridge University Press, 2006. Interweaves decolonization and U.S.-Soviet rivalry for influence in the Third World into the story of the Cold War.

White, Richard. *The Middle Ground: Indians, Empires, and Republics in the Great Lakes Region, 1650–1815*. Cambridge: Cambridge University Press, 1991. Describes borderlands where European rivals and Indian nations negotiated coexistence before American independence altered the balance of power.

Williams, William Appleman. *Empire as a Way of Life*. New York: Oxford University Press, 1980. An iconoclastic analysis that traces U.S. imperial designs to the early 1800s and links continental to overseas expansion.

Woodruff, William. *America's Impact on the World: A Study of the Role of the U.S. in the World Economy, 1750–1970*. New York: Wiley, 1975. Emphasizing technology, finance, and trade, this study contains useful data on how the U.S. was shaped by global developments, then influenced them.

Journals

49th Parallel

www.49thparallel.bham.ac.uk. Based in the UK, this is an interdisciplinary e-journal devoted to North American studies. Its focus is strongly twentieth century, and it publishes innovative and challenging academic work.

American Historical Review

The official publication of the American Historical Association, the *AHR* brings together articles, roundtables, and book reviews from all fields of historical study. In addition to articles with global perspectives on the United States, since the 1990s it has featured periodic "*AHR* Forums" on special topics, many of which are useful for situating American history among global developments. See, for example, the following *AHR* Forums:

"American Exceptionalism in an Age of International History," *AHR* 96, no. 4 (October 1991): 1031–1072.

"The New British History in Atlantic Perspective," *AHR* 104, no. 2 (April 1999): 426–500.

"Borders and Borderlands," *AHR* 104, no. 3 (June 1999): 813–841.

"Revolutions in the Americas," *AHR* 105, no. 1 (February 2000): 92–152.

"Crossing Slavery's Boundaries," *AHR* 105, no. 2 (April 2000): 451–484.

"Creating National Identities in a Revolutionary Era," *AHR* 106, no. 4 (October 2001): 1214–1289.

"Amalgamation and the Historical Distinctiveness of the United States," *AHR* 108, no. 5 (December 2003): 1362–1414.

"Oceans of History," *AHR* 111, no. 3 (June 2006): 717–780.

"The Problem of American Homicide," *AHR* 111, no. 1 (February 2006): 75–114.

"Historical Perspectives on Anti-Americanism," *AHR* 111, no. 4 (October 2006): 1041–1129.

"On Transnational History," *AHR* 111, no. 5 (December 2006): 1440–1464.

"Entangled Empires in the Atlantic World," *AHR* 112, no. 3 (June 2007): 710–799 and no. 5 (December 2007): 1414–1431.

American Quarterly

http://www.americanquarterly.org. This official journal of the American Studies Association has been absorbed in recent years in theoretical debates over defining "postnational" and "transnational" approaches to the study of American culture. See especially, Janice Radway, "What's in a Name? Presidential Address to the American Studies Association, 20 November 1998," *American Quarterly* 51 (March 1999): 1–32, and later articles that continued the debate.

American Studies

www2.ku.edu/~amerstud. A tri-annual interdisciplinary journal sponsored by the Mid-America American Studies Association and the University of Kansas. See especially the theme issue on "Globalization, Transnationalism, and the End of the American Century," 41, nos. 2–3 (Summer/Fall 2000).

American Studies International

www.gwu.edu/~asi. Published since 1962, *ASI* has served as a forum for exchange about the study of the United States by scholars throughout the world. *ASI* publishes scholarly articles, bibliographical essays, book reviews, and announcements of conferences and programs. In 2005 *ASI* was absorbed by *American Studies*. See especially the following theme issues of *ASI:*

"American Studies? A Dialogue Across the Americas," 37, no. 3 (October 1999).
"Asia and America at Century's End," 38, no. 2 (June 2000).
"Global Feminisms, American Studies," 38, no. 3 (October 2000).

Common-Place

www.common-place.org. Sponsored by the American Antiquarian Society and the Gilder-Lehrman Institute, this online journal covers early America (to about 1860) and offers lively feature articles, book reviews, and first-person essays by scholars and teachers that describe their research discoveries and curricular projects. See especially the following special issues:

"Early Cities of the Americas," 2, no. 2 (July 2003).
"Pacific Routes," 5, no. 2 (January 2005).

Comparative American Studies

www.maney.co.uk. Published in print in the UK but also available to subscribers online, *Comparative American Studies* is an international journal that extends scholarly debates in American studies beyond the United States, repositioning discussions about American culture within an international, comparative framework. Intended for a theoretically inclined scholarly audience, it focuses on literature, recent politics, and popular culture.

History Compass

www.blackwell-compass.com/subject/history. This online journal offers state-of-the-field essays and bibliographies in many areas of history, serving as a good entry point for nonspecialists. Many articles also contain teaching guides or suggestions.

History Now

www.historynow.org. An online quarterly journal of the Gilder Lehrman Institute of American History, this publication brings the latest scholarship to teachers and students. Its theme issues feature brief essays by recognized scholars, lesson plans for school teachers, and links to bibliographies, web sources, and other materials. For internationalized content, see especially issues 3 (March 2005) on immigration and 12 (June 2007) on the age of exploration.

The History Teacher

www.thehistoryteacher.org. Addressed to teachers from the secondary level through college, this quarterly journal includes overviews of recent trends in scholarship, reports on new curricula and teaching techniques, and reviews of textbooks and other classroom materials. In recent years it has devoted increased attention to world history and to globally informed U.S. history.

Itinerario

www.let.leidenuniv.nl/history/itinerario. Covering the history of European overseas expansion and its cross-cultural effects, *Itinerario* is an online international journal published three times a year by the Institute for the History of European Expansion (IGEER) of Leiden University, the Netherlands. Focusing on the period before 1800, it contains articles, interviews, and book reviews.

Journal of American History

The major U.S. journal for American history, the *JAH* undertook an internationalizing campaign in the 1990s that included greater input from historians abroad and more attention to comparative and transnational topics. See especially articles in the following special issues:

"Internationalizing the *Journal of American History*," *JAH* 79, no. 2 (September 1992).
"The Declaration of Independence in Translation," *JAH* 85, no. 4 (March 1999).
"Rethinking the Nation-State: Mexico and the United States," *JAH* 86, no. 2 (September 1999).
"The Nation and Beyond: Transnational Perspectives on the United States," *JAH* 86, no. 3 (December 1999).
Also see the following "Roundtables":
"Cinqué and the Historians: How a Story Takes Hold," *JAH* 87, no. 3 (December 2000).
"Empires and Intimacies: Lessons from (Post) Colonial Studies," *JAH* 88, no. 3 (December 2001).
"History and September 11," *JAH* 89, no. 2 (September 2002).
"Brown v. Board of Education, Fifty Years After," *JAH* 91, no. 1 (June 2004).
"Contemporary Anti-Americanism," *JAH* 93, no. 2 (September 2006).

Journal of World History

http://www.uhpress.hawaii.edu/journals/jwh. This journal addresses teaching as well as scholarship and offers articles, review essays, and book reviews on global and globally informed regional history. Articles on Atlantic history, slavery, race, migration, industrialization, and other topics include comparative or other material that can be very useful to globally minded U.S. history teachers.

OAH Magazine of History

www.oah.org/pubs/magazine. Now appearing quarterly, this publication of the Organization of American Historians makes scholarship relevant to secondary-school and college history classrooms. Its thematic issues include summaries of recent scholarship, articles on particular events or topics, teaching strategies, and lesson plans. For invaluable globally informed articles, see especially the series entitled "America on the World Stage" (Chapter 24 in this book) and the special issues on the Spanish Frontier in North America (vol. 14, no. 4, Summer 2000) and Atlantic History (vol. 18, no. 3, April 2004).

Safundi: The Journal of South African and American Studies

www.safundi.com. An innovative interdisciplinary journal published in print and online, *Safundi* contains articles, reviews, and teaching essays that link and compare U.S. and South African cultural and historical topics. Its website also maintains a database of comparative syllabi.

Social Education

www.socialstudies.org/publications/se. Social Education is the official journal of the National Council for the Social Studies. Published seven times annually, it includes topical overviews, teaching strategies, and classroom materials useful to K–12 and college social studies teachers.

World History Connected

http://worldhistoryconnected.org. An "e-journal of learning and teaching," *WHC* is aimed at world history teachers and students. It presents innovative classroom-ready scholarship, keeps readers current on the latest research and debates, discusses learning and teaching methods and practices, offers teaching resources, and reports on exemplary teaching. Many of its articles and reviews include material that suggests how to compare or connect American history to global developments.

Syllabi

AP Central

http://apcentral.collegeboard.com/apc/Controller.jpf. Includes four annotated sample syllabi for AP U.S. History.

Center for History and New Media—Syllabus Finder

http://chnm.gmu.edu/tools/syllabi. A searchable database of over 1 million syllabi at the Center for History and New Media and over 500,000 syllabi via Google.

History Matters—Syllabus Central

http://historymatters.gmu.edu/browse/syllabus. This feature provides annotated syllabi that offer creative approaches to teaching, with particular emphasis on innovative ways of organizing the U.S. survey and integrating technology.

Websites/Organizations

For the most complete reference guide to Internet resources in U.S. history, see Dennis A. Trinkle and Scott A. Merriman, eds., *The American History Highway: A Guide to Internet Resources on U.S., Canadian, and Latin American History* (Armonk, NY: M.E. Sharpe, 2007).

American Council on Education

http://www.acenet.edu//AM/Template.cfm?Section=Home. The ACE is a coordinating body for American institutions of higher education. Through its Center for International Initiatives, the ACE offers programs and services that enhance internationalization on U.S. campuses and situate U.S. higher education in a global context. Among its publications are works on globalizing the campus and curriculum.

American Historical Association

www.historians.org. The American Historical Association website shares important information for scholars and teachers (primarily at the college and high school levels) in the field of history. One section, "Resources for Teachers," includes essays and reports on professional development, history standards, and textbooks as well as links to projects such as "Teaching and Learning in the Digital Age," which contains ideas and documents for introductory survey courses. On this website, see also the report to the ACE entitled "Internationalizing Student Learning Outcomes in History," and the syllabus and other documents related to an NEH/AHA Institute on "Rethinking America in Global Perspective" held in summer 2008. Finally, the AHA's project "The Next Generation of History Teachers," reprinted on its website, advocates training in world and comparative history for future K–12 teachers.

America's History in the Making

www.learner.org/resources/series208.html. Produced by Oregon Public Broadcasting, this video course covers the pre-Columbian period to Reconstruction and is designed for middle and high school teachers. It features eight half-hour video programs with faculty guide, online textbook, and supporting website.

Anarchy Archives: Online Research Center on the History and Theory of Anarchism

http://dwardmac.pitzer.edu/Anarchist_Archives/index.html. This site connects the anarchist movement in the United States to worldwide anarchist developments, with links to major anarchists and links to complete pamphlets and contemporary periodicals. There is also a bibliography and time line.

AP Central

http://apcentral.collegeboard.com/apc/Controller.jpf. This site contains essential information and aids for those who teach AP U.S. and World History, and much that is useful for non-AP teachers interested in globalizing their U.S. courses. Go to the AP U.S. History Course Home Page (*http://apcentral.collegeboard.com/apc/public/courses/teachers_corner/3501.html*) for links to detailed course outlines, sample syllabi, AP exam information, teaching resource materials (web guides and teaching units), "state of the field" articles by noted historians, and essays on teaching the AP U.S. history course. Follow the link for Teachers' Resources Reviews for evaluations of textbooks and websites. You may also want to join an electronic discussion group for AP U.S. history teachers. Since the College Board has taken an interest in a more globally informed approach to U.S. history, expect additional materials to be posted on this site.

Avalon Project at Yale Law School: Documents in Law, History, and Diplomacy

http://yale.edu/lawweb/avalon/avalon.htm. This site features extensive document collections in law, history, economics, and diplomacy, with special emphasis on the eighteenth to the twenty-first centuries. A subject guide for the documents is included.

Best of History Websites

www.besthistorysites.net/about.shtml. Contains links to over 1,200 history-related websites, including K–12 history lesson plans, teacher guides, activities, games, and quizzes.

Bridging World History

www.learner.org/channel/courses/worldhistory. This integrated course guide offers teacher and classroom materials to support the teaching of world history. It divides world history into 26 units and for each unit includes content overviews, themes, questions, pdf versions of readings, maps, audio glossaries, and video segments. Although it is somewhat short on North American content, the following units contain useful American history materials:

Unit 16: Food, Demographics, and Culture
Unit 17: Ideas Shape the World (Revolutions)
Unit 19: Global Industrialization
Unit 25: Global Popular Culture

Canadian-American Center, University of Maine, Orono

www.umaine.edu/canam/cartography/britishatlantic.html. Includes a series of 50 downloadable, high-resolution maps on Atlantic trade and the settlement of British America. These maps, which are extremely useful for adopting an Atlantic perspective to colonial history, are supplements to Stephen J. Hornsby's *British Atlantic, American Frontier: Spaces of Power in Early Modern British America* (2005).

Carrie: A Full-Text Electronic Library

http://vlib.iue.it/carrie. A central clearinghouse for sites that feature collections of online documents. It includes such sites as EuroDocs (for European history) and AMDOCS (for U.S. history). There is also an important link to documents on World War I.

Center for World History, University of California, Santa Cruz

http://cwh.ucsc.edu. This site includes teaching resources for world history and for an internationalized U.S. history. Of special interest is a graduate student collaborative project on globalizing the U.S. history survey, which includes syllabi, rationales, sample lectures, and a critique.

Cold War: From Yalta to Malta (CNN)

www.cnn.com/SPECIALS/cold.war. Links to the national security archive, interactive maps, and a chronology. Click on "Educator's Guide" for help with curriculum materials.

Columbus and the Age of Discovery

http://muweb.millersville.edu/~columbus. Contains over 1,100 texts and articles on Columbus and European expansion with links to discovery literature and the Library of Congress 1492 exhibition.

Contemporary Postcolonial and Postimperial Literature in English

www.postcolonialweb.org. An extensive and excellent introduction to the important field of postcolonial studies, with essays that define postcolonial studies, globalization, and other topics. There are links to other essays and to such subjects as demography, religion, economics, science and technology, bibliography, and web links—all organized by country. There is also a link to diaspora studies.

Digital History

www.digitalhistory.uh.edu. This collaborative site includes an online U.S. history textbook and special links for teachers to lessons plans, resource guides, historical exhibits, flash movies, primary sources (including speeches), and games. Current offerings are especially strong on race and ethnic history, the Civil War, and the history of technology.

Discovery Education

http://school.discoveryeducation.com. This project of the Discovery Channel offers a "Lesson Plan Library" for grades K–12 on dozens of topics in U.S. history, many of them keyed to videos, with links to readings and other websites.

EDSITEment

http://edsitement.neh.gov. This is a sponsored project of the National Endowment for the Humanities in partnership with the Thinkfinity project, funded by the Verizon Foundation. The EDSITEment website includes dozens of online lesson plans in American and world history that integrate Internet materials, including documents. (See Chapter 31 in this book.)

FirstWorldWar.Com: The War to End All Wars

www.firstworldwar.com. This site offers an abundant trove of materials for teaching about World War I, with links to primary source documents, posters, audio files, video clips, a time line, websites, maps, and diaries.

Gilder Lehrman Institute of American History

www.gilderlehrman.org/teachers. This site offers teaching modules on major topics in American history, quizzes, and primary source documents, many taken from the Gilder Lehrman Institute's valuable collection. Also included is information about Teaching American History grants and summer professional development opportunities.

H-Net Online: Humanities and the Social Sciences

www.h-net.org. A website produced by an extensive international and interdisciplinary collaboration of scholars and teachers. There are links to peer-reviewed essays in various fields of world and U.S. history and to multimedia materials. H-Net is perhaps best known for its growing list of specialized online discussion groups. By joining such free discussion groups as H-USA, H-Women, H-Teach, H-Survey, H-Slavery, and H-World, teachers can read comments from other scholars and ask questions themselves.

History.com

www.history.com. The History Channel website has links to U.S. and world history speeches, maps, a world timeline, and 1–8 minute video clips.

History Cooperative

www.historycooperative.org. A joint site managed by the Organization of American History, the University of Illinois Press, and the National Academy Press for members of the OAH. The site provides full text of current issues of journals, including the *Journal of World History* and the *History Teacher.* There are additional connections to historical map collections and history links on the Internet.

History Matters: The U.S. Survey Course on the Web

http://historymatters.gmu.edu. Designed for high school and college teachers and students, this site features web links and online resources for U.S. history, including syllabi. The History Matters archive includes annotated reviews of historical exhibits and websites. Of unusual interest is the "Secrets of Great History Teachers"—transcripts of interviews with prominent faculty. Also features a digital blackboard for teaching assignments using web resources, primary source documents, guides on how to use historical evidence, and links to websites.

The History Place: The Past into the Future

www.historyplace.com. Established by Philip Gavin in 1996 for those interested in history, this site contains movie reviews (on popular films), various opinions on historical subjects, slide shows, and much material on World War II and Europe. More on international slavery and comparative revolutions is promised.

Hyperwar: A Hypertext History of the Second World War

www.ibiblio.org/hyperwar. Public domain materials in English on World War II. There are extensive secondary and primary sources (mainly generated by the U.S. government), broken down by theater of operations.

Immigration to the United States, 1789–1930

http://ocp.hul.harvard.edu/immigration. Part of the Harvard University Open Collections Program, this site contains a generous selection of materials from Harvard's collections on American immigration. Included are 1,800 books and pamphlets, 9,000 photographs, 200 maps, and 13,000 pages of manuscript collections, including records of the Immigration Restriction League. The collection is searchable by topics, people, themes, organizations, and keywords. The site also features a useful timeline of landmarks in U.S. immigration history.

Internet History Sourcebooks

www.fordham.edu/halsall. A site to serve teachers in U.S. and European history with links to hundreds of primary source documents. The Modern History Sourcebook is especially useful.

Interpreting the Declaration of Independence by Translation

http://chnm.gmu.edu/declaration. Includes the *Journal of American History*'s March 1999 roundtable on the Declaration of Independence in translation, plus several translations.

James Ford Bell Library: Trade Products in Early Modern History

http://bell.lib.umn.edu/Products/Products.html. A clever site, useful for both students and teachers, that explores world trade in the early modern period by links to various commodities, among them beavers, coffee, porcelain, tobacco, sea otters, and codfish.

Library of Congress

www.loc.gov/index.html. A general gateway to the numerous exhibitions and rich online resources available at the Library of Congress (LOC). Click on "Library Catalogs" for information about the Library's holdings, and "Teachers" for links to lesson plans and activities. "American Memory" contains millions of documents, photos, maps, and audio/video clips on American history and culture. "Exhibitions" houses archived LOC exhibits since 1992, including those on Columbus, Benjamin Franklin, Lewis and Clark, and Women at the Front in World War II. "Today in History" and "Portraits of the World" provide links to websites about individual countries and their histories.

MERLOT History Portal

www.history.merlot.org. MERLOT stands for Multimedia Educational Resource for Learning and Online Teaching. A collaboration initiated by the California State University system and later joined by libraries, professional societies, and other state universities, MERLOT features a collection of peer-reviewed online history learning materials suitable for higher education. Its resources include model lesson plans for modules in the U.S. History Survey and links to history learning materials on the web, including topical websites, historical simulations, lesson plans, and digital archives.

The National Archives

www.archives.gov. Click on "Educators and Students," then "Teaching with Documents" for teacher-submitted lesson plans with supporting National Archives documents. Among the lesson topics are Eli Whitney's cotton gin, the Amistad case, the Dawes Act, the anti-Chinese movement, the Zimmerman telegram, and Pearl Harbor. Among other useful links and materials is "Start Your Research," on how to use online materials and research tools. There are also links to the various presidential libraries and their materials.

National Center for History in the Schools, UCLA

http://nchs.ucla.edu. This site contains online versions of the National History Standards for U.S. and world history, along with summaries of teaching units.

National Council for History Education

www.nche.net. The NCHE is a nonprofit corporation dedicated to promoting the importance of history in schools and in society. This site includes information about their publications and annual conference. It also features useful links to dozens of Internet history resources.

National Council for the Social Studies

www.ncss.org. Founded in 1921, National Council for the Social Studies is the largest association in the country devoted solely to social studies education. This site contains archived lesson plans and "teaching with documents" units, many of which were published originally in *Social Education.* Also included are teaching resources culled from other websites. Note: some of these materials are available to NCSS members only.

National History Education Clearinghouse

http://teachinghistory.org. Launched in February 2008, this project is supported by a grant from the U.S. Department of Education. It is partnered by the Center for History and New Media at George Mason University, the History Education group at Stanford University, the American Historical Association, and the National History Center. Eventually, the site promises to include seven features: history education news, teaching materials, best practices, policy and research, professional development for teachers, and information about Teaching American History grants.

National Humanities Center/TeacherServe

www.nhc.rtp.nc.us/tserve/tsaboutus.htm. A site sponsored by the National Humanities Center (an independent institute for advanced studies in the humanities), TeacherServe is expressly designed to help teachers with course planning and with incorporating important scholarship into courses. Sections on religion and American culture and the environment and American history offer several important content essays for teachers.

Naval Historical Center

www.history.navy.mil. This official Naval Historical Center website offers links to online photo collections, bibliographies, online publications, naval history by period, and wars and conflicts.

Organization of American Historians

www.oah.org. The website of the main organization for scholars and teachers of U.S. history includes most back issues of the *OAH Magazine of History,* with many downloadable articles and lesson plans. Its section on teaching resources includes information on teacher certification and state-based standards. You can read the complete *La Pietra Report* of 2000 on internationalizing U.S. history. And the publications link allows you to purchase teaching units, with documents and lesson plans, aimed at grades 7–12, co-produced by the OAH and the National Center for History in the Schools. Among the units with international content are "Asian Immigration to the United States," "U.S. Indian Policy: From Removal to Reservations," "The Philippine-American War," and "The Vietnam War—An American Dilemma."

PBS Teachers

www.pbs.org/teachers/socialstudies. Developed by the Public Broadcasting Service to help teachers, this site includes film references, online courses for the social sciences, a PBS teachers newsletter, and curriculum materials such as lesson plans and assignments. There is valuable information for those interested in teaching, learning, and professional development online, as well as an extensive guide to PBS educational videos on U.S. history, world history, and other subjects.

Primary Source

www.primarysource.org/default.php. A New England–based nonprofit organization, Primary Source promotes history and humanities education by connecting scholars with schoolteachers and conducting professional development programs. A special focus is providing global content for curricular innovation on race, multiculturalism, and international education. The site contains curricular units, primary source materials, and useful bibliographies, including books for teachers, for students, and videos, on several themes in U.S. history. Look for the bibliography on "American History in International Perspective."

Small Planet: The Age of Imperialism

www.smplanet.com/imperialism/toc.html. A site dedicated to providing multimedia teaching resources for instructors to explore expansion into Asia and the Pacific, with links to lesson plans, narrative text, a bibliography, and images.

The Smithsonian

www.si.edu. A master website for the Smithsonian in Washington, D.C., its collections and exhibits, and museums that are part of the larger Smithsonian complex. This site can connect teachers to the African Art Museum, the American Indian Museum, the American History Museum, and the Air and Space Museum, among others. Especially valuable is the "History and Culture" link that offers access to exhibits and collections on transportation in the United States, Lewis and Clark, Japanese Americans, and other topics. In "Bearing Witness to History," there are photos and brief descriptions of artifacts from September 11, 2001. There are additional links to African, African-American, Asian-Pacific, Latino, and European history.

UNESCO Transatlantic Slave Trade

www.vgskole.net/prosjekt/slavrute/welcome.htm. The UNESCO ASPnet Slave Route Project offers links to the history of the transatlantic slave trade (from the sixteenth through the nineteenth centuries) that connect users to bibliography, films, maps, documents, and teaching guides for secondary school teachers. There are also regional links to Europe, Africa, and the Americas.

U.S. Department of State International Information Programs

http://usinfo.state.gov/products/pubs/histryotln/index.htm. This online "Outline of U.S. History" (2005) is a thoroughly revised and updated version by Professor Alonzo Hamby of Ohio University of the text originally published by the State Department in 1949–50. It shows how the U.S. government presents the nation's history to foreign audiences.

Women and Social Movements in the United States, 1600–2000

http://womhist.alexanderstreet.com/projectmap.htm. This website provides learning modules in the form of document projects, each of which is organized around a specific question about a single social movement. Some projects have an international or cross-cultural dimension. Also included are lesson ideas, document-based questions, and links to other websites on U.S. and European women's history. Some materials require a subscription.

World History Archives

www.hartford-hwp.com/archives. Links to documents and sites that explore world history from a non-Eurocentric, working-class, and social justice perspective.

World History Association

www.thewha.org. Devoted to research and teaching in world history, the WHA has placed on its website archived copies of its newsletter, *World History Bulletin,* a list of recommended world history books, and links to other world history sites.

World History for Us All

http://worldhistoryforusall.sdsu.edu/dev/default.htm. A project of San Diego State University in cooperation with the National Center for History in the Schools at UCLA, this site offers a comprehensive model curriculum for teaching world history in middle and high schools. It divides world history into nine "Big Eras" and for each provides a narrative, Powerpoint slides, detailed unit descriptions, lesson plans, activities, and resources. Big Eras 3–5 contain information on pre-contact America and Big Eras 6–9 incorporate material from post-1500 North America.

World History Matters

http://worldhistorymatters.org. A project of the Center for History and New Media, George Mason University, this is a portal to two sites, World History Sources and Women

in World History. Each contains reviews of online primary source archives, guides to analyzing primary sources, teaching modules, and sample document lesson plans.

World War II Sites

http://connections.smsd.org/veterans/wwii_sites.htm. Links by topic to sites about World War II, divided into sites for students and sites for teachers. There are links to audio files, oral histories, and a teacher's guide on the Holocaust.

World Wide Web Virtual Library: Naval and Maritime

http://vlnavmar.usnaweb.org. Links to a wide range of teaching materials on shipping and naval history. A sample of some of the links includes piracy, submarines, ships, and aviation.

Videos

American Social History Project/Center for Media and Learning

www.ashp.cuny.edu. These 30-minute documentaries for college and high-school classrooms emphasize the role of workers in the U.S. past. Among those with international content:

"Tea Party Etiquette"
"Five Points" (Irish immigration)
"Savage Acts: Wars, Fairs and Empire" (Spanish-American War)

BBC

www.bbcamericashop.com.

"The Great War, 1918"
"The War of 1812"
"The World at War" (World War II)

Discovery Channel

http://teacherstore.discovery.com. Contains information on titles and purchase of Discovery Channel DVDs. Among them are:

"Abolishing Slavery in America"
"The Cuban Missile Crisis"
"Destination: America"
"How the West Was Lost"

The History Channel

http://store.aetv.com/html/home/index_branded.jhtml.

"Bay of Pigs Declassified"
"Conquest of America"
"Desperate Crossing" (The Mayflower)
"The First Americans"
"The Iran-Contra Scandal"
"The Irish in America"
"Italians in America"
"Pearl Harbor"
"Ship of Slaves"
"The U.S. in Latin America: Yankee Go Home"

PBS

www.pbs.org.

American Experience. This excellent documentary series includes titles that examine international themes. Among them are:

"Remember the Alamo"
"Journey to America"
"Hawaii's Last Queen"
"Emma Goldman"
"The Hunt for Pancho Villa"
"The Great War—1918"
"Influenza 1918"
"Marcus Garvey: Look for Me in the Whirlwind"
"America and the Holocaust"
"Pearl Harbor"
"D-Day"
"Love in the Cold War"
"Race for the Superbomb"
"Vietnam: A Television History"
"Nixon's China Game"

People's Century (PBS/BBC)—This 26-part television series weaves historical analysis with revealing personal testimony from those who lived through key events of the twentieth century. The focus is mainly on the United States and Europe, but the episodes bring in a considerable amount of narrative and testimony from around the globe, giving new perspective to familiar events. See, for example:

"Age of Hope, 1900"
"Lost Peace, 1919"
"Great Escape, 1927"
"Breadline, 1929"
"Brave New World, 1945"
"Boomtime, 1948"
"Endangered Planet, 1959"
"Skin Deep, 1960"
"Young Blood,1968"
"Half the People, 1969"
"God Fights Back, 1979"

Other Relevant PBS Videos and Video Series

"Africans in America"
"Columbus and the Age of Discovery"
"Destination America"
"Lewis and Clark"
"Liberty! The American Revolution"
"Rebels and Redcoats"
"Slavery and the Making of America"
"The U.S.-Mexican War"
"The War" (World War II)
"The War That Made America" (Seven Years' War)

Other Videos

www.500nations.tv/home.htm.

"500 Nations" (10-part documentary on Native Americans)

Editors and Contributors

Editors

Carl Guarneri teaches American and world history at Saint Mary's College of California. He earned his doctorate at Johns Hopkins University in 1979 and has also taught U.S. history at Bates College, the University of Paris VIII, and Colgate University. Through his publications, presentations, and seminars, Guarneri has played a leading role in the movement to globalize the teaching and studying of U.S. history. He participated in the La Pietra conferences on internationalizing American history (1997–2000) and has co-directed two NEH institutes on "Rethinking America in Global Perspective." Guarneri is the author of *America in the World: United States History in Global Context* (2007) and the editor of a survey course reader, *America Compared: American History in International Perspective* (2nd ed., 2005).

James Davis teaches world history, U.S. history, the humanities, and film history at Mt. San Jacinto College in California, after working as an Air Force historian for ten years. He received his Ph.D. in Comparative History from Brandeis University in 1981. Davis has been president of the Academic Senate and the Faculty Association and has received the Teacher of the Year Award, all while at Mt. San Jacinto College. He has participated in six NEH institutes and programs and has delivered conference papers for the American Historical Association and the Community College Humanities Association.

Contributors

Kevin Arlyck, *Brooklyn, New York, Middle Schools*
Thomas Bender, *New York University, New York City*
Brett Berliner, *Morgan State University, Baltimore, Maryland*

Melinda K. Blade, *Academy of Our Lady of Peace, San Diego, California*
Elaine Breslaw, Professor Emerita, *Morgan State University, Baltimore, Maryland*
Karen E. Carter, *Georgetown University, Washington, D.C.*
Derek Catsam, *University of Texas of the Permian Basin, Odessa, Texas*
Erin Cook, *Martin Luther King, Jr. Papers Project, Stanford University, Stanford, California*
Ken Cruikshank, *McMaster University, Hamilton, Ontario, Canada*
Alan Dawley (deceased), *The College of New Jersey, Ewing, New Jersey*
Carl N. Degler, Professor Emeritus, *Stanford University, Stanford, California*
John J. DeRose, *Whitefish Bay High School, Whitefish Bay, Wisconsin*
Maureen A. Flanagan, *Michigan State University*
Eric Foner, *Columbia University, New York City*
Paul R. Frazier, *Brookfield Academy College Preparatory High School, Brookfield, Wisconsin*
Kevin Gaines, *University of Michigan, Ann Arbor*
Alison Games, *Georgetown University, Washington, D.C.*
David L. Ghere, *University of Minnesota, Minneapolis, Minnesota*
Sally Gilbert, *Georgetown Day School, Washington, D.C.*
Maurice Godsey, *Princeton High School, Cincinnati, Ohio*
Dirk Hoerder, *University of Bremen, Bremen, Germany*
Clair W. Keller, *Iowa State University, Ames, Iowa*
Robin D.G. Kelley, *New York University, New York City*
M. Alison Kibler, *Franklin and Marshall College, Lancaster, Pennsylvania*
Dennis J. Maika, *Fox Lane High School, Bedford, New York.*

Donald W. Meinig, *Syracuse University, Syracuse, New York*

Thomas J. Osborne, *Santa Ana College, Santa Ana, California*

Stan Pesick, *Oakland Unified School District, Oakland, California*

Horacio N. Rocque Ramírez, *University of California, Santa Barbara*

Emily S. Rosenberg, *University of California, Irvine*

Norman L. Rosenberg, *Macalaster College, St. Paul, Minnesota*

Kathy Schollenberger, *Georgetown Day School, Washington, D.C.*

Erik Seeman, *State University of New York at Buffalo*

Peter N. Stearns, *George Mason University, Fairfax, Virginia*

James Tagg, *University of Lethbridge, Lethbridge, Alberta, Canada*

Dennis J. Townsend, *Providence High School, Charlotte, North Carolina*

Ian Tyrrell, *University of New South Wales, Sydney, Australia*

Laurence Veysey (deceased), *University of California, Santa Cruz*

Mark Wallace, *Gateway Senior High School, Monroeville, Pennsylvania*

Barbara Winslow, *Brooklyn College, Brooklyn, New York*

Lawrence A. Wolf, *Hilliard Darby High School, Hilliard, Ohio*

Henry Yu, *University of British Columbia, Vancouver, Canada, and University of California, Los Angeles*

Index